T0180763

Communications in Computer and Information Science   1947

Rationale

The CCIS series is devoted to the publication of proceedings of computer science conferences. Its aim is to efficiently disseminate original research results in informatics in printed and electronic form. While the focus is on publication of peer-reviewed full papers presenting mature work, inclusion of reviewed short papers reporting on work in progress is welcome, too. Besides globally relevant meetings with internationally representative program committees guaranteeing a strict peer-reviewing and paper selection process, conferences run by societies or of high regional or national relevance are also considered for publication.

Topics

The topical scope of CCIS spans the entire spectrum of informatics ranging from foundational topics in the theory of computing to information and communications science and technology and a broad variety of interdisciplinary application fields.

Information for Volume Editors and Authors

Publication in CCIS is free of charge. No royalties are paid, however, we offer registered conference participants temporary free access to the online version of the conference proceedings on SpringerLink (http://link.springer.com) by means of an http referrer from the conference website and/or a number of complimentary printed copies, as specified in the official acceptance email of the event.

CCIS proceedings can be published in time for distribution at conferences or as post-proceedings, and delivered in the form of printed books and/or electronically as USBs and/or e-content licenses for accessing proceedings at SpringerLink. Furthermore, CCIS proceedings are included in the CCIS electronic book series hosted in the SpringerLink digital library at http://link.springer.com/bookseries/7899. Conferences publishing in CCIS are allowed to use Online Conference Service (OCS) for managing the whole proceedings lifecycle (from submission and reviewing to preparing for publication) free of charge.

Publication process

The language of publication is exclusively English. Authors publishing in CCIS have to sign the Springer CCIS copyright transfer form, however, they are free to use their material published in CCIS for substantially changed, more elaborate subsequent publications elsewhere. For the preparation of the camera-ready papers/files, authors have to strictly adhere to the Springer CCIS Authors' Instructions and are strongly encouraged to use the CCIS LaTeX style files or templates.

Abstracting/Indexing

CCIS is abstracted/indexed in DBLP, Google Scholar, EI-Compendex, Mathematical Reviews, SCImago, Scopus. CCIS volumes are also submitted for the inclusion in ISI Proceedings.

How to start

To start the evaluation of your proposal for inclusion in the CCIS series, please send an e-mail to ccis@springer.com.

Sławomir Nowaczyk · Przemysław Biecek ·
Neo Christopher Chung · Mauro Vallati ·
Paweł Skruch · Joanna Jaworek-Korjakowska ·
Simon Parkinson · Alexandros Nikitas et al.
Editors

Artificial Intelligence

ECAI 2023 International Workshops

XAI^3, TACTIFUL, XI-ML, SEDAMI, RAAIT, AI4S, HYDRA, AI4AI
Kraków, Poland, September 30 – October 4, 2023
Proceedings, Part I

 Springer

For the full list of editors *see next page*

ISSN 1865-0929   ISSN 1865-0937 (electronic)
Communications in Computer and Information Science
ISBN 978-3-031-50395-5   ISBN 978-3-031-50396-2 (eBook)
https://doi.org/10.1007/978-3-031-50396-2

Editors

Sławomir Nowaczyk (iD)
Halmstad University
Halmstad, Sweden

Przemysław Biecek (iD)
Warsaw University of Technology
Warsaw, Poland

Neo Christopher Chung (iD)
Warsaw University
Warsaw, Poland

Mauro Vallati
University of Huddersfield
Huddersfield, UK

Paweł Skruch
AGH University of Science and Technology
Kraków, Poland

Joanna Jaworek-Korjakowska
AGH University of Science and Technology
Kraków, Poland

Simon Parkinson
University of Huddersfield
Huddersfield, UK

Alexandros Nikitas
University of Huddersfield
Huddersfield, UK

Martin Atzmüller
Universität Osnabrück
Osnabrück, Germany

Tomáš Kliegr (iD)
University of Economics Prague
Prague, Czech Republic

Ute Schmid
University of Bamberg
Bamberg, Germany

Szymon Bobek (iD)
Jagiellonian University
Kraków, Poland

Nada Lavrac
Jožef Stefan Institute
Ljubljana, Slovenia

Marieke Peeters
HU University of Applied Sciences Utrecht
Utrecht, The Netherlands

Roland van Dierendonck
Rotterdam University of Applied Sciences
Rotterdam, The Netherlands

Saskia Robben
Amsterdam University of Applied Sciences
Amsterdam, The Netherlands

Eunika Mercier-Laurent
University of Reims Champagne-Ardenne
Reims, France

Gülgün Kayakutlu (iD)
Istanbul Technical University
Istanbul, Türkiye

Mieczyslaw Lech Owoc (iD)
Wroclaw University of Economics and Business
Wrocław, Poland

Karl Mason
University of Galway
Galway, Ireland

Abdul Wahid
University of Galway
Galway, Ireland

Pierangela Bruno
University of Calabria
Rende, Italy

Francesco Calimeri (iD)
University of Calabria
Rende, Italy

Francesco Cauteruccio
Marche Polytechnic University
Ancona, Italy

Giorgio Terracina
University of Calabria
Rende, Italy

Diedrich Wolter (iD)
University of Bamberg
Bamberg, Germany

Jochen L. Leidner
Coburg University of Applied Sciences
Coburg, Germany

Michael Kohlhase
FAU Erlangen-Nürnberg
Erlangen, Germany

Vania Dimitrova (iD)
University of Leeds
Leeds, UK

Preface

The European Conference on Artificial Intelligence (ECAI) is the premier European conference on Artificial Intelligence. In 2023, ECAI took place in Kraków, Poland, from the 30th of September till the 4th of October. The program included workshops on specialised topics of high relevance for the scientific community. They were held during the first two days of the conference, in parallel with tutorials and side events such as the Doctoral Consortium or STAIRS (the 10th European Starting AI Researchers' Symposium). This two-volume set includes the proceedings of the following workshops:

1. XAI^3: Joint workshops on XAI methods, challenges and applications
2. TACTFUL: Workshop on Trustworthy AI for safe & secure traffic control in connected & autonomous vehicles
3. XI-ML: International Workshop on Explainable and Interpretable Machine Learning
4. SEDAMI: The Semantic Data Mining Workshop
5. RAAIT: Workshop on Responsible Applied Artificial Intelligence
6. AI4S: Workshop on Artificial Intelligence for Sustainability
7. HYDRA: HYbrid models for coupling Deductive and inductive ReAsoning
8. AI4AI: AI for AI Education

Each section of this book contains the papers from one of the workshops, following a preface from the organisers. We would like to thank all participants and invited speakers, the Program Committees and reviewers, and the ECAI conference and workshop chairs—we appreciate your efforts in making the workshops successful events. We are also grateful to Springer for their help in publishing the proceedings.

October 2023

Sławomir Nowaczyk
on behalf of the volume editors

Organization

ECAI Workshop Chairs

Tom Lenaerts   Université Libre de Bruxelles, Belgium
Paolo Turrini   University of Warwick, UK

XAI^3 Workshop Chairs

Sławomir Nowaczyk   Halmstad University, Sweden
Biecek Przemysław   Warsaw University of Technology, Poland
Neo Christopher Chung   University of Warsaw, Poland

TACTFUL Workshop Chairs

Mauro Vallati   University of Huddersfield, UK
Paweł Skruch   AGH University of Science and Technology in Kraków, Poland
Joanna Jaworek-Korjakowska   AGH University of Science and Technology in Kraków, Poland
Simon Parkinson   University of Huddersfield, UK
Alexandros Nikitas   University of Huddersfield, UK

XI-ML Workshop Chairs

Martin Atzmueller   Osnabrück University & DFKI, Germany
Tomáš Kliegr   Prague University of Economics and Business, Czechia
Ute Schmid   University of Bamberg, Germany

SEDAMI Workshop Chairs

Szymon Bobek   Jagiellonian University, Poland
Martin Atzmueller   Osnabrück University & DFKI, Germany
Nada Lavrac   Jožef Stefan Institute, Slovenia

RAAIT Workshop Chairs

Marieke Peeters	HU University of Applied Sciences Utrecht, The Netherlands
Roland van Dierendonck	Rotterdam University of Applied Sciences, The Netherlands
Saskia Robben	Amsterdam University of Applied Sciences, The Netherlands

AI4S Workshop Chairs

Eunika Mercier-Laurent	University of Reims Champagne Ardenne, France
Gülgün Kayakutlu	Istanbul Technical University, Turkey
Mieczyslaw Lech Owoc	Wrocław University of Economics and Business, Poland
Karl Mason	University of Galway, Ireland
Abdul Wahid	University of Galway, Ireland

Hydra Workshop Chairs

Pierangela Bruno	University of Calabria, Italy
Francesco Calimeri	University of Calabria, Italy
Francesco Cauteruccio	Polytechnic University of Marche, Italy
Giorgio Terracina	University of Calabria, Italy

AI4AI Workshop Chairs

Diedrich Wolter	University of Bamberg, Germany
Jochen L. Leidner	Coburg University of Applied Sciences, Germany
Michael Kohlhase	FAU Erlangen-Nürnberg, Germany
Ute Schmid	University of Bamberg, Germany
Vania Dimitrova	University of Leeds, UK

Contents – Part I

XI-ML

Contents – Part II

AI4S

Hydra

AI4AI

XAI^3

XAI³: Explainable Artificial Intelligence Methods, Challenges, and Applications, ECAI, Cracow, 1 October 2023

Preface

Explainability is gaining an increasing momentum and criticality in artificial intelligence (AI) research. Operating characteristics of modern AI models, primarily powered by deep neural networks (DNNs), are notoriously difficult to understand due to an extremely large number of parameters, non-linearity, complex architectures, and end-to-end training. As we attempt to translate the success of AI into high-risk and high-impact domain areas such as medicine and industry, we are interested in evaluating current XAI practices and developing a new generation of XAI methods. To this end, we organised joint workshops on XAI methods, challenges, and applications (XAI³) at the 26th European Conference on Artificial Intelligence (ECAI 2023).

So far, XAI methods have been primarily developed in a post-hoc manner where the original DNNs are unchanged. These methods attempt to interpret the decision-making process of pre-trained models. For example, when the computer vision model (e.g., ResNet-50) classifies a picture, the saliency map seeks to quantify and visualize which input pixels have contributed to that particular classification. In the majority of cases, XAI has been application-agnostic with the hope that methods for natural images and languages would readily translate into specific application domains. However, that approach has not worked particularly well, as evident in limited real-world cases of XAI in medicine or industrial processes. In this workshop, we seek to investigate challenges and opportunities for the new generation of explainable AI (XAI) methods that are reliable, robust, and trustworthy. We envision the next generation of XAI methods must be motivated by and directly benefit specific application domains.

At the XAI³ workshop, we planned three tracks: medical, industry, and future challenges, where we will explore the challenges and opportunities in creating useful XAI methods for medical applications, integrating explainability in highly automated industrial processes, and evaluating current and future XAI methods. We welcomed contributions from researchers, academia, and industries primarily from a technical and application point of view, but also from an ethical and sociological perspective.

In **medical applications**, explainability is as important as classification performance. Doctors and patients are unlikely to trust a blackbox algorithm, as false positives and false negatives could lead to great burdens. This challenge is compounded by substantial differentiation in subpopulations, technology, and medical practices. So far, AI methods have generally produced neither superhuman performances nor accurate explanations. In high risk medical applications, it appears that those two aspects are closely related, as understanding edge cases and biases via XAI methods could improve inference and prediction. Therefore, as discussed in the XAI³ workshop, inherently interpretable models are emerging as potentially powerful approaches that could provide both explainability and high performance. XAI may be utilized to improve our understanding of AI in medicine and modify the model architectures and behaviors accordingly. Alternatively, XAI methods could be utilized in human-computer interactions where explanations in conjunction with diagnosis or prognosis could help humans to make more informed decisions. Furthermore, recent legislations and regulations around the world (e.g., EU General Data Protection Regulation) emphasize "right to an explanation" when computer algorithms are used in decision making process. Therefore, XAI will become an indispensable element in translating the success of AI into medical applications.

Industry 4.0, the fourth industrial revolution, is characterised by a high degree of automation and the use of AI for optimising key processes of manufacturing, logistics and more. Building on this foundation, Industry 5.0, known as "Smart Factory," allows humans and machines to collaborate seamlessly, driving sustainability, resiliency, and benefits to people and society. As a result, today's industry is characterised by the widespread integration of cutting-edge technologies into highly automated and interconnected processes, where data is collected from many sources, fused, and analysed in real time to make decisions and optimise operations. However, it is equally essential to ensure that the resulting systems are transparent, reliable, and explainable to humans in various roles, from operators through managers and overseers, all the way to certification authorities. Integration of explainable AI (XAI) is crucial to ensure trustworthiness, safety, security, and accountability. The workshop brought industrial AI professionals together with explainability experts to discuss the latest developments in XAI and their practical applications, providing an opportunity for attendees to learn about the latest research, best practices, and challenges in this area. It was an opportunity to bridge researchers and engineers to discuss emerging topics and the newest trends. The integration of explainability in Industry 4.0 and 5.0 is crucial to ensure AI systems' reliability, trustworthiness and transparency.

The more research is conducted on the topics of XAI, the more new problems and **future challenges** open up. Among these challenges, one of the key importance includes the issue of the evaluation of explanations, an issue that is very important but also very complex. Important, because without evaluation it is difficult to compare the growing number of model exploration techniques. Complex, because explanations are used by different stakeholders, in different contexts, and thus it is difficult to capture with a single metric how good an explanation is. It is not only the multiplicity of stakeholders that is a challenge, but also their different levels of knowledge regarding machine learning techniques or even algorithmic operation. A related topic is the issue of explanation stability and fidelity in explaining the actual model. During the workshop, we brought together researchers conducting research dedicated to the evaluation of XAI techniques, as well as researchers applying these techniques in a variety of disciplines (such as the social sciences). Not only new dimensions of the evaluation of XAI methods were presented, but also the results of evaluations of selected methods. We know now that a single explanation is not enough and model exploration requires a multifaceted perspectives on a model. The presented papers will serve as a reference in the construction of further benchmarks evaluating explanatory methods.

The organisers would like to thank the authors, keynote speakers, and Program Committee members for their contributions to the workshop. We hope and believe that the workshop has been a valuable resource for participants and contributed to identifying new ideas, applications, and future research papers in XAI. The workshop provided a premier forum for sharing findings, knowledge, insights, experience, and lessons learned from practical and theoretical work. The intrinsic interdisciplinary nature of the workshop promoted the interaction between different competencies, thus paving the way for an exciting and stimulating environment involving researchers and practitioners.

Keynote Talks

The workshop included three keynote talks.

Christin Seifert from University of Marburg: *Can we trust XAI? Current status and challenges of evaluating XAI methods.*

The XAI community develops methods to make black-box models more transparent, with transparency catering to multiple stakeholders. In the case of post-hoc, local XAI methods, the user-facing output is a prediction and its accompanying explanation. The user should refer to the explanation to understand why a prediction was (not) made. But how can we evaluate whether an explanation is correct, understandable, useful to the user and truthful to the model? And how can we compare multiple XAI methods in a harmonised way to measure and ensure scientific progress? In this talk, I discussed different evaluation approaches, methods, and metrics, that have been developed – mostly bottom-up – in the XAI community. I then revisited other scientific fields, such as machine learning and information retrieval and their de facto evaluation standards. Finally, I presented obstacles and challenges towards a unified evaluation framework for XAI.

Concha Bielza and Pedro Larrañaga from Technical University of Madrid: *Explanation Capabilities of Bayesian Networks in Dynamic Industrial Domains.*

This talk described how Bayesian network models can provide natural explanations in temporal domains from the industry. After a brief introduction to Bayesian networks in static settings, discrete-time versions for temporal domains were presented, which include dynamic Bayesian networks and the popular hidden Markov models. The more recent continuous-time Bayesian networks and their supervised classification counterparts, both in uni- and multi-dimensional settings, were explained. How Bayesian networks can be used in dynamic clustering was also covered. In all cases, real examples from industry illustrated the versatile capabilities of Bayesian networks to intrinsically explain the model as a whole, predictions (reasoning), instances (evidences) and decisions. This is the so-called XBN framework, that encourages efficient communication with end users and supports understanding of how and why certain predictions were made, gaining new industrial insights.

Issam El Naqa from Moffitt Cancer Center: *Towards Trustworthy AI for Clinical Oncology.*

Artificial intelligence (AI) and Machine learning (ML) algorithms are currently transforming biomedical research, especially in the context of cancer research and clinical care. Despite the anticipated potential, their application in oncology and healthcare has been limited in scope with less than 5% of major healthcare providers implementing any form of AI/ML solutions. This is partly attributed to concerning issues that AI/ML-driven technologies instead of reducing healthcare disparities would exacerbate existing racial and gender equity due to inherent bias and lack of prediction transparency. In this work, we presented different approaches for detecting and mitigating such bias in AI/ML algorithms. We further showed examples of implementing these approaches in oncology applications from our work and others and discussed their implications for the future of AI/ML.

Acknowledgements. This work was in part supported by the INFORM consortium, CHIST-ERA grant [CHIST-ERA-19-XAI-007] funded by General Secretariat for Research and Innovation (GSRI) of Greece [T12EPA5-00053], CHIST-ERA grant [CHIST-ERA-19-XAI-012] funded by Swedish Research Council, National Science Centre (NCN) of Poland [2020/02/Y/ST6/00071, Sonata Bis 2019/34/E/ST6/00052], Agence Nationale de la Recherche (ANR) of France [ANR-21-CHR4-0006]. It also received partial supports from the IDUB program (POB3) from the Faculty of Mathematics, Informatics, and Mechanics, University of Warsaw.

October 2023

Sławomir Nowaczyk
Przemysław Biecek
Neo Christopher Chung

Organization

Workshop Chairs

Sławomir Nowaczyk   Halmstad University, Sweden
Przemysław Biecek   Warsaw University of Technology, Poland
Neo Christopher Chung   University of Warsaw, Poland
Hubert Baniecki   University of Warsaw, Poland

Workshop Organisers

Albert Bifet   Telecom-ParisTech
Szymon Bobek   Jagiellonian University
Lennart Brocki   University of Warsaw
Giuseppe Casalicchio   Ludwig Maximilian University of Munich
Joao Gama   University of Porto
Mathieu Hatt   LaTIM
Grzegorz J. Nalepa   Jagiellonian University
Panagiotis Papadimitroulas   BIOEMTECH
Sepideh Pashami   Halmstad University
Rita P. Ribeiro   University of Porto
Dawid Rymarczyk   Jagiellonian University
Jacek Tabor   Jagiellonian University
Bruno Veloso   University of Porto
Bartosz Zieliński   Jagiellonian University

Clash of the Explainers: Argumentation for Context-Appropriate Explanations

Leila Methnani$^{(\boxtimes)}$ (iD), Virginia Dignum (iD), and Andreas Theodorou (iD)

Umeå University, Umeå, Sweden
{leila.methnani,andreas.theodorou}@umu.se, virginia@cs.umu.se

Abstract. Understanding when and why to apply any given eXplainable Artificial Intelligence (XAI) technique is not a straightforward task. There is no single approach that is best suited for a given context. This paper aims to address the challenge of selecting the most appropriate explainer given the context in which an explanation is required. For AI explainability to be effective, explanations and how they are presented needs to be oriented towards the stakeholder receiving the explanation. If—in general—no single explanation technique surpasses the rest, then reasoning over the available methods is required in order to select one that is context-appropriate. Due to the transparency they afford, we propose employing argumentation techniques to reach an agreement over the most suitable explainers from a given set of possible explainers.

In this paper, we propose a modular reasoning system consisting of a given mental model of the relevant stakeholder, a reasoner component that solves the argumentation problem generated by a multi-explainer component, and an AI model that is to be explained suitably to the stakeholder of interest. By formalizing supporting premises—and inferences—we can map stakeholder characteristics to those of explanation techniques. This allows us to reason over the techniques and prioritise the best one for the given context, while also offering transparency into the selection decision.

Keywords: Explainability · Transparency · Argumentation

1 Introduction

Now that the need for eXplainable Artificial Intelligence (XAI) has been firmly established [2], the development of state-of-the-art techniques, such as Local Interpretable Model-agnostic Explanations (LIME) [30] and SHapley Additive exPlanations (SHAP) [22], is continuously being pursued. While researchers and practitioners have benefited from model interpretations offered by such techniques, issues remain that make them tricky to adopt. One identified pitfall of current XAI methods is the failure to make their limitations clear; misleading explanations can be inconspicuous, and may result in downstream actions that are unjustified [20,28,31]. Moreover, with this large suite of XAI methods comes

S. Nowaczyk et al. (Eds.): ECAI 2023 Workshops, CCIS 1947, pp. 7–23, 2024.
https://doi.org/10.1007/978-3-031-50396-2_1

the need to understand each in order to make an informed choice about which to select, and then further interpret the results received. The assumption here is that these explainees will have the expertise to make such informed choices and analyses. In reality, current explanations mostly serve system developers—who have limited temporal constraints (i.e. how fast the explanation is to be produced and can be consumed) and require a large amount of in-depth information [24].

Thus, we propose an XAI system built to support the selection of an XAI method using symbolic reasoning, taking into account what the explainee may *value* and *need* in order to determine the optimal method and explanations to present. In this work, we focus only on selecting the best suited explainer. While an aggregated view of many potential explanations could perhaps be more appropriate depending on context, it is possible to mislead the stakeholder when attempting to augment one explanation using other explanations generated by incompatible techniques [28].

Moreover, it is important to consider the context within which explanations are needed and the context within which they will be used. When we refer to *context-sensitivity*, we mean capturing the frame that surrounds the request for an explanation. This includes capturing relevant knowledge about available explanation techniques, such as strengths and weaknesses, as well as relevant knowledge about the target audience, referred to as the *stakeholder*, including their understanding of the AI system and their intentions behind seeking an explanation for its decision-making. Too few techniques are developed with the intention of modelling the stakeholder's view of the system and with consideration for their explainability needs [6]. Still, explainability begins with considering *who* is in need of an explanation. Often, the "who" is not entirely aware of what type of explanation is best suited to their needs, which introduces the added challenge of selecting an optimal explanation technique that can be sufficiently interpreted for the context at hand. Thus, more transparency, i.e. providing insights into 'why' an explanation has been selected, is required.

Contribution Our main contribution is a framework for the formalisation of and reasoning over: i)the characteristics of explanation techniques; ii) the properties that make them well-suited—or ill-suited—towards various contexts; and iii) the contexts in which the produced explanations are to be used. With such a formalisation, transparency into the selection of existing explainer methods that also maps needs to their capabilities is afforded. This is proposed by our introduction of the reasoning component on top of a multi-explainer system. The intention is to take an appropriate mental model of a target explainee into account when offering explanations, removing any assumption that the user is sufficiently informed of all the strengths and weaknesses of each explanation method and the technicalities required to interpret the output. For the purposes of this paper only, we assume that these explainee mental models are given and accurately portray their existing knowledge and intentions.

In this paper, we begin with an overview in Sect. 2 of the concepts that underpin our proposed solution; we define terms central to explainable artificial intelligence (XAI) and human-centric XAI (HCXAI), as well as computational reasoning and argumentation for both making and justifying decisions. In Sect. 4, we describe our working example and describe an experimental setup. Finally in Sect. 5, we conclude that reasoning over multiple explanations can be used to map explainers to explainee characteristics. We further motivate the need for evaluating this work in a human-subject study to validate the transparency effects with target human stakeholders.

2   Background

2.1   Explainable Artificial Intelligence

It is widely agreed that no one 'true' explanation exists and that stakeholders have diverse needs when it comes to explainability and interpretability of AI models [3]. There can be many explanations for a single outcome, each contributing towards a particular explanatory dimension [28].

To build on this notion of *explanatory dimensions* we first need to unpack what is meant by an *explanation*. Here, we adopt the definition offered by Guidotti *et al.* In their survey, they describe an explanation to be 'an interface' between humans and a decision maker that is ... both an accurate proxy of the decision maker and comprehensible to humans" [17]. Markus *et al.* characterise explainability similarly by highlighting the properties of *interpretability*—relating to clarity and parsimony—and *fidelity*—relating to completeness and soundness [23]. The importance of each property, they argue, is dependent on the reason that explainability is demanded in the first place. Today, a vast amount of XAI methods have been—and continue to be—developed towards different explanatory demands. Models can be developed to be *intrinsically* explanatory and interpretable to humans. Consider decision trees, for instance, as such intrinsically interpretable Machine Learning (ML) models; decision-making steps can be intuitively followed and understood for simple trees[1]. When such interpretable models suffer in terms of predictive power, the need for more complex models may arise, motivating the employment of *black-box* models that are not intuitively understandable. *Post-hoc* XAI methods become useful in this case, where explanations can be offered after model training has been completed. More useful still, are *model-agnostic* methods, which are those that are not innately baked into a specific ML model and can—in principle—be applied to any ML model. The benefits of taking a model-agnostic approach include the freedom to choose any machine learning model for the prediction task at hand and *still* being able to offer an explanation to stakeholders after the fact. It offers practitioners the added benefit of comparing interpretability across machine learning methods as well, which can be insightful in terms trade-offs. These qualities make post-hoc, model-agnostic XAI approaches desirable, and we therefore focus on these methods only.

---

[1] It is worth noting that as decision trees scale, their interpretability may also decline due to the sheer size of the structure.

Post-hoc methods can be *global* or *local*. If an understanding of the overall behaviour of an AI system is required, then global explanation techniques can be employed. For an understanding of how a single decision came to be, local techniques can be used. In this paper, we consider both classes of XAI techniques as the context within which explanations are needed will drive the choice of class.

2.2 Human-Centred Explainable Artificial Intelligence

Effectively applying XAI techniques requires, according to Pitman and Munn, practitioners to "start from the consumer's place of understanding and build upon it" [28]. This is precisely what Human-centred Explainable Artificial Intelligence (HCXAI) intends to do by putting the human at the core of XAI design [13].

HCXAI moves beyond superficial consideration of who the target human might be; by employing human-computer interaction (HCI) techniques such as *value-sensitive design* (VSD) [12] and *participatory design* [15], HCXAI aims to involve the human stakeholder directly for a holistic understanding of relevant design requirements. VSD is rooted in consideration for human values when designing technology. Participatory design aims to build technology together with those who hold a stake in it. These approaches often result in the formulation of *mental models* of relevant human stakeholders.

Here, we define a mental model to be the stakeholder's cognitive representation of how any given system works. This includes what the stakeholder knows about the system's components, the interactions between them, as well as the processes that transform them [7]. Additionally, we consider what is known about the stakeholder themselves; this includes their *needs* to fulfil a role and adhere to values, amongst others. Mental models are important to consider in the context of explainable AI in particular for numerous reasons. For one, there is no universal explanation best suited for all stakeholders and their needs. Furthermore, individuals within stakeholder groups may also have slightly different requirements based on their personal experience with AI and XAI in particular. Similarly, as we humans explain concepts amongst ourselves, we tailor our explanations based on the explainee and what they are already expected to understand about the concept, building on top of that expected knowledge. Attention is given to context, which we understand as the relevant elements that shape the setting within which an explanation is required. This calls for the consideration of relevant explainee characteristics mapped to XAI techniques to inform more suitable selections of explanations.

2.3 Reasoning and Argumentation

Transparency into the various elements that contribute towards the choice of an explanation technique offers stakeholders the value of making more informed decisions when it comes to AI and its applications in industry. Transparency is afforded through the neat and intuitive way of forming *inferences*—drawing conclusions—derived from a knowledge base of *facts* already assumed to be true.

The availability of such a knowledge base of truths together with well-formulated and documented rules of inference can help stakeholders in their interpretation of any given explanation.

Argumentation is considered pivotal to the way humans arrive at conclusions and thus make decisions [10]. Arguments are formulated to defend and persuade given claims and further support actions that can be taken. Offering "the correct" argument is not of the essence, which is fitting in the context of offering explanations—we do not necessarily have one *correct* approach to explaining a decision outcome, but rather many; some approaches are more suitable than others depending on the context.

Computational argumentation can therefore offer a solid foundation for human-centric AI, where the intention is to augment human cognition. Thus, we choose to adopt a computational argumentation approach to reasoning over the choice of explanation when given a system of multiple explainers suited for presenting different motivations for the outcome of a single machine learning model.

Consider Dung's Abstract Argumentation (AA) framework [11]. Formally, the AA framework takes the form of a pair $S = \langle Ar, R \rangle$ where Ar is the set of arguments, and R is a binary relation of *attacks*, where $R \subseteq Ar \times Ar$. For $a, b \in Ar$, $R(a, b)$ indicates that the argument a represents an attack on the argument b.

To compute a reasonable *position* given by the argumentation framework S, an *extension* set E can be built, where $E \subseteq Ar$. E is considered *conflict-free* if no member within it attacks another. That is there exists no elements a and b within E such that $R(a, b)$. An argument a that is attacked by b through the relation $R(a, b)$ is said to be defended by c if $R(c, a)$ and thus *acceptable* as an argument with respect to the position. Conflict-free positions that contain acceptable arguments are said to be *admissible*. [33]

Label-based approaches to solving arguments also exist [4]. Arguments that are free from the effect of any attack are labelled *IN*. IN arguments are accepted and render any argument they attack to be *OUT*. Therefore, we can reject all arguments that are labelled OUT. Arguments that are neither IN nor OUT are undecided and labelled *UNDEC*. This label-based approach can be depicted visually using a graphical representation of the argument framework. The AA framework can be constructed as a graph; the nodes represent arguments and directed edges represent attack relations. Starting with a graph of the abstract argument, the label-based approach can be used to remove those nodes labelled as OUT, together with any outgoing edges from OUT nodes, and retain those nodes that are labelled as IN. What is left is a neat visual depiction of an accepted position as shown in Fig. 1. Visualisations of the AA framework as a graph support the value of transparency, offering a representation of the argumentation flow that is often easily digestible for humans.

3   Related Work

In his work summarising XAI insights from the social sciences, Miller [24] describes some requirements for the selection of the "best" explanation in AI. From a social sciences perspective, the question asked by the explainee is of utmost importance, and often driven by anomalies or surprising observations. As users interact with system, they learn and generalise, adjusting their need for certain explanations along the way. This motivates the need for selection mechanisms that take into account both the question asked by the explainee, and the mental model they have of the system. Further motivation is given for maintaining a model of both the explainee and the explainer, with early work in XAI such as Cawsey's EDGE system [8] or Weiner's BLAH system [35] that both promote explanations that are oriented towards the users and what they seem to *know* about the system. The focus, however, is consistently on selecting and evaluating individual explanations rather than motivating the existing methods that generate them, which is also of significant importance.

Considering the time and expertise currently required to select an XAI method that generates relevant explanations, motivation exists to automate the whole XAI pipeline, as in Automated Machine Learning (AutoML). The objective with AutoML is to automate the ML pipeline end to end as a means of enabling domain experts to create ML solutions without much of the technical pre-requisites [18]. In their work, Cugny *et al.* [9] propose a framework for AutoXAI, also motivated by the need for contextualising XAI solutions and relieving the data scientist of the tedious tasks required to do so. There are three main components in their framework: (1) the user who offers elements of the context, (2) the context adapter that selects a subset of explainers that match these specified needs, and (3) a hyper parameter optimiser that performs a search over hyperparameters to reduce loss based on explanation evaluation function aggregates. As with most XAI techniques, this framework is also oriented towards the practitioner—namely data scientists—as its primary user. In our work, we motivate consideration for a wider scope that includes expert and non-expert users alike. Moreover, the authors raise ethical issues that may follow from the explanation selection, namely the bias that may arise from preference configurations within their framework. Biases that may arise from stakeholder preferences is one consideration that encourages our choice of argumentation and reasoning; they support making the facts, opinions, and beliefs that drive such preferences explicit and clear.

The Gorgias Argumentation Framework is a structured argumentation framework that accounts for beliefs and how they shape the conditions that lead to a given position. Gorgias allows for the generation of priority arguments, where preference or relative strength between arguments can be expressed. These assigned strengths then determine their attack or defense influence over other arguments. In their work, Kakas *et al.* explore Gorgias output in relation to XAI and the need for "socially useful" explanations, arguing that the properties such as being (1) attributive in the rules of an argument and (2) contrastive in the set of preferences presented are supported by argumentation frameworks such as Gorgias [32]. In their work developing Visual Gorgias, Vassiliades *et al.* [34] describe how an added visualisation layer that offers graphical representations can support the user's understanding of the argumentation framework and the decisions that were made.

4   Modular Multi-explainer and Reasoning System

In this section, we describe our proposed solution—a modular explanation selection system for determining context-appropriate explanations. We consider contextual factors such as the stakeholder receiving the explanation, timeliness of the explanation, the model that needs to be explained, the application domain, etc. A high-level overview of the system is offered by the illustration in Fig. 3. One critical component is a given mental model of the relevant stakeholder. Here, we will assume that the mental model is already defined and provided. It captures a representation of the stakeholder's cognitive state with respect to the context including elements such as values and requirements. This representation contributes towards a Knowledge Base (KB) of *facts* and *beliefs* that the reasoner component can access to make inferences over an appropriate explanation offered by multiple *explainers*. We consider multiple explanation techniques to comprise of the multi-explainer component of this system. Each explainer has characteristics that support particular values, requirements, and other knowledge characteristics of the users that employ them. Thus, we can extend our KB with facts about these explainers, and construct relations in the form of *attacks* as captured by Dung's AA framework. Our final component is ML system itself, which can—in principle—be any dataset and model of the stakeholder's choice. In our system, we promote the selection of post-hoc and model-agnostic explainers for the multi-explainer component, thus allowing for the desirable flexibility of choosing any ML model to explain. End-to-end, we make available any supporting premises—and inferences—that map stakeholder characteristics to those of the explanation techniques to make the process not only transparent, but also *contestable*. The latter refers to the property of providing information as to why this was the best decision possible [1]. In our argumentation framework, we demonstrate that we have selected the best possible explanation—given the conditions presented to the system—through our attack system.

We see a system like this being utilised when companies are in need of a formal and standardised approach to fulfilling the explainability demands of their stakeholders based on regulatory and other policy requirements. While a system like this is by no means intended to replace the interview and participatory design processes that an organisation is expected to engage in with their stakeholders, it offers a means of concretising those findings and making any biases explicit. In the context of this paper, the decision problem we are concerned with is that of selecting an explanation technique when an explanation is demanded. Capturing and presenting various assumptions about the context to the stakeholder supports their understanding of organisational decision making around AI. It can also support organisations in their due diligence whenever their AI ecosystem is audited. Presenting reasoning around explainability becomes increasingly important when you consider the fact that AI explanations can be 'weaponised.' It is possible, for example, to induce over-confidence in an AI system by generating explanation that are misleading [14,26,31]. We propose our framework as a means of designing for accountability and avoiding "ethics washing."

4.1   Use Case: Predicting Current Housing Prices

To best explain our work, we offer an example use case and describe a modular Multi-explainer and Reasoning System (MxRS) component by component. Consider the scenario of buying and selling houses. A real-estate agency has deployed an AI system trained on historical housing data of the region. The agency is performing evaluations for a customer interesting in selling their house. This customer is also seeking an explanation for the price point offered by the prediction system. The agency has an in-house team of AI architects who design, develop, and maintain their AI ecosystem together with a suite of XAI techniques. Now, the agency must make a decision on how to explain the outcome to the customer; a choice that is contextual and stakeholder dependent. For the purposes of our use case, we define an instance of a system using our proposed architecture component by component. We use this theoretical implementation to ground our discussion throughout.

The Stakeholder Mental Model(s) and Building Context. Collecting the knowledge required to construct a mental model can be achieved through many means; for instance, using sensors, direct user input, or a mix of the two. The HCXAI community advocates for conversational explainable AI, where users can engage in conversation when seeking explanations from a given AI system [21,24]. Neurosymbolic techniques can therefore be employed to extract symbolic rules from the user's natural language prompts if such a dialogue were to be developed as the interface between our proposed system and the user. The extracted symbolic knowledge can then be used by the MxRS to construct a mental model for the stakeholders and populate the knowledge base for the system to reason over an appropriate explanation technique to employ.

The appropriate solution will depend on (at least) both stakeholders presented in our use case. Facts and beliefs about each side should be considered for the context at hand. Let us take the first stakeholder to be the real-estate agency that has deployed the housing price prediction model and the second to be the customer interested in selling their house; the former must present the latter with an explanation as to why the selling price is not as high as they had expected.

Consider that the real-estate agency has two XAI techniques at their disposal when explaining their model outcomes. The first one is LIME, a local interpretability technique that is considered to be human-friendly and intuitive to decipher, the second is counterfactual, describing how the variables need to be adjusted to obtain a different outcome. For this scenario, we assume that both these methods are valid. The real estate agency expresses a preference for computationally cheap methods over those that generate short explanations, which are considered more human-friendly. They also express a preference for using more trustworthy techniques over those that generate short explanation due to the observation that their customers have expressed doubt towards their services; they want to boost the customer's trust. They want to demonstrate to their trustworthiness to the customer by being transparent about their methods; those that are susceptible to adversarial attack is a stronger argument against trustworthiness than instability.

To build the argumentation framework around this decision problem of selecting a context-appropriate explainer, we must first identify the knowledge related to this selection process. In the housing prices scenario, we consider the requirements from the two stakeholders, the real estate agency and the customer, which include:

- The real estate agency has preference for computationally cheap methods.
- The customer puts high values on the trustworthiness of an explanation.
- The customer requires a 'human-friendly' explanation.

Let us also list some contextual facts and some beliefs about the context in general:

- It has been shown that LIME is susceptible to adversarial attack that can intentionally mislead explainees by hiding biases [31].
- An explanation is human-friendly' if it is short (presenting only one or two causes) and contrastive, i.e., it compares the current context with some context in which the event would not have happened. [24, 26]
- Simpler explanations that boost the likelihood of the explainee understanding and accepting an explanation may better support trust than offering a more likely explanation. [24]

Contextual Information About the ML System. In our MxRS, the ML component is more than just an ML Model and its output; multiple explainers would in fact require access to the dataset, as depicted by Fig. 3. Explainers may, for example, generate alternative outputs based on permutation or in order to select samples as example-based explanations. So we define our ML system component to consist of metadata, data, and the trained ML model. Metadata capture information about the dataset that may be relevant to the context and used to populate the KB. This can include information extracted from a datasheet, describing the dataset [16], or a model card reporting on the trained model [25].

In our use case, the dataset is historical housing data of the region within which the stakeholder is looking to buy and sell. Making predictions for house prices is considered a regression problem solved by models such as *eXtreme Gradient Boosting* (XGBoost) [5]. XGBoost is a tree-based ensemble learning method that has high predicting power for regression problems.

The Multi-Explainer Component. The multi-explainer component consists of at least two *explainer* sub-components. Each explainer provides its own means of extracting or producing explanations from the ML model. For example, one explainer may be providing local explanations by using the Local Interpretable Model-agnostic Explanations (LIME) [30] method and another may offer counterfactual explanations using Diverse Counterfactual Example (DiCE) [27].

In principle, a multi-explainer component can comprise multiple instances of the same explanation technique, only with different parameter settings. Then, the explanations offered will be intrinsic and/or model-specific, therefore requiring modifications and substitutions within the ML System module of our architecture. Such an approach is outside the scope of this paper but relevant to consider for future iterations.

Each explainer also contains a list of arguments for why its produced explanations are the best for each explanation request. It offers those arguments to the reasoner component. We would also like to highlight the ability to take into consideration various characteristic of explanation techniques themselves within explainer arguments. Such characteristics of interest may include the computational costs of generating an explanation using any given method, the environmental impact of said computation, or even access to interpretable visualisations for example. These pros and cons may be mapped to stakeholder requirements and contribute to the argumentation computation.

The Reasoner Component. The reasoner component is made up of a KB and an argumentation solver. The KB is populated with relevant facts and beliefs offered by the previously described multi-explainer component, as well as those offered by the mental model of the stakeholder, to be described in the upcoming subsection. The argumentation solver computes admissible positions given the arguments posed. Our working example uses notation from both Dung's Abstract Argumentation Framework [11] and Gorgias Preference-based Argumentation Framework [19]; introducing preferences offers a value-based approach that is appropriate in various applications of our systems due to emphasis on human-centricity when solving for context-appropriate explanations. If the context requires consistency and involves arguments constructed from imperfect information, then admissibility-based semantics are desirable [4]. In principle, however, an instance of our proposed system can be implemented with any argumentation semantics; while the outcome of the system will be determined by it, transparency will illuminate biases in the designer's choice.

Using syntax from the Gorgias framework, we can represent knowledge of rules, conflicts, and preferences using predicate symbols. Labelled rules are constructed using the form *rule(Label, Head, Body)*. Here, the Head is a literal, the Body is a list of literals, and the Label is a compound term made up of the rule's name along with selected variables from the Head and Body [29]. To represent negative literals, Gorgias uses the form *neg(L)*. An attack is characterised both by the complements and preferences defined in the framework. That is, argument a is said to attack argument b if they have complementary conclusions, and argument a contains rules of higher or equal priority to argument b. To follow, we put the scenario described in our use case above into Gorgias syntax to construct the argumentation framework and solve for the queries neg(use(X=lime)) and use(X=counterfactual) respectively.

```
%% Arguments, where X is an explainer
rule(r1(X), use(X), [is_sparse(X)]).
rule(r2(X), neg(use(X)), [neg(is_computationally_cheap(X)
    )]).
rule(r3(X), use(X),[is_trustworthy(X)]).
rule(r4(X), is_trustworthy(X), [is_stable(X)].
rule(r5(X), neg(is_trustworthy(X)), [
    susceptible_to_adversarial_attack(X)].
```

```
%% Preference Rules
rule(pr1(X), prefer(r2(X), r1(X)), []). % prefer
    computational costs short explanations.
rule(pr2(X), prefer(r3(X), r2(X)), []). % prefer
    trustworthiness over  computational costs.
rule(pr3(X), prefer(r5(X), r4(X)), []). % susceptibility
    to adversarial attack is stronger argument than
    stability.
```

```
%% Facts / Beliefs
rule(f1, is_sparse(X = counterfactual), []).
rule(f2, is_sparse(X = lime), []).
rule(f3, is_computationally_cheap(X = lime), []).
rule(f4, neg(is_computationally_cheap(X = counterfactual)
    ), []).
rule(f5, susceptible_to_adversarial_attack(X = lime), [])
    .
rule(f6, neg(is_stable(X = lime)), []).
```

The set of arguments, presented as rules $r1$ through to $r5$, together with the preference rules pr1 through to pr3, already encapsulate bias in the designer's choice and presenting these rules and reasoning steps to any stakeholder (customers, auditors, system engineers, etc.) will make the designer's assumptions clear. Starting with $r1$, we see that the agency has a rule to use methods that produce short explanations, which is characterised by *sparsity*. If it is not computationally cheap, $r2$ says not to use the method. Using trustworthy methods is depicted by $r3$. What constitutes a trustworthy method is determined by the *stability* of the method, as described by $r4$, while $r5$ states that a method's trustworthiness is compromised if it is susceptible to adversarial attack. We can also see that the agency has a preference to save on computational costs over generating short explanations, as described by $pr1$. More important still is the preference for trustworthiness; $pr2$ says it is a stronger argument over computational cost. With regards to trustworthiness, $pr3$ states that susceptibility to adversarial attack is a stronger argument against it than stability is for it. Then, we can populate the knowledge base with facts and/or beliefs about the available explainers, for instance $f5$, that states LIME is susceptible to adversarial attack.

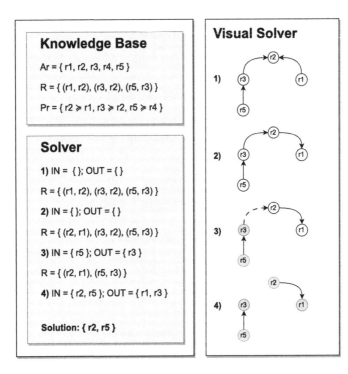

Fig. 1. An example solution using labellings, where the argument not to use LIME holds in the described argumentation framework. The example is further described in Sect. 4.1.

In Fig. 1, the KB consists of an argument set Ar, binary relations R representing attacks, and preferences Pr that depict priority of some arguments over others. The example depicted in the figure solves for the argument against using LIME as an explainer in the described context; i.e. the framework is queried to see if r2(X=lime): neg(use(X=lime)) holds. The arguments and relations generated using this query are $Ar = \{r1, r2, r3, r5\}$ and $R = \{(r1, r2), (r3, r2), (r5, r3)\}$. The argument $r4$ is not generated because it does not hold that LIME is stable. The preferences are $Pr = \{r2 \succeq r1, r3 \succeq r2, r5 \succeq r4\}$. Graphically, we can represent these arguments as nodes and the attacks as directed edges. Priority arguments are handled by countering an incident attack. So, in step 2, we can flip the edge in the graph and update the attack relations to apply this priority preference. Recall from Sect. 2 that an argument without any effective attacks is considered IN (that is, any attack is labelled OUT). Thus, in step 3, the argument $r5$ can be trivially marked as IN (coloured green in Fig. 1) and any argument that

$r5$ attacks will be marked as OUT (coloured red in Fig. 1). Uncoloured nodes are UNDEC. We can disregard attacks coming from OUT arguments, as indicated by the dotted edges in Fig. 1. Removing those outgoing edges in step 4 allows us to consider $r2$ an argument that is IN—it considered *defended* by $r5$. It follows that any argument attacked by $r2$ is OUT. Finally, we can see that only two arguments remain, concluding an admissible and accepted position $\{r2, r5\}$, which contains the argument r2(X=lime): neg(use(X=lime)), that is, not to use LIME in the given context, holds.

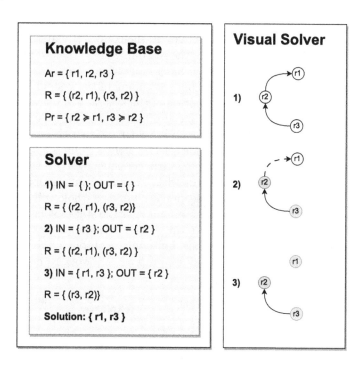

Fig. 2. An example solution using laballeings, where the argument to use counterfactual explanations holds in the described argumentation framework. The example is further described in Sect. 4.1.

In Fig. 2, we demonstrate the same process, but with the query use(X=counterfactual), showing that it also holds. The agency may therefore select a counterfactual method to generate explanations for the explainee in this given context. The agency may apply DiCE, for example, and present the customer with a diverse set of feature-perturbed instances of their house that would have received the price they were expecting. In natural language, such an explanation would be interpreted as follows, "you would have received the price range you are looking for if your house had an additional balcony." Such an explanation shows how the number of balconies influences housing prices in the given geographic location, for example, and can support the explainee in understanding what renovations may—or may not—support them in achieving their target price. This explanation is more context-appropriate considering the explainee's question of why their expectations on housing prices were not met by the agency's evaluation; LIME may have offered an explanation that depicts the number of balconies as an influential factor on price, but would not have offered the additional information required to satisfy the explainee's question about a specific target price bracket.

It may be that an empty set $E = \emptyset$ is returned by the solver. In such a case, we propose that the system always present a default explanation as a fallback. Here, we are of the position that some explanation is better than none. We prioritise both ensuring an explanation is always available regardless of the context, and that the system is transparent at all times, even when only a trivial solution exists. The opportunity to offer a log showing the reasoning steps that result in $E = \emptyset$ also exists here, allowing users to better understand where conflicts in arguments arise and how that might impact their understanding of the system as a whole.

Notice that the stakeholder's perception of the system will not only be influenced by the explanations presented, but also by the transparency by which an explanation is selected. By offering the stakeholder insights through the provision of all reasoning steps for explanation selection, the system is also influencing their understanding of an explanation context-dependency, thereby influencing the state of the stakeholder's mental model. Therefore, interaction with both the ML model and our explanation selection system as a whole will result in the need for continuous updates to the mental model of the stakeholder, as depicted in our high-level diagram in Fig. 3. At this stage, considerations for how such updates can be done have not been made, but doing so through interactivity and accounting for user feedback is one way we propose this work to move forward.

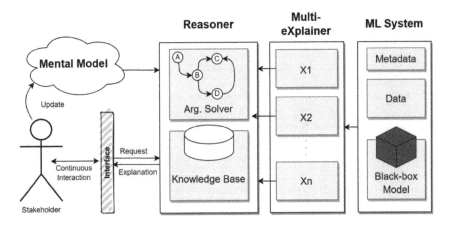

Fig. 3. A high-level illustration of our proposed explanation selection system comprising of: (a) the mental model; (b) the Reasoner component that consists of a Argumentation Solver and a Knowledge Base; (c) the multi-explainer component consisting of many explainers; and (d) the Machine Learning system consisting of any available meta-data, a dataset, and the trained model itself that is to be explained (black-box).

5   Conclusion and Future Work

In selecting a suitable explainer, there is no one-size-fits-all solution. There are increasingly many methods to select from when it comes to explaining AI outcomes. Some are more appropriate than others given the context, which includes the AI system(s) being used, the mental model of the explainee and the questions they ask, and potentially also legal or sectorial requirements on what are suitable explanations. Still, the path to selecting context-appropriate solutions is not always conflict-free considering the facts and beliefs that give shape to the context. Using argumentation to reason over available explanation techniques and select that which will generate a context-appropriate explanation is therefore desirable. Moreover, making those reasoning steps accessible and readily available for the target stakeholder offers transparency into explanation selection, making XAI applications themselves less of an opaque practice.

Beyond selecting explanations, evaluating the quality of the selection and the explanation requires grounding in studies with human subjects. Therefore, we propose the development of a Minimum Viable Product (MVP) and a user study as the necessary next steps to determining the effectiveness of our approach in collaboration with target stakeholders. Future work includes such an MVP implementation, along with an investigation of how neurosymbolic AI techniques can be utilised for extracting additional contextual knowledge and beliefs as a supplement to traditional methods of participatory design for constructing stakeholder mental models.

Ethical Statement. The authors have no competing interests, research involving human participants and/or animals, or issues of informed consent to disclose.

References

1. Aler Tubella, A., Theodorou, A., Dignum, V., Michael, L.: Contestable black boxes. In: Gutiérrez-Basulto, V., Kliegr, T., Soylu, A., Giese, M., Roman, D. (eds.) RuleML+RR 2020. LNCS, vol. 12173, pp. 159–167. Springer, Cham (2020). https://doi.org/10.1007/978-3-030-57977-7_12
2. Arrieta, A.B., et al.: Explainable artificial intelligence (XAI): concepts, taxonomies, opportunities and challenges toward responsible AI. Inf. Fusion **58**, 82–115 (2020)
3. Arya, V., et al.: One explanation does not fit all: a toolkit and taxonomy of AI explainability techniques. arXiv preprint arXiv:1909.03012 (2019)
4. Baroni, P., Caminada, M., Giacomin, M.: An introduction to argumentation semantics. Knowl. Eng. Rev. **26**(4), 365–410 (2011)
5. Bell, A., Solano-Kamaiko, I., Nov, O., Stoyanovich, J.: It's just not that simple: an empirical study of the accuracy-explainability trade-off in machine learning for public policy. In: 2022 ACM Conference on Fairness, Accountability, and Transparency, pp. 248–266 (2022)
6. Bhatt, U., Andrus, M., Weller, A., Xiang, A.: Machine learning explainability for external stakeholders. arXiv preprint arXiv:2007.05408 (2020)
7. Carroll, J.M., Olson, J.R.: Mental models in human-computer interaction. Handbook of Human-Computer Interaction, pp. 45–65 (1988)

8. Cawsey, A.: Planning interactive explanations. Int. J. Man Mach. Stud. **38**(2), 169–199 (1993)

9. Cugny, R., Aligon, J., Chevalier, M., Roman Jimenez, G., Teste, O.: AutoXAI: a framework to automatically select the most adapted XAI solution. In: Proceedings of the 31st ACM International Conference on Information & Knowledge Management, pp. 315–324 (2022)

10. Dietz, E., Kakas, A., Michael, L.: Argumentation: a calculus for human-centric AI. Front. Artif. Intell. **5**, 955579 (2022)

11. Dung, P.M.: On the acceptability of arguments and its fundamental role in non-monotonic reasoning, logic programming and n-person games. Artif. Intell. **77**(2), 321–357 (1995)

12. Ehn, P.: Scandinavian design: on participation and skill. In: Participatory Design, pp. 41–77. CRC Press (2017)

13. Ehsan, U., Riedl, M.O.: Human-centered explainable AI: towards a reflective sociotechnical approach. In: Stephanidis, C., Kurosu, M., Degen, H., Reinerman-Jones, L. (eds.) HCII 2020. LNCS, vol. 12424, pp. 449–466. Springer, Cham (2020). https://doi.org/10.1007/978-3-030-60117-1_33

14. Ehsan, U., et al.: Human-centered explainable AI (HCXAI): beyond opening the black-box of AI. In: CHI Conference on Human Factors in Computing Systems Extended Abstracts, pp. 1–7 (2022)

15. Friedman, B., Kahn, P.H., Borning, A., Huldtgren, A.: Value sensitive design and information systems. In: Doorn, N., Schuurbiers, D., van de Poel, I., Gorman, M.E. (eds.) Early engagement and new technologies: Opening up the laboratory. PET, vol. 16, pp. 55–95. Springer, Dordrecht (2013). https://doi.org/10.1007/978-94-007-7844-3_4

16. Gebru, T., et al.: Datasheets for datasets. Commun. ACM **64**(12), 86–92 (2021)

17. Guidotti, R., Monreale, A., Ruggieri, S., Turini, F., Giannotti, F., Pedreschi, D.: A survey of methods for explaining black box models. ACM Comput. Surv. **51**(5), 1–42 (2018)

18. He, X., Zhao, K., Chu, X.: AutoML: a survey of the state-of-the-art. Knowl.-Based Syst. **212**, 106622 (2021)

19. Kakas, A., Michael, L.: Abduction and argumentation for explainable machine learning: a position survey. arXiv preprint arXiv:2010.12896 (2020)

20. Kaur, H., Nori, H., Jenkins, S., Caruana, R., Wallach, H., Wortman Vaughan, J.: Interpreting interpretability: understanding data scientists' use of interpretability tools for machine learning. In: Proceedings of the 2020 CHI Conference on Human Factors in Computing Systems, pp. 1–14 (2020)

21. Lakkaraju, H., Slack, D., Chen, Y., Tan, C., Singh, S.: Rethinking explainability as a dialogue: a practitioner's perspective. arXiv preprint arXiv:2202.01875 (2022)

22. Lundberg, S.M., Lee, S.I.: A unified approach to interpreting model predictions. In: Advances in Neural Information Processing Systems, vol. 30 (2017)

23. Markus, A.F., Kors, J.A., Rijnbeek, P.R.: The role of explainability in creating trustworthy artificial intelligence for health care: a comprehensive survey of the terminology, design choices, and evaluation strategies. J. Biomed. Inform. **113**, 103655 (2021). https://doi.org/10.1016/j.jbi.2020.103655, https://www.sciencedirect.com/science/article/pii/S1532046420302835

24. Miller, T.: Explanation in artificial intelligence: insights from the social sciences. Artif. Intell. **267**, 1–38 (2019)

25. Mitchell, M., et al.: Model cards for model reporting. In: Proceedings of the Conference on Fairness, Accountability, and Transparency, pp. 220–229 (2019)

26. Molnar, C.: Interpretable Machine Learning, 2 edn (2022). https://christophm. github.io/interpretable-ml-book
27. Mothilal, R.K., Sharma, A., Tan, C.: Explaining machine learning classifiers through diverse counterfactual explanations. In: Proceedings of the 2020 Conference on Fairness, Accountability, and Transparency, pp. 607–617 (2020)
28. Munn, M., Pitman, D.: Explainable AI for Practitioners. O'Reilly Media Inc, California (2022)
29. Noël, V., Kakas, A.: GORGIAS-C: extending argumentation with constraint solving. In: Erdem, E., Lin, F., Schaub, T. (eds.) LPNMR 2009. LNCS (LNAI), vol. 5753, pp. 535–541. Springer, Heidelberg (2009). https://doi.org/10.1007/978-3-642-04238-6_54
30. Ribeiro, M.T., Singh, S., Guestrin, C.: "why should i trust you?" explaining the predictions of any classifier. In: Proceedings of the 22nd ACM SIGKDD International Conference on Knowledge Discovery and Data Mining, pp. 1135–1144 (2016)
31. Slack, D., Hilgard, S., Jia, E., Singh, S., Lakkaraju, H.: Fooling lime and shap: adversarial attacks on post hoc explanation methods. In: Proceedings of the AAAI/ACM Conference on AI, Ethics, and Society, pp. 180–186 (2020)
32. Spanoudakis, N.I., Gligoris, G., Kakas, A.C., Koumi, A.: Gorgias cloud: on-line explainable argumentation. In: System demonstration at the 9th International Conference on Computational Models of Argument (COMMA 2022) (2022)
33. Thimm, M.: Strategic argumentation in multi-agent systems. KI-Künstliche Intelligenz **28**(3), 159–168 (2014)
34. Vassiliades, A., Papadimitriou, I., Bassiliades, N., Patkos, T.: Visual Gorgias: a mechanism for the visualization of an argumentation dialogue. In: 25th Pan-Hellenic Conference on Informatics, pp. 149–154 (2021)
35. Weiner, J.: Blah, a system which explains its reasoning. Artif. Intell. **15**(1–2), 19–48 (1980)

EcoShap: Save Computations by only Calculating Shapley Values for Relevant Features

Parisa Jamshidi[ID], Sławomir Nowaczyk[(✉)][ID], and Mahmoud Rahat[ID]

Center for Applied Intelligent Systems Research (CAISR), Halmstad University,
Halmstad, Sweden
{parisa.jamshidi,slawomir.nowaczyk,mahmoud.rahat}@hh.se

Abstract. One of the most widely adopted approaches for eXplainable
Artificial Intelligence (XAI) involves employing of Shapley values (SVs)
to determine the relative importance of input features. While based on
a solid mathematical foundation derived from cooperative game theory,
SVs have a significant drawback: high computational cost. Calculating
the exact SV is an NP-hard problem, necessitating the use of approximations, particularly when dealing with more than twenty features. On
the other hand, determining SVs for all features is seldom necessary
in practice; users are primarily interested in the most important ones
only. This paper introduces the Economic Hierarchical Shapley values
(ecoShap) method for calculating SVs for the most crucial features only,
with reduced computational cost. EcoShap iteratively expands disjoint
groups of features in a tree-like manner, avoiding the expensive computations for the majority of less important features. Our experimental
results across eight datasets demonstrate that the proposed technique
efficiently identifies top features; at a 50% reduction in computational
costs, it can determine between three and seven of the most important
features.

Keywords: Feature Importance · Shapley Value · Explainable
Artificial Intelligence (XAI)

1 Introduction

In recent years, researchers are increasingly focusing on explaining machine
learning models due to their ever-growing practical applications in industry,
business, society, healthcare, and justice. Especially in safety-critical systems, it
is essential to be able to interpret the output of a prediction model correctly. This
builds trust among users, allows humans to understand the machine's decision-
making process, and provides insight into the model's potential enhancements
[1–3]. Among many diverse approaches to XAI, including feature importance,
prototype explanations, rule-based systems, counterfactual analysis, and model
distillation [4–6], explanations based on feature importance are arguably the
most popular.

© The Author(s) 2024
S. Nowaczyk et al. (Eds.): ECAI 2023 Workshops, CCIS 1947, pp. 24–42, 2024.
https://doi.org/10.1007/978-3-031-50396-2_2

It is so because feature importance provides a straightforward and intuitive understanding and enables a deeper comprehension of the relationship between input features and prediction targets. This approach can increase transparency and build trust in the model by highlighting the most important features, especially for users without a technical background. It can also help data scientists identify and revise biased, irrelevant, or redundant features, improving model accuracy and reducing overfitting. Finally, only with humans understanding how and why ML made its decisions can AI provide knowledge discovery through actionable and robust insights exploiting super-human performance achievable in some tasks. Generally, feature importance scores are used to assess the influence each input feature has on a particular model predicting a specific variable. The fact that they are often easier to understand than other XAI techniques makes them a popular choice for many users [7–9].

Among the different approaches to feature importance, those based on cooperative game theory (CGT) have gained recognition in recent years. In contrast to other approaches, CGT concepts are axiomatically motivated. An example of this type of solution is the Shapley value (SV), built on a very strong theoretical foundation and characterized by fairness, symmetry, and efficiency [10]. However, computing the SV is NP-hard; even with significant progress related to calculating approximate Shapley values [11], the computational complexity still limits potential usage areas [12].

In this paper, we propose a method to calculate a limited number of the highest Shapley values, instead of all of them, in significantly reduced time. The solution builds on a recent idea introduced by [13], where SVs are calculated for a group of features instead of one feature at a time. We exploit the (typically assumed to hold) superadditivity property and the lower computational cost associated with calculating SVs for groups of features at once. This way, our approach allows calculating SVs for the most important features at a fraction of the cost (across eight popular ML datasets, we can always find the single most important feature in 30% of the calculations; and in half of the time, we can compute from three to seven highest ranked features).

The idea is motivated by the notion that, in most applications, only a select few of the most important features warrant in-depth analysis; the SVs for all the others are of little value. The primary goal for the user is to evaluate the impact a specific input feature has on predicting the target variable; thus, the explanations should highlight critical features and facilitate relative comparisons among them. SVs for low-importance features are rarely needed. In practice, simply not being among the top ones conveys sufficient information. Let us consider the three specific examples of uses of explanations mentioned earlier.

First, XAI increases transparency and fosters trust in the model. This is typically achieved by comparing the user's (human expert's) expectations against the ML model's internal mechanisms. Trust is undermined when the model disregards features deemed important or assign considerable weight to features known to be irrelevant. Clearly, both of these scenarios can be identified based on SVs for the most important features. While a user may have intuitions concerning the relative significance of key features (e.g., that the top feature should be at least twice as important as the second one), it is difficult to envision similar phenomena for the lowest-ranked features. The second use of XAI involves model debugging and enhancement. Virtually all actions in this context can be carried out based on SVs for the top features as well. For instance, by dropping irrelevant features, a model can be simplified and made computationally cheaper – but precise SVs are not needed, only information regarding which features fall outside of the retained range. Another enhancement technique entails increasing the quality of key features, by allocating additional preprocessing and cleaning efforts where they yield the most benefit – on the highest-ranked features. Finally, knowledge creation or discovery of insights is, essentially, the opposite of trust building. It relies on finding discrepancies between the model's operation and expert understanding. Specifically, in cases where the model outperforms the human, these discrepancies are discovery opportunities. Both unexpectedly high-importance features and those with unexpectedly low importance are valuable in this context – and both can be efficiently detected using ecoShap.

The remainder of the paper is organized as follows. In Sect. 2, we first present the background of this work in terms of Shapley values in the ML setting, the assumptions made, and the proposed method. In Sect. 3, we cover the experimental setting and dataset that was used. In Sect. 4, we present some computational results of the experiments and finish the paper with some conclusions and future works.

2 Methodology

2.1 Background

Lloyd Shapley introduced one of the most influential solution concepts in cooperative games, now referred to as the Shapley value [14]. When a group of players agrees to cooperate, the SV helps determine a fair payoff for each individual, considering that each player may have contributed to varying extents.

Although extensively studied from a theoretical standpoint, calculating the SV is an NP-hard problem [15]. Due to its strong theoretical properties, the SV has emerged as a favored explanation method for black-box models. Considerable efforts have been dedicated to approximate the SVs in cases where exact solutions are impractical. Nevertheless, even with those approximations, employing SVs for larger datasets continues to pose significant computational challenges.

Shapley Values. In a cooperative game, SVs are formally defined as a fair way to distribute payoffs to players according to their marginal contributions. The Shapley value ϕ_i^{Sh} for player i is calculated as follows:

$$\phi_i^{Sh}(v) = \sum_{S \subseteq N \setminus \{i\}} \frac{|S|! \, (|N| - |S| - 1)!}{|N|!} \Big(v\big(S \cup \{i\}\big) - v(S) \Big), \qquad (1)$$

where N is a set of all players, S is a partial coalition, and $v(S)$ is the payoff (sometimes referred to as value or worth) created by coalition $S \subseteq N$ (so-called "characteristic function"). This formula computes the average marginal contribution of player i over all possible orderings of the players.

In recent years, SVs have been widely adopted in various machine learning settings, including explainable machine learning, feature selection, data valuation, multi-agent reinforcement learning, and ensemble model evaluation, all of which have specific cooperative game formulations, see for example [16,17]. In this paper, we are particularly interested in using SVs to find the most important features in supervised machine learning problems, so we formulate cooperative games based on that setting. In principle, though, the core idea of the proposed approach could be extended to most, if not all, other formulations as well.

Let $\mathcal{D} = \left\{ (\boldsymbol{x}^i, y^i) \,|\, i = 1 : M \right\}$ be a dataset, where the target variable y can be either categorical or continuous for classification or regression, respectively. Each instance $\boldsymbol{x}_i \in \mathcal{R}^n$ is described by n features $\boldsymbol{F} = [f_1, \cdots, f_n]$, and $\mathcal{A} : \mathcal{R}^n \to y$ is a black box model to predict the outputs.

Let $v(S) = g(y^i, \hat{y}^i)$, where $g(\cdot)$ is the goodness of fit function, y^i is the ground truth and $\hat{y}^i = \mathcal{A}^S(\boldsymbol{x}^i)$ is the target predicted by $\mathcal{A}^S$, namely the model trained on a subset of features $S \subseteq \boldsymbol{F}$. The ϕ_i^{Sh} is SV of a single feature i, calculated according to Eq. 1. Then, ϕ_G^{Sh} is SV of a group of features G, where $G \subseteq \boldsymbol{F}$. To calculate ϕ_G^{Sh}, we consider all features in G as a single unit:

$$\phi_G^{Sh}(v) = \sum_{S \subseteq F \setminus G} \frac{|S|! \, (|F| - |S| - |G|)!}{(|F| - |G|)!} \Big(v(S \cup G) - v(S) \Big). \qquad (2)$$

As can be seen from Eq. 2, calculating ϕ_G^{Sh} for $|G| \gg 1$ is significantly faster than ϕ_i^{Sh} from Eq. 1. Since coalitions are elements of the power set of $N \setminus \{G\}$, the power set of remaining players would therefore have much fewer elements when calculating the SV of a group than a single feature. The larger the group of players G is, the fewer elements in the power set and the fewer model evaluations are required according to Eq. 2.

2.2   EcoShap Assumptions

Intuitively, the Shapley value of a feature represents the extent of the contribution made by that feature to the machine learning model. SV for a group of features captures the combined contribution of all these features together. As a result, it is reasonable to expect that the SV for a set of features will be at least as high as the individual SVs of each of those features.

Incorporating additional features does not diminish the performance of an optimal machine learning model. An ideal model should be able to discern features that negatively affect the result and disregard them. In practice, of course, less robust machine learning algorithms fall prey to spurious features and overfit. However, with a sufficiently powerful model, one can expect that the introduction of more features will either cause the SV of the group to increase or maintain its current level.

Algorithm 1. EcoShap Algorithm

Require:
    F - list of all features
    K - the number of most important features wants to find
Ensure:
    Top features - The top K most important features
1: *Top features* $\leftarrow$ []
2: $G^* \leftarrow [F]$
3: $\mathcal{G} \leftarrow [G^*]$
4: $count_k \leftarrow 0$
5: **while** $count_k < K$ **do**
6:     **if** $len(G^*) == 1$ **then**
7:         *Top features*$[count_k] \leftarrow G^*$
8:         $count_k += 1$
9:     **else**
10:       $G_1, G_2 \leftarrow Divide(G^*)$
11:       Calculate $\phi_{G_1}^{Sh}, \phi_{G_2}^{Sh}$
12:       $\mathcal{G}.add(G_1)$
13:       $\mathcal{G}.add(G_2)$
14:     **end if**
15:     $\mathcal{G}.remove(G^*)$
16:     $G^* \leftarrow$ The member of $\mathcal{G}$ with the highest SV
17: **end while**
18: **Return** *Top features*

This corresponds to an assumption of the superadditive characteristic function. Formally, if S and T are disjoint coalitions players ($S \cap T = \varnothing$), then

$$v(G_1 \cup G_2) \geq v(G_1) + v(G_2). \tag{3}$$

It means the value of two disjoint coalitions working together is at least as big as when they work separately. Of course, in game theory, superadditivity is not required for many coalition games; however, it seems natural for the machine learning formulation. From the above directly follows the following constraint:

$$v(G) \geq \max_{f_i \in G} v(f_i). \tag{4}$$

Thus, if we calculate SV for a group of features G, and it is lower than some "threshold of interest", there is no need to calculate individual SVs for any of the $f_i \in G$ since no feature in that group can be "good enough".

2.3 EcoShap Algorithm

Our proposed approach follows the binary search tree idea. First, we intuitively describe how to find the single most important feature. We then generalize the approach to more features in ecoShap Algorithm 1.

In the first step, the set of all features F is randomly split into two disjoint subsets of equal sizes, G_1 and G_2. Given that we can identify which of these two subsets contains the most important feature f^*, then – by ignoring the other subset – we would be able to find f^*, recursively, in $log_2|F|$ steps by splitting one of the groups until we reach a leaf, i.e., a group comprising just one feature.

In the general case, of course, it is not possible to (efficiently) determine that with absolute certainty. However, it is easy to determine which branch is more likely to contain the most important feature(s) based on the SV of each group. As mentioned in Sect. 2.2, a group has a value greater than or equal to the maximum value of the features belonging to that group. Thus, we calculate SV for each of the two groups. Let us assume that the first subgroup has value $\phi_{G_1}^{Sh}$ and the second has value $\phi_{G_2}^{Sh}$, and without loss of generality $\phi_{G_1}^{Sh} < \phi_{G_2}^{Sh}$.

We can then suppose that G_2 contains f^* and select that one to split first. Nevertheless, we store G_1 in a priority queue called $\mathcal{G}$, in case we need to revisit it later. Generally, we expect that f^* belongs to the group with the highest SV among all the already evaluated groups. We call it G^*, and in each step, G^* will split into two disjoint groups.

Continuing our example, if at some point we reach a state where $\phi_{G_1}^{Sh}$ is the largest SV, we will "backtrack" and split it as well. Since there is no upper bound on the SV of a group, it is conceivable that a number of individually weak features combine into a powerful impact on the model. While somewhat harmful to the computational performance of our algorithm, this backtracking procedure guarantees such phenomena do not affect the correctness – and they happen relatively rarely in practice, according to the experimental evaluation.

We repeat such splitting of G^* until we find the single feature f_i. As long as f_i has the highest value among all the unexpanded nodes in the current tree (please note that we do not need to evaluate this over all the leaves of the fully-expanded tree), we can be sure that f_i has a higher SV than the features belonging to the other leaves. Therefore, it is the most important feature, i.e., $f_i = f^*$. For clarity, this example is visualized in Fig. 1.

$$f_i \equiv f^*, \quad if \quad \forall_{G \in \mathcal{G}} \quad \phi_{f_i}^{Sh} > \phi_G^{Sh}. \tag{5}$$

After finding the single feature f^* with the highest Shapley value ϕ_*^{Sh}, we can identify the next-in-line G^* on the remainder of the tree. This is the group that should be expanded next. As before, while there is no guarantee that it contains the second-best feature, we also cannot exclude that possibility. And whenever we find a single feature with the second-highest value among all leaves, we can be sure that it is the second-important feature.

Overall, whenever we find a single feature with a higher value than all the remaining groups within the $\mathcal{G}$ at any point in the search, we can be sure that this feature is more important than all the "yet unexplored" features, allowing us to efficiently calculate an arbitrary number of SVs.

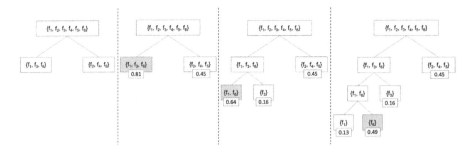

Fig. 1. A raw example of using ecoShap to find the most important feature(f_6) among the six features.

3 Experiments

3.1 Datasets

We used eight well-known machine learning datasets of moderate size for the experiments. Four variants are very similar to each other, corresponding to data of Wave Energy Converters from four different cities. This allows us to compare the behavior of ecoShap on datasets with consistent characteristics. Note that we remove all categorical features from all datasets to avoid the arbitrary choice of encoding. An overview of the datasets used can be found in Table 1.

Table 1. Summary of datasets

Datasets	Abbreviation	#features	#Instances
House Price[a]	HP	36	1460
Wave Energy Converters from Sydney[b] [18]	WEC_A	48	72000
Wave Energy Converters from Adelaide[b] [18]	WEC_P	48	72000
Wave Energy Converters from Perth[b] [18]	WEC_S	48	72000
Wave Energy Converters from Tasmania[b] [18]	WEC_T	48	72000
Online News Popularity[b] [19]	ONP	59	39797
Superconductivity Data[b] [20]	SC	81	21263
Year Prediction on MSD[b] [18]	MSD	90	515345

[a] https://www.kaggle.com/
[b] https://archive.ics.uci.edu/ml/index.php

We intentionally selected relatively small datasets for the experimental evaluation to more clearly illustrate the behavior near the budget threshold. In practice, ecoShap is especially well-suited for datasets with hundreds or thousands of features, where "classical" Shapley approaches are infeasible. More formally, the complexity of ecoShap grows logarithmically with the number of features, whereas existing methods require a linear number of SV computations.

3.2   Baseline Shapley Value

All experiments were conducted using our custom Python[1] implementation of the Monte Carlo permutation method (MCshap) to approximate SVs. The implementation permits the approximation of the SV for either a single feature or a group of features, utilizing the same core algorithm. Given that the concept of calculating SVs for groups of features is relatively novel, we are not aware of any existing implementation that offers such versatility.

The MCshap method involves randomly permuting the feature values based on a subset of the training set, known as the "background," and computing the difference in model predictions with and without the feature under evaluation. As ML models are trained with all features, directly excluding a feature during prediction is impossible. The permutation simulates such exclusion by replacing actual values with random values from the background samples. It effectively disrupts any existing meaningful patterns while preserving the structure of the data. The global SV for any feature is determined by repeating the above procedure for multiple test instances and calculating the mean absolute value. Consequently, the SV depends not only on the feature itself, but also on the test and background instances used in the computations.

3.3   Experimental Setup

To assess the global feature importance, ecoShap requires a trained model, a test set, and background data. The datasets have been randomly divided into training (75%) and testing (25%) sets, except for the MSD dataset, in which the train and test split is predefined. Two models, namely, Extreme Gradient Boosting (XGBoost[2]) [21] and Random Forest Regression[3]) [22], have been trained on each dataset. To estimate the global SV, we randomly select 100 data points as the test set and 100 data points as the background from the test set and training set, respectively.

We use ecoShap and MCshap to find different numbers of important features, repeating every experiment 50 times on each dataset. It is worth mentioning that both models performed similarly, though, for brevity, only the result of XGB is reported.

As mentioned in Sect. 2.1, calculating the SV is an NP-hard problem. Computing the exact SV for real-world datasets, particularly those with more than 20–25 features, is infeasible [15], and the lack of ground truth presents a significant challenge.

Therefore, we compare against the MCshap baseline to demonstrate that the ecoShap method does not introduce significant additional errors, beyond those inherent in the Monte Carlo approximation. We used MCshap 50 times to approximate the SVs of each dataset and considered their average as an SV of each feature. We refer to these values as close-to-ground-truth and use them to evaluate the ecoShap.

---

[1] https://www.python.org/.

[2] https://github.com/dmlc/xgboost.

[3] https://scikit-learn.org/stable/modules/generated/sklearn.ensemble.RandomFores tRegressor.html.

4   Results

In this section, we showcase the results of experiments that emphasize the advantages of the ecoShap method. We start by illustrating the computational efficiency of the ecoShap and explore how different dataset characteristics influence its performance. Finally, we verify the precision of the ecoShap results by comparing them to the baseline MCshap method.

4.1   Measuring Computational Efficiency of EcoShap

The initial experiment aims to demonstrate the computational effectiveness of the proposed ecoShap method in identifying the most important features. Specifically, we investigate the relationship between the computational cost and the number of highest-ranked features found. The findings for two representative datasets (MSD and SC) are presented in Fig. 2, while comprehensive results for all datasets can be found in Figs. 5 and 6.

The most straightforward way to compare the two methods is the number of times they need to call the SV function. Clearly, MCshap needs to calculate SV for all features and then sort them; thus, even to find the single most important feature, MCshap must call the SV function as many times as there are features. In contrast, ecoShap uses significantly fewer calls to identify the first feature, but computing SV for additional features incurs an extra cost. The leftmost panels of Fig. 2 illustrate (top one for MSD and bottom for SC datasets) the number of times each method calls the SV function (y-axis) to find the required number of important features (x-axis). The intersection of the blue line (corresponding to ecoShap) with the horizontal red line (MCshap) represents the break-even point for the proposed method, signifying that fewer function calls are required to calculate SVs for that many top features.

It is worth noting, though, that the ecoShap method often considers a group of features as a single entity for calculating SV; and somewhat counterintuitively, the computational cost for a group is smaller than for a single feature(see Sect. 2.2). Consequently, considering both a group and a single feature as a unit of computation underestimates the computational benefits of the ecoShap method.

To achieve a fairer comparison, therefore, we examine the time required by each method. A direct comparison of the time consumption reveals that the advantage of the ecoShap approach over MCshap is even more pronounced. As indicated in the middle panels of Fig. 2 (labeled b1 and b2), ecoShap discovers even more features up to the intersection point, confirming that the number of SV function calls is biased. However, measuring time directly introduces experimental uncertainties, particularly in an environment with shared resources, and creates undesired correlations with specific hardware, making future comparisons more challenging.

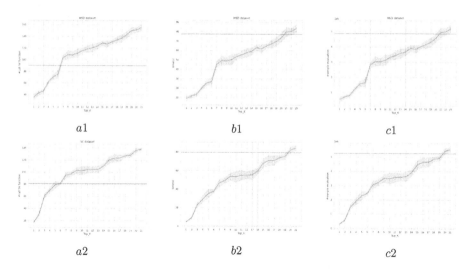

Fig. 2. Comparing MCshap (red line) and ecoShap (blue line) in terms of *a*) the number of calls to the SV function, *b*) computation time, and *c*) the number of samples evaluated; per number of features to discover, for the MSD (top) and SC (bottom) datasets. (Color figure online)

Consequently, as a final and most equitable comparison, we propose using the total number of sample evaluations by the ML model across the whole SV calculation process. Since estimating the SV for a group of features requires fewer permutations and fewer sample evaluations than for a single feature, this metric provides a more comprehensive and fair assessment. These findings are shown in the far-right panels of Fig. 2 (labeled c1 and c2). When comparing subfigures b1 against c1 and b2 against c2, the fidelity of the number of sample evaluations is superior to the SV function calls and is more reliable than direct time measurements.

4.2   EcoShap Performance on Budget

The first experiment focused on comparing the time efficiency of ecoShap and MCshap using different evaluation metrics. In this section, we explore how many top-ranked features ecoShap can calculate SVs for, while still conserving computations in comparison to MCshap. To this end, we consider the MCshap computational costs to be the "full budget." Table 2 shows the number of features that ecoShap can identify by allocating different percentages of the budget (from 10% to 100%) for each of the eight datasets.

Likewise, we are also interested in determining the amount of budget necessary to identify various numbers of important features. Table 3 illustrates the percentage of computations (MCshap full budget) required to find between one and ten most important features for each of the eight datasets.

Table 2. The average number of features found based on the budget percentage

Budget Percentage	Dataset							
	HP	WEC_A	WEC_P	WEC_S	WEC_T	ONP	SC	MSD
10%	0.18	0.0	0.0	0.0	0.0	0.12	1.18	0.42
20%	1.32	0.0	0.0	0.0	0.0	1.04	2.0	3.02
30%	2.18	0.22	0.38	0.18	0.22	2.16	2.6	4.32
40%	3.24	1.8	2.1	1.52	1.64	4.54	3.9	5.98
50%	4.44	3.44	4.3	3.08	3.74	7.1	5.64	6.02
60%	5.46	5.64	7.12	5.82	6.22	8.94	7.58	7.54
70%	6.68	8.14	10.24	9.14	8.96	11.86	11.98	11.4
80%	8.2	12.5	12.5	12.9	11.8	15.04	14.28	15.26
90%	10.7	15.76	15.4	15.22	14.76	18.88	17.06	18.52
100%	13.68	16.6	15.98	16.26	16.14	24.18	19.18	19.64

These experiments demonstrate that ecoShap can always identify the top three most important features by using up to half of the budget, often much less. In some instances, it can discover as many as seven of the most significant features at half of the budget. These experiments demonstrate the computational advantages of ecoShap in identifying essential features with a limited budget.

4.3   Dataset Characteristics

Interestingly, there is a noticeable variation in the results across different datasets. This is evident even in the simplest scenario, where the objective is to find the first most important feature. In some datasets, ecoShap can discover the top feature by spending less than 10% of the budget, while in others, it requires more than 35% of the budget.

This relation between each dataset's features SV pattern and the budget used by ecoShap can be explained based on the algorithm's design. EchoShap can find the most important feature faster when the SV of the first feature is significantly higher than those of the remaining features. For instance, in the case of the SC dataset, ecoShap identified the first important feature with as little as 5% of the budget – because it has a notably higher SV than other features. The SV of the second feature is roughly half that of the first one. In contrast, the SV of the first sixteen significant features of the WEC_T dataset are all very similar to each other, and ecoShap expended more than 35% of the budget to identify the first one.

Intuitively, the more similar the SVs are, the more budget ecoShap will need to recognize the order of features. This phenomenon is a result of the ecoShap algorithm, which partitions feature groups based on their SV values. When the SV of the first important feature, f^*, is significantly higher than that of other features, it strongly impacts the SV of its group. Thus, any group it is placed

Table 3. The mean and (std) of the budget rate were used to find the first to the tenth important features in eight datasets.

Top features	Datasets							
	HP	WEC_A	WEC_P	WEC_S	WEC_T	ONP	SC	MSD
Top 1	0.1139	0.3457	0.3466	0.3465	0.3676	0.1295	0.0566	0.1024
	(0.0201)	(0.0614)	(0.0754)	(0.0503)	(0.0635)	(0.0256)	(0.0108)	(0.0195)
Top 2	0.2098	0.4264	0.4033	0.4268	0.3792	0.27	0.1159	0.1519
	(0.0291)	(0.0702)	(0.0708)	(0.0684)	(0.0628)	(0.0474)	(0.0178)	(0.0213)
Top 3	0.3377	0.4292	0.4107	0.4479	0.4456	0.3334	0.288	0.1625
	(0.0421)	(0.0696)	(0.073)	(0.0702)	(0.0754)	(0.0484)	(0.0366)	(0.0232)
Top 4	0.4291	0.4717	0.4613	0.5716	0.4991	0.3504	0.3682	0.239
	(0.0538)	(0.0777)	(0.0682)	(0.0717)	(0.0711)	(0.0484)	(0.0356)	(0.0314)
Top 5	0.5101	0.5884	0.4972	0.5765	0.5163	0.3807	0.4477	0.3187
	(0.0577)	(0.0737)	(0.0608)	(0.0725)	(0.0709)	(0.0454)	(0.0431)	(0.0328)
Top 6	0.6744	0.6211	0.5147	0.5817	0.6019	0.4309	0.4823	0.3255
	(0.0782)	(0.0701)	(0.0616)	(0.074)	(0.0783)	(0.0495)	(0.051)	(0.0348)
Top 7	0.6981	0.6345	0.6079	0.5928	0.6249	0.4616	0.5659	0.5964
	(0.0829)	(0.0692)	(0.0732)	(0.0709)	(0.0679)	(0.0513)	(0.0531)	(0.0538)
Top 8	0.7192	0.6615	0.6298	0.6084	0.6315	0.5245	0.6132	0.6187
	(0.0799)	(0.0724)	(0.069)	(0.0665)	(0.0673)	(0.0593)	(0.0483)	(0.0551)
Top 9	0.874	0.7218	0.642	0.6957	0.6743	0.6102	0.6222	0.637
	(0.0741)	(0.0607)	(0.0677)	(0.0717)	(0.0713)	(0.0605)	(0.0469)	(0.0574)
Top 10	0.8852	0.7466	0.7005	0.7299	0.7774	0.6304	0.6553	0.658
	(0.0801)	(0.0576)	(0.0712)	(0.0702)	(0.0763)	(0.0602)	(0.0529)	(0.0535)

into becomes G^* most of the time. As a result, the algorithm does not need to evaluate any other groups and can always split the group containing f^*. On the other hand, if multiple features share similar high SVs, ecoShap needs to analyze several unwanted groups, and finding f^* will require more SV calculations.

When considering more than just the top feature, the differences in slope in Fig. 3 can be similarly explained. For example, in the MSD dataset, there is a substantial increase in computational cost between the 5th and 6th features, which is much larger than that between the 4th and 5th features. A comparison with the corresponding SV plot (Fig. 4) reveals a more significant difference between the SVs of the 6th and 7th features than that between the 6th and 5th features.

4.4 Backtracking Cost

As discussed in Sect. 2.3, the proposed algorithm can backtrack when the wrong branch is chosen. In this experiment, we investigate ecoShap's backtrack ability. For simplicity, we limit ourselves to the single most important feature. We first compute the expected number of SV function calls required to identify the most

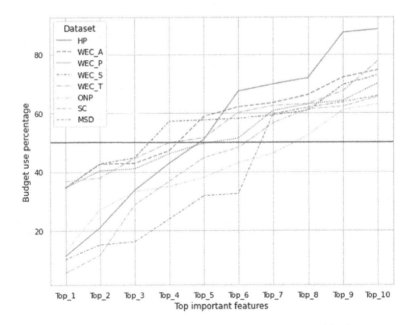

Fig. 3. The percentage of the budget used to find the first to the tenth important features in eight datasets. The red line indicates half of the budget. Each intersection of the red line with the other lines shows how many features ecoShap found by spending half of the budget across each dataset. (Color figure online)

significant feature, assuming the correct branch is always selected (i.e., an oracle is used). In Table 4, we then compare this to the mean number of calls made by ecoShap, for each dataset.

For example, the algorithm finds the first important feature of the HP dataset by calling the SV function close to 12 times while the expected value is 10.44). It shows that the algorithm almost always selects the branch containing the most important feature for the split. Meanwhile, the true number of calls for the WEC_T dataset exceeds the expected value by a factor of three. This indicates that the algorithm explored many incorrect branches before finding the first feature. These results are consistent with earlier findings and supported by Fig. 4.

4.5   The Accuracy of the EcoShap

As the final step, we consider the accuracy of the proposed method. In principle, given our assumptions, ecoShap should not introduce any error in the calculations. In practice, though, due to the stochastic nature of all the algorithms involved, there is a possibility of errors accumulating in unfavorable ways. This section aims to demonstrate that these effects are negligible.

Given that there is no definitive ground truth for the SVs, we compare ecoShap results with their close-to-ground-truth (CtGT) MCshap counterparts to demonstrate that our proposed method does not significantly deviate from its

Table 4. Expected versus actual number of SV function calls.

Dataset	#feature	Expected value	Mean number of calls
HP	36	10.44	11.52 ± 1.42
WEC_A	48	11.33	37.92 ± 3.67
WEC_P	48	11.34	38.76 ± 4.4
WEC_S	48	11.35	38.4 ± 3.27
WEC_T	48	11.36	39.76 ± 3.57
ONP	59	11.83	26.16 ± 2.94
SC	81	12.84	17.28 ± 1.64
MSD	90	13.16	35.04 ± 2.97

baseline in approximating SVs. We use the "features on the whole budget" (FoB) metric, which refers to the most important features that ecoShap can identify using the MCshap computational budget. As a measure of accuracy, we use the sum of absolute errors (SAE) of the FoB features, defined as:

$$SAE = \sum_{f \in FoB} |ecoShap(f) - CtGT(f)| \qquad (6)$$

Table 5. The mean and standard deviation of the SAE for each dataset.

Dataset	#feature	#FoB	SAE
HP	36	14	0.0011 ± 0.0002
WEC_A	48	17	0.0011 ± 0.0002
WEC_P	48	16	0.0010 ± 0.0002
WEC_S	48	16	0.0011 ± 0.0002
WEC_T	48	16	0.0010 ± 0.0002
ONP	59	24	0.0005 ± 0.0000
SC	81	19	0.0019 ± 0.0003
MSD	90	20	0.0934 ± 0.0171

Table 5 presents the mean and standard deviation of the SAE for each dataset, indicating that there is essentially no approximation error caused by ecoShap. For example, in the HP dataset, the sum of errors for 14 features is 0.0011, which is quite negligible.

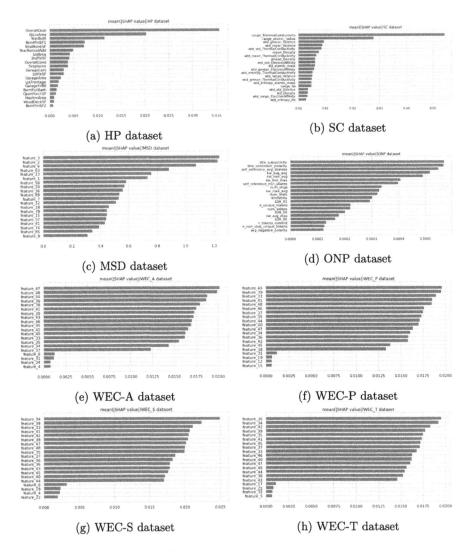

Fig. 4. Barplots of the mean |SHAP values| of the first 20 important features for eight datasets using the SHAP library

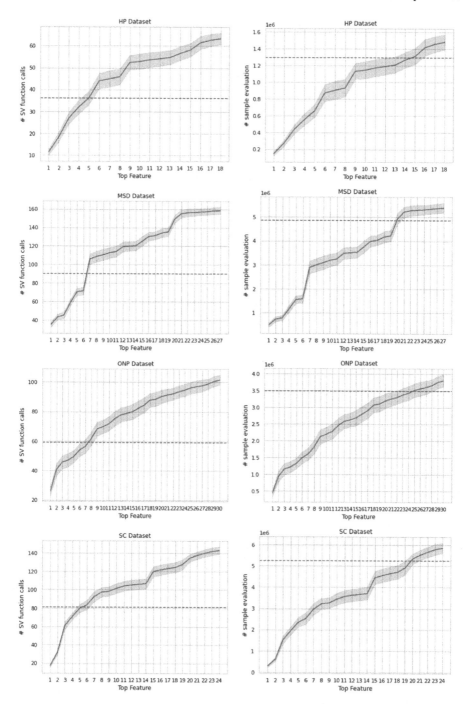

Fig. 5. Comparing MCshap (red line) and ecoShap (blue line) in terms of the number of calls to the SV function(left) and the number of samples evaluated(right); per the number of features to discover for HP, MSD, ONP, and SC datasets, respectively. (Color figure online)

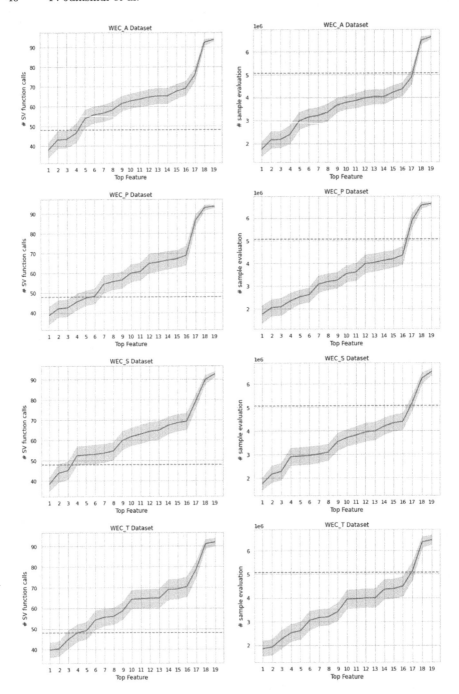

Fig. 6. Comparing MCshap (red line) and ecoShap (blue line) in terms of the number of calls to the SV function(left) and the number of samples evaluated(right); per the number of features to discover for WEC_A, WEC_P, WEC_S, and WEC_T datasets, respectively. (Color figure online)

5   Conclusion

In this paper, we introduced the Economic Hierarchical Shapley value (ecoShap) method, which efficiently identifies the most important features and calculates their Shapley values, with computational savings of up to 95%. By utilizing group-wise efficient computation of Shapley values in the early stages of the search process, ecoShap serves as a filter, bypassing the unnecessary calculation of Shapley values for less important individual features.

Our method can be used based on the desired number of important features or the computational budget. Experimental results indicate that ecoShap performs much better in datasets whose features are well separated and feature importance levels differ. Additionally, ecoShap has consistently identified between three and seven most important features across all evaluated datasets while using less than half of the available budget. To verify the accuracy of ecoShap, it was compared with the close-to-ground-truth results obtained from a baseline, demonstrating that there is no significant approximation error introduced.

It is worth noting that in the current version of ecoShap, features are randomly split into groups. One idea for future work is to develop more effective grouping approaches, for example, based on correlations, that will allow ecoShap to avoid unnecessary divisions and perform an even smarter search.

Acknowledgments. This work was partially supported by the CHIST-ERA grant CHIST-ERA-19-XAI-012, funded by the Swedish Research Council.

References

1. Doshi-Velez, F., Kim, B.: Towards a rigorous science of interpretable machine learning. arXiv preprint arXiv:1702.08608 (2017)
2. Lipton, Z.C.: The mythos of model interpretability: in machine learning, the concept of interpretability is both important and slippery. Queue **16**(3), 31–57 (2018)
3. Ribeiro, M.T., Singh, S., Guestrin, C.: " why should I trust you?" explaining the predictions of any classifier. In: Proceedings of the 22nd ACM SIGKDD International Conference on Knowledge Discovery and Data Mining, pp. 1135–1144 (2016)
4. Domingos, P.: A few useful things to know about machine learning. Commun. ACM **55**(10), 78–87 (2012)
5. Kusner, M.J., Loftus, J., Russell, C., Silva, R.: Counterfactual fairness. In: Advances in Neural Information Processing Systems, vol. 30 (2017)
6. Van Looveren, A., Klaise, J.: Interpretable counterfactual explanations guided by prototypes. In: Oliver, N., Pérez-Cruz, F., Kramer, S., Read, J., Lozano, J.A. (eds.) ECML PKDD 2021. LNCS (LNAI), vol. 12976, pp. 650–665. Springer, Cham (2021). https://doi.org/10.1007/978-3-030-86520-7_40
7. Ribeiro, M.T., Singh, S., Guestrin, C.: Model-agnostic interpretability of machine learning. arXiv preprint arXiv:1606.05386 (2016)
8. Sundararajan, M., Najmi, A.: The many shapley values for model explanation. In: International Conference on Machine Learning, pp. 9269–9278. PMLR (2020)
9. Karlaš, B., et al.: Data debugging with shapley importance over end-to-end machine learning pipelines. arXiv preprint arXiv:2204.11131 (2022)

10. Shapley, L.S., et al.: A Value for N-person Games: Princeton University Press, Princeton (1953)
11. Lundberg, S.M., Lee, S.-I.: A unified approach to interpreting model predictions. In: Advances in Neural Information Processing Systems, vol. 30 (2017)
12. Sundararajan, M., Dhamdhere, K., Agarwal, A.: The shapley taylor interaction index. In: International Conference on Machine Learning, pp. 9259–9268. PMLR (2020)
13. Harris, C., Pymar, R., Rowat, C.: Joint shapley values: a measure of joint feature importance. arXiv preprint arXiv:2107.11357 (2021)
14. Shapley, L.S.: "Notes on the n-person game – ii: the value of an n-person game," RAND Corporation, Santa Monica, Calif., Technical Report (1951)
15. Ancona, M., Oztireli, C., Gross, M.: Explaining deep neural networks with a polynomial time algorithm for shapley value approximation. In: International Conference on Machine Learning, pp. 272–281. PMLR (2019)
16. Rozemberczki, B., et al.: The shapley value in machine learning. arXiv preprint arXiv:2202.05594 (2022)
17. Wang, G.: Interpret federated learning with shapley values. arXiv preprint arXiv:1905.04519 (2019)
18. Dua, D., Graff, C.: UCI machine learning repository (2017). http://archive.ics.uci.edu/ml
19. Fernandes, K., Vinagre, P., Cortez, P.: A proactive intelligent decision support system for predicting the popularity of online news. In: Pereira, F., Machado, P., Costa, E., Cardoso, A. (eds.) EPIA 2015. LNCS (LNAI), vol. 9273, pp. 535–546. Springer, Cham (2015). https://doi.org/10.1007/978-3-319-23485-4_53
20. Hamidieh, K.: A data-driven statistical model for predicting the critical temperature of a superconductor. Comput. Mater. Sci. **154**, 346–354 (2018)
21. Chen, T., Guestrin, C.: Xgboost: a scalable tree boosting system. In: Proceedings of the 22nd ACM SIGKDD International Conference on Knowledge Discovery and Data Mining, pp. 785–794 (2016)
22. Geurts, P., Ernst, D., Wehenkel, L.: Extremely randomized trees. Mach. Learn. **63**, 3–42 (2006)

Evaluation of Human-Understandability of Global Model Explanations Using Decision Tree

Adarsa Sivaprasad[1]([✉]) [ID], Ehud Reiter[1] [ID], Nava Tintarev[2] [ID], and Nir Oren[1] [ID]

[1] Department of Computing Science, University of Aberdeen, Aberdeen, UK
{.sivaprasad.22,e.reiter,n.oren}@abdn.ac.uk
[2] Maastricht University, Maastricht, Netherlands
n.tintarev@maastrichtuniversity.nl

Abstract. In explainable artificial intelligence (XAI) research, the predominant focus has been on interpreting models for experts and practitioners. Model agnostic and local explanation approaches are deemed interpretable and sufficient in many applications. However, in domains like healthcare, where end users are patients without AI or domain expertise, there is an urgent need for model explanations that are more comprehensible and instil trust in the model's operations. We hypothesise that generating model explanations that are narrative, patient-specific and *global* (holistic of the model) would enable better understandability and enable decision-making. We test this using a decision tree model to generate both local and global explanations for patients identified as having a high risk of coronary heart disease. These explanations are presented to non-expert users. We find a strong individual preference for a specific type of explanation. The majority of participants prefer global explanations, while a smaller group prefers local explanations. A task based evaluation of mental models of these participants provide valuable feedback to enhance narrative global explanations. This, in turn, guides the design of health informatics systems that are both trustworthy and actionable.

Keywords: Global Explanation · End-user Understandability · Health Informatics

1 Introduction

The field of explainable artificial intelligence (XAI) has witnessed significant advancements, primarily focusing on the interpretability of models. However, the interpretability of an AI model for developers does not seamlessly translate into end-user interpretability [3]. Even inherently interpretable models like decision trees (DT) and decision lists are challenging to use in applications due to the complexity and scale of data. Hence popular explanation techniques interpret black box models by considering an individual input and corresponding prediction - *local explanations.* Model-agnostic explanations such as Shapley values

S. Nowaczyk et al. (Eds.): ECAI 2023 Workshops, CCIS 1947, pp. 43–65, 2024.
https://doi.org/10.1007/978-3-031-50396-2_3

and Local Interpretable Model-Agnostic Explanations (LIME) offer insights into the features contributing to an individual prediction, revealing the importance of specific characteristics in decision-making. Nevertheless, they do not capture the complete model functioning, comprehensive utilization of data, and, most importantly, the interactions among features. They lack the ability to facilitate generalization or provide a complete mental model of the system's workings.

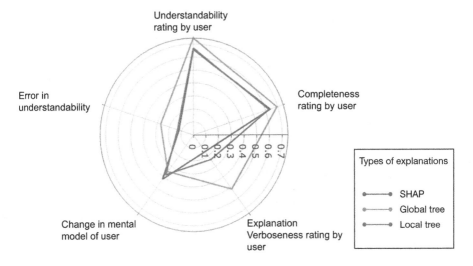

Fig. 1. A comparison of Local SHAP, Local and Global tree explanation of CHD risk prediction using decision tree model. Different evaluation parameters are computed based on end-user feedback of the explanation.

In critical domains such as healthcare and financial predictions, the interpretability of AI models by end-users holds significant importance. The understandability of the underlying AI model and the trust in its predictions can have life-altering implications for stakeholders. Enabling user intervention and action to modify predicted outcomes require explanations that address the *How* and *Why* questions, as well as convey causal relationships [18,21]. Achieving this necessitates an overall comprehension of the model. Further, the explanation should not only align the user's mental model with the AI system's model but also be perceived as understandable and trustworthy. We propose that a global model explanation hold greater potential for providing understandability and building trust compared to local model explanations. This study is a preliminary step towards testing this.

What qualifies as a global explanation and what methodologies would provide an overall understandability is relatively less researched. The comparison between global model explanations and local explanations for end users, along with various presentation aspects such as narrative and visualization, bears significance when building explanation-centric applications. This study delves into the understandability of local and global explanations, specifically in the context of a coronary heart prediction model. We address the following research question:

1. For non-expert users, do global explanations provide a better understanding of the AI's reasoning in comparison to (only) local explanations?
2. As the complexity of the explanation increases is there a difference in understandability and user preference for local and global explanations?

We use decision tree (DT) models which are interpretable by design, and construct local and global explanations with varying levels of complexity. We gauge the perceived understandability of these models and evaluate their effectiveness based on predefined tasks. We also measure the changes in users' mental models following exposure to the explanations. Figure 1 shows different evaluation parameters. The experiment identifies preferences in explanation types among different participant groups. It is found that while complexity does not have a significant effect on perceived understandability and completeness of explanation, errors in understanding increase with complexity. The obtained results offer valuable insights for designing narrative explanations for end-users and highlight the majority of participant preference for global explanations in healthcare risk models.

2   Related Work

In healthcare, a risk score is a quantifiable measure to predict aspects of a patient's care such as morbidity, the chance of response to treatment, cost of hospitalisation etc. Risk scoring is utilised for its predictive capabilities and in managing healthcare at scale. A predicted risk score is representative of the probability of an adverse outcome and the magnitude of its consequence. Article 22 of the General Data Protection Regulation (GDPR) mandates human involvement in automated decision-making and in turn understandability of a risk prediction model. Hence the use of risk scores requires the effective communication of these scores to all stakeholders - doctors, patients, hospital management, health regulators, insurance providers etc. With statistical and black-box AI models used in risk score computations, this is an added responsibility of the AI model developer to ensure the interpretability of these systems to all stakeholders.

Current regulations such as model fact tables [25] are useful for clinicians and approaches of local model interpretation [15,24] to model developers. For a non-expert end-user who has limited domain knowledge and who is not trained to understand a fact table, these approaches will not explain a recommendation given to them. Further, explaining a risk prediction model to the end user should address the perceived risk from numeric values and previous knowledge of the user, any preferences and biases. In other words, the explanation presentation should address socio-linguistic aspects [18] involved.

Researchers have recognized that a good explanation should aim to align the user's mental model with the mental model of the system, promoting faithful comprehension and reducing cognitive dissonance [18]. Achieving such effectiveness is very context-dependent [1]. However, aspects of explanation presentation generalise across a broad spectrum of applications. The significance of narrative-style explanations is emphasised by [23] while [26], highlights the effectiveness of a combined visual and narrative explanation. Recent studies have evaluated existing systems in use [6,16] and calls for focus on the design choices for explanation presentation in health informatics. Further, with tools available in the public domain such as QRisk[1] from National Health Service (NHS), evaluating the impact and actionability of explanation approaches in use would enable improving them and ensure their safe usage.

Before looking into evaluating black-box models, it would be worthwhile to explore what constitutes a good explanation in interpretable models such as DTs, decision lists [13] etc. DT algorithms are methods of approximating a discrete-valued target by recursively splitting the data into smaller subsets based on the features that are most *informative* for predicting the target. DTs can be interpreted as a tree or as a set of if-else rules which is a useful representation for human understanding. The most successful DT models like Classification and Regression Trees (CART) [5] and C4.5 [22] are greedy search algorithms. Finding DTs by optimising for say a fixed size, is NP-hard, with no polynomial-time approximation [9]. Modern algorithms have attempted this by enforcing constraints such as the independence of variables [10] or using all-purpose optimization toolboxes [2,4,27].

In [12] authors attempt the optimisation of the algorithm for model interpretability to derive decision lists. The reduced size of the rules opens up the option of interpreting the decisions in their entirety and not in the context of a specific input/output alone - a global explanation. The authors highlight the influence of complexity on the understandability of end-users. However, decision list algorithms still do not scale well for larger datasets. Optimal Sparse Decision Trees (OSDT) [8] and later improved with Generalized and Scalable Optimal Sparse Decision Trees (GOSDT) [14] algorithms produce optimal decision trees over a variety of objectives including F-score, AUC, and partial area under the ROC convex hull. GOSDT generates trees with a smaller number of nodes while maintaining accuracy on par with state-of-art models.

On explaining DTs for end-users, current studies have investigated local explanations using approaches such as counterfactuals [28], the integration of contextual information and identified narrative style textual explanations [17]. All these attempts to answer the *why* questions based on a few input features and specific to a particular input. Extending these insights to global explanations should help better understanding of the model by end-users and allow generalisation of the interpretations, driving actionability.

---

[1] https://qrisk.org/index.php.

3   Experiment Design

Our main research question is to determine what type of explanation are most relevant for non-expert end-users to be able to understand underlying risk model. We evaluate a local and global explanation by measuring user's perceived understanding and completeness. We also measure whether the user's mental model had changed after reading an explanation.

3.1   Dataset and Modeling

For the experiment, we used the Busselton dataset [11], which consists of 2874 patient records and information about whether they developed coronary heart disease (CHD) within ten years of the initial data collection. This study is similar to the data collected by NHS to develop QRISK3 [7]. Computing a risk score demands that we also explain the risk score, data used, probability measures of the scoring algorithm in addition to model prediction. We limit the scope of this study to only explaining the model prediction and use the CHD observation from the dataset as target variable for prediction. Using GOSDT [14] algorithm, we fit the data to obtain decision tress. GOSDT handles both categorical and continuous variables. While the optimum model may have multiple closeby splits for numeric values, such splits can reduce the readability of the tree. Hence we preprocess the data by converting most of the features into categorical variables. We follow the categories as mandated by National Health Service (NHS). The data is pre-processed as described in Appendix A, with 2669 records and 11 features.

The GOSDT algorithm generated a comprehensive decision tree for the dataset, comprising 19 leaf nodes at a depth of 5, achieving an accuracy of 90.9% (Fig. 4 in Appendix A). For the purpose of human evaluation and comparison of local and global explanations, it was necessary to have multiple DTs with comparable structures. Hence, we created subsets of the data by varying the ranges and combinations of *Age* and *Gender*. By working with reduced data points, the size of the constructed trees was significantly reduced. To ensure larger trees for evaluation purposes, we enforced a consistent depth of 4. Ultimately, we selected four trees for the evaluation task as shown in Table 1.

As mentioned in [20], a higher complexity of explanation rules in clinical setting leads to longer response times and decreased satisfaction with the explanations for end-user. The authors refer to unique variables within the rules as cognitive chunks, which contribute to complexity in understanding. In our experiment, global explanations naturally contain more cognitive chunks. To prevent bias in the results, we incorporated two levels of difficulty for each explanation type. The easy level consisted of trees with similar structures, both local and global, featuring 5 nodes and decision paths of equal length with an identical number of cognitive chunks. For ease of understanding, we henceforth refer to a particular combination of explanation type and difficulty level as a specific scenario, namely - local-easy, global-easy, local-hard, and global-hard. A local-SHAP explanation was generated utilizing the same tree as the local-easy scenario. We use kernel SHAP [15] to obtain feature importance for the local-easy tree for specific patient input. The SHAP explanation is treated as a baseline for evaluation.

The hard scenario for both explanation types, consist of larger trees of similar structures. The tree had 8 nodes for local-hard scenario and 9 nodes in case of global-hard scenario. For global explanations, the explanation presentation involves more cognitive chunks, potentially introducing bias by making the global-hard scenario challenging to comprehend. Nevertheless, we proceeded with evaluating this scenario in our experiment.

Another factor to consider when generating explanation is the possible contradiction between model explanation and general assumptions. For instance, a node *BMI = Normal* appearing in decision rules for low CHD risk is expected but not in those for high risk. Communicating this contradiction in explanation would be important in its understandability. We also include this in our experiment. Explanation scenarios categorized as hard involved contradictory explanations, which could prove more challenging for comprehension. We addressed these cases using semifactual [19] explanations, employing phrase *even-if*. We assess the impact of such risk narrations on understandability. Table 1 provides a summary of the four trees used for explanation generation.

Table 1. Description of DTs and type of explanation generated.

Age	Gender	Leaf count	Accuracy	Explanation Type
70–79	Female	6	78.4	Local Easy
60–84	Female	6	82.5	Global Easy
60–70	Male	9	77.3	Local Hard
65–70	male	10	85.4	Global Hard

3.2   Generation of Explanation

For a given CHD prediction model and a corresponding patient input, the local explanation is a set of necessary conditions and predicted decisions of high/low risk. For the decision tree model in Fig. 2a, given particular patient info as input, the decision rule that is triggered to predict high risk is highlighted in blue. The path followed for the decision can be represented textually as shown in Fig. 2b. This is one possible representation. A more natural language expression of the rule is treated as a local explanation for the experiment. The language generation is rule-based. Details of the generation algorithm and an example of the evaluated explanation are given in Appendix B.

The global tree explanation is a list of all the decision rules of the tree. For a particular patient, a combination of the global explanation and the specific rule triggered corresponding to the given patient input is treated as the global

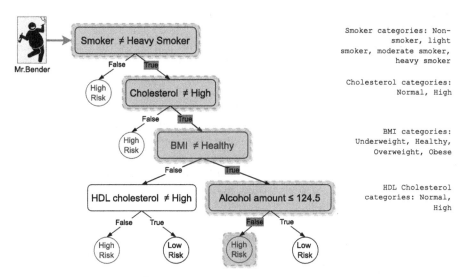

(a) The decision path followed along a given DT for a particular patient Mr Bender. The tree is learned from different categorical features of a patient dataset and the black square boxes represent decision nodes learned by the model. On the right, all the possible values of each feature are listed (except Alchohol amount which is numeric). This tree has 6 leaf nodes each a possible decision of *high* or *low risk*. For a given input corresponding to Mr Bender, the model predicts *high risk* following the decision path highlighted in Blue.

Mr.Bender has High risk of CHD **since** (BMI **is** not Healthy) **and** (daily alcohol consumption **is** greater than 124.5ml) **even if is** (not Heavy Smoker) **and** (Cholesterol **is** not High).

(b) A local explanation of the decision in 2a.

A patient has High risk of CHD if:

1. (**Is** Heavy Smoker).
2. (Cholesterol **is** High) **even if** (not Heavy Smoker).
3. (HDL cholesterol **is** High) **even if is** (not Heavy Smoker) **and** (Cholesterol **is** not High) **and** (BMI **is** Healthy).
4. (BMI **is** not Healthy) **and** (daily alcohol consumption **is** greater. than 124.5ml) **even if** (not Heavy Smoker) **and** (Cholesterol **is** not High).

Mr.Bender has High risk of CHD **since** he follows Rule 4.

(c) A global explanation of the DT and the decision in 2a.

Fig. 2. An example of local and global narrative explanation of a DT. Note that this is one way of generating a global tree explanation (Appendix B). Listing all the nodes or stating all possible categorical values of features are design choices that will affect understandability.

prediction explanation. Once again, this is a choice we make for this experiment. A list of all decision nodes similar to feature importance in SHAP could also be a possible global tree explanation. For the patient in Fig. 2a, the corresponding global explanation is shown in Fig. 2c. As the tree size becomes large, the number of rules and the number of features in each rule increase. This means the explanation size and the cognitive chunks in the explanation increase. The best way to frame natural language explanations, for these different cases, is a separate research problem that we do not address here. Further, we restrict the rules in global explanation to those corresponding to a single risk category - high risk. Since the particular case involves only two categories, this still provides coverage to possible predictions while keeping the explanation less verbose. The narration generation involves the same algorithm as in the case of local explanation.

In addition to the model accuracy, note that each leaf node has a probability and confidence associated with that particular decision. For a particular node, the probability is the ratio of training data points that fits the criteria of that node to the number of data points in its previous node. A low probability node denotes that, the particular decision was rare based on the training data. The statistical significance of this prediction denotes its confidence. Both these measures are used for generating decision narration. Appendix B shows examples of the usage. To express the probabilities, we use verbal mapping proposed by [26]. An additional usage of *possibly* is introduced to accommodate cases involving low confidence and high probability.

The SHAP explanation does not have associated confidence. We filter features with SHAP score greater that 0 and present them as bulleted points in descending order of importance.

3.3   Evaluation

For evaluation, a within-subject survey is conducted with participants recruited on Prolific platform. We conducted a pilot study among peers and the feedback was used to improve the readability of the explanations and assess the time taken for the tasks.

The survey involves 5 patient scenarios namely local-SHAP, local-easy, local-hard, global-easy and global-hard. Each scenario consists of 2 pages. On the first page, the participant is provided with information about a patient. This consists of their features: age, gender, height, weight, BMI, blood pressure, different cholesterol values, smoking, and drinking habit. They are asked to enter the assumptions on what patient features may contribute to the AI model's prediction. This captures the mental model of the participant regarding CHD. Appendix C shows examples of the pages used in the survey.

On the next page, participants are presented with the same patient, the risk of CHD (high or low) as predicted by the AI system along with an explanation. They are asked to enter feature importance once again based on their understanding of the explanation. They are also asked to rate the explanation on three parameters: completeness, understandability, and verboseness, using a 5-

Table 2. Evaluation criteria for comparison of different explanation types.

Measure	Definition
Completeness rating (CR)	User rating for the prompt: This explanation helps me completely understand why the AI system made the prediction
Understandability rating (UR)	User rating for the prompt: Based on the explanation I understand how the model would behave for another patient
Verboseness rating (VR)	User rating for the prompt: This explanation is long and uses more words than required
Change in mental model (CMM)	Difference in perceived feature importance before and after viewing model explanation
Error in Understanding (EU)	Difference between model feature importance and perceived feature importance after viewing explanation

level Likert scale. Text feedback on each explanation and overall feedback at the end of the survey is collected.

The evaluation of each explanation has 3 parameters from a Likert rating based on participant perceptions. In addition, based on the task of choosing feature importance we compute two additional parameters: change in mental model and correctness of understanding. Change in mental model is defined as the updation of perceived feature importance before and after explanation. Let $U = (u_1, u_2, ..., u_N)$ where $u_i \in \{0, 1\}, 1 \leq i \leq N$ be the selected feature importance before explanation where N is the total number of features. Let $V = (v_1, v_2, ..., v_N)$ where $v_i \in \{0, 1\}, 1 \leq i \leq N$ be the selected feature importance after explanation. *Change in mental model* is computed as

$$D_m = \frac{d(U, V)}{N}$$

where d is the *Hamming distance* between U and V.

For each explanation, based on the features that are shown in the narration, we also know the *correct* feature importance. In the case of SHAP, these are the features with a SHAP score greater than 0. For local explanations, these are the features in the decision path, and for global explanations, it is all the features in the tree. If the correct feature importance $C = (c_1, c_2, ..., c_N)$ where $c_i \in \{0, 1\}, 1 \leq i \leq N$, we compute the *error in understanding* w.r.t to the system mental model as

$$D_c = \frac{d(V, C)}{N}.$$

Since for each feature, the participant selects a yes/no for importance, these measures do not capture the relative importance among features. Table 2 summarises all the evaluation parameters.

4   Results and Discussion

Fifty participants were recruited from the Prolific platform for the experiment, ensuring a balanced gender profile. All participants were presented with five patient-explanation scenarios and were requested to evaluate each of them. The survey took an average of 26 min to complete, and participants received a compensation of £6 each, as per the minimum pay requirement. However, one participant was excluded from the analysis due to indications of low-effort responses, spending less than 1 min on multiple scenarios. The demographic details of the selected participants are summarized in Table 3. Based on the responses, we computed the evaluation parameters mentioned in the previous section. The Likert scale ratings for *Completeness*, *Understandability*, and *Verboseness* are assigned values from 0 to 1, 0 corresponding to 'Strongly Disagree' and 1 to 'Strongly Agree'. We also calculate, *Change in the mental model* and *Error in understanding* from the selection of feature importance. The calculated scores are also normalised to range from 0 to 1. The mean values across all participants are presented in Table 4.

Table 3. Demographic distribution of survey participants.

Feature	Category: Proportion
Age	18–30: 81.63%, 30–40: 16.33%, 40–65: 2.04%
Gender	Male: 51.02% , Female: 48.98%
First language	English: 38.8%, Others: 61.2%

Table 4. Evaluation parameters across all the scenarios. Maximum is highlighted in bold and minimum in italics. CR - Completeness rating, UR - Understandability rating, VR - Verboseness rating, CMM - Change in mental model, EU - Error in Understanding.

	Local SHAP	Local Easy	Local Hard	Global Easy	Global Hard
CR	0.64	0.69	*0.63*	0.68	**0.69**
UR	*0.66*	0.71	0.67	0.72	**0.74**
VR	*0.16*	0.26	0.23	**0.56**	0.52
CMM	**0.42**	*0.28*	0.38	0.34	0.35
EU	0.12	*0.07*	0.13	0.19	**0.30**

While local-easy scenario has the lowest error in understandability (EU), participants rated all the models comparably in terms of Understandability (UR) and Completeness (CR). The Change in the Mental Model (CMM) exhibited uniformity across all types of explanations, except for local-SHAP and local-easy. To assess the significance of these results, we performed the Wilcoxon test, for all combinations of explanation types. Since multiple comparisons are performed, we apply Bonferroni Correction on p-value and a threshold of 0.01 is chosen. In comparing local and global explanations, local-SHAP is excluded and the ratings for both levels of difficulty in each case are averaged. The results are shown in Table 5. The observations that hold for a stricter threshold of 0.001 are highlighted with ∗.

Table 5. Significance of difference between types of explanation. CR - Completeness rating, UR - Understandability rating, VR - Verboseness rating, CMM - Change in mental model, EU - Error in Understanding. The values which are significant (Bonferroni Corrected p-value threshold of 0.01) are highlighted in **bold**. P-value ≤ 0.001 are highlighted with ∗.

	CR	UR	VR	CMM	EU
Local vs Global	0.42	0.44	**0.00**∗	0.53	**0.00**∗
Local Easy vs Global Easy	0.84	0.85	**0.00**∗	0.05	**0.00**∗
Local Hard vs Global Hard	0.35	0.42	**0.00**∗	0.36	**0.00**∗
Local Easy vs Local Hard	0.38	0.24	0.76	**0.00**∗	**0.00**∗
Global Easy vs Global Hard	0.50	0.53	0.56	0.43	**0.00**∗
Local SHAP vs Local Hard	0.63	0.76	0.10	0.23	0.42
Local SHAP vs Local Easy	0.18	0.28	0.03	**0.00**∗	0.11
Local SHAP vs Global Hard	0.02	0.30	**0.00**∗	0.09	**0.00**∗
Local SHAP vs Global Easy	0.16	0.28	**0.00**∗	**0.01**	0.02

Global explanations resulted in a lower average understandability based on the feature selection (EU) and it was observed that harder scenarios resulted in higher errors for both local and global explanations. For each type of explanation, the patient features wrongly selected was investigated (Tables 11, 12). Incorrect feature selection related to *cholesterol* caused the majority of errors. Participants chose the wrong cholesterol-related feature, possibly due to a lack of attention or limited understanding of medical terminology. Improving the presentation of explanations and providing more contextual information could potentially address this issue. Importantly, when presented with semifactual explanations of hard scenarios both local and global explanations led to almost half or more participants excluding the corresponding feature. This clearly points to the ambiguity of such narration.

The error analysis does not explain the contradiction between the understandability ratings and the correctness of feature selection. Interestingly, a considerable number of participants expressed a preference for longer, global explanations, even if they did not fully comprehend them. Significant rating of global explanations as more verbose adds to this contradiction. To delve deeper into this phenomenon, participant clustering was performed based on the ratings and computed scores. Using the k-means algorithm, three distinct groups of participants were identified and manually validated. Figure 3 displays the average rating across different parameters for each group.

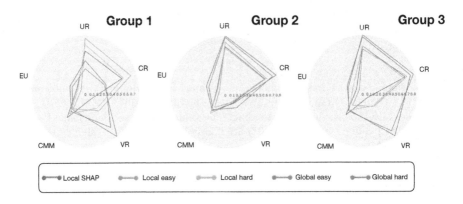

Fig. 3. Average rating for different explanation type across the participant groups

- Group 1: Strongly prefer and understand local explanations. The cluster consists of 11 participants who rate patient-specific local tree explanations highest on completeness and understandability.
- Group 2: Majority group that rates global explanation as most understandable: This cluster consist of 22 people who has the least significance in preference between global, local explanation or difference based on the difficulty level. They rate Global explanation highest on completeness and understandability
- Group 3: This cluster consist of 16 people who strongly prefer global explanations but critical about the narration. This cluster is more detail oriented and rates global explanations as more understandable and complete. This group was critical on the narration and presentation of explanation in the feedback form. The average error in feature selection for global explanation for this group, is lower than Group 2.

It is evident that within the clusters, the ratings on each parameters has significant preferential pattern between each type of explanation. Group 1, 3 has strong polarity on the preferences and their rating tend to *Strongly agree* or *Strongly disagree*. Both these Groups identify Global explanations as verbose. This shows that, in healthcare setting, the effectiveness of an explanation to an end-user, is very dependent on their individual preference.

4.1   Local vs. Global

While there is no significant difference between local and global explanations overall, strong differences emerge at the Group level. Group 1 rates the local explanation as complete, while both Groups 2, and 3 favour the global explanation for completeness. Similar preferences are observed in participants' perception of understandability within each group. When a stricter p-value threshold of 0.001 is applied, the significance of the difference in user rating for understandability and correctness holds only in Group 1. The results of the Wilcoxon test for combinations of explanation types within Groups are given in Appendix D.

- *The results indicate that certain people strongly prefer specific type of explanation. This preference does not necessarily translate to understandability.*
- *In all groups, a higher error in feature selection is observed for global explanations, mainly due to the semifactual explanation and wrongly interpreting features related to Cholesterol*

Among participants belonging to Group 2, the factors driving their preference for global explanations remain unclear. Demographics data examination (Table 6) offers no apparent patterns, leading us to propose the influence of unique cognitive styles within the groups. Further investigations are warranted to unveil the underlying reasons for these preferences and errors. While users may perceive explanations as understandable, it is vital to recognize that this perception may not necessarily translate into accurate decision-making. The lack of significant changes in mental models substantiate this, indicating the need for continued exploration to optimize explanation presentations for healthcare AI models.

Table 6. Demographic distribution of participants within each group. All the features are not available for all participants. Missing data are excluded in the counts.

	Group1	Group2	Group3
Number of participants	11	22	16
Male to female ratio	4:7	9:13	12:4
Count of full time employed	2	8	5
Student to non-student ratio	8:2	10:9	8:7
Number of native english speakers	4	11	4
Ethnicity, white to black ratio	9:2	11:10	11:3

4.2 Tree Explanation vs. SHAP

The overall ratings of SHAP explanations are comparable to those of local-hard explanations but lower than those of local-easy explanations generated from the same underlying decision tree. This suggests that the comprehensibility and interpretability of SHAP explanations are slightly lower than those of the local-easy explanations. However, this may be attributed to the presentation bias, as all participants were exposed to the SHAP explanation first. It is noted that the presentation style of SHAP explanations, using bulleted points, is generally considered less verbose even though it does not impact the error in understandability or perceived understandability and completeness. Hence the simpler readability of the SHAP explanation is not seen to have impacted its overall understandability.

4.3   Easy vs. Hard

The ratings provided by the participants on the Likert scale did not reveal any significant distinction between the explanation scenarios characterized as easy and hard. However, an examination of the impact of difficulty levels on the error in feature selection uncovered significant results. Hard scenarios, whether global or local explanations, exhibited significantly higher error rates, even within participant groups.

– *The explanation understanding is strongly dependent on the complexity of the feature interaction being explained.*

When participants encountered explanations that deviated from their preexisting notions of feature dependence, it introduced confusion, becoming a major contributor to error in hard scenarios. We observed that harder scenarios, on average, caused larger changes in the mental model of participants. However, this alone was insufficient to mitigate the observed errors. Furthermore, the consistent error patterns across different participant groups present an opportunity to enhance the current framework of narration and presentation of explanations, benefiting all participants.

5   Limitations and Future Work

The experiment provides evidence for the usefulness of global explanations in health informatics. Identifying cognitive styles that lead to particular explanation preferences and errors in comprehension, is pivotal to applying global explanations in real-life applications. The current experiment has been carried out on a small dataset. Evaluating these findings on a larger data set with more data points and larger features will be undertaken in future studies. We recognise that regression models are commonly used in risk prediction. Expanding the scope of the narrative global explanation within the context of regression and assessing its comparative utility against the local explanation will enable the integration of our findings into established risk predictive tools.

Further, the evaluation in this study was crowdsourced and hence the participants are not representative of real-life patients. Most of the participants fall in the age category that does not have a risk of heart disease as predicted by the model. This may have biased their rating. We aim to rectify this by conducting the evaluation on a representative patient population, which would also require addressing ethical concerns.

The current study has not focussed on generating effective global explanations. The use of semifactuals has not addressed the mismatch with the user's mental models. Further, the presentation of Explanation features is seen to have introduced errors. Effective communication and presentation techniques would be vital in reducing errors. Though we have used a linguistic representation of probability and confidence, the evaluations in this regard remain undone. For risk communication at scale, this is a crucial component. Further research is warranted to delve deeper into these aspects and refine the design and implementation of explanation systems.

Acknowledgement. We would like to thank Dr. Sameen Maruf and Prof. Ingrid Zukerman for generously sharing their expertise in utilizing the dataset, continuous support and valuable feedback in designing the experiment. We thank Nikolay Babakov and Prof. Alberto José Bugarín Diz for their feedback throughout the development of this research. We also thank the anonymous reviewers for their feedback which has significantly improved this work. A. Sivaprasad is ESR in the NL4XAI project which has received funding from the European Union's Horizon 2020 research and innovation programme under the Marie Skłodowska-Curie Grant Agreement No. 860621.

A   Construction and Selection of DT

B   Generating Explanation Narration

Steps in generating narration (Figs. 5, 6 and 7):

1. Filter the rules corresponding to high risk leaves.
2. Sort the decision rules in order of their leaf node confidence and insert verbal mapping of relative probability.
3. Reorder the features and place contradictory features at the end preceded by even-if.
4. combine the features with *and*
5. Add header with *age, gender*

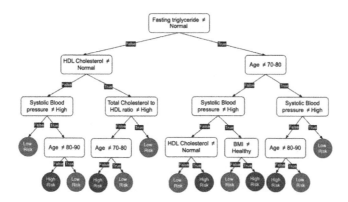

Fig. 4. Depth 5 Decision tree generated on 2134 datapoints. Training accuracy = 90.9%, test accuracy on 534 records = 85%.

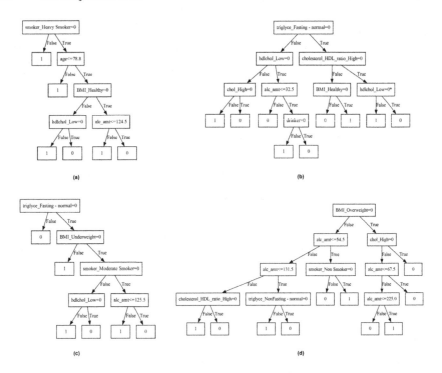

Fig. 5. DTs for different scenarios. (a) Local easy scenario: Decision tree generated on 116 data points. Training accuracy = 78.4%, (b) Local Hard scenario: Decision tree generated on 163 data points. Training accuracy = 77.3%, (c) Global easy scenario: Decision tree generated on 382 data points. Training accuracy = 82.5% (d) Global Hard scenario: Decision tree generated on 108 data points. Training accuracy = 85.4%.

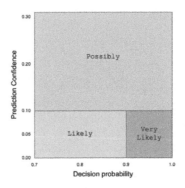

Fig. 6. Verbal mapping of relative probabilities.

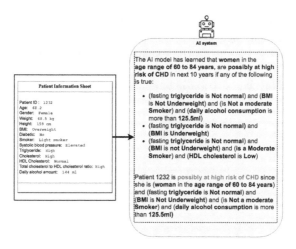

Fig. 7. An example for generated global explanation. This model corresponds to Global-easy scenario.

Table 7. Category definitions for Data preprocessing.

Feature	Categories
Smoking	Non-smoker, light smoker: (less than 10), moderate smoker - (10 to 19)/day, heavy smoker- (20 or over)/day
BMI	Underweight (less than 18.5), Healthy - (18.5 to 24.9), Overweight - (25 to 29.9), Obese - (30 or over)
Cholesterol	Normal: ≤ 5, High: above 5
Cholestrol HDL ratio	Normal: ≤ 6, High: above 6
Triglycerides	Fasting - normal (0 to 1.7), Non Fasting - normal (1.7 to 2.3), High (2.3 to 10)
HDL	Normal: ≤ 1, High: above 1
Systolic Blood Pressure	Low: (0 to 90), Normal: (90 to 120), Elevated: (120 to 140), High: (140 to 250)
Diastolic Blood pressure	Low: (0 to 60), Normal: (60 to 80), Elevated: (80 to 90), High: (90 to 150)

C   User Survey on Prolific

For each scenario, a participant first see the patient information as shown in Fig. 8. The participant is asked to pick all the features they think might be influential in predicting the patient's risk of CHD. This captures the participants mental model regarding CHD prediction before viewing any explanation (Table 7).

In the next page, a participant is shown the explanation followed by questions to rate the explanation. The are asked to redo the task of picking all the features they think were influential in predicting the patient's risk of CHD as shown in Fig. 9. This captures the participant's understanding of AI's mental model. This is followed by questions to get the users rating based on a 5 point Likert scale. The questions correspond to 3 parameters being measured:

1. Completeness: This explanation helps me completely understand why the AI system made the prediction
2. Understandability: Based on the explanation, I understand how the model would behave for another patient
3. Verboseness: This explanation is long and uses more words than require

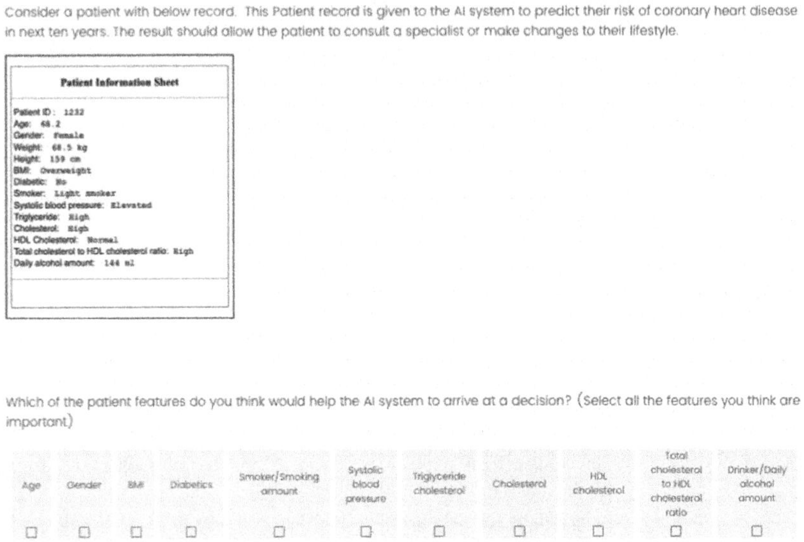

Fig. 8. First page of a scenario shown to participants with a patient info. They question captures the participant's mental model of CHD prediction before viewing explanation.

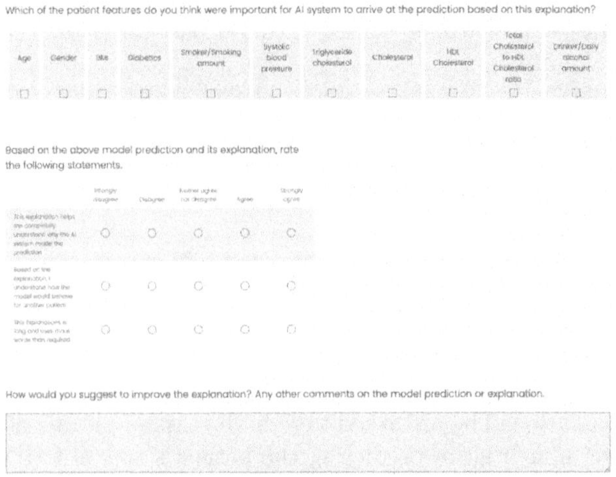

Fig. 9. The first question evaluates participant's understanding of the explanation. The Remaining questions capturing their feedback on explanation.

D   Comparison of Local and Global Explanation Ratings

Results of Wilcoxon test, for combinations of explanation types within participant Groups. After Bonferroni Correction, p-values less than 0.01 are chosen as significant (Tables 8, 9 and 10).

Table 8. Significance of difference between different types of explanation for Group 1 rounded to 2 decimal places. Significant p-value are in **bold**. P-value ≤ 0.001 are highlighted with *.

	CR	UR	VR	CMM	EU
Local vs Global	**0.00***	**0.00***	**0.00***	0.81	**0.00**
Local easy vs Global easy	**0.00**	**0.01**	**0.00**	0.93	**0.00**
Local Hard vs Global Hard	0.05	0.05	0.03	0.62	0.07
Local easy vs Local Hard	0.20	0.21	0.50	0.04	0.19
Global easy vs Global Hard	0.34	0.65	0.16	0.56	0.66
Local SHAP vs Local Hard	0.53	0.79	0.04	0.29	0.79
Local SHAP vs Local easy	0.04	0.34	**0.01**	**0.01**	0.18
Local SHAP vs Global Hard	0.21	0.03	**0.01**	0.21	0.10
Local SHAP vs Global easy	0.03	0.07	**0.00**	0.02	0.35

Table 9. Significance of difference between different types of explanation for Group 2 rounded to 2 decimal places. Significant p-value are in **bold**. P-value ≤ 0.001 are highlighted with *.

	CR	UR	VR	CMM	EU
Local vs Global	0.02	**0.01**	0.13	0.89	**0.00***
Local easy vs Global easy	0.22	0.08	0.10	0.38	**0.00***
Local Hard vs Global Hard	0.06	0.08	0.65	0.29	**0.00***
Local easy vs Local Hard	0.40	0.60	0.92	0.02	0.19
Global easy vs Global Hard	0.53	0.24	0.21	0.42	0.35
Local SHAP vs Local Hard	0.84	0.99	0.51	0.81	0.92
Local SHAP vs Local easy	0.27	0.71	0.97	0.05	0.58
Local SHAP vs Global Hard	**0.00**	0.02	0.80	0.71	**0.01**
Local SHAP vs Global easy	0.03	0.07	0.10	0.20	0.02

Table 10. Significance of difference between different types of explanation for Group 3 rounded to 2 decimal places. Significant p-value are in **bold**. P-value ≤ 0.001 are highlighted with *.

	CR	UR	VR	CMM	EU
Local vs Global	**0.01**	0.05	**0.00***	0.17	**0.00***
Local easy vs Global Hard	0.02	0.10	**0.00**	0.03	**0.00***
Local Hard vs Global Hard	0.27	0.27	**0.00***	0.94	**0.01**
Local easy vs Local Hard	0.60	0.62	0.77	0.14	**0.00**
Global easy vs Global Hard	0.66	0.26	0.14	0.96	0.40
Local SHAP vs Local Hard	0.56	0.62	0.13	0.25	0.06
Local SHAP vs Local easy	0.60	0.60	0.07	**0.01**	0.29
Local SHAP vs Global Hard	0.05	0.23	**0.00***	0.15	**0.00***
Local SHAP vs Global easy	0.03	0.05	**0.00***	0.23	**0.01**

Table 11. Error in selecting patient feature after explanation. Type I error (False Positive) - Wrong selection overall.

	Local SHAP	Local easy	Local hard	Global easy	Global hard
Age					
Gender	3				
BMI			2		
Diabetics	5	2		1	
Cholesterol	5	2	2	8	
HDL cholesterol					15
Triglyceride cholesterol	1				
Total cholesterol to HDL cholesterol ratio	2	1	1	6	
Systolic blood pressure	5	1		2	5
Smoking/Smoking amount			2		
Dinker/Drinking amount					2

Table 12. Error in selecting patient feature after explanation. Type II error (False Negative) - Missing correct feature.

	Local SHAP	Local easy	Local hard	Global easy	Global hard
Age	6	6	1	8	9
Gender		8	13	22	23
BMI	14	1		1	3
Diabetics					
Cholesterol					31
HDL cholesterol	10		23	37	
Triglyceride cholesterol			20	4	35
Total cholesterol to HDL cholesterol ratio					11
Systolic blood pressure					
Smoking/Smoking amount	4	17		10	27
Dinker/Drinking amount	12		9	3	

References

1. Adadi, A., Berrada, M.: Peeking inside the black-box: a survey on explainable artificial intelligence (XAI). IEEE Access **6**, 52138–52160 (2018). https://doi.org/10.1109/ACCESS.2018.2870052

2. Bertsimas, D., Dunn, J.: Optimal classification trees. Mach. Learn. **106**(7), 1039–1082 (2017). https://doi.org/10.1007/s10994-017-5633-9

3. Biran, O., Cotton, C.V.: Explanation and justification in machine learning: a survey. In: IJCAI-17 Workshop on Explainable AI (XAI), vol. 8 (2017)

4. Blanquero, R., Carrizosa, E., Molero-Río, C., Morales, D.R.: Optimal randomized classification trees. Comput. Oper. Res. **132**, 105281 (2021). https://doi.org/10.1016/j.cor.2021.105281

5. Breiman, L., Friedman, J.H., Olshen, R.A., Stone, C.J.: Classification and regression trees (1984)

6. Glik, D.C.: Risk communication for public health emergencies. Annu. Rev. Publ. Health **28**(1), 33–54 (2007). https://doi.org/10.1146/annurev.publhealth.28.021406.144123, pMID: 17222081

7. Hippisley-Cox, J., Coupland, C., Brindle, P.: Development and validation of qrisk3 risk prediction algorithms to estimate future risk of cardiovascular disease: prospective cohort study. BMJ **357** (2017). https://doi.org/10.1136/bmj.j2099

8. Hu, X., Rudin, C., Seltzer, M.: Optimal sparse decision trees. In: Wallach, H., Larochelle, H., Beygelzimer, A., d'Alché-Buc, F., Fox, E., Garnett, R. (eds.) Advances in Neural Information Processing Systems, vol. 32. Curran Associates, Inc. (2019)

9. Hyafil, L., Rivest, R.L.: Constructing optimal binary decision trees is np-complete. Inf. Process. Lett. **5**(1), 15–17 (1976)

10. Klivans, A.R., Servedio, R.A.: Toward attribute efficient learning of decision lists and parities. In: Shawe-Taylor, J., Singer, Y. (eds.) COLT 2004. LNCS (LNAI), vol. 3120, pp. 224–238. Springer, Heidelberg (2004). https://doi.org/10.1007/978-3-540-27819-1_16

11. Knuiman, M.W., Vu, H.T., Bartholomew, H.C.: Multivariate risk estimation for coronary heart disease: the Busselton health study. Aust. N. Z. J. Publ. Health **22**(7), 747–753 (1998)

12. Lakkaraju, H., Bach, S.H., Leskovec, J.: Interpretable decision sets: a joint framework for description and prediction. In: Proceedings of the 22nd ACM SIGKDD International Conference on Knowledge Discovery and Data Mining. KDD '16, pp. 1675–1684. Association for Computing Machinery, New York, NY, USA (2016). https://doi.org/10.1145/2939672.2939874

13. Letham, B., Rudin, C., McCormick, T., Madigan, D.: Interpretable classifiers using rules and Bayesian analysis: building a better stroke prediction model. Ann. Appl. Stat. **9**, 1350–1371 (2015). https://doi.org/10.1214/15-AOAS848

14. Lin, J., Zhong, C., Hu, D., Rudin, C., Seltzer, M.: Generalized and scalable optimal sparse decision trees. In: III, H.D., Singh, A. (eds.) Proceedings of the 37th International Conference on Machine Learning, vol. 119, pp. 6150–6160. PMLR, 13–18 July 2020

15. Lundberg, S.M., Lee, S.I.: A unified approach to interpreting model predictions. In: Proceedings of the 31st International Conference on Neural Information Processing Systems. NIPS'17, pp. 4768–4777. Curran Associates Inc., Red Hook, NY, USA (2017)

16. Markus, A.F., Kors, J.A., Rijnbeek, P.R.: The role of explainability in creating trustworthy artificial intelligence for health care: a comprehensive survey of the terminology, design choices, and evaluation strategies. J. Biomed. Inform. **113**, 103655 (2021). https://doi.org/10.1016/j.jbi.2020.103655

17. Maruf, S., Zukerman, I., Reiter, E., Haffari, G.: Influence of context on users' views about explanations for decision-tree predictions. Comput. Speech Lang. **81**, 101483 (2023). https://doi.org/10.1016/j.csl.2023.101483

18. Miller, T.: Explanation in artificial intelligence: insights from the social sciences. Artif. Intell. **267**, 1–38 (2019). https://doi.org/10.1016/j.artint.2018.07.007

19. Moreno-Ríos, S., García-Madruga, J.A., Byrne, R.M.: Inferences from semifactual 'even if' conditionals. Acta Physiol. (OXF) **128**(2), 197–209 (2008). https://doi.org/10.1016/j.actpsy.2007.12.008

20. Narayanan, M., Chen, E., He, J., Kim, B., Gershman, S., Doshi-Velez, F.: How do humans understand explanations from machine learning systems? An evaluation of the human-interpretability of explanation. CoRR abs/1802.00682 (2018)

21. Pearl, J., Mackenzie, D.: The Book of Why: The New Science of Cause and Effect, 1st edn. Basic Books Inc., New York (2018)

22. Quinlan, J.R.: C4.5: Programs for Machine Learning. Morgan Kaufmann Publishers Inc., San Francisco, CA, USA (1993)

23. Reiter, E.: Natural language generation challenges for explainable AI. In: Proceedings of the 1st Workshop on Interactive Natural Language Technology for Explainable Artif. Intell. (NL4XAI 2019), pp. 3–7. Association for Computational Linguistics (2019). https://doi.org/10.18653/v1/W19-8402

24. Ribeiro, M., Singh, S., Guestrin, C.: "why should I trust you?": Explaining the predictions of any classifier. In: Proceedings of the 2016 Conference of the North American Chapter of the Association for Computational Linguistics: Demonstrations, pp. 97–101. Association for Computational Linguistics, San Diego, California (2016). https://doi.org/10.18653/v1/N16-3020

25. Sendak, M.P., Gao, M., Brajer, N., Balu, S.: Presenting machine learning model information to clinical end users with model facts labels. NPJ Digit. Med. **3** (2020)

26. Spiegelhalter, D.: Risk and uncertainty communication. Annu. Rev. Stat. Appl. **4**(1), 31–60 (2017). https://doi.org/10.1146/annurev-statistics-010814-020148

27. Verwer, S., Zhang, Y.: Learning optimal classification trees using a binary linear program formulation. In: Proceedings of the AAAI Conference on Artificial Intelligence, vol. 33, no. 01, pp. 1625–1632 (2019)

28. Wachter, S., Mittelstadt, B.D., Russell, C.: Counterfactual explanations without opening the black box: automated decisions and the GDPR. CoRR abs/1711.00399 (2017)

The Blame Problem in Evaluating Local Explanations and How to Tackle It

Amir Hossein Akhavan Rahnama^(✉)

KTH Royal Institute of Technology, Stockholm, Sweden
amiakh@kth.se

Abstract. The number of local model-agnostic explanation techniques proposed has grown rapidly recently. One main reason is that the bar for developing new explainability techniques is low due to the lack of optimal evaluation measures. Without rigorous measures, it is hard to have concrete evidence of whether the new explanation techniques can significantly outperform their predecessors. Our study proposes a new taxonomy for evaluating local explanations: robustness, evaluation using ground truth from synthetic datasets and interpretable models, model randomization, and human-grounded evaluation. Using this proposed taxonomy, we highlight that all categories of evaluation methods, except those based on the ground truth from interpretable models, suffer from a problem we call the "blame problem." In our study, we argue that this category of evaluation measure is a more reasonable method for evaluating local model-agnostic explanations. However, we show that even this category of evaluation measures has further limitations. The evaluation of local explanations remains an open research problem.

Keywords: Explainable AI · Explainability in Machine Learning · Local model-agnostic Explanations · Evaluation of Local Explanations · Local Explanations · Interpretability

1 Introduction

One of the most popular areas within explainable AI is the study of local model-agnostic explanation techniques[1] [17]. Local explanations, originally called explanations for individual instances [42], differ from global explanations. Global explanations are the information intrinsically available in the interpretable models, such as the weights of linear models or the feature importance scores in tree models [13]. Moreover, they provide information about the internal logic of their models at the dataset level, i.e., for all data instances. On the other hand, local explanations are information about the prediction of an individual instance [38]. One of the main arguments for the need for local explanations is that obtaining a global explanation of complex black-box models for all instances might be hard [38,39].

---

[1] For brevity, we refer to them as local explanations in our study.

© The Author(s), under exclusive license to Springer Nature Switzerland AG 2024
S. Nowaczyk et al. (Eds.): ECAI 2023 Workshops, CCIS 1947, pp. 66–86, 2024.
https://doi.org/10.1007/978-3-031-50396-2_4

There are numerous different ways to represent local explanations. However, feature attribution is the most common representation in the literature of explainable AI [17]. The feature attribution explanation technique allocates importance scores to each feature, showing their contribution to the predicted output of a black-box model[2].

The need for rigorous evaluation of local explanations has been amplified after several studies have shown that local explanations can fail. For example, in [40], the author argues that we should not use local explanation techniques in high-stake decision-making domains by showing numerous failure cases of these techniques. In [31], the authors show that local explanation techniques can fail to consider feature interaction in their output explanations. Meanwhile, the number of proposed local explanation techniques is growing rapidly. In only one study, [8], the authors have listed 29 local explanation techniques.

Even though we share the same concern with the authors of [31,40], we believe that the real problem that hinders the adaptation of these techniques into high-stake domains is *the lack of optimal measures to evaluate them*. In the absence of strict and rigorous measures, there has been a surge in studies that propose new explainability techniques, yet it is unclear whether the newly introduced explanation techniques can significantly improve upon their predecessors and, if so, in what type of tasks or problems. In [26], the authors share their concerns about the poor evaluation of local *model-based* explanation techniques of neural network models. In their words, "interpretability research suffers from an over-reliance on intuition-based approaches that risk-and in some cases have caused illusory progress and misleading conclusions.".

In an ideal world, each instance will have a local ground truth importance score[3]. These include information about the importance of each feature in the explained instance to the black box's predicted output. We expect this local ground truth to be unique for data instances with substantially different feature values and predicted output. However, we are faced with a contradiction: if we can extract such information from a black box model, why do we call that model a black box, and hence, what is the need for local explanations? Therefore, we can naturally assume a limit to how fine-grained and accurate these ground truth importance scores can be.

Faced with this problem, researchers in explainable machine learning have introduced and extensively used alternative measures to circumvent this challenging problem. However, we have noticed that these measures' assumptions and limitations are mostly stated implicitly. As a result, researchers can draw misleading conclusions about the accuracy of local explanations when using these evaluation measures. Because of this, in our study, we propose to categorize these evaluation measures based on the assumptions they are based on:

---

[2] See Sect. 3 for a formal definition of these techniques.

[3] For brevity, we refer to local ground truth importance scores as ground truth. Note that these ground truth vectors differ from the common ground truth in machine learning, which are discrete class labels for the data points.

- **Robustness Measures** are based on the *assumption* that nullifying important (unimportant) features should cause large (insignificant) changes to the predicted output of a black-box model for the explained instance. Another sub-category of these measures is based on the assumption that adding a small variation (noise) to the explained instance needs to cause minimal changes to their explanation.
- **Ground Truth from Synthetic Data** is based on the *assumption* that local explanations must provide feature importance scores similar to the prior importance scores generated by the synthetic data generators.
- **Ground Truth from Interpretable Models** is based on the *assumption* that local explanations must be able to allocate similar importance scores to the local ground truth importance scores obtained from simpler and more interpretable models.
- **Model Randomization** evaluation measures are based on the assumption that local explanations of a randomized (contaminated) model must be substantially different from those obtained for the original black-box model.
- **Human-grounded Evaluation** is based on the *assumption* that if human subjects need to be able to replay the model prediction of a black-box model using local explanations or the content of local explanations need to be similar to the human reasoning process for local explanation to be accurate.

The main contribution of our study is to highlight the different ways we evaluate local explanations. This is in contrast to some studies that have primarily focused on one class of evaluation measures, namely Robustness measures [32]. Moreover, we show all categories of evaluation measures suffer from a range of implicit limitations, the most influential of which is a "blame problem.". In our definition, *the blame problem is when we are unsure whether we should allocate the poor performance of local explanations to themselves or the black-box model*. What becomes straightforward through our proposed systematic categorization is the realization that the "blame problem" is a recurring problem in all the above categories of evaluation methods, except when we evaluate local explanations via extracting ground truth using interpretable models. However, even in this category, we face further limitations. To our knowledge, no study has highlighted the blame problem or systematically investigated these different categories of evaluation measures. Moreover, the relationship between different evaluation measures across these categories is poorly studied. We provide a synthetic example of such investigations.

The rest of the paper is organized as follows. Section 2 discusses the related work. In Sect. 3, we provide the formal definition of local model-agnostic explanations. In Sect. 4, we briefly discuss how global explanations of black-box models are evaluated, as these methods precede local explanations. In Sect. 5, we present our proposed categories of evaluation measures along with their strengths and limitations. We conclude our study and provide directions for future studies in Sect. 6.

2   Related Work

Several well-written surveys on the local model-agnostic explanation techniques exist in the literature of explainability [17,30]. In Molnar et al. [31], the authors provide general pitfalls of local explanation models. However, the study focuses on the limitations of the explanation techniques and not the evaluation measures.

In [11], the evaluation methods of local explanations are categorized into Human-grounded, Application-grounded, and Functionally-grounded evaluation. Human-grounded evaluations use expert human subjects to replay the black-box prediction, whereas functionally grounded evaluation uses systematic proxy measures to evaluate local explanations. Application-grounded Evaluation is similar to Human-grounded assessment. However, the experiments involve lay humans, not experts. The first four categories of evaluation we discuss in our study fall into the Functionally-grounded evaluation measure.

In the rest of this section, we provide an overview of the studies that have provided critical overviews or surveys of the evaluation measures. The discussion of related work for each category of evaluation measures will be presented in their respective subsections of Sect. 5.

In [33,47], the authors have focused on providing systematic surveys of the evaluation measures for local explanations. In these surveys, the authors aim to provide a reference for the type of evaluation measures used in the literature on explainability. We consider these studies reliable references for knowing what measures were used to evaluate explanations in the literature. However, our study aims to highlight implicit assumptions and limitations behind these evaluation measures and their respective limitations.

In [18], the author argues that robustness analysis of local explanations is useful for obtaining explanations that can generalize to real-world problems. In [19], the authors propose an evaluation toolkit for evaluating the local model-based explanations of neural networks. In [3], the authors propose an open benchmark to evaluate local explanations. Most of the measures included in the two aforementioned studies are based on the robustness analysis (See Sect. 5.1 for more details on robustness analysis).

In [26], the authors state four criticisms of how local model-based explanations of neural networks are evaluated. Firstly, they criticize the excessive use of visualization, such as saliency maps, as a means to evaluate explanations[4]. Moreover, they state that the design principles behind most explanation techniques are not rigorously verified in their respective studies. Thirdly, they criticize the lack of quantifiable measures in some evaluation studies. Lastly, they highlight that while some studies claim to provide explanations that are interpretable to humans, they include limited or no studies that involve human subjects. The study provides general guidelines for improving the quality of research in explaining neural networks. Unlike the study of [26], whereauthors propose gen-

---

[4] Other studies have shown that saliency maps are unreliable for evaluating explanations [1,14].

eral guidelines for a more rigorous study of local model-agnostic explanations, our study aims to showcase the implicit assumptions and the limitations of these evaluation methods used in the literature on eXplainable AI (XAI).

3   Local Explanations

This section briefly defines our formal notion of local model-agnostic explanations[5]. Let $X \in \mathbb{R}^{N \times M}$ and $f : \mathbb{R}^{N \times M} \to \mathbb{R}^N$. Let $f(x)$ be the black-box model f predicted output for a designated class given instance x, namely $f(x)$. An explanation technique g provides ϕ_j, the local feature importance of feature j in x_j for the output $f(x)$. The feature importance can be ϕ_j zero, which indicates that the feature has no contribution to the predicted output, or negative (positive), which indicates that it negatively (positively) affects the predicted output of black-box of instance x, namely $f(x)$. A sub-category of local model-agnostic explanations, e.g. LIME [39] and SHAP [28] additionally satisfy the completeness property [29] where

$$f(x) = \sum_{j=1}^{M} \phi_j x_j \tag{1}$$

The completeness property states that the predicted output $f(x)$ equals an additive set of importance scores. The local explanation is created by all the individual feature importance scores into $\Phi_{x,f}^c = [\phi_1, ..., \phi_M] \in \mathbb{R}^M$.

Local explanations should not be confused with global explanations. In Local explanations, we explain an individual instance, whereas global explanations provide a single importance scores vector for all instances. In local explanations, each unique instance can have a unique local explanation. On the other hand, global explanations are the feature importance scores for the entire dataset that are equal for all instances.

Numerous local model-agnostic explanations, such as LIME [39], SHAP [28] obtain their $\Phi_{x,f}^c$ from the weight of an interpretable surrogate g. The surrogate model is trained on interpretable representations of explained instances that are interpretable to humans. For example, in the text datasets, binary representations are used where the existence of a token in a sentence is set to one. See Fig. 1 for an example of how LIME builds its interpretable surrogate.

We want to emphasize that local model-agnostic explanation techniques differ from local (model-based) explanations of neural network models. In those explanations, we need to assume that the model is differentiable since the explanations are obtained based on the derivative of the model $f(x)$ with respect to the input instance x, i.e., df/dx [41,44]. Even though some of the evaluation measures used in evaluating model-based gradient explanations are similar to the ones used for evaluating local model-agnostic explanations, e.g., robustness analysis, we focus only on the taxonomy of the evaluations of local model-agnostic explanations in our study.

---

[5] For brevity, we might refer to local model-agnostic explanations as local explanations in our study.

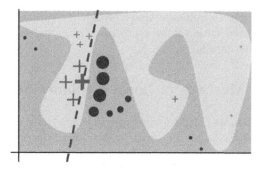

Fig. 1. LIME explanations are obtained from the weight of the surrogate linear regression model shown by a dotted line. Compared to the original explained model, this model focuses on the model trained in the neighborhood around the explained instance (red bold plus sign). Source: [39] (Color figure online)

4   History

The problem of evaluating local explanations is significantly harder than the evaluation of global explanations. This section examines how global explanations have been evaluated in the literature of explainability. Even though these studies have inspired some of the evaluation studies of local explanations, we discuss why these methods cannot be directly used to evaluate local explanations.

The first approach to evaluate global explanations is by dropping features from the entire dataset and retraining the model [20]. Based on this, the feature importance scores of *accurate* global explanations must equal the difference between the new and original models' accuracy. While this method is imperfect, the evaluation can be considered a controlled experiment. However, this cannot be easily translated into local explanations. Local explanations can be different for each instance. Therefore, dropping an entire set of features is not possible. In [21], the authors propose separately nullifying the important features from each image instance and retraining the model with this new dataset. However, this breaks the properties of a controlled experiment as this process can be sensitive to the type of nullification and the emergence of further complex covariance relationships among the nullified features.

The second approach to evaluating global explanations is based on the fidelity measure. Some studies aimed to replace black-box models with interpretable global explanations, especially in the form of rule classifiers [9,10,13]. In such studies, the fidelity measure, i.e., the difference between the accuracy of global explanations and the black-box models, showed the quality of those explanations. For the case of evaluating local explanations, the fidelity metric cannot be directly applied. Because in the local explanation techniques, the interpretable surrogate and the black-boxmodels are trained on two different datasets and labels. We want to emphasize that the fidelity measure proposed in [45] should not be confused with the measure used in global explanations studies. See Sect. 5.1 for more details.

5   Evaluation Methods of Local Explanations

In the previous section, we clarified why applying the former approaches to evaluating global explanations is not directly translatable to the problem of evaluating local explanations. As we mentioned in Sect. 1, the most straightforward way to evaluate local explanations is to measure their similarity to ground truth importance scores. However, such ground truth needs to be obtained from a black-box model. Remember that we need local explanations because we do not understand black-box models. Therefore, directly evaluating local explanations using local ground truth importance scores is challenging, if not impossible.

Therefore, all evaluation measures of local explanations need to make certain assumptions. This section provides a taxonomy of evaluation measures, which are categorized based on the assumptions and the ways they circumvent this impossible task. These methods range from Robustness Measures (Sect. 5.1) and Evaluation based on Ground Truth (Sect. 5.2) to Human-grounded evaluation (Sect. 5.4). In each section, we focus on the implicit assumptions and limitations of each measure in a critical manner. In the last section, we provide an example where some evaluation measures from different categories are compared in a synthetic dataset.

5.1   Robustness Measures

The robustness measures of local explanations can be divided into two subcategories. In the first category, measures evaluate local explanations by nullifying important (unimportant) features of local explanations. Importance by Preservation, Importance by Deletion [12] are examples of this first category. The main underlying **assumption** is that nullifying features deemed important (unimportant) from the local explanation in the explained instance need to cause significant (insignificant) changes in the predicted scores of the explained instance [32].

Formally, let f be a black-box model and E the set of top-K features ranked by their importance scores obtained from a local explanation technique g in *descending* order, for instance, x. The user selects the variable K. Now, Let x' be the explained instance after the features in E are replaced by a baseline value, such as the average feature value in the dataset. The importance By Deletion measure is then measured as $\frac{|f(x')-f(x)|}{|x-x'|}$. Importance by Preservation is calculated similarly; however, in this case, E is the set of top-K features ranked by their importance scores in an *ascending* order. Robust explanations have relatively large (small) Importance by Deletion (Preservation) values [4,32].

In the second category, measures compare the similarity (distance) of the local explanations of the explained instance with the local explanations of an instance that includes a small noise (variation) of the explained instance. Continuity [2, 32, 45] is an example of such measures. The second category of the measure is based on the **assumption** that there needs to be a proportional difference between how much the local explanations of an explained instance changes based on the magnitude of the change in the explained instance.

The continuity measure is an example of this category of robustness measure proposed by [4]. Let x_j be an instance located in an Euclidean ball with a maximum radius of ϵ, $B_\epsilon(x)$, from the explained instance $x \in X$. We define the continuity for x_i based on the explanation technique g as follows:

$$\tilde{L}(x_i) = \arg\max_{x_j \in B_\epsilon(x)} \frac{||g(x) - g(x_j)||_2}{||x - x_j||_2} \tag{2}$$

where ϵ and the size of B is set by the user and $||$ is a norm function.

As it is clear from their definitions, the robustness measures have no further **assumptions** about the data and model explained. Moreover, none of these categories of robustness measures include any notion of ground truth for evaluating local explanations. This can make the evaluation process more accessible and can be the reason that they are widely used in evaluating local explanations of black-box models [22, 28, 29, 39]. Because of this, we consider them as *indirect* measures for evaluating local explanations.

However, they rely heavily on the role of the black-box model as an oracle to provide accurate and certain predictions. Even though we are unaware of studies that have addressed the limitations of the robustness analysis, except partially the work of [42], we have identified more limitations associated with them:

Firstly and most importantly, *blaming* the local explanation for their lack of robustness is not straightforward. It is equally probable that after nullifying features, the black-box model is providing us with wrongful predictions with high certainty, similar to the case of adversarial examples. We provide examples of this problem in each category of robustness measures. For showing this limitation in the first subcategory of robustness measures, Fig. 2 shows the evaluation process of superpixels, similar to those used by LIME and SHAP explanations. The example includes the image of the class bird with predicted label *indigo bunting*. We can see that nullifying features from these superpixels can generate wrong predictions. For example, in the first image of the bottom row, consider when LIME correctly allocates significant importance scores to the superpixels of the body of the bird. Using Importance by Deletion, we nullify these pixels and record the change in the predicted output of the ResNET model. The model still predicts the label of the instances of the class "bird." Therefore, we blame LIME for inaccurate explanations. We can see that using wrongful information to evaluate explanations may result in blaming explanations for producing explanations that are not robust. However, the model should be blamed for its role as an inaccurate oracle.

To see that the blame problem also exists with the second sub-category of robustness measures, we will show the example provided by [2] (Fig. 3). In this example, instances with added Gaussian noise are created to evaluate the Con-

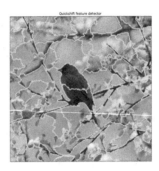

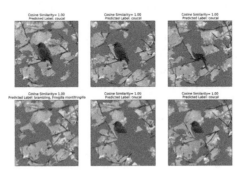

Fig. 2. (Above): The explained bird image from the ImageNet dataset with the predicted label of *indigo bunting* by the ResNET model. (Below). Let us evaluate the importance of superpixels that include the body of the bird (first image from the bottom row) by removing those pixels. Since the model can still predict the class of the image as a bird, we will wrongfully blame the explanations for inaccurate explanations because of an inaccurate oracle. Source: [36]

tinuity robustness of the explained instance (shown with dotted circle). Since the instance lies close to the decision boundary, the prediction of these instances will include a significant change in the predicted output and potentially in their local explanations. Because of this, we blame the local explanations for their lack of robustness, yet the underlying reason is that the black-box model does not satisfy the Lipshizt condition around the explained.

Secondly, there is also a lack of agreement on nullifying features and accounting for that bias in evaluating explanations. In [43], the authors show that the choice of the nullification method can severely affect the selection of the most robust explanation technique.

Lastly, there is no global optimal robustness value or an acceptable threshold for selecting robustness explanations. In other words, how much change in the predicted score of a black-box model after nullifying an important (unimportant) feature can deem the explanation robust? [4]. In numerous studies, we see how the scale of change after nullifying features can be extremely large between the

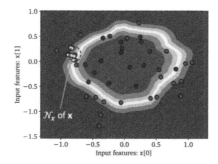

Fig. 3. For evaluating the robustness of the explained instance (shown with a dotted circle), several instances with added Gaussian noise are created around that instance. Since the explained instance lies close to the decision boundary, it can have a potentially large value for Continuity (hence low robustness concerning this measure). However, the model does not satisfy the Lipshitz condition in the neighborhood around the explained instance. Yet again, we blame explanations for their lack of robustness, whereas the model is at fault. Source: [36]

same model trained on different datasets or two models trained on a single dataset, as shown in [22].[6]

Some studies have aimed to address the limitations of the robustness measures. In [20,21], the authors propose to retrain the model after replacing the important (unimportant) features before evaluating the robustness of explanations. Their proposed method aims to tackle the first aforementioned problem above, namely to minimize the problem of uncertain predictions by the oracle. However, this raises the blame problem again: what if the newly trained model does not represent the original black-box model we aimed to explain?

Overall, we need to emphasize that the conclusions we can draw from evaluating local explanations with robustness measures are very limited due to the absence of ground truth. In the next Section, we provide an overview of the methods that introduce the notion of ground truth to evaluate local explanations directly.

5.2 Evaluations Using Ground Truth

As mentioned in the previous section, robustness measures can be applied to evaluate local explanations of any model trained on any dataset. However, these measures only measure the accuracy of explanations indirectly. Unlike the robustness measure, using the ground truth-based evaluation measure, we can measure the accuracy of local explanations directly without using the black-box model as an oracle.

In the upcoming subsections, we show that evaluation based on the ground truth can be categorized into two subcategories: extracting ground truth from synthetic datasets (Sect. 5.2) and extracting ground truth from interpretable

---

[6] See Table 2 of the study and the scale of values that explanations show for robustness.

models (Sect. 5.2). In Sect. 5.2, we show the important role of the similarity metric when evaluating local explanations with these ground truth-based approaches.

Ground Truth from Synthetic Data. The studies that aim to obtain ground truth from synthetic data are based on the following **assumption**: if the model we explain is too complex. The extraction of ground truth from them is challenging. However, we can obtain ground truth from synthetic dataset generators. We create synthetic datasets that include prior importance scores for each feature, and then we train the black-box model on this dataset and obtain local explanations. The similarity between the feature importance from the local explanations and the prior importance scores can measure the accuracy of local explanations in this setting. The main benefit of this approach is that we still evaluate the explanations of a black-box model since there is no limitations on the model, and we can also measure the accuracy of local explanations directly.

In [16], the authors proposed their method Seneca-RC that generates data from a polynomial function that can include varying operators such as *sin* or *cos* in its polynomial terms. After that, a sample dataset is generated based on the chosen polynomial function. Lastly, the algorithm returns the ground truth importance scores for the explained instance x based on the following steps: 1) the closest instance $x*$ to x on the decision boundary of an explained model, f, is found, and 2) the derivative of the ground truth polynomial is evaluated at this point and returned as true importance scores for x. The main benefit of using SenecaRC is that it has a simple logic based on the derivative for various polynomial-based data generation processes. We show an example of Seneca-RC in Sect. 5.5. The same study proposes other methods for obtaining ground truth for rule-based, saliency maps, and text-based explanations.

In [7], the authors evaluate the local explanation techniques using the following synthetic datasets with polynomial features:

1. 2-dimensional XOR as binary classification. The input vector X is generated from a 10-dimensional standard Gaussian. The response variable Y is generated from $P(Y = 1|X) \propto \exp\{X_1 X_2\}$.
2. Orange Skin. The input vector X is generated from a 10-dimensional standard Gaussian. The response variable Y is generated from $P(Y = 1|X) \propto \exp\{\sum_{i=1}^{4} X_i^2 - 4\}$. Figure 4 (a) shows an example of this dataset with instance ground truth over the decision plane of Multi-layer perceptron trained on this dataste.
3. Nonlinear additive model. Generate X from a 10-dimensional standard Gaussian. The response variable Y is generated from $P(Y = 1|X) \propto \exp\{-100 \sin(2X_1) + 2|X_2| + X_3 + \exp\{-X_4\}\}$.
4. Switch feature. Generate X_1 from a mixture of two Gaussians centered at ± 3 respectively with equal probability. If X_1 is generated from the Gaussian centered at 3, the $2 - 5th$ dimensions generate Y like the orange skin model. Otherwise, the $6 - 9th$ dimensions are used to generate Y from the nonlinear additive model.

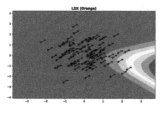   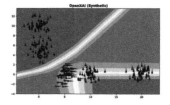

(a) Orange Skin Dataset from [7]   (b) Gaussian Dataset from [3] (4 clusters)

Fig. 4. Ground Truth from Synthetic Datasets represented on the decision plane of a multi-layer perception in two trained on this dataset. The arrow represents the ground truth importance scores. Note that the representation of the model does not agree with prior ground truth importance scores.

In this study, after the model is trained on these datasets, local explanations must provide feature importance scores close to the weight of the respective features in the label-generating function. We have found some limitations of the datasets proposed in [7]. Firstly, as we can see in Fig. 4, the ground truth of Orange Skin is equal for all instances irrespective of their position on the decision plane. Similar cases happen in XOR and Nonlinear additive models, as no specific rule changes the label generation formula for specific instances. Even though Switch Feature (dataset 4) can be considered a baseline for local ground truth definitions as the label generation is based on each instance's feature value since the two Gaussian collide around the value of 0, all the features $2 - 9$ can all be considered important.

In [3], the authors propose a synthetic dataset with Gaussian clusters without covariance between each cluster to solve the problem of datasets such as the Switch feature (Fig. 4 (b)). The dataset allocates random feature masks that control which features can contribute to the predicted output. As shown in the figure, these ground truth importance scores disagree with the model's decision plane. For example, the cluster on the top left disregards the importance of the feature along the x-axis, whereas the nearest decision boundary has used this feature to separate instances, which means that it is important to the model.

Overall, the main limitation of obtaining ground truth from synthetic datasets in [3,7,16] is that it suffers from the blame problem. We are blaming local explanations even though proving that the explained model has learned a representation that follows our prior importance scores is difficult. As highlighted in the work of [6], local explanations must be truthful to the model and not the data-generating process. In this case, we again fall into the same problem: we cannot directly blame the explanation technique for inaccurate explanations.

Another (important) limitation of this category of evaluation measures is that synthetic datasets do not exhibit the complexities of benchmark datasets. Therefore, we do not gain an understanding of the effects complex datasets have on the accuracy of local explanations.

Ground Truth from Interpretable Models. One of the limitations of the studies that use ground truth from datasets is that there is no guarantee that the explained model has learned a representation by the data. As mentioned in the previous section, explanation techniques must explain the model, not the data. Some studies have aimed to tackle this limitation by extracting ground truth from models directly, however, from simpler and more interpretable models. Their **assumption** is as follows: even though we cannot extract ground truth from the black-box model, we can extract them from the more transparent interpretable models. The main benefit of this approach is that we are extracting the ground truth straight from the model's representation and have no assumptions about the datasets. The main strength of this category of evaluation measures is we are confident that these ground truth importance scores are obtained directly from the model and its representation we aim to explain. In these types of evaluations, similar to the methods in Sect. 5.2, we can evaluate the local explanations directly.

In [3,25], the ground truth for local explanations is extracted from the weight of Logistic Regression models. Formally, given weights $w \in \mathbb{R}^{M+1}$ and an instance $x_n \in \mathbb{R}^M$, a logistic regression model is defined as:

$$P(y_n = c || x_n, w) = \frac{1}{1 + e^{-\sum_{m=0}^{M} w^m x_n^m}} \tag{3}$$

where $x_n^0 = 1$. Based on this, the vector of w is used as the ground truth importance score for all instances. One major drawback of this ground truth is that it is similar for all instances regardless of their feature values.

In [37], the authors highlight that the approach used by [3,25] is a baseline for a global explanation and not local explanations as shown earlier in [13,30]. Their study proposes extracting the ground truth for local explanation techniques using additive terms of linear additive prediction functions. For example, by transforming the prediction function of Logistic Regression to log odds ratio, they extract the additive terms as the ground truth importance scores. These scores are referred to as Model-Intrinsic Additive Scores (MIAS). More formally,

$$log \frac{P(y_n = c || x_n, w)}{P(y_n = \neg c || x_n, w)} = \sum_{m=0}^{M} w^m x_n^m \tag{4}$$

where $\neg c$ is the complement of class c, the authors propose $\lambda_n^m = w^m x_n^m$ as MIAS, the ground truth for local explanations. We can see that in their definition, the feature value of each instance plays a role in the local ground truth importance scores. As we mentioned earlier, local explanations can be unique for different instances, and therefore, the optimal local ground truth needs to include terms specific to each instance as well. The authors show that their proposed method can be used to evaluate local explanations of other interpretable models, such as Linear Regression and Gaussian Naive Bayes.

There is an advantage to the evaluation methods of this category. Since ground truth importance scores are extracted from the explained model without inducing any change, we can finally blame the inaccuracy of local explanations for themselves. These evaluation methods follow a more principled approach in which they only rely on the explained model, not as an oracle, but as a source to extract ground truth importance scores.

However, there are other limitations associated with this class of evaluation measures. The main limitation of methods that extract ground truth from interpretable models is the explanation techniques were initially developed for explaining black-box models. Therefore, it is not straightforward to conclude that if local explanations accurately explain these interpretable models, they will successfully provide accurate explanations of black-box models. Moreover, ground truth importance scores must be defined separately for each explained model class. Section 5.5 highlights this in an example of a synthetic dataset.

The Role of Similarity Metric. Measuring the local explanations directly using ground truth is highly sensitive to the choice of similarity metric. This is a critical issue that has not gained the attention of the studies in the Explainable AI community. The Euclidean distance [4], cosine similarity [39], and Spearman's rank correlation [15], F1-Score [16] are among the set of measures usually used in the evaluation studies of local explanations.

For illustration, we provide an example of comparing two local explanations using Euclidean and Cosine similarity and Spearman's rank correlation taken from [37]. This example shows that using different similarity metrics can lead to selecting different local explanations based on explanation accuracy. Suppose we need to measure the accuracy of two different local explanations $\phi_1 = [0.21, 0.1, 0.32]$ and $\phi_2 = [0.21, 0.3, 0.12]$ to the local ground truth score $\lambda = [0.32, 0.2, 0.42]$. We compare the similarity of these explanations with the ground truth:

$$EuclideanS(\lambda, \phi_1) = 0.179 \qquad EuclideanS(\lambda, \phi_2) = 0.28$$
$$SpearmanC(\lambda, \phi_1) = 1 \qquad SpearmanC(\lambda, \phi_2) = -1$$
$$CosineS(\lambda, \phi_1) = 0.99 \qquad CosineS(\lambda, \phi_2) = 0.81$$

Based on Spearman's rank correlation, the ranking of ϕ_1 correlates perfectly with λ, while the ranking of ϕ_2 negatively correlates with λ. Using this rank-based metric, we can thus conclude that explanation ϕ_1 is more accurate than ϕ_2. The Euclidean[7], and Cosine Similarity instead votes in favor of ϕ_2 as the more accurate explanation. This is because Euclidean similarity takes the difference between importance and ground truth scores similarly for all features. On the other hand, cosine similarity only considers the angle between the two vectors. For Spearman's rank correlation, the order of features based on their importance is the most important aspect.

---

[7] In this example, the Euclidean similarity is defined as $1/(\epsilon + d)$ where d is the Euclidean distance and ϵ is the machine epsilon of Python.

Even though cosine similarity can be the most optimal measure for data domains such as text and image, we argue that for tabular datasets, rank-based measures such as Spearman's rank correlation might be more suitable for evaluating local explanations. This is large because feature importance is presented to users sorted based on their importance scores in descending order in tabular datasets. In this representation, the similarity among the features with the largest importance scores becomes more important. In addition, the rank-based measures enable comparing feature importance scores with substantially different mechanisms for explanations, e.g., LIME and SHAP versus Permutation Importance. However, the optimal choice of similarity for evaluating local explanations remains an open research question.

5.3   Evaluation with Model Randomization

In some studies, local explanations are evaluated based on comparing the local explanations of an accurate black-box model versus after some randomization (contamination) induced on the same black-box model. The **assumption** is that local explanations need to show significantly different explanations for these two models. In this category of evaluation methods, we no longer have access to or include ground truth in evaluating local explanations.

In [1], the authors propose two randomization tests. In the first test, they randomly re-initialize the weights of the neural networks model sequentially. In the second test, they independently randomize the weights of a single layer one at a time. They show that most of the local explanation techniques of neural network models, both model-agnostic and model-based, provide similar explanations for the original and randomized models. They conclude that these methods are inaccurate for explaining the investigated neural network models.

In this category of evaluation measures, we face the blame problem again. Studies have shown that black-box models, including deep neural networks, tend to memorize and extract accurate knowledge even from random or corrupted labels [23,46]. Because of this, there is no guarantee that randomizations can largely obfuscate the workings of the black-box models enough to cause changes to the local explanations. We can blame local explanations in these scenarios even though the explained models can still provide meaningful predictions after introducing randomization.

5.4   Human-Grounded Evaluation

The main focus of our study so far was on the limitations of the functionally grounded evaluations of local explanations. In this section, we briefly describe a set of limitations in the studies that perform human-grounded evaluation of local explanations.

The human-based evaluations were initially suggested by [24]. The authors proposed several ways in which human users can evaluate the explanation. One of the most common methods is called model replay, i.e. a task in which the human subjects are asked to replay the model, i.e., to predict the prediction of the instance explained [34, 35, 39] using local explanations. The **assumption** is that if the human subjects can replay the model promptly, the explanations can be considered accurate. In these studies, it is customary to divide human subjects into experts of the task at hand or lay humans.

One of the main benefits of such methods is that there is also no need to obtain the ground truth for explanations before our evaluation process. On the other hand, there is a limitation associated with them: we cannot subjectively measure how much of the mimicking is performed using human subjects' prior knowledge of data or the model. If human subjects have a poor understanding of the model or data in the task, the poor model replay will still be blamed on local explanations for their inaccuracy.

In other studies [29], the notion of consistency with human subjects is considered a metric for evaluating explanations. The measure represents the similarity between human explanations and algorithmic local explanations. The main assumption behind such methods is that if the similarity is large between the local explanations and human explanations, the local explanations are accurate. However, these methods also suffer from limitations. There are no analysis presented to evaluate whether there are complete agreements between the logic of the explained model and human subjects in the way they solve the task at hand. Studies have shown that humans and machine learning models rely on different knowledge in performing tasks [5]. Because of this, we will blame local explanations again even though the main underlying problem is that the model has learned the task with a significantly different logic.

5.5   Synthetic Example

As we said earlier, all evaluation measures have different assumptions and study different characteristics of local explanations. In simple words, they are orthogonal to one another. However, in this section, we show an example, taken from [37], where all of these measures can be compared against one another from synthetic datasets proposed by [16], the ground truth proposed [3], robustness measures [12, 22] and the MIAS scores of [37]. This is because we use synthetic datasets trained on a Logistic Regression model.

Let $Y = 2x_0 - x_1$ be the data generation process where features x_0 contribute positively and x_1 negatively to the label (Fig. 5). Let Seneca-RC use this function to generate its synthetic datasets. We sample one thousand instances from Seneca-RC's data generation process where no extra redundant features are added, and we set the noise level to 0.3. We train a Logistic Regression model on this generated dataset. The decision boundary shows that overall, the model has correctly identified that both features are important for separating instances from different classes (Class 1 is represented by the blue color). We also see arrows on top of each instance. The arrows represent the baseline importance scores that each evaluation method uses for evaluating the explanation of local explanations. Note that these arrows do not represent the local explanations but the baselines each evaluation measure uses for evaluating the local explanations.

The Seneca-RC ground truth importance scores are all equal to the vector, $[1, -1]$, irrespective of the position of the instance in the prediction space or the decision boundary of the model. This is because the derivative of the data generation process concerning each feature is a constant value. As mentioned earlier, there can be a discrepancy between the label generation function and the model representation, which is evident in this case.

The ground truth of OpenXAI [3] is also constant across all instances. This is because the model weights are used as the baseline for evaluating all local explanations in this approach. Based on this, all instances receive equal ground truth scores regardless of their position in the decision space.

Unlike the other methods in our example, robustness measures do not technically have the ground truth for each instance. However, the rationale behind these measures is to measure the effect of nullification of each feature on the prediction of the model's predicted output. Because of this, the arrow on top of instances is created as follows: each feature is nullified separately, and the absolute change in the predicted scores of the model concerning class one is recorded. We have nullified each feature using the average values of that feature in the dataset as it is generally practiced in tabular datasets [27,31,32]. In the figure, we can see that for most instances, the robustness arrow does not set any importance to the second feature on the y-axis, even though it plays an important role in the linear boundary of logistic regression and the data generation process. Moreover, an instance will receive zero robustness by default along an axis, i.e., for a feature, if its feature values are similar to the empirical

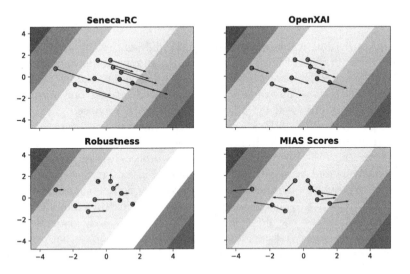

Fig. 5. Comparison of the baseline importance scores that Seneca-RC, OpenXAI along with robustness measures and Model-intrinsic Additive Score (MIAS). The Seneca-RC algorithm generated the dataset. The baseline importance score for each instance is visualized as vectors on the top of each instance.

average of each feature. This is because nullifying those features will not affect the predicted output.

The Model-Intrinsic Additive Scores (MIAS) allocate different values for instances based on the feature value and their location on the decision plane of the Logistic Regression model. MIAS score of Logistic Regression models sets importance to both features in explaining the log odds ratio of the model. We can also see that the instances will have arrows toward the subspace with maximum log odds of their predicted class visualized by the shades in the background. Moreover, the MIAS vectors of instances close to the decision boundary are more different since the uncertainty in the model's predicted output is larger in those parts of the plane. This satisfied the uniqueness property as discussed in Sect. 1.

Overall, among the evaluation methods we discussed here, we argue that MIAS scores are the most reliable ground truth for evaluating local explanations of Logistic Regression since 1) Their baseline is sensitive to the decision boundary of the model, and 2) MIAS scores allocate unique ground truth scores for different instances depending on their position in the decision plane of Logistic Regression.

6   Conclusion

Our study presented a taxonomy of the evaluation methods for local model-agnostic explanations: robustness analysis, extracting ground truth from synthetic data and interpretable models, evaluation with model randomization, and human-grounded evaluation. We provide a detailed discussion of each evaluation method's assumptions, strengths, and limitations. Through our study, we highlighted that the significant limitation of all of the categories of evaluation measures is the presence of a "blame problem" where we are unsure of blaming the inaccuracy of local explanations on the explanation techniques or the black-box model or human subjects (in the case of human-based evaluation methods).

Even though robustness analysis poses no assumption or the type of model or data used for obtaining local explanations, it can only evaluate the local explanations indirectly. The main limitation of robustness analysis is that we can no longer directly blame the explanations for their lack of robustness or the explained model if it provides wrongful predictions.

Extracting ground truth from a synthetic dataset measures the local explanations directly by setting prior importance scores in the data generation process. However, there are no guarantees that the explained model has learned these prior importance scores. In this case, we will blame the local explanations for inaccuracy instead of the black-box model.

Extracting ground truth from an interpretable model solves the limitation of the synthetic datasets approaches by obtaining ground truth directly from the interpretable model. The number of studies that use this approach is limited, but to our knowledge, they represent the most principled approach to evaluating local model-agnostic explanations. They are the only category of evaluation methods that bypass the blame problem. However, they come with their limitations as well. Since explanation techniques are built to explain black-box models, it is hard to conclude that they are accurate for these models by only looking at local explanations' accuracy of interpretable models.

Evaluation using model randomization assumes that local explanations must provide significantly different explanations after randomizing the model weights or parts of the black-box model. Several studies have shown that randomization in black-box models does not necessarily reduce or change their predictive power. In this case, we can blame the local explanations for their inaccuracy, whereas we need to blame the black-box model.

Using human-grounded evaluation measures to evaluate local explanations can circumvent the need for ground truth importance scores. However, we can end up blaming local explanations for the inherently wrong intuition of the human subjects of the datasets and task at hand or that humans and models are solving the task at hand with different logic.

The thesis of our study is that none of the available evaluation methods in the literature of explainability is optimal, even though they can circumvent the blame problem in the case of ground truth via interpretable models. Moreover, beyond the blame problem, we need to be aware of the trade-offs these evaluation measures offer. Finding the optimal measure for evaluating local model-agnostic explanations remains an open research problem.

References

1. Adebayo, J., Gilmer, J., Muelly, M., Goodfellow, I., Hardt, M., Kim, B.: Sanity checks for saliency maps. In: Advances in Neural Information Processing Systems, vol. 31 (2018)
2. Agarwal, C., et al.: Rethinking stability for attribution-based explanations. arXiv preprint arXiv:2203.06877 (2022)
3. Agarwal, C., et al.: OpenXAI: towards a transparent evaluation of model explanations. In: Advances in Neural Information Processing Systems, vol. 35, pp. 15784–15799 (2022)
4. Alvarez-Melis, D., Jaakkola, T.S.: On the robustness of interpretability methods. arXiv preprint arXiv:1806.08049 (2018)
5. Arnold, T., Kasenberg, D.: Value alignment or misalignment - what will keep systems accountable? In: AAAI Workshop on AI, Ethics, and Society (2017)
6. Chen, H., Janizek, J.D., Lundberg, S., Lee, S.-I.: True to the model or true to the data? arXiv preprint arXiv:2006.16234 (2020)
7. Chen, J., Song, L., Wainwright, M., Jordan, M.: Learning to explain: an information-theoretic perspective on model interpretation. In International Conference on Machine Learning, pp. 883–892. PMLR (2018)
8. Covert, I., Lundberg, S.M., Lee, S.-I.: Explaining by removing: a unified framework for model explanation. J. Mach. Learn. Res. **22**, 209-1 (2021)
9. Craven, M., Shavlik, J.: Extracting tree-structured representations of trained networks. In: Advances in Neural Information Processing Systems, vol. 8 (1995)
10. Craven, M.W., Shavlik, J.W.: Using sampling and queries to extract rules from trained neural networks. In: Machine Learning Proceedings 1994, pp. 37–45. Elsevier (1994)
11. Doshi-Velez, F., Kim, B.: Towards a rigorous science of interpretable machine learning. arXiv preprint arXiv:1702.08608 (2017)

12. Fong, R.C., Vedaldi, A.: Interpretable explanations of black boxes by meaningful perturbation. In: Proceedings of the IEEE International Conference on Computer Vision, pp. 3429–3437 (2017)
13. Freitas, A.A.: Comprehensible classification models: a position paper. ACM SIGKDD Explor. Newsl. **15**(1), 1–10 (2014)
14. Geirhos, R., Zimmermann, R.S., Bilodeau, B., Brendel, W., Kim, B.: Don't trust your eyes: on the (un) reliability of feature visualizations (2023)
15. Ghorbani, A., Abid, A., Zou, J.: Interpretation of neural networks is fragile. In: Proceedings of the AAAI Conference on Artificial Intelligence, vol. 33, pp. 3681–3688 (2019)
16. Guidotti, R.: Evaluating local explanation methods on ground truth. Artif. Intell. **291**, 103428 (2021)
17. Guidotti, R., Monreale, A., Pedreschi, D., Giannotti, F.: Principles of explainable artificial intelligence. In: Sayed-Mouchaweh, M. (ed.) Explainable AI Within the Digital Transformation and Cyber Physical Systems, pp. 9–31. Springer, Cham (2021). https://doi.org/10.1007/978-3-030-76409-8_2
18. Hancox-Li, L.: Robustness in machine learning explanations: does it matter? In: Proceedings of the 2020 Conference on Fairness, Accountability, and Transparency, pp. 640–647 (2020)
19. Hedström, A., et al.: Quantus: an explainable AI toolkit for responsible evaluation of neural network explanations and beyond. J. Mach. Learn. Res. **24**(34), 1–11 (2023)
20. Hooker, G., Mentch, L., Zhou, S.: Unrestricted permutation forces extrapolation: variable importance requires at least one more model, or there is no free variable importance. Stat. Comput. **31**(6), 1–16 (2021)
21. Hooker, S., Erhan, D., Kindermans, P.-J., Kim, B.: A benchmark for interpretability methods in deep neural networks. In: Advances in Neural Information Processing Systems, vol. 32 (2019)
22. Hsieh, C.-Y., et al.: Evaluations and methods for explanation through robustness analysis (2021)
23. Jiang, L., Zhou, Z., Leung, T., Li, L.-J., Fei-Fei, L.: Mentornet: learning data-driven curriculum for very deep neural networks on corrupted labels. In: International Conference on Machine Learning, pp. 2304–2313. PMLR (2018)
24. Kim, B., Khanna, R., Koyejo, O.O.: Examples are not enough, learn to criticize! Criticism for interpretability. In: Advances in Neural Information Processing Systems, vol. 29 (2016)
25. Krishna, S., et al.: The disagreement problem in explainable machine learning: a practitioner's perspective. arXiv preprint arXiv:2202.01602 (2022)
26. Leavitt, M.L., Morcos, A.: Towards falsifiable interpretability research. arXiv preprint arXiv:2010.12016 (2020)
27. Liu, Y., Khandagale, S., White, C., Neiswanger, W.: Synthetic benchmarks for scientific research in explainable machine learning. arXiv preprint arXiv:2106.12543 (2021)
28. Lundberg, S.M., Lee, S.-I.: A unified approach to interpreting model predictions. In: Advances in Neural Information Processing Systems, vol. 30 (2017)
29. Lundberg, S.M., et al.: From local explanations to global understanding with explainable AI for trees. Nat. Mach. Intell. **2**(1), 56–67 (2020)
30. Molnar, C., Casalicchio, G., Bischl, B.: Interpretable machine learning – a brief history, state-of-the-art and challenges. In: Koprinska, I., et al. (eds.) ECML PKDD 2020. CCIS, vol. 1323, pp. 417–431. Springer, Cham (2020). https://doi.org/10.1007/978-3-030-65965-3_28

31. Molnar, C., et al.: General pitfalls of model-agnostic interpretation methods for machine learning models. In: Holzinger, A., Goebel, R., Fong, R., Moon, T., Müller, K.R., Samek, W. (eds.) xxAI 2020. LNCS, vol. 13200, pp. 39–68. Springer, Cham (2022). https://doi.org/10.1007/978-3-031-04083-2_4

32. Montavon, G., Samek, W., Müller, K.-R.: Methods for interpreting and understanding deep neural networks. Digit. Sig. Process. **73**, 1–15 (2018)

33. Nauta, M., et al.: From anecdotal evidence to quantitative evaluation methods: A systematic review on evaluating explainable ai. ACM Comput. Surv. **55**(13s), 1–42 (2023)

34. Nguyen, D.: Comparing automatic and human evaluation of local explanations for text classification. In: Proceedings of the 2018 Conference of the North American Chapter of the Association for Computational Linguistics: Human Language Technologies, Volume 1 (Long Papers), pp. 1069–1078 (2018)

35. Poursabzi-Sangdeh, F., Goldstein, D.G., Hofman, J.M., Vaughan, J.W.W., Wallach, H.: Manipulating and measuring model interpretability. In: Proceedings of the 2021 CHI Conference on Human Factors in Computing Systems, pp. 1–52 (2021)

36. Rahnama, A.H.A., Boström,H.: A study of data and label shift in the lime framework. arXiv preprint arXiv:1910.14421 (2019)

37. Rahnama, A.H.A., Bütepage, J., Geurts, P., Boström, H.: Can local explanation techniques explain linear additive models? Data Min. Knowl. Discov. pp. 1–44 (2023)

38. Ribeiro, M.T., Singh, S., Guestrin, C.: Model-agnostic interpretability of machine learning. arXiv preprint arXiv:1606.05386 (2016)

39. Ribeiro, M.T., Singh, S., Guestrin, C.: "Why should I trust you?" explaining the predictions of any classifier. In: Proceedings of the 22nd ACM SIGKDD International Conference on Knowledge Discovery and Data Mining, pp.1135–1144 (2016)

40. Rudin, C.: Please stop explaining black box models for high stakes decisions. Stat **1050**, 26 (2018)

41. Selvaraju, R.R., Cogswell, M., Das, A., Vedantam, R., Parikh, D., Batra, D.: Gradcam: Visual explanations from deep networks via gradient-based localization. In: Proceedings of the IEEE International Conference on Computer Vision, pp. 618–626 (2017)

42. Strumbelj, E., Kononenko, I.: An efficient explanation of individual classifications using game theory. J. Mach. Learn. Res. **11**, 1–18 (2010)

43. Sturmfels, P., Lundberg, S., Lee, S.-I.: Visualizing the impact of feature attribution baselines. Distill **5**(1), e22 (2020)

44. Sundararajan, M., Taly, A., Yan, Q.: Axiomatic attribution for deep networks. In: International Conference on Machine Learning, pp. 3319–3328. PMLR (2017)

45. Yeh, C.-K., Hsieh, C.-Y., Suggala, A., Inouye, D.I., Ravikumar, P.K.: On the (in)fidelity and sensitivity of explanations. In: Advances in Neural Information Processing Systems, vol. 32 (2019)

46. Zhang, C., Bengio, S., Hardt, M., Recht, B., Vinyals, O.: Understanding deep learning (still) requires rethinking generalization. Commun. ACM **64**(3), 107–115 (2021)

47. Zhou, J., Gandomi, A.H., Chen, F., Holzinger, A.: Evaluating the quality of machine learning explanations: a survey on methods and metrics. Electronics **10**(5), 593 (2021)

Explainable Anomaly Detection in Industrial Streams

Jakub Jakubowski[1,2]($\boxtimes$) (ID), Przemysław Stanisz[2], Szymon Bobek[3] (ID), and Grzegorz J. Nalepa[3] (ID)

[1] Department of Applied Computer Science, AGH University of Science and Technology, 30-059 Krakow, Poland
`jjakubow@agh.edu.pl`
[2] ArcelorMittal Poland, 31-752 Krakow, Poland
[3] Jagiellonian University, Faculty of Physics, Astronomy and Applied Computer Science, Institute of Applied Computer Science, and Jagiellonian Human-Centered AI Lab (JAHCAI), and Mark Kac Center for Complex Systems Research, ul. prof. Stanisława Łojasiewicza 11, 30-348 Kraków, Poland

Abstract. Anomaly detection in industrial environment is a complex task, which requires to consider multiple characteristics of the data from industrial sensors and anomalies itself. Such data is often highly imbalanced and the availability of labels is limited. The data is generated in streaming fashion, which means that it is unbounded and potentially infinite. The industrial process may evolve over time due to degradation of the asset, maintenance actions or modifications. The manual verification and definition of anomaly source is a tideous task, which requires human to carefully investigate each anomalous observation. An anomaly detection system should consider all above challanges. In this paper we propose a system, which addresses the discussed issues. It is applicable for industrial data stream scenarios and comprises of unsupervised anomaly detection model, resampling module and explanation module. We consider two different approaches towards the utilization of machine learning model – online and offline. We present our work in relation to a cold rolling process use case, which is one of the steps in production of steel strips.

Keywords: Anomaly detection · Data streams · Explainable Artificial Intelligence

1 Introduction

Significant progress in the domains of Industrial Internet of Things, Machine Learning (ML), and Big Data has presented a remarkable prospect for the development of innovative intelligent systems that can effectively assist industrial procedures. An inherent concern in industrial systems, which can be tackled through the utilization of Industry 4.0 technologies, revolves around real-time anomaly detection. Anomalies refer to deviations from the typical operational states that possess the potential to significantly disrupt production processes, leading to unplanned downtime, compromised product quality, or increased safety hazards.

S. Nowaczyk et al. (Eds.): ECAI 2023 Workshops, CCIS 1947, pp. 87–100, 2024.
https://doi.org/10.1007/978-3-031-50396-2_5

The implementation of an anomaly detection system is a complex task, requiring one to carefully consider various challenges. First, the anomalies usually constitute a very small fraction of the data, which makes the dataset heavily imbalanced. Additionally, it is difficult to determine all potential kinds of anomalies, even for existing industrial sites, as the anomalies tend to be very diverse. Second, except for the rarity of anomalies, another problem might be the rarity of some operating conditions. By operating conditions, we understand different states of the machine, which are caused not due to deviations in the process itself, but the deviations in the characteristics of the environment which influence the observed data. In case of cold rolling, the different operating conditions can be regarded as the processing of different products, which differ by thickness, width, reduction or steel composition. The family of products in a manufacturing site is often composed of certain number of popular products and some number of rare products (operating conditions), which are not well represented in the data. This is another dimension of data imbalance in the industrial setting. If the problem is not carefully considered, then the anomaly detection system could treat all rare operating conditions as anomalies, even if the issue does not originate in any malfunctions of the production site. Third, data in industrial processes are continuously generated at high speeds, creating large volumes of data that need to be processed in a limited amount of time [9]. The industrial setting may evolve with time due to various reasons, e.g., production of new type of product, slow degradation of the manufacturing line, changes in the asset. This evolution of the data over time is often referred to as concept drift [9]. Last, the ML models are often considered as black boxes, and humans are not able to follow the reasoning of the algorithm. For anomaly detection in an industrial environment, this might be a big issue, as we usually deal with high-dimensional data, where the source of anomaly might not be visible superficially. Therefore, the system should provide not only an alarm in case of anomaly but also some kind of explanation of its reasoning. This is especially important if there might be multiple sources of anomalies in the system.

To address the issues described above, we propose a system for the detection of anomalies in streaming data from industrial processes, which comprises of anomaly detection model, resampling module and explanation module. We do not restrict the proposed solution to any specific type of industrial equipment; however, we focus on the type of anomaly detection tasks, where we deal with high-dimensional data and unknown number of potential anomaly sources. We present the solution on the use-case of cold rolling process, which is one of the stages in steel production. However, we believe our method is suitable for other industries such as manufacturing, energy, mining, but also transportation or whenever there is an evolving system.

The remainder of the paper is organized as follows. In Sect. 2 we briefly discuss the current state of knowledge in the related fields. In Sect. 3 we present our use case, which is the steel rolling process. In Sect. 4 we present the proposed system for anomaly detection. In Sect. 5 we conclude the work and discuss the potential directions of further research.

2 Related Works

In this section we provide a brief overview of anomaly detection, data streams, and explainable artificial intelligence.

2.1 Anomaly Detection

Anomaly detection, often referred to as outlier or novelty detection, is a process of identifying the data points that significantly differ from the rest of the data in terms of their characteristics. In real-life applications anomalies may be a symptom of invalid data, e.g. missing or extreme values, but also an indication of system malfunctions. The possibility to detect early signs of anomalies is very important for the industry, as they can gain significant benefits from preventing the anomalous states of machines. The potential issues that may arise due to such states include the breakdown of an asset (which leads to increased maintenance costs and unplanned downtime), production of downgraded material, and safety hazards. Each of the listed problems can cause significant financial or reputational losses; therefore, we believe that potential savings significantly surpass the cost of implementation of anomaly detection system.

The special characteristics of the anomalies, that is, their rarity, diversity, and inpredictability, are a major issue from point of view of machine learning models. Additionally, the availability of labels in real-life situations might be limited, which hinders the utilization of supervised learning methods. The discussed problems can be solved by switching from supervised ML methods to semi-supervised or unsupervised methods. These methods require little or no labeled data for training the models, which solves the problem of a limited number of labels. Unsupervised anomaly detection methods, depending on their characteristics, can be divided into similarity-based, one-class classification, isolation-based or deep learning categories [17]. Similarity-based algorithms, such as clustering algorithms or LOF [5] classify the points based on their neighborhood. If an observation does not have sufficient number of neighbors, it is classified as anomaly. A classification of one class such as OCSVM [21] aims to determine the characteristics of a normal class; if the observation does not follow the learned pattern, it is considered anomalous. The example of an isolation-based method is Isolation Forest [16]. The aim of the algorithm is to partition a dataset in such a way that an observations are isolated with the smallest possible number of partitionings. The points which require fewer divisions (which is equivalent to a smaller average depth of a tree) are given higher anomaly scores. The state-of-the-art deep learning methods, which are used for anomaly detection, are autoencoders [20] (AEs) and generative adversarial networks [12] (GANs). The general idea of AE is to encode the observations into latent representations and then decode them to obtain the original observation. The observations which are not well-reconstructed can be treated as anomalies. GANs use networks known as discriminator and generator in order to distinguish between normal and abnormal data.

2.2   Data Streams

Data streams learning is a field of machine learning that focuses on processing data in real-time, which is more suitable for data coming from a industrial environment than traditional batch learning. The main characteristics of a data stream are [11]:

- The data is generated continuously, which means that the stream is infinite in nature.
- The data distribution may vary over time.
- The labels for the new data may be delayed or inaccessible.

To account for the characteristics listed above, a machine learning model in streaming setting should meet some specific requirements. Most importantly, the model should meet the following criteria [7,9]:

- Data are processed only once upon arrival.
- The data are processed with limited memory and time, preferably before the new observation arrives.
- Its time and memory requirements do not depend on the number of observed data points (the complexity of the model should not increase with time).
- It has similar performance to its batch learning equivalent.
- It possesses the ability to adapt to new data, but can also remember relevant information from the past.

The majority of the state-of-the-art ML models, e.g. Random Forest, Support Vector Machine, or k-Means, are not designed for the online learning, as they require access to all data at time of training. For the purpose of online learning, alternative implementations of well-known ML algorithms were proposed, e.g., the alternative to Random Forest is Adaptive Random Forest [18], which uses Hoeffding Tree [6] as a single classifier.

However, offline learning algorithms might also be used in a streaming environment, provided that they meet the requirements listed above. Particularly, these algorithms should be re-trained upon any relevant changes in the data distribution are observed (concept drift), which can be monitored using drift detection methods e.g., Early Drift Detection Method (EDDM) [2], Adaptive Windowing (ADWIN) [4] or others. To achieve this, one needs to store some part of the most recent data in the memory, which will be accessible when the need for retraining occurs. What is also important is that the retraining of the model should have negative influence on the online predictions, i.e., the retraining of the model should not block the threads used for processing new observations.

One of the challenges, when dealing with streaming data, is the problem of pattern forgetting. It is the situation where the ML model loses the knowledge it has gained at some point in the past, which is still relevant. The simplest scenario is when we retrain the offline model upon concept drift and we lose all the knowledge of the previous model. There are several approaches which can be used to tackle this problem. One solution is to use the ensemble of the models, where each model is a separate instance, and the prediction is made using, e.g., majority vote [15]. When one of the models is outdated, it is re-trained, but the other models retain their knowledge. Another approach is to use domain adaptation, instead of retraining the model on new data. The domain adaptation aims at aligning the source domain (on which the model was trained) with the target domain (on which the predictions are made) [8]. Research on the use of domain adaptation for concept drift handling is not well established but yields promising results [14,23].

2.3 Explainable Artificial Intelligence

Explainable Artificial Intelligence (XAI) methods aim to gain some insight into the decisions of the models regarded as black-boxes. For complex models that use deep learning or a tree ensemble, the human has no cognitive ability to follow the decision process of the ML model, which might raise some issues. In the anomaly detection problem, when we have a complex system under observation with multivariate data, the model's user may not be able to easily determine the reason for the anomaly. The utilization of XAI methods can help indicate which measurements are perceived by the anomaly detection model as anomalous and thus guide the model's user to perform necessary corrective actions.

The field of XAI has gained a lot of attention in recent years due to the rapid development of ML methods, especially deep learning. The taxonomy of XAI is very broad and divides explainability methods based on factors such as type of explanation (feature importance, counterfactual, example-based etc.), the scope of explanation (local, global), applicability (model-specific, model-agnostic), or stage of computation (ante hoc, post hoc) [22]. Some of the state-of-the-art XAI methods include LIME [19], SHAP [18] or Counterfactual Explanations [24]. However, for streaming data, it must be taken into account that some of the methods like LIME or SHAP require access to background data, which might not always be available. In such cases the XAI methods, which do not have such requirement, like Counterfactual Explanations, should be considered. Another robust option for streaming setting is to use the surrogate models, which are interpretable, so that human can follow their reasoning. For streaming data, some of the algorithms could be considered as AMRules [1], which generates rules for each prediction or Hoeffding Tree [6], which builds a single decision tree that should be relatively easy to follow.

3 Cold Rolling

3.1 Mill Description

Our use case is related to a steel manufacturing process, more specifically cold rolling, which is most often preceded by hot rolling and pickling. It is a manufacturing method that aims at reshaping the steel strip by reducing its thickness. Additional results of the process include the increase in the strength of the material (which causes the necessity of annealing afterwards) and impartition of desired surface finish. A set of rollers typically consists of two work rolls (which are in direct contact with a steel strip) and two backup rolls. Remaining equipment of the mill, which is worth mentioning, includes uncoiler, recoiler, lubrication system, bending system, and electrical motors.

The manufacturing procedure begins with the unwinding of the steel coil on the uncoiler, and the strip gradually moves alongside the mill. The head of the strip is placed between the work rolls, and interstand tensions are applied to the strip. When the head of the strip is gripped by recoiler, the process accelerates and actual rolling begins. The reduction of strip thickness is achieved by applying pressure towards the strip with the use of work rolls. The whole manufacturing process is controlled by a programmable logic controller (PLC) with a human user able to manually perform some corrections. The superior task of the PLC is to achieve predefined thickness at the mill exit, while preserving process boundaries. The dynamics of this process necessitates rapid responses to minor fluctuations in the measured thickness. Proper maintenance is extremely important to guarantee the safety and quality of the process. The deviations of the rolling parameters from the normal working conditions may lead to many problems, e.g., flatness issues, scratches, thickness deviations, or strip breaks.

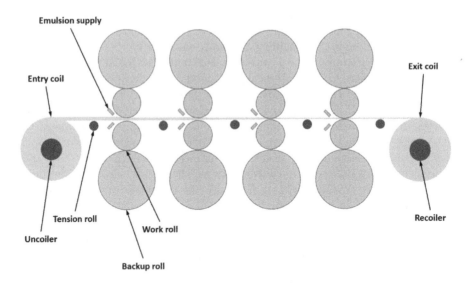

Fig. 1. Schematic diagram of tandem cold mill with 4 rolling stands [13].

The cold rolling mill investigated in our investigation is located in Kraków, Poland and is a part of ArcelorMittal company. It consists of four pairs of rollers, which gradually decrease the thickness of the steel from about 30% to 80% in total. The simplified diagram of our use-case production site is presented in Fig. 1. From the production line, we receive the sensor measurements at 1 Hz sampling frequency. The most relevant features include the metadata of the steel (grade, dimensions), work roll speeds, applied reductions, rolling forces, rolls bending, tensions, gaps, lubrication parameters (flow, pressure, temperature) and motor load (voltage, current). The observed values of the process may vary greatly depending on factors, e.g., the demanded rolling schedule, the wear of the work rolls, the condition of the lubricant, or the human corrections.

With respect to anomaly detection in the cold rolling process, there are few aspects of the data set which require a more detailed explanation. Most of the rolling parameters highly depend on the material being rolled, so the working conditions can change drastically from coil to coil if there is significant change in steel metadata. Additionally, the wear of the work rolls is a relatively rapid process and the replacement procedure of the work rolls is usually performed few times per day. As the characteristics of the work rolls may be different, their replacement may lead to a noticeable change in the observed working conditions.

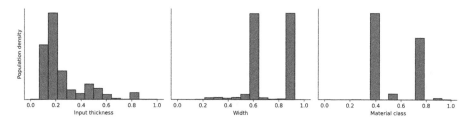

Fig. 2. Distribution of selected product metadata

3.2 Data Description

From a data point of view, an important issue is the fact that the data is highly imbalanced. This imbalance reveals itself in two dimensions. The first is the ratio of anomalies to normal observation, which is usually below 1%, which is a typical case in anomaly detection tasks. The second is high imbalance in the coil metadata – generally there are few types of 'common' products, which are often rolled and are well represented in the data. Apart from them, there are dozens of uncommon products, which are produced irregularly and in small amounts, leading to poor representation in the data. Figure 2 presents the distribution of the main characteristics of the product. In such a scenario, there is a risk of overfitting the model to the products well represented in the data, with the other ones automatically considered as anomalies (which is not at all certain). To tackle this issue, a resampling algorithm should be included in the training of the anomaly detection model, to ensure that all kinds of product are sufficiently represented in the training data. On the other hand, the problem of rarity of explanations can be easily solved using unsupervised methods, where the model learns only the normal behavior of the mill and assumes data that do not fit to the learned distribution, to be anomalies.

4 Proposed System

We propose a system that can be used for the detection of anomalies in data streams. Although we focus on the process of cold rolling, which is our use case, we believe that the following approach can be adapted to wide range of industrial applications. Our objective is to propose a flexible solution, which is not restricted to any specific ML methods, so that selection of algorithms can be done individually depending on the use case. We consider two different approaches towards detection of anomalies in streaming data. The first approach assumes that we do not store any observations in the memory and the algorithm works using an online learning methodology. The second approach assumes we are able to store some limited amount of data in the system memory and offline learning algorithms can be applied (with option to adapt them upon concept drifts). The proposed system is the extension of the anomaly detection method we have proposed in [13].

4.1 Main Assumptions

Regardless of the selected approach, the main assumptions of the system remain the same. The system consists of five main components, i.e., data stream, anomaly detection model, resampling module, XAI module, and human operator. Additionally, in the offline learning, we use a buffer, which stores the selected data, and concept drift detection, to detect changes in data distribution.

Data Stream. The data arrive at the system at any time interval, i.e., we do not need to have any specific sampling frequency. Each observation contains the sensor measurements from the line, which are processed by the system. It is assumed that the obviously invalid observations, e.g., sensor temperature indication $0K$ due to sensor fault, are filtered during preprocessing and not processed by the anomaly detection model.

Anomaly Detection. The anomaly detection model is designed as an unsupervised learning algorithm, which processes each observation received from the data stream. First, the model predicts the label of the observation (normal or anomalous). If the sample is considered normal, the model passes this observation to a resampling module for further processing. On the other hand, if the sample is predicted to be anomalous, it is passed to the XAI module and is not considered in future training. The label of the observation is assigned on the basis of the anomaly score. The mean anomaly score μ and its standard deviation σ are stored as a moving average. When the predicted anomaly score exceeds the selected threshold, e.g., $\mu + 3\sigma$, the observation is marked as anomaly.

Resampling Module. The task of the resampling module is to increase the number of rare products and decrease the number of popular products, which the anomaly detection model observes during training. To achieve this resampling module should utilize selected clustering algorithm, which classifies each observation to one of N operating conditions (clusters). The resampling is then performed based on the population of each cluster; minority clusters are oversampled, while majority clusters are undersampled. Potential methods for resampling include, but are not limited to, random sampling or C-SMOTE [3].

XAI Module. Explainable Artificial Intelligence methods are used to determine the source of the anomaly, so that the human can easily understand the reasoning of the anomaly detection model and take the necessary corrective actions. In a complex process with hundreds of measurements, a simple anomaly indication is not enough, as the human operator may not be able to recognize the symptoms of the anomaly by himself quickly. Highlighting most relevant features related to the anomaly prediction can ease the job of the operator and shorten time required to implement corrections in the system. In terms of generating explanations, anomaly detection seems to be fairly easy task, as there are only two possible labels (normal or anomaly), which actually limits the scope of explanation. The explanation should answer why the model has predicted that the observation is anomaly rather than a normal observation. We assume that only anomalies are explained, since it makes little sense to explain why the sample is normal rather than anomaly. For XAI methods, we propose to use explanations in the form of feature importance, e.g., SHAP [18], counterfactuals [24], or rules [1]. However, other methods which apply to the given task can also be considered.

Operator. The task of the operator is to watch for the anomaly signals raised by the model and to take the necessary actions to resolve the problem. As described above, the operator is equipped not only with the prediction of the model, but also with the explanation, so that his job is to assess the situation based on the received information. We also consider including the operator in the loop, so that he will be able to indicate the incorrect predictions of the anomaly detection system (e.g. false positives), which could shorten the process of adapting to concept drifts. However, the implementation of such human-in-the-loop functionality is outside of the scope of this system.

4.2   Online Learning.

In the online learning we run the training procedure each time the observation arrives at the system. As described in Sect. 4.1, the training procedure begins when the sample is labeled by the model as normal observation. The sample is then passed to the resampling module, which will generate more similar instances or dismiss the observation. Otherwise, the sample might be omitted from the training (undersampled). Although there is no concept drift detection method included in the main components of the online learning system, some of the algorithms may utilize those methods, e.g., Adaptive Random Forest [10]. In the online learning approach, we assume that no observations are stored in the memory, so they are discarded soon after the training procedure ends. The online learning system is presented in Fig. 3.

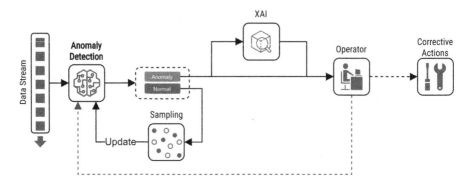

Fig. 3. Online learning system

4.3 Offline Learning

In the offline learning approach, we assume that the static model (or ensemble of models) is used to predict anomalies. The model is initially trained on the acquired data, and the anomaly score is monitored by the concept drift detection method. Each normal observation is passed to the resampling module, similarly to the online learning approach, and over- or undersampled. The selected samples are then stored in a limited size memory, to be used for future training. When the concept drift is detected, the model is discarded and the new one is trained on the data from the buffer. For ensemble models, each individual model is equipped with its own drift detection method, so that only outdated models are discarded, not the whole ensemble. The offline learning system is presented in Fig. 4.

4.4 Preliminary Results

In this section we present the preliminary results of our studies. Some of our results on the topic of anomaly detection in streaming data from cold rolling process were presented in our previous study [13]. The results have shown that the concept drift is a major issue in learning the characteristics of cold rolling process, as the data tends to deviate significantly. Figure 5 presents the evolution of the anomaly score in the analyzed period using three different learning approaches: offline learning, offline learning with concept drift detection (and

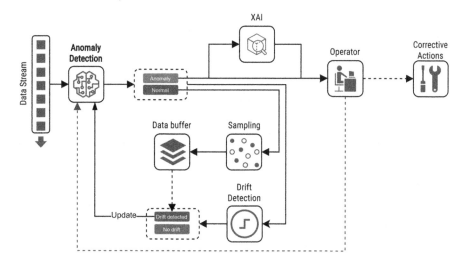

Fig. 4. Offline learning system

model retraining) and online learning. As the anomaly detection model is put into production (after initial training), the anomaly score is comparable among all the considered approaches. However the offline models deteriorate with time, which is reflected by increased anomaly score. The retraining of the offline model allows to reduce the anomaly score and hence adapt to new characteristics of the data.

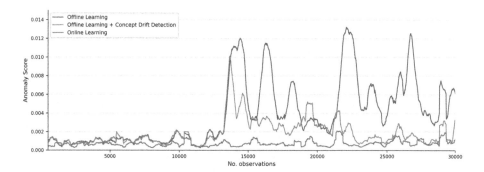

Fig. 5. Evolution of mean anomaly score (sliding window) for different learning approaches.

To present the use of XAI methods in the anomaly detection system, we have employed SHAP [18] method, which was used to show which features are responsible for high anomaly scores. The SHAP method assigns an importance value to every feature. In our case, where the target prediction is the anomaly score (high values indicate anomalies), the higher SHAP value of a given feature corresponds to its higher contribution to anomaly score. Figure 6 presents an example of the anomaly, which was predicted by the anomaly detection model together with the SHAP values of some selected features. In this example, anomaly score greatly increases on the 200th observation, meaning an anomaly is detected. By observing the SHAP values of each feature, we can find out that the rolling speed at first stand has supposably high contribution to the anomaly score. The other two presented features does not show any significant impact on the increased value of anomaly score.

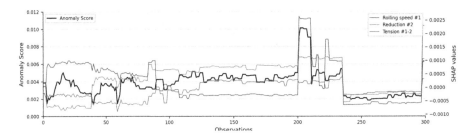

Fig. 6. Example of anomaly score predictions and SHAP values assigned to selected features

5   Conclusion

In this paper, we have proposed a system for anomaly detection in industrial data streams. The proposed system comprises such components as anomaly detection model, resampling module, and XAI module. Each module is designed to deal with specific tasks for data streams and anomaly detection. The anomaly detection model uses an unsupervised learning approach to classify the incoming observations as normal or anomalous. Based on the assigned label, the samples are passed to either resampling module (normal) or XAI module (anomaly). The resampling module is used to balance the data set so that rare operating modes are not underrepresented during model training. The output of the resampling module is used for training the anomaly detection model. The XAI module is used to explain the reasoning of the model when the sample is classified as anomaly. This is done to help the human operator understand the reasons behind the anomaly and allow him to quickly take corrective actions. In our system, two distinct approaches are considered. First, the online learning approach, which uses data for training as soon as it arrives at the system and discards it later. Second, the offline learning approach, which trains the model in an offline manner and allows retraining it when the drift is detected. We have shown some of our preliminary results on the cold rolling use case, with the emphasis on the comparison of different learning approaches. Moreover, we have presented how the SHAP method can be used to gain insight into model's reasoning.

In future work, we plan to implement the described system in an object-oriented way, so that each component is easily replaceable. We decide for this approach, so that we are not limited to any specific methods, but rather a group of potential methods from which the system can be built. Additionally, we want to extend our system to include the human-in-the-loop functionality, so that the operator will have direct impact on the training of the model.

Acknowledgements. Project XPM is supported by the National Science Centre, Poland (2020/02/Y/ST6/00070), under CHIST-ERA IV programme, which has received funding from the EU Horizon 2020 Research and Innovation Programme, under Grant Agreement no 857925.

The research has been additionally supported by a grant from the Priority Research Area (DigiWorld) under the Strategic Programme Excellence Initiative at Jagiellonian University.

References

1. Almeida, E., Ferreira, C., Gama, J.: Adaptive model rules from data streams. In: Blockeel, H., Kersting, K., Nijssen, S., Železný, F. (eds.) ECML PKDD 2013. LNCS (LNAI), vol. 8188, pp. 480–492. Springer, Heidelberg (2013). https://doi.org/10.1007/978-3-642-40988-2_31
2. Baena-García, M., Campo-Avila, J.D., Fidalgo, R., Bifet, A., Gavalda, R., Morales-Bueno, R.: Early drift detection method (2005)
3. Bernardo, A., Gomes, H.M., Montiel, J., Pfahringer, B., Bifet, A., Valle, E.D.: C-smote: continuous synthetic minority oversampling for evolving data streams. In: 2020 IEEE International Conference on Big Data (Big Data), pp. 483–492 (2020). https://doi.org/10.1109/BigData50022.2020.9377768
4. Bifet, A., Gavaldà, R.: Learning from time-changing data with adaptive windowing (2007)
5. Breunig, M.M., Kriegel, H.P., Ng, R.T., Sander, J.: LOF: identifying density-based local outliers. SIGMOD Rec. **29**(2), 93–104 (2000). https://doi.org/10.1145/335191.335388
6. Domingos, P., Hulten, G.: Mining high-speed data streams. In: Proceedings of the Sixth ACM SIGKDD International Conference on Knowledge Discovery and Data Mining. KDD '00, pp. 71–80. Association for Computing Machinery, New York, NY, USA (2000). https://doi.org/10.1145/347090.347107
7. Domingos, P., Hulten, G.: Catching up with the data: research issues in mining data streams (2001)
8. Farahani, A., Voghoei, S., Rasheed, K., Arabnia, H.R.: A brief review of domain adaptation. In: Stahlbock, R., Weiss, G.M., Abou-Nasr, M., Yang, C.-Y., Arabnia, H.R., Deligiannidis, L. (eds.) Advances in Data Science and Information Engineering. TCSCI, pp. 877–894. Springer, Cham (2021). https://doi.org/10.1007/978-3-030-71704-9_65
9. Gama, J.: Knowledge Discovery from Data Streams. Chapman and Hall/CRC Data Mining and Knowledge Discovery Series, CRC Press, Boca Raton (2010)
10. Gomes, H.M., et al.: Adaptive random forests for evolving data stream classification. Mach. Learn. **106**, 1469–1495 (10 2017). https://doi.org/10.1007/s10994-017-5642-8

11. Gomes, H.M., Read, J., Bifet, A., Barddal, J.P., Gama, J.: Machine learning for streaming data. ACM SIGKDD Explor. Newsl. **21**, 6–22 (11 2019). https://doi.org/10.1145/3373464.3373470
12. Goodfellow, I., et al.: Generative adversarial nets. In: Ghahramani, Z., Welling, M., Cortes, C., Lawrence, N., Weinberger, K. (eds.) Advances in Neural Information Processing Systems, vol. 27. Curran Associates, Inc. (2014)
13. Jakubowski, J., Stanisz, P., Bobek, S., Nalepa, G.J.: Towards online anomaly detection in steel manufacturing process. In: Mikyška, J., de Mulatier, C., Paszynski, M., Krzhizhanovskaya, V.V., Dongarra, J.J., Sloot, P.M. (eds.) ICCS 2023. LNCS, vol. 10476, pp. 469–482. Springer, Cham (2023). https://doi.org/10.1007/978-3-031-36027-5_37
14. Karimian, M., Beigy, H.: Concept drift handling: a domain adaptation perspective. Expert Syst. Appl. **224**, 119946 (2023). https://doi.org/10.1016/j.eswa.2023.119946
15. Krawczyk, B., Minku, L.L., Gama, J., Stefanowski, J., Woźniak, M.: Ensemble learning for data stream analysis: a survey. Inf. Fusion **37**, 132–156 (9 2017). https://doi.org/10.1016/j.inffus.2017.02.004
16. Liu, F.T., Ting, K.M., Zhou, Z.H.: Isolation forest. In: 2008 Eighth IEEE International Conference on Data Mining, pp. 413–422 (2008). https://doi.org/10.1109/ICDM.2008.17
17. Lu, T., Wang, L., Zhao, X.: Review of anomaly detection algorithms for data streams. Appl. Sci. **13**(10) (2023). https://doi.org/10.3390/app13106353
18. Lundberg, S.M., Lee, S.I.: A unified approach to interpreting model predictions. In: Guyon, I., et al. (eds.) Advances in Neural Information Processing Systems, vol. 30, pp. 4765–4774. Curran Associates, Inc. (2017)
19. Ribeiro, M.T., Singh, S., Guestrin, C.: "why should i trust you?": Explaining the predictions of any classifier. In: Proceedings of the 22nd ACM SIGKDD International Conference on Knowledge Discovery and Data Mining. KDD '16, pp. 1135–1144. Association for Computing Machinery, New York, NY, USA (2016). https://doi.org/10.1145/2939672.2939778
20. Rumelhart, D.E., Hinton, G.E., Williams, R.J.: Learning Internal Representations by Error Propagation, pp. 318–362. MIT Press, Cambridge, MA, USA (1986)
21. Schölkopf, B., Williamson, R., Smola, A., Shawe-Taylor, J., Platt, J.: Support vector method for novelty detection. In: Proceedings of the 12th International Conference on Neural Information Processing Systems. NIPS'99, pp. 582–588. MIT Press, Cambridge, MA, USA (1999)
22. Speith, T.: A review of taxonomies of explainable artificial intelligence (XAI) methods. In: Proceedings of the 2022 ACM Conference on Fairness, Accountability, and Transparency. FAccT '22, pp. 2239–2250. Association for Computing Machinery, New York, NY, USA (2022). https://doi.org/10.1145/3531146.3534639
23. Tang, J., Lin, K.Y., Li, L.: Using domain adaptation for incremental SVM classification of drift data. Mathematics **10**(19) (2022). https://doi.org/10.3390/math10193579
24. Wachter, S., Mittelstadt, B., Russell, C.: Counterfactual explanations without opening the black box: automated decisions and the GDPR (2017). https://doi.org/10.48550/ARXIV.1711.00399

Towards Explainable Deep Domain Adaptation

Szymon Bobek[1] , Sławomir Nowaczyk[2(✉)] , Sepideh Pashami[2] ,
Zahra Taghiyarrenani[2] , and Grzegorz J. Nalepa[1]

[1] Jagiellonian Human-Centered Artificial Intelligence Laboratory (JAHCAI),
Mark Kac Center for Complex Systems Research,
and Institute of Applied Computer Science, Jagiellonian University,
31-007 Kraków, Poland
{szymon.bobek,grzegorz.j.nalepa}@uj.edu.pl
[2] Center for Applied Intelligent Systems Research,
Halmstad University, Halmstad, Sweden
{slawomir.nowaczyk,sepideh.pashami,zahra.taghiyarrenani}@hh.se

Abstract. In many practical applications data used for training a machine learning model and the deployment data does not always preserve the same distribution. Transfer learning and, in particular, domain adaptation allows to overcome this issue, by adapting the source model to a new target data distribution and therefore generalizing the knowledge from source to target domain. In this work, we present a method that makes the adaptation process more transparent by providing two complementary explanation mechanisms. The first mechanism explains how the source and target distributions are aligned in the latent space of the domain adaptation model. The second mechanism provides descriptive explanations on how the decision boundary changes in the adapted model with respect to the source model. Along with a description of a method, we also provide initial results obtained on publicly available, real-life dataset.

Keywords: Explainable AI (XAI) · Domain adaptation · artificial intelligence

1 Introduction

Domain adaptation (DA) aligns different but related domains to leverage all the available knowledge together. Typically, a source domain with an abundance of training data is used to enable models to generalize effectively in another domain, called a target domain [5]. This capability makes domain adaptation a suitable approach for overcoming the challenges of limited labeled data in many practical applications, and it has demonstrated significant success in addressing real-world problems [13]. The main challenge of DA is how to map both input data distributions, given the data shift between the source and target domains, into a common latent space. Deep domain adaptation [14], which covers a lot of recent work, aims at learning this transferable representation using deep learning. Similar to any deep learning model [1], deep domain adaptation techniques are

S. Nowaczyk et al. (Eds.): ECAI 2023 Workshops, CCIS 1947, pp. 101–113, 2024.
https://doi.org/10.1007/978-3-031-50396-2_6

considered black-box models, and understanding the adaptation process between source and target domains is challenging. In particular, explaining the adaptation process is an important step in many practical settings for ensuring trust and acceptance from the end user.

The success of domain adaptation depends on the difficulty of transferring knowledge from the source domain to a "different but related" target domain [12]. Neither of these two terms ("different" and "related") is generally well-defined; those concepts highly depend on the task at hand and are often impossible for domain experts, not well-versed in data science, to grasp fully. Surprisingly, these concepts have received limited attention in the existing literature [15]. In particular, there is a lack of discussions on these aspects from an explainability perspective – how to convey to humans key knowledge about the adaptation performed by a model. We claim that explainability can help in describing, in a meaningful way, the domains' variations, discrepancies, and similarities.

When performing DA, one of the most common techniques is to learn a shared feature representation that aligns both domains with each other. The final prediction model operates within this shared feature space. Understanding how this shared feature space is constructed is crucial to comprehend the differences between the domains and how the DA model addresses these differences. It is particularly important to focus only on regions of feature space that affect decision boundary in the adapted model, i.e., regions from the target domain that are incorrectly classified by the source model; discrepancies that are irrelevant to the decision-making should be hidden not to distract the expert. The second important aspect of domain adaptation is how the decision boundary differs between the original model (trained only using the source domain) and the adapted model (trained using both domains). Given that the additional data is likely to affect the decision-making, possibly by identifying new discriminative patterns, a full-picture explanation needs also to highlight those changes.

This paper proposes a model-agnostic explanation, which allows us to analyze the adapted model from two complementary perspectives explained above. First, it provides an explanation of the feature extraction process by generating an approximation of the transform that the DA performs to align two domains. Second, it gives insight into the changes in a decision boundary in the adapted model, compared to the source model. This work is the first attempt at explaining the meta-level of the domain adaptation mechanism. The expert can directly use this knowledge to gain more understanding of the technical aspect of adaptation (model debugging) but also to obtain information about semantic relations between domains that the adaptable mechanism encoded and the explainable method revealed (knowledge discovery). For example, if rich knowledge about the source domain exists, but little is known about the target domain, such a descriptive summary linking source and target domains through the lenses of an adapted model clearly brings new insights and opportunities for data analysis.

The rest of the paper is organized as follows. In Sect. 2 we describe current trends at the intersection of explainable AI and DA. In Sect. 3 we introduce the theoretical background of our method and demonstrate it on a simple 2D use-case. The more advanced case-study that involves explanation of a domain adaptation in the area of network intrusion detection is presented in Sect. 4.

Finally, we summarize our work in Sect. 5 and provide future possible extensions and application of our method.

2 Related Work

Explainable Domain Adaptation has been approached from different perspectives in the literature. In this section, we focus on the use of explainable methods as a tool for performing DA. Typically, some explanation is provided for every domain, explaining the model or data, and then the explanations are used to adapt the domains. In this regard, the authors of [11] propose an explanation-guided training strategy, specifically focusing on the Cross-domain Few-shot learning mechanism. To achieve this, they utilize LRP (Layerwise relevance propagation) to construct a weight vector that indicates the relative importance of features in the prediction process and feeds it into the classifier. By downscaling the weights of features with lower LRP values, they ensure that the classifier pays more attention to the features deemed more important. The authors of [18] also employ the concept of explainability, specifically saliency maps, as a tool for conducting domain adaptation. The proposed method in [18] utilizes saliency maps to create a strong influence on classifier prediction, forcing it to prioritize attention to specific regions. As a result of being forced to focus primarily on these salient regions, the model will focus more on features that are domain-invariant while neglecting features that are domain-specific (such as background information). The emphasis on domain-invariant features facilitates the mapping of the source and target domains so that source domain information can be used to make accurate predictions in the target domain. Such an approach focuses primarily on explaining the domains rather than explaining how they are adapted.

Designing DA methods that are inherently explainable is another direction, although very few papers have been published in this area. The proposed method in [7] explains the prediction of the output of the test samples based on the prototypes of source and target domains. The method focuses on aligning the prototypes between the domains, ensuring that prototypes belonging to the same class are closer to each other and farther from prototypes of other classes. Furthermore, a prototype projection layer is introduced to map the prototype vectors into visually interpretable images, enhancing human understanding of the model's inner workings. Such methods provide explanations for final predictions. However, they adapt source and target domains according to their predefined rules. Thus, the explanations provided by such approaches are aligned with what is injected into the DA model for adaptation.

In the paper [16], the authors present a method to explain DA by highlighting the impact of source samples on predicting a target sample. To achieve this, they introduce an interpretable deep classifier and integrate it into the framework of Domain-Adversarial Neural Networks (DANN). The classifier works by measuring the distance between source and target samples resulting in interpretability. In summary, the proposed method provides insights into the role of source samples in the DA process.

All of the aforementioned works focus either on explaining the final adapted model or using explanations in the process of adaptation to enhance it. In our work, we focus on explaining the adaptation itself; hence we provide explanations in the form of transform vectors that approximate the adaptation process and describe shifts in decision boundaries between source and adapted models. In the next section, we describe how we achieve that in more detail.

3 Method

In our work, we focus on descriptive explanation mechanisms that capture two aspects of domain adaptation: domain alignment and decision boundary update. In Fig. 1, we present how our explanation modules fit into the architecture of the most common domain adaptation model. The first module is responsible for explaining the latent space adaptation mechanism by providing a transform (or a set of transforms) that the feature extractor performs on the original data to align source and target domains in the latent space. The second module is responsible for explaining how the decision boundary changes in the adapted model in comparison to the source model.

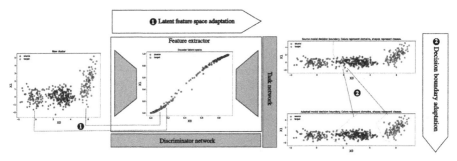

Fig. 1. Explainability modules in the architecture of the domain-adapted model. The first module describes the transform performed by the feature extractor in order to align domains in latent space. The section module describes the changes in the decision boundary.

In both cases, the explanation Φ for an adapted model M_a with respect to the source model M_s is defined as a vector $\Phi^{M_s \rightarrow M_a} = (v_1, v_2, \ldots, v_n)$, where $v_i \in \mathbb{R}$ is a value associated with the feature i. In the case of the feature space adaptation, the $(v_1, v_2, \ldots, v_n)$ represents a transform vector that aligns the source and target domains in the latent space, while in case of the decision boundary adaptation, the vector represents the change in the separation hyperplanes in the source and the adapted model. In the next paragraphs, we describe how the explanations for these two modules are constructed.

3.1 Explanation of a Feature Space Adaptation

One of the tasks of adaptable models such as DANN is the discovery of latent space representation of the input data that makes the source and target domains indistinguishable. This stage is often referred to as feature extraction because the latent space becomes the new feature space for both source and target domains. In our work, our aim is to explain what is an interpretation of such an alignment in the input space, i.e., what transform $(v_1, v_2, \ldots, v_n)$ of the target domain input space makes it indistinguishable from the source input space.

To solve this problem, we first select unaligned samples from source and target domains. We are interested in samples $X_e = \{x_i \in X_s \cup X_t : M_s(x_1) \neq M_a(x_i)\}$, where X_s are source domain samples and X_t are target domain samples. Next, we build a classifier C that is trained to distinguish samples from X_e as either source domain samples or target domain samples. In this step, we do not use latent space representation of the samples, where they are indistinguishable, but operate on original input space.

Based on the classifier C, we define counterfactual sub-spaces for each sample from the target domain. The counterfactual subspace for a sample $x_i : C(x_i) = l$ is a set of samples $X_{cf}^i \subseteq X_e$ such that for the majority of samples from X_{cf}^i the $C(x_j) \neq C(x_i)$. The counterfactual sub-spaces are constructed with LUX explainer [2], which uses a decision tree to partition input space into homogeneous areas with respect to class label and returns counterfactual sub-spaces by traversing the decision tree in a search for partitions that contain a majority of samples from opposite class, i.e., $C(x_j) \neq C(x_i)$. It is worth noting that we do not define a counterfactual as the nearest sample from the input space with the opposite class label, as this approach is prone to noise. Instead, we are interested in finding all of the groups of counterfactual samples, which form more stable and representative counterfactuals than single nearest instances. This is also motivated by the fact that later in our method we move the analysis to the latent space, where similarities from input space do not have to be preserved. This step can also be used to obtain an explanation of the differences between the domains in the input space, as shown in Fig. 2.

In the subsequent step, we transform each sample x_i and its associated counterfactual subspace X_{cf}^i into latent representations, becoming $\overline{x}_i$ and $\overline{X}_{cf}^i$ respectively. Then we select the nearest neighbor $\overline{x}_{cf} \in \overline{X}_{cf}^i$ of $\overline{x}_i$, which now forms a pair $(\overline{x}_i, \overline{x}_{cf})$ and so can be easily traced back to its original input space representation (x_i, x_{cf}). Finally, for each sample, we calculate the transform vector $(v_1, v_2, \ldots, v_n)$ as a difference between its real representation and the real representation of a nearest latent counterfactual: $x_i - x_{cf}$. Due to the fact that the transform performed in the adaptation model might not be linear, we cluster detected instance-based transforms according to cosine similarity as depicted in Fig. 2.

In the case of low-dimensional space, the visualization as presented in Fig. 2 is satisfactory as a way of presenting the explanation. In higher-dimensional spaces, we adapted the SHAP waterfall plots to depict the transformations. In Fig. 3, the example waterfall plot for the transform of one of the clusters from Fig. 2 is presented.

It is worth noting that the waterfall plot from Fig. 3 transfers the information about the counterfactual explanations, as it is built based on the counterfactual sub-spaces X_{cf} discussed earlier in this section. In other words, the transform depicted in the plot is a generalized version of a counterfactual explanation for a whole cluster of data.

The transform clusters defined in this stage are used as input for the phase of explaining the decision boundary adaptation.

3.2   Explanation of a Decision Boundary Adaptation

In the explanation of a decision boundary adaptation, we focus on describing how the decision boundary changed between the source model M_s and the adapted

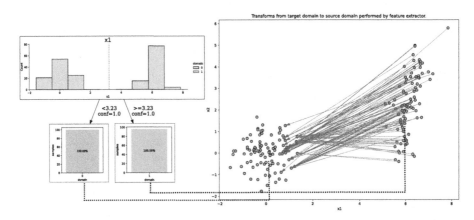

Fig. 2. Visualization of a transform-based explanation for feature space adaptation. On the left-hand side, there is a decision tree generated by the LUX algorithm that divides the space into two homogeneous subspaces and helps in defining counterfactuals. On the right-hand side, there are transforms in the input space, conditioned on their representation in latent space.

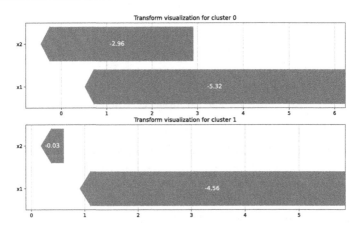

Fig. 3. Visualization of a transform-based explanation for feature space adaptation with SHAP-like waterfall plot. Three important pieces of information can be read from the plot: 1) how many transform clusters are there in the data 2) what are cluster centroids defined by the origins of bars in the plot, and 3) the transform itself depicted as colored bars which define a shift in dimension represented by a particular feature. (Color figure online)

model M_a. The decision boundaries of M_s and M_a are assumed to be non-linear and possibly complex; therefore, we approximate it locally with a linear interpretable model such as LIME. To achieve that, we use transform clusters defined in previous steps as initial samples for which we calculate two approximations of decision boundaries with a local linear surrogate model: one for M_s and one for M_a. As a result, we obtain two vectors of coefficients $(\theta_1^s, \theta_2^s, \ldots, \theta_n^s)$ and $(\theta_1^a, \theta_2^a, \ldots, \theta_n^a)$ which define the hyperplanes perpendicular to them. Such a situation for the toy example used in this section is presented in Fig. 4. The yellow lines represent decision boundaries for the source model (solid line) and the adapted model (dashed line). The other straight lines represent the linear approximations of the decision boundaries for particular transform cluster points (different colors for different transform clusters). The arrows are associated with each transform clusters and are vectors perpendicular to the decision boundary, which locally approximate the M_s and one for M_a boundaries. From the visualization of the vectors, one can immediately notice that for both of the transform clusters, the decision boundary has flipped by more than $180°$.

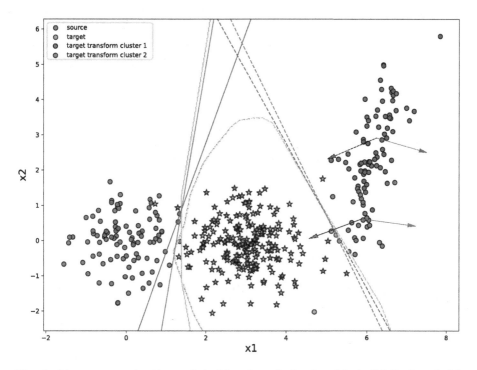

Fig. 4. Linear approximations of decision boundaries for M_s (solid line) and M_a (dashed lines) and corresponding vectors that define these hyperplanes. Arrows represent the contribution of features according to LIME for clusters of transforms. Dotted lines – adapted model, solid lines – source model.

Although such a visualization is straightforward for simple cases, it becomes infeasible for the multidimensional case. In such a situation, we adapted the summary plot from SHAP plots that shows the variant and invariant features for the domain adaptation procedure, as shown in Fig. 5. The smaller the value associated with the feature, the smaller the change of the decision boundary related to this feature in the source and adapted models. For instance, in Fig. 5 one can observe that for both transform clusters the x2 attribute is considered invariant, while x1 variant feature. This means that the biggest change in the decision boundary in the adapted model was made along the feature x1 , which is also visible in Fig. 4.

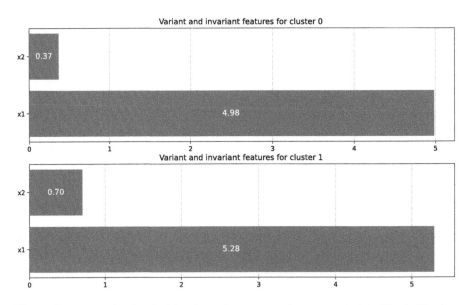

Fig. 5. Summary plot for decision boundary comparison presented in Fig. 4. The low values are associated with invariant features, while high values denote the variant features.

In the following section, we demonstrate the method on a real-life, multidimensional dataset.

4   Case Study

For the evaluation study, we selected real-life multidimensional datasets, CICIDS17 [9] and InSDN [4], from the computer network security area. These two datasets are collected using the same network monitoring tools resulting in homogeneous feature sets [17]. Despite sharing the same feature set, these two datasets differ greatly from one another due to two factors: they are collected from two different networks, and the existing attacks in each dataset are different. This characteristic of these datasets makes them suitable for performing DA. As a source domain dataset, we used the CICDS17 dataset, and as a target domain dataset, we used the InSDN dataset.

Datasets include samples for different attacks (5 attacks) that can be used for multilabel network intrusion classification. However, in order to have the same label set in different domains (while keeping the divergence between them), we changed it to binary classification. We altered the labels of all of the different types of attacks to be *abnormal* state focusing on building a classifier that distinguishes this state from *normal* state.

First, we trained a model on the source dataset (CICDS17) and evaluated it on both source and target dataset (InSDN). We obtained F1 scores of 0.96 (macro average 0.95) and 0.22 (macro average 0.25), respectively, which indicated that in order to achieve adequate performance on the target dataset, an adaptation to a new domain is required. We used the CCSA algorithm [8] to perform the adaptation and achieved F1 scores for the source and target domain of an adapted model equal to 0.96 (macro average 0.96) and 0.99 (macro average 0.99), respectively, proving that the adaptation was performed correctly.

Next, we applied our method to explain the adaptation process. We distinguished the sets of samples X_e from the target domain that are misclassified by the source model. Then we created the interpretable classifier C (the left plot in Fig. 6) that distinguishes between the domains in the input space. This classifier was later used to generate the counterfactual sub-spaces X_{cf}^i based on which we obtained explanations in the form of cluster transforms. The generated cluster of transforms are presented in the right-hand graph in Fig. 6.

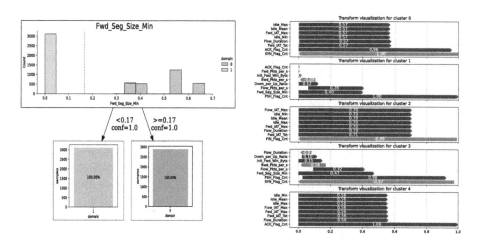

Fig. 6. Explainable decision tree (on the left) describing the most discriminative feature that allows for distinguishing between source and target domains. Transform visualization for the top five most important features (on the right) depicting how the adaptation aligns domains in a feature space.

From these results, several conclusions can be drawn. First, the most discriminative feature that makes the two domains different is the `Fwd_Seg_Size_Min` feature. In the target domain, the value of this feature is much lower than in the source domain. Our method detected five distinct cluster transforms (the optimal number of clusters was obtained by the analysis of silhouette score and K-means clustering). These clusters depicted in the waterfall plot in Fig. 6 show how samples from the target domain are transformed to the source domain in the input space.

It can be seen that `Fwd_Seg_Size_Min` , the most discriminative feature, is not present as the most important feature in the transforms-based explanations. One can conclude that the domain alignment that is performed in the latent space is a much more complex operation, and it cannot be derived only by looking at the differences between the samples in the input space. Furthermore, the cluster transforms reveal additional information on how the alignment is done with respect to the semantics of the samples. For instance, the datasets used by us in this case study were originally multi-labeled datasets, which we converted to a binary classification problem. Each of the labels in the original dataset corresponded to an attack performed on the network infrastructure, which we interpreted as anomalous behavior.

We traced back which classes from the original dataset were mapped with each other by the domain adaptation mechanism; it appeared that the only class from the target domain that was incorrectly classified by the source model was 'DDoS' attack. Additionally, by analyzing instances linked by the transforms obtained from our method, we discovered that the 'DDoS' attack from the target domain (which was missing in the source domain) was aligned with the 'Patator' attack in the source domain (not present in target domain). Such information can be used by the expert to judge whether the alignment performed by the domain adaptation mechanism is consistent with background knowledge. In this case, one can argue that this alignment does make sense, as the 'Patator' attack, which is a brute-force password cracking mechanism, may resemble DDoS or DoS attacks. The transform clusters give more details on how such alignment was performed. For example, when analyzing the cluster transform 1 in Fig. 6, we can observe that there exist several features for which the transform was minimal, such as `Init_Fwd_Win_Byts` or `ACK_Flag_Cnt` . This means that samples from source and target domains had similar values for these parameters. According to the analysis of the source domain dataset [10], these features happen to be the most important features for identifying 'Patator' attacks. Thanks to transform clusters and available knowledge about the source domain, we can derive a conclusion that the type of attack that is associated with cluster transform 1 resembles 'Patator' attacks from the source domain, and the alignment done by the adaptation mechanism is semantically sound.

In Fig. 7, linear decision boundaries approximations for source and adapted model for cluster transform 1 was presented. It can be seen that the biggest difference between decision boundaries (right plot) is observed in features related to the number of packages sent over the network per second. This is again consistent with the background knowledge about the difference between 'Patator' and 'DDoS' attacks. The former is performed from a single computer, and the latter is a distributed attack that results in larger packet intensity.

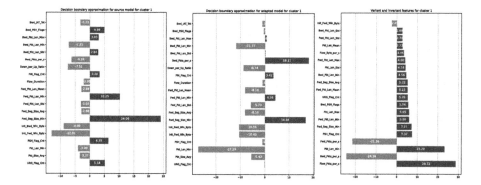

Fig. 7. Linear decision boundary approximation in source model for transform cluster 1 (left plot). Linear decision boundary approximation in the adapted model for transform cluster 1 (middle plot). Variant and invariant features between domains (right plot).

Similarly to transform cluster analysis, the feature which is the most discriminative from the perspective of data distribution (i.e. Fwd_Seg_Size_Min) is not present as important in decision boundary explanations. Because the model fits decision boundary with a different objective than separating domains, this suggests a conclusion that domain adaptation explanation cannot be done purely based on data distribution analysis.

5 Summary

In this paper, we proposed explainability mechanisms for feature-based domain adaptation algorithms. The explanations provide two complementary perspectives on the domain adaptation process: (1) feature alignment and (2) decision boundary updates. Our initial investigation has shown that it is not enough to look at domain adaptation through the perspective of differences between data distributions of source and target domains. Instead, looking deeper into how these distributions are aligned by the adaptation mechanism and observing in which directions the decision boundaries are changing can give a new opportunity to relate the two domains on a more semantic level and open the possibilities to transfer background knowledge from the source to the target domain.

Although the work presented in this paper contributes the most towards the theoretical analysis of XAI applications in the domain adaptation area, the potential practical value is much broader. One of the possible applications of the method we presented herein is to distinguish domain shifts from anomalies in a data-stream scenario. The problem of differentiating between these two phenomena in data streams was recently reported in [6]. The usage of explainable domain adaptation can help in detecting anomalies or failures in industrial applications, separating them from domain shifts.

Furthermore, in the case of consecutively changing domains, especially in industrial settings, where each domain represents a new generation of products or processes, one can use explainable domain adaptation to build a predictive model on top of the discovered feature adaptation transforms and use it to tune future new models better.

Finally, one of the important research paths related to explainable domain adaptation is exploring more sophisticated ways of visualizing explanations. We plan to evaluate methods that are more interactive and better suited for multidimensional dataset analysis, such as interactive parallel coordinate plots (IPCP) [3], and combine them with explanations obtained from our method.

Acknowledgment. The paper is funded from the XPM project funded by the National Science Centre, Poland under the CHIST-ERA programme (NCN UMO2020/02/Y/ST6/00070) and the Swedish Research Council under grant CHIST-ERA19-XAI-012 and by a grant from the Priority Research Area (DigiWorld) under the Strategic Programme Excellence Initiative at Jagiellonian University.

References

1. Berenji, A., Nowaczyk, S., Taghiyarrenani, Z.: Data-centric perspective on explainability versus performance trade-off. In: Crémilleux, B., Hess, S., Nijssen, S. (eds.) IDA 2023. LNCS, vol. 13876, pp. 42–54. Springer, Cham (2023). https://doi.org/10.1007/978-3-031-30047-9_4

2. Bobek, S., Nalepa, G.J.: Introducing uncertainty into explainable AI methods. In: Paszynski, M., Kranzlmüller, D., Krzhizhanovskaya, V.V., Dongarra, J.J., Sloot, P.M.A. (eds.) ICCS 2021. LNCS, vol. 12747, pp. 444–457. Springer, Cham (2021). https://doi.org/10.1007/978-3-030-77980-1_34

3. Bobek, S., et al.: Virtual reality-based parallel coordinates plots enhanced with explainable AI and data-science analytics for decision-making processes. Appl. Sci. **12**(1) (2022). https://doi.org/10.3390/app12010331, https://www.mdpi.com/2076-3417/12/1/331

4. Elsayed, M.S., Le-Khac, N.A., Jurcut, A.D.: INSDN: a novel SDN intrusion dataset. IEEE Access **8**, 165263–165284 (2020)

5. Ganin, Y., et al.: Domain-adversarial training of neural networks. J. Mach. Learn. Res. **17**(59), 1–35 (2016). http://jmlr.org/papers/v17/15-239.html

6. Jakubowski, J., Stanisz, P., Bobek, S., Nalepa, G.J.: Towards online anomaly detection in steel manufacturing process. In: Mikyška, J., de Mulatier, C., Paszynski, M., Krzhizhanovskaya, V.V., Dongarra, J.J., Sloot, P.M. (eds.) ICCS 2023. LNCS, vol. 10476, pp. 469–482. Springer, Cham (2023). https://doi.org/10.1007/978-3-031-36027-5_37

7. Kamakshi, V., Krishnan, N.C.: Explainable supervised domain adaptation. In: 2022 International Joint Conference on Neural Networks (IJCNN), pp. 1–8. IEEE (2022)

8. Motiian, S., Piccirilli, M., Adjeroh, D.A., Doretto, G.: Unified deep supervised domain adaptation and generalization. CoRR abs/1709.10190 (2017). http://arxiv.org/abs/1709.10190

9. Sharafaldin, I., Lashkari, A.H., Ghorbani, A.A.: Toward generating a new intrusion detection dataset and intrusion traffic characterization. ICISSp **1**, 108–116 (2018)

10. Sharafaldin, I., Lashkari, A.H., Ghorbani, A.A.: Toward generating a new intrusion detection dataset and intrusion traffic characterization. In: International Conference on Information Systems Security and Privacy (2018)

11. Sun, J., Lapuschkin, S., Samek, W., Zhao, Y., Cheung, N.M., Binder, A.: Explain and improve: cross-domain few-shot-learning using explanations. arXiv preprint arXiv:2007.08790, **1**(3), 8 (2020)

12. Taghiyarrenani, Z., Fanian, A., Mahdavi, E., Mirzaei, A., Farsi, H.: Transfer learning based intrusion detection. In: 2018 8th International Conference on Computer and Knowledge Engineering (ICCKE), pp. 92–97 (2018). https://doi.org/10.1109/ICCKE.2018.8566601

13. Taghiyarrenani, Z., Nowaczyk, S., Pashami, S., Bouguelia, M.R.: Multi-domain adaptation for regression under conditional distribution shift. Expert Syst. Appl. **224**, 119907 (2023). https://doi.org/10.1016/j.eswa.2023.119907, https://www.sciencedirect.com/science/article/pii/S0957417423004086

14. Wang, M., Deng, W.: Deep visual domain adaptation: a survey. Neurocomputing **312**, 135–153 (2018). https://doi.org/10.1016/j.neucom.2018.05.083, https://www.sciencedirect.com/science/article/pii/S0925231218306684

15. Zamir, A., Sax, A., Shen, W., Guibas, L., Malik, J., Savarese, S.: Taskonomy: disentangling task transfer learning. In: Proceedings of the Twenty-Eighth International Joint Conference on Artificial Intelligence. IJCAI-19, pp. 6241–6245. International Joint Conferences on Artificial Intelligence Organization (2019). https://doi.org/10.24963/ijcai.2019/871

16. Zhang, Y., Yao, T., Qiu, Z., Mei, T.: Explaining cross-domain recognition with interpretable deep classifier. arXiv preprint arXiv:2211.08249 (2022)

17. Zoppi, T., Ceccarelli, A., Bondavalli, A.: Towards a general model for intrusion detection: An exploratory study. In: Koprinska, I., et al. (eds.) ECML PKDD 2022. CCIS, vol. 1753, pp. 186–201. Springer, Cham (2022). https://doi.org/10.1007/978-3-031-23633-4_14

18. Zunino, A., et al.: Explainable deep classification models for domain generalization. In: Proceedings of the IEEE/CVF Conference on Computer Vision and Pattern Recognition, pp. 3233–3242 (2021)

Tactful

TACTFUL 2023: The 1st Workshop on Trustworthy AI for Safe and Secure Traffic Control in Connected and Autonomous Vehicles

Connected and Autonomous Vehicles and System Technologies will be the product of a rapidly developing Artificial Intelligence (AI)-centric breakthrough that will most likely transform the very way transport is perceived, mobility is serviced, travel eco-systems 'behave', and cities and societies as a whole operate. At least on paper this breakthrough promises some critical safety, mobility and sustainability rewards spanning from accident prevention, reduced traffic congestion and lessened greenhouse gas emissions to energy savings, improved surveillance, increased ease of use, and improved traffic management and control. However, these promising benefits are not without significant technological challenges. On the one hand, there is the need to ensure the autonomous driving capabilities of individual vehicles. On the other hand, the complex machine-led and interconnected dynamics of a high-tech mobility paradigm built around Connected and Autonomous Vehicles (CAVs) make our transport futures more susceptible to data exploitation and vulnerable to cyber-attacks, increasing the risks of privacy breaches and cyber security violations for road users.

There is a wealth of literature addressing trustworthy issues and cyber security threats and vulnerabilities on the technology and operational level in terms of how CAVs can be compromised and how the threat can be overcome and mitigated. However, these studies are often performed in a 'bottom-up' isolated manner. I.e., they focus on specific aspects of the technology that can be compromised without considering why the technology might be exploited and for what purpose within the smart traffic infrastructure. This has resulted in discrete research studies lacking a joined-up perspective of their adversarial use and how they can be mitigated. In the meanwhile, the risk of a substantial cyber-attack on smart transport infrastructure is continuously increasing.

The aim of TACTFUL 2023, held in conjunction with the 26th European Conference on Artificial Intelligence (ECAI) in Krakow, Poland, was to provide a venue to present approaches related to any aspect of autonomous driving and on the use of CAV/AV functionalities for traffic control, including driving algorithms, security vulnerabilities, exploit potential, and how to mitigate them by leveraging on AI to increase resilience and robustness of intelligent transport systems. Topics of interest included, among the others, AI ethics in AVs and CAVs, The role of AI interpretability in traffic control with CAVs, Vulnerabilities associated with underpinning technology and connectivity, Threat modelling in CAVs and smart traffic control, Cyber Threat Analysis in urban traffic control and mobility, Intersection between safety and security, Security by design in urban traffic control and mobility, AI and Traffic Control, Knowledge representation and reasoning in autonomous driving, Smart cities and interaction with CAVs, and Policy developments for safety and secure CAVs and smart traffic control.

We encouraged submissions of regular papers (long or short). All submitted papers were peer reviewed by three reviewers from the Program Committee, and selected for presentation at the workshop and inclusion in the proceedings on the basis of these reviews. In this proceedings, the three best papers accepted for the workshop are included. The TACTFUL workshop run for half a day, were a total of 5 papers were presented and innovative ways of using AI in concert with connected and autonomous vehicles were discussed and presented.

October 2023

Pawel Skruch
Marek Dlugosz
Moi Hoon Yap
Joanna Jaworek-Korjakowska
Alexandros Nikitas
Mateusz Orlowski
Simon Parkinson
Mauro Vallati

Finding Time Optimal Routes for Trains Using Basic Kinematics and A

Dimitris Manolakis$^{(\boxtimes)}$ and Ioannis Refanidis

University of Macedonia, 156, Egnatia Street, Thessaloniki, Greece
{dmanolakis,yrefanid}@uom.edu.gr

Abstract. This paper tackles the problem of finding time optimal routes for trains over a railway network. The problem is defined as follows: A train has a known length. The position of the train is defined over parts of one or more consecutive track segments. There are a maximum speed, a maximum acceleration and a maximum deceleration capability for the train. Each track segment has a maximum allowed speed for any train being over it. A problem instance is defined by an initial and a goal state, which are two positions accompanied with desired speeds (being usually, but not necessarily, zero). In this paper we are interested in minimizing the total duration of reaching the goal state from the initial one; other metrics such as fuel consumption could be considered.

We solve this problem using basic kinematics and A*. We present two algorithms: The first one computes analytically in continuous space the optimal speed profile of the train for a problem defined over a given path. The second algorithm extends the first one over arbitrary graphs. A* empowered with a simple admissible heuristic is employed to find the optimal combination of speed profile and path.

Keywords: Scheduling · Heuristic search · Kinematics

1 Introduction

Railways are key components in the transportation systems of many countries around the world, with many European development economists considering a modern rail infrastructure as a significant indicator of a country's economic advancement [12]. Moreover, the European Commission aims for rail networks to absorb the majority of medium-distance passenger transport by 2050 [10]. Increasing the efficiency of transport in the railway infrastructure can greatly improve speed and reliability, reduce costs and energy consumption.

In recent years, research on train scheduling has grown significantly. Companies such as the Swiss Federal Railways invest in research through the Flatland challenge, on tasks which include train schedule optimization (railway timetable generation) [2], as well as applications of multi-agent reinforcement learning on the re-scheduling problem (RSP) [3].

Supported by University of Macedonia.

S. Nowaczyk et al. (Eds.): ECAI 2023 Workshops, CCIS 1947, pp. 119–137, 2024.
https://doi.org/10.1007/978-3-031-50396-2_7

In this paper we present algorithms to generate time-optimal routes for single trains over arbitrary railway networks, using basic kinematics. The main contribution of this paper is a realistic approach to compute the amount of time a train needs to traverse a certain path, making use of a variety of train and path characteristics, particularly train max speed, acceleration and deceleration; train length; and maximum allowed speed per railway segment, while aiming at minimizing journey duration. Our approach employs continuous domains (a train can be anywhere in the railway network and have any speed and acceleration or deceleration, while satisfying the physical constraints), whereas it uses basic kinematic equations to compute the state of a train over time. The aim is to approximate real-world conditions on railway networks, which, in turn, will improve the optimization of the train-scheduling problem and contribute to the development of an application that can be effectively used on real-world railway networks. The project's structure and originality allows a lot of possible extensions, including more features of a train (e.g., load; engine power; variable maximum acceleration/deceleration depending on speed) or the environment (e.g., slopes of the ground), as well as alternative optimization criteria (e.g., fuel consumption).

This paper contributes in two directions: First, we present an algorithm to compute the precise duration needed for the train to arrive at any position over a given path, while respecting the physical constraints of the train and the maximum allowed speed for any segment of the network. Second, we empower the first algorithm with A* search and a common straight line distance admissible heuristic function in order to find the optimal route between a source and a target state over any given railway network.

The rest of the paper is organized as follows. Section 2 presents a review of the background literature, whereas Sect. 3 provides the problem formulation. Sections 4 and 5 present the algorithms which are used, in order to compute the optimal speed profile over a given path and the shortest (in terms of time) combination of path and speed profile over a railway network, respectively. Finally, Sect. 6 concludes the paper and poses future challenges.

2   Related Work

A great amount of effort has been invested in solving the train-scheduling problem for multiple trains on a single or multiple railway tracks, with an emphasis on conflict resolution in the planning phase. Optimization is used in order to generate timetables, with many works [4,6,11,14,15,20] presenting surveys on the subject. The train scheduling problem on a single track line has been modeled as a job shop scheduling problem and solved with a branch and bound algorithm [18], while the same algorithm has also been used on railway networks [7]. The patent US20110046827A1 [21] showcases a method for controlling speed in an automatic train operation, making use of kinematic equations in order to estimate and control speed. However, the train's length is not included in the problem formulation reducing the complexity significantly since for example, a train cannot be in multiple segments with overlapping speed limits.

On the other hand, many researchers have proposed and evaluated many heuristic search approaches and artificial intelligence techniques. Genetic algorithms (GA) were used in order to further reduce the number of trains (previously assigned individually on routes) on a network basis [16], while in [19] a GA was designed for application on railway scheduling problems, achieving a good performance on real-world instances from the Spanish Manager of Railway Infrastructure (ADIF). Samà et al. [17] formulated the routing selection problem as a linear programming model and adopted an ant colony optimization algorithm to solve it. Ant colony optimization algorithms were also attempted to solve a simulated dynamic multi-objective railway rescheduling problem [8]. Bożejko et al. [5] applied the Dijkstra algorithm on railway networks in order to determine the fastest routes for rail freight transportation.

The resurgence of neural networks in the modern era of artificial intelligence gave way to the application of deep learning and learning methods in general on the train-scheduling problem. Reinforcement learning is applied in [13], where deep neural networks are used in order to approximate Q-values, formulating the problem as a Markov decision process. Šemrov et al. [9] proposed a Q-learning algorithm for train rescheduling and compared the implementation with the rescheduling methods that do not rely on learning, showing that the solutions are at least equivalent or superior. Two deep Q-learning methods (a decentralized and a centralized approach) were applied and evaluated on the train dispatching problem [1], showcasing their advantages over the classical linear Q-learning method.

3   Problem Formulation

A railway network graph is modeled as a directed graph $G = (V, E)$, where V is the set of the vertices and E the set of the edges. A track segment, $s = (u, v)$, is an edge of E. Each track segment s is labeled with its length $l(s) \in \mathbb{R}^+$, and the maximum allowed speed $vmax(s) \in \mathbb{R}^+$ a train can reach while traversing it. A track segment can be connected at its ends with any number of other track segments; no inner connections are allowed. A *path* is a list of consecutive segments $(s_1, s_2, ..., s_k), k \geq 1$, such that $s_i = (u_i, v_i)$ and for each i in $\{1..k-1\}$ we have $v_i = u_{i+1}$. Furthermore, for every $1 \leq i < j \leq k$, $u_i \neq u_j$, that is the sequence of segments do not cross (but potentially, $u_1 = v_k$, $k > 1$, in which case we have a cycle).

A train T is described by its length $l(T) \in \mathbb{R}^+$, its maximum speed $vmax(T) \in \mathbb{R}^+$, its maximum acceleration $maxacc(T) \in \mathbb{R}^+$, and its maximum deceleration $maxdec(T) \in \mathbb{R}^+$. We use the functions $head(T)$ to denote the head point of T, and $tail(T)$ to denote the tail point of T.

The position of a train T, denoted by $pos(T)$, is defined as a pair (S, x), where $S = (s_1, s_2, ..., s_k)$, with $k \geq 1$, is a path (that is, the train may span over multiple consecutive segments). Furthermore, $tail(T) \in s_1$ but $tail(T) \neq v_1$, and $head(T) \in s_k$ but $head(T) \neq u_k$. x is the distance of $head(T)$ from v_k across s_k. In case $k = 1$, $head(T)$ is considered to be closer to v_1 than $tail(T)$.

The state of a train T, denoted by $state(T)$, is the pair $(pos(T), speed(T))$, where $speed(T)$ is its current speed. We assume that $speed(T) \geq 0$, meaning that the train can move only forwards. We use also the notation $speed(T, t)$ to denote the speed of train T at a particular time point t. A valid state is a state that satisfies the following constraints:

$$0 \leq speed(T) \leq vmax(T)$$

and for each $i \in [1..k]$, where $(s_1, s_2, ..., s_k)$ is the list of segments over which the train spans,

$$speed(T) \leq vmax(s_i)$$

A *Problem* is defined by a tuple $(T, G, init, goal)$, where T is a train, with its given attributes, G is a directed graph with speed limits on its segments, $init$ is the initial state and $goal$ is the goal state.

A speed profile $SP_{t_1:t_2}$, or simply SP, is an infinite set of pairs $\{(state, t) :$ for every t such that $t_1 \leq t \leq t_2\}$, for some time points t_1 and t_2, such that $t_1 \leq t_2$. A speed profile $SP_{t_1:t_2}$ is valid if and only if (a) it consists of valid states for every t in $[t_1, t_2]$; (b) for every pair $(state', t')$ and $(state'', t'')$ in $SP_{t_1:t_2}$, if $t' \rightarrow t''$ then $state' \rightarrow state''$, where convergence between states is defined in the obvious way, that is, the difference in train position and speed between the two states tends to zero; and (c) for every pair $(state', t')$ and $(state'', t'')$ in $SP_{t_1:t_2}$, such that $t' < t''$, if $speed(T, t') < speed(T, t'')$ then $(speed(T, t'') - speed(T, t'))/(t'' - t') \leq maxacc(T)$, whereas if $speed(T, t') > speed(T, t'')$ then $(speed(T, t') - speed(T, t''))/(t'' - t') \leq maxdec(T)$. Note that the third constraint subsumes the second one.

The duration of $SP_{t_1:t_2}$ is defined as $t_2 - t_1$. Moreover, we define three functions: $mint(SP_{t_1:t_2})$ that returns the minimum time label (t_1) in the speed profile; $maxt(SP_{t_1:t_2})$ that returns the maximum time label (t_2) in the speed profile; and $stateAt(SP_{t_1:t_2}, t)$ that returns the state $state(T)$ of T at time t, where $t_1 \leq t \leq t_2$.

Given a *Problem*, a pair $(path, SP)$ is a solution to the *Problem* if (a) the segments in $init$ comprise the prefix of $path$; (b) the segments in $goal$ comprise the suffix of path; (c) the speed profile is valid; (d) $init = stateAt(mintime(SP))$; and (e) $goal = stateAt(maxtime(SP))$. The optimal solution to *Problem* is the pair $(path, SP)$ with the minimum duration.

Moving on, we will make use of two simple examples with the aim of showcasing the operation of the algorithms. It is important to note that our approach makes use of algorithms of low complexity. In more detail, finding an optimal speed profile can be done in time linear in the length of the path, while the process of finding the optimal path has the same worst case algorithmic complexity as the Dijkstra algorithm. For that reason, an extensive experimental study was deemed to be unnecessary.

Example 1. We present an example of an optimal speed profile between an initial and a goal state over a given path (so, we do not have to search over alternative paths). Since the path is given, we are interested only in the speed profile. Table 1 details the path, while Table 2 gives the train T characteristics, as well as the initial and the goal states for this example.

Table 1. Path layout (Example 1)

Segment s	Length l_s (m)	$vmax(s)$ (m/s)
s_0	150	20
s_1	150	40
s_2	700	50
s_3	800	80
s_4	1000	85
s_5	200	40
s_6	300	60
s_7	700	50
s_f	150	30

Table 2. Train T characteristics; *init* and *goal* states for Example 1

Parameters	Value
Length $l(T)$	$150\,\mathrm{m}$
Maximum speed $vmax(T)$	$75\,\mathrm{m/s}$
Acceleration $maxacc(T)$	$1.5\,\mathrm{m/s^2}$
Deceleration $maxdec(T)$	$1\,\mathrm{m/s^2}$
init	$((s_0, 150), 0)$
goal	$((s_f, 0), 0)$

Figure 1 presents the optimal speed profile for the particular problem. Note that there are two vertical axes in the figure, the left (red) denoting the speed and the right (green) denoting the distance travelled by the train for any particular time. The distance in this diagram is measured in length units from the initial position of $head(T)$, which (in this example) is at the start of s_0 ($head(T) = u_0$) and is considered the 0 in the green axis. The vertical dotted lines show the time point in which $head(T)$ enters each segment (of course the tail of the train is still in previous segments).

It is worth noting that whenever the train leaves a segment with a speed limit that is lower than the speed limits of the segments of its new position, it starts accelerating (if not already accelerating). On the other hand, before the train enters a segment with a speed limit that is lower than its current speed, the train starts decelerating earlier enough, even several segments before the low speed limit segment. The same happens with the goal state, where (in the

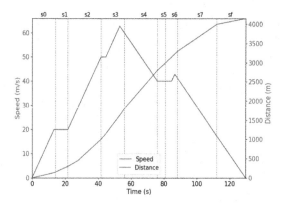

Fig. 1. Speed and Position vs. time graph

current example) the train should be idle: the train may start decelerating early enough.

Furthermore, in order for the speed profile to minimize the duration of the journey, the train must continuously maintain the maximum possible speed. This implies that whenever the train accelerates or decelerates, it does so at the maximum possible acceleration and deceleration rates. Thus why in Fig. 1 the periods of acceleration have the same ascending slope, and the same happens with the periods of deceleration, which all have the same descending slope.

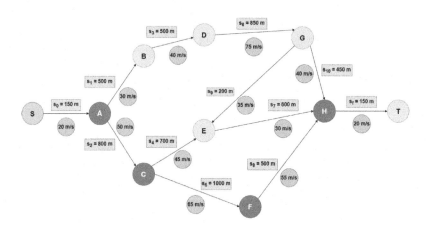

Fig. 2. Calculating the shortest path from A to H

Example 2. Figure 2 presents an example railway network, consisting of 10 vertices and 12 edges. Each edge s is labeled with $l(s)$ and $vmax(s)$. The train T characteristics, as well as the goal state, remain the same as in Table 2, while $init = ((s_0, 0), 0)$.

The nodes marked with a green colour form the optimal solution path, with the corresponding optimal speed profile having a total duration of about 91 s. In this case, the solution path is not the shortest one in terms of length; indeed, path $[S, A, C, E, H, T]$ is 200 m shorter than the solution path $[S, A, C, F, H, T]$. We will return to this example in Sect. 5.

4   Computing Optimal Speed Profile Over a Given Path

This section presents the computation of the optimal speed profile between *init* and *goal*, assuming that there is a single path that can be used to reach the goal state, with no junctions across it. Before presenting the details of the computation, we give an overview of it.

There are three possible modes for a train: (a) Maintaining a steady speed; (b) accelerating; and, (c) decelerating. The train maintains a steady speed if it cannot accelerate and there is no need to decelerate. The need for deceleration arises from a subsequent segment (not necessarily the immediate next one) with a lower speed limit than the current speed of the train, or a goal state with a smaller goal speed (usually zero) than the current train speed. Acceleration occurs whenever the train is in a list of segments having all of them higher speed limits that its current speed, provided that there is no need to decelerate. Deceleration has priority over acceleration, which in turn has priority over maintaining steady speed. The computation's crucial part is to determine the point where deceleration should start.

The computation proceeds forwards. For each segment over the given path, it computes the optimum speed profile until $head(T)$ reaches the end of the segment, taking into account the already computed speed profiles over the previous segments of the given path. In case the new segment has a lower speed limit than the train speed when entering the segment, it is assumed that the train enters the new segment with a speed equal to its speed limit and, then, the algorithm computes where and when the train should have started decelerating, in order to satisfy the lower speed limit. This computation has as result changing the speed profile(s) of the previous segment(s).

Example 3. We present an example of the event in which the speed profile is recalculated, since the train reached a segment that has a speed limit lower than its current speed. Tables 3 and 4 provide the path and the train T characteristics, as well as the *initial* and the *goal* states for this example.

Figure 3 presents the speed profile at the end of segment s_4; till that point the train mostly accelerates or maintains a steady speed due to the high speed limits of the previous segments. So, according to Fig. 3, the train is ready to exit s_4 with a speed over 70 m/s. However, the speed limit for the next segment is 10 m/s hence, the train needs to decelerate significantly. Considering that T enters s_4 with a speed of about 64 m/s, as well as $l(s_4)$ and $maxdec(T)$, deceleration must start earlier enough. Hence, the process is backtracked at previous segments until the deceleration line crosses the speed profile. The result of this procedure is shown in Fig. 4. The train's deceleration starts at s_2 in order to reach the speed limit of s_f at the time it enters it, resulting in a slower speed profile. As a result, time expands from the deceleration starting point and onwards.

Table 3. Path layout (Example 3)

Segment s	Length $l(s)$ (m)	$vmax(s)$ (m/s)
s_0	150	20
s_1	150	20
s_2	800	50
s_3	700	65
s_4	600	85
s_f	150	10

Table 4. Train T characteristics, *init* and *goal* states for Example 3.

Parameters	Value
Length $l(T)$	$150\,\mathrm{m}$
Maximum speed $vmax(T)$	$78\,\mathrm{m/s}$
Acceleration $maxacc(T)$	$1.5\,\mathrm{m/s^2}$
Deceleration $maxdec(T)$	$0.5\,\mathrm{m/s^2}$
init	$((s_0, 0), 0)$
goal	$((s_f, 0), 0)$

Algorithm 1 details the main procedure that iteratively detects events during the train's journey. An event happens in three cases: (a) $head(T)$ enters a new segment; (b) $tail(T)$ exits a segment; and (c) the train reaches the effective *speedLimit* (which is the trains's speed limit or the minimum speed limit of the segments where the train spans). The input to this algorithm includes the train attributes, the given path with its segments' attributes as well as, the *init* and *goal* states. The position of train T in *init* comprises a prefix of the path, whereas the position of train in *goal* comprises a suffix of the path. The output of the algorithm is the optimal speed profile SP, in terms of journey duration. A speed profile is represented as a finite list of pairs $(state(T), t)$, with the train being in the same mode between subsequent states. Time at *init* is considered 0. $SP[i]$ denotes the ith node of SP, with $SP[0] = (init, 0)$ and the last node of SP, denoted as $SP[-1]$, being of the form $(goal, t_{total})$ where t_{total} is the duration of the journey. Between $SP[i]$ and $SP[i+1]$ the train remains in the same mode (acceleration, deceleration or steady speed), which is determined from the difference between the train speeds in the two subsequent nodes.

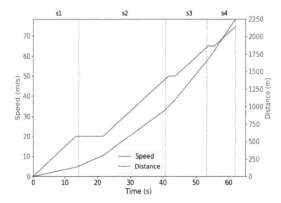

Fig. 3. Speed Profile until reaching the end of s_4 (before backtrack).

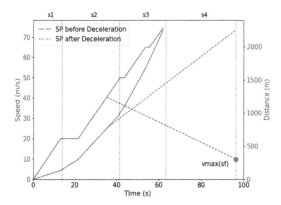

Fig. 4. Speed Profile until reaching the end of s_4 (after backtrack).

Concerning *goal*, the *head*(T) position can be at any point of the last seg-ment. Without loss of generality, we assume that in *goal* the train must reach the end of the last segment (if this is not the case, we can split the last segment in two ones). Furthermore, we assume an additional segment, after the last one, with a speed limit equal to the desired speed of the train in *goal*. In this way, the goal can be restated as having the train ready to enter this additional segment with a speed equal to its speed limit.

Note that in general the problem may not have a solution. This may happen in two cases: The first one is when the goal speed is too high and the train cannot accelerate early enough (because of either a low initial state speed or low speed limits in the segments before the goal) in order to reach it. The second scenario is when the initial speed is very high and the train cannot decelerate early enough, in order to enter a segment with a low speed limit or to reach the goal state with the desired slow speed.

Algorithm 1. Finding the optimal speed profile

Input: $Path = (s_0, .., s_f), T,$
$init = ((s_0, .., s_k), initX), initV),$
$goal = ((s_m, .., s_f), goalX), goalV)$

Output: SP

1: Initialize $currentV, hSgm, tSgm,$
   $hExit, tExit, currentAcc, SP, t_{total}$
2: $speedLimit \leftarrow getSL(T, (s_{tSgm}, ..., s_{hSgm}))$
3: $(t_{min}, t_1, t_2, t_3) \leftarrow getMinT(currentAcc, currentV,$
   $tExit, hExit, speedLimit)$
4: **while** $SP[-1] \neq goal$ **do**
5:    Proceed by t_{min}
6:    $p \leftarrow currentV * t_{min} + (1/2) * currentAcc * t_{min}^2$
7:    $currentV \leftarrow currentV + t_{min} * currentAcc$
8:    $hExit \leftarrow hExit - p, tExit \leftarrow tExit - p$
9:    $t_{total} \leftarrow t_{total} + t_{min}$
10:   **if** $t_2 = t_{min}$ **then**
11:       $hSgm \leftarrow hSgm + 1, hExit \leftarrow l(s_{hSgm})$
12:       $speedLimit \leftarrow getSL(T, (s_{tSgm}, ..., s_{hSgm}))$
13:       **if** $currentV > speedLimit$ **then**
14:           Apply Algorithm 2
15:           **if** Algorithm 2 returns False **then**
16:               EXIT
17:           **end if**
18:       **end if**
19:   **end if**
20:   **if** $t_1 = t_{min}$ **then**
21:       $tSgm \leftarrow tSgm + 1, tExit \leftarrow l(s_{tSgm})$
22:       $speedLimit \leftarrow getSL(T, (s_{tSgm}, ..., s_{hSgm}))$
23:       **if** $currentV < speedLimit$ **then**
24:           $currentAcc = maxacc(T)$
25:       **end if**
26:   **end if**
27:   **if** $t_3 = t_{min}$ AND $currentV = speedLimit$ **then**
28:       $currentAcc = 0$
29:   **end if**
30:   $SP.append((Path_{tSgm:hSgm}, hExit), currentV, t_{total})$
31:   **if** $dist(SP[-1]) = dist(goal)$ AND $currentV \neq goalV$ **then**
32:       EXIT
33:   **end if**
34:   $(t_{min}, t_1, t_2, t_3) \leftarrow getMinT(currentAcc,$
   $currentV, tExit, hExit, speedLimit)$
35: **end while**
36: **return** SP

Algorithm 1 begins with initiliazing all the necessary variables. $currentV$ tracks the train's current speed and is initialized to be equal to the starting speed $initV$ of the $init$ state. $hSgm$ and $tSgm$ represent the indices of the segments in which $head(T)$ and $tail(T)$ reside respectively. At the $init$ state the train is in $(s_0, .., s_k)$ hence, $hSgm = k$ and $tSgm = 0$. $hExit$ and $tExit$ concern the distance of $head(T)$ and $tail(T)$ from the end of segments $hSgm$ and $tSgm$ respectively. The initial values for $hExit$ is $initX$ which are provided by $init$. If $hExit = 0$, $hSmg$ is incremented by one and $hExit$ is set to be equal to the length of next segment $l(s_{hSgm})$. $tExit$ is initialized using the following equation:

$$tExit \leftarrow l(s_0) - (\sum_{i=0}^{k} l(s_i) - hExit - l(T))$$

$currentAcc$ keeps the train's acceleration and is initialized to be equal to $maxacc(T)$. The $init$ state is stored in $SP[0]$. t_{total} is used to keep track of the duration so far and is initialized with 0. For the initialization of the $speedLimit$ that is in effect for the first event, the $getSl()$ function is used, that takes as input the train characteristics and the segments it is currently in. In case $speedLimit$ is equal to $currentV$, $currentAcc$ is set to 0.

Having initialized all variables, $getMinT()$ is called to detect which type of event is upcoming, by computing the time $t_{min} = min(t_1, t_2, t_3)$ needed to reach each one of them. t_1 is the time needed for the tail to exit its segment; t_2 is the time needed for the head to enter a new segment; and t_3 is the time needed for the train to reach the $speedLimit$, provided that it is in accelerating mode. When the train is accelerating, t_1 and t_2 are computed as the roots of the quadratic equation:

$$(1/2) * currentAcc * t^2 + currentV * t - distance = 0$$

$maxRoot()$ returns the positive root (there is always one). t_3 is computed as the time needed in order to accelerate from $currentV$ to the $speedLimit$ with an acceleration of $maxacc(T)$.

Having completed the preliminary computations, the while-loop updates all the relevant variables such as $currentV$, the distance travelled p that is used to update $tExit$ and $hExit$. Based on the type of the event that occurred, either $hSgm$ and $hExit$ or $tSgm$ and $tExit$ or none of them are updated. The train's $currentAcc$ is also updated accordingly; to 0 if the train reached the $speedLimit$ and to $maxacc(T)$ if $currentV$ is lower than the $speedLimit$.

---

function GETSL$(T, (s_{tSgm}, ..., s_{hSgm}))$
    $lowestVmax \leftarrow min(s_i), i \in [tSgm..hSgm]$
return $min(lowestVmax, vmax(T))$
end function

---

function GETMINT($currentAcc, currentV,$
$tExit, hExit, speedLimit$)
    if $currentAcc > 0$ **then**
        $t_1 \leftarrow MaxRoot((1/2) * currentAcc, currentV,$
$- tExit)$
        $t_2 \leftarrow MaxRoot((1/2) * currentAcc, currentV,$
$- hExit)$
    else
        $t_1 \leftarrow tExit/currentV$
        $t_2 \leftarrow hExit/currentV$
    end if
    if $currentAcc > 0$ AND $speedLimit > currentV$ **then**
        $t_3 \leftarrow \frac{speedLimit - currentV}{currentAcc}$
    else
        $t_3 \leftarrow Infinite$
    end if
    return $min(t_1, t_2, t_3), t_1, t_2, t_3$
end function

---

function MAXROOT(a, b, c)
    $\Delta \leftarrow b^2 - 4ac$
    $t \leftarrow \frac{-b + \sqrt{\Delta}}{2a}$
    return t
end function

The most complicated case occurs when $head(T)$ is about to enter a new segment ($t_2 = t_{min}$) with $currentV$ higher than the new segment's speed limit $vmax(s_{hSgm})$, that is the new $speedLimit$. In this case the speed profile must be recomputed by adding a deceleration point at the latest possible time, when the train should start decelerating in order to reach the new segment with a speed equal to $speedLimit$ (denoted as v_0 in Algorithm 2). Intermediate speed profile entries are removed from SP. Algorithm 2 handles this case, by backtracking in previous states stored in SP, searching for the optimal point to decelerate. In order to access information stored in an entry i of SP, we use $dist(SP[i])$ for the total travelled distance, $speed(SP[i])$ for the train's current speed. Finally, $length(SP)$ denotes the total number of entries in SP.

The algorithm searches for previous speed profile segments during which the train was either accelerating or maintaining its speed, starting from the most recent one. A speed profile segment is defined by two consecutive speed profile nodes. The train's mode in a speed profile segment is determined by comparing its speed at the two defining speed profile nodes, (denoted by v_1 and v_2). If $v_1 > v_2$, meaning that at this segment the train was already decelerating, the for-loop continues to the previous speed profile segment (deceleration cannot start at a speed profile segment where the train was already decelerating) until an appropriate segment of the speed profile is found. If $v_2 \geq v_1$, d_1 becomes the cumulative travelled distance till $SP[j]$, while d represents the cumulative travelled distance at $SP[-1]$. The next step is to find whether the optimal deceleration point x_{dec} lies between these two positions, as well as computing the train's speed $v^\#$ at that point, with $d_1 \leq x_{dec} \leq d$ and $v_1 \leq v^\# \leq v_2$. There are two modes for the train's motion in this segment, since it will accelerate or keep steady until it reaches x_{dec} at time $t_1^\#$ with a speed of v_1 and then decelerate until d at time $t_2^\#$ with a speed of v_0.

Algorithm 2. Finding the deceleration point

---

  for $j \leftarrow length(SP) - 2 \; to \; 0$ **do**
    $v_0 \leftarrow speedLimit$
    $v_1 \leftarrow speed(SP[j])$, $v_2 \leftarrow speed(SP[j+1])$
    if $v_2 \geq v_1$ **then**
      if $v_2 = v_1$ **then**
        $a = 0$
      else
        $a = maxacc(T)$
      end if
      $d_1 \leftarrow dist(SP[j])$, $d \leftarrow dist(SP[-1])$
      $x_{dec} \leftarrow \frac{v_0^2 - v_1^2 + 2(ad_1 + bd)}{2(a+b)}$
      $v^\# \leftarrow \sqrt{v_1^2 + 2a(x_{dec} - d_1)}$
      if $v^\# > v_1$ **then**
        $SP \leftarrow SP[0:j]$
        $t_1^\# \leftarrow \frac{v^\# - v_1}{a}$, $t_2^\# \leftarrow \frac{v^\# - v_0}{b}$
        Add two new states in SP
        $currentV \leftarrow v_0$, $currentAcc \leftarrow 0$
        Return True
      end if
      if $v^\# = v_1$ **then**
        $SP \leftarrow SP[0:j]$
        if $x_{dec} > d_1$ **then**
          $t_1^\# \leftarrow \frac{x_{dec} - d_1}{v^\#}$, $t_2^\# \leftarrow \frac{v^\# - v_0}{b}$
          Add two new states in SP
        else
          $t^\# \leftarrow \frac{v^\# - v_0}{b}$
          Add one new state in SP
        end if
        $currentV \leftarrow v_0$, $currentAcc \leftarrow 0$
        Return True
      end if
    end if
  end for
  return False

If $v^\# > v_1$, this means that the deceleration point lies between d_1 and d. Existing SP nodes after $SP[j]$ are removed, while two new SP nodes are added, $SP[j+1]$ at the beginning of deceleration and $S[j+2]$ at the end of it. In case $v^\# = v_1$, the train maintains steady speed between $SP[j]$ and $S[j+1]$. In case $x_{dec} = d_1$, $SP[j+1]$ is removed, so $SP[j+2]$ becomes $SP[j+1]$. Finally, execution returns of Algorithm 2 on Algorithm 1 with the train at the start of the new segment having a speed equal to the new *speedLimit* and and *currentAcc* = 0. If Algorithm 2 returns False, Algorithm 1 terminates since the train started the path with a speed high enough that a deceleration to *speedLimit* is not possible.

Algorithm 1 ends by saving the new state in SP, proceeding by t_{min}. It is also checked whether the train has arrived at the position of the *goal* state but with a speed different than *goalV*, which means that it is impossible to reach it thus, the algorithm terminates.

5 Shortest Path Finding

Algorithm 3. Shortest path with A*

Input: $T, G, init = ((s_0, .., s_k), initX), initV)$,
$goal = ((s_m, .., s_f), goalX), goalV)$
Output: $SP_{dict}[min(openDict)]$, $min(openDict)$

1: Initialize *start*, *openDict*.
2: $openDict \leftarrow generatePaths(G, start)$
3: $openDict \leftarrow expandPaths(G, openDict)$
4: For $path \in openDict$, $openDict[path] = f(path)$
5: Update SP_{dict}.
6: **while** *openDict* is not empty **do**
7:     $current \leftarrow min(openDict)$.
8:     $openDict \leftarrow openDict - current$
9:     $current \leftarrow generatePaths(G, current)$
10:    $successors \leftarrow expandPaths(G, current)$
11:    For $path \in successors$, $successors[path] = f(path)$
12:    Update SP_{dict}.
13:    $openDict \leftarrow openDict \cup successors$
14:    $lastState \leftarrow (SP_{dict}[min(openDict)])[-1]$
15:    **if** $lastState = goal$ **then**
16:       return $SP_{dict}[min(openDict)]$, $min(openDict)$.
17:    **end if**
18: **end while**

In this section we employ the A* algorithm to compute the shortest path in terms of time for the general form of the problem, that is over an arbitrary graph. Algorithm 3 takes as input a *Problem* (T, G, init, goal) and outputs the solution, that is the pair (*path*, *SP*) (if it exists). *openDict* contains all the discovered paths and is initialized to include only the *start* path, that is a sequence of nodes $(u_0, u_1, ..., u_k, s_k)$, defined by the segments $(s_0, .., s_k)$ in *init*. For each path in *openDict*, *generatePaths()* iterates through the outgoing edges (of the last vertex of the path), generating new paths (which are extensions of the current path, with a single or more segments added to it) that are stored temporarily in *neighbors*, before entering *openDict*. In the example of Fig. 2, $s_k = s_0$ with $s_0 = (S, A)$ hence, the *start* path is (S, A). Using the neighboring nodes B and C, extended paths (S, A, B) and (S, A, C) are created.

---

function GENERATEPATHS$(G, path)$
    $node \leftarrow path[-1]$
    for (u, v) *in* $G.edges$ **do**
        if $u = node$ **then**
            $path \leftarrow (node, v)$
            $neighbors.insert(path)$
        end if
    end for
    return *neighbors*
end function

---

function EXPANDPATHS$(G, paths)$
    for *path in paths* **do**
        $v \leftarrow path[-1]$
        while v not a junction AND $v \neq v_f$ **do**
            $extension \leftarrow generatePaths(G, v)$
            $v \leftarrow extension[-1]$
            $path \leftarrow path \cup v$
        end while
        $expandedPaths.insert(path)$
    end for
    return *expandedPaths*
end function

In the next step, these paths are further expanded until the first junction, by applying the *expandPaths()* function. This function takes as input a list of *paths* and for each *path* (saved as a sequence), it iteratevily expands it by applying the *generatePaths()* function on its last node v. If v has a single outgoing edge, it has a single neighbor and the *generatePaths()* function returns only one path (of two nodes) that is stored in the set *extension*. The last element of *extension* is the new node, that is added to the *path*. Moreover, if v has multiple outgoing edges or it is the *destination* node (the end of segment s_f, that is v_f), the path is not expanded. The *expandedPaths* are stored in *openDict*. In our example this means that the path (S, A, B) is expanded into (S, A, B, D, G) while path (S, A, C) remains unchanged, since node C has more than one outgoing edges.

As mentioned previously, Algorithm 1 stores train states in the list SP. In contrast, Algorithm 3 handles multiple paths, each one having its own SP list. Whenever a path is expanded, its SP is used as the starting point. This functionality is implemented by using the dictionary SP_{dict} that stores the SP arraylist for each path. $openDict$ is a another dictionary as well; the keys identify all the discovered paths, while the values concern the f values for a particular path.

A* scores all paths in $openDict$ with their f value. The g function makes use of Algorithm 1, in order to calculate the traversal time for each path, reaching the end of the path with the maximum possible speed, irrelevant to the next segments. In our example, the g values for paths $[A, B, D, G]$ and $[A, C]$ are 59.16 and 33.15 seconds respectively. The f function values for each path are computed in the usual way using an admissible heuristic function h that that computes the time needed to travel the straight line distance between the last node of a path and the *destination* node using $maxv(T)$.

Note that $min(openDict)$ denotes the key of $openDict$ with the lowest f value. The *successors* dictionary contains the expansions of the *current* path with neighboring nodes. In our example this means that path $[A, C]$ generates the paths $[A, C, E]$ and $[A, C, F]$. Path $[A, C, F]$ is expanded to path $[A, C, F, H]$ and path $[A, C, E]$ is expanded to path $[A, C, E, H]$ since there is no junction at nodes F and E. After the calculations of the f, g and h values, SP_{dict} is updated with the new paths and their SP arraylists, while $openDict$ and *successors* are merged. Finally, if *lastState*, that is the final state in the SP of the current shortest path, is the *goal* state, the algorithm terminates and returns the speed profile of the solution path as well as, the optimal *path*.

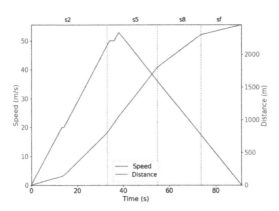

Fig. 5. Speed and Position vs. time graph for the optimal path

Figure 5 presents the optimal speed profile for the shortest path $[A, C, F, H]$ that has a duration of 91.02 s.

6   Conclusions and Future Challenges

Our work resulted in the development and the implementation of two algorithms for the tasks of computing the optimal speed profile over a given path, as well as, that of computing the shortest path in terms of journey duration, over arbitrary directed graphs. We provided a realistic problem formulation that makes use of train characteristics, including its length, maximum speed, acceleration and deceleration capabilities, while also including path characteristics, such as the speed limits that apply in the path segments. The algorithm handles cases in which the train is in multiple segments concurrently, with multiple effective speed limits, as well as cases where speed profiles must be recomputed recursively because of the need for deceleration.

The main advantage of the presented approach is that it employs basic kinematics, without resorting to micro-simulation, but taking advantage from kinematic equations that are solved for any segment of the journey where the train maintains a constant acceleration. Thus, the proposed approach is able to find optimal speed profiles in time linear in the length of a path, whereas it exhibits the same worst case algorithmic complexity as the Dijkstra algorithm to find the optimal path and speed profile over arbitrary graphs (of course, A* usually results in much lower average complexity).

Future challenges include the extension of our work in order to handle more physical characteristics of the problem, such as railway machine power profile, train load, ground slopes, optimizing other metrics, like fuel consumption. Offline and online scheduling of multiple trains, in order to satisfy particular transportation needs, is another significant, while optimizing the aforementioned metrics, is another significant future challenge. Finally, integrating our work with an information system with real data about railway networks, such as openrailwaymap.org, is needed to have a fully functional product.

Acknowledgements. This paper is a result of research conducted within the "MSc in Artificial Intelligence and Data Analytics" of the Department of Applied Informatics of University of Macedonia. The presentation of the paper is funded by the University of Macedonia Research Committee

References

1. Agasucci, V., Grani, G., Lamorgese, L.: Solving the train dispatching problem via deep reinforcement learning. J. Rail Transp. Plann. Manage. **26**, 100394 (2023). https://doi.org/10.1016/j.jrtpm.2023.100394, https://www.sciencedirect.com/science/article/pii/S2210970623000264
2. AIcrowd: train schedule optimisation challenge (2018). https://www.aicrowd.com/challenges/train-schedule-optimisation-challenge
3. AIcrowd: flatland 3 (2021). https://www.aicrowd.com/challenges/flatland-3
4. Assad, A.A.: Models for rail transportation. transportation research part a: general **14**(3), 205–220 (1980). https://doi.org/10.1016/0191-2607(80)90017-5, https://www.sciencedirect.com/science/article/pii/0191260780900175

5. Bożejko, W., Grymin, R., Pempera, J.: Scheduling and routing algorithms for rail freight transportation. Procedia Eng. **178**, 206–212 (2017). https://doi.org/ 10.1016/j.proeng.2017.01.098, https://www.sciencedirect.com/science/article/pii/ S187770581730098X, relStat-2016: Proceedings of the 16th International Scientific Conference Reliability and Statistics in Transportation and Communication October 19-22, 2016. Transport and Telecommunication Institute, Riga, Latvia

6. Cordeau, J.F., Toth, P., Vigo, D.: A survey of optimization models for train routing and scheduling. Transp. Sci. **32**(4), 380–404 (1998). https://doi.org/10.1287/trsc. 32.4.380

7. D'Ariano, A., Pacciarelli, D., Pranzo, M.: A branch and bound algorithm for scheduling trains in a railway network. Euro. J. Oper. Res. **183**(2), 643–657 (2007). https://doi.org/10.1016/j.ejor.2006.10.034, https://www.sciencedirect. com/science/article/pii/S0377221706010678

8. Eaton, J., Yang, S., Gongora, M.: Ant colony optimization for simulated dynamic multi-objective railway junction rescheduling. IEEE Trans. Intell. Transp. Syst. **18**(11), 2980–2992 (2017). https://doi.org/10.1109/TITS.2017.2665042, https:// ieeexplore.ieee.org/abstract/document/7875408

9. Šemrov, D., Marsetič, R., Žura, M., Todorovski, L., Srdic, A.: Reinforcement learning approach for train rescheduling on a single-track railway. Transp. Res. Part B: Methodol. **86**, 250–267 (2016). https://doi.org/10.1016/j.trb.2016.01.004, https:// www.sciencedirect.com/science/article/pii/S0191261516000084

10. European-Comission: white paper on transport : roadmap to a single european transport area - towards a competitive and resource-efficient transport system. Publications Office of the European Union, Luxembourg (2011)

11. Fang, W., Yang, S., Yao, X.: A survey on problem models and solution approaches to rescheduling in railway networks. IEEE Trans. Intell. Transp. Syst. **16**(6), 2997–3016 (2015). https://doi.org/10.1109/TITS.2015.2446985, https://ieeexplore.ieee. org/abstract/document/7160720

12. Firzli, N.J.: Transportation infrastructure and country attractiveness. Revue Analyse Financière (2013). https://www.academia.edu/6494981

13. Gong, I., Oh, S., Min, Y.: Train scheduling with deep q-network: a feasibility test. Appl. Sci. **10**(23), 8367 (2020). https://doi.org/10.3390/app10238367

14. Huisman, D., Kroon, L.G., Lentink, R.M., Vromans, M.J.C.M.: Operations research in passenger railway transportation. Stat. Neerl. **59**(4), 467–497 (2005). https://doi.org/10.1111/j.1467-9574.2005.00303.x

15. Lusby, R.M., Larsen, J., Ehrgott, M., Ryan, D.: Railway track allocation: models and methods. OR Spectrum **33**(4), 843–883 (2009). https://doi.org/10.1007/ s00291-009-0189-0

16. Nirmala, G., Ramprasad, D.: A genetic algorithm based railway scheduling model. Int. J. Sci. Res. (IJSR) (2014)

17. Samà, M., Pellegrini, P., D'Ariano, A., Rodriguez, J., Pacciarelli, D.: Ant colony optimization for the real-time train routing selection problem. Transp. Res. Part B: Methodol. **85**, 89–108 (2016). https://doi.org/10.1016/j.trb.2016.01.005, https:// www.sciencedirect.com/science/article/pii/S0191261515301077

18. Szpigel, B.: Optimal train scheduling on a single line railway. Oper. Res. **72**, 343–352 (1973)

19. Tormos, P., Lova, A., Barber, F., Ingolotti, L., Abril, M., Salido, M.A.: A genetic algorithm for railway scheduling problems. Metaheuristics for Scheduling in Industrial and Manufacturing Applications, pp. 255–276 (2008). https://doi.org/10. 1007/978-3-540-78985-7_10

20. Törnquist, J.: Computer-based decision support for railway traffic scheduling and dispatching: a review of models and algorithms. Dagstuhl Research Online Publication Server 2 (2006). https://doi.org/10.4230/OASIcs.ATMOS.2005.659
21. Yoon, Y.H., Bang, Y.: Apparatus and method for controlling speed in automatic train operation (2010), https://patents.google.com/patent/US20110046827A1/ar

Deep Reinforcement Learning of Autonomous Control Actions to Improve Bus-Service Regularity

Josef Bajada[1]([✉]) [iD], Joseph Grech[1], and Thérèse Bajada[2] [iD]

[1] Department of Artificial Intelligence, Faculty of ICT, University of Malta,
Msida MSD2080, Malta
`{josef.bajada,joseph.grech.20}@um.edu.mt`
[2] Institute for Climate Change and Sustainable Development, University of Malta,
Msida MSD2080, Malta
`therese.bajada@um.edu.mt`

Abstract. Bus Bunching is caused by irregularities in demand across the bus route, together with other factors such as traffic. The effect of this problem is that buses operating on the same route start to catch up with each other, severely impacting the regularity and the quality of the service. Control actions such as Bus Holding and Stop Skipping can be used to regulate the service and adjust the headway between two buses. Traditionally, this phenomenon is mitigated either reactively online through simple rule-based control, or preemptively through analytical scheduling solutions, such as mathematical optimization. Over time, both approaches degrade to an irregular service.

In this work, we investigate the use of Deep Reinforcement Learning algorithms to train a policy that determines which actions should take place at specific control points to regularise the bus service. While prior studies are typically restricted to one control action, we consider both Bus Holding and Stop Skipping. We replicate benchmarks found in the latest literature, and also introduce traffic to increase the realism of the simulation. Furthermore, we also consider scenarios where the service is already unstable and buses are already bunched together, a first of this kind of study. We compare the performance of the RL-based policies with a no-control policy and a rule-based policy. The learnt policies not only keep a significantly lower headway variance and mean waiting time, but also recover from unstable scenarios and restore service regularity.

Keywords: Deep Reinforcement Learning · PPO · TRPO · Autonomous Control · Bus Bunching · Bus Service Regularity

1 Introduction

Bus bunching is a phenomenon of public transport services operating on a schedule and a fixed route [12,21], which occurs when the buses in front start to fall behind due to various factors such as passenger demand at upcoming bus stops, or traffic conditions. When the buses behind start to catch-up, not enough time would have passed from when the previous bus last picked up passengers from the upcoming stops, which makes the buses behind catch-up even faster. After some time, unless there is an intervention, the bus behind gets close to the bus in front of it, causing the two buses serving the same route to arrive together [7]. Figure 1 illustrates the effect of bus bunching on service regularity.

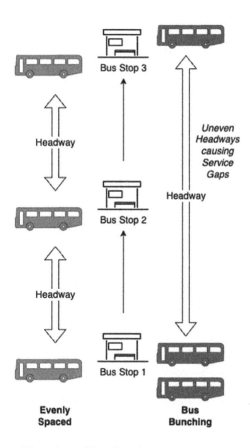

Fig. 1. The effect of bus bunching on service regularity.

On high-frequency and high demand routes, public transport operators publish expected arrival rates for each specific bus stop, rather than a fixed schedule with absolute arrival times. This gives them some flexibility to apply control actions in an attempt to regularise the service. These include *Bus Holding* [8,28], where the bus waits at specific control points, *Speed Adjustments*, where the bus cruising speed is adjusted to restore the gap between two buses [9], *Stop Skipping*, where the bus is instructed to skip the next stop [25], and imposing *Boarding Limits*, such that not all passengers waiting at a specific bus stop board the first bus [10,30]. While these actions help to regulate the *headway*, the distance or temporal gap between two buses, they have a negative effect on other aspects, such as the *waiting time* passengers spend on bus stops, or the overall trip duration. One has to find the right balance in the trade-off between regularising the service and the time passengers spend commuting.

In this work we present a formal model for the bus bunching problem. We then propose a method with which an effective automated policy for a specific route can be found. We trained a policy using Deep Reinforcement Learning (DRL), which adapts to the dynamic and stochastic properties of the route, while considering both bus capacity constraints and different passenger demand levels at each bus stop. We also introduce traffic as an extra dynamic factor. While other similar studies typically only consider a single action, such as Bus Holding [24] or Stop Skipping [14], we incorporate both actions. Furthermore, while other techniques aim to maintain a stable service with minimal headway variance [6,8,24,29], we also train our policy to recover from unstable situations that are unavoidable in real-life due to the stochastic and dynamic nature of the environment.

We trained our DRL model on a simulated environment using the SUMO[1] microsocopic urban mobility simulator. The simulation is configured with the information that is typically available to transport planners, such as traffic counts and passenger arrival rates. Our results show that our DRL model can learn a robust bus-dispatching policy that adapts to the route's characteristics. It not only maintains a low headway variance, but also recovers from bunched scenarios to restore the regularity of the service.

We also analyse the effect of the policy on the waiting time, and show that with the trained policy we maintain a low mean waiting time, even under traffic conditions, when compared to leaving the service run its course without any corrective actions, or when a simple rule-based policy is applied. Finally, we measure the occupancy dispersion of the buses, to determine whether they are filling up to capacity along the route or the load is being distributed evenly.

The proposed approach only requires a limited amount of real-time telemetry, primarily the location of each bus, together with a basic communication mechanism to control or instruct the bus to perform an action at the next control point. This means that this approach can be adopted to a bus fleet that has a mix of both human-driven and autonomous vehicles.

2   Background

2.1   The Bus Bunching Problem

We define the bus bunching problem as the tuple $\langle B, C, A \rangle$. $B = (b_1, b_2, ..., b_n)$ is the list of buses operating on a route simultaneously, $C = (c_1, c_2, ..., c_m)$ is the list of bus stops in the route, and A is the set of discrete corrective actions. For the scope of this work they are defined as $\{Hold, Skip, Proceed\}$. The *Hold* action has a predefined holding duration. If necessary, a longer holding time can be achieved by multiple consecutive discrete *Hold* actions while the bus is at the

---

[1] https://www.eclipse.org/sumo/.

same stop. The *Skip* action instructs the bus not to board any passengers from the next bus stop. The *Proceed* action allows the bus to take its natural course of disembarking and embarking passengers, leaving from the stop immediately after. Each of these actions is applied on a specific bus, $b \in B$, when it reaches specific control points, which in our case are the instants when a bus approaches a stop $c \in C$.

Each bus, $b \in B$, has a maximum passenger capacity, $\Phi(b)$, where $\Phi : B \to \mathbb{N}_{>0}$, and the current occupancy level, $\phi(b)$, where $\phi : B \to \mathbb{N}$ and $0 \le \phi(b) \le \Phi(b)$. Each bus stop c has an arrival rate, $\lambda(c)$, which indicates the passenger demand of that stop. The set of passengers waiting at a stop c at some point in time t, is denoted, $\eta_t(c)$. The demand, $d_t(c) = |\eta_t(c)|$, corresponds the number of passengers waiting at bus stop c at some instant in time t. For each passenger, $\rho \in \eta_t(c)$, the waiting time, $\omega(\rho)$ is the time elapsed from when ρ arrived at stop c to the time p embarked on some bus, b.

$\hat{\omega}_t(c)$ corresponds to the maximum waiting time for stop c at some instant in time t, that is the longest a passenger has been waiting at that stop, as defined in Eq. 1:

$$\hat{\omega}_t(c) = \max_{\rho \in \eta_t(c)} \omega(\rho) \tag{1}$$

The headway $h(b_i, b_j)$ is the gap between bus b_i and bus b_j. This gap is typically either calculated in terms of time, or in terms of distance. The *forward headway*, $h^-(b_i) = h(b_{i-1}, b_i)$ is the headway to bus b_i from the preceding bus in front of it, b_{i-1}, while the *backward headway*, $h^+(b_i) = h(b_i, b_{i+1})$ is the headway from bus b_i to the one following it b_{i+1}.

The *dwell time*, $\theta(b, c)$, is the time spent by bus b at stop c, including disembarking and embarking passengers. This depends primarily on the number of passengers waiting to embark a bus at the bus stop c, $\psi_e(c)$, together with the number of passengers who want to disembark from bus b at stop c, $\psi_d(b, c)$. A *Hold* action naturally inflates the dwell time.

The problem can be modelled as a Markov Decision Process (MDP) [27]. Each state, $s \in S$, corresponds to the set of relevant observations, where S is the set of all possible states. Each state contains the relevant information, such as positions of the buses, forward and backward headways, number of passengers waiting at each bus stop, waiting times, and bus capacities. Given the set of all possible actions, A, the expression $p(s', r|s, a)$ represents the probability of an action, $a \in A$, applied within state, s, of transitioning to a new state $s' \in S$ and obtaining the immediate reward $r \in \mathbb{R}$. This reward indicates whether the situation improved or degraded from the previous state. The reward function for r depends on the objective being optimized. This is typically defined in terms of some service quality measure, such as the headway variability or change in waiting time. In this work we focus on the difference between the forward and backward headway. The chosen reward function is discussed later in Sect. 4.3.

A discount factor, $\gamma \in [0, 1]$ can be used to determine how much weight future rewards should be given future time steps importance that rewards obtained in future time steps should be given. A low discount factor indicates that we are only interested in the immediate or short-term effects of the chosen actions, while a high discount factor indicates that we are also interested in how decisions impact the long-term future of our state trajectory.

The solution is an $n \times m$ matrix of partially-ordered actions, where each action, $a(b, c) \in A$, corresponds to the action taken by bus $b \in B$ at bus stop $c \in C$. Ordering constraints between actions can be defined using the temporal precedence operator, $\prec$. Given that $t(a)$ refers to the instant in time when action a takes place, $t(a) \prec t(a')$ states that action a must happen before a'. Each bus stop must be visited in sequence according to the pre-established route, and thus: $\forall b, c_i : t(a(b, c_i)) \prec t(a(b, c_{i+1}))$. If bus overtaking is not allowed, $\forall b_i, c : t(a(b_i, c)) \prec t(a(b_{i+1}, c))$, that is, bus b_i has to visit a bus stop c before the following bus b_{i+1} visits the same bus stop c. Such a solution can be optimised in terms of various metrics, such as the standard deviation of the headway across all stops and buses, σ_h, as defined in Eq. 2, the mean of the maximum registered waiting time of each bus stop, as shown in Eq. 3, and the occupancy dispersion, ϕ_d, the variance-to-mean ratio of the occupancy of all buses, shown in Eq. 4.

$$\sigma_h = \sqrt{\frac{\sum_{i=1}^{n}(|h^-(b_i) - h^+(b_i)| - \mu)}{n}},$$
$$\text{s.t. } \mu = \frac{1}{n}\sum_{i=1}^{n}(|h^-(b_i) - h^+(b_i)| \tag{2}$$

$$\bar{\omega} = \frac{1}{m}\sum_{i=1}^{m}\max_t \hat{w}_t(c_i) \tag{3}$$

$$\phi_d = \frac{\sigma_\phi^2}{\mu_\phi}, \text{ s.t. } \sigma_\phi^2 = \frac{1}{n}\sum_{i=1}^{n}(\phi(b_i) - \mu_\phi)^2,$$
$$\text{and } \mu_\phi = \frac{1}{n}\sum_{i=1}^{n}\phi(b_i) \tag{4}$$

To generate the solution, one could take a search-based approach, where the schedule of when each action is likely to take place is computed. In this approach, alternative actions are considered to improve the solution according to some objective function, which is typically optimised using a mixed-integer programming approach. Another approach is to find a policy, π, which given the current state of the service at a specific control point, determines which is the best action to apply. While the former is model-based and requires accurate predictions of the effects of each action on the schedule, the second requires a high-fidelity simulation of the transport network to train the policy. Given that the probabilistic properties of a transport network are typically non-stationary, both approaches can be improved and adjusted with real-world data such as seasonal traffic counts, observed delays, and passenger demand. In this work we adopt the second approach and make use of Reinforcement Learning (RL) to find such a policy.

2.2 Reinforcement Learning

RL is a family of machine learning techniques that aims to solve sequential decision making problems. It is typically modelled in terms of states, actions that correspond to transitions between states, and rewards, scalar signals that can be positive or negative. Some of the RL techniques, such as SARSA and Q-Learning [27], are referred to as model-free, because they infer the model implicitly through the data collected from observations. On the other hand, model-based RL is also possible, using algorithms such as Dyna-Q and Monte Carlo Tree Search [27], where the dynamics of the model are either provided by experts, or learnt from observations.

Another characteristic of modern state-of-the-art RL techniques is that they make use of function approximation techniques to manage large, and potentially infinite state spaces, including ones with continuous values. These techniques incorporate ideas from supervised learning approaches, and often make use of Deep Learning techniques such as Convolutional Neural Networks (CNNs) [18] and Recurrent Neural Networks (RNNs) [4,5,20]. The trade-off of these approaches, however, is that one needs to have a sufficiently large source of data, often taking the form of a simulated environment, to explore the effects of different sequences of actions. The result of this process is a policy that chooses which action is best to take in a specific situation. RL algorithms typically learn policies that optimise the *return*, that is the cumulative discounted reward, rather than just the immediate reward of an action. This means that a policy can learn to sacrifice some immediate reward, or even incur some immediate penalty, to reach a state that has a higher expected return.

While some RL algorithms, such as DQN [18] and A2C only support discrete action spaces, others like DDPG and TD3 [13] support continuous action spaces. TRPO [22] and PPO [23] support both. For the scope of this work, we will only be using a discrete action space. Furthermore, the chosen algorithms are model-free, and thus require only the observation for the current state, the set of possible actions, and the appropriate reward function.

3 Related Work

The bus bunching problem was originally defined in [21], and since then, various approaches to mitigate it have been proposed. More recently, with the advent of real-time telematic data, it is possible to react more quickly to irregularities in the service. [11] formulate the bus bunching problem as a vehicle holding problem, and take a quadratic programming approach. They assume a deterministic environment, with a rolling horizon. Similarly, [16] also takes a quadratic programming approach to find the optimal holding time for a vehicle at a single control point. In this case, stochastic service attributes were considered such as passenger boarding and alighting times. [26] revisited this quadratic programming approach, but this time using multiple control points and potentially holding multiple vehicles concurrently. However, these optimization approaches fail to account for uncertainties due to traffic or variations in demand.

Instead of bus holding, which has the adverse effect of delaying the whole service, [25] proposed Stop Skipping. They model the problem as a nonlinear integer programming problem, and assume that passenger boarding and alighting follow predefined binomial and Poisson distributions. They use an exhaustive search approach, assuming that the problem will not grow beyond a tractable size.

[8] introduced the idea of using real-time headway measurements as input for a dynamic bus holding strategy. This holding takes place at predefined control points and operates on a single bus line operated on a regular schedule, assuming time-independent conditions. They proposed the use of a simple policy where the headway is increased when buses are too close, and decreased when buses are too far away. Under the simplifying assumptions used at that time, it was proven that granular control actions at specific control points can mitigate significant deviation from the schedule. However, the local and myopic nature of the strategy, without considering what else is bound to happen on the route, only makes this approach effective when disturbances are small. To address this issue, [9] proposed to use bus-to-bus cooperation, where the forward and backwards headways are monitored continuously, and buses slow down to adjust these headways, aiming to maintain an equilibrium. Nonetheless, more complex environment properties, such as passenger demand or traffic were not taken into consideration. A similar approach was also reconsidered more recently by [2], where rather than using specific control points, a follow-the-leader bus-to-bus communication system ensures that the desired headway is maintained.

[10] analysed the effects of both vehicle holding and also imposing boarding limits, applied over a rolling horizon. Imposing boarding limits has the opposite effect of bus holding, and avoids holding back the service, thus decreasing the waiting time of passengers at bus stops further ahead. An optimisation approach, based on the MINOS solver, was used, which assumes deterministic passenger demand and travel times. Despite these limitations they report significant improvements in terms of total waiting times, when compared to a no control strategy.

[19] acknowledged that advancements in telematics and telecommunications offered opportunities for more real-time control. They used data collected from 18 bus routes in Porto, Portugal, to train an Artificial Neural Network and predict headways depending on the current state and the chosen corrective action, being either Bus Holding or Stop Skipping. They managed to reduce the number of bus bunching events by 67.59%, with the neural network choosing to perform Bus Holding for 81.86% of the control actions. This is one of the few studies where both actions were considered simultaneously.

[3] take a different approach, and use a predictive-control strategy to mitigate bus bunching. They predict future headways using data collected from a busy real-world bus route, formulated as a time series. Historical data is used to determine the likely headway trajectory for the specified prediction horizon. They evaluate various prediction techniques, including linear regression, kernel regression, multilayer perceptrons, and autoregressive-moving-average models.

They adopt the same headway-based bus holding strategy introduced by [8]. However, they do not take into account the stochastic effects of high passenger demand, and also observe that the control actions themselves will impact the accuracy of the predictions of the chosen models. They acknowledge that a reinforcement learning approach that accounts for future control actions is probably more appropriate.

More recently, researchers have started to explore a Reinforcement Learning approach to solving the bus bunching problem. [28] propose to use multi-agent deep reinforcement learning based on PPO. They use a reward function which promotes headway regularisation. They introduce different passenger arrival rates per bus-stop, which is more realistic, since parts of a bus route are typically more popular then others. However, they only consider a single action, bus holding, and do not take into consideration traffic conditions. Furthermore, their scenarios always start out with evenly spaced buses, with the aim of maintaining such regularity. [15] use a Q-Learning algorithm to determine whether to apply bus holding at a specific bus stop. They also account for passenger demand by specifying different passenger arrival rates for each bus stop. While they do not consider traffic, it is one of the few studies that takes into consideration traffic signals. [24] use a distributed deep reinforcement learning approach, trained using historical traffic data. They use a distributed PPO algorithm implementation, where each bus is controlled separately in a multi-agent fashion. Rather than enforcing the use of Bus Holding actions, they introduce the concept of control force between two stops. This determines to which direction the bus needs to adjust its headway, using either bus holding or other ways such as speed control, or early departure. While their experiments were based on historical data, these strategies proved to be effective in maintaining a reasonably stable headway and minimising schedule deviation.

4   Proposed Solution

We propose to use an RL approach to learn a policy that maintains the service stable with no bus bunching and minimal waiting time. We first trained a policy with simple scenarios that do not include traffic and where the buses start evenly spaced. Subsequently, we trained a policy with a mix of scenarios where sometimes buses start evenly spaced, while in others the buses start already bunched, all of which include traffic. Both policies were evaluated separately.

The scenarios were generated using the SUMO simulation framework, through which the road network, location of the bus stops, passenger arrival rates, bus routes and behaviour of different vehicles, were defined. SUMO also provides a programmatic Traffic Control Interface, TraCI[2], through which the behaviour of vehicles and the observation data we need to collect for our states can be obtained. The simulator was wrapped within a Gymnasium environment[3],

---

[2] https://sumo.dlr.de/docs/TraCI.html.
[3] https://github.com/Farama-Foundation/Gymnasium.

such that off-the-shelf RL algorithm implementations can instruct our simulator to execute the respective actions. The Stable Baselines3[4] implementations of TRPO and PPO were used to train our policy.

Following the same approach of prior studies [1,10,29], we use a circular route, where buses restart the route as soon as they finish the prior lap. We use the same scenario described in [28] with 12 bus stops and 6 buses. Each bus stop has a different passenger arrival rate, as shown in Table 1, with passenger arrival events generated using a Poisson distribution. Apart from the circular route, the road network also includes feeder roads through which vehicles enter and leave the scenario, generating traffic which interferes with the bus service. When training with traffic, a car is added to the simulation every 2.25 min, and assigned one of 4 possible speeds randomly: 12km/h, 24km/h, 36km/h, and 60km/h, and loops around the same loop used by the buses for 1 to 3 times, to create stochastic traffic congestion levels. The default bus cruising speed was configured to 20km/h, in line with the conditions described in [28].

Table 1. Passenger arrival rates for each bus stop. (Adopted from [28].)

Bus Stop	Rate (per minute)
1	0.5
2	0.5
3	0.8
4	1.0
5	1.0
6	3.0
7	4.0
8	2.0
9	1.0
10	0.65
11	0.55
12	0.5

Since we only apply actions at specific control points (when the bus is approaching a bus stop), the RL time-steps are less granular than the time-steps of the SUMO simulation. After each action, the environment proceeds with running the simulation until the next control point is reached. This takes places when a bus is approaching one of the bus stops on its route. At this point the observation and the reward obtained from the previous action is passed to the RL algorithm, which then selects the next action.

---

[4] https://stable-baselines3.readthedocs.io.

In order to train a robust policy that can handle both stable and unstable scenarios, we alternate between scenarios that start with buses evenly spaced, and scenarios where the buses are already bunched together. This is a departure from the work of [28] where buses always start evenly distributed, and it serves to train the policy with a more diverse distribution of states. In our scenarios, buses are not allowed to overtake each other.

4.1   Baseline Control Strategies

Two baseline control strategies were implemented. The first one is a *no-control policy*, where buses are left to fulfil their routes according to the demand without any intervention. The second one is a *rule-based control policy*, where the system reacts to significant deviations in the forward or backwards headway, and applies control actions to recover. A minimum threshold level, H is selected, and a control action is taken if the forward or backwards headway is less than this threshold. This is similar in principle to the Naive Hard-holding Control used in [28], with the difference that in their case, they only apply Holding control if the forward headway, $h^-(b_i)$ is smaller than the threshold, H, while in our case we also apply Stop Skipping if the backward headway, $h^+(b_i)$ is smaller than the threshold, H. For this work H was set to 0.433km, which was equivalent to half of the ideal headway of 0.886km for the route. These values were obtained from [28] and scaled to the length of our route.

4.2   Observation and Action Spaces

The observation data consists of the following elements for the selected bus, b_i, for which an action $a(b_i, c)$ needs to be taken when approaching bus stop c, at some time step t: The stop, c, that the bus, b_i, is at, the forward headway, $h^-(b_i)$, and backward headway, $h^+(b_i)$, for the selected bus, b, the estimated dwell time, $\theta(b_i, c)$, according to the number of people embarking to and alighting from bus b_i at stop c, the number of passengers on the bus, $\phi(b_i)$, together with the number of passengers on the previous bus, $\phi(b_{i-1})$ and the next bus, $\phi(b_{i+1})$, the number of persons waiting at each stop, $(\psi_e(c_1), \psi_e(c_2), ..., \psi_e(c_m))$, the maximum passenger waiting time at each stop $(\hat{\omega}_t(c_1), \hat{\omega}_t(c_2), ..., \hat{\omega}_t(c_n))$, and the speed factor of the selected bus, together with those of the previous and next buses, which measures how slow the buses are traveling due to traffic, with respect to their predefined cruising speed, which is calculated as shown in Eq. 5.

$$f_t(b) = v_t(b)/v_c(b) \tag{5}$$

where $v_t(b)$ is the current velocity of bus b, and $v_c(b)$ is the cruising velocity for bus b without traffic, which in our experiments was set to 20km/h for all buses.

The action space is discrete and consists of 3 actions, Hold (0), Skip (1), and Proceed (2). In case of the Hold action, the holding duration was set to 135 s.

4.3   Reward Function

The reward function is based on the difference between the forward and backward headway. The reasoning here is that a balanced headway should result in a higher reward, thus guiding the RL algorithm to prefer actions that distribute the headway evenly. The equation for the reward function is defined below:

$$R_t = -|h_t^-(b) - h_t^+(b)| \tag{6}$$

where $h_t^-(b)$ is the forward headway of bus b at time step t, for which the action was taken, and $h_t^+(b)$ is the backward headway. Naturally, $R_t <= 0$, reaching its maximum, 0, when the forward and backward headways for the same bus are equal, $h_t^-(b) = h_t^+(b)$.

4.4   The Reinforcement Learning Algorithms

We use the Trust Region Policy Optimisation (TRPO) [22] algorithms, and the Proximal Policy Optimisation (PPO) [23] algorithms. The latter combines ideas from the Advantage Actor Critic (A2C) algorithm [17] to parallelize learning and Trust Region Policy Optimisation (TRPO) [22]. These two algorithms empirically proved to be more stable, and converge more reliably than other discrete RL algorithms, such as DQN and DDQN (the results for these methods are omitted for brevity). The algorithm implementations internally use a Multi-Layer Perceptron Actor-Critic policy, based on the PyTorch library[5], and optimised using the Adam algorithm. We used the default Stable Baselines3 configuration of 2 fully connected layers of 64 units per layer, with the *tanh* activation function. Table 2 shows the training configuration for each algorithm and scenario.

Table 2. Training configuration for both TRPO and PPO under different scenarios. (NT = no traffic, T+A = traffic and alternating bunched and un-bunched scenarios)

Algorithm	Episodes	Time (hrs)	Learning Rate	Batch Size	Discount Factor (γ)
TRPO (NT)	720	7.5	0.001	128	0.99
TRPO (T+A)	1000	12.8	0.001	128	0.99
PPO (NT)	720	7.1	0.001	64	0.99
PPO (T+A)	1000	11	0.001	64	0.99

Since actions are only applied at specific control points, the duration of a time step from an RL algorithm perspective, is the time needed for some bus to reach any stop from the instant when another bus departs from its stop. Thus, the duration of each time step is not constant. Through trial and error it was observed that bus bunching starts to manifest itself after about 200 time steps.

---

[5] https://pytorch.org.

Thus, the episode length was set to 250 time steps, to ensure the phenomenon manifests itself in each episode. Training was done on an Intel® Core™ i7-10710U CPU at 1.10Ghz, and 16Gb RAM, running Windows 10 64 bit. The implementation of the environment was done in Python. The source code for these experiments is publicly available[6].

The trained policies were evaluated and compared to a no-control policy, where the buses were left to fulfil their route without any intervention, and a rule-based control policy, applying Hold and Skip actions according to the forward and backward headway deviations, as described in Sect. 4.1. The headway of each bus at each bus stop, together with the mean waiting times and occupancy dispersion levels were recorded at each control point.

5   Results

The trained policies were evaluated on the three criteria described in Sect. 2.1; headway standard deviation as a measure of headway regularity throughout the route, mean of the maximum waiting time at each stop, as a measure of service quality, and occupancy dispersion, as a measure of capacity availability throughout the route. These were measured for three scenarios, without any traffic, with traffic and buses starting evenly spaced (as in [28]), and with traffic and buses starting already bunched together. The latter scenario tests the policy's ability to recover from the scenario and regularise the headway.

As shown in Fig. 2, with no control, headway starts to become highly irregular after some time for both no traffic and traffic scenarios. While the rule-based policy manages to keep the headway variance under control initially, it still degrades over time. Both TRPO and PPO produce a policy that keeps the headway variance low over time, even under traffic. For the scenario where the buses start already bunched, the no control policy never recovers, and buses stay travelling as one for the remaining of time of the run. Rule-based control manages to restore some of the headway between the buses, until the same degradation observed in the other scenarios takes place. The policies produced by TRPO and PPO both recover from the bunched scenario and restore the stability of the service within a shorter time period when compared to the Rule-based policy, with TRPO stabilising the headway almost twice as fast as PPO.

Figure 3 shows the effect of the different policies on the maximum waiting time. With no control, it starts to increase as the network regularity degrades, for both no traffic and traffic scenarios. The rule-based policy manages to maintain a lower mean waiting time, although it has higher fluctuations than the RL-based policies, especially when traffic is introduced. On the other hand, both the TRPO and PPO-based policies maintain a low mean of the maximum waiting times throughout, with TRPO having a slightly lower waiting time on average. For the scenario where the buses start bunched, the mean of the maximum waiting time for the no control policy immediately goes up and fluctuates between 22 and 38 min. The three other policies, manage to bring the waiting time within

---

[6] https://github.com/josephgrech01/BusBunchingRL.

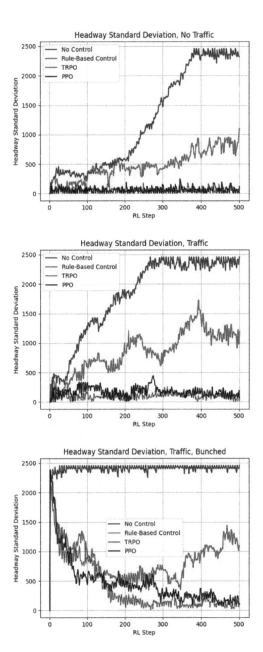

Fig. 2. Headway Standard Deviation for three scenarios (no traffic, with traffic but starting evenly spaced, and traffic starting bunched), with No Control, Rule-based Control, TRPO and PPO-based policies. The RL steps on the x-axis correspond to the number of control points at which a control action was taken.

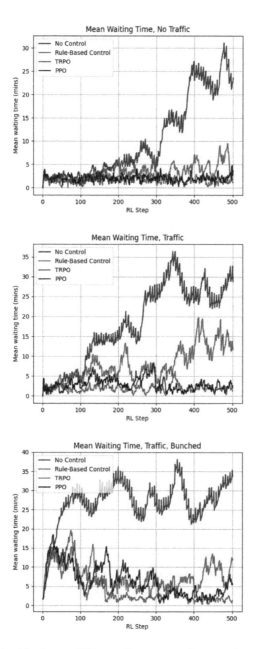

Fig. 3. Mean of the Maximum Waiting Time at each stop, for three scenarios (no traffic, with traffic but starting evenly spaced, and traffic starting bunched), with No Control, Rule-based Control, TRPO and PPO-based policies. The RL steps on the x-axis correspond to the number of control points at which a control action was taken.

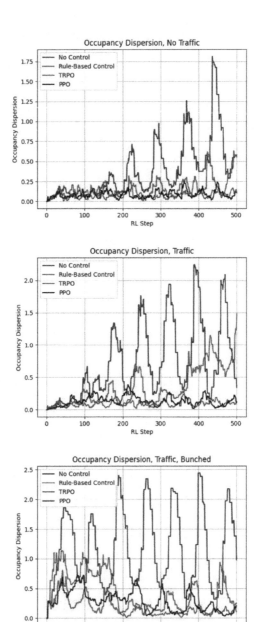

Fig. 4. Occupancy Dispersion for three scenarios (no traffic, with traffic but starting evenly spaced, and traffic starting bunched), with No Control, Rule-based Control, TRPO and PPO-based policies. The RL steps on the x-axis correspond to the number of control points at which a control action was taken.

acceptable levels, with TRPO maintaining the lowest and most stable levels fluctuating mostly around the 3 min mark.

Finally, Fig. 4 shows the occupancy dispersion levels under the different policies. With no control, the occupancy levels start to get unbalanced and fluctuate heavily as time goes by and the network destabilises itself, for both the no traffic and traffic scenarios. The Rule-based control policy also has a similar effect but to a much lesser extent. TRPO and PPO both maintain a very low occupancy dispersion, indicating that passengers are relatively well distributed across the buses circulating on the route. For the scenario where the buses start bunched, the no control policy keeps fluctuating between extremes, reflecting the fact that the front bus would be full and the one behind would be empty. Interestingly, the rule based control policy manages to recover the occupancy dispersion faster than all the other policies, but still retains the fluctuating behaviour. The PPO-based policy takes longer to regularise the occupancy dispersion and also suffers from the same fluctuating behaviour. On the other hand, although TRPO does not recover as fast as the other two polices, it recovers completely after 200 steps and does not exhibit any fluctuating behaviour, which is a desirable characteristic for a reliable service.

6   Conclusion

In this work we have presented a formal definition of the bus bunching problem, a combinatorial problem where actions need to be assigned to control points with the objective to minimise service quality criteria such as headway variance, waiting time and occupancy dispersion. We proposed to use TRPO and PPO to find an effective policy that selects the right actions to take at control points, with a reward function formulated from the difference between the forward and backward headway of the bus on which the action is being taken. We compared the performance of these algorithms with a No Control policy and a Rule-based Control policy. While previous studies typically focus on the application of one action, such as Bus Holding, we propose the use of both Bus Holding and Stop Skipping. Furthermore, we introduce a high level of traffic which intentionally interferes with the simulated bus service, making the environment more dynamic and stochastic. Finally, apart from training our policy to maintain headway regularity, we also train the policy to recover from bunched scenarios, making this study a first of its kind. Our results show that our proposed RL-based policies not only maintain a low headway variance, but also achieves a low waiting time, a low occupancy disperation, and are capable of recovering from scenarios where the buses are bunched together, thus restoring regularity, with TRPO outperforming PPO in most metrics.

This work opens up various avenues for possible further research. Firstly, the current work limited the actions to Bus Holding and Stop Skipping. Another possibility is to use boarding limits, where the chosen action also determines the maximum target dwell time, from which the boarding limit for a stop can be inferred. One could also explore how speed adjustments could be used to adjust the service regularity. Another possibility is to investigate the effect of using a multi-objective reward function that includes the waiting time or the travel time, apart from the headway. Another limitation of this study is that the passenger arrival rates were fixed, following those defined in prior work by [28]. A more realistic approach would be to have time-varying arrival rates which take into account the time of day and also the days of the week, which can be simulated using a non-homogeneous Poisson process. This could be combined with training on larger bus routes with even higher passenger demand. Finally, since in reality bus routes often overlap, and the same subset of bus stops are used by multiple routes, we also plan to investigate the possibility of applying the same approach on a more complex multi-route bus bunching problem.

References

1. Alesiani, F., Gkiotsalitis, K.: Reinforcement learning-based bus holding for high-frequency services. In: 2018 21st International Conference on Intelligent Transportation Systems (ITSC), pp. 3162–3168. IEEE (2018)
2. Ampountolas, K., Kring, M.: Mitigating bunching with bus-following models and bus-to-bus cooperation. IEEE Trans. Intell. Transp. Syst. **22**(5), 2637–2646 (2021)
3. Andres, M., Nair, R.: A predictive-control framework to address bus bunching. Transp. Res. B Methodol. **104**, 123–148 (2017)
4. Bakker, B.: Reinforcement learning with long short-term memory. In: Advances in Neural Information Processing Systems, vol. 14 (2001)
5. Bakker, B.: Reinforcement learning by backpropagation through an LSTM model/critic. In: 2007 IEEE International Symposium on Approximate Dynamic Programming and Reinforcement Learning, pp. 127–134. IEEE (2007)
6. Bie, Y., Xiong, X., Yan, Y., Qu, X.: Dynamic headway control for high-frequency bus line based on speed guidance and intersection signal adjustment. Comput. Aided Civil Infrastruct. Eng. **35**(1), 4–25 (2020)
7. Chioni, E., Iliopoulou, C., Milioti, C., Kepaptsoglou, K.: Factors affecting bus bunching at the stop level: a geographically weighted regression approach. Int. J. Transp. Sci. Technol. **9**(3), 207–217 (2020)
8. Daganzo, C.F.: A headway-based approach to eliminate bus bunching: systematic analysis and comparisons. Transp. Res. B Methodol. **43**(10), 913–921 (2009)
9. Daganzo, C.F., Pilachowski, J.: Reducing bunching with bus-to-bus cooperation. Transp. Res. B Methodol. **45**(1), 267–277 (2011)
10. Delgado, F., Munoz, J.C., Giesen, R.: How much can holding and/or limiting boarding improve transit performance? Transp. Res. B Methodol. **46**(9), 1202–1217 (2012)
11. Eberlein, X.J., Wilson, N.H., Bernstein, D.: The holding problem with real-time information available. Transp. Sci. **35**(1), 1–18 (2001)
12. Fuentetaja, R., Borrajo, D., Linares, C.: Public transport bunching: a critical review with focus on methods and findings for implications for policy and future research. In: Australasian Transport Research Forum 2022 (2022)
13. Fujimoto, S., Hoof, H., Meger, D.: Addressing function approximation error in actor-critic methods. In: International conference on machine learning, pp. 1587–1596. PMLR (2018)

14. Gkiotsalitis, K., Stathopoulos, A.: Demand-responsive public transportation rescheduling for adjusting to the joint leisure activity demand. Int. J. Transp. Sci. Technol. **5**(2), 68–82 (2016)
15. He, S.X., He, J.J., Liang, S.D., Dong, J.Q., Yuan, P.C.: A dynamic holding approach to stabilizing a bus line based on the q-learning algorithm with multistage look-ahead. Transp. Sci. **56**(1), 31–51 (2022)
16. Hickman, M.D.: An analytic stochastic model for the transit vehicle holding problem. Transp. Sci. **35**(3), 215–237 (2001)
17. Mnih, V., et al.: Asynchronous methods for deep reinforcement learning. In: International Conference on Machine Learning, pp. 1928–1937. PMLR (2016)
18. Mnih, V., et al.: Playing Atari with deep reinforcement learning. arXiv preprint arXiv:1312.5602 (2013)
19. Moreira-Matias, L., Cats, O., Gama, J., Mendes-Moreira, J., De Sousa, J.F.: An online learning approach to eliminate bus bunching in real-time. Appl. Soft Comput. **47**, 460–482 (2016)
20. Mousavi, S.S., Schukat, M., Howley, E.: Deep reinforcement learning: an overview. In: Bi, Y., Kapoor, S., Bhatia, R. (eds.) IntelliSys 2016. LNNS, vol. 16, pp. 426–440. Springer, Cham (2018). https://doi.org/10.1007/978-3-319-56991-8_32
21. Newell, G.F., Potts, R.B.: Maintaining a bus schedule. In: Australian Road Research Board (ARRB) Conference, 2nd, 1964, Melbourne, vol. 2, no. 1 (1964)
22. Schulman, J., Levine, S., Abbeel, P., Jordan, M., Moritz, P.: Trust region policy optimization. In: International Conference on Machine Learning, pp. 1889–1897. PMLR (2015)
23. Schulman, J., Wolski, F., Dhariwal, P., Radford, A., Klimov, O.: Proximal policy optimization algorithms. arXiv preprint arXiv:1707.06347 (2017)
24. Shi, H., Nie, Q., Fu, S., Wang, X., Zhou, Y., Ran, B.: A distributed deep reinforcement learning-based integrated dynamic bus control system in a connected environment. Comput. Aided Civil Infrastruct. Eng. **37**(15), 2016–2032 (2022)
25. Sun, A., Hickman, M.: The real-time stop-skipping problem. J. Intell. Transp. Syst. **9**(2), 91–109 (2005)
26. Sun, A., Hickman, M.: The holding problem at multiple holding stations. In: Hickman, M., Mirchandani, P., Vob, S. (eds.) Computer-aided Systems in Public Transport. Lecture Notes in Economics and Mathematical Systems, vol. 600, pp. 339–359. Springer, Berlin, Heidelberg (2008). https://doi.org/10.1007/978-3-540-73312-6_17
27. Sutton, R.S., Barto, A.G.: Reinforcement Learning: An Introduction. MIT Press (2018)
28. Wang, J., Sun, L.: Dynamic holding control to avoid bus bunching: a multi-agent deep reinforcement learning framework. Transp. Res. C Emerg. Technol. **116**, 102661 (2020)
29. Wu, W., Liu, R., Jin, W.: Modelling bus bunching and holding control with vehicle overtaking and distributed passenger boarding behaviour. Transp. Res. B Methodol. **104**, 175–197 (2017)
30. Zhao, S., Lu, C., Liang, S., Liu, H.: A self-adjusting method to resist bus bunching based on boarding limits. Math. Prob. Eng. **2016**, 1–7 (2016)

Identifying Critical Scenarios in Autonomous Driving During Operation

Lorenz Klampfl$^{(\boxtimes)}$ and Franz Wotawa

CD Laboratory for Quality Assurance Methodologies for Autonomous Cyber
-Physical Systems, Institute of Software Technology, Graz University of Technology,
Graz, Austria
{lklampfl,wotawa}@ist.tugraz.at

Abstract. Ensuring autonomous driving systems' safety, reliability, and trustworthiness is paramount to preventing incorrect or unexpected system behaviors and hazardous scenarios. However, due to the complexity of such systems and the immense search space of possible scenarios, testing could be infeasible, necessitating the need to detect critical situations during operation. This paper proposes a hybrid approach that combines qualitative reasoning and object detection to prevent and discover critical driving scenarios. The proposed approach relies on identifying spatiotemporal patterns of detected objects in the driving environment that are indicative of critical scenarios, such as specific changes in movement or physical impossibilities. We evaluate the approach's effectiveness on real-world driving data and demonstrate its ability to identify critical driving situations successfully. Moreover, we discuss the challenges associated with the approach and outline future research activities.

Keywords: Qualitative reasoning · Autonomous driving · Quality assurance of safety-critical systems

1 Introduction

Autonomous driving has emerged as a critical application area of artificial intelligence (AI) in recent years. With the development and integration of advanced sensors, algorithms, and software, advanced driver assistant systems (ADAS) and autonomous driving (AD) have achieved remarkable progress toward the vision of safe, efficient, and comfortable transportation. However, ensuring their safety and reliability remains a significant challenge due to the complexity and diversity of driving scenarios. The need for extensive testing and validation to ensure the trustworthiness and dependability of such systems has been widely recognized in the research community, e.g., Koopman and Wagner [16] or Wotawa [24]. However, testing such systems is challenging due to the enormous search space that must be examined, making it infeasible to test all possible parameters and combinations. With this in mind, new methodologies have been introduced over the last few years, focusing on the virtual validation of ADAS/AD. It is worth

Fig. 1. Real-world example where the mirroring of an approaching object is detected instead of the actual object.

noting that these methods have improved testing and validation significantly compared to simple road testing, but these approaches also have their limitations. For example, let us consider a driving scenario consisting of 50 parameters that describe the static properties, e.g., weather conditions, road networks, or traffic signs, and dynamic properties like other traffic participants. Assuming that each parameter takes at least five values, the entire search space is 5^{50}, roughly $9 \cdot 10^{34}$. Therefore, verifying the correct behavior of the system in all of the resulting scenarios is not feasible even with virtual verification methods. Thus, revealing a wrong behavior during the operation is likely that testing could not detect. Unfortunately, several fatal incidents, like the Uber self-driving car accident in 2018 or the Tesla autopilot crash in 2016, highlighted the difficulty of detecting and correctly responding to unexpected events during autonomous driving.

Figure 1 illustrates an interesting real-world example we discovered during our experiments. The image is extracted from our dataset on which we performed object detection with a modified version of YOLOv4 [3]. As seen, the mirroring of the approaching object within a building fooled the object detection algorithm. Moreover, the object detector only detected the mirrored object but not the actual object. The showcased example might lead to unwanted actions based on the internal control logic of the integrated system. An example could be that the autonomous car tries to evade a possible collision with the wrongly detected car and drives on the left side of the road to ensure a safe distance. However, precisely with this action, it would collide with the actual car that the object detector missed. The mentioned incidents and real-world examples emphasize the need to prevent critical scenarios during operations where the safety of passengers, pedestrians, and other road users is at risk. Hence, trustworthy systems require strict verification during development and the validation of the system behavior during operation to prevent hazardous situations and harm.

Therefore, this paper proposes a hybrid approach that utilizes qualitative reasoning (QR) complementary to object detection and object tracking in the

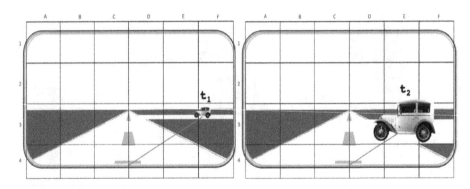

Fig. 2. Simplified view from the front window of a car driving straight towards a junction together with an approaching car at two different time steps.

autonomous driving domain. The proposed method uses spatiotemporal properties of detected objects and formalized expectations to identify possible critical situations. QR provides the necessary concepts to efficiently implement formal representations of a general view of the autonomous system and its environment and common sense interpretations of critical and non-critical situations.

In Fig. 2, we illustrate with a simplified example the use of qualitative representations. Let us assume that an autonomous car drives straight on the road and recognizes a car at time t_1 driving towards a T-junction. When approaching the detected car, its visual appearance enlarges at time t_2. In addition, the angle of the bearing line between the car's center view and the detected object stays constant over the two consecutive time steps. With the help of two qualitative properties like *object_size* (*"increased"*), and *object_angle* (*"constant"*), we could reason that we are on a potential collision course if we do not take any countermeasures.

The paper aims to demonstrate the necessity of quality assurance during the operation of autonomous systems and the applicability of qualitative reasoning (QR) as a suitable methodology. We first give an overview of related work in applying QR in the automotive driving domain and identify related challenges. Moreover, we outline how to utilize qualitative reasoning to solve some of the discovered challenges. Then, in more detail, we introduce a simple qualitative model capable of detecting situations where the autonomous system is on a collision path with other traffic participants. In addition, we present the first results obtained from applying our proposed methodology to the Audi Autonomous Driving Dataset (A2D2) [10].

2   Related Work

With recent advancements in the development of ADAS/AD, more and more of these systems are integrated into new vehicles. This can be mostly accredited to significant improvements in the field of computer vision algorithms and especially those liable for detecting and tracking objects within the autonomous car's vicinity. Reliably perceiving and interpreting the surroundings is inevitable to take appropriate actions and avoid hazardous situations with other traffic participants. Object detection algorithms like YOLOv4 [3] or Faster R-CNN [18] and object tracking algorithms, e.g., SORT [2], achieved remarkable results in various benchmarks and are capable of detecting and tracking objects with high accuracy. However, even if we could guarantee that all objects are correctly detected and classified, the autonomous car still must take adequate actions to ensure safe behavior.

Therefore, quality assurance for ADAS/AD is of uttermost importance, and several publications have been published in the last decade, including Schuldt et al. [20], or Wotawa and colleagues [26]. It is important to note that simple road testing is infeasible in practice, as expressed by Kalra and Paddock [12], who calculated that an autonomous vehicle has to operate 275 million miles for verification. With this, testing activities focus more on developing sophisticated methods within virtual environments and simulation. For instance, Klück and colleagues [15] and Klampfl et al. [13] proposed methods utilizing genetic algorithms for testing ADAS. However, also virtual testing methods need to consider various scenario properties, e.g., different traffic participants, road conditions, or dynamic entities like different velocities, resulting in numerous diverse driving scenarios that must be explored. Thus, in addition to testing during development, we require methods that assure the safety of autonomous systems during operation.

To ensure that an autonomous system operates as intended, it is necessary to have a mechanism to distinguish between desirable and undesirable behaviors. One way to accomplish this is through qualitative reasoning and identifying relations between the system and its perceived environment. Spatial and temporal reasoning are important capabilities for formalizing relationships between detected objects and the autonomous system being validated. Therefore, qualitative reasoning can provide a solid foundation for checking if correct actions are performed or if countermeasures need to be triggered. Qualitative reasoning has already been applied successfully in the context of autonomous driving. In [21,22] Suchan and colleagues introduce a modular framework for visual sensemaking using answer set programming (ASP) [5] as well as a qualitative model for tracking objects in traffic, including occlusion handling. Furthermore, Wotawa and Klampfl pursued a similar idea and introduced logic models for explaining object motion in a sequence of images [25] as well as three application scenarios where qualitative reasoning can be utilized in the autonomous driving domain, i.e., assuring the safety, improving computer vision, and the testing of autonomous systems [14]. In addition, Gilpin [11] proposed methods for monitoring autonomous driving systems and comparing their behavior with driving knowledge, regulatory knowledge, and safety requirements.

3   Methodology

Qualitative reasoning (QR) has a long research history in the field of artificial intelligence and is often used when dealing with uncertain or incomplete information. Rather than dealing with precise numerical values, qualitative reasoning focuses on understanding and making sense of information based on its qualitative properties and relationships with other variables. QR has applications in various fields, including computer sciences, engineering, and social sciences. For example, it can be used in physics to understand the behavior of systems besides unknown precise measurements. Within the last decades, many subclasses like qualitative spatial reasoning, qualitative temporal reasoning, and qualitative simulation were established. Especially for systems where spatial information is utilized for performing a certain task, e.g., robotics or autonomous vehicles, spatial reasoning can support drawing the correct conclusions since, in most cases, not a complete a priori quantitative knowledge is necessary, but qualitative abstractions [4]. Additionally to the theory behind spatial and temporal reasoning like for example, the research carried out by Forbus [6], research on fundamental reasoning mechanisms have been conducted, e.g., [1,19], or [22], covering logic and constraints as well as advanced logic reasoning methods like answer set programming.

This paper's contribution continues the research performed in the area of qualitative reasoning, spatial reasoning, and temporal reasoning. It proposes using advanced logic reasoning methods, i.e., ASP, complementary to established methods in computer vision to identify critical situations in driving scenarios and, with this, ensure the safety of autonomous systems and vehicles during operation. Moreover, we want to answer whether qualitative knowledge about detected objects within the vicinity of the autonomous vehicle is sufficient to draw an appropriate conclusion about the movement of the objects and, with this, identify possible collision paths to trigger countermeasures to avoid danger. We suggest that the angle between the bearing line of the autonomous car's center to the object of interest and the change in distance to the object are suitable candidates for indicating if a situation is critical. To evaluate our proposal, we use the output of object detection and tracking algorithms as a knowledge base for extracting the respective qualitative measures and applying the ASP model to compute the respective answer sets stating if a scenario can lead to a potential risk for traffic participants.

The following paragraphs outline the basic definitions of detecting critical situations during autonomous driving operations. We start defining the autonomous driving runtime verification setup comprising a set of observations obtained from measurements in the ego vehicle and the set of properties that must hold for ordinary driving situations not considered critical.

Definition 1 (Runtime Verification Setup (RVS)). *A runtime verification setup (RVS) is a tuple $(OBS, PROP)$ comprising a set of observations OBS and a set of properties $PROP$. Both sets comprise knowledge specified in first-order logic (or any similar representation).*

In the above definition of an RVS, properties are assumed to specify constraints that must hold during ordinary operation. These properties utilize data and information from the sensors, e.g., the bearing angle to objects outside the car obtained from computer vision systems. A property specifies, for example, that the bearing angle is not allowed to be constant over successive time steps. Formally, we can specify this as follows: $\forall t \in TIME, o \in OBJECTS, \alpha \in ANGLE : \neg(ba(o, \alpha, t) \wedge ba(o, \alpha, succ(t)))$. If there are observations $OBS = \{ba(car, 45, 100), ba(car, 45, 110)\}$ and assuming that $succ(100) = 110$, this property is obviously not fulfilled, and we have detected a critical situation. This example leads to the following definition of criticality.

Definition 2 (Critical situation). *Given an RVS* $(OBS, PROP)$. *$(OBS, PROP)$ is considered a critical situation if and only if $OBS \cup PROP$ is inconsistent (i.e., not satisfiable).*

Hence, we can formalize detecting critical situations as not confirming to given pre-defined runtime properties. We can distinguish properties accordingly to their underlying source of origin, which might be useful for formalization.

- *Spatial and temporal knowledge:* This class of properties includes all rules that deal with spatial and temporal knowledge. Stating that the bearing angle is not allowed to be constant over time or indicating that the distance with an object in the front should not be less than a predefined value are examples of this type of property.
- *General driving knowledge:* We may also indicate that an autonomous vehicle should not violate traffic regulations. For example, the vehicle should not exceed the speed limit on highways or in rural areas.
- *Physical impossibilities:* Sensors might indicate the existence of objects irrelevant to autonomous driving or not in conformance with the laws of physics. In [7], handling such physical impossibilities for restricting the search space of diagnosis was introduced. Similarly, we may come up with rules like stating that an object cannot appear immediately in front of a car without being tracked over time. In addition, we might specify that cars or similar objects cannot fly. Hence, detecting a car at a place within the field of view requiring cars to fly would allow us to raise an issue with vision and may lead to ignoring such objects in analysis.
- *Safety-specific knowledge:* Due to circumstances like bad lightning conditions, sensors may not consistently track objects over time. Such objects may be ignored, leading to crashes. Hence, we may indicate a rule stating that object detection is not working appropriately under some conditions, requiring slower driving or the ego vehicle to consider unstable object detection as a real object and use estimations for tracking it. Of course, there is more safety-specific knowledge someone should consider for detecting critical scenarios.

It is worth noting that we do not require full-blown first-order logic to check properties for a particular ego vehicle and situation. In particular situations, all variables are replaced by constants representing the current parameters and objects. Hence, satisfiability checks only require propositional SAT solving for which efficient solvers exist. However, first-order logic allows for a more easy representation of knowledge. Hence, we suggest using ASP solvers like Clingo [8] that come with an automated grounding procedure.

In contrast to other research like [22,23], we do not consider sophisticated knowledge representations. Instead, we focus on simple properties that can be efficiently checked during operation for detecting critical situations fulfilling soft real-time requirements.

In the next section, the experiment design with its details is explained before showing the first results of the method and indicating the challenges and limitations we faced during the implementation and testing phase.

4   Experiment Design

To demonstrate the successful application of our proposed methodology, we set up an experiment framework comprising an object detector, an object tracking algorithm, data pre-processing and post-processing pipelines, and qualitative reasoning models. The next section gives a detailed overview of the individual framework components.

4.1   Data Processing

To perform object detection and tracking, a comprehensive dataset that includes a variety of different traffic participants, as well as driving scenarios, is needed. Fortunately, with the recent advances in the field of ADAS/AD, numerous datasets were collected for research, development, and testing purposes, e.g., KITTI [9] or the A2D2 dataset [10]. For our experiments, we decided to use the latter for the following reasons. First, it is a large-scale dataset containing different high-resolution sensor data, including not only cameras but also LiDARs and the vehicle's bus giving insights into the vehicle state, e.g., velocities, accelerations, and positions. Second, the dataset provides time series data within three different cities, i.e., Gaimersheim, Munich, and Ingolstadt, with more than 15,000 camera images and LiDAR scans each, which is especially crucial for performing object tracking and identifying movement patterns of objects.

To fully utilize the dataset, we implemented dedicated data processing pipelines responsible for performing four main tasks:

1. **Data Synchronization:** Although each sensor data, i.e., camera images, LiDAR scans, vehicle bus data, has a unique timestamp indicating the time of data retrieval, it was necessary to synchronize the different sensor data due to the fact of different component working frequencies. For instance, vehicle bus data was not always available at the exact image and LiDAR timestamps. To compensate for this, we applied interpolation to the vehicle data, e.g., velocities, and positions, to acquire estimates at the respective time

steps of the images and LiDAR scans. It should be noted that this was only necessary for the vehicle bus data. Camera images and LiDAR scans were already synchronized.

2. **Camera/LiDAR Data Transformations:** With the objective of using information included in the LiDAR scans complementary to camera images, there was the need to transform each point included in the LiDAR scan to the correct coordinate frame to be able to map it onto the image. For implementing the respective transformations, we adapted the code base provided with the dataset and which can be found on the A2D2 homepage.[1] In summary, we applied different rotation and translation matrices on each LiDAR point so that it can be represented in the desired view.

3. **Object Detection and Tracking:** Object detection, classification, and tracking are indispensable for ADAS/AD to perceive other traffic participants as well as static objects like traffic signs within the environment of the autonomous car. When talking about object detection and tracking, there is always a trade-off that has to be made between performance in the sense of how fast frames are processed and accuracy. Since our proposed method should ensure safety during operation, object detection needs to be executed in real-time. YOLOv4 [3] is a well-established open-source object detection model that is known for its high performance and accuracy and, therefore, a perfect candidate. Since the purpose is not to develop new object detection algorithms, we used a model pre-trained on the COCO [17] dataset and integrated it into our experiment framework. For the purpose of tracking and assigning unique IDs to each object detected, we integrated the lightweight object tracking algorithm SORT [2]. SORT is based on a combination of Kalman filtering and the Hungarian algorithm and is able to track multiple objects within a scene in real-time.

4. **Distance Extraction:** For reasoning about the spatiotemporal behavior of detected objects, it is necessary to have at least an estimate of the object's distance relative to the vehicle. To obtain distance values, we extracted distance values provided by the LiDAR scans. In more detail, we looked at all LiDAR points within the object bounding box and obtained the distance values from the respective points.

All of the above-mentioned parts were implemented in Python version 3.10 using a Macbook Pro with a 2.9 GHz Intel Core i7 processor, 16 GB memory, and an integrated Radeon Pro 560 graphics card.

4.2   QR Model and Solver

An autonomous car must have the capability to react correctly to unseen and unknown situations. In the best case, the car should perform common sense reasoning and infer the appropriate actions based on previously experienced situations, similar to what we do as humans when driving. However this is a challenging task, but the first steps to achieve this goal might be the implementation

---

[1] https://www.a2d2.audi/a2d2/en.html.

of different logical models representing knowledge about possible situations, like the simplified introductory example where we could reason that a dangerous situation will occur if no countermeasures are taken due to the constant bearing angle and the enlargement of the object's appearance. Qualitative spatial and temporal models have already been explored in research to support and enhance perception systems and autonomous driving (see Sect. 2). Inspired by previous work in this area, we introduce logical models for certain situations that are indicative of critical situations. In Listing 1.1, a simple model showing the application of qualitative reasoning implemented in answer set programming (ASP) [5] is shown.

ASP is a programming paradigm that adopts a declarative approach and draws upon logic programming and non-monotonic reasoning. Essentially, an ASP model comprises logical rules, integrity constraints, i.e., rules that lead to a contradiction, and facts, including constants and observations.

For simplicity and space reasons, the depicted ASP model shows only one specific implementation for the case of a detected object in front of us. However, in the same manner, additional situations, like objects that are passing by the vehicle or approaching traffic participants, can be represented and encoded. For defining the objects and their corresponding properties, e.g., the unique object ID, the point in time where it appears, or the bearing angle relative to our vehicle, specific predicates like $objID/1$ are defined (see source code line 1). Due to space reasons, we omitted the definition of other predicates used in the implementation since they follow the same principle. In source code line 2, a $sit/6$ predicate is defined. Based on the observations illustrated in Listing 1.2, for each detected object, all possible situation combinations are derived. In more detail, this means that we get for each object a situation predicate indicating the *Start* and *End* of the situation, as well as the corresponding properties of the specific object.

Within source code lines 3, we define the predicate $crit\_sit/3$, which encodes a possible problematic situation in the following way: First, we retrieve all generated situations of the detected objects with their specific parameters. Second, we define constraints that need to be fulfilled to be considered severe. For instance, in our example, we want to identify objects that are in front of us and with which we are on a potential collision path. This is the case if the bearing angle is either constant over consecutive time steps, like in the introductory example, or if it is in the range of $-20°$ and $+20°$ when assuming that $0°$ is represented by the vertical center line of our camera image. It should be noted that the set boundary conditions are estimates, and adaption and calibration would be needed for other scenarios or the actual integration within a vehicle.

After defining our ASP model, we can pass the model and our observations from Listing 1.2 to an answer set solver to compute statements describing at which frames our vehicle is on a collision path with detected traffic participants. For our implementation, we rely on the Potassco answer set solver[2] and would acquire one answer set, namely $crit\_sit(5, 1, 10)$, indicating that there is a poten-

---

[2] https://potassco.org/.

Listing 1.1. Simplified ASP model for applying qualitative reasoning and identifying objects over consecutive time steps that are on a collision path with the vehicle.

```
1   objID(ObjID)  :- obs(ObjID,_,_,_,_,_).
2   sit(ObjID,Start,End,A2,A2_q,Dy2)  :- objID(ObjID),
        frame(F1), frame(F2), F1 < F2,
        angle(ObjID,F2,A2), angle_q(ObjID,F2,A2_q),
        dy(ObjID,F2,Dy2), Start = F1, End = F2.
3   crit_sit(ObjID,Start,End)  :-
        sit(ObjID,Start,End,A2,A2_q,Dy2), Dy2 = "decr",
        1{A2 <= 20; A2_q = "const"},
        1{A2 >= -20 ; A2_q = "const"}.
```

Listing 1.2. Observations provided to the ASP model in Listing 1.1 and retrieved from the data piplines described Section 4.1.

```
1   obs(5,"car",1,11,"incr","decr").
2   obs(5,"car",10,19,"incr","decr").
3   obs(5,"car",20,22,"incr","decr").
```

tially hazardous situation with an object having the unique identifier 5 within time 1 and 10 if no countermeasures are taken, e.g., braking or changing direction. In the upcoming section, we will present our results obtained when applying our ASP model to the A2D2 real-world dataset.

5   Results

For the purpose of evaluating our method, we applied our ASP model to the A2D2 dataset. In more detail, on the pre-processed data for driving in the city of Gaimersheim. The drive comprises a total number of 15,688 images and LiDAR scans. Since no ground truth is provided for this data, we rely solely on the objects detected by our implemented object recognition algorithm YOLOv4 and SORT algorithm for tracking each observed object. Figure 3 gives an overview of the number of objects detected (blue), the number of unique objects identified (orange), and the number of critical scenarios obtained through our ASP model (green).

In total, we identified 79,592 objects within all images captured by the camera sensor. As it can be seen, with a total number of 71,921 detections, the object class *car* is the most prominent within the used dataset. With this, it is not surprising that also the number of unique objects extracted by the SORT tracking algorithm is the highest for the category *car*, i.e., 1,922 out of 2,270 unique objects are represented by cars. When having a closer look at the critical situations obtained by our logic model, we discovered 183 instances where the vehicle is on a potential collision path with a car. Respectively, seven times with an object classified as a truck, one time with a bus, and five times with a person.

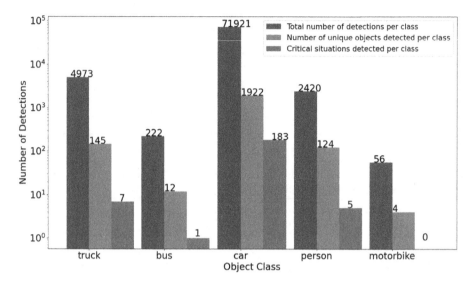

Fig. 3. Bar graph showing the number of detected objects, unique objects, and critical situations per object class.

Before looking at a real-world example where we extracted a potentially hazardous situation, let us consider the situation illustrated in Fig. 4. The drawing shows a simplified situation at a junction from a top-view perspective, with the ego vehicle in yellow and the object of interest in black. Furthermore, $-\alpha$ and $+\alpha$ indicate the previously mentioned angle threshold from $-20°$ and $+20°$. The angle β represents the calculated bearing angle relative to the ego vehicle. In addition, the two black dashed arrows show the indented driving paths of the ego vehicle and the object of interest.

Let us consider three discrete points in time, t_1 where the objects are at their initial positions, t_3 where the objects are at their final destinations, and t_2 somewhere in the middle of both. When executing this scenario, we can certainly infer that at some point in time, i.e., between t_1 and t_3, both objects are on a potential collision course if, for instance, the steering control would malfunction and therefore not be able to follow the path planned by the control logic. This is, for instance, a situation that we are interested in identifying when applying our ASP models to real-world data or during operation.

Fortunately, during conducting our experiments and applying our model to the A2D2 dataset, we were able to identify numerous potential critical scenarios (see Fig. 3). One example is shown in Fig. 5 and displays a situation discussed in Fig. 4. The figure shows three frames at three consecutive points in time. Within each image, the current bearing angle relative to the ego vehicle is indicated with

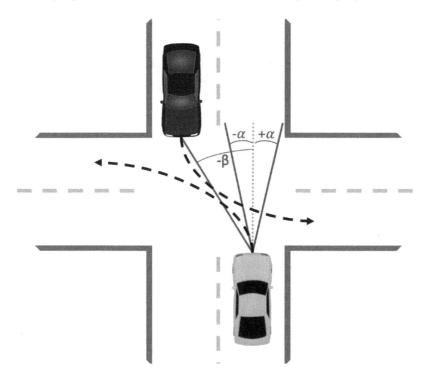

Fig. 4. Simplified top view schematic of the situation shown in Fig. 5.

a blue line. Similarly, the red lines represent the range of $-20°$ and $+20°$ and mark the threshold where we consider a detected object as critical if no actions are taken. In addition, each image contains the results from the object detection algorithm, indicated by a bounding box, and estimates for the distance to the object.

When looking at the situation's first frame (t_1), we see that the ego vehicle is approaching a junction with another object approaching the same junction from the opposite direction. Although we do not know the intended path of the detected object in advance, we can state that there is no potential risk for a crash, i.e., the object is outside our set threshold. Moreover, when looking at the following frame, i.e., t_2, we see that the detected object crosses our projected path, and we would face a potentially hazardous situation if we drove straight. In this case, our ASP model would compute the respective output and could, for instance, trigger a warning to the vehicle's passenger. However, since the dataset does not contain data where actually a crash happens, the situation gets resolved in the last image displayed (t_3) since the planned paths of the ego vehicle as well as of the detected object are the same as illustrated in Fig. 4.

Fig. 5. Example result obtained from applying our ASP model on the A2D2 dataset. *Left:* no collision is expected with the detected object at time t_1. *Middle:* on collision path at time t_2. *Right:* critical situation resolved at t_3.

Given that no ground truth is available, indicating if our identified scenarios are indeed critical within the calculated time frame, we relied on manually evaluating our observations. For this, we selected critical and non-critical representatives from each object class and investigated the results by looking at the video sequence including the critical and non-critical objects. Evaluating in total 20 critical and 20 non-critical situations, we can state that for the selected candidates, our method positively delivered correct results. In contrast to the dangerous situation illustrated in Fig. 5, non-critical scenarios included for instance parked objects on the side of the street where the bearing angle increased within consecutive frames when the object was on the right side relative to the ego vehicle, and respectively decreased when parked on the left side.

Despite successfully applying our ASP model and identifying critical situations within the A2D2 real-world dataset, we faced some challenges during the implementation process as well as some limitations were identified that need to be tackled in future work. In the next section, we give a short overview of those and explain how they were solved and which remain currently open.

6   Challenges and Limitations

Throughout the process of establishing our experiment framework and during the execution of our first test runs, we encountered some major and minor challenges and limitations. Especially when working with real-world sensor data, one has to deal with noise and different update frequencies of the included components and sensors. Although the A2D2 dataset was collected with a sophisticated sensor setup and additional components for time stamping, e.g., GNSS clocks, embedded computers, and gateways, pre-processing before being able to use it for our experiments was necessary. While this was relatively easily possible for some vehicle bus data, e.g., velocities or acceleration, through interpolation algorithms, for some signals like longitude and latitude values, this was not straightforward. In particular, longitude and latitude values were not updated as frequently as other bus signals, resulting in a delayed position reporting of the vehicle. Unfortunately, within the scope of this paper, we have not found an acceptable solution for this problem. However, since using position data in addition to the already used object-related measures could further improve the accuracy of our method as well as can be used to implement additional logic models, for instance, for identifying if objects are within a building like illustrated in Fig. 1, we plan to solve this problem in our future work.

As described in the previous sections, we used the bearing angle relative to the ego vehicle as well as distance estimations for encoding critical situations with other traffic participants in our ASP model. However, since the bearing angle and distances are calculated based on the center of the bounding boxes computed by the object detector and tracking algorithm, we might encounter imprecise angles and distances at some points in time. For instance, on some occasions, we received increasing angles and distance values, although the values theoretically should be decreasing. This can be accredited to the fact that the camera sensors of the vehicle capture images at a frame rate of 30 frames per second. Hence when detecting an object in two consecutive frames, the situation is basically still the same since only 30 milliseconds have passed. However, if the bounding box is not exactly the same as in the previous frame, this results in imprecise angle and distance measures, i.e., decreasing instead of increasing. To compensate for this problem, we implemented a sliding window approach that eliminated, for most cases, the resulting variances for the angle to the object as well as the distance.

Let us assume that X is a time series dataset with length N, and let W be the size of the sliding window. The sliding window approach involves dividing the time series into overlapping windows of size W and sliding the window over the time series with a certain stride, i.e., S where $S < W$. The resulting sliding window can be denoted by a tuple $(i, i + W - 1)$, where i is the index of the first element in the window. By using the sliding window approach and calculating the change rate of angles and distances over each window, we were able to reduce the short-term fluctuations while ensuring that no frame is ignored.

When talking about limitations, it must be mentioned that our proposed approach is currently implemented with a fixed angle α (see Fig. 4). However, this might not be appropriate for driving scenarios where a lot of objects are near the ego vehicle, e.g., driving within a city or traffic jams, since in such cases, it is often the case that detected objects are very close and therefore would be permanently within the critical threshold. A possible solution for this, which will be tackled in future work, might be to adapt the critical angle range depending on the driving environment or, alternatively, to calculate it dynamically dependent on the distance of the nearest detected objects. Furthermore, the current approach evaluates only the criticality with respect to one object at a time. However, it would be desirable to implement additional logical models that are able to evaluate the criticality of the complete scenario, including all objects involved. For instance, we might encounter a situation where although no critical situation is identified when looking at all objects separately, the overall situation is critical because of the combination of maneuvers performed by the individual traffic participants. As a last limitation it should be mentioned that validation of the output produced with our ASP model was done manually by having a look on the specific frames where a critical situation was identified. Nonetheless, as a next step we want to evaluate our approach based on simulated scenarios in order to automatically obtain ground truth data for the sensors used on the one hand, and certainty if a scenario was really critical on the other hand. All of the mentioned unresolved challenges and limitations will be tackled in future work.

7   Conclusion

In this paper, we motivated the use of qualitative reasoning to identify critical scenarios in autonomous driving. We highlighted the necessity of quality assurance during operation in addition to strict testing and verification methods within the development phase of such systems. Furthermore, we argued that by explaining spatiotemporal patterns of detected objects in the vicinity of the autonomous vehicle, it is possible to distinguish potentially dangerous situations from uncritical ones. In more detail, we used the bearing angle between the detected object and the autonomous vehicle and estimates for the distance extracted from the output of implemented object detection and tracking algorithms. Furthermore, we used answer set programming for encoding our logic models. To test our approach, we set up an experiment framework consisting of an object detector algorithm, an object tracking algorithm, a data preprocessing pipeline, and an ASP model. We performed the evaluation on the well-known A2D2 dataset, where we successfully showed that scenarios could be identified as critical based on qualitative reasoning principles.

We plan to extend the introduced qualitative model to be able to not only capture critical objects separately but also take into account situations where each object on its own presents no danger but the combination of maneuvers performed by the detected objects does. Furthermore, we want to carry out more exhaustive experiments based on different datasets and especially on simulated scenarios in order to validate our method automatically.

Acknowledgments. The financial support by the Austrian Federal Ministry for Digital and Economic Affairs, the National Foundation for Research, Technology, and Development, and the Christian Doppler Research Association is gratefully acknowledged.

References

1. Bennett, B.: Modal logics for qualitative spatial reasoning. Logic J. IGPL **4**(1), 23–45 (1996). https://doi.org/10.1093/jigpal/4.1.23
2. Bewley, A., Ge, Z., Ott, L., Ramos, F., Upcroft, B.: Simple online and realtime tracking. In: 2016 IEEE International Conference on Image Processing (ICIP), pp. 3464–3468 (2016). https://doi.org/10.1109/ICIP.2016.7533003
3. Bochkovskiy, A., Wang, C.Y., Liao, H.Y.M.: YOLOv4: optimal speed and accuracy of object detection (2020). https://doi.org/10.48550/ARXIV.2004.10934, https://arxiv.org/abs/2004.10934
4. Cohn, A.G., Hazarika, S.M.: Qualitative spatial representation and reasoning: an overview. Fund. Inform. **46**(1–2), 1–29 (2001)

5. Eiter, T., Ianni, G., Krennwallner, T.: Answer Set Programming: A Primer. In: Tessaris, S., et al. (eds.) Reasoning Web 2009. LNCS, vol. 5689, pp. 40–110. Springer, Heidelberg (2009). https://doi.org/10.1007/978-3-642-03754-2_2
6. Forbus, K.D.: Qualitative process theory. Artif. Intell. **24**(1), 85–168 (1984). https://doi.org/10.1016/0004-3702(84)90038-9, https://www.sciencedirect.com/science/article/pii/0004370284900389
7. Friedrich, G., Gottlob, G., Nejdl, W.: Physical impossibility instead of fault models. In: Proceedings of the National Conference on Artificial Intelligence (AAAI), pp. 331–336. Boston (1990), also appears in Readings in Model-Based Diagnosis (Morgan Kaufmann, 1992)
8. Gebser, M., Kaminski, R., Kaufmann, B., Schaub, T.: Multi-shot ASP solving with clingo. Theory Pract. Logic Program. **19**(1), 27–82 (2019). https://doi.org/10.1017/S1471068418000054
9. Geiger, A., Lenz, P., Stiller, C., Urtasun, R.: Vision meets robotics: the KITTI dataset. Int. J. Robot. Res. (IJRR) **32**(11), 1231–1237 (2013). https://doi.org/10.1177/0278364913491297
10. Geyer, J., et al.: A2D2: audi autonomous driving dataset (2020). https://www.a2d2.audi
11. Gilpin, L.H.: Anomaly detection through explanations. Ph.D. thesis, Massachusetts Institute of Technology, Cambridge, MA (2020)
12. Kalra, N., Paddock, S.M.: Driving to safety: how many miles of driving would it take to demonstrate autonomous vehicle reliability? Transp. Res. A: Policy Pract. **94**, 182–193 (2016). https://doi.org/10.1016/j.tra.2016.09.010, www.sciencedirect.com/science/article/pii/S0965856416302129
13. Klampfl, L., Klück, F., Wotawa, F.: Using genetic algorithms for automating automated lane-keeping system testing. J. Softw. Evol. Process e2520 (2022). https://doi.org/10.1002/smr.2520, https://onlinelibrary.wiley.com/doi/abs/10.1002/smr.2520
14. Klampfl, L., Wotawa, F.: On the use of qualitative reasoning in autonomous driving. In: 35th International Workshop on Qualitative Reasoning; 23 July 2022 (2022). https://www.esade.edu/faculty-research/en/institute-for-data-driven-decisions/research/juice-research-group/35th-international-workshop-on-qualitative-reasoning,
15. Klück, F., Zimmermann, M., Wotawa, F., Nica, M.: Genetic algorithm-based test parameter optimization for ADAS system testing. In: Proceedings of the 19th IEEE International Conference on Software Quality, Reliability and Security (QRS), pp. 418–425 (2019). https://doi.org/10.1109/QRS.2019.00058
16. Koopman, P., Wagner, M.: Challenges in autonomous vehicle testing and validation. SAE Int. J. Trans. Safety **4**, 15–24 (2016). https://doi.org/10.4271/2016-01-0128
17. Lin, T.-Y., et al.: Microsoft COCO: common objects in context. In: Fleet, D., Pajdla, T., Schiele, B., Tuytelaars, T. (eds.) ECCV 2014. LNCS, vol. 8693, pp. 740–755. Springer, Cham (2014). https://doi.org/10.1007/978-3-319-10602-1_48
18. Ren, S., He, K., Girshick, R., Sun, J.: Faster R-CNN: towards real-time object detection with region proposal networks. IEEE Trans. Pattern Anal. Mach. Intell. **39**(6), 1137–1149 (2017). https://doi.org/10.1109/TPAMI.2016.2577031
19. Renz, J., Nebel, B.: Qualitative spatial reasoning using constraint calculi. In: Aiello, M., Pratt-Hartmann, I., Van Benthem, J. (eds.) Handbook of Spatial Logics, pp. 161–215. Springer, Netherlands, Dordrecht (2007). https://doi.org/10.1007/978-1-4020-5587-4_4

20. Schuldt, F., Reschka, A., Maurer, M.: A method for an efficient, systematic test case generation for advanced driver assistance systems in virtual environments. In: Winner, H., Prokop, G., Maurer, M. (eds.) Automotive Systems Engineering II, pp. 147–175. Springer, Cham (2018). https://doi.org/10.1007/978-3-319-61607-0_7

21. Suchan, J., Bhatt, M., Varadarajan, S.: Out of sight but not out of mind: an answer set programming based online abduction framework for visual sensemaking in autonomous driving. In: Proceedings of the Twenty-Eighth International Joint Conference on Artificial Intelligence, IJCAI 2019. 10–16 August 2019, Macao, China, pp. 1879–1885. International Joint Conferences on Artificial Intelligence Organization (2019). https://doi.org/10.24963/ijcai.2019/260

22. Suchan, J., Bhatt, M., Varadarajan, S.: Commonsense visual sensemaking for autonomous driving - on generalised neurosymbolic online abduction integrating vision and semantics. Artif. Intell. **299**, 103522 (2021). https://doi.org/10.1016/j.artint.2021.103522, www.sciencedirect.com/science/article/pii/S0004370221000734

23. Suchan, J., Bhatt, M., Wałega, P., Schultz, C.: Visual explanation by high-level abduction: on answer-set programming driven reasoning about moving objects. In: Proceedings of the AAAI Conference on Artificial Intelligence, vol. 32, no. 1 (2018). https://doi.org/10.1609/aaai.v32i1.11569, https://ojs.aaai.org/index.php/AAAI/article/view/11569

24. Wotawa, F.: Testing autonomous and highly configurable systems: challenges and feasible solutions. In: Watzenig, D., Horn, M. (eds.) Automated Driving, pp. 519–532. Springer, Cham (2017). https://doi.org/10.1007/978-3-319-31895-0_22

25. Wotawa, F., Klampfl, L.: Explaining object motion using answer set programming. In: Helic, D., Leitner, G., Stettinger, M., Felfernig, A., Raś, Z.W. (eds.) ISMIS 2020. LNCS (LNAI), vol. 12117, pp. 298–307. Springer, Cham (2020). https://doi.org/10.1007/978-3-030-59491-6_28

26. Wotawa, F., Peischl, B., Klück, F., Nica, M.: Quality assurance methodologies for automated driving. Elektrotech. Informationstechnik **135**(4–5), 322–327 (2018). https://doi.org/10.1007/s00502-018-0630-7

XI-ML

Preface: Third International Workshop on Explainable and Interpretable Machine Learning (XI-ML)

Martin Atzmueller[1,2] ⓘ, Marina Höhne[3] ⓘ, Tomáš Kliegr[4] ⓘ, and Ute Schmid[5] ⓘ

[1] Semantic Information Systems Group, Osnabrück University, Germany
martin.atzmueller@uni-osnabrueck.de
[2] German Research Center for Artificial Intelligence (DFKI), Osnabrück, Germany
[3] University of Potsdam and Data Science in Bioeconomy Group, ATB, Germany
mhoehne@atb-potsdam.de
[4] Department of Information and Knowledge Engineering, Faculty of Informatics and Statistics, Prague University of Economics and Business, Czech Republic
tomas.kliegr@vse.cz
[5] Cognitive Systems, University of Bamberg, Bamberg, Germany
ute.schmid@uni-bamberg.de

1 Introduction

Explainable Artificial Intelligence (XAI), algorithmic transparency, interpretability, accountability and finally, explainability of algorithmic models and decisions are important and prominent research themes. The XI-ML workshop on explainable and interpretable machine learning tackles these themes, in particular, from the modeling and learning perspective. Here, it specifically targets interpretable methods and models being able to explain themselves and their output, respectively. Overall, the workshop aims to provide an interdisciplinary forum to investigate fundamental issues in explainable and interpretable machine learning as well as to discuss recent advances, trends, and challenges in the targeted scope.

With this third edition of the workshop, we aimed to provide a discussion platform for the topics of explainable and interpretable learning in the scope of XAI. The main emphasis of the call was on explainability approaches within which the editors were acquainted in their prior research. This included symbolic, intrinsically explainable methods such as rule learning and pattern mining (cf. e. g., [2, 4]), as well as representations of complex data [6, 13] like networks/graphs and time series. An equally important emphasis was put on cognitive approaches [1, 9, 12], human concept learning and contrastive explanation [11]. The workshop did not intend to cover only supervised (classification approaches) but also research on XAI in the unsupervised domain such as clustering [14], or subgroup discovery [8]; this also relates to challenges and pitfalls in those areas, specifically regarding, training and evaluation [7]. The third focus area was explanations of black box models as well as applications of all of the above (i. e., [3, 5, 10]).

The first edition of the XI-ML (Explainable and Interpretable Machine Learning) workshop was held on September 21, 2020, at the 43rd German Conference on Artificial Intelligence, Bamberg, Germany. The second edition of the workshop was held on September 20, 2022, in co-location with the 45th German Conference on Artificial Intelligence, Trier, Germany (virtually). This third edition of the workshop was held on September 30, 2023, colocated with the European Conference on Artificial Intelligence (ECAI), Krakow, Poland.

For the workshop, there were 16 accepted papers out of 25 submissions in total. Below, we structure these according to the general topics and/or their specific methodological foci in the context of explainable and interpretable machine learning, as well as individual applications. These 16 accepted papers were presented within four internally topically related sessions:

Explanations Through Trees, Rules, and Subgroups

- Julia Herbinger, Susanne Dandl, Fiona Katharina Ewald, Sofia Maria Loibl and Giuseppe Casalicchio Leveraging: Model-based Trees as Interpretable Surrogate Models for Model Distillation
- Tanmay Chakraborty, Christian Wirth and Christin Seifert: Post-hoc Rule Based Explanations for Black Box Bayesian Optimization
- Dan Hudson and Martin Atzmueller: Subgroup Discovery with SD4Py
- Ruth Cohen Arbiv1, Laurence Lovat, Avi Rosenfeld, and David Sarne1: Optimizing Decision Trees for Enhanced Human Comprehension

Domain- and Application-Specific Explainability Methods

- Emanuel Slany, Stephan Scheele and Ute Schmid: Bayesian CAIPI: A Probabilistic Approach to Explanatory and Interactive Machine Learning
- Munkhtulga Battogtokh, Michael Luck, Cosmin Davidescu and Rita Borgo: Simple Framework for Interpretable Fine-grained Text Classification
- Francisco N. F. Q. Simoes, Thijs van Ommen and Mehdi Dastani: Causal Entropy and Information Gain for Measuring Causal Control
- Nghia Duong-Trung, Duc-Manh Nguyen and Danh Le-Phuoc: Temporal Saliency Detection Towards Explainable Transformer-based Timeseries Forecasting

Interdisciplinary Approaches

- Stefanie Krause and Frieder Stolzenburg: Commonsense Reasoning and Explainable Artificial Intelligence Using Large Language Models
- Foivos Charalampakos and Iordanis Koutsopoulos: Exploring Multi-Task Learning for Explainability
- Ondřej Vadinský and Petr Zeman: Towards Evaluating Policy Optimisation Agents using Algorithmic Intelligence Quotient Test
- Federico Sabbatini and Roberta Calegari: Achieving Complete Coverage with Hypercube-Based Symbolic Knowledge-Extraction Techniques

Image and Prompt-Based Medical Explanations and Feature-Based Importance Methods

- Kirill Bykov, Klaus-Robert Müller and Marina Höhne: Mark My Words: Dangers of Watermarked Images in ImageNet
- Fatemeh Nazary, Yashar Deldjoo and Tommaso Di Noia: ChatGPT-HealthPrompt. Harnessing the Power of XAI in Prompt-Based Healthcare Decision Support using ChatGPT
- Eric Loff, Sören Schleibaum, Jörg P. Müller and Benjamin Säfken: Explaining Taxi Demand Prediction Models based on Feature Importance
- Meike Nauta, Johannes H. Hegeman, Jeroen Geerdink, Jörg Schlötterer, Maurice van Keulen and Christin Seifert: Interpreting and Correcting Medical Image Classification with PIP-Net

Acknowledgments. We would like to thank the ECAI 2023 organization team for their support throughout the event.

References

1. Ai, L., Muggleton, S.H., Hocquette, C., Gromowski, M., Schmid, U.: Beneficial and harmful explanatory machine learning. Mach. Learn. **110**, 695–721 (2021). https://doi.org/10.1007/s10994-020-05941-0
2. Atzmueller, M., Puppe, F., Buscher, H.P.: Exploiting background knowledge for knowledge-intensive subgroup discovery. In: Proceedings of the IJCAI, pp. 647–652. Edinburgh, Scotland (2005)
3. Beranová, L., Joachimiak, M.P., Kliegr, T., Rabby, G., Sklenák, V.: Why was this cited? Explainable machine learning applied to covid-19 research literature. Scientometrics **127**(5), 2313–2349 (2022)
4. Fürnkranz, J., Kliegr, T.: A brief overview of rule learning. In: Bassiliades, N., Gottlob, G., Sadri, F., Paschke, A., Roman, D. (eds.) RuleML 2015. LNCS, vol 9202. Springer, Cham (2015). https://doi.org/10.1007/978-3-319-21542-6_4
5. Gautam, S., Höhne, M.M.C., Hansen, S., Jenssen, R., Kampffmeyer, M.: This looks more like that: enhancing self-explaining models by prototypical relevance propagation. Pattern Recognit. **136**, 109172 (2023)
6. Górriz, J., et al.: Computational approaches to explainable artificial intelligence: advances in theory, applications and trends. Inf. Fusion **100** (2023). https://doi.org/10.2139/ssrn.4415369
7. Hedström, A.. et al.: Quantus: an explainable ai toolkit for responsible evaluation of neural network explanations and beyond. J. Mach. Learn. Res. **24**(34), 1–11 (2023)
8. Iferroudjene, M., Lonjarret, C., Robardet, C., Plantevit, M., Atzmueller, M.: Methods for explaining top-n recommendations through subgroup discovery. Data Min. Knowl. Discov. 1–40 (2022)

9. Kliegr, T., Bahník, Š., Fürnkranz, J.: A review of possible effects of cognitive biases on interpretation of rule-based machine learning models. Artif. Intell. **295** (2021)

10. Müller, D., März, M., Scheele, S., Schmid, U.: An interactive explanatory ai system for industrial quality control. In: Proceedings of the AAAI. vol. 36, pp. 12580–12586 (2022)

11. Rabold, J., Siebers, M., Schmid, U.: Generating contrastive explanations for inductive logic programming based on a near miss approach. Mach. Learn. **111**(5), 1799–1820 (2022). https://doi.org/10.1007/s10994-021-06048-w

12. Schmid, U., Wrede, B.: What is missing in XAI so far? An interdisciplinary perspective. KI-Künstliche Intelligenz **36**(3–4), 303–315 (2022). https://doi.org/10.1007/s13218-022-00786-2

13. Schwenke, L., Atzmueller, M.: Constructing global coherence representations: identifying interpretability and coherences of transformer attention in time series data. In: Proceedings of the 8th IEEE International Conference on Data Science and Advanced Analytics, DSAA 2021, Porto, Portugal, 6–9 October 2021, pp. 1–12. IEEE (2021)

14. Žárský, J., Lopez, G., Kliegr, T.: Explainability of text clustering visualizations—twitter disinformation case study. IEEE Comput. Graph. Appl. **42**(4), 8–19 (2022)

Organization

Editors

Martin Atzmueller	Osnabrück University & DFKI, Germany
Marine Höhne	University of Potsdam & ATB, Germany
Tomáš Kliegr	Prague University of Economics and Business, Czech Republic
Ute Schmid	University of Bamberg, Germany

Program Committee of XI-ML 2023

Martin Atzmueller	Osnabrück University & DFKI, Osnabrück, Germany
Tanya Braun	University of Münster, Germany
David Cerna	Czech Academy of Sciences, Czech Republic
Bettina Finzel	Otto-Friedrich-Universität Bamberg, Germany
Johannes Fürnkranz	Johannes Kepler University Linz, Austria
Jose Hernandez-Orallo	Universitat Politècnica de València, Spain
Marina Höhne	University of Potsdam & ATB, Germany
Marcin Joachimiak	Lawrence Berkeley National Laboratory, USA
Jiří Kléma	Czech Technical University, Czech Republic
Tomáš Kliegr	Prague University of Economics and Business, Czech Republic
Jaroslav Kuchař	Czech Technical University, Prague, Czech Republic
Sebastian Lapuschkin	Fraunhofer Heinrich Hertz Institute, Germany
Anna Saranti	University of Natural Resources and Life Sciences, Vienna
Ute Schmid	University of Bamberg, Germany
Dietmar Seipel	University of Wuerzburg, Germany
Ahmet Soylu	OsloMet - Oslo Metropolitan University, Norway
Ondrej Šuch	University of Matej Bel, Slovakia
Ondřej Vadinský	Prague University of Economics and Business, Czech Republic
Kristoffer Wickstrøm	UiT The Arctic University of Norway, Norway

Achieving Complete Coverage with Hypercube-Based Symbolic Knowledge-Extraction Techniques

Federico Sabbatini[1]([envelope]) [ID] and Roberta Calegari[2] [ID]

[1] Department of Pure and Applied Sciences (DiSPeA),
University of Urbino "Carlo Bo", Urbino, Italy
f.sabbatini1@campus.uniurb.it
[2] Department of Computer Science and Engineering (DISI), University of Bologna,
Bologna, Italy
roberta.calegari@unibo.it

Abstract. Symbolic knowledge-extraction (SKE) techniques are currently employed for various purposes, particularly addressing the challenge of explaining opaque models by generating human-understandable explanations. The existing literature encompasses a diverse range of techniques, each relying on specific theoretical assumptions and possessing its own advantages and disadvantages. Amongst the available choices, hypercube-based SKE techniques are notable for their adaptability and versatility. However, they may suffer from limited completeness when utilised for making predictions. This research aims to augment the predictive capabilities of hypercube-based SKE techniques, striving for a completeness rate of 100%. Furthermore, the study includes experiments that assess the effectiveness of the proposed enhancements.

Keywords: Explainable artificial intelligence · Symbolic knowledge extraction · PSyKE

1 Introduction

Ensuring the explainability of predictions made by machine learning (ML) models is crucial, especially in critical domains where the outcomes significantly impact human well-being, such as health, wealth, and safety. To address the opacity of ML predictors, the explainable artificial intelligence (XAI) community proposes two primary approaches [8]: *(i)* utilizing inherently human-interpretable models, such as decision trees with limited depth [13]; or *(ii)* employing symbolic knowledge-extraction (SKE) techniques to extract post-hoc explanations from trained opaque models [12]. This paper focuses on SKE techniques.

Over the past few decades, numerous SKE algorithms have been proposed in the literature. While these techniques exhibit diversity, certain common characteristics can be identified amongst the most widely adopted approaches. For

S. Nowaczyk et al. (Eds.): ECAI 2023 Workshops, CCIS 1947, pp. 179–197, 2024.
https://doi.org/10.1007/978-3-031-50396-2_10

example, G-REX [11], TREPAN [4] and CART [2] offer human-understandable knowledge in the form of decision trees. However, it should be noted that TREPAN is only applicable to binary input feature classification tasks. On the other hand, G-REX and CART can be utilised also for regression tasks and accept inputs that are either discrete or continuous.

SKE techniques often exhibit a recurring pattern of employing hypercubic[1] partitioning of the input feature space [22,24]. This approach aims to generate interpretable predictions. The identification of specific regions within the input feature space, characterised by interval inclusion constraints – typically one constraint per input feature –, forms the basis of these methods. Consequently, the outputs of these techniques can be easily understood by human users. Each hypercubic region that is identified is associated with a comprehensible output value, which could be a class label, a constant value, or a linear combination of the input features.

SKE algorithms based on hypercubes can be executed using either a top-down or a bottom-up workflow [15]. The bottom-up approach is particularly susceptible to non-exhaustivity issues, referring to the potential inability to generate predictions for instances belonging to certain subregions of the input space. Generally, the bottom-up strategy involves iteratively expanding the hypercubes created in the input feature space, one cube and one dimension at a time. The cubes are initially defined as multidimensional points, and achieving convergence (i.e., complete coverage of the input feature space) may require a significant number of iterations, especially for data sets with numerous input features. Consequently, the presence of non-exhaustivity in bottom-up hypercube-based SKE techniques depends on the complexity of the data set being analyzed. An example of an SKE algorithm that suffers from this drawback is ITER [9].

Due to the time-consuming process of iterative hypercube expansion, bottom-up algorithms like ITER may terminate after a specific number of user-defined iterations, even if they have not yet achieved convergence. This means that certain subregions of the input space remain uncovered by the identified hypercubes, resulting in the inability to predict instances belonging to these uncovered subregions. As a result, the completeness of SKE becomes a crucial factor to consider when evaluating the quality of a technique [7].

The significance of completeness in assessing the quality of knowledge extracted through SKE methods is also emphasised in [18,19], where two metrics are introduced to evaluate knowledge quality. These metrics utilise other indices commonly employed to assess the quality of SKE techniques, namely correctness and compactness [7]. Correctness measures the ability of the SKE technique to replicate the predictions of the underlying opaque predictor. On the other hand, compactness is a measure of human readability, as knowledge with a smaller dimension is more understandable for end users compared to knowledge with a large size.

---

[1] We use the term "hypercube" also for referring to actual hyperrectangles, as commonly made in the literature [9, for instance].

In this paper, we address the significance of obtaining comprehensive interpretable models by introducing a set of vicinity-based extensions for hypercube-based SKE methods. These extensions aim to provide human-interpretable predictions even for instances that do not belong to any identified hypercube. The proposed extension is not limited to a specific SKE algorithm or task. Therefore, it can be applied to any type of SKE technique that relies on hypercubic partitioning of the input feature space, regardless of whether it involves classification or regression tasks with categorical, discrete, or continuous outputs.

The paper is organised as follows: Section 2 resumes background notions on SKE, Sect. 3 describes the proposed extensions, and Sect. 4 shows the effectiveness of our proposal via several experiments on real world data sets. Finally, Sect. 5 summarises our conclusions.

2 Symbolic Knowledge Extraction

Knowledge-extraction mechanisms usually aim to reverse-engineer an opaque model in order to understand the rationale behind the output predictions it provides [10]. SKE algorithms may be categorised along several dimensions, including (but not limited to) the expressive power of the extracted knowledge (e.g., propositional, fuzzy, oblique rules) and the *translucency* extent of the technique [1]. According to the translucency dimension, SKE methods may be classified as *decompositional* or *pedagogical*.

A group of pedagogical SKE techniques [9,14,20,25] rely on hypercubic partitioning of the input feature space to establish input/output relationships between queries made to opaque models and their corresponding output predictions. These techniques fall into a category that typically generates human-interpretable outcomes in the form of propositional rules presented as a list or tree structure. In the following, we delve into the specifics of these hypercube-based SKE methods to elucidate the potential causes of their non-exhaustivity. Additionally, we highlight the advantages of employing the presented extension to achieve complete coverage, addressing the limitations of these techniques.

2.1 Iter

ITER [9] is a bottom-up SKE technique originally designed for regression tasks described by continuous input features. It is based on the creation of a user-defined number of small hypercubes randomly placed inside the input feature space (i.e., multidimensional points) and on the iterative expansion of these cubes until the whole input space is covered (i.e., convergence) or it is not possible to further expand them. Hypercubes are always non-overlapping, to avoid ambiguity in the prediction phase.

The expansion step of ITER may terminate without reaching convergence after a user-defined number of iterations. In this case some portions of the input feature space remain unassociated with the found hypercubes and the resulting interpretable model will be unable to provide predictions for all instances belonging to these unassociated regions.

The non-exhaustivity of ITER is thus due to the slow convergence of its expansion phase, given that at each iteration only one cube is expanded along a single dimension and such expansion is generally represented by a small user-defined amount of input space.

2.2   GridEx and GridREx

GridEx [25] is a top-down algorithm to perform knowledge extraction from any kind of opaque predictor. It has been designed to overcome the non-exhaustivity issues deriving from the usage of ITER. To do so, GridEx recursively splits the input feature space in a set of symmetric, disjoint partitions according to some criteria. In particular, GridEx identify 3 classes of input space regions: negligible if there are no training samples belonging to them; permanent if they contain training samples and the associated predictive error is below the user-defined threshold; and eligible if they contain samples and the corresponding error is above the threshold. From a workflow standpoint, negligible regions are discarded, permanent regions are converted into human-readable rules and eligible regions are further split during the recursive phase of the algorithm.

A consequence of the splitting strategy adopted by GridEx is the possibility to produce a non-exhaustive input space partitioning when applied to data sets having sparse data points, due to the discarded negligible regions. In this case GridEx cannot predict instances falling inside these input space portions.

GridREx [14] is an extension of GridEx aimed at achieving better predictive performance. Since GridEx associates constant output values to the identified hypercubes, it introduces an undesired discretisation impinging the predictive performance of the interpretable model. GridREx overcomes this drawback by substituting the constant output of each hypercube with a regression law expressing a linear combination of the input features. However, it shares with GridEx the same splitting strategy and thus the same issues related to the non-exhaustivity due to negligible regions.

2.3   CREEPY

CREEPY [20] is a top-down SKE technique producing a hypercubic partitioning of the input feature space organised as a binary tree. It is based on an underlying explainable clustering algorithm that may be selected by users, together with the corresponding parameters. Available clustering techniques are EXACT [16] and CREAM [17].

The tree structure produced by this algorithm is created by recursively splitting input space regions into two subregions: a hypercube and a difference cube, obtained by subtracting the hypercubic subregion from the starting region. As a consequence, each node of the tree is associated with a constraint describing a hypercube. The two child nodes are then associated with inclusion in/exclusion from that hypercube.

Since CREEPY produces human-intelligible rules by traversing the binary tree, it is always possible to provide an output prediction for a given query and therefore it is a complete technique by design.

3 Vicinity-Based Extensions to Achieve Complete Coverage

In order to address the completeness of the interpretable models obtained through SKE techniques, we have developed an extension that can be applied to any SKE algorithm utilizing hypercubic input space partitioning for predictions. The problem of drawing predictions for uncovered queries has already been investigated in the literature [5, 27]. In particular, [5] emphasises the need for a more sophisticated strategy than majority-based assignments and proposes an alternative method based on rule stretching. On the other hand, [27] exploits Euclidean distance to assign a point to the nearest hypercube, selected amongst a set of possibly *nested* hypercubes.

It is important to note that our proposed extension does not impact the prediction phase for data points that fall within the identified hypercubes during knowledge extraction. These instances can be predicted as intended by the design of the SKE algorithm. Instead, our focus is solely on predicting instances that are included in regions not covered by any hypercube, referred to as *uncovered instances* hereafter.

The core concept behind this extension is to assign each uncovered instance to an existing hypercube based on a vicinity criterion. This approach ensures that the readability extent of the interpretable model obtained through SKE remains unchanged, as it is directly related to the size of knowledge represented by the number of identified hypercubes, which remains unaltered with our extension. Additionally, employing a vicinity criterion enables the assignment of outliers to the closest hypercube. Experimental tests have shown that the proposed extension, which in the following we refer to as *brute prediction*, can enhance the predictive performance of the interpretable model by accurately assigning uncovered instances to the correct hypercube.

Brute prediction depends on the closest hypercube w.r.t. the query. The distance between a data point and a cube may be calculated according to more than one definition. In the following several strategies are defined, each one presenting a trade-off between computational complexity and expected predictive performance. In particular, we propose to assimilate the distance between a point and a cube to the Euclidean distance between the point and the *relevant points* of the cube. The selection of Euclidean distance derives from the need to maintain the highest possible degree of human interpretability for the SKE outputs. Indeed, the most natural method to assess distance for humans is in terms of "straight lines" between two points. Other commonly used metrics are the Manhattan distance or the Chebyshev distance. We briefly recall that the Manhattan distance between a pair of points is calculated as the sum of the absolute differences of the points' Cartesian coordinates ("city block" strategy).

On the other hand, the Chebyshev distance between two points is the greatest distance amongst those calculated for each point dimension ("chessboard" strategy). In our opinion, these alternatives hinder the immediacy of the knowledge representation, even if they may be more computationally efficient.

In our proposed extension we consider the following points of the hypercube as relevant: the centre, barycentre, vertices, and edge points. This allows us to employ different approaches for brute prediction, such as centre-based, density-based, corner-based, and perimeter-based methods. Additionally, we introduce an additional majority criterion that disregards the identified hypercubes and instead relies solely on the average output observed for the instances provided during the extraction phase of the SKE technique. This criterion can be used as an alternative prediction strategy.

To establish the different strategies for brute prediction, we begin by formalising the concepts of a data set and a hypercube. We define a data set D as a collection of n-dimensional points, where n represents the number of input features in the data set. For the purpose of this definition, without loss of generality, we will ignore the output feature since the hypercubes created using SKE techniques are based on the dimensions of the input features alone. The domain of data set D, i.e. $Dom(D)$, is defined as the Cartesian product of the domains of each input feature f of D:

$$Dom(D) = Dom(f_1) \times Dom(f_2) \times \cdots \times Dom(f_n). \tag{1}$$

Hypercube-based SKE algorithms work upon continuous input features, therefore

$$Dom(f_i) \subseteq \mathbb{R} \qquad \forall i = 1, \ldots, n. \tag{2}$$

As a consequence

$$Dom(D) \subseteq \mathbb{R}^n. \tag{3}$$

A hypercube H is defined as a portion of the input feature space:

$$H \subseteq D. \tag{4}$$

The corresponding domain is thus a subset of the domain of data set D. We denote with h_1, h_2, ..., h_n the n individual dimensions of the cube, with the following domains:

$$Dom(h_i) \subseteq Dom(f_i) \qquad \forall i = 1, \ldots, n. \tag{5}$$

It is worthwhile to notice that hypercubes (and their corresponding domains) are usually strict subsets of the data set (and its corresponding domain), except for the *surrounding cube*, defined as the cube enclosing all the instances of the data set. Therefore, this cube coincides with the data set and its domain coincides with the one of the data set.

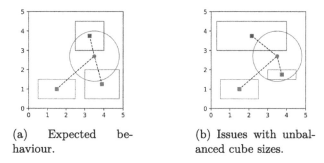

(a) Expected be-
haviour.

(b) Issues with unbal-
anced cube sizes.

Fig. 1. Example of centre-based distance calculation.

3.1   Majority-Based Assignment

The simplest option to provide predictions for data instances belonging to uncovered input space regions is to consider a surrounding hypercube enclosing all the possible queries. This enables SKE techniques to exhibit a default behaviour when there are no cubes providing the needed prediction. To minimise the predictive error of this default prediction it is necessary to consider the most common output values observed in the whole data set. When performing classification tasks, it is possible to consider as default output the most common class label in the data set. Conversely, for regression tasks the output feature can be averaged over all the data points to provide a constant value. Alternatively, it is possible to express the output value as a linear function of the input features approximating the data point distribution within the whole data set.

With this majority-based criterion brute predictions may be provided in constant time, regardless of the number of input features describing the data set, and without calculating any distance between queries and hypercubes found via SKE. However, the default output value is strongly subject to the data used to extract knowledge. For instance, if a balanced data set with 3 classes is randomly split into training and test sets and only the training set is used to extract knowledge (as usually done), the default value will be determined based on the class label distribution after the random train/test splitting, leading to arbitrary brute predictions.

3.2   Centre-Based Assignment

A slightly more complex solution, albeit with comparable computational complexity, resides in the calculation of the Euclidean distance between the query and the centre of each identified hypercube. The brute prediction is then provided based on the hypercube whose centre is the closest to the query.

We define the centre of a hypercube H as the multidimensional point whose coordinates are the centres of the cube's dimensions:

$$Centre(H) = (Centre(h_1), Centre(h_2), ..., Centre(h_n)). \qquad (6)$$

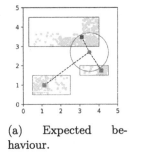
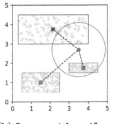

(a) Expected be-
haviour.

(b) Issues with uniform
density cubes.

Fig. 2. Example of density-based distance calculation.

We finally define the centre of a hypercube dimension h as the dimension mid-point:

$$Centre(h) = \frac{max(h) + min(h)}{2}. \tag{7}$$

The centre-based criterion requires the calculation and comparison of a single distance for each hypercube since the only relevant point is the cube centre. However, it may be not a proper strategy when there are cubes having very different sizes. In this case, small cubes are arbitrarily privileged since instances belonging to uncovered regions have more probability of being closer to the centre of small cubes than to those of large cubes.

An example of an expected centre-based assignment is reported in Fig. 1a, where the point belonging to the uncovered region (red point) is associated with the closest cube (the blue one). The issue due to high diversity in the cube sizes is reported in Fig. 1b, where the point is associated with the green hypercube, given the vicinity to its centre, even if the point is visibly closer to the blue hypercube.

3.3 Density-Based Assignment

Centre-based brute predictions may be theoretically enhanced by adding aware-ness of the data set instance distribution within the identified hypercubes. In this case we move towards a density-based assignment of the uncovered queries since the brute prediction is based on the distance between a query and the barycentres of the cubes identified via SKE.

We define the barycentre of a hypercube H as the multidimensional point whose coordinates are the barycentres of the cube's dimensions:

$$Barycentre(H) = (Barycentre(h_1), Barycentre(h_2), ..., Barycentre(h_n)). \tag{8}$$

We finally define the barycentre of a hypercube dimension h as the mean value calculated for that dimension on the data set instances enclosed within the hyper-cube:

$$Barycentre(h) = \overline{h}. \tag{9}$$

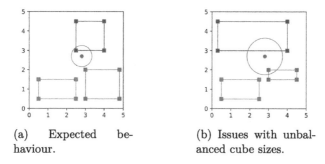

(a) Expected behaviour.

(b) Issues with unbalanced cube sizes.

Fig. 3. Example of corner-based distance calculation.

The density-based criterion for brute prediction has the same computational complexity as the centre-based criterion. In both cases, only a single distance calculation and comparison are required for each identified hypercube in the SKE technique. However, the density-based criterion may encounter drawbacks when it comes to assigning instances to hypercubes that have a uniform distribution of data points. In such cases, the barycentres of the hypercubes are equivalent to the centres, resulting in similar issues as those described for the centre-based brute prediction.

Examples of density-based assignments are shown in Fig. 2a (expected assignment) and Fig. 2b (incorrect assignment due to hypercubes with uniform density).

3.4   Corner-Based Assignment

Given that manual assignments of uncovered instances to hypercubes performed by human users would take into account the distance of the data point to the edges of the cube, we formalise accordingly a corner-based criterion considering the cube vertices.

We define the corners of a hypercube H as the set of points obtained via the Cartesian product of the sets of corners corresponding to the individual cube's dimension:

$$Corners(H) = \bigtimes_{i=1}^{n} Corners(h_i). \tag{10}$$

We finally define the corners of a hypercube dimension h as the set containing its minimum and maximum values:

$$Corners(h) = \{min(h), max(h)\}. \tag{11}$$

The computational complexity of corner-based brute prediction is no longer constant. For each assignment, it is necessary to calculate the distance between the uncovered instance and each corner of each identified hypercube. Therefore,

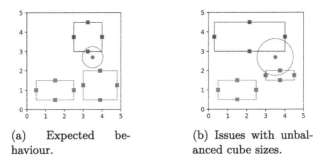

(a) Expected behaviour.

(b) Issues with unbalanced cube sizes.

Fig. 4. Example of midpoint-based distance calculation.

the complexity of corner-based brute prediction is directly related to the dimensionality of the hypercubes, which corresponds to the number of input features in the data set, denoted as n. The number of corners in an n-dimensional hypercube is equal to 2^n. This means that as the dimensionality of the hypercube increases, the number of corners and the computational complexity of corner-based brute prediction also increase. However, corner-based brute prediction remains feasible even with high-dimensional data sets. It is worth noting that when using the corner-based strategy, there can be challenges when assigning instances to hypercubes of different sizes. In such cases, smaller cubes may be privileged, leading to potential issues in the assignment process. The assignment may become arbitrary and dependent on the positioning of the hypercubes within the input space. Examples of corner-based assignments are reported in Figures 3a and 3b, which demonstrate the expected behavior and highlight the issues that can arise when hypercubes of significantly different sizes are present.

3.5   Midpoint-Based Assignment

Alternatively, other relevant multidimensional points laying on the hypercube edges may be selected to compute the Euclidean distances. For instance, one can use edge midpoints instead of vertices.

We define the midpoints of a hypercube H as the set obtained through the union of the Cartesian products of an edge midpoint with the corners of all the other cube edges:

$$Midpoints(H) = \bigcup_{i=1}^{n} \left\{ \{Centre(h_i)\} \times \bigtimes_{j \in \{1,\dots,n\} \setminus \{i\}} Corners(h_j) \right\}. \quad (12)$$

The computational complexity of midpoint-based brute prediction is slightly higher than that of corner-based assignments. This strategy involves calculating the distance between the uncovered instance and every midpoint of each identified hypercube. The number of midpoints in an n-dimensional hypercube is equal to the number of edges, which is given by $n \cdot 2^{n-1}$. However, it is worth noting that the negative effects on computational complexity become noticeable

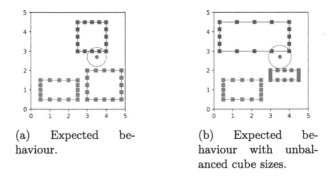

(a) Expected behaviour.

(b) Expected behaviour with unbalanced cube sizes.

Fig. 5. Example of perimeter-based distance calculation, $p = 5$.

when the dimensionality of the hypercube exceeds 6. Therefore, midpoint-based assignments can still be computationally feasible for data sets with dimensions up to a certain threshold. Similar to corner-based assignments, midpoint-based assignments also face challenges when dealing with hypercubes of significantly different sizes. The issues arising from these cubes are shared between the two strategies, as shown in Fig. 4.

3.6 Perimeter-Based Assignment

The notion of midpoint-based assignment may be relaxed in order to enable a more fine-grained sampling of edge points and to overcome the issues of cubes having different sizes. We then introduce the p parameter to indicate how many equispaced points have to be selected on edges and modify Eq. (12) accordingly:

$$Perimeter(H, p) = \bigcup_{i=1}^{n} \left\{ Equispaced(h_i, p) \times \mathop{\times}_{j \in \{1, \ldots, n\} \setminus \{i\}} Corners(h_j) \right\},$$
(13)

where $Equispaced(h, p)$ denotes the set of p equispaced points for the hypercube dimension h.

The accuracy of perimeter-based brute prediction is greater with greater values of p, however, the computational complexity grows together with p. Indeed, the number of relevant points identified for a single n-dimensional cube is equal to $p \cdot n \cdot 2^{n-1}$ (i.e., p points per edge). This value is actually reduced in practice, given that duplicate points corresponding to the cube edges are ignored. An n-dimensional cube has $(n-1) \cdot 2^n$ duplicate points. The number of relevant points without duplicates is thus $p \cdot n \cdot 2^{n-1} - (n-1) \cdot 2^n$, equivalent to $(p-2) \cdot n \cdot 2^{n-1} + 2^n$. Perimeter-based assignments are exemplified in Fig. 5.

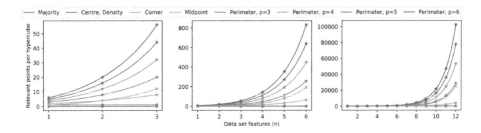

Fig. 6. Computational complexity of the proposed vicinity-based assignments.

It is worthwhile to notice that with $p = 1$ this strategy corresponds to the midpoint-based brute prediction, whereas with $p = 2$ it corresponds to the corner-based one.

3.7   On the Computational Complexity

The computational complexity of each brute prediction strategy described in this work is reported in Fig. 6. The figure shows the complexity of perimeter-based assignments for different values of the p parameter, up to 6.

Unfortunately, there is an important trade-off between the quality of the brute prediction and the corresponding computational complexity. Indeed, as described in this section, the simplest and fastest strategies to be applied are the most prone to provide predictive errors, e.g., when the sizes of hypercubes are strongly unbalanced. On the other hand, perimeter-based predictions have more probability to give the correct results. However, this strategy becomes quite unfeasible for $p = 3$ when $n > 6$, given that the overall amount of relevant points *of a single cube* would be greater than 576 (corresponding to the calculation and comparison of as many distances for each query to predict). For the same reason the perimeter-based strategy is not recommended with $p \in \{4, 5\}$ if $n > 5$ and with $p = 6$ if $n > 4$.

Obviously, the complexity of the adopted strategy also depends on the number of cubes identified via the SKE technique, given that the reported measurements have to be multiplied by the number of cubes. SKE algorithms usually output a limited amount of hypercubes to preserve human readability and therefore the overall complexity of the vicinity-based assignments is not strongly altered. However, there may be applications where the hypercube amount is bound to the domain itself and it has a heavy impact on the computational complexity of vicinity-based brute prediction, e.g., classification tasks for handwritten digits or characters. Even by assuming an optimal hypercubic partitioning of the input feature space, resulting in only a single cube per possible output class, 10 or 26 different cubes are identified, respectively, thus causing a non-negligible impact on the overall computational complexity.

4   Experiments

To evaluate the effectiveness of our proposed extension, we performed a number of experiments with the aid of the PSyKE[2] Python framework [3,21,23,26].

We selected the Iris data set[3] [6] to exemplify our proposed vicinity-based brute prediction strategies since it can be easily visualised as a bidimensional projection. In particular, we privileged the petal length and width input features, given that these are the most relevant input features to perform the classification.

The experimental setup is the following. The sepal length and width input features have been first removed from the data set. Then, the 150 available data instances were split into 2 halves, one to train an opaque model and extract knowledge, the other to test the predictive performance of both the model and the knowledge.

A k-nearest neighbours with $k = 7$ (7-NN) has been selected as opaque underlying model for the GridEx hypercube-based knowledge extractor. Data samples and decision boundaries of the 7-NN and the GridEx extractor are shown in Fig. 7.

From Fig. 7c it is possible to notice that GridEx identifies 3 different hypercubes, one per output class of the data set. The cubes do not cover the whole input feature space, yet they enclose the majority of data samples. Only 2 instances of Virginica Iris are outside the boundaries of the cubes (green stars with blue and magenta contour in Fig. 7c) and thus they cannot be predicted through the interpretable model provided by GridEx.

In Fig. 7 the proposed vicinity-based brute predictions are exemplified. In particular, Fig. 7d shows the majority-based assignment of the 2 uncovered instances. Since the random train/test splitting produced a training set where the Versicolor output class label is predominant, both uncovered instances are wrongly classified as Versicolor Iris. This very simple strategy is thus easy to compute but not accurate from a predictive standpoint.

Figure 7e and 7f reports the assignment obtained according to the centre- and density-based strategies, respectively. In both cases only one uncovered instance is correctly classified as Virginica Iris (the magenta one), whereas the other is misclassified as Versicolor Iris (the blue one).

The inverse situation is present by adopting a corner-based brute prediction, as depicted in Fig. 7g. According to the distance between uncovered instances and cubes' corners, the blue instance is incorrectly associated with the Versicolor class and the magenta one is correctly classified as a Virginica Iris.

Both instances are misclassified by adopting midpoint-based assignments (cf. Fig. 7h).

Finally, Fig. 7i shows the effectiveness of perimeter-based brute prediction. Indeed, both uncovered instances are correctly classified by adopting this strategy with $p = 5$.

---

[2] https://github.com/psykei/psyke-python.
[3] https://archive.ics.uci.edu/dataset/53/iris.

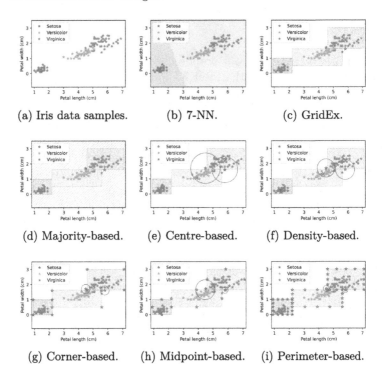

Fig. 7. Example of vicinity-based assignments for GridEx on the Iris data set.

4.1 Experiments on Real World Data Sets

A quantitative assessment of the predictive performance obtained for the distance-based brute prediction on the Iris data set is reported in Table 1. In this case the data set has been used without removing input features. The same training/test splitting strategy (50% + 50%) has been adopted. A new 7-NN has been trained accordingly, achieving an accuracy score of 0.96. A set of non-exhaustive hypercube-based SKE techniques (i.e., ITER and 2 instances of GridEx, having different parameters) are compared with 2 instances of CREEPY, used as benchmark for hypercube-based SKE methods complete by design. The parameters of each algorithm are reported in the table. In particular, ITER requires the size of the single updates, the maximum number of iterations (it), the number of starting points, and an error threshold (θ). GridEx requires a splitting strategy, a maximum depth (δ) and an error threshold (θ). We selected for GridEx adaptive strategies based on the input feature relevance: we let the 2 algorithm instances perform 5 or 8 slices along features with relevance greater than 0.5 or 0.85, respectively, and only a single slice along all the others. Finally, CREEPY requires an underlying explainable clustering technique, a maximum depth (δ) and an error threshold (θ).

Table 1. Predictive performance of brute predictions for the Iris data set.

	k-NN	ITER	GridEx	GridEx	CREEPY	CREEPY
Parameters	$k = 7$	update $= 0.1$ $it = 100$ points $= 1$ $\theta = 0.1$	adaptive split if relev. < 0.5: 1 split else 5 $\delta = 1$ $\theta = 0.1$	adaptive split if relev. < 0.85: 1 split else 8 $\delta = 1$ $\theta = 0.1$	Clustering: ExACT $\delta = 2$ $\theta = 0.1$	Clustering: CREAM $\delta = 2$ $\theta = 0.1$
Accuracy	0.96	0.97	0.96	0.90	0.92	0.93
Rules		3	6	3	3	3
Completeness		0.93	0.92	0.92	1.00	1.00
Majority		0.91	0.88	0.83		
Centre		0.97	0.96	0.91		
Density		0.97	0.96	0.91		
Corner		0.97	0.96	0.91		
Midpoint		0.97	0.96	0.91		
Perimeter, $p = 3$		0.97	0.96	0.91		
Perimeter, $p = 5$		0.97	0.96	0.91		

For each SKE instance the fidelity w.r.t. the 7-NN expressed as classification accuracy, the number of extracted rules and the completeness expressed as percentage of test set covered by the identified hypercubes are reported in Table 1. For the non-exhaustive SKE techniques, several vicinity-based brute prediction strategies have been tested and the corresponding results are reported in the same table.

From the table, it is possible to notice that CREEPY outperforms the other techniques on 2 different dimensions, indeed it has the smallest amount of rules and the highest completeness. However, thanks to the proposed brute prediction strategies, ITER and GridEx may achieve complete coverage of the input feature space as well. As a result, ITER becomes the best algorithm in the examined pool, since it maximises both the completeness and the accuracy of its predictions with only 3 extracted rules. As for GridEx, an instance is able to outperform CREEPY in terms of accuracy but produces a double amount of rules, whereas the other exhibits the same rule amount but smaller classification accuracy. The proposed extension to draw predictions for uncovered instances is thus effective in obtaining better overall results.

We conclude this experimental section with a regression case study on the Combined Cycle Power Plant (CCPP) data set [28]. A random forest (RF) regressor based on 20 decision trees (DT) with unbounded depth (δ) and leaf amount (λ) has been selected as opaque model. The pool of SKE techniques is composed of GridEx, GridREx, CREEPY adopting CREAM clustering, and 2 different instances of ITER. We omitted the results of CREEPY adopting ExACT clustering, since it showed the same input space partitioning obtained by adopting CREAM, with the same performance measurements, by setting $\delta = 3$. Results are reported in Table 2, where predictive performance is expressed through the R^2 score.

Table 2. Predictive performance of brute predictions for the CCPP data set.

	RF	ITER	ITER	GridEx	GridREx	CREEPY
		upd. = 0.03	upd. = 0.07	adaptive split	adaptive split	CREAM clust
	DT = 20	$it = 100$	$it = 150$	if relev. < 0.7:	if relev. < 0.7:	$\delta = 2$
Parameters	$\lambda = \infty$	points = 1	points = 2	1 split else 3	1 split else 3	$\theta = 0.1$
	$\delta = \infty$	$\theta = 10$	$\theta = 10$	$\delta = 1$	$\delta = 1$	output: linear
				$\theta = 1$	$\theta = 1$	functions
R^2	0.96	0.62	0.86	0.98	0.93	0.97
Rules		4	13	3	9	4
Completeness		0.58	0.93	0.99	0.99	1.00
Majority		0.31	0.77	0.97	0.93	
Centre		0.65	0.86	0.98	0.93	
Density		0.61	0.84	0.98	0.93	
Corner		0.60	0.81	0.98	0.93	
Midpoint		0.62	0.87	0.98	0.93	
Perimeter, $p = 3$		0.62	0.87	0.98	0.93	
Perimeter, $p = 5$		0.63	0.86	0.98	0.93	

In this case study GridEx is superior to CREEPY from the predictive performance and rule amount standpoints. However, only CREEPY provides complete knowledge. Our proposed extension enables GridEx to achieve 100% completeness as well. GridEx empowered with brute prediction capabilities outperforms CREEPY and it is thus the best SKE technique in the pool.

Amongst all the proposed vicinity-based strategies, from our experiments, the majority-based criterion appears to be the simplest but also the least performing in terms of prediction accuracy. Conversely, the other alternatives do not exhibit very noticeable differences in the measured predictive performance. For this reason we suggest applying one of the least computationally expensive strategies to empower non-exhaustive hypercube-based SKE techniques.

5 Conclusions

In this paper, we introduce a vicinity-based extension for SKE techniques that ensures 100% completeness in predictions. This extension can be applied to any hypercube-based SKE method and offers flexibility to users in selecting the desired trade-off between computational complexity and predictive performance. We define different strategies based on *vicinity* for the extension, allowing users to tailor the approach to their specific needs. Additionally, we provide an analytical study of the computational complexity associated with the proposed extension. Furthermore, we present experimental results that demonstrate the effectiveness of the extension in practical applications.

Our future work aims to enhance the selection of relevant points within hypercubes to achieve smaller sets of points while maintaining comparable or even improved predictive performance with reduced computational complexity.

Specifically, we plan to consider points on the surface of the hypercubes and to develop mechanisms for coarse-grained sampling of relevant points in low-importance regions of the cubes, such as cube edges near the boundaries of the data set domain or perimeter sampling for very small cubes. These advancements will further refine and optimise the extension of SKE techniques.

Acknowledgments. This work has been supported by European Union's Horizon Europe AEQUITAS research and innovation programme under grant number 101070363.

References

1. Andrews, R., Diederich, J., Tickle, A.B.: Survey and critique of techniques for extracting rules from trained artificial neural networks. Knowl. Based Syst. **8**(6), 373–389 (1995). https://doi.org/10.1016/0950-7051(96)81920-4
2. Breiman, L., Friedman, J., Stone, C.J., Olshen, R.A.: Classification and Regression Trees. CRC Press, Boca Raton (1984)
3. Calegari, R., Sabbatini, F.: The PSyKE technology for trustworthy artificial intelligence. In: Dovier, A., Montanari, A., Orlandini, A. (eds.) XXI International Conference of the Italian Association for Artificial Intelligence, AIxIA 2022, Udine, Italy, November 28 – December 2, 2022, Proceedings, vol. 13796, pp. 3–16 (2023). https://doi.org/10.1007/978-3-031-27181-6_1
4. Craven, M.W., Shavlik, J.W.: Extracting tree-structured representations of trained networks. In: Touretzky, D.S., Mozer, M.C., Hasselmo, M.E. (eds.) Advances in Neural Information Processing Systems 8. Proceedings of the 1995 Conference, pp. 24–30. The MIT Press (1996). https://papers.nips.cc/paper/1152-extracting-tree-structured-representations-of-trained-networks.pdf
5. Eineborg, M., Boström, H.: Classifying uncovered examples by rule stretching. In: Rouveirol, C., Sebag, M. (eds.) Inductive Logic Programming, 11th International Conference, ILP 2001, Strasbourg, France, September 9–11 2001, Proceedings. LNCS, vol. 2157, pp. 41–50. Springer, Heidelberg (2001). https://doi.org/10.1007/3-540-44797-0_4
6. Fisher, R.A.: The use of multiple measurements in taxonomic problems. Ann. Eugenics **7**(2), 179–188 (1936). https://onlinelibrary.wiley.com/doi/abs/10.1111/j.1469-1809.1936.tb02137.x, https://doi.org/10.1111/j.1469-1809.1936.tb02137.x
7. Garcez, A.S.d., Broda, K., Gabbay, D.M.: Symbolic knowledge extraction from trained neural networks: a sound approach. Artif. Intell. **125**(1–2), 155–207 (2001)
8. Guidotti, R., Monreale, A., Ruggieri, S., Turini, F., Giannotti, F., Pedreschi, D.: A survey of methods for explaining black box models. ACM Comput. Surv. **51**(5), 1–42 (2018). https://doi.org/10.1145/3236009
9. Huysmans, J., Baesens, B., Vanthienen, J.: ITER: an algorithm for predictive regression rule extraction. In: Tjoa, A.M., Trujillo, J. (eds.) DaWaK 2006. LNCS, vol. 4081, pp. 270–279. Springer, Heidelberg (2006). https://doi.org/10.1007/11823728_26
10. Kenny, E.M., Ford, C., Quinn, M., Keane, M.T.: Explaining black-box classifiers using post-hoc explanations-by-example: the effect of explanations and error-rates in XAI user studies. Artif. Intell. **294**, 103459 (2021). https://doi.org/10.1016/j.artint.2021.103459

11. Konig, R., Johansson, U., Niklasson, L.: G-REX: a versatile framework for evolutionary data mining. In: 2008 IEEE International Conference on Data Mining Workshops (ICDM 2008 Workshops), pp. 971–974 (2008). https://doi.org/10.1109/ICDMW.2008.117

12. Rocha, A., Papa, J.P., Meira, L.A.A.: How far do we get using machine learning black-boxes? Int. J. Pattern Recogn. Artif. Intell. **26**(02), 1261001-(1–23) (2012). https://doi.org/10.1142/S0218001412610010

13. Rudin, C.: Stop explaining black box machine learning models for high stakes decisions and use interpretable models instead. Nat. Mach. Intell. **1**(5), 206–215 (2019). https://doi.org/10.1038/s42256-019-0048-x

14. Sabbatini, F., Calegari, R.: Symbolic knowledge extraction from opaque machine learning predictors: GridREx & PEDRO. In: Kern-Isberner, G., Lakemeyer, G., Meyer, T. (eds.) Proceedings of the 19th International Conference on Principles of Knowledge Representation and Reasoning, KR 2022, Haifa, Israel, July 31–August 5, 2022 (2022). https://doi.org/10.24963/kr.2022/57. https://proceedings.kr.org/2022/57/

15. Sabbatini, F., Calegari, R.: Bottom-up and top-down workflows for hypercube- and clustering-based knowledge extractors. In: Proceedings of the V International Workshop on Explainable and Transparent AI and Multi-Agent Systems, EXTRAAMAS 2023, London, UK, 29 May 2023, vol. 14127. Springer, Cham. (2023, to appear). https://doi.org/10.1007/978-3-031-40878-6_7

16. Sabbatini, F., Calegari, R.: Explainable clustering via ExACT. In: Proceedings of the II International Workshop on Knowledge Diversity, KoDis 2023, Rhodes, Greece, 2–8 September 2023 (2023). https://ceur-ws.org/Vol-3548/paper3.pdf

17. Sabbatini, F., Calegari, R.: Explainable clustering with CREAM. In: Proceedings of the 20th International Conference on Principles of Knowledge Representation and Reasoning, pp. 593–603 (2023). https://doi.org/10.24963/kr.2023/58

18. Sabbatini, F., Calegari, R.: The ICE score to evaluate symbolic knowledge quality. In: Proceedings of the XXXVIII Annual AAAI Conference on Artificial Intelligence, AAAI24, Vancouver, Canada, 20–27 February 2024 (2023, submitted to)

19. Sabbatini, F., Calegari, R.: On the evaluation of the symbolic knowledge extracted from black boxes. In: AAAI 2023 Spring Symposium Series, San Francisco, California (2023, to appear)

20. Sabbatini, F., Calegari, R.: Unveiling opaque predictors via explainable clustering: the CReEPy algorithm. In: Proceedings of the 2nd Workshop on Bias, Ethical AI, Explainability and the role of Logic and Logic Programming, BEWARE-23, Rome, Italy, November 6, 2023, (2023, to appear)

21. Sabbatini, F., Ciatto, G., Calegari, R., Omicini, A.: On the design of PSyKE: a platform for symbolic knowledge extraction. In: Calegari, R., Ciatto, G., Denti, E., Omicini, A., Sartor, G. (eds.) WOA 2021–22nd Workshop "From Objects to Agents". CEUR Workshop Proceedings, vol. 2963, pp. 29–48. Sun SITE Central Europe, RWTH Aachen University (2021). https://ceur-ws.org/Vol-2963/paper14.pdf, 22nd Workshop "From Objects to Agents" (WOA 2021), Bologna, Italy, 1–3 September 2021. Proceedings (2021)

22. Sabbatini, F., Ciatto, G., Calegari, R., Omicini, A.: Hypercube-based methods for symbolic knowledge extraction: towards a unified model. In: Ferrando, A., Mascardi, V. (eds.) WOA 2022–23rd Workshop "From Objects to Agents", CEUR Workshop Proceedings, Sun SITE Central Europe, RWTH Aachen University, vol. 3261, pp. 48–60 (2022). https://ceur-ws.org/Vol-3261/paper4.pdf

23. Sabbatini, F., Ciatto, G., Calegari, R., Omicini, A.: Symbolic knowledge extraction from opaque ML predictors in PSyKE: platform design experiments. Intelligenza Artificiale **16**(1), 27–48 (2022). https://doi.org/10.3233/IA-210120

24. Sabbatini, F., Ciatto, G., Calegari, R., Omicini, A.: Towards a unified model for symbolic knowledge extraction with hypercube-based methods. Intelligenza Artificiale **17**(1), 63–75 (2023). https://doi.org/10.3233/IA-230001

25. Sabbatini, F., Ciatto, G., Omicini, A.: GridEx: an algorithm for knowledge extraction from black-box regressors. In: Calvaresi, D., Najjar, A., Winikoff, M., Främling, K. (eds.) Explainable and Transparent AI and Multi-Agent Systems. Third International Workshop, EXTRAAMAS 2021, Virtual Event, 3–7 May 2021, Revised Selected Papers, LNCS, vol. 12688, pp. 18–38. Springer, Cham (2021). https://doi.org/10.1007/978-3-030-82017-6_2

26. Sabbatini, F., Ciatto, G., Omicini, A.: Semantic Web-based interoperability for intelligent agents with PSyKE. In: Calvaresi, D., Najjar, A., Winikoff, M., Främling, K. (eds.) Explainable and Transparent AI and Multi-Agent Systems, LNCS, vol. 13283, pp. 124–142. Springer, Cham (2022). https://doi.org/10.1007/978-3-031-15565-9_8

27. Salzberg, S.: A nearest hyperrectangle learning method. Mach. Learn. **6**, 251–276 (1991). https://doi.org/10.1023/A:1022661727670

28. Tüfekci, P.: Prediction of full load electrical power output of a base load operated combined cycle power plant using machine learning methods. Int. J. Electr. Power Energy Syst. **60**, 126–140 (2014). https://www.sciencedirect.com/science/article/pii/S0142061514000908, https://doi.org/10.1016/j.ijepes.2014.02.027

Interpreting and Correcting Medical Image Classification with PIP-Net

Meike Nauta[1]([✉])[iD], Johannes H. Hegeman[1,2][iD], Jeroen Geerdink[2][iD], Jörg Schlötterer[3,4][iD], Maurice van Keulen[1], and Christin Seifert[1,4][iD]

[1] University of Twente, Enschede, The Netherlands
{m.nauta,m.vankeulen}@utwente.nl
[2] Hospital Group Twente, Almelo & Hengelo, The Netherlands
{h.hegeman,j.geerdink}@zgt.nl
[3] University of Mannheim, Mannheim, Germany
[4] University of Marburg, Hessian.AI, Marburg, Germany
{joerg.schloetterer,christin.seifert}@uni-marburg.de

Abstract. Part-prototype models are explainable-by-design image classifiers, and a promising alternative to black box AI. This paper explores the applicability and potential of interpretable machine learning, in particular PIP-Net, for automated diagnosis support on real-world medical imaging data. PIP-Net learns human-understandable prototypical image parts and we evaluate its accuracy and interpretability for fracture detection and skin cancer diagnosis. We find that PIP-Net's decision making process is in line with medical classification standards, while only provided with image-level class labels. Because of PIP-Net's unsupervised pretraining of prototypes, data quality problems such as undesired text in an X-ray or labelling errors can be easily identified. Additionally, we are the first to show that humans can manually correct the reasoning of PIP-Net by directly disabling undesired prototypes. We conclude that part-prototype models are promising for medical applications due to their interpretability and potential for advanced model debugging.

Keywords: Explainable AI · prototypes · medical imaging · interpretable machine learning · hybrid intelligence

1 Introduction

Deep learning has shown great promise in medical imaging tasks, as neural networks can outperform clinicians in fracture detection [17] or have equivalent performance in medical diagnosis [20]. Machine learning (ML) models are usually evaluated in terms of predictive performance, e.g., classification accuracy. However, performance metrics do not capture whether the evaluated model is right for the right reasons [18]. ML models can replicate biases and other confounding patterns from the input data when these are discriminative for the downstream task. For example, COVID-19 detectors were found to rely on markers, image

© The Author(s), under exclusive license to Springer Nature Switzerland AG 2024
S. Nowaczyk et al. (Eds.): ECAI 2023 Workshops, CCIS 1947, pp. 198–215, 2024.
https://doi.org/10.1007/978-3-031-50396-2_11

edges, arrows and other annotations in chest X-rays [11], and [4] showed that deep learning models can predict hip fractures indirectly through confounding patient and healthcare variables rather than directly detecting the fracture in the image. This so-called "Clever Hans" behaviour [18] makes a medical classifier right for the *wrong* reasons, by basing its predictions on clinically irrelevant artefacts that are not representative for the actual data distribution [12,32]. Such shortcut learning will therefore lead to a lack of generalisation and in turn unsatisfactory performance once deployed in clinical practice [12].

Detecting shortcut learning and other undesired reasoning is challenging since neural networks are black boxes [1]. Explainable AI (XAI) aims to provide insight into the reasoning of a predictive model. A commonly used explanation method in medical imaging is the feature attribution map [7], a heatmap that highlights relevant regions in an input image [36]. These explanation methods are, however, *post-hoc*, i.e., they reverse-engineer an already trained predictive model. With the explanation method detached from the predictive model, the explanation is not guaranteed to truthfully mimic the internal calculations of the black box. Additionally, such heatmaps do not explain the *full* reasoning process but only give an intuition, making them irrelevant to tasks in realistic scenario's [10,33, 37]. Specifically, it has been shown that feature attribution maps do not fulfil clinical requirements to correctly explain a model's decision process [14].

Recently, as an alternative to post-hoc explanations, intrinsically interpretable models are proposed based on prototypical parts [8,26,27,35]. Their reasoning follows the recognition-by-components theory [6] by analysing whether patches in an input image are similar to a learned prototypical part. Importantly, part-prototype models do not require any part annotations and only rely on image-level class labels. Most of these models have been developed for fine-grained natural image recognition, including recognising bird species and car types. Only a few works apply part-prototype models to medical images: ProtoPNet [8] is also applied to chest X-rays [38] and MRI scans [24], ProtoMIL [34] is developed for histology slide classification and [5] adapted ProtoPNet for mammography by including a loss based on fine-grained expert image annotations.

In this work, we show the applicability and potential of PIP-Net for understanding and *correcting* medical imaging classification, and thus contribute towards explanatory interactive model debiasing [3,29,40]. PIP-Net [27] is a next-generation interpretable ML method that lets users understand its sparse reasoning with prototypical parts and will abstain from a decision for out-of-distribution input. In addition, its intuitive design empowers users to make adjustments in the model's reasoning. We investigate to what extent PIP-Net can be used for revealing and correcting *shortcut learning* when applied to fracture detection and skin cancer diagnosis. Generally, one can identify three ways of debugging models: either by adapting the dataset to neutralise the bias (e.g. [28]), by adapting the model's loss function (e.g. [5,31]), or by adapting the predictive model directly. Steering a model's reasoning through a loss function requires manual annotations that indicate where a model should or should not focus. Although such additional annotations could improve predictive accuracy, providing such annotations by physicians is complex and time-consuming, and therefore expensive and often unfeasible. Instead, the interpretable scoring sheet of PIP-Net allows debugging the model directly by simply disabling shortcut prototypes.

In summary, we show that PIP-Net applied to medical imaging:

- learns an interpretable, sparse scoring sheet with semantically meaningful prototypical parts (Sect. 4.1 and 4.2),
- can reveal data quality problems, including spurious artefacts and labelling errors (Sect. 4.3),
- learns interpretable reasoning that is in line with medical domain knowledge and classification standards (Sect. 5),
- can reveal shortcut learning and subsequently be 'debugged' by clinicians by disabling undesired prototypes (Sect. 6).

2   Background on PIP-Net

PIP-Net [27] is a deep learning model designed with interpretability integrated into its architecture and training mechanism. It consists of a convolutional neural network (CNN) with loss terms that disentangle the latent space and optimise the model to learn semantically meaningful components, while only having access to image-level class labels and thus not relying on additional part annotations. The learned components are "prototypical parts" (prototypes) which are visualised as image patches. Subsequently, PIP-Net classifies images by connecting the learned prototypes to classes via a sparse, linear layer. The linear decision making process is therefore globally interpretable as a scoring sheet where the presence of a prototypical part in an input image adds to the evidence for a particular class. In case no relevant part-prototypes are found, all output scores stay zero. Hence, PIP-Net can abstain from a decision for out-of-distribution input. An overview of the architecture is shown in Fig. 1. In contrast to ProtoPNet [8] that requires a fixed number of prototypes per class, PIP-Net has a novel training mechanism and is optimised for sparsity *and* accuracy. It therefore learns the suitable number of prototypes itself. Training of PIP-Net consists of two stages: in the first stage, the latent space is automatically disentangled into prototypes that are learned self-supervised with contrastive learning. In this stage, no image labels are needed and hence would allow the use of additional unlabelled data, which is highly relevant due to expensive labelling effort in the medical domain. The second training stage learns the weights in the sparse classification layer while finetuning the prototypes based on image-level labels.

3   Datasets and Experimental Setup

We evaluate the predictive accuracy and interpretability of PIP-Net with two open benchmark datasets on skin cancer diagnosis (ISIC [9]) and bone abnormality detection in bone X-rays (MURA [30]), and two real-world data sets from a

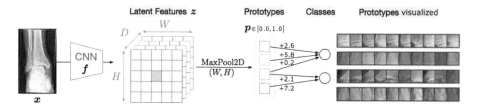

Fig. 1. PIP-Net consists of a CNN backbone (e.g. ConvNeXt with $D = 768$) with a novel training mechanism to disentangle the latent space and learn prototypical representations z. The feature representations are pooled to a vector of prototype presence scores p. Prototypes and classes are connected via a sparse linear layer. Model outputs during inference are not normalised and allow the outputs to be interpreted as a simple scoring sheet. A prototype can be visualised as an image patch by upsampling the corresponding patch in z.

Dutch hospital on hip and ankle fracture detection (HIP resp. ANKLE). Table 1 shows descriptions of the datasets and Fig. 2 some example images.

Data Preprocessing: We sample a random split of 20% of the HIP and ANKLE datasets as test sets. For ISIC, we use the same 361 malignant images in the test set as [28] and randomly sample a similar fraction from the benign images. The MURA dataset contains a fixed training and validation split (which we use as test set as the hidden test set competition is closed). All images are resized to 224×224 and augmented with TrivialAugment [25]. We account for imbalanced data with class over-sampling using a weighted sampler. Code including the data preprocessing is available at https://github.com/M-Nauta/PIPNet.

In radiography, usually multiple X-rays (with different views) are taken for one *study*. Therefore, images in MURA, HIP and ANKLE are annotated at the study level. In this work, we assign the study label to each image individually and prevent data leakage by splitting data in train and test sets *per study*. Conceptually, we think that PIP-Net could also be used for interpretable multi-instance classification by doing a max-pooling operation over all latent image representations z in a study, rather than a single image embedding (see Fig. 1). PIP-Net can then indicate in which image and at which location evidence for a certain class is found. We leave experimental investigation on multi-instance PIP-Net for future work.

Model Training: We use a ConvNeXt-tiny [21] backbone, adapted to output feature maps of size 13×13 and pretrained on ImageNet, as it is shown that CNNs pretrained on natural images and with adequate fine-tuning outperform, or perform just as well as, CNNs trained for radiology from scratch [39]. Similar to the training process for PIP-Net on natural images, we train PIP-Net with a learning rate of 0.05 for the linear classification layer, and 0.0001 for the backbone. We use a batch size of 64 and adapt the number of epochs, such that the number of weight updates is similar for all datasets. We apply roughly 2,000 updates for

Table 1. Description of the datasets, including their number of samples. All used datasets are binary labelled (indicating presence or absence of abnormality).

	Description	Label present/absent
ISIC	Public skin cancer dataset from the International Skin Imaging Collaboration (ISIC) [9]. Specifically selected as it is known to contain confounding artefacts [28,31]: half of the images of benign lesions contain elliptical, coloured patches (colour calibration charts [23]), whereas the malignant lesion images contain none.	# **Train images:** 2,192 / 16,998 # **Test images:** 361/2,736
MURA	Public dataset with musculoskeletal radiographs [30] from different body parts, including the shoulder, humerus, elbow, forearm, wrist, hand, and finger. The bone X-rays are labelled as 'normal' or 'abnormal'. Images with the 'abnormal' label have any abnormal finding, including the presence of a fracture, hardware, lesions and joint diseases.	# **Train images:** 14,873 / 21,935 # **Test images:** 1,530 / 1,667
HIP	Dataset from hospital Ziekenhuisgroep Twente (ZGT). Included were hip/pelvis radiographic studies (2005–2018), patients ≥ 21y old). Studies were labelled based on an administrative code and by analysing radiology reports with a rule-based approach. Images from follow-up studies were excluded. A sample of the selected studies (127 with fracture and 204 without) was manually verified by a radiologist. Images were anonymised by removing Protected Health Information (PHI). All radiographic images were converted from DICOM format [15] to JPG.	# **Train images:** 3,468/4,080 # **Test images:** 859 / 1,005
ANKLE	Dataset from ZGT. Selected were ankle studies (2005–2020) based on administrative code for "ankle fracture" or "ankle distortion" (no fracture). Images from follow-up studies were excluded, PHI information removed and images converted from DICOM to JPG.	# **Train images:** 12,233 / 8,602 # **Test images:** 3,033/ 2,169

pretraining the prototypes and 10,000 updates for the second training stage. This calculation results in 6 (pretrain) and 34 (training) epochs for ISIC, 4 and 18 epochs for MURA, 16 and 85 epochs for HIPS and 6 and 31 epochs for ANKLE. Results reported in this paper are based on a slightly older version of PIP-Net. On natural images, the final published version of PIP-Net gives similar or higher prediction accuracy and similar prototypes when compared to this older version, hence we don't expect significant differences.

4 Interpretable and Accurate Image Classification

We evaluate the applicability and potential of PIP-Net for binary medical image classification by first analysing its classification performance (Sect. 4.1), followed by evaluating the interpretability of the learned prototypes (Sect. 4.2) and exploring its capabilities to reveal data quality issues (Sect. 4.3). In Sect. 5 we then evaluate to what extent the learned reasoning is aligned with medical domain knowledge, and the possibilities for manually correcting shortcut learning are investigated in Sect. 6.

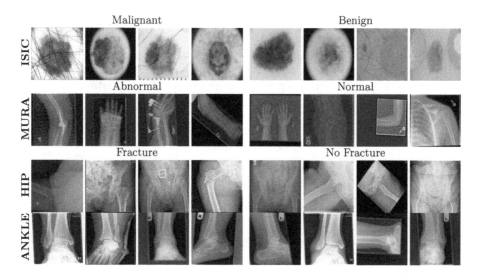

Fig. 2. Example images from medical datasets (resized to 224 × 224).

Table 2. PIP-Net's performance on the test sets. Reporting accuracy (Acc), F1 score, sensitivity (Sens), and specificity (Spec). Sensitivity corresponds to the absent-class. Sparsity is the ratio of weights in the classification layer with a value of zero. # Proto indicates how many prototypes have at least one non-zero weight to a class, and therefore indicates the global explanation size of PIP-Net. The local explanation size indicates the average number of found ($p > 0.1$) and relevant (to any of the classes) prototypes in a single test image.

Dataset	Acc	F1	Sens	Spec	Sparsity	# Proto	Local size
ISIC	94.1%	72.6%	97.7%	67.0%	92.3%	119	13.8
MURA	82.1%	84.2%	91.3%	72.0%	95.1%	75	7.6
HIP	94.0%	94.4%	93.2%	94.9%	93.6%	99	7.4
ANKLE	77.3%	74.0%	77.8%	76.9%	98.1%	29	2.5

4.1 Classification Performance and Sparsity

Table 2 reports the predictive performance of PIP-Net, and shows that PIP-Net can successfully classify images from all four medical datasets. The ISIC predictive performance is comparable to a standard black box classifier which achieves a sensitivity of 0.90 and a specificity of 0.75 (results from [28]). Additionally, PIP-Net achieves a high sparsity ratio, thereby lowering the explanation size. These results show that the training mechanism of PIP-Net, originally developed for multi-class classification of natural images [27], also works well for medical binary classification. Figure 3 shows that the sparsity of PIP-Net's classification layer slowly increases during training, while predictive performance is relatively stable. Therefore, the number of training iterations mainly influences the trade-off between explanation size and prototype purity (see also next Sect. 4.2). While a smaller explanation size is generally favourable, it limits the amount of distinct visual concepts that can be represented by separate (pure) prototypes. The tradeoff between explanation size and prototype purity can be tuned based on visual inspection of the prototypes or automated purity evaluation with part annotations (as done in the original PIP-Net paper [27]).

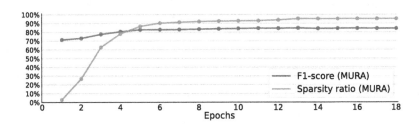

Fig. 3. MURA Plot of PIP-Net's sparsity ratio and F1-score during training.

4.2 Perceived Prototype Purity

An important aspect of interpretability of learned medical prototypes, is the purity of the set of image patches corresponding to a prototype. A pure prototype clearly represents a single visual concept, such as a metal screw and does not mix multiple concepts, e.g., fractures and metal parts. We visually assess the prototypes of the MURA, ANKLE and HIP datasets for fractures and abnormalities. Figure 4 (top and center row), visualises image patches for the most relevant (i.e., highest weight in the classification layer) prototypes for the ANKLE and HIP dataset. It can be seen that image patches for one prototype, either fully trained or only pretrained, look similar, and generally correspond to semantically meaningful concepts. Our findings on medical data are therefore in accordance with high prototype purity for natural images as reported for PIP-Net [27].

Figure 4 (bottom row) visualises the 10 most relevant prototypes per class for the MURA dataset. Images in MURA are labelled as *normal* or *abnormal* without any additional description. Hence, either the presence of a fracture, hardware lesions or other diseases could be the reason for the *abnormal* label. The part-prototypes of PIP-Net can provide fine-grained insight into the model's learned reasoning. Figure 4, bottom left, shows that most prototypes relevant to the *abnormal* class represent metal parts, such as operative plates, screw fixation and shoulder prostheses. Prototypes for the *normal* class mainly focus on bones and joints, but PIP-Net also reveals spurious correlations, such as rotated text (cf. Figure 4 bottom center, 6th row). This potential is further investigated in Sect. 6.

To facilitate easier interpretation of the prototypes, Fig. 5 shows representative images from which the prototype image patches are extracted. While the

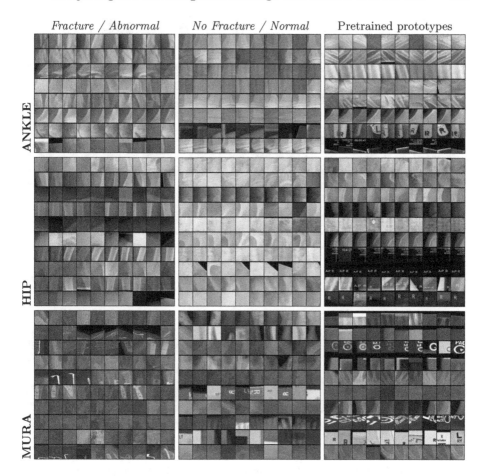

Fig. 4. Top-10 image patches for the most relevant prototypes per class. One row corresponds to one prototype. **ANKLE** showing 8 relevant prototypes, since only 8 are relevant for the *fracture* class. **HIP** and **MURA** showing top-10 prototypes. Last column: showing prototypes after pretraining that are eventually not relevant for the classification task, including markers, tags and background.

MURA dataset contains images from different body parts, which are shuffled during training, it can be seen that a prototype often relates to a single body part. This is however not always the case, as shown in Fig. 5(d) where a prototype represents different types of hardware in different body parts. The optimal trade-off between prototype purity and sparsity can be decided by the user upon visual inspection and tuned with the number of training iterations.

4.3 Prototypes for Data Quality Inspection

Since PIP-Net first learns prototypes in a self-supervised fashion, the pretrained prototypes can inform the user about artefacts and patterns hidden in the training data. Even when these are not discriminative for the prediction task, such

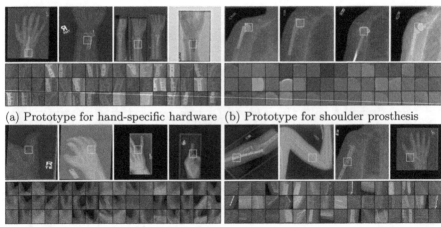

(a) Prototype for hand-specific hardware (b) Prototype for shoulder prosthesis

(c) Prototype for joint disease in finger (d) Prototype for various metalware

Fig. 5. MURA Prototypes relevant to class *abnormal*, visualised with a set of image patches and four representative images indicating where the prototype is detected.

HIP   **ANKLE**

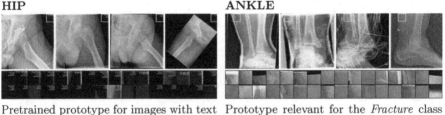

Pretrained prototype for images with text Prototype relevant for the *Fracture* class
in the upper-right corner   that represents orthopedic cast and splint

Fig. 6. An inspection of PIP-Net's prototypes can reveal data quality issues.

as the prototypes shown in Fig. 4 (third column), they can facilitate data quality inspection. For example, visual inspection of the prototypes could be used for anomaly detection, or to check whether all individually identifiable information is removed to ensure sufficient anonymisation. Additionally, PIP-Net could assist in quickly identifying labelling errors. For example, the top-left image in Fig. 5(a) has the ground-truth label *normal* in MURA but is mislabelled since the presence of metal, a reason for abnormality, is detected. Two examples of data quality issues discovered with PIP-Net are shown in Fig. 6. Visual analysis of the pretrained prototypes from the HIP dataset reveals that a few images contain text in the upper-right corner. Similarly, on the ANKLE dataset we find a prototype that relates to orthopedic cast and splint (although it is also activated by a few images with soft tissue, as shown in the rightmost image). X-rays with cast and splints should have been excluded from the dataset as they are taken as part of a follow-up study. Such data collection problems can be easily solved

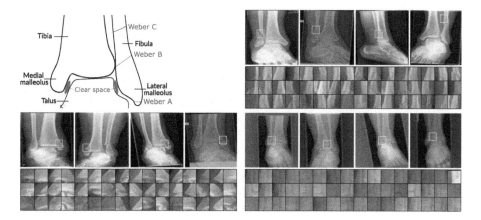

Fig. 7. ANKLE Correspondence to ankle fracture classification standard, related to three highly relevant prototypes. Visualised with a set of image patches and four representative images indicating where the prototype is detected.
Top left: Weber classification standard; Top right: Prototype relevant to *fracture*, corresponding to Weber B and, with lower presence scores, to Weber C; Bottom left: Prototype relevant to *fracture*, consistently found at the distal end of the medial malleolus, a common location for fractures; Bottom right: Prototype relevant to *no fracture*, located at the joint where the fibula, tibula and talus meet.

with PIP-Net by removing the images where the prototype is found, in order to prevent that casts and splints become a shortcut for fracture recognition.

5   Alignment of Prototypes with Domain Knowledge

This section evaluates how well the prototypes align with medical domain knowledge. We evaluate prototypes from the ANKLE and HIP datasets by comparing them with medical literature and classification standards, supported by the expert knowledge of a trauma surgeon from hospital ZGT. We find that a learned prototype of PIP-Net is generally consistently found at the same location in the body and that most, but not all, of these locations are medically relevant.

5.1   ANKLE Dataset

Figure 7 visualises a representative subset of PIP-Net's most relevant prototypes for ankle fracture recognition. The sketch on the top left illustrates the anatomy of the ankle and additionally indicates the three types of fibula fractures according to the Weber classification standard [41]. The most frequently occurring prototype is shown in Fig. 7 (top right) and consistently locates fibula fractures. The prototype corresponds to Weber B fractures, which is the most common fracture type [13]. The prototype is also activated by Weber C fractures (most-right image), although with a lower prototype presence score. The prototype in

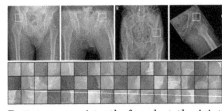 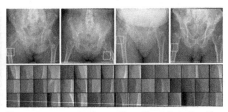

Prototype consistently found at the joint where the femoral head and the socket meet

Prototype consistently found at the trochanter minor, an indication for a pertrochanteric fracture

Fig. 8. HIP Visualisations of the two most relevant prototypes for the *fracture* class. Visualised with a set of image patches and four representative images indicating where the prototype is detected.

Fig. 7 (bottom left) is consistently found at the distal end of the medial malleolus, which is reasonable as this is a common location for fractures [13]. These different prototypes show that PIP-Net's reasoning can distinguish between different types of fractures, even though the model is only trained on binary labels.

Lastly, Fig. 7 (bottom right) shows a highly relevant prototype for the *no fracture* class. It focuses on the ankle joint where the tibia, fibula and talus meet, and is only detected in the anteroposterior (AP) views. Another prototype (not shown here) finds the same area in lateral views. It is reasonable that the model checks that this area does not contain any fracture, as Weber B fractures usually end at this joint. Additionally, clear space widening is a radiographic sign which has been shown to be relevant to the diagnosis of ankle fractures [19]. We conclude that PIP-Net learns prototypes for ankle fracture detection that are in line with existing domain knowledge. However, we also find that a few prototypes with a lower but non-zero weight are focusing on regions that do not seem to have any medical relevance, such as soft tissue at the top of the foot or ankle. Further future investigation of the prototypes could analyse what discriminative information these image patches hold.

5.2   HIP Dataset

Figure 8 shows the two most relevant prototypes for the *fracture* class. The prototype visualised on the left is consistently located at the joint where the femoral head and the socket meet. Although all images contain fractures, the actual fracture is often located slightly below the femoral head. Instead of, or potentially, *in addition to* locating the fracture, the white lines in the image patches might be a sign of arthritis and degeneration of the bone. This indicates a decrease in bone mass and correlates with age, making it a plausible indicator for fractures. The second most relevant prototype, visualised in Fig. 8 (right), is also consistently found at the same location and is identified in images that include a fracture. The prototype correctly locates the fracture in some images (e.g. two left images showing a pertrochanteric fracture), while focusing below the actual fracture for others (two right images showing a femoral neck fracture). As future work, further investigation can be conducted to identify whether evidence for the fracture is present at these exact locations, or that a learned shortcut is discovered.

6 Revealing and Correcting Shortcut Learning

In this section, we investigate shortcut learning by PIP-Net for the ISIC dataset, which is known to contain coloured patches which spuriously correlate with benign lesions [28,31]. Additionally, we investigate a shortcut that was found in the HIP dataset. We evaluate whether the shortcuts can be suppressed by disabling the corresponding prototypes.

6.1 ISIC Dataset

To evaluate whether PIP-Net bases its decision making process on the presence of coloured patches, a known bias, we first analyse how many learned prototypes correspond to a coloured patch. We use the segmentation masks from [31] to locate coloured patches and calculate their overlap with image segments where a prototype is detected[1]. We label a prototype as related to a coloured patch when at least 20% of the image patches where the prototype is found (prototype presence score $p > 0.1$) has overlap with the patch segmentation mask. We then find that 43 prototypes are related to the spurious coloured patches. Figure 9 (left) visualises 10 of these prototypes, which have a positive weight to the *benign* class.

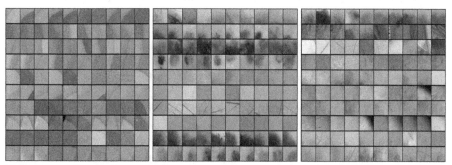

Relevant to *Benign*, located on coloured patches   Relevant to *Benign*, not on coloured patches   Relevant to *Malignant*

Fig. 9. ISIC Top-10 image patches for the 10 most relevant prototypes per class. One row corresponds to one prototype.

---

[1] If segmentation masks were not available, patch-related prototypes could efficiently be collected manually, since the sparsity of PIP-Net results in a reasonable number of relevant prototypes (only 119 for ISIC).

Table 3. ISIC Classification performance for different data subsets. Reporting Accuracy (Acc), Sensitivity (Sens), and Specificity (Spec). All images with patches are correctly classified as benign. Inserting spurious patches into malignant images tricks the model into classifying malignant images as benign, revealing unreliable behaviour when used in clinical practice. Disabling patch-related prototypes repairs this behaviour.

ISIC	Original PIP-Net			Adapted PIP-Net		
Data subset	Acc	Sens	Spec	Acc	Sens	Spec
Full test set	94.1%	97.7%	67.0%	93.5%	96.7%	69.3%
Excl. images w/patches	89.9%	95.6%	67.0%	88.9%	93.8%	69.3%
Benign w/ patches	100.0%	100.0%	n.a.	99.9%	99.9%	n.a.
Malignant w/ inserted patches	9.1%	n.a.	9.1%	65.7%	n.a.	65.7%

To validate that PIP-Net bases its decision on these patch-prototypes, we apply PIP-Net to an artificial test set where coloured patches are pasted into *malignant* images, using the same dataset as [28]. Table 3 shows that the accuracy for these malignant images (specificity) drops from 67% to only 9% when the coloured patch is inserted, confirming that the patch shortcut is indeed exploited. When used in clinical practice, a patient with a malignant lesion could then be misdiagnosed purely because of the presence of a coloured patch. Concluding, these findings motivate the usage of interpretable models: only judging a model based on its predictive performance would not have revealed the shortcut learning.

We investigate whether the shortcut learning in PIP-Net can be corrected by setting the weights of all patch-related prototypes to zero. Disabling all patch-related prototypes reduces the global explanation size from 113 to 75 prototypes in total. The bottom row of Table 3 shows that this manual intervention is effective: the adapted PIP-Net reaches almost the same accuracy on the adapted malignant patches compared to their original, non-adapted counterparts. Additionally, the accuracy of benign images with patches is barely changed. Disabling the patch-related prototypes reduces their local explanation size from 13.6 to 2.6 prototypes, but PIP-Net still finds sufficient evidence to classify the benign images correctly. This is supported by the visualised prototypes in Fig. 9 (centre and right) which indicate that PIP-Net also learned other class-relevant prototypes. In addition to these *global* explanations, Fig. 10 shows two *local* explanations for a test image from both the original and adapted model.

6.2   HIP Dataset

Based on visual inspection of the learned prototypes for the HIP dataset, we found that 20 of the 42 prototypes that were relevant to the *fracture* class, were only activated on a specific image view, as shown in Fig. 11 (left). These views are only taken in the emergency room for immobile patients, and are not part of standard X-ray examinations performed in the outpatient clinic. As immobility

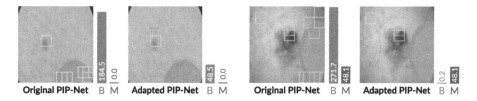

Fig. 10. ISIC Local explanations indicating where prototypes were found, shown for both the original PIP-Net and its adapted version where patch-prototypes are disabled. Left: benign image with patch, right: malignant image with inserted patch.

is highly correlated with the presence of a hip fracture, it is likely that any deep learning method will use this correlation as a shortcut. We follow a similar approach as for the ISIC dataset, and disable all prototypes that are related to this particular view. Whereas the adapted PIP-Net still found sufficient evidence for correct classifications in the ISIC dataset, it outputs zero scores for roughly half of the images with that specific view, as shown in Fig. 11 (left). These results indicate that PIP-Net had indeed learned a shortcut, as it was basing its decision for some of these images solely on that particular type of view. Once this shortcut information is suppressed, the output scores will be zero and the model will abstain from a decision. Adapting the model after suppressing shortcut information opens interesting opportunities for future research, such as partial retraining with constraints or integrating human-in-the-loop feedback.

Fig. 11. HIP Shortcut learning by PIP-Net for predicting *fracture*. Left: Shortcut prototype that detects a particular view that is only made for immobile patients in the emergency room. In some images, the edge of the bed is still visible. Center: The adapted model does not find evidence anymore for the *fracture* class. Right: output-score for the *fracture* class decreases to zero after suppressing shortcut prototypes.

7 Conclusion

We demonstrated the wide applicability of PIP-Net by successfully employing it for real-world binary medical image classification. We see a controlling role for PIP-Net in the medical domain to support human decision making by providing another pair of eyes, underpinned by explanations. Mawatari et al. [22] already showed that the diagnostic performance of radiologists for detecting hip fractures in X-ray images improves when they are additionally provided with the prediction of a trained neural network. Rather than only showing predictions, PIP-Net can also show its reasoning based on interpretable prototypical parts. Visual analysis showed that image patches corresponding to a learned prototype are coherent and semantically meaningful. We also found that prototypes focus on specific areas that are relevant according to medical classification standards.

Additionally, PIP-Net can reveal hidden biases and shortcuts in the data that may cause unintended behaviour. The interpretable design of PIP-Net can support the user in quickly identifying these data quality problems. Lastly, we explored whether shortcut learning can be suppressed by directly adapting the reasoning of the model and have shown that disabling prototypes can be an effective way of repairing the reasoning of PIP-Net. This capability empowers users not only to uncover improper reasoning, but to take immediate action for correcting it. In contrast, commonly applied black-box models require model adaptations with unclear outcome and costly retraining cycles.

8   Future Work

Future research could explore whether retraining the last classification layer *after* disabling the prototypes could improve predictive performance further. We identify this as a promising research opportunity given that the last layer of a standard, uninterpretable neural network can be successfully retrained with only a small subset of the data where the spurious correlation is not present [16].

Rather than only disabling undesired prototypes *after* fully training the model, we see an interesting research opportunity to have a human *in* the loop who identifies and disables undesired prototypes in an earlier stage, such that the model can adapt itself immediately. It might be even more effective when users can also *add* desired prototypes. When provided with a manual hint, PIP-Net could then automatically refine the prototype in the subsequent learning process. This would allow, for example, to already start with a set of prototypes based on established medical standards. Such an approach would enable a bidirectional feedback loop: an ML model learns prototypes and could start to augment existing medical standards, while medical experts can additionally suggest extra prototypes to the model and disable undesired prototypes. An immediate step towards augmenting existing medical standards could be the detailed inspection of the prototypes found in Sect. 5 and whether they indeed contain yet unknown discriminative features. This work is therefore a step towards hybrid AI [2], where artificial intelligence complements human intelligence.

References

1. Adadi, A., Berrada, M.: Peeking inside the black-box: a survey on explainable artificial intelligence (xai). IEEE Access **6**, 52138–52160 (2018)
2. Akata, Z., et al.: A research agenda for hybrid intelligence: Augmenting human intellect with collaborative, adaptive, responsible, and explainable artificial intelligence. Computer **53**(8), 18–28 (2020). https://doi.org/10.1109/MC.2020.2996587
3. Anders, C.J., Weber, L., Neumann, D., Samek, W., Müller, K.R., Lapuschkin, S.: Finding and removing clever hans: Using explanation methods to debug and improve deep models. Inform. Fusion **77**, 261–295 (2022). https://doi.org/10.1016/j.inffus.2021.07.015, https://www.sciencedirect.com/science/article/pii/S1566253521001573
4. Badgeley, M.A., et al.: Deep learning predicts hip fracture using confounding patient and healthcare variables. npj Digital Med. **2**(1), 1–10 (Apr 2019). https://doi.org/10.1038/s41746-019-0105-1, https://www.nature.com/articles/s41746-019-0105-1
5. Barnett, A.J., et al.: A case-based interpretable deep learning model for classification of mass lesions in digital mammography. Nature Mach. Intell. **3**(12), 1061–1070 (2021)
6. Biederman, I.: Recognition-by-components: a theory of human image understanding. Psychol. Rev. **94**(2), 115 (1987)
7. Borys, K., Schmitt, Y.A., Nauta, M., Seifert, C., Krämer, N., Friedrich, C.M., Nensa, F.: Explainable ai in medical imaging: An overview for clinical practitioners - saliency-based xai approaches. Europ. J. Radiol. **162**, 110787 (2023). https://doi.org/10.1016/j.ejrad.2023.110787, https://www.sciencedirect.com/science/article/pii/S0720048X23001018
8. Chen, C., Li, O., Tao, D., Barnett, A., Rudin, C., Su, J.: This looks like that: Deep learning for interpretable image recognition. In: NeurIPS (2019). https://proceedings.neurips.cc/paper/2019/hash/adf7ee2dcf142b0e11888e72b43fcb75-Abstract.html
9. Codella, N., et al.: Skin lesion analysis toward melanoma detection 2018: a challenge hosted by the international skin imaging collaboration (ISIC). arXiv:1902.03368 [cs] (2019). http://arxiv.org/abs/1902.03368
10. Colin, J., Fel, T., Cadene, R., Serre, T.: What i cannot predict, i do not understand: a human-centered evaluation framework for explainability methods. In: Advances in Neural Information Processing Systems (Oct 2022)
11. DeGrave, A.J., Janizek, J.D., Lee, S.I.: Ai for radiographic covid-19 detection selects shortcuts over signal. Nature Machi. Intell. **3**(7), 610–619 (2021)
12. Geirhos, R., et al.: Shortcut learning in deep neural networks. Nature Mach. Intell. **2**(11), 665–673 (2020)
13. Han, S.M., et al.: Radiographic analysis of adult ankle fractures using combined danis-weber and lauge-hansen classification systems. Sci. Rep. **10**(1), 7655 (2020)
14. Jin, W., Li, X., Hamarneh, G.: Evaluating explainable AI on a multi-modal medical imaging task: can existing algorithms fulfill clinical requirements? Proc. AAAI Conf. Artif. Intell.**36**(11), 11945–11953 (Jun 2022). https://doi.org/10.1609/aaai.v36i11.21452, https://ojs.aaai.org/index.php/AAAI/article/view/21452
15. Kahn, C.E., Carrino, J.A., Flynn, M.J., Peck, D.J., Horii, S.C.: Dicom and radiology: past, present, and future. J. Am. Coll. Radiol. **4**(9), 652–657 (2007)
16. Kirichenko, P., Izmailov, P., Wilson, A.G.: Last layer re-training is sufficient for robustness to spurious correlations. arXiv preprint arXiv:2204.02937 (2022)

17. Langerhuizen, D.W.G., et al.: What are the applications and limitations of artificial intelligence for fracture detection and classification in orthopaedic trauma imaging? a systematic review. Clin. Orthopaedics Related Res. Ⓡ477(11), 2482 (Nov 2019). https://doi.org/10.1097/CORR.0000000000000848

18. Lapuschkin, S., Wäldchen, S., Binder, A., Montavon, G., Samek, W., Müller, K.R.: Unmasking clever hans predictors and assessing what machines really learn. Nature Commun. **10**(1), 1096 (2019). https://doi.org/10.1038/s41467-019-08987-4, https://www.nature.com/articles/s41467-019-08987-4, number: 1 Publisher: Nature Publishing Group

19. Lau, B.C., Allahabadi, S., Palanca, A., Oji, D.E.: Understanding radiographic measurements used in foot and ankle surgery. J. Am. Acad. Orthop. Surg. **30**(2), e139–e154 (2022). https://doi.org/10.5435/JAAOS-D-20-00189

20. Liu, X., et al.: A comparison of deep learning performance against healthcare professionals in detecting diseases from medical imaging: a systematic review and meta-analysis. The Lancet Digital Health **1**(6), e271–e297 (Oct 2019). https://doi.org/10.1016/S2589-7500(19)30123-2, http://www.sciencedirect.com/science/article/pii/S2589750019301232

21. Liu, Z., Mao, H., Wu, C.Y., Feichtenhofer, C., Darrell, T., Xie, S.: A convnet for the 2020s. In: Proceedings of the IEEE/CVF Conference on Computer Vision and Pattern Recognition (CVPR), pp. 11976–11986 (June 2022)

22. Mawatari, T., et al.: The effect of deep convolutional neural networks on radiologists' performance in the detection of hip fractures on digital pelvic radiographs. European J. Radiol. **130**, 109188 (2020). https://doi.org/10.1016/j.ejrad.2020.109188, https://www.sciencedirect.com/science/article/pii/S0720048X20303776

23. Mishra, N.K., Celebi, M.E.: An overview of melanoma detection in dermoscopy images using image processing and machine learning. arXiv preprint arXiv:1601.07843 (2016)

24. Mohammadjafari, S., Cevik, M., Thanabalasingam, M., Basar, A.: Using protopnet for interpretable alzheimer's disease classification. In: Canadian Conference on AI (2021)

25. Müller, S.G., Hutter, F.: Trivialaugment: Tuning-free yet state-of-the-art data augmentation. In: Proceedings of the IEEE/CVF International Conference on Computer Vision (ICCV), pp. 774–782 (October 2021)

26. Nauta, M., van Bree, R., Seifert, C.: Neural prototype trees for interpretable fine-grained image recognition. In: 2021 IEEE/CVF Conference on Computer Vision and Pattern Recognition (CVPR), pp. 14928–14938 (2021). https://doi.org/10.1109/CVPR46437.2021.01469

27. Nauta, M., Schlötterer, J., van Keulen, M., Seifert, C.: Pip-net: patch-based intuitive prototypes for interpretable image classification. In: Proceedings of the IEEE/CVF Conference on Computer Vision and Pattern Recognition (CVPR) (June 2023)

28. Nauta, M., Walsh, R., Dubowski, A., Seifert, C.: Uncovering and correcting shortcut learning in machine learning models for skin cancer diagnosis. Diagnostics 12(1) (2022). DOI: 10.3390/diagnostics12010040, https://www.mdpi.com/2075-4418/12/1/40

29. Pahde, F., Dreyer, M., Samek, W., Lapuschkin, S.: Reveal to revise: An explainable AI life cycle for iterative bias correction of deep models (2023)

30. Rajpurkar, P., et al.: Mura: large dataset for abnormality detection in musculoskeletal radiographs. arXiv preprint arXiv:1712.06957 (2017)

31. Rieger, L., Singh, C., Murdoch, W.J., Yu, B.: Interpretations are useful: Penalizing explanations to align neural networks with prior knowledge. In: Proceedings of the 37th International Conference on Machine Learning, ICML 2020, 13–18 July 2020, Virtual Event. Proceedings of Machine Learning Research, vol. 119, pp. 8116–8126. PMLR (2020). http://proceedings.mlr.press/v119/rieger20a.html

32. Ross, A.S., Hughes, M.C., Doshi-Velez, F.: Right for the right reasons: training differentiable models by constraining their explanations. In: IJCAI (2017). https://doi.org/10.24963/ijcai.2017/371, https://doi.org/10.24963/ijcai.2017/371

33. Rudin, C.: Stop explaining black box machine learning models for high stakes decisions and use interpretable models instead. Nature Mach. Intell. 1(5), 206–215 (2019)

34. Rymarczyk, D., Pardyl, A., Kraus, J., Kaczyńska, A., Skomorowski, M., Zieliński, B.: Protomil: multiple instance learning with prototypical parts for whole-slide image classification. In: Amini, M.R., Canu, S., Fischer, A., Guns, T., Kralj Novak, P., Tsoumakas, G. (eds.) Machine Learning and Knowledge Discovery in Databases, pp. 421–436. Springer International Publishing, Cham (2023)

35. Rymarczyk, D., Struski, Ł., Górszczak, M., Lewandowska, K., Tabor, J., Zieliński, B.: Interpretable image classification with differentiable prototypes assignment. In: Computer Vision - ECCV 2022. pp. 351–368. Springer Nature Switzerland, Cham (2022)

36. Salahuddin, Z., Woodruff, H.C., Chatterjee, A., Lambin, P.: Transparency of deep neural networks for medical image analysis: a review of interpretability methods. Comput. Biol. Med. 140, 105111 (2022). https://doi.org/10.1016/j.compbiomed.2021.105111, https://www.sciencedirect.com/science/article/pii/S0010482521009057

37. Shen, H., Huang, T.H.: How useful are the machine-generated interpretations to general users? a human evaluation on guessing the incorrectly predicted labels. Proc. AAAI Conf. Human Comput. Crowdsourc. 8(1), 168–172 (Oct 2020). https://doi.org/10.1609/hcomp.v8i1.7477, https://ojs.aaai.org/index.php/HCOMP/article/view/7477

38. Singh, G., Yow, K.C.: An interpretable deep learning model for Covid-19 detection with chest x-ray images. IEEE Access 9, 85198–85208 (2021). https://doi.org/10.1109/ACCESS.2021.3087583

39. Tajbakhsh, N., Shin, J.Y., Gurudu, S.R., Hurst, R.T., Kendall, C.B., Gotway, M.B., Liang, J.: Convolutional neural networks for medical image analysis: full training or fine tuning? IEEE Trans. Med. Imaging 35(5), 1299–1312 (2016). https://doi.org/10.1109/TMI.2016.2535302

40. Teso, S., Kersting, K.: Explanatory interactive machine learning. In: Proceedings of the 2019 AAAI/ACM Conference on AI, Ethics, and Society, pp. 239–245. AIES '19, Association for Computing Machinery, New York, NY, USA (2019). https://doi.org/10.1145/3306618.3314293, https://doi.org/10.1145/3306618.3314293

41. Yufit, P., Seligson, D.: Malleolar ankle fractures. a guide to evaluation and treatment. Orthopaedics Trauma 24(4), 286–297 (2010). https://doi.org/10.1016/j.mporth.2010.03.010, https://www.sciencedirect.com/science/article/pii/S1877132710000357

Causal Entropy and Information Gain for Measuring Causal Control

Francisco Nunes Ferreira Quialheiro Simoes[(✉)] [ID], Mehdi Dastani [ID], and Thijs van Ommen [ID]

Department of Information and Computing Sciences, Utrecht University, Utrecht, Netherlands
{f.simoes,m.m.dastani,t.vanommen}@uu.nl

Abstract. Artificial intelligence models and methods commonly lack causal interpretability. Despite the advancements in interpretable machine learning (IML) methods, they frequently assign importance to features which lack causal influence on the outcome variable. Selecting causally relevant features among those identified as relevant by these methods, or even before model training, would offer a solution. Feature selection methods utilizing information theoretical quantities have been successful in identifying statistically relevant features. However, the information theoretical quantities they are based on do not incorporate causality, rendering them unsuitable for such scenarios. To address this challenge, this article proposes information theoretical quantities that incorporate the causal structure of the system, which can be used to evaluate causal importance of features for some given outcome variable. Specifically, we introduce causal versions of entropy and mutual information, termed causal entropy and causal information gain, which are designed to assess how much control a feature provides over the outcome variable. These newly defined quantities capture changes in the entropy of a variable resulting from interventions on other variables. Fundamental results connecting these quantities to the existence of causal effects are derived. The use of causal information gain in feature selection is demonstrated, highlighting its superiority over standard mutual information in revealing which features provide control over a chosen outcome variable. Our investigation paves the way for the development of methods with improved interpretability in domains involving causation.

Keywords: Causal Inference · Information Theory · Interpretable Machine Learning · Explainable Artificial Intelligence

1 Introduction

Causality plays an important role in enhancing not only the prediction power of a model [19] but also its interpretability [4]. Causal explanations are more appropriate for human understanding than purely statistical explanations [12]. Accordingly, comprehending the causal connections between the variables of a

S. Nowaczyk et al. (Eds.): ECAI 2023 Workshops, CCIS 1947, pp. 216–231, 2024.
https://doi.org/10.1007/978-3-031-50396-2_12

system can enhance the interpretability of interpretable machine learning (IML) methods themselves.

Interpretable models such as linear regression or decision trees do not, despite their name, always lend themselves to *causal* interpretations. To illustrate this point, consider running multilinear regression on the predictors X_1, X_2 and outcome Y within a system whose variables are causally related as depicted in the graph of Fig. 1. The regression coefficients β_1 and β_2 of X_1 and X_2 might yield large values, which may be (and are often in practice) interpreted as suggesting a causal relationship. However, a causal interpretation of β_1 would not be appropriate. Although X_1 might provide predictive power over Y, this does not imply a causal relationship, since this predictive power is due to the confounder W. Consequently, intervening on X_1 would not impact the outcome Y.

In current model-agnostic methods, a causal interpretation is often desirable but rarely possible. In partial dependence plots (PDPs) [6], the partial dependence of a model outcome $\hat{Y}$ on a variable X_i coincides with the backdoor criterion formula [15] when the conditioning set encompasses all the other covariates $X_{j \neq i}$ [24]. Consequently, there is a risk of disregarding statistical dependence or, conversely, finding spurious dependence, by conditioning on causal descendants of X_i [24]. Therefore, PDPs (along with the closely related individual conditional expectation (ICE) lines [7]) generally lack a causal interpretation. Similarly, when utilizing (Local Interpretable Model-Agnostic Explanations) LIME [18] to evaluate the importance of a feature for an individual, a causal interpretation cannot be guaranteed. LIME fits a local model around the point of interest and assesses which features, when perturbed, would cause the point to cross the decision boundary of the model. However, intervening on a feature in such a way as to cross the model's decision boundary does not guarantee an actual change in the outcome in reality. This is because the model was trained on observational data, and that feature may merely be correlated with the outcome through a confounding factor, for example, rather than having a causal effect on the outcome.

In both cases just described, it is the presence of confounders, selection bias, or an incorrect direction of causality seemingly implied by the model that can lead to misleading predictions and interpretations. We need a way to select which features are causally relevant — *i.e.* give us control over the chosen outcome variable. Information theoretical quantities such as mutual information are often used to assess the relevance of a feature with respect to a given outcome variable [2,20,25], but this relevance is still purely statistical. This is a common issue when using standard information theoretical quantities in situations that require consideration of the underlying causal relationships. A version of mutual information which takes into account the causal structure of the system would solve this problem. This is what we set out to develop in this work.

In our research, we extend traditional conditional entropy and mutual information to the realm of *interventions*, as opposed to simple conditioning. This extension drew inspiration from the conceptual and philosophical work presented in[1] [8]. We dub these constructs "causal entropy" and "causal information gain". They are designed to capture changes in the entropy of a given variable in response to manipulations affecting other variables. We derive fundamental results connecting these quantities to the presence of causal effect. We end by illustrating the use of causal information gain in selecting a variable which allows us to control an outcome variable, and contrast it with standard mutual information.

The novelty of our work consists of providing rigorous definitions for causal entropy and causal information gain, as well as deriving some of their key properties for the first time. These contributions set the foundations for the development of methods which correctly identify features which provide causal control over an outcome variable.

This paper is organized as follows. In Sect. 2, we introduce the definitions of quantities from the fields of causal inference and information theory that will be used throughout the rest of the paper. Section 3 includes a simple example of a structural causal model where standard entropy and mutual information are inadequate for obtaining the desired causal insights. In Sect. 4, we define causal entropy and explore its relation to total effect. Section 5 discusses the definition of causal information gain and investigates its connection with causal effect. Furthermore, it revisits the example from Sect. 3, showing that causal entropy and causal information gain allow us to arrive at the correct conclusions about causal control. In Sect. 6, we compare the definitions and results presented in this paper with those of previous work. Finally, in Sect. 7, we discuss the obtained results and propose future research directions.

2   Formal Setting

In this section we present the definitions from causal inference and information theory which are necessary for the rest of this paper. All random variables are henceforth assumed to be discrete and have finite range.

2.1   Structural Causal Models

One can model the causal structure of a system by means of a "structural causal model", which can be seen as a Bayesian network [10] whose graph G has a causal interpretation and each conditional probability distribution (CPD) $P(X_i \mid \mathrm{PA}_{X_i})$ of the Bayesian network stems from a deterministic function f_{X_i} (called "structural assignment") of the parents of X_i. In this context, it is common to separate the parent-less random variables (which are called "exogenous" or "noise" variables) from the rest (called "endogenous" variables). Only the endogenous variables are represented in the structural causal model graph. As is commonly done [16], we assume that the noise variables are jointly independent and that exactly one noise variable N_{X_i} appears as an argument in the structural assignment f_{X_i} of X_i. In full rigor[2] [16]:

---

[1] The reader is referred to Sect. 6 for a detailed discussion about this.

[2] We slightly rephrase the definition provided in [16] to enhance its clarity.

Definition 1 (Structural Causal Model). *Let X be a random variable with range R_X and $\mathbf{W}$ a random vector with range $R_\mathbf{W}$. A structural assignment for X from $\mathbf{W}$ is a function $f_X \colon R_\mathbf{W} \to R_X$. A structural causal model (SCM) $\mathcal{C} = (\mathbf{X}, \mathbf{N}, S, p_\mathbf{N})$ consists of:*

1. *A random vector $\mathbf{X} = (X_1, \dots, X_n)$ whose variables we call* endogenous.
2. *A random vector $\mathbf{N} = (N_{X_1}, \dots, N_{X_n})$ whose variables we call* exogenous *or* noise.
3. *A set S of n structural assignments f_{X_i} for X_i from (PA_{X_i}, N_{X_i}), where $PA_{X_i} \subseteq \mathbf{X}$ are called* parents *of X_i. The causal graph $G^\mathcal{C} := (\mathbf{X}, E)$ of $\mathcal{C}$ has as its edge set $E = \{(P, X_i) : X_i \in \mathbf{X}, \ P \in PA_{X_i}\}$. The PA_{X_i} must be such that the $G^\mathcal{C}$ is a directed acyclic graph (DAG).*
4. *A jointly independent probability distribution $p_\mathbf{N}$ over the noise variables. We call it simply the* noise distribution.

We denote by $\mathcal{C}(\mathbf{X})$ the set of SCMs with vector of endogenous variables $\mathbf{X}$. Furthermore, we write $X := f_X(X, N_X)$ to mean that $f_X(X, N_X)$ is a structural assignment for X.

Notice that for a given SCM the noise variables have a known distribution $p_\mathbf{N}$ and the endogenous variables can be written as functions of the noise variables. Therefore the distributions of the endogenous variables are themselves determined if one fixes the SCM. This brings us to the notion of the entailed distribution (See Footnote 2) [16]:

Definition 2 (Entailed distribution). *Let $\mathcal{C} = (\mathbf{X}, \mathbf{N}, S, p_\mathbf{N})$ be an SCM. Its* entailed distribution *$p^\mathcal{C}_\mathbf{X}$ is the unique joint distribution over $\mathbf{X}$ such that $\forall X_i \in \mathbf{X}, \ X_i = f_{X_i}(PA_{X_i}, N_{X_i})$. It is often simply denoted by $p^\mathcal{C}$. Let $\mathbf{x}_{-i} := (x_1, \dots, x_{i-1}, x_{i+1}, \dots, x_n)$. For a given $X_i \in \mathbf{X}$, the marginalized distribution $p^\mathcal{C}_{X_i}$ given by $p^\mathcal{C}_{X_i}(x_i) = \sum_{\mathbf{x}_{-i}} p^\mathcal{C}_\mathbf{X}(\mathbf{x})$ is also referred to as* entailed distribution *(of X_i).*

An SCM allows us to model interventions on the system. The idea is that an SCM represents how the values of the random variables are generated, and by intervening on a variable we are effectively changing its generating process. Thus intervening on a variable can be modeled by modifying the structural assignment of said variable, resulting in a new SCM differing from the original only in the structural assignment of the intervened variable, and possibly introducing a new noise variable for it, in place of the old one. Naturally, the new SCM will have an entailed distribution which is in general different from the distribution entailed by the original SCM.

The most common type of interventions are the so-called "atomic interventions", where one sets a variable to a chosen value, effectively replacing the distribution of the intervened variable with a point mass distribution. In particular, this means that the intervened variable has no parents after the intervention. This is the only type of intervention that we will need to consider in this work. Formally (See Footnote 2) [16]:

Definition 3 (Atomic intervention). *Let* $C = (\mathbf{X}, \mathbf{N}, S, p_{\mathbf{N}})$ *be an SCM,* $X_i \in \mathbf{X}$ *and* $x \in R_{X_i}$. *The atomic intervention* $do(X_i = x)$ *is the function* $C(\mathbf{X}) \rightarrow C(\mathbf{X})$ *given by* $C \mapsto C^{do(X_i=x)}$, *where* $C^{do(X_i=x)}$ *is the SCM that differs from* C *only in that the structural assignment* $f_{X_i}(PA_{X_i}, N_{X_i})$ *is replaced by the structural assignment* $\tilde{f}_{X_i}(\tilde{N}_{X_i}) = \tilde{N}_{X_i}$, *where* $\tilde{N}_{X_i}$ *is a random variable with range* R_{X_i} *and*[3] $p_{\tilde{N}_{X_i}}(x_i) = \mathbf{1}_x(x_i)$ *for all* $x_i \in R_{X_i}$. *Such SCM is called the* post-atomic-intervention SCM. *One says that the variable* X_i *was* (atomically) intervened on. *The distribution* $p^{do(X_i=x)} := p^{C^{do(X_i=x)}}$ *entailed by* $C^{do(X_i=x)}$ *is called the* post-intervention distribution *(w.r.t. the atomic intervention* $do(X_i = x)$ *on* C).

We can also define what we mean by "X having a total causal effect on Y". Following [14,16], there is such a total causal effect if there is an atomic intervention on X which modifies the initial distribution of Y (See footnote 2) [16]:

Definition 4 (Total Causal Effect). *Let* X, Y *be random variables of an SCM* C. X *has a* total causal effect *on* Y, *denoted by* $X \rightarrow Y$, *if there is* $x \in R_X$ *such that* $p_Y^{do(X=x)} \neq p_Y$.

In this work, all variables of the form X_i, Y_i or Z_i are taken to be endogenous variables of some SCM C.

2.2   Entropy and Mutual Information

Since the quantities defined and studied in this article build upon the standard entropy and mutual information, it is important for the reader to be familiar with these. In this subsection we will state the definitions of entropy, conditional entropy and mutual entropy. In the interest of space, we will not try to motivate these definitions. For a pedagogical introduction the reader is referred to [5,11]. We will also clarify what we precisely mean by causal control.

Definition 5 (Entropy and Conditional Entropy [5]). *Let* X *be a discrete random variable with range* R_X *and* p *be a probability distribution for* X. *The entropy of* X *w.r.t. the distribution* p *is*[4]

$$H_{X \sim p}(X) := - \sum_{x \in R_X} p(x) \log p(x). \tag{1}$$

Entropy is measured in bit. *If the context suggests a canonical probability distribution for* X, *one can write* $H(X)$ *and refers to it simply as the* entropy of X. *The* conditional entropy $H(Y \mid X)$ *of* Y *conditioned on* X *is the expected value w.r.t.* p_X *of the entropy* $H(Y \mid X = x) := H_{Y \sim p_{Y|X=x}}(Y)$:

$$H(Y \mid X) := \mathbb{E}_{x \sim p_X}\left[H(Y \mid X = x)\right]. \tag{2}$$

---

[3] We denote by $\mathbf{1}_x$ the indicator function of x, so that $\mathbf{1}_x(x_i) = \begin{cases} 1, & x_i = x \\ 0, & \text{otherwise} \end{cases}$.

[4] In this article, log denotes the logarithm to the base 2.

This means that the conditional entropy $H(Y \mid X)$ is the entropy of $H(Y)$ that remains on average if one conditions on X.

An essential concept closely associated with entropy is that of "uncertainty." This qualitative concept is often present when interpreting information-theoretical quantities. The entropy of a variable X purports to measure the uncertainty regarding X. In this paper, we use another qualitative concept called "causal control" (or simply "control"). The (causal) control that variable X has over variable Y is the level of uncertainty remaining about Y after intervening on X. It indicates how close we are to fully specifying Y by intervening on X. This understanding of the term "control" has been implicitly utilized in the philosophy of science literature [3,17].

Remark 1. Notice that $H(Y \mid X = x)$ is seen as a function of x and the expected value in Equation (2) is taken over the random variable x with distribution p_X. This disrespects the convention that random variables are represented by capital letters, but preserves the convention that the specific value conditioned upon (even if that value can be randomly realized — *i.e.* is a random variable) is represented by a lower case letter. Since we cannot respect both, we will follow the common practice and opt to use lower case letters for random variables in these cases.

There are two common equivalent ways to define mutual information (often called information gain).

Definition 6 (Mutual Information [5]). *Let X and Y be discrete random variables with ranges R_X and R_Y and distributions p_X and p_Y, respectively. The mutual information between X and Y is the KL divergence between the joint distribution $p_{X,Y}$ and the product distribution $p_X p_Y$, i.e.:*

$$I(X;Y) := \sum_{x,y \in R_X \times R_Y} p_{X,Y}(x,y) \log \frac{p_{X,Y}(x,y)}{p_X(x)p_Y(y)}. \tag{3}$$

Or equivalently:

$$I(X;Y) := H(Y) - H(Y \mid X) \tag{4}$$
$$= H(X) - H(X \mid Y).$$

The view of mutual information as entropy reduction from Equation (4) will be the starting point for our definition of causal information gain.

3 Running Example - Comparing Control over an Outcome

We provide a simple example showcasing how the standard entropy and mutual information can fail to assess which variable gives us more control over a chosen outcome variable. We will later (Sect. 5) check that using causal entropy and causal information gain enable us to correctly make this assessment.

Example 1. Let us consider an ice-cream shop where the sales volume Y on a given day can be categorized as low ($Y = 0$), medium ($Y = 1$), or high ($Y = 2$). We would like to find a way to control Y. Assume that the sales volume is influenced by two factors: the temperature W, characterized as warm ($W = 1$) or cold ($W = 0$), and whether the ice-cream shop is being advertised, represented by the binary variable X_2. Additionally, we introduce a discrete variable X_1 to represent the number of individuals wearing shorts, which can be categorized as few ($X_1 = 0$), some ($X_1 = 1$), or many ($X_1 = 2$). Naturally, higher temperatures have a positive influence on the variable X_1. We do not consider any other variables.

One can crudely model this situation using an SCM with endogenous variables X_1, X_2, W and Y, as specified in Fig. 1. The chosen structural assignments and noise distributions reflect the specific scenario where: the temperature W is warm about half of the time; the number X_1 of people wearing shorts is highly determined by the weather conditions; and the ice-cream shop is advertised occasionally. W, X_2 and all noise variables of the SCM are binary variables, while $X_1, Y \in \{0, 1, 2\}$. Assume we cannot intervene on W. We would like to decide which of the variables X_1 or X_2 provide us with the most control over Y. It is clear that being able to intervene on X_1 gives us no control whatsoever over Y. Any observed statistical dependence between X_1 and Y comes purely from the confounder W. Consequently, interpreting a non-zero correlation or mutual information between X_1 and Y as indicative of a causal connection between these variables would be a mistake, and an instance of conflation between correlation and causation.

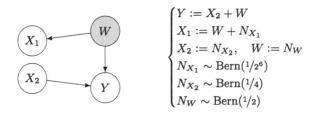

$$\begin{cases} Y := X_2 + W \\ X_1 := W + N_{X_1} \\ X_2 := N_{X_2}, \quad W := N_W \\ N_{X_1} \sim \mathrm{Bern}(1/2^6) \\ N_{X_2} \sim \mathrm{Bern}(1/4) \\ N_W \sim \mathrm{Bern}(1/2) \end{cases}$$

Fig. 1. An SCM[3]. It models the real-world scenario described in Example 1, where Y is the sales volume of an ice-cream shop, W is the temperature, X_1 is the amount of people wearing shorts, and X_2 stands for the advertisement efforts of the ice-cream shop. The notation $N_Z \sim \mathrm{Bern}(q)$ signifies that the random variable Z follows the Bernoulli probability distribution with parameter q. Grayed out variables cannot be intervened on. [3](The careful reader may notice that there is no noise variable N_Y for Y, which seems to conflict with Definition 1. Such apparent conflicts are resolved by seeing a deterministic assignment function such as $Y := X_2 + W$ as having a trivial additive dependence on a noise variable N_Y with a point mass distribution at 0.)

If we naively use the mutual information to assess whether one should intervene on X_1 or X_2 for controlling Y, one wrongly concludes that one should use

X_1. Intuitively, this happens because knowing X_2 provides us with less information about Y than W, and X_1 is very close to W. The (approximate) values can be consulted[5] in Table 1.

Table 1. Information theoretical values for Fig. 1.

$H(Y) \approx 1.41$	$H(Y \mid X_1) \approx 0.85$	$H(Y \mid X_2) = 1$
$I(Y;W) \approx 0.60$	$I(Y;X_1) \approx 0.56$	$I(Y;X_2) \approx 0.41$

Notice that $I(Y;W) > I(Y;X_1)$, as it should be: W has more information about Y than X_1 has. We also see that $I(Y;X_2) < I(Y;X_1)$. If mutual information were a suitable criterion for selecting the variable to intervene on, the contrary would be expected. In the context of our real-world scenario, intervening on the number X_1 of people wearing shorts would not be a logical approach for controlling ice cream sales. Instead, allocating more resources to advertising efforts (represented by X_2) would be more appropriate.

The issue is that the mutual information $I(Y;X_1)$ includes the information that one has about Y by *observing* X_1 which flows through the confounder W. But what we want is a metric quantifying how much control we can have over Y by *intervening* on X_1. We will see that the generalization of mutual information studied in this paper ("causal information gain") satisfies these requirements.

4   Causal Entropy

The causal entropy of Y for X will be the entropy of Y that is left, on average, after one atomically intervenes on X. In this section we give a rigorous definition of causal entropy and study its connection to causal effect.

We define causal entropy in a manner analogous to conditional entropy (see Definition 5). It will be the average uncertainty one has about Y if one sets X to x with probability $p_{X'}(x)$, where X' is a new auxiliary variable with the same range as X but independent of all other variables, including X. In contrast with the non-causal case, here one needs to make a choice of distribution over X' corresponding to the distribution over the atomic interventions that one is intending to perform.

Definition 7 (Causal entropy, H_c). *Let Y, X and X' be random variables such that X and X' have the same range and X' is independent of all variables in C. We say that X' is an* intervention protocol *for X.*

The causal entropy $H_c(Y \mid do(X \sim X'))$ *of Y given the intervention protocol X' for X is the expected value w.r.t. $p_{X'}$ of the entropy $H(Y \mid do(X = x)) :=$ $H_{Y \sim p_Y^{do(X=x)}}(Y)$ of the interventional distribution $p_Y^{do(X=x)}$. That is:*

$$H_c(Y \mid do(X \sim X')) := \mathbb{E}_{x \sim p_{X'}} [H(Y \mid do(X = x))] \tag{5}$$

---

[5] The details of the computations can be found in Appendix A.

We will now see that, unsurprisingly, if there is no total effect of X on Y, then the causal entropy is just the initial entropy $H(Y)$. Perhaps more unexpectedly, the converse is not true: it is possible to have $H_c(Y \mid X \sim X') = H(Y)$ while $X \rightarrow Y$. One way this can happen is due to the non-injectivity of entropy when seen as a mapping from the set of distributions over Y, *i.e.* it may happen that $p_Y^{do(X=x)} \neq p_Y$ but $H_{Y \sim p_Y^{do(X=x)}}(Y) = H_{Y \sim p_Y}(Y)$.

Proposition 1. *If there is no total effect of X on Y, then $H_c(Y \mid do(X \sim X')) = H(Y)$ for any intervention protocol X' for X. The converse does not hold.*

Proof. The proof can be found in Appendix B.   □

If there is a total causal effect of X on Y, there cannot be a total causal effect of Y on X (if X is a cause of Y, Y cannot be a cause of X) [16]. This immediately yields the following corollary.

Corollary 1. *If $H_c(Y \mid do(X \sim X')) \neq H(Y)$ for some intervention protocol X' for X, then $H_c(X \mid do(Y \sim Y')) = H(X)$ for any intervention protocol Y' for Y.*

Proof. Suppose that $H_c(Y \mid X \sim X') \neq H(Y)$. By the contrapositive of Proposition 1, this means that there is a total effect of X on Y. Hence there is no total effect of Y on X, which again by Proposition 1 yields the desired result.   □

5   Causal Information Gain

Causal information gain extends mutual information to the causal context. The causal information gain of Y for X will be the average decrease in the entropy of Y after one atomically intervenes on X. We start this section by giving a rigorous definition of causal information gain, and proceed to study its connection with causal effect. We end this section by revisiting Example 1 armed with this new information theoretical quantity. We will confirm in this example that causal information is the correct tool for assessing which variable has the most causal control over the outcome, as opposed to standard mutual information.

Recall the entropy-based definition of mutual information in Equation (4). The mutual information between two variables X and Y is the average reduction in uncertainty about Y if one observes the value of X (and vice-versa, by symmetry of the mutual information). This view of mutual information allows for a straightforward analogous definition in the causal case, so that one can take causal information gain $I_c(Y \mid do(X \sim X'))$ to signify the average reduction in uncertainty about Y if one sets X to x with probability $p_{X'}(x)$.

Definition 8 (Causal Information Gain, I_c). *Let Y, X and X' be random variables such that X' is an intervention protocol for X. The causal information gain $I_c(Y \mid do(X \sim X'))$ of Y for X given the intervention protocol X' is the* *difference between the entropy of Y w.r.t. its prior and the causal entropy of Y given the intervention protocol X'. That is:*

$$I_c(Y \mid do(X \sim X')) := H(Y) - H_c(Y \mid do(X \sim X')). \qquad (6)$$

A few properties of causal information gain can be immediately gleaned from its definition. First, in contrast with mutual information, causal information gain is *not* symmetric. Also, similarly to causal entropy, one needs to specify an intervention protocol with a distribution to be followed by interventions on X.

We can make use of the relation between causal entropy and causal effect to straightforwardly deduce the relation between causal information gain and causal effect.

Proposition 2. *If $I_c(Y \mid do(X \sim X')) \neq 0$ for some protocol X' for X, then $X \rightarrow Y$. The converse does not hold.*

Proof. The implication in this proposition follows directly from Definition 8 and the contrapositive of the implication in Proposition 1. The converse does not hold simply because it is equivalent to the converse of the contrapositive of the implication in Proposition 1, which also does not hold. □

Corollary 2. *Let X' and Y' be intervention protocols for X and Y, respectively. At least one of $I_c(Y \mid do(X \sim X'))$ or $I_c(X \mid do(Y \sim Y'))$ is zero.*

Proof. Suppose both $I_c(Y \mid do(X \sim X'))$ and $I_c(X \mid do(Y \sim Y'))$ are non-zero. Then by Corollary 2 we have both $X \rightarrow Y$ and $Y \rightarrow X$, which is not possible in the context of an SCM. □

It is worth noting that the last part of Corollary 2 contradicts [17]. In that work, it is stated without proof that "causation is equivalent to non-zero specificity", wherein the term "specificity" coincides with what we refer to as causal information gain given a uniformly distributed intervention protocol.

5.1 Comparison of Causal Information Gain and Mutual Information in Running Example

Consider again Example 1. Compare the causal entropy and causal information gain values[6] in Table 2 with the conditional entropy and mutual information values from Table 1.

We see that using causal information gain allows us to correctly conclude that using X_1 to control Y would be fruitless: intervening on X_1 does not change the entropy of Y. This is reflected by the fact that the causal information gain of Y for X_1 is zero. Since X_1 has no causal effect on Y, this result was to be expected by the contrapositive of Corollary 2. On the other hand, X_2 does

---

[6] In this particular case it does not matter what intervention protocol X' we choose, since $H_c(Y \mid do(X_1 = x_1)) = H(Y) \approx 1.41$ for all x_1 and $H_c(Y \mid do(X_2 = x_2)) = 1$ for all x_2.

Table 2. Causal information theoretical values for Fig. 1.

$H_c(Y \mid do(X_1 \sim X_1')) \approx 1.41$	$H_c(Y \mid do(X_2 \sim X_2')) = 1$
$I_c(Y \mid do(X_1 \sim X_1')) = 0$	$I_c(Y \mid do(X_2 \sim X_2')) \approx 0.41$

provide us with some control over Y: intervening on X_2 decreases the entropy of Y by 0.4 bit on average. In the real-world scenario described in Example 1, utilizing causal information gain to determine which variable to intervene on for controlling the sales volume Y would lead us to make the correct decision of intensifying advertising efforts (X_2). Furthermore, it would enable us to conclude that manipulating the number of people wearing shorts (X_1) provides no control whatsoever over Y. Thus, causal information gain could be used in this case to assess whether statistical dependence between Y and another variable in this causal system can be interpreted to have causal significance.

6 Related Work

Previous work has aimed to provide causal explanations of machine learning models through "counterfactual explanations" [13,21]. These explanations reveal what the model would have predicted under different feature values. However, they do not offer insights into the causal significance of a feature in influencing the outcome variable. Instead, they merely inform us about the behavior of the model itself. In other words, counterfactual explanations inform us about the changes required for the model to produce a different prediction, but not the changes necessary for the outcome to differ in reality. While counterfactual explanations can be useful, for instance, in advising loan applicants on improving their chances of approval [13], they fall short in providing causal interpretations for tasks such as scientific exploration [23], where it is crucial to understand the actual causal relationships between features and the chosen outcome. As discussed in Sect. 1, the quantities investigated in this paper can precisely address this need.

Information theoretical quantities aimed at capturing aspects of causality have been previously proposed. An important example is the work in [9]. In that paper, the authors suggest a list of postulates that a measure of causal strength should satisfy, and subsequently demonstrate that commonly used measures fall short of meeting them. They then propose their own measure (called "causal influence"), which does satisfy the postulates. Causal influence is the KL divergence of the original joint distribution and the joint distribution resulting from removing the arrows whose strength we would like to measure, and feeding noise to the orphaned nodes. Thus although it utilizes information theory, it does not purport to generalize entropy or mutual information to the causal context. One information-theoretical measure mentioned in [9] is closer to ours. It is called "information flow" [1]. Similarly to causal information gain, this quantity is a causal generalization of mutual information. Their goal was to come up with a generalization of mutual information that would be a measure of "causal independence" in much the same way as standard mutual information is a measure of statistical independence. They take the route of starting from the definition of mutual information as the KL divergence between the joint distribution and the product of the marginal distributions (Equation (3)), and proceed to "make it causal" by effectively replacing conditioning with intervening everywhere. In contrast, we treat entropy as the main quantity of interest, and start from the definition of mutual entropy as the change in entropy due to conditioning (Equation (4)), and proceed to define its causal counterpart as the change in entropy due to intervening. This then results in a quantity that is the appropriate tool for evaluating the control that a variable has over another.

The basic idea of extending the concept of mutual information to the causal context as the average reduction of entropy after intervening was introduced in the philosophy of science literature, as part of an attempt to capture a property of causal relations which they refer to as "specificity" [8]. This property can be thought of as a measure of the degree to which interventions on the cause variable result in a deterministic one-to-one mapping [22]. This means that maximal specificity of a causal relationship is attained when: (a) performing an atomic intervention on the cause variable results in complete certainty about the effect variable's value; and (b) no two distinct atomic interventions on the cause variable result in the same value for the effect variable [8]. Notice that (a) means precisely that the cause variable provides maximal causal control over the effect variable. The causal extension of mutual information proposed in [8] was named "causal mutual information". They call "causal entropy" the average entropy of the effect variable after performing an atomic intervention on the cause variable. Their "causal mutual information" is then the difference between the initial entropy of the effect variable and the causal entropy. Although they do not say so explicitly, their definition of causal entropy assumes that one only cares about the entropy that results from interventions that are equally likely: the average of post-intervention entropies is taken w.r.t. a uniform distribution — hence their "causal entropy" is the same as the causal entropy defined in this paper, but restricted to uniform intervention protocols. This was also noted in [17], where the authors propose that other choices of distribution over the interventions would result in quantities capturing causal aspects that are distinct from the standard specificity. In this paper we both generalized and formalized the information theoretical notions introduced in [8]. We provided rigorous definitions of causal entropy and causal information gain which allow for the use of non-uniform distributions over the interventions. Our causal entropy can thus be seen as a generalized version of their causal entropy, while our causal information gain can be seen as a generalization of their causal mutual information[7]. Armed

---

[7] The term causal mutual information may be misleading given the directional nature of the relationship between cause and effect. We thus prefer the term causal information gain, drawing inspiration from the alternate name "information gain", which is frequently employed in discussions about decision trees when referring to mutual information.

with concrete, mathematical definitions, we are able to study key mathematical aspects of these quantities.

7 Discussion and Conclusion

The motivation behind extending traditional entropy and mutual information to interventional settings in the context of interpretable machine learning (IML) arises from the necessity to determine whether the high importance assigned to specific features by machine learning models and IML methods can be causally interpreted or is purely of a statistical nature.

Information theoretical quantities are commonly used to assess statistical feature importance. We extended these quantities to handle interventions, allowing them to capture the control one has over a variable by manipulating another. The proposed measures, namely causal entropy and causal information gain, hold promise for the development of new algorithms in domains where knowledge of causal relationships is available or obtainable. It is worth noting that the utility of these measures extends well beyond the field of IML, as both information-theoretical quantities and the need for causal control are pervasive in machine learning.

Moving forward, a crucial theoretical endeavor involves establishing a fundamental set of properties for the proposed causal information-theoretical measures. This can include investigating a data processing inequality and a chain rule for causal information gain, drawing inspiration from analogous properties associated with mutual information. Other important research directions involve the extension of these definitions to continuous variables, as well as investigating the implications of employing different intervention protocols. Furthermore, the design and study of appropriate estimators for these measures constitute important avenues for future research, as well as their practical implementation. Ideally, these estimators should be efficient to compute even when dealing with high-dimensional data and complex, real-world datasets. Additionally, they ought to be applicable to observational data. In cases where the structural causal model is known, this could be accomplished by utilizing a framework such as *do*-calculus [14] when devising the estimators. This could allow for their application in extracting causal insights from observational data.

A Computations for the Running Example

We have

$$H(Y) = p_Y(0)\log(\frac{1}{p_Y(0)}) + p_Y(1)\log(\frac{1}{p_Y(1)}) + p_Y(2)\log(\frac{1}{p_Y(2)})$$

$$= \frac{3}{8}\log(\frac{8}{3}) + \frac{1}{2}\log(2) + \frac{1}{8}\log(8) = 2 - \frac{3}{8}\log(3) \approx 1.41\,(\text{bit}),$$

and

$$H(Y \mid W) = H(Y \mid W = 0) = \frac{3}{4}\log(\frac{4}{3}) + \frac{1}{4}\log(4) \approx 0.81 \,(\text{bit}),$$

where we used that $H(Y \mid W = 0) = H(Y \mid W = 1)$, so that taking the average is unnecessary.

Notice that $X_1 = 0$ implies $W = 0$, in which case $Y = X_2$. Hence $H(Y \mid X_1 = 0) = H(Y \mid W = 0) \approx 0.81 \,(\text{bit})$. By a similar argument, $H(Y \mid X_1 = 2) = H(Y \mid W = 1) \approx 0.81 \,(\text{bit})$. Now, denote $q = \frac{1}{64}$. It is easy to check that $p_{Y|X_1=1}(0) = \frac{3q}{4}$, $p_{Y|X_1=1}(1) = \frac{3}{4} - \frac{q}{2}$ and $p_{Y|X_1=1}(2) = \frac{1}{4}(1 - q)$. Then

$$H(Y \mid X_1 = 1) = -\frac{3q}{4}\log(\frac{3q}{4}) - (\frac{3}{4} - \frac{q}{2})\log(\frac{3}{4} - \frac{q}{2}) - \frac{1}{4}(1-q)\log(\frac{1}{4}(1-q)) \approx 0.89 \,(\text{bit}).$$

We can then compute:

$$H(Y \mid X_1) = p_{X_1}(0)\overbrace{H(Y \mid X_1 = 0)}^{0.81} + p_{X_1}(1)\overbrace{H(Y \mid X_1 = 1)}^{0.89} + p_{X_1}(1)\overbrace{H(Y \mid X_1 = 2)}^{0.81}$$
$$= \frac{1}{2} \times (1 - q) \times 0.81 + \frac{1}{2} \times 0.89 + \frac{q}{2} \times 0.81 \approx 0.85 \,(\text{bit}).$$

We also have:

$$H(Y \mid X_2) = p_{X_2}(0)\overbrace{H(Y \mid X_2 = 0)}^{1} + p_{X_2}(1)\overbrace{H(Y \mid X_2 = 1)}^{1} = 1 \,(\text{bit}),$$

It immediately follows that $I(Y; W) \approx 0.60$, $I(Y; X_1) \approx 0.56 \,(\text{bit})$ and $I(Y; X_2) \approx 0.41 \,(\text{bit})$.

Moving on to the causal information theoretical quantities, we have $H(Y \mid do(X_1 = x_1)) = H(Y) \approx 1.41 \,(\text{bit})$ for every $x_1 \in R_{X_1}$ and $H(Y \mid do(X_2 = x_2)) = H(W) = 1 \,(\text{bit})$ for every $x_2 \in R_{X_2}$. Hence $H_c(Y \mid do(X_1 \sim X_1')) \approx 1.41 \,(\text{bit})$ and $H_c(Y \mid do(X_2 \sim X_2')) = 1 \,(\text{bit})$ for any intervention protocols X_1', X_2'. It follows that $I_c(Y \mid do(X_1 \sim X_1')) = 0 \,(\text{bit})$ and $I(Y \mid do(X_2 \sim X_2')) \approx 0.41 \,(\text{bit})$.

B   Proof of Proposition 1

Proof. Suppose X has no causal effect on Y. Then $\forall x \in R_X$, $p_Y^{do(X=x)} = p_Y$. The expression for the causal entropy then reduces to $\mathbb{E}_{x \sim X'} H(Y) = H(Y)$. This shows the implication in the proposition.

We will check that the converse does not hold by giving an example where X has a causal effect on Y but $H_c(Y \mid X \sim X') = H(Y)$. Consider the SCM with three binary endogenous variables X, Y and M specified by:

$$\begin{cases} f_M(N_M) = N_M \\ f_X(M, N_X) = \begin{cases} (N_X + 1) \mod 2, M = 1 \\ N_X, M = 0 \end{cases} \\ f_Y(M, N_X) = \begin{cases} X, M = 1 \\ (X + 1) \mod 2, M = 0 \end{cases} \\ N_X, N_M \sim \text{Bern}(q), \text{ for some } q \in (0, 1). \end{cases} \quad (7)$$

Then $p_Y^{do(X=0)} \sim \text{Bern}(q)$ and $p_Y^{do(X=1)} \sim \text{Bern}(q)$. Also,

$$p_Y = p_{X|M=1}(1)p_M(1) + p_{X|M=0}(0)p_M(0) = 1 - q \quad \Rightarrow \quad Y \sim \text{Bern}(1 - q) \ (8)$$

Hence $p_Y \neq p_Y^{do(X=1)}$, meaning that $X \to Y$. And since both post-intervention distributions have the same entropy $H_{Y \sim \text{Bern}(q)}(Y) = H_{Y \sim \text{Bern}(1-q)}(Y)$, then the causal entropy will also be $H_c(Y \mid X \sim X') = H_{Y \sim \text{Bern}(1-q)}(Y) = H(Y)$ (for any chosen of X').   □

References

1. Ay, N., Polani, D.: Information flows in causal networks. Adv. Complex Syst. **11**(01), 17–41 (2008)
2. Beraha, M., Metelli, A.M., Papini, M., Tirinzoni, A., Restelli, M.: Feature selection via mutual information: new theoretical insights. CoRR abs/1907.07384 (2019). http://arxiv.org/abs/1907.07384
3. Bourrat, P.: Variation of information as a measure of one-to-one causal specificity. Eur. J. Philos. Sci. **9**(1), 1–18 (2019)
4. Confalonieri, R., Coba, L., Wagner, B., Besold, T.R.: A historical perspective of explainable artificial intelligence. Wiley Interdisc. Rev.: Data Min. Knowl. Disc. **11**(1), e1391 (2021)
5. Cover, T.M., Thomas, J.A.: Elements of Information Theory. Wiley-Interscience (2006)
6. Friedman, J.H.: Greedy function approximation: a gradient boosting machine. Ann. Stat., 1189–1232 (2001)
7. Goldstein, A., Kapelner, A., Bleich, J., Pitkin, E.: Peeking inside the black box: visualizing statistical learning with plots of individual conditional expectation. J. Comput. Graph. Stat. **24**(1), 44–65 (2015)
8. Griffiths, P.E., Pocheville, A., Calcott, B., Stotz, K., Kim, H., Knight, R.: Measuring causal specificity. Philos. Sci. **82**(4), 529–555 (2015)
9. Janzing, D., Balduzzi, D., Grosse-Wentrup, M., Schölkopf, B.: Quantifying causal influences. Ann. Stat. **41**(5), 2324–2358 (2013)
10. Koller, D., Friedman, N.: Probabilistic graphical models: principles and techniques. MIT press (2009)
11. MacKay, D.J., Mac Kay, D.J.: Information Theory, Inference and Learning Algorithms. Cambridge University Press, Cambridge (2003)
12. Miller, T.: Explanation in artificial intelligence: insights from the social sciences. Artif. Intell. **267**, 1–38 (2019)

13. Mothilal, R.K., Sharma, A., Tan, C.: Explaining machine learning classifiers through diverse counterfactual explanations. In: Proceedings of the 2020 Conference on Fairness, Accountability, and Transparency, pp. 607–617 (2020)
14. Pearl, J.: Causality. Cambridge University Press, Cambridge (2009)
15. Pearl, J., Glymour, M., Jewell, N.P.: Causal inference in statistics: a primer. John Wiley & Sons (2016)
16. Peters, J., Janzing, D., Schölkopf, B.: Elements of causal inference: foundations and learning algorithms. The MIT Press (2017)
17. Pocheville, A., Griffiths, P., Stotz, K.: Comparing causes - an information-theoretic approach to specificity, proportionality and stability. In: 15th Congress of Logic, Methodology, and Philosophy of Science (2015)
18. Ribeiro, M.T., Singh, S., Guestrin, C.: Why should i trust you? Explaining the predictions of any classifier. In: Proceedings of the 22nd ACM SIGKDD International Conference on Knowledge Discovery and Data Mining, pp. 1135–1144 (2016)
19. Schölkopf, B., Janzing, D., Peters, J., Sgouritsa, E., Zhang, K., Mooij, J.: On causal and anticausal learning. arXiv preprint arXiv:1206.6471 (2012)
20. Vergara, J.R., Estévez, P.A.: A review of feature selection methods based on mutual information. Neural Comput. Appl. **24**, 175–186 (2014)
21. Wachter, S., Mittelstadt, B., Russell, C.: Counterfactual explanations without opening the black box: automated decisions and the GDPR. Harv. JL Tech. **31**, 841 (2017)
22. Woodward, J.: Causation in biology: stability, specificity, and the choice of levels of explanation. Biol. Philos. **25**(3), 287–318 (2010)
23. Zednik, C., Boelsen, H.: Scientific exploration and explainable artificial intelligence. Mind. Mach. **32**(1), 219–239 (2022)
24. Zhao, Q., Hastie, T.: Causal interpretations of black-box models. J. Bus. Econ. Stat. (2019)
25. Zhou, H., Wang, X., Zhu, R.: Feature selection based on mutual information with correlation coefficient. Appl. Intell., 1–18 (2022)

Leveraging Model-Based Trees as Interpretable Surrogate Models for Model Distillation

Julia Herbinger[1,2], Susanne Dandl[1,2], Fiona K. Ewald[1,2], Sofia Loibl[1], and Giuseppe Casalicchio[1,2(✉)]

[1] Department of Statistics, LMU Munich, Ludwigstr. 33, 80539 Munich, Germany
`Giuseppe.Casalicchio@stat.uni-muenchen.de`
[2] Munich Center for Machine Learning (MCML), Munich, Germany

Abstract. Surrogate models play a crucial role in retrospectively interpreting complex and powerful black box machine learning models via model distillation. This paper focuses on using model-based trees as surrogate models which partition the feature space into interpretable regions via decision rules. Within each region, interpretable models based on additive main effects are used to approximate the behavior of the black box model, striking for an optimal balance between interpretability and performance. Four model-based tree algorithms, namely SLIM, GUIDE, MOB, and CTree, are compared regarding their ability to generate such surrogate models. We investigate fidelity, interpretability, stability, and the algorithms' capability to capture interaction effects through appropriate splits. Based on our comprehensive analyses, we finally provide an overview of user-specific recommendations.

Keywords: Interpretability · Model distillation · Surrogate model · Model-based tree

1 Introduction

Various machine learning (ML) algorithms achieve outstanding predictive performance, but often at the cost of being complex and not intrinsically interpretable. This lack of transparency can impede their application, especially in highly regulated industries, such as banking or insurance [8]. A promising class of post-hoc interpretability methods to provide explanations for these black boxes are so-called surrogate models, which are intrinsically interpretable models – such as linear models or decision trees – that approximate the predictions of black box models [21]. The learned parameters of surrogate models (e.g., the coefficients of a linear model or the tree structure) are thereby used to provide insights into the black box model. The usefulness of these explanations hinges on how well they approximate the predictions of the original ML model. If a surrogate

---

J. Herbinger and S. Dandl—Contributed equally to this work.

S. Nowaczyk et al. (Eds.): ECAI 2023 Workshops, CCIS 1947, pp. 232–249, 2024.
https://doi.org/10.1007/978-3-031-50396-2_13

model is too simple to accurately approximate a complex black box model on the entire feature space, it cannot reliably explain the general behavior of the underlying ML model. This is especially the case if the underlying ML model comprises feature interactions and highly non-linear feature effects. Other existing methods have, therefore, focused on local surrogate models to explain single observations. The idea is that while simple surrogate models may not accurately approximate the complex ML model on the entire feature space, they might be a good approximation in the immediate vicinity of a single observation. However, such local explanations cannot be used to explain the general model behavior. We would require to produce and analyze multiple local explanations to get an understanding of the general model behavior, which is inconvenient because the sheer number of local models increases run-time while impeding interpretability.

One promising idea to trade-off between global and local explanations is to train a global surrogate model that automatically finds regions in the feature space where the ML model's predictions can be well described by interpretable surrogate models using only main effects.[1] [14] introduced surrogate locally-interpretable models (SLIM) using model-based trees (MBTs) to find distinct and interpretable regions in the feature space where the ML model's predictions can be well described by a simple additive model that consists only of feature main effects in each leaf node. As such, SLIM generates regional additive main effect surrogate models which approximate the underlying ML model predictions and can be combined into a global surrogate model. Other MBT algorithms have already been introduced before SLIM, but not as a surrogate model for post-hoc interpretation, for example, model-based recursive partitioning (MOB) [28], conditional inference trees (CTree) [11], and regression trees with unbiased feature selection and interaction detection (GUIDE) [17]. All these MBT algorithms are decision trees and usually differ in their splitting procedure and the objective used for splitting. While the well-known CART algorithm [3] estimates constant values in the leaf nodes, MBTs fit interpretable models – such as a linear model.

Contributions. This paper aims to inspect SLIM, MOB, CTree, and GUIDE and their suitability as *regional additive main effect surrogate models*[2] which approximate the underlying ML model predictions well. We specifically focus on main effect models because they enable good interpretability of the models in the leaf nodes. In the ideal case, interactions should then be handled by splits, so that the leaf node models are free from interaction effects. In a simulation study, we apply the four MBT approaches as post-hoc surrogate models on the ML model predictions and compare them with regard to fidelity, interpretability, and stability – as tree algorithms often suffer from poor stability [4]. We analyze their differences and provide recommendations that help users to choose the

---

[1] In regions where only a few feature interactions are present, an additive main effect model is expected to be a good approximation.

[2] Meaning surrogate models that partition the feature space into interpretable regions and fit an additive main effect model within each region (e.g., a linear model using only first-order feature effects).

suitable modeling technique based on their underlying research question and data.

Reproducibility and Open Science. The scripts to reproduce all experiments can be found at https://github.com/slds-lmu/mbt_comparison. It also contains the code for the SLIM and GUIDE algorithms, displaying (to the best of our knowledge) the first implementations of these approaches available in R. For the MOB and CTree algorithms the implementations of the R package **partykit** [12] were used.

2   Related Work

The purpose of surrogate models is to approximate the predictions of a black box model as accurately as possible and to be interpretable at the same time [21]. Global or local surrogate models are used based on whether the goal is to achieve a global interpretation of the black box model (model explanation) or to explain predictions of individual input instances (outcome explanation) [19].

Global Surrogate Models. The concept of global surrogate models is also known as model distillation, which involves training a simpler and more interpretable model (the distilled model) to mimic the predictions of a complex black box model. If the performance is good enough (i.e., high fidelity), the predictions of the black box model can be explained using the interpretable surrogate model. The main challenge is to use an appropriate surrogate model that balances the trade-off between high performance and interpretability [21]. For example, linear models are easily interpretable, but may not capture non-linear relationships modeled by the underlying ML model. Some researchers explore tree-based or rule-based approaches for model distillation [2,5,20]. Others propose promising models like generalized additive models plus interactions (GA2M) that include a small number of two-way interactions in addition to non-linear main effects to achieve both high performance and interpretability [18].

Local Surrogate Models.   Local interpretable model-agnostic explanations (LIME) [23] is probably the most prominent local surrogate model. It explains a single prediction by fitting a surrogate model in the local neighborhood around the instance of interest. This can, for example, be achieved by randomly sampling data points following the distribution of the training data and weighting the data points according to the distance to the instance of interest. This local approach offers an advantage over global surrogate models, as it allows for a better balance between model complexity and interpretability by focusing on a small region of the feature space, thereby achieving a higher fidelity in the considered locality. However, the selection of an appropriate neighborhood for the instance of interest remains a challenging task [16]. A major drawback of LIME is its instability, as a single prediction can obtain different explanations due to different notions and possibilities to define the local neighborhood. Several modifications of LIME have been proposed to stabilize the local explanation, including S-LIME [29] and OptiLIME [27].

Regional Surrogate Models. The idea of regional surrogate models is to partition the feature space into appropriate regions in which fitting a simple interpretable model is sufficient. For example, K-LIME [7] uses an unsupervised approach to obtain K partitions via K-means clustering. In contrast, locally interpretable models and effects based on supervised partitioning (LIME-SUP) [13] – also known as SLIM [14] – use a supervised approach (MBT) to partition the feature space according to a given objective.

To the best of our knowledge, the suitability of well-established model-based tree algorithms (e.g., MOB, CTree, and GUIDE) as surrogate models has not been investigated so far.

3 Background: Model-Based Trees

In the following, the general framework underlying MBTs is introduced and the different algorithms are presented.

3.1 General Notation

We consider a p−dimensional feature space $\mathcal{X}$ and a target space $\mathcal{Y}$ (e.g., for regression $\mathcal{Y} = \mathbb{R}$ and for classification $\mathcal{Y}$ is finite and categorical with $|\mathcal{Y}| = g$ classes). The respective random variables are denoted by $X = (X_1, \ldots, X_p)$ and Y. The realizations of n observations are denoted by $(y^{(1)}, \mathbf{x}^{(1)}), \ldots, (y^{(n)}, \mathbf{x}^{(n)})$. We further denote $\mathbf{x}_j$ as the j-th feature vector containing the observed feature values of X_j. Following [28] and [26], let $\mathcal{M}((y, \mathbf{x}), \theta)$ be a parametric model, that describes the target y as a function of a feature vector $\mathbf{x} \in \mathcal{X}$ and a vector of parameters $\theta \in \Theta$. As a surrogate model the notation $\mathcal{M}((\hat{y}, \mathbf{x}), \theta)$ is used, i.e. the surrogate estimates the predictions of the black box model $\hat{y}$. Thus, y denotes the observed ground truth, $\hat{y}$ the black box model predictions, and $\hat{\hat{y}}$ the surrogate model predictions. For regional surrogate models, the feature space is partitioned into B distinct regions $\{\mathcal{B}_b\}_{b=1,\ldots,B}$ with the corresponding locally optimal vector of parameters θ_b in each partition $b = 1, \ldots, B$.

3.2 Model-Based Tree (MBT) Algorithms

In this section, the four MBT algorithms SLIM, MOB, CTree, and GUIDE are described, and theoretical differences are explained. All MBTs can be described by the following recursive partitioning algorithm:

1. Start with the root node containing all n observations.
2. Fit the model $\mathcal{M}$ to all observations in the current node to estimate $\hat{\theta}_b$.
3. Find the optimal split within the node.
4. Split the current node into two child nodes until a certain stop criterion[3] is met and repeat steps 2–4.

---

[3] For example, until a certain depth of the tree, a certain improvement of the objective after splitting, or a certain significance level for the parameter instability is reached.

Table 1. Comparison of MBT algorithms

Algorithm	Split point selection	Test	Implementation
SLIM	exhaustive search	–	–
MOB	two-step	score-based fluctuation	R **partykit**
CTree	two-step	score-based permutation	R **partykit**
GUIDE	two-step	residual-based χ^2	binary executable

SLIM uses an exhaustive search to select the optimal split feature and split point. Due to the exhaustive search, SLIM might suffer from a selection bias similar to CART.[4] MOB, CTree, and GUIDE apply a 2-step procedure to combat the selection bias [25]:

1. Select the feature with the highest association with the target y to perform the splitting (partitioning). The hypothesis tests used to determine the most significant association differ between the MBT algorithms.
2. Search for the best split point only within this feature (e.g., by exhaustive search or again by hypothesis testing).

We will use all four algorithms as surrogate MBTs in conjunction with a linear main effect model $\mathcal{M}((\hat{y}, \mathbf{x}), \theta_b) = \theta_{0,b} + \theta_{1,b}x_1 + ... + \theta_{p,b}x_p$ with $\theta_b = (\theta_{0,b}, ..., \theta_{p,b})^T$ for a (leaf) node b such that the splits are based on feature interactions. The assumption here is that if the main effects in the nodes are well-fitted, any lack of fit must come from interactions. Therefore, each feature can be used for splitting as well as for regressing (i.e., to train the linear main effect model in each node). In the following, the four approaches are presented in more detail. Table 1 gives a concise comparison of them.

SLIM. The SLIM algorithm performs an exhaustive search to find the optimal split point based on a user-defined objective function. [14] use the sum of squared errors – similar to CART but fit more flexible parameterized models (such as an L_1-penalized linear model) instead of constant values. The computational effort for estimating all possible child models that are trained at each potential split point becomes very large with an increasing number of possible partitioning features. For this reason, [14] developed an efficient algorithm for estimating them for the case of linear regression, linear regression with B-spline transformed features, and ridge regression (see [14] for more details).

To avoid overfitting and to obtain a small interpretable tree, [14] use the approach of post-pruning. In order to keep the computational effort as low as possible, we use an early stopping mechanism: a split is only performed if the

---

[4] According to [11] an algorithm for recursive partitioning is called unbiased when, under the conditions of the null hypothesis of independence between target y and features $\mathbf{x}_1, ..., \mathbf{x}_p$, the probability of selecting feature $\mathbf{x}_j$ is $1/p$ for all $j = 1, ..., p$ regardless of the measurement scales or the number of missing values.

objective after the best split improves by at least a fraction of $\gamma \in [0, 1]$ (compared to the objective in the parent node). To the best of our knowledge, no openly accessible implementation of SLIM exists and we implemented SLIM in R as part of this work.

MOB. After an initial model is fitted in step 2, MOB examines whether the corresponding parameter estimates $\hat{\theta}_b$ are stable. To investigate this, the score function of the parametric model trained in the node is considered, which is defined by the gradient of the objective function with respect to the parameter vector θ_b. To test the null hypothesis of parameter stability, the M-fluctuation test is used [28]. The feature for which the M-fluctuation test detects the highest instability (smallest p-value) is chosen for splitting. The choice of the optimal split point with respect to this feature is then made by means of an exhaustive search, analogous to SLIM. MOB uses the Bonferroni-adjusted p-value of the M-fluctuation test as an early stopping criterion. That means a split is only performed if the instability is significant at a given significance level α. MOB generally distinguishes between regressor features, which are only used to fit the models in the nodes, and features, which are only used for splitting. However, [28] do not explicitly exclude overlapping roles as assumed here. MOB is implemented in the **partykit** R package [12].

CTree. CTree – similarly to MOB – tries to detect parameter instability by measuring the dependency between potential splitting features and a transformation $h()$ of the target. A common transformation used in MBTs is the score function, which is also used for MOB. Also, other transformations such as the residuals could be used. However, [25] argues that the score function is generally preferred since it performs best in detecting parameter instabilities.

CTree uses a standardized linear association test to test the independence between the transformation $h()$ and the potential split features. In the linear model case with continuous or categorical split features, this is equal to the Pearson correlation and one-way ANOVA test, respectively [25]. The final test statistic follows an asymptotic χ^2–distribution under the null hypothesis. The feature with the smallest p-value is selected as the splitting feature. As for MOB, a Bonferroni-adjusted p-value is used as an early stopping criterion [11].

Unlike SLIM and MOB, the split point is selected by a statistical hypothesis test. The discrepancy between two subsets is measured with a two-sample linear test statistic for each possible binary split. The split that maximizes the discrepancy is chosen as the split point [11]. [25] state that the linear test used in CTree has higher power in detecting smooth relationships between the scores and the splitting features compared to the M-fluctuation test in MOB. MOB, on the other hand, has a higher ability in detecting abrupt changes. An implementation of CTree is also part of the **partykit** R package [12].

GUIDE. GUIDE [17] uses a categorical association test to detect parameter instabilities. Specifically, a χ^2–independence test between the dichotomized residuals at 0 (only the sign of the residuals matter) of the fitted model and the categorized features are performed and the p-values of these so-called curvature tests are calculated. In addition to the curvature tests, GUIDE explicitly searches for interactions by using again χ^2–independence tests. If the smallest p-value comes from a curvature test, the corresponding feature is chosen as the partitioning feature. If the smallest p-value is from an interaction test, the categorical feature involved, if any, is preferably chosen as the splitting feature. If both involved features are categorical, the feature with the smaller p-value of the curvature test is chosen for splitting. In the case of two numerical features, the choice is made by evaluating the potential child models after splitting with respect to both features. Subsequently, a bootstrap selection bias correction is performed. In the original GUIDE algorithm developed by [17], categorical features are only used for splitting due to the large number of degrees of freedom that are needed for the parameter estimation of categorical features. GUIDE is only available as a binary executable under https://pages.stat.wisc.edu/~loh/guide.html. We incorporated GUIDE as an option for the SLIM implementation in R. Pruning is therefore carried out in the same way as for SLIM.

4   Comparison Study

Here, we first define desirable properties of MBTs when used as surrogate models on the predictions of an ML model. To quantify these properties and compare them for the different MBT algorithms, we define several evaluation measures. Then, we compare SLIM, MOB, CTree, and GUIDE based on these measures for different experimental settings and provide recommendations for the user.

4.1   Desirable Properties and Evaluation Measures

The following properties of MBTs are desirable:

- **Fidelity**: To derive meaningful interpretations, the predictions of the ML model need to be well approximated by the MBT.
- **Interpretability**: To provide insights into the inner workings of the ML model, the MBT needs to be interpretable and hence not too complex to be understood by a human.
- **Stability**: Since MBTs are based on decision trees, they might be unstable in the sense that they are not robust to small changes in the training data [4]. However, stable results are needed for reliable interpretations.

These properties are measured using the evaluation metrics below.

Fidelity. To evaluate the fidelity of an MBT as a surrogate model, we use the R^2, which is defined by

$$R^2 \left(\left\{ \hat{y}, \hat{\hat{y}} \right\} \right) = 1 - \frac{\sum_{i=1}^n \left(\hat{\hat{y}}^{(i)} - \bar{\hat{y}} \right)^2}{\sum_{i=1}^n \left(\hat{y}^{(i)} - \bar{\hat{y}} \right)^2},$$

where $\hat{\tilde{y}}^{(i)}, i = 1, ..., n$ are the predictions of the MBT model and $\bar{\tilde{y}}$ is the arithmetic mean of the ML model predictions $\hat{y}^{(i)}$. Fidelity is measured on training data but also on test data in order to evaluate the MBT's fidelity on unseen data.

Interpretability. If different MBTs fit the same interpretable models within the leaf nodes (as done in the following experiments), the interpretability comparison of MBTs reduces to the complexity of the respective tree structure. Therefore, the number of leaf nodes is used here to evaluate the interpretability, since fewer leaf nodes lead to shallower trees which are easier to understand and interpret.

Stability. We consider an MBT algorithm stable if it partitions the feature space in the same way after it has been applied again on slightly different training data. To compare two MBTs, an additional evaluation data set is used that is partitioned according to the decision rules learned by each of the two MBTs. If the partitioning is identical for both MBTs, the interpretation of the decision rules is also assumed to be identical, which suggests stability.

To measure the similarity of regions found by MBTs trained on slightly different data, the Rand index (RI) [22], which was introduced for clustering approaches, is used. The RI defines the similarity of two clusterings $\mathcal{A}, \mathcal{B}$ of n observations each by the proportion of the number of observation pairs that are either assigned to the same partition in both clusterings (n_{11}) or to different partitions in both clusterings (n_{00}) measured against the total number of observation pairs [6]:

$$\mathrm{RI}(\mathcal{A}, \mathcal{B}) = \frac{n_{11} + n_{00}}{\binom{n}{2}}.$$

When comparing MBTs, the clusterings in the RI are defined by the regions based on the decision rules learned by the MBTs. Since the number of leaf nodes influences the RI, we only compute RIs for MBTs with the same number of leaf nodes. A high RI for a pair of MBTs with the same number of leaf nodes indicates that the underlying MBT algorithm is stable for the analyzed scenario.

Additionally, the range of the number of leaf nodes is used as a measure of stability. It is assumed that MBTs are more unstable if the number of leaf nodes for different simulation runs varies strongly.

4.2 Experiments

Here, we empirically evaluate the four presented MBT algorithms with respect to fidelity, interpretability, and stability as surrogate models to interpret the underlying ML model. Therefore, we define three simple scenarios (linear smooth, linear categorical, linear mixed) which mainly differ regarding the type of interactions. Thus, we evaluate how well the MBT algorithms can handle these different types of interactions to provide recommendations for the user at the end of this section, depending on the underlying data and research question.

Simulation Setting. Since the measures for interpretability and fidelity strongly depend on the early stopping configuration of γ for SLIM and GUIDE and α for MOB and CTree, the simulations are carried out for three different values of each of these parameters for all three scenarios and for a sample size of $n = 1500$ of which $n_{train} = 1000$ observations are used for training and $n_{test} = 500$ observations for testing. All MBT algorithms are fitted as surrogate models on the predictions of a correctly specified linear model (lm) or generalized additive model (GAM) and on an XGBoost model with correctly specified interactions. Further specifications of the hyperparameters for the XGBoost algorithm for each scenario can be found in Online Appendix B.1 [10]. Table 2 provides an overview of all $3 \times 3 \times 2 = 18$ variants for each of the four MBT algorithms. Hyperparameters that are fixed in all variants are a maximum tree depth of 6 and a minimum number of observations per node of 50. We perform 100 repetitions.

Table 2. Definition of variants for all simulation settings.

Varied factors	levels
Scenario	linear smooth, linear categorical, linear mixed
Early stopping config	$\alpha \in \{0.05, 0.01, 0.001\}, \gamma \in \{0.05, 0.1, 0.15\}$
Surrogate model	lm/GAM, XGBoost

Fidelity and interpretation measures are calculated in each simulation run. The RIs are calculated after the simulation based on pairwise comparisons of the final regions of an evaluation data set. More detailed steps on the quantification of the RI for the stated simulation settings are explained in Online Appendix A [10].

Linear Smooth

Scenario Definition. The DGP in this scenario includes one smooth two-way interaction between two numeric features and is defined as follows: Let $X_1, X_2, X_3 \sim \mathcal{U}(-1, 1)$, then the DGP based on the n drawn realizations is given by $y = f(\mathbf{x}) + \epsilon$ with $f(\mathbf{x}) = \mathbf{x}_1 + 4\mathbf{x}_2 + 3\mathbf{x}_2\mathbf{x}_3$ and $\epsilon \sim \mathcal{N}(0, 0.01 \cdot \sigma^2(f(\mathbf{x})))$.

Results. Aggregated results on interpretability and fidelity are provided for all four MBT algorithms as surrogate models on the respective black box model in Table 3. Since the DGP is rather simple, all MBTs have a high fidelity but they also require a very high number of leaf nodes since the smooth interactions can only be well approximated by many binary splits. To compare the fidelity, we focus on configuration $\gamma = \alpha = 0.05$ since this configuration leads to a similar mean number of leaf nodes for all four algorithms. We see that, for a similar number of leaf nodes, the fidelity is equally high for the four MBTs, whereby the fidelity of MOB and CTree deviate less over the repetitions.

The number of leaf nodes fluctuates considerably more for SLIM and GUIDE than for MOB and CTree even when γ and α are fixed. In general, we can see that the R^2, which measures fidelity, increases with an increasing number of leaf nodes for all models, reflecting the trade-off between fidelity and interpretability.

Table 3. Simulation results on 100 simulation runs for all four MBTs as surrogate models on the scenario linear smooth with sample sizes $n_{train} = 1000$ and $n_{test} = 500$ for different values of γ and α. The mean (standard deviation) fidelity on the training data for the lm is 0.9902 (0.0006) and for the XGBoost 0.9858 (0.0008). On the test data set the respective fidelity values for the lm are 0.9901 (0.0008) and for the XGBoost 0.9768 (0.0018).

Black box	MBT	γ/α	Number of Leaves			R^2_{train}		R^2_{test}	
			mean	min	max	mean	sd	mean	sd
lm	SLIM	0.15	2.06	2	3	0.9650	0.0043	0.9631	0.0046
lm	SLIM	0.10	12.11	5	16	0.9965	0.0052	0.9958	0.0060
lm	SLIM	0.05	15.70	14	16	0.9995	0.0001	0.9993	0.0001
lm	GUIDE	0.15	2.07	2	3	0.9651	0.0044	0.9632	0.0049
lm	GUIDE	0.10	12.03	5	16	0.9965	0.0051	0.9957	0.0060
lm	GUIDE	0.05	15.75	14	16	0.9995	0.0001	0.9993	0.0001
lm	MOB	0.001	15.78	14	16	0.9994	0.0001	0.9993	0.0001
lm	MOB	0.010	15.78	14	16	0.9994	0.0001	0.9993	0.0001
lm	MOB	0.050	15.78	14	16	0.9994	0.0001	0.9993	0.0001
lm	CTree	0.001	15.22	13	17	0.9993	0.0001	0.9992	0.0001
lm	CTree	0.010	15.22	13	17	0.9993	0.0001	0.9992	0.0001
lm	CTree	0.050	15.22	13	17	0.9993	0.0001	0.9992	0.0001
XGBoost	SLIM	0.15	2.31	2	6	0.9665	0.0069	0.9629	0.0079
XGBoost	SLIM	0.10	7.33	2	14	0.9850	0.0060	0.9814	0.0062
XGBoost	SLIM	0.05	14.30	8	17	0.9948	0.0010	0.9909	0.0017
XGBoost	GUIDE	0.15	2.26	2	5	0.9664	0.0067	0.9628	0.0077
XGBoost	GUIDE	0.10	6.92	2	14	0.9847	0.0061	0.9811	0.0062
XGBoost	GUIDE	0.05	14.15	8	17	0.9945	0.0010	0.9906	0.0017
XGBoost	MOB	0.001	10.89	8	13	0.9944	0.0005	0.9904	0.0011
XGBoost	MOB	0.010	11.96	9	15	0.9946	0.0005	0.9906	0.0011
XGBoost	MOB	0.050	12.86	11	15	0.9948	0.0005	0.9908	0.0011
XGBoost	CTree	0.001	12.09	9	15	0.9940	0.0006	0.9900	0.0012
XGBoost	CTree	0.010	13.21	10	15	0.9943	0.0006	0.9902	0.0013
XGBoost	CTree	0.050	14.09	11	17	0.9944	0.0006	0.9904	0.0012

Considering stability, SLIM and GUIDE provide – for each configuration of γ – similar results for the number of leave nodes (interpretability) and for the R^2 values (fidelity). While these measures are rather sensitive with regard to the value of γ, the variation of α has a much smaller impact on the results for MOB and CTree. Moreover, Fig. 1 shows the RIs of the four algorithms applied to the XGBoost model for tree pairs with identical numbers of leaf nodes. For a lower number of leaf nodes, MOB and CTree seem to generate more stable trees for this scenario. This effect diminishes with an increasing number of nodes and is also not apparent for the linear model (see Fig. 1 in Online Appendix B.2 [10]).

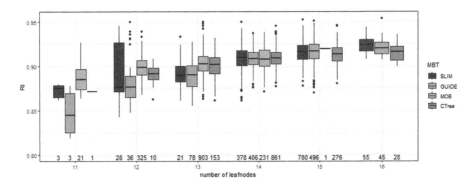

Fig. 1. RI for the four MBT algorithms when used as surrogate models for an XGBoost model for the scenario linear smooth with $n_{train} = 1000$ and $n_{test} = 500$, $\alpha = \gamma = 0.05$. The numbers below the boxplots indicate the number of tree pairs, for which both trees have the respective number of leaf nodes. Higher values are better.

Linear Categorical

Scenario Definition. Here, a scenario definition based on [9] with linear main effects and interactions between numerical and binary features (i.e., subgroup-specific linear effects) is regarded: Let $X_1, X_2 \sim \mathcal{U}(-1, 1)$, $X_3 \sim Bern(0.5)$, then the DGP based on n drawn realizations is defined by $y = f(\mathbf{x}) + \epsilon$ with $f(\mathbf{x}) = \mathbf{x}_1 - 8\mathbf{x}_2 + 16\mathbf{x}_2\mathbb{1}_{(\mathbf{x}_3=0)} + 8\mathbf{x}_2\mathbb{1}_{(\mathbf{x}_1 > \bar{\mathbf{x}}_1)}$ and $\epsilon \sim \mathcal{N}(0, 0.01 \cdot \sigma^2(f(\mathbf{x})))$. In this scenario, the DGP is not determined by a smooth interaction but can be fully described by main effect models in four regions. Assuming that the ML model accurately approximates the real-world relationships, if the regions of the MBTs are defined by a (first-level) split with respect to the binary feature $\mathbf{x}_3$ and by a (second-level) split at the empirical mean of feature $\mathbf{x}_1$, the final regions only contain main effects of the given features as defined in the DGP.

Results. Aggregated results on interpretability and fidelity are provided for all four MBT algorithms as surrogate models on the respective black box model in Online Appendix B.3 [10]. In all scenarios – independent of the early stopping configurations – SLIM and GUIDE lead to fewer leaves than MOB and CTree. This can be explained by the chosen split features. SLIM and GUIDE perform splits with respect to features x_1 and x_3, which lead to the subgroup-specific linear effects defined by the DGP and thus, only need a few splits to well approximate the DGP. In contrast, MOB and CTree rather choose x_2 for splitting, resulting in many splits to achieve a comparable fidelity. Hence, MOB and CTree lead to a worse fidelity and due to many more leaf nodes to a worse interpretability than SLIM and GUIDE for this scenario.

Figure 2 shows that, while the number of leaf nodes for SLIM and GUIDE is always four for the regarded setting ($\alpha = \gamma = 0.05$, see Online Appendix B.3 [10] for an overview), the number of leaf nodes for MOB and CTree varies strongly for the different simulation runs. It is also noticeable that MOB performs better than CTree with the same number of leaf nodes. A possible explanation is that the fluctuation test used within the splitting procedure of MOB performs better in detecting abrupt changes than the linear test statistic used in CTree [25]. Online Appendix B.3 [10] also shows that SLIM and GUIDE show a better mean fidelity compared to MOB and CTree when applied to a GAM.

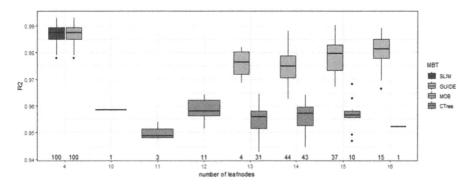

Fig. 2. Test accuracy R^2 vs. number of leaf nodes for the four MBT algorithms as surrogate models for XGBoost for scenario linear categorical with $n_{train} = 1000$ and $n_{test} = 500$, $\alpha = \gamma = 0.05$. The numbers below the boxplots indicate the number of trees (from 100 simulation runs) which have the respective number of leaf nodes for the regarded algorithm.

Linear Mixed

Scenario Definition. The third scenario combines the linear smooth and the linear categorical scenarios. Hence, the DGP is defined by linear main effects, interaction effects between categorical and numerical features, and smooth interactions: Let $X_1, X_2 \sim \mathcal{U}(-1,1)$, $X_3, X_4 \sim Bern(0.5)$, then the DGP based on n drawn realizations is defined by $y = f(\mathbf{x}) + \epsilon$ with $f(\mathbf{x}) = 4\mathbf{x}_2 + 2\mathbf{x}_4 + 4\mathbf{x}_2\mathbf{x}_1 + 8\mathbf{x}_2\mathbb{1}_{(\mathbf{x}_3=0)} + 8\mathbf{x}_1\mathbf{x}_2\mathbb{1}_{(\mathbf{x}_4=1)}$ and $\epsilon \sim \mathcal{N}(0, 0.01 \cdot \sigma^2(f(x)))$.

Results. Aggregated results on interpretability and fidelity are provided for all four MBT algorithms as surrogate models on the respective black box model in Online Appendix B.3 [10]. To compare the different MBT algorithms, we choose the early stopping configurations, which lead to a similar mean number of leaf nodes ($\gamma = \alpha = 0.05$). Figure 3 shows that SLIM and GUIDE achieve a slightly better trade-off between fidelity and interpretability than MOB and CTree in this scenario. This can be reasoned as follows: SLIM and GUIDE split more often with respect to the binary features compared to the other two MBT algorithms (see Fig. 4). Thus, SLIM and GUIDE use the categorical features more often to reveal the subgroups defined by them, while MOB and particularly CTree split almost exclusively with respect to the numerical features and hence perform slightly worse for the same mean number of leaf nodes.

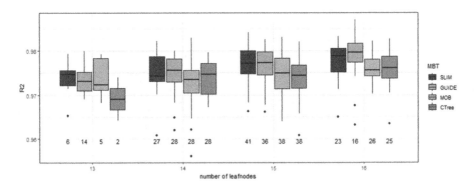

Fig. 3. Test accuracy R^2 vs. number of leaf nodes for the four MBT algorithms when used as a surrogate model on the xgboost model for scenario linear mixed with $n_{train} = 1000$ and $n_{test} = 500$, $\alpha = \gamma = 0.05$. The numbers below the boxplots indicate the number of trees (from 100 simulation runs) which have the respective number of leaf nodes for the regarded algorithm.

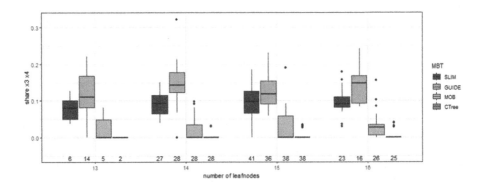

Fig. 4. Relative amount of partitions which use features $\mathbf{x}_3, \mathbf{x}_4$ for splittings vs. the number of leaf nodes for the four MBT algorithms when the XGBoost model is used as a surrogate model for the scenario linear mixed with $n = 1500, \alpha = \gamma = 0.05$.

However, MOB and CTree provide on average more stable results regarding the RI for a fixed number of leaf nodes compared to SLIM and GUIDE (see Fig. 5).

4.3 Recommendations

Based on our analyses in this work, we provide some general recommendations on how to choose the MBT algorithm based on the underlying data and research question. The recommendations are based on the given assumption that we are interested in partitioning the feature space in such a way that we receive interpretable and distinct regions where regional relationships are reduced to additive (linear) main effects of the features. Hence, the feature space is partitioned such that feature interactions are reduced.

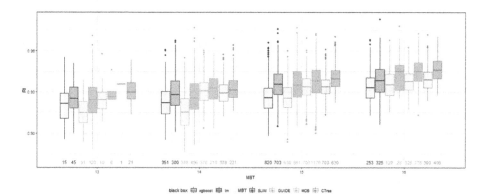

Fig. 5. RI for the four MBT algorithms when used as a surrogate model for the scenario linear mixed with $n_{train} = 1000$ and $n_{test} = 500$, $\alpha = \gamma = 0.05$. The numbers below the boxplots indicate the number of tree pairs (from 4950 pairs), for which both trees have the respective number of leaf nodes. Higher values are better.

If features cannot be separated into modeling and partitioning features (as is the case here), we recommend to

1. use SLIM and GUIDE on subgroup detection tasks (scenario linear categorical and linear mixed) since they provide a better trade-off between fidelity and interpretability than MOB and CTree. CTree performed worst in these settings. This is often the case when there is a higher number of categorical features with low cardinality included in the dataset (which interact also with numeric features in the data set).
2. use MOB and CTree in scenarios with smooth interactions (scenario linear smooth and linear mixed) for which these algorithms produce more stable trees while performing as well as SLIM and GUIDE. These settings are more likely for data sets with a high number of numerical features that are interacting with each other. However, smooth interactions can often only be modeled

well by a large number of binary splits, which makes MBTs difficult to interpret on such data. Thus, depending on the underlying feature interactions, MBTs might not be the best choice. Global modeling approaches such as GA2M [18] or compboost [24] should be considered or at least compared to MBTs in this case.

If features can be separated into modeling and partitioning features (e.g., based on domain-specific knowledge), we recommend using MOB which has been developed and analyzed in detail for these settings and showed good fidelity and stable results [1,15].

4.4   Extensions Beyond Linearity

When the main effects learned by the black box model are non-linear, the MBTs will not only split according to feature interactions but also according to non-linear main effects to approximate the main effects within regions by linear effects. This leads to deeper trees, which again are less interpretable. An alternative to fitting linear models within MBTs would be to use, for example, polynomial regression, splines, or GAMs. These models are able to account for non-linearity such that splits can be placed according to feature interactions. However, not all MBTs provide this flexibility to adapt the fitted model within the recursive partitioning algorithm (at least not out-of-the-box). [14] provide these alternatives, including efficient estimation procedures for SLIM. We apply SLIM with more flexible models fitted within the regions on a non-linear setting in Online Appendix B.5 [10] to demonstrate the differences and improved interpretability compared to the usage of linear models. We leave adaptions and analyses of GUIDE, MOB, and CTree for these scenarios to future research.

It is also helpful to add a regularization term for settings with many potential noise features to obtain more interpretable and potentially more stable results. SLIM again allows adding any regularization term (e.g., Lasso regularization for feature selection) out of the box. Such an analysis can be found in Online Appendix B.6 [10] for the MBTs as surrogate models for the (correctly specified) linear model and as a standalone model on the DGP. Further analyses using other ML models and diverse hyperparameters are also a matter of future research.

5   Discussion

While SLIM and GUIDE performed strongly in most of our simulation settings, they often showed less stable results compared to MOB and CTree in our analyses. In some scenarios, the tree size varied greatly for both algorithms. This observation might depend on the chosen hyperparameter configuration. Thus, SLIM and GUIDE could be improved by tuning the early stopping hyperparameters or by adding a post-pruning step to receive more stable results.

Furthermore, SLIM might be sensitive regarding a selection bias which is common in recursive partitioning algorithms based on exhaustive search. In contrast, MOB, CTree, and GUIDE circumvent that problem by a two-step approach in their splitting procedure which is based on parameter stability tests [25]. How the selection bias influences the trees fitted in these settings as well as the investigation of an extended setup of more complex scenarios and real-world settings are interesting open questions to analyze in future work.

In conclusion, it can be said that MBT algorithms are a promising addition – although not a universal solution – to interpreting the black box models by surrogate models. By combining decision rules and (non-linear) main effect models, we might achieve high fidelity as well as high interpretability at the same time. However, interpretability decreases very quickly with a high number of regions. Thus, the trade-off between fidelity and interpretability remains, and the compromise to be found depends on the underlying use case.

References

1. Alemayehu, D., Chen, Y., Markatou, M.: A comparative study of subgroup identification methods for differential treatment effect: performance metrics and recommendations. Stat. Methods Med. Res. **27**(12), 3658–3678 (2018). https://doi.org/10.1177/0962280217710570
2. Bastani, O., Kim, C., Bastani, H.: Interpreting blackbox models via model extraction. arXiv preprint arXiv:1705.08504 v6 (2019). https://doi.org/10.48550/arXiv.1705.08504
3. Breiman, L., Friedman, J., Stone, C.J., Olshen, R.A.: Classification and regression trees. CRC Press (1984). https://doi.org/10.1201/9781315139470
4. Fokkema, M.: Fitting prediction rule ensembles with R package pre. J. Stat. Softw. **92**(12) (2020). https://doi.org/10.18637/jss.v092.i12
5. Frosst, N., Hinton, G.: Distilling a neural network into a soft decision tree. arXiv preprint arXiv:1711.09784 (2017)
6. Gates, A.J., Ahn, Y.Y.: The impact of random models on clustering similarity. J. Mach. Learn. Res. **18**, 1–28 (2017). https://jmlr.org/papers/v18/17-039.html
7. Hall, P., Gill, N., Kurka, M., Phan, W.: Machine learning interpretability with H2O driverless AI. H2O.ai (2017). http://docs.h2o.ai/driverless-ai/latest-stable/docs/booklets/MLIBooklet.pdf
8. Henckaerts, R., Antonio, K., Côté, M.P.: When stakes are high: balancing accuracy and transparency with model-agnostic interpretable data-driven surrogates. Expert Syst. Appl. **202**, 117230 (2022). https://doi.org/10.1016/j.eswa.2022.117230
9. Herbinger, J., Bischl, B., Casalicchio, G.: REPID: regional effect plots with implicit interaction detection. In: International Conference on Artificial Intelligence and Statistics, pp. 10209–10233 (2022). https://proceedings.mlr.press/v151/herbinger22a/herbinger22a.pdf
10. Herbinger, J., Dandl, S., Ewald, F.K., Loibl, S., Casalicchio, G.: Online appendix for leveraging model-based trees as interpretable surrogate models for model distillation (2023). https://github.com/slds-lmu/mbt_comparison/blob/main/Online_Appendix.pdf
11. Hothorn, T., Hornik, K., Zeileis, A.: Unbiased recursive partitioning: a conditional inference framework. J. Comput. Graph. Stat. **15**(3), 651–674 (2006). https://doi.org/10.1198/106186006X133933

12. Hothorn, T., Zeileis, A.: partykit: a modular toolkit for recursive partytioning in R. J. Mach. Learn. Res. **16**, 3905–3909 (2015). https://www.jmlr.org/papers/v16/hothorn15a.html
13. Hu, L., Chen, J., Nair, V.N., Sudjianto, A.: Locally interpretable models and effects based on supervised partitioning (LIME-SUP). arXiv preprint arXiv:1806.00663 (2018)
14. Hu, L., Chen, J., Nair, V.N., Sudjianto, A.: Surrogate locally-interpretable models with supervised machine learning algorithms. arXiv preprint arXiv:2007.14528 (2020)
15. Huber, C., Benda, N., Friede, T.: A comparison of subgroup identification methods in clinical drug development: simulation study and regulatory considerations. Pharm. Stat. **18**(5), 600–626 (2019). https://doi.org/10.1002/pst.1951
16. Laugel, T., Renard, X., Lesot, M.J., Marsala, C., Detyniecki, M.: Defining locality for surrogates in post-hoc interpretablity. Workshop on Human Interpretability for Machine Learning (WHI) - International Conference on Machine Learning (ICML) (2018)
17. Loh, W.Y.: Regression tress with unbiased variable selection and interaction detection. Statistica Sinica **12**(2), 361–386 (2002). http://www.jstor.org/stable/24306967
18. Lou, Y., Caruana, R., Gehrke, J., Hooker, G.: Accurate intelligible models with pairwise interactions. In: Ghani, R., et al (eds.) Proceedings of the 19th ACM SIGKDD International Conference on Knowledge Discovery and Data Mining, pp. 623–631. ACM, New York, NY, USA (2013). https://doi.org/10.1145/2487575.2487579
19. Maratea, A., Ferone, A.: Pitfalls of local explainability in complex black-box models. In: Proceedings of the 13th International Workshop on Fuzzy Logic and Applications (WILF) (2021). https://ceur-ws.org/Vol-3074/paper13.pdf
20. Ming, Y., Qu, H., Bertini, E.: RuleMatrix: visualizing and understanding classifiers with rules. IEEE Trans. Vis. Comput. Graph. **25**(1), 342–352 (2018). https://doi.org/10.1109/TVCG.2018.2864812
21. Molnar, C.: Interpretable Machine Learning, 2 edn. (2022). https://christophm.github.io/interpretable-ml-book
22. Rand, W.M.: Objective criteria for the evaluation of clustering methods. J. Am. Stat. Assoc. **66**(336), 846–850 (1971). https://doi.org/10.1080/01621459.1971.10482356
23. Ribeiro, M.T., Singh, S., Guestrin, C.: Why should I trust you?: Explaining the predictions of any classifier. In: Proceedings of the 22nd ACM SIGKDD International Conference on Knowledge Discovery and Data Mining, pp. 1135–1144. KDD '16, Association for Computing Machinery, New York, NY, USA (2016). https://doi.org/10.1145/2939672.2939778
24. Schalk, D., Thomas, J., Bischl, B.: compboost: modular framework for component-wise boosting. JOSS **3**(30), 967 (2018). https://doi.org/10.21105/joss.00967
25. Schlosser, L., Hothorn, T., Zeileis, A.: The power of unbiased recursive partitioning: a unifying view of CTree, MOB, and GUIDE. arXiv preprint arXiv:1906.10179 (2019)
26. Seibold, H., Zeileis, A., Hothorn, T.: Model-based recursive partitioning for subgroup analyses. Int. J. Biostat. **12**(1), 45–63 (2016). https://doi.org/10.1515/ijb-2015-0032
27. Visani, G., Bagli, E., Chesani, F.: OptiLIME: optimized LIME explanations for diagnostic computer algorithms. arXiv preprint arXiv:2006.05714 v3 (2022)

28. Zeileis, A., Hothorn, T., Hornik, K.: Model-based recursive partitioning. J. Comput. Graph. Stat. **17**(2), 492–514 (2008). https://doi.org/10.1198/106186008X319331
29. Zhou, Z., Hooker, G., Wang, F.: S-LIME: stabilized-LIME for model explanation. In: Proceedings of the 27th ACM SIGKDD Conference on Knowledge Discovery & Data Mining, pp. 2429–2438. Association for Computing Machinery, New York, NY, USA (2021). https://doi.org/10.1145/3447548.3467274

Temporal Saliency Detection Towards Explainable Transformer-Based Timeseries Forecasting

Nghia Duong-Trung[1]($\boxtimes$) ⓘ, Duc-Manh Nguyen[2] ⓘ, and Danh Le-Phuoc[2] ⓘ

[1] German Research Center for Artificial Intelligence (DFKI), Alt-Moabit 91 C,
10559 Berlin, Germany
nghia_trung.duong@dfki.de
[2] Technische Universität Berlin, Straße des 17. Juni 135, 10623 Berlin, Germany
{duc.manh.nguyen,danh.lephuoc}@tu-berlin.de

Abstract. Despite the notable advancements in numerous Transformer-based models, the task of long multi-horizon time series forecasting remains a persistent challenge, especially towards explainability. Focusing on commonly used saliency maps in explaining DNN in general, our quest is to build attention-based architecture that can automatically encode saliency-related temporal patterns by establishing connections with appropriate attention heads. Hence, this paper introduces Temporal Saliency Detection (TSD), an effective approach that builds upon the attention mechanism and applies it to multi-horizon time series prediction. While our proposed architecture adheres to the general encoder-decoder structure, it undergoes a significant renovation in the encoder component, wherein we incorporate a series of information contracting and expanding blocks inspired by the U-Net style architecture. The TSD approach facilitates the multiresolution analysis of saliency patterns by condensing multi-heads, thereby progressively enhancing the forecasting of complex time series data. Empirical evaluations illustrate the superiority of our proposed approach compared to other models across multiple standard benchmark datasets in diverse far-horizon forecasting settings. The initial TSD achieves substantial relative improvements of 31% and 46% over several models in the context of multivariate and univariate prediction. We believe the comprehensive investigations presented in this study will offer valuable insights and benefits to future research endeavors.

Keywords: Time Series Forecasting · Saliency Patterns · Explainability · Pattern Mining

1 Introduction

Time series forecasting empowers decision-making on chronological data, and performs an essential role in various research and industry fields such as healthcare [34], energy management [48], industrial automation [60], planning for

S. Nowaczyk et al. (Eds.): ECAI 2023 Workshops, CCIS 1947, pp. 250–268, 2024.
https://doi.org/10.1007/978-3-031-50396-2_14

infrastructure construction [43], economics and finance [44]. Time series observations can be a single sequence addressed by traditional time series forecasting approaches such as autoregressive integrated or exponentially weighted moving averages. However, actual time series data may consist of several channels as predictors for future forecasting and thus require more effective approaches. Multi-horizon prediction allows us to estimate a long sequence, optimizing intervened actions at multiple time steps in the future where performance improvements are precious. Hence, a significant challenge for time series forecasting is to develop practical models dealing with the heterogeneity of multi-channel time series data and produce accurate predictions in multi-horizon.

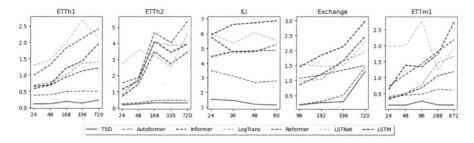

Fig. 1. Multivariate time series forecasting comparison. The lower lines indicate better forecasting capacity. y-axis indicates the MSE loss while x-axis presents the prediction horizon.

Following the great success of attention mechanisms in machine translation, recent research has adapted it for time series forecasting [6,13,21,63,64,66]. Self-attentions consider the local information that the models only utilize point-wise dependencies. Benefiting from the self-attention mechanism, Transformers achieve significant efficiencies in dependency modeling for sequential data, allowing for constructing more powerful large models. However, the forecasting problem is highly challenging in the long term and when many variables affect the target. First, detecting temporal dependencies directly from long-horizon time series is unreliable because the dependencies can be spread across many variables, and each variable tends to be different. Second, the canonical Transformer with self-attention requires high-power computing for long-term forecasting because of the quadratic complexity of the sequence length. Thus, to solve the computational hardware bottleneck, the previous Transformer-based predictive models mainly focused on improving the full self-attention to a sparse version. For the information aggregation, Autoformer adopts the time delay block to aggregate the similar sub-series from underlying periods rather than selecting scattered points by dot-product. The Auto-Correlation mechanism can simultaneously benefit the computation efficiency and information utilization from the inherent sparsity and sub-series-level representation aggregation. Despite the significantly improved performance, this approach has to sacrifice information usage because point connections lead to long-term time series forecasting bottlenecks that make it difficult to explain the trained models.

Towards explainability, saliency maps have been widely used to highlight important input features in model predictions to explain model behaviors in computer vision [9,27,62] and recently also apply for time series. In fact, [11] introduces the saliency-guided architecture that shows it works CNN and LSTM. However, it is still being determined whether such an approach will work with the recent transformer-based approach above, especially with the ones using sparsifying techniques. For example, [12] pointed out that attention-based methods can be insufficient for interpreting multivariate time-series data, e.g., saliency maps fail to reliably and accurately identify feature importance over time in time series data. We hypothesize that we need a technique to automatically encode the *saliency-related temporal patterns* via connecting to the suitable attention heads. Thus, we attempt to go beyond heuristic approaches such as Informer, e.g., sparse point-wise connection, Autoformer, e.g., sub-level-wise connection, and propose a generic architecture to empower forecasting models with automatic segment-wise interpolation. Inspired by saliency detection theory [65] in images and video recognition [19,53], we propose a method to weigh the proper attention to possible emerging temporal patterns.

This method is realized as a learning architecture called Temporal Saliency Detection, which can be categorized into Transformer-family for far-horizon time series forecasting. Our proposed architecture still follows a general encoder-decoder structure but renovates the encoder component with a series of information contracting and expanding blocks inspired by U-Net style architecture [39]. The fundamental architecture of a U-net model comprises two distinct paths. The first path, referred to as the contracting path, encoder, or analysis path, closely resembles a conventional convolutional network and is responsible for extracting pertinent information from the input data. On the other hand, the second path, known as the expansion path, decoder, or synthesis path, encompasses up-convolutions and feature concatenations derived from the contracting path. This expansion process facilitates learning localized extracted information and concurrently enhances the output resolution. Subsequently, the augmented output passes through a final convolutional layer to generate the fully synthesized data. The resultant network exhibits an almost symmetrical configuration, endowing it with a U-like shape. To this end, similar to the latent diffusion models for high-resolution image synthesis [38], by allowing the attention mechanism and the information contraction to work in concert, our architecture can construct temporal saliency patterns through segment-wise aggregation. While U-Net style architecture [46] can pay the way for temporal saliency patterns to emerge like in [30], the challenge is how to match the performance of heuristics point-wise or sub-series-wise methods (e.g., Informer, LogTrans, and Autoformer). The experiments in Section 4 show that our approach can be competitive with several state-of-the-art methods as visually summarized in Fig. 1. The contributions of the paper are summarized as follows:

- We introduce the Temporal Saliency Detection model as a harmonic combination between encoder-decoder structure and U-Net architecture to empower the far-horizon time series forecasting towards explainability.
- Our proposed approach discovers and aggregates temporal information at the segment-wise level. TSD consistently performs the prediction capacity in ten different multivariate-forecasting horizons.
- At the current initial investigation, TSD achieves a **31%** and **46%** relative improvement over compared models under multivariate and univariate time series forecasting on standard benchmarks.

2   Related Work

Long and Multi Horizon Time Series Forecasting has been a well-established research topic with a steadily growing number of publications due to its immense importance for real applications [25,26]. Classical methods such as ARIMA [1], RNN [37,58,61], LSTM [2] and Prophet [50] serve as a standard baselines for forecasting. One of the most ubiquitous approaches in a wide variety of forecasting systems is deep time series which have been proven effective in both industries [24,28] and academic [7,51]. Amazon time series forecasting services build around DeepAR [42], which combines RNNs and autoregressive sliding methods to model the probabilistic future time points. Attention-based RNNs approaches capture temporal dependency for short and long term predictions [36,45,47]. CNN's models for time series forecasting also provide a noticeable solution for periodically high-dimensional time series [17,18,56]. Another deep stack of fully-connected layers based on backward and forward residual links, named N-BEATS, was proposed by [29] and later improved by [3], called N-HITS, have empowered this research direction. Those forecasting approaches focus on temporal dependency modeling by current knowledge, recurrent connections, or temporal convolution.

Transformers Based on the Self-attention Mechanism, originating from the machine translation domain, have been successfully adapted to address different time series problems [5,17,20,22,45,47]. Attention computation allows direct pair-wise comparison to any uncommon occurrence, e.g., sale seasons, and can model temporal dynamics inherently. However, pair-wise interactions make attention-based models suffer from the quadratic complexity of sequence length. Recent research, Reformer [14], Linformer [57], and Informer [66], proposes multiple variations of the canonical attention mechanisms have achieved superior forecasting while in parallel reducing the complexity of pair-wise interactions. Another exciting paper that belongs to the attention-based family of models is the Query Selector [15], where the idea of computing a sparse approximation of an attention matrix is exploited. Note that these forecasting models still rely on point-wise computation and aggregation. Nevertheless, those models have improved the self-attention mechanism from a full to a sparse version by sacrificing information utilization. In this context, we call them as *sparsification architectures*. Along the same line, YFormer [23] adjusted the Informer model by integrating a U-Net architecture into Informer's *ProbSparse Self-attention* module. While it is also inspired by U-Net like us, YFormer inherits the problem of sacrificing the information utilization of Informer. Originated from the medical image segmentation problem, U-Net is capable of condensing input information to several intermediate embeddings and up-sampling them to the same resolutions as the input [10,16,39]. Apart from the image domain, the U-Net approach has proven noticeable results for sequence modeling [49] and time series segmentation [33].

Auto-correlation Mechanism. A noticeable encoder-decoder architecture that utilizes Fourier transform is Autoformer [59] with decomposition capacities and an attention approximation. Autoformer is based on the series periodicity addressed in the stochastic process theory, where trend, seasonal, and other components are blended [4]. Hence, the model does not depend on temporal dependency as with the transformer-based solutions, but the auto-correlation emerging from data. The series-wise connections replace the point-wise representation.

Saliency has emerged as a prominent and effective method for enhancing interpretability, providing insights into why a trained model produces specific predictions for a given input. One approach to leveraging saliency is through saliency-guided training, which aims to diminish irrelevant features' influence by reducing the associated gradient values. This is achieved by masking input features with low gradients and then minimizing the KL divergence between the outputs generated from the original input and the masked input, in addition to the main loss function. The effectiveness of the saliency approach has been demonstrated across various domains, including image analysis, language processing, and time series data [41,52]. Another saliency technique involves extracting a series of images from sliding windows within time series data and defining a learnable mask based on these series images and their perturbed counterparts. This approach, series saliency, acts as an adaptive data augmentation method for training deep models [31]. In exploring perturbed versions of data, Parvatharaju *et al.* introduced a method called perturbation by prioritized replacement. This technique learns to emphasize the timesteps that contribute the most to the classifier's prediction, indicating their importance [32]. Saadallah *et al.* tackled the challenge of searching for an optimal network architecture by considering candidate models from various deep neural network architectures. They dynamically selected the most suitable architecture in real-time using concept drift detection in time series data. Saliency maps were utilized to compute the region of competence for each candidate network [40].

3 Attention with Temporal Saliency

3.1 Problem Definition and Notation

A time series is composed of N univariate time series where each $i = 1 \ldots N$, we have y_t^i as a value of the univariate time series i at time t. Given the look-back window τ, x_t^i are exogenous inputs as associated co-variate values, e.g., day-of-the-week and hour-of-the-day. We can formulate the one-step-ahead prediction model as follows:

$$\hat{y}_{i,t+1} = f(y_{t-\tau \triangleright t}^i, x_{t-\tau \triangleright t}^i) \tag{1}$$

where $y_{t-\tau \triangleright t}^i = \{y_{t-\tau}^i, ..., y_t^i\}$ and $x_{t-\tau \triangleright t}^i = \{x_{t-\tau}^i, ..., x_t^i\}$.

As a common practice in transformer-based model, e.g., [57] and [59], the inputs $y_{t-\tau \triangleright t}^i, x_{t-\tau \triangleright t}^i$ are encoded under a vector of hidden states z to serve as the inputs for an attention block as the below step. The size $|z|$ is aligned with the number of input tokens for the transformer-based encoding block.

To prepare for the description of our architecture in the next section, we introduce two fundamental building blocks $\mathrm{Conv}^{\downarrow}$ and $\mathrm{Conv}^{\uparrow}$, with two following equations, e.g., downsampling and upsampling blocks, respectively. They are two parameterized sub-modules used in U-Net [39] style architecture. They both have two parameters, namely, $\mathcal{H}$ and d, which are the hidden input states and the drop-out parameter.

$$\mathrm{Conv}^{\downarrow}(\mathcal{H}, d) = \mathrm{DropOut}(\mathrm{MaxPool}(\mathrm{ReLU}(\mathrm{Conv1d}(\mathcal{H}))), d) \tag{2}$$

$$\mathrm{Conv}^{\uparrow}(\mathcal{H}, d) = \mathrm{DropOut}(\mathrm{ConvT1d}(\mathrm{ReLU}(\mathrm{Conv1d}(\mathcal{H}))), d) \tag{3}$$

where ConvT1d is shorted for ConvTranspose1d.

3.2   Architecture for Temporal Saliency Detection

This section will introduce our proposed learning architecture illustrated in Fig. 2.

The description will be followed from left to right according to the input flow. The critical novel aspect of this architecture is that the Temporal Saliency Detection ($\mathcal{TSD}$) block can work in tandem with the Temporal Self-Attention ($\mathcal{TSA}$) block. During the training process, the weights in both these blocks can be automatically adjusted to reveal temporal saliency maps in a similar fashion to semantic segmentation in computer vision. While our implementation is proven to outperform its competitors by a large margin, the saliency aspect will open the door for supporting the interpretability of our models as a natural next step for this work.

Time Series Tokenization. To prepare the input for the below $\mathcal{TSA}$ block, our architecture will encode time series into a Linear Embedding z to make it compatible with token inputs of the attention module $\mathcal{TSA}$. Next, we use convolution block Conv1d to encode z from input time series $(y_{t-\tau \triangleright t}^i, x_{t-\tau \triangleright t}^i)$. Note the number of the tokens $|z|$ is a hyper-parameter for our architecture (see Ablation study in Sect. 5).

$$z = \mathrm{Conv1d}(y_{t-\tau \triangleright t}^i, x_{t-\tau \triangleright t}^i) \tag{4}$$

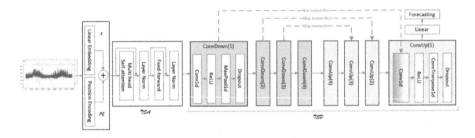

Fig. 2. The high-level design of the Temporal Saliency Detection (TSD) model.

Temporal Self-Attention ($\mathcal{TSA}$). We use a multi-attention block to encode the correlation of temporal pattern, similar to [57]. Here, we only use one multi-attention block to mitigate the memory problem of dot products similar to Informer and the like. The subsequent convolution blocks can be adjusted to avoid the quadratic memory consumption of multiple attention blocks of vanilla transformers. Our evaluation results and ablation study show that this block alone can work in concert with $\mathcal{TSD}$ to adjust the learning weights allowing temporal saliency patterns to emerge so that our trained models could outperform those of specification architectures in similar memory consumption. Also, as a common practice, we add the position encoding PE [54] to z to create $\mathcal{TSA}$ as follows.

$$\mathcal{TSA} = \text{LN}(\text{FFN}(\text{LN}(\text{SelfAttention}(z + \text{PE})))) \tag{5}$$

where LN(.), FFN(.) and SelfAttention(.) are LinearNorm, FeedForward and Self-Attention blocks, respectively.

Temporal Saliency Detection ($\mathcal{TSD}$). Inspired by saliency map generation using U-Net in semantic segmentation, this block consists of two mirroring paths: contracting and expanding with $\text{Conv}^{\downarrow}$ and $\text{Conv}^{\uparrow}$ blocks, respectively. The below equations define such $\mathcal{L}$ block pairs. $\mathcal{L}$ is also considered as a hyper-parameter that can be empirically adjusted based on the data and the memory availability of the training infrastructure. Figure 2 illustrates $\mathcal{L} = 4$.

$$\text{ConvDown}^i = \text{Conv}^{\downarrow}(\text{ConvDown}^{i-1}, d_i) \tag{6}$$

where $i = 2, ..., \mathcal{L}$ and $\text{ConvDown}^1 = \text{Conv}^{\downarrow}(TSA, d_1)$.

$$\text{ConvUp}^i = \text{Conv}^{\uparrow}(\text{ConvDown}^i \oplus \text{ConvUp}^{i+1}, d^i) \tag{7}$$

where $i = 1, ..., \mathcal{L} - 1$ and $\text{ConvUp}^{\mathcal{L}} = \text{Conv}^{\uparrow}(\text{ConvDown}^{\mathcal{L}}, d^{\mathcal{L}})$. $\oplus$ is the concatenation operator.

Note that the skip connections are specified as the concatenations between ConvDown^i and ConvUp^{i+1}. These skip connections are used to connect different patterns that emerged from different time scales. They also help avoid information loss due to the compression process that sparsification architectures suffer.

Moreover, [55] indicated that such skip connections could be well integrated well with attention heads of $\mathcal{TSA}$. In this design, we can see the features for z after the $\mathcal{TSA}$ might be at different scales or magnitudes. This can be due to some components of z or later $\mathcal{TSA}$ having very sharp or very distributed attention weights when summing over the features of the other components. Additionally, at the individual feature/vector entries level, concatenating across multiple attention heads-each of which might output values at different scales-can lead to the entries of the final vector having a wide range of values. Hence, these skip connections and the up-down sampling process work hand-in-hand to enable the temporal saliency patterns to emerge while canceling the noise. In the sequel, we have the definition of $\mathcal{TSD}$ block as follows.

$$\mathcal{TSD} = \text{LN}(\text{ConvUp}^1) \tag{8}$$

Regarding $\mathcal{L}$ in our implementation for evaluated datasets, both contracting or expanding paths contain three or four repeated blocks, i.e., $\mathcal{L} = 3$ or $\mathcal{L} = 4$. Note that $\mathcal{L}$ can be seen as a counterpart of the k parameters in 'top-k' components for sparsification architectures such as Informer and Autoformer. In our evaluation and ablation studies, $\mathcal{L}$ and associated parameters are more intuitive and easier to adjust to optimize the model performance empirically.
Forecasting. The forecasting operation involves one-step-ahead prediction $\hat{y}_{i,t+1}$ powered by $\mathcal{TSD}$ that can dynamically uses to compute a new hidden state y_{t+1}^i for each element $i = 1...N$ from the τ previous states $y_{t-\tau \triangleright t}^i$ from t.

4 Experiment

4.1 Datasets

To have a fair comparison with the current best approaches, we select the public data files from the Informer's Github page[1], including ETTh1, ETTh2, and ETTm1, and Autoformer's Github[2], e.g., Exchange and ILI. We evaluate all baselines and our model on a wide range of prediction horizons within {24, 36, 48, 60, 96, 168, 288, 336, 672, 720}.

ETT: Electricity Transformer Temperature is a real-world dataset for electric power deployment. The dataset is further converted into different granularity, e.g., ETTh1 and ETTh2 for 1-h-level and ETTm1 for 15-min-level. Each data point consists of six predictors and one oil temperature target value.

ILI: Influenza-like illness dataset[3] reports weekly recorded influenza patients from the Center for Disease Control and Prevention of the United States. It measures the ratio of illness patients over the total number of patients in a week. Each data point consists of six predictors and one target value.

---

[1] https://github.com/zhouhaoyi/Informer2020.
[2] https://github.com/thuml/Autoformer.
[3] https://gis.cdc.gov/grasp/fluview/fluportaldashboard.html.

Exchange: The dataset is a collection of daily exchange rates of different countries from 1990 to 2016 [17]. Each data point consists of seven predictors and one target value.

We follow the splitting protocol mentioned in the Autoformer paper [59] by the ratio of 7:1:2 for all datasets. Figure 3 visualizes the challenge of real-world finance Exchange, disease ILI, and energy consumption ETT datasets. To be more precise, we choose time series that exhibit either a trend or are exceptionally challenging to predict.

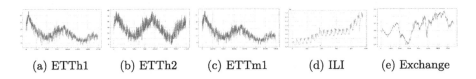

    (a) ETTh1   (b) ETTh2   (c) ETTm1   (d) ILI   (e) Exchange

Fig. 3. A visualization of datasets' forecasting targets.

4.2 Experimental Setup

Baselines. We compared our TSD model with six baseline approaches. Regarding multivariate time series forecasting, we designed the experiments similar to the Autoformer model [59], a standard benchmark for much following-up time series forecasting research. More concretely, we compare TSD with Autoformer [59], Informer [66], LogTrans [20], Reformer [14], LSTNet [17], and LSTM [8]. We reused the experimental reports in the Autoformer paper after randomly double-checking by re-running several experiments not to repeat all implementations on all datasets. Additionally, regarding univariate time series prediction, we designed the experiments similar to the Informer model [66]. Here, we compare our model with Informer, Reformer, LogTrans, DeepAR [42], Yformer [23], and Query Selector [15]. The Git repository is available at[4].

Hyperparameter Optimization. We conduct a grid search over the hyperparameters, and the ranges are given in the following. We set the number of the encoder as one while mainly focusing on the Conv-down-up architecture design, which is the core power of the TSD model. The hidden state sequence z size is selected from $\{512, 1024, 1280, 1536\}$ while the number of heads is $\{8, 16, 32\}$. The number of up-sampling and down-sampling blocks is $\{3, 4, 5\}$. The dropout values are searched from $\{0.05, 0.1, 0.2, 0.3\}$. We performed a grid search of the learning rate of $\{0.00001, 0.00002, 0.000001, 0.000005, 0.0000001\}$. Furthermore, we apply a scheduling reduction of learning rate by a factor γ of $\{0.97, 0.95, 0.87, 0.85\}$ with a step size of $\{2, 5, 8\}$. The training epoch range is $\{15, 20, 25, 30, 35\}$. The number of heads in self-attention is from $\{8, 16\}$. Regarding the optimizer, we select AdamW.

---

[4] https://github.com/duongtrung/time-series-temporal-saliency-patterns.

Metrics and Implementation Details. We trained the TSD model regarding optimizing the mean absolute error MAE $= \frac{1}{n}\sum_{i=1}^{n}|\mathbf{y} - \hat{\mathbf{y}}|$ and mean squared error MSE $= \frac{1}{n}\sum_{i=1}^{n}(\mathbf{y} - \hat{\mathbf{y}})^2$ losses on each prediction horizon. We conducted most of Pytorch implementation on high-performance computing nodes equipped with a GeForce RTX 2080Ti 32 GB. We ran all experiments three times and reported the average results.

4.3   Results and Analysis

We select datasets under a wide range of horizon lengths from 24 to 720-time points to compare prediction capacity in the challenging multivariate scenario. Regarding the multivariate time series forecasting, Table 1 summarizes the experimental results of all models and benchmarks, while Fig. 1 visualizes a relative comparison in trends. As for this experimental scenario, TSD has achieved remarkable performance in all benchmarks and all forecasting horizons, as illustrated in Table 2. Especially under the optimization for the MSE loss, TSD outperforms six baselines in all 23 different forecasting lengths. Autoformer achieves better results in only 4 MAE cases out of 46 cases in both MSE and MAE. However, these better results fall into short forecasting horizons, e.g., (48, 168) and (96, 192) in ETTh2 and Exchange, respectively. The trends of ETTh1, ETTh2, ILI, and ETTm1 in Fig. 1 have proven the consistent prediction power of TSD in far horizons. Especially, under the MSE loss, compared to the previous best state-of-the-art performance, TSD gives average **65%** reduction in ETTh1, **29%** in ETTh2, **65%** in ETTm1, **18%** in Exchange, and **56%** in ILI. A similar reduction is observed regarding the MAE loss. The error reduction harmonizes with trends and nature of the data as shown in Fig. 1. ETTh1 and ETTm1 share a general downward trend, and the data part corresponding to the test set has a small fluctuation amplitude. Contrary to ETTh1 and ETTm1, the ILI dataset tends to increase, and the corresponding test set data has a larger fluctuation amplitude. Due to the unforeseen interaction between countless economic phenomena, the Exchange dataset is comparatively challenging. Therefore, a reduction of **18%** is achieved. Overall, 46 reported results in 10 different forecasting horizons, TSD yields a **31%** reduction in both MSE and MAE losses. It proves TSD's superiority against several current best models for many complex real-world multivariate forecasting applications, including early disease warning, long-term financial planning, and resource consumption arrangement.

As for the univariate scenario, i.e. $N = 1$, TSD has also achieved consistent performance in all benchmarks and all forecasting horizons. TSD yields the best scores in 28 out of 30 experimental cases within five different horizons. Note that TSD has noticeably outperformed DeepAR, the back-bone model for Amazon Forecast Service. The Query Selector model is a robust approach outperforming Informer in all three datasets in both losses. However, compared to our model, the Query Selector is only better in two cases, e.g., ETTm1 at 672 horizons for MSE and MAE. The relative error reduction in both MSE and MAE losses is **46%**.

Table 1. Multivariate time series forecasting results. A lower MSE or MAE indicates better forecasting. The best scores are in **bold**.

Model		TSD		Autoformer		Informer		LogTrans		Reformer		LSTNet		LSTM	
Data & Metric		MSE	MAE	MSE	MAE	MSE	MAE	MSE	MAE	MSE	MAE	MSE	MAE	MSE	MAE
ETTh1	24	**0.115**	**0.285**	0.384	0.425	0.577	0.549	0.686	0.604	0.991	0.754	1.293	0.901	0.650	0.624
	48	**0.119**	**0.279**	0.392	0.419	0.685	0.625	0.766	0.757	1.313	0.906	1.456	0.960	0.702	0.675
	168	**0.191**	**0.313**	0.490	0.481	0.931	0.752	1.002	0.846	1.824	1.138	1.997	1.214	1.212	0.867
	336	**0.141**	**0.285**	0.505	0.484	1.128	0.873	1.362	0.952	2.117	1.280	2.655	1.369	1.424	0.994
	720	**0.233**	**0.416**	0.498	0.500	1.215	0.896	1.397	1.291	2.415	1.520	2.143	1.380	1.960	1.322
ETTh2	24	**0.189**	**0.270**	0.261	0.341	0.720	0.665	0.828	0.750	1.531	1.613	2.742	1.457	1.143	0.813
	48	**0.242**	0.538	0.312	**0.373**	1.457	1.001	1.806	1.034	1.871	1.735	3.567	1.687	1.671	1.221
	168	**0.320**	0.493	0.457	**0.455**	3.489	1.515	4.070	1.681	4.660	1.846	3.242	2.513	4.117	1.674
	336	**0.309**	**0.462**	0.471	0.475	2.723	1.340	3.875	1.763	4.028	1.688	2.544	2.591	3.434	1.549
	720	**0.314**	**0.472**	0.474	0.484	3.467	1.473	3.913	1.552	5.381	2.015	4.625	3.709	3.963	1.788
ETTm1	24	**0.145**	**0.306**	0.383	0.403	0.323	0.369	0.419	0.412	0.724	0.607	1.968	1.170	0.621	0.629
	48	**0.143**	**0.293**	0.454	0.453	0.494	0.503	0.507	0.583	1.098	0.777	1.999	1.215	1.392	0.939
	96	**0.268**	**0.390**	0.481	0.463	0.678	0.614	0.768	0.792	1.433	0.945	2.762	1.542	1.339	0.913
	288	**0.157**	**0.316**	0.634	0.528	1.056	0.786	1.462	1.320	1.820	1.094	1.257	2.076	1.740	1.124
	672	**0.149**	**0.313**	0.606	0.542	1.192	0.926	1.669	1.461	2.187	1.232	1.917	2.941	2.736	1.555
Exchange	96	**0.184**	0.369	0.197	**0.323**	0.847	0.752	0.968	0.812	1.065	0.829	1.551	1.058	1.453	1.049
	192	**0.262**	0.445	0.300	**0.369**	1.204	0.895	1.040	0.851	1.188	0.906	1.477	1.028	1.846	1.179
	336	**0.293**	**0.422**	0.509	0.524	1.672	1.036	1.659	1.081	1.357	0.976	1.507	1.031	2.136	1.231
	720	**1.307**	**0.758**	1.447	0.941	2.478	1.310	1.941	1.127	1.510	1.016	2.285	1.243	2.984	1.427
ILI	24	**1.514**	**1.103**	3.483	1.287	5.764	1.677	4.480	1.444	4.400	1.382	6.026	1.770	5.914	1.734
	36	**1.449**	**1.086**	3.103	1.148	4.755	1.467	4.799	1.467	4.783	1.448	5.340	1.668	6.631	1.845
	48	**1.186**	**0.971**	2.669	1.085	4.763	1.469	4.800	1.468	4.832	1.465	6.080	1.787	6.736	1.857
	60	**1.140**	**0.946**	2.770	1.125	5.264	1.564	5.278	1.560	4.882	1.483	5.548	1.720	6.870	1.879

4.4   Discussions

When applying prediction principles to sequential data, e.g., natural language or time series, contextual information weighs a lot, primarily when long-range dependencies exist. In this context, the issues of gradient vanishing and explosion, model size, and dependencies depend on the length of the sequential data. Transformer's self-attention approach successfully addressed those mentioned issues by designing a novel encoder-decoder architecture [54]. Developed upon that architecture, the Probsparse self-attention was introduced to overcome the memory bottleneck of the transformer while acceptably handling extremely long input sequences. Table 4 presents the evolutional simplification of general encoder-decoder pairs throughout the research. Employing model design, the complexity of an encoder-decoder architecture is significantly reduced. For instance, the number of encoders and decoders in the Informer model was reduced from 6 to 4 and 6 to 2, respectively. However, the long-term forecasting problem of time series remains challenging, although various self-attention mechanisms were adopted. In far-horizon forecasting, a model, instead of attending to several single points, treat sub-series level and aggregates dependencies discovery and representation. Consequently, the auto-correlation mechanism was developed [59], which yielded a 38% relative improvement on compared models.

The number of encoders and decoders was noticeably reduced from 4 to 2 and 2 to 1, respectively. One point to note is that the authors of those mentioned models do not provide any ablation study on why they chose the number of encoders and decoders. However, the core idea is to balance forecasting accuracy and computation efficiency. As discussed in Sect. 1, our hypothesis is to automatically encode the correct temporal pattern to the suitable self-attention heads and to learn saliency patterns emerging from the sequential data. Hence, one encoder is enough to output a self-attention representation. Unlike the existing methods, we completely replace a general decoder with a U-sharp architecture, effectively addressing the image segmentation task. Generally speaking, we also want to *segment* time series in automatic processing and discovery.

Table 2. Univariate time series forecasting results. A lower MSE or MAE indicates better forecasting. The best scores are in bold.

Models		TSD		Informer		Reformer		LogTrans		DeepAR		Yformer		Query Selector	
Dataset & Metric		MSE	MAE	MSE	MAE	MSE	MAE	MSE	MAE	MSE	MAE	MSE	MAE	MSE	MAE
ETTh1	24	**0.018**	**0.102**	0.098	0.247	0.222	0.389	0.103	0.259	0.107	0.280	0.082	0.230	*0.043*	0.161
	48	**0.043**	**0.166**	0.158	0.319	0.284	0.445	0.167	0.328	0.162	0.327	0.139	0.308	*0.072*	0.211
	168	**0.082**	**0.225**	0.183	0.346	1.522	1.191	0.207	0.375	0.239	0.422	0.111	0.268	*0.093*	0.237
	336	**0.094**	**0.237**	0.222	0.387	1.860	1.124	0.230	0.398	0.445	0.552	0.195	0.365	*0.126*	0.284
	720	**0.129**	**0.291**	0.269	0.435	2.112	1.436	0.273	0.463	0.658	0.707	0.226	0.394	*0.213*	0.373
ETTm1	24	**0.011**	**0.082**	0.030	0.137	0.095	0.228	0.065	0.202	0.091	0.243	0.024	0.118	*0.013*	0.087
	48	**0.019**	**0.110**	0.069	0.203	0.249	0.390	0.078	0.220	0.219	0.362	0.048	0.173	*0.034*	0.140
	96	**0.038**	**0.161**	0.194	0.372	0.920	0.767	0.199	0.386	0.364	0.496	0.143	0.311	*0.070*	0.210
	288	**0.057**	**0.199**	0.401	0.554	1.108	1.245	0.411	0.572	0.948	0.795	*0.150*	0.316	0.154	0.324
	672	0.341	1.052	0.512	0.644	1.793	1.528	0.598	0.702	2.437	1.352	0.305	0.476	**0.173**	**0.342**
ETTh2	24	**0.075**	**0.210**	0.093	0.240	0.263	0.437	0.102	0.255	0.098	0.263	*0.082*	0.221	0.084	0.223
	48	**0.073**	**0.213**	0.155	0.314	0.458	0.545	0.169	0.348	0.163	0.341	0.139	0.334	*0.111*	0.262
	168	**0.110**	**0.270**	0.232	0.389	1.029	0.879	0.246	0.422	0.255	0.414	*0.111*	0.337	0.175	0.332
	336	**0.121**	**0.273**	0.263	0.417	1.668	1.228	0.267	0.437	0.604	0.607	*0.195*	0.391	0.208	0.371
	720	**0.123**	**0.273**	0.277	0.431	2.030	1.721	0.303	0.493	0.429	0.580	*0.226*	0.382	0.258	0.413

5 Ablation Study

5.1 Pooling Selection

TSD comprises u-pair blocks of down-sampling and up-sampling that play a central role in current architecture. At each block l, we propose to use a pooling layer with a kernel size of $k_l = 3$ to help the layer focus a specific scale if its input. It helps reduce the input's width, release memory usage, reduce learnable parameters, alleviate the effects of overfitting, and limit the computation. We carefully explore max and average pooling operations and the model's stability under various far-horizon. Table 3 presents the empirical evaluation of pooling configurations. This ablation shows that max pooling is more stable in long-term forecasting, e.g., from a horizon of 60 and beyond.

Table 3. Empirical evaluation of eight different horizons with two pooling settings. The best scores are in **bold**.

Data	Horizon	MaxPool		AveragePool	
		MSE	MAE	MSE	MAE
ILI	24	**1.514**	**1.103**	1.577	1.108
	36	1.449	1.086	**1.429**	**1.042**
	48	**1.186**	0.971	1.239	**0.962**
	60	**1.140**	**0.946**	1.146	0.947
Exchange	96	**0.184**	**0.369**	0.985	1.263
	192	**0.262**	**0.445**	0.347	0.453
	336	**0.293**	**0.422**	0.455	0.513
	720	**1.307**	**0.758**	1.620	1.787

Table 4. The simplification of models' architecture and its reason. Referring to *Attention*, we mean the model developed by [54].

Model	# encoder	# decoder	Reason of simplification
Attention	6	6	Replacement of recurrent layers with encoder-decoder pairs
Informer	4	2	Introduction of Probsparseself-attention
Autoformer	2	1	Introduction of auto-correlationmechanism
Our model	1	1	Introduction of saliency detection mechanism

5.2 Architecture Variations

In this ablation, we test several variations of TSD architecture and its performance in three alternative layouts: $\{3, 4, 5\}$ conv-down-up blocks. We believe that the advantages of TSD architecture are rooted in its flexibility in multi-block design for a specific dataset. Table 5 compares TSD alternatives qualitatively. All hyperparameters are the same, excluding the block design. Most importantly, the best model design is to have a balance between forecasting accuracy and computation costs. Therefore, in this paper, we chose a TSD architecture with four conv-down-up blocks for all experiments.

6 Future Work

Although the concept of TSD demonstrates remarkable experimental outcomes, it requires a thorough hyperparameter search, as outlined in Sect. 4.2. The predefined range of hyperparameters heavily relies on domain expertise provided by an expert in the field. Specifically, the investigation involves determining the appropriate layer size in the convolutional blocks, establishing the optimal sequence of layers and examining its impact on prediction, and exploring potential interactions between the number of heads and conv-down-up blocks. This

Table 5. Evaluation of architectural variations of our proposed model. The best scores are in **bold**.

Model	Horizon	3 conv-down-up blocks		4 conv-down-upblocks		5 conv-down-upblocks	
		MSE	MAE	MSE	MAE	MSE	MAE
ILI	24	1.519	**1.081**	**1.514**	1.103	1.537	1.107
	36	**1.396**	**1.080**	1.449	1.086	1.405	1.128
	48	1.224	**0.958**	**1.186**	0.971	1.278	0.978
	60	1.126	**0.924**	1.140	0.946	**1.125**	0.930
Exchange	96	0.643	1.442	**0.184**	**0.369**	3.109	1.406
	192	1.818	1.676	**0.262**	**0.445**	0.287	0.458
	336	0.934	1.343	**0.293**	**0.422**	0.463	0.494
	720	1.411	0.937	**1.307**	**0.758**	1.505	1.040

process entails over 700 manual trial-and-error iterations in selecting the hyperparameter ranges, further enhancing performance. We acknowledge that hyperparameter optimization remains a limitation of the model.

While U-Net architectures are predominantly employed in biomedical image segmentation to automate identifying and detecting target regions or subregions, our study demonstrates that TSD can be effectively utilized for time series data. It is essential to highlight that a thorough analysis of U-Net variants [35, 46], encompassing inter-modality and intra-modality categorization, holds significance in gaining deeper insights into the challenges associated with time series forecasting and saliency detection. This analysis recommends a valuable avenue for future research endeavors in this field.

This study scrutinizes the efficacy of automatically encoding saliency-related temporal patterns by establishing connections with appropriate attention heads by incorporating information contracting and expanding blocks inspired by the U-Net style architecture. To substantiate our claims, we utilize an embarrassingly simple TSD forecasting baseline. It is crucial to note that the contributions of this work do not solely lie in proposing a state-of-the-art model; instead, they stem from posing a significant question, presenting surprising comparisons, and elucidating the effectiveness of TSD, as asserted in existing literature, from various perspectives. Our comprehensive investigations will prove advantageous for future research endeavors in this domain. The initial TSD model exhibits limited capacity, and its primary purpose is to serve as a straightforward yet competitive baseline with robust interpretability for subsequent research. TSD sets a new baseline for all pursuing multi-discipline work on popular time series benchmarks.

7   Conclusion

This research introduces an effective time series forecasting model called Temporal Saliency Detection, inspired by advancements in machine translation and down-and-up samplings in the context of image segmentation tasks. The proposed TSD model leverages the U-Net architecture and demonstrates superior predictability compared to existing models. This work's fundamental premise is the need for a technique to encode saliency-related temporal patterns through appropriate attention head connections automatically. The outcomes of our study underscore the significance of automatically learning saliency patterns from time series data, as the proposed TSD model significantly outperforms several state-of-the-art approaches and benchmark methods. In the multivariate scenario, our experiments reveal that TSD achieves a remarkable 31% reduction in MSE and MAE losses across 46 reported results encompassing ten diverse forecasting horizons. Similarly, in the univariate forecasting setting, TSD yields a noteworthy 46% reduction in both MSE and MAE losses. The authors conducted an ablation analysis to ensure the proposed model's effectiveness and expected behavior. However, it is worth noting that further potential for improvement is evident, suggesting the need for hyperparameter optimization and the exploitation of U-net variants. These findings underscore the efficacy and promise of the TSD model in the context of time series forecasting while also highlighting avenues for future research and refinement.

Acknowledgements. This work is supported by the German Research Foundation (DFG) under the COSMO project (grant No. 453130567), and by the European Union's Horizon WINDERA under the grant agreement No. 101079214 (AIoTwin), and RIA research and innovation programme under the grant agreement No. 101092908 (Smart-Edge).

References

1. Ariyo, A.A., Adewumi, A.O., Ayo, C.K.: Stock price prediction using the Arima model. In: 2014 UKSim-AMSS 16th International Conference on Computer Modelling and Simulation, pp. 106–112. IEEE (2014)
2. Bahdanau, D., Cho, K., Bengio, Y.: Neural machine translation by jointly learning to align and translate. arXiv preprint arXiv:1409.0473 (2014)
3. Challu, C., Olivares, K.G., Oreshkin, B.N., Garza, F., Mergenthaler, M., Dubrawski, A.: N-HiTS: neural hierarchical interpolation for time series forecasting. arXiv preprint arXiv:2201.12886 (2022)
4. Duarte, F.S., Rios, R.A., Hruschka, E.R., de Mello, R.F.: Decomposing time series into deterministic and stochastic influences: a survey. Digit. Sig. Proc. **95**, 102582 (2019)
5. Fan, C., et al.: Multi-horizon time series forecasting with temporal attention learning. In: Proceedings of the 25th ACM SIGKDD International Conference on Knowledge Discovery & Data Mining, pp. 2527–2535 (2019)
6. Gao, C., Zhang, N., Li, Y., Bian, F., Wan, H.: Self-attention-based time-variant neural networks for multi-step time series forecasting. Neural Comput. Appl. **34**(11), 8737–8754 (2022)
7. Hewamalage, H., Bergmeir, C., Bandara, K.: Recurrent neural networks for time series forecasting: current status and future directions. Int. J. Forecast. **37**(1), 388–427 (2021)

8. Hochreiter, S., Schmidhuber, J.: Long short-term memory. Neural Comput. **9**(8), 1735–1780 (1997)
9. Hu, B., Tunison, P., RichardWebster, B., Hoogs, A.: Xaitk-saliency: an open source explainable AI toolkit for saliency. In: Proceedings of the AAAI Conference on Artificial Intelligence, vol. 37, pp. 15760–15766 (2023)
10. Ibtehaz, N., Rahman, M.S.: MultiResUNet: rethinking the U-Net architecture for multimodal biomedical image segmentation. Neural Netw. **121**, 74–87 (2020)
11. Ismail, A.A., Corrada Bravo, H., Feizi, S.: Improving deep learning interpretability by saliency guided training. In: Ranzato, M., Beygelzimer, A., Dauphin, Y., Liang, P., Vaughan, J.W. (eds.) Advances in Neural Information Processing Systems, vol. 34, pp. 26726–26739. Curran Associates, Inc. (2021)
12. Ismail, A.A., Gunady, M., Bravo, H.C., Feizi, S.: Benchmarking deep learning interpretability in time series predictions. In: Proceedings of the 34th International Conference on Neural Information Processing Systems, NIPS 2020. Curran Associates Inc., Red Hook, NY, USA (2020)
13. Jin, X., Park, Y., Maddix, D., Wang, H., Wang, Y.: Domain adaptation for time series forecasting via attention sharing. In: International Conference on Machine Learning, pp. 10280–10297. PMLR (2022)
14. Kitaev, N., Kaiser, Ł., Levskaya, A.: Reformer: the efficient transformer. arXiv preprint arXiv:2001.04451 (2020)
15. Klimek, J., Klimek, J., Kraskiewicz, W., Topolewski, M.: Long-term series forecasting with query selector-efficient model of sparse attention. arXiv preprint arXiv:2107.08687 (2021)
16. Kohl, S., et al.: A probabilistic U-Net for segmentation of ambiguous images. In: Advances in Neural Information Processing Systems, vol. 31 (2018)
17. Lai, G., Chang, W.C., Yang, Y., Liu, H.: Modeling long-and short-term temporal patterns with deep neural networks. In: The 41st International ACM SIGIR Conference on Research & Development in Information Retrieval, pp. 95–104 (2018)
18. Lara-Benítez, P., Carranza-García, M., Riquelme, J.C.: An experimental review on deep learning architectures for time series forecasting. Int. J. Neural Syst. **31**(03), 2130001 (2021)
19. Li, H., Chen, G., Li, G., Yu, Y.: Motion guided attention for video salient object detection. In: Proceedings of the IEEE/CVF International Conference on Computer Vision, pp. 7274–7283 (2019)
20. Li, S., et al.: Enhancing the locality and breaking the memory bottleneck of transformer on time series forecasting. In: Advances in Neural Information Processing Systems, vol. 32, pp. 5243–5253 (2019)
21. Lim, B., Arık, S.Ö., Loeff, N., Pfister, T.: Temporal fusion transformers for interpretable multi-horizon time series forecasting. Int. J. Forecast. **37**, 1748–1764 (2021)
22. Ma, J., Shou, Z., Zareian, A., Mansour, H., Vetro, A., Chang, S.F.: CDSA: cross-dimensional self-attention for multivariate, geo-tagged time series imputation. arXiv preprint arXiv:1905.09904 (2019)
23. Madhusudhanan, K., Burchert, J., Duong-Trung, N., Born, S., Schmidt-Thieme, L.: Yformer: U-Net inspired transformer architecture for far horizon time series forecasting. arXiv preprint arXiv:2110.08255 (2021)
24. Makridakis, S., Spiliotis, E., Assimakopoulos, V.: Predicting/hypothesizing the findings of the M5 competition. Int. J. Forecast. **38**, 1337–1345 (2021)
25. Masini, R.P., Medeiros, M.C., Mendes, E.F.: Machine learning advances for time series forecasting. J. Econ. Surv. **37**, 76–111 (2021)

26. Meisenbacher, S., et al.: Wiley review of automated time series forecasting pipelines. Interdisc. Rev. Data Min. Knowl. Disc. **12**, e1475 (2022)
27. Morrison, K., Mehra, A., Perer, A.: Shared interest... sometimes: understanding the alignment between human perception, vision architectures, and saliency map techniques. In: Proceedings of the IEEE/CVF Conference on Computer Vision and Pattern Recognition, pp. 3775–3780 (2023)
28. Olivares, K.G., Meetei, N., Ma, R., Reddy, R., Cao, M.: Probabilistic hierarchical forecasting with Deep Poisson Mixtures. In: NeurIPS 2021 Workshop on Deep Generative Models and Downstream Applications (2021)
29. Oreshkin, B.N., Carpov, D., Chapados, N., Bengio, Y.: N-BEATS: neural basis expansion analysis for interpretable time series forecasting. arXiv preprint arXiv:1905.10437 (2019)
30. Pan, Q., Hu, W., Chen, N.: Two birds with one stone: series saliency for accurate and interpretable multivariate time series forecasting. In: Zhou, Z.H. (ed.) Proceedings of the Thirtieth International Joint Conference on Artificial Intelligence, IJCAI-21, pp. 2884–2891. International Joint Conferences on Artificial Intelligence Organization, August 2021
31. Pan, Q., Hu, W., Chen, N.: Two birds with one stone: series saliency for accurate and interpretable multivariate time series forecasting. In: IJCAI, pp. 2884–2891 (2021)
32. Parvatharaju, P.S., Doddaiah, R., Hartvigsen, T., Rundensteiner, E.A.: Learning saliency maps to explain deep time series classifiers. In: Proceedings of the 30th ACM International Conference on Information & Knowledge Management, pp. 1406–1415 (2021)
33. Perslev, M., Jensen, M., Darkner, S., Jennum, P.J., Igel, C.: U-Time: a fully convolutional network for time series segmentation applied to sleep staging. In: Advances in Neural Information Processing Systems, vol. 32, pp. 4415–4426 (2019)
34. Picetalli, F., Giampaolo, F., Prezioso, E., Camacho, D., Acampora, G.: Artificial intelligence and healthcare: forecasting of medical bookings through multi-source time-series fusion. Inf. Fusion **74**, 1–16 (2021)
35. Punn, N.S., Agarwal, S.: Modality specific U-Net variants for biomedical image segmentation: a survey. Artif. Intell. Rev. **55**(7), 5845–5889 (2022)
36. Qin, Y., Song, D., Chen, H., Cheng, W., Jiang, G., Cottrell, G.W.: A dual-stage attention-based recurrent neural network for time series prediction. In: IJCAI (2017)
37. Rangapuram, S.S., Seeger, M.W., Gasthaus, J., Stella, L., Wang, Y., Januschowski, T.: Deep state space models for time series forecasting. In: Advances in Neural Information Processing Systems, vol. 31 (2018)
38. Rombach, R., Blattmann, A., Lorenz, D., Esser, P., Ommer, B.: High-resolution image synthesis with latent diffusion models. CoRR abs/2112.10752 (2021)
39. Ronneberger, O., Fischer, P., Brox, T.: U-Net: convolutional networks for biomedical image segmentation. In: Navab, N., Hornegger, J., Wells, W.M., Frangi, A.F. (eds.) MICCAI 2015. LNCS, vol. 9351, pp. 234–241. Springer, Cham (2015). https://doi.org/10.1007/978-3-319-24574-4_28
40. Saadallah, A., Jakobs, M., Morik, K.: Explainable online deep neural network selection using adaptive saliency maps for time series forecasting. In: Oliver, N., Pérez-Cruz, F., Kramer, S., Read, J., Lozano, J.A. (eds.) ECML PKDD 2021. LNCS (LNAI), vol. 12975, pp. 404–420. Springer, Cham (2021). https://doi.org/10.1007/978-3-030-86486-6_25
41. Saadallah, A., Jakobs, M., Morik, K.: Explainable online ensemble of deep neural network pruning for time series forecasting. Mach. Learn. **111**(9), 3459–3487 (2022)

42. Salinas, D., Flunkert, V., Gasthaus, J., Januschowski, T.: DeepAR: probabilistic forecasting with autoregressive recurrent networks. Int. J. Forecast. **36**(3), 1181–1191 (2020)
43. Sartirana, D., et al.: Data-driven decision management of urban underground infrastructure through groundwater-level time-series cluster analysis: the case of Milan (Italy). Hydrogeol. J. **30**, 1157–1177 (2022). https://doi.org/10.1007/s10040-022-02494-5
44. Sezer, O.B., Gudelek, M.U., Ozbayoglu, A.M.: Financial time series forecasting with deep learning: a systematic literature review: 2005–2019. Appl. Soft Comput. **90**, 106181 (2020)
45. Shih, S.Y., Sun, F.K., Lee, H.: Temporal pattern attention for multivariate time series forecasting. Mach. Learn. **108**(8), 1421–1441 (2019)
46. Siddique, N., Paheding, S., Elkin, C.P., Devabhaktuni, V.: U-Net and its variants for medical image segmentation: a review of theory and applications. IEEE Access **9**, 82031–82057 (2021)
47. Song, H., Rajan, D., Thiagarajan, J.J., Spanias, A.: Attend and diagnose: clinical time series analysis using attention models. In: Thirty-Second AAAI Conference on Artificial Intelligence (2018)
48. Stefenon, S.F., et al.: Time series forecasting using ensemble learning methods for emergency prevention in hydroelectric power plants with dam. Electric Power Syst. Res. **202**, 107584 (2021)
49. Stoller, D., Tian, M., Ewert, S., Dixon, S.: Seq-U-Net: a one-dimensional causal U-Net for efficient sequence modelling. In: Bessiere, C. (ed.) Proceedings of the Twenty-Ninth International Joint Conference on Artificial Intelligence, IJCAI-20, pp. 2893–2900. International Joint Conferences on Artificial Intelligence Organization, July 2020
50. Taylor, S.J., Letham, B.: Forecasting at scale. Am. Stat. **72**(1), 37–45 (2018)
51. Tealab, A.: Time series forecasting using artificial neural networks methodologies: a systematic review. Fut. Comput. Inf. J. **3**(2), 334–340 (2018)
52. Tomar, S., Tirupathi, S., Salwala, D.V., Dusparic, I., Daly, E.: Prequential model selection for time series forecasting based on saliency maps. In: 2022 IEEE International Conference on Big Data (Big Data), pp. 3383–3392. IEEE (2022)
53. Ullah, I., et al.: A brief survey of visual saliency detection. Multimedia Tools Appl. **79**(45), 34605–34645 (2020)
54. Vaswani, A., et al.: Attention is all you need. In: Advances in Neural Information Processing Systems, pp. 5998–6008 (2017)
55. Wang, H., Cao, P., Wang, J., Zaïane, O.R.: UCTransNet: rethinking the skip connections in U-Net from a channel-wise perspective with transformer. In: Thirty-Sixth AAAI Conference on Artificial Intelligence, AAAI 2022, Thirty-Fourth Conference on Innovative Applications of Artificial Intelligence, IAAI 2022, The Twelveth Symposium on Educational Advances in Artificial Intelligence, EAAI 2022 Virtual Event, 22 February–1 March 2022, pp. 2441–2449. AAAI Press (2022)
56. Wang, K., et al.: Multiple convolutional neural networks for multivariate time series prediction. Neurocomputing **360**, 107–119 (2019)
57. Wang, S., Li, B.Z., Khabsa, M., Fang, H., Ma, H.: Linformer: self-attention with linear complexity. arXiv preprint arXiv:2006.04768 (2020)
58. Wen, R., Torkkola, K., Narayanaswamy, B., Madeka, D.: A multi-horizon quantile recurrent forecaster. arXiv preprint arXiv:1711.11053 (2017)
59. Xu, J., Wang, J., Long, M., et al.: Autoformer: decomposition transformers with auto-correlation for long-term series forecasting. In: Advances in Neural Information Processing Systems, vol. 34 (2021)

60. Yang, Y., Fan, C., Xiong, H.: A novel general-purpose hybrid model for time series forecasting. Appl. Intell. **52**, 2212–2223 (2021). https://doi.org/10.1007/s10489-021-02442-y

61. Yu, R., Zheng, S., Anandkumar, A., Yue, Y.: Long-term forecasting using tensor-train RNNs. arXiv (2017)

62. Yun, H., Lee, S., Kim, G.: Panoramic vision transformer for saliency detection in 360° videos. In: Avidan, S., Brostow, G., Cissé, M., Farinella, G.M., Hassner, T. (eds.) Computer Vision, ECCV 2022. LNCS, vol. 13695, pp. 422–439. Springer, Cham. https://doi.org/10.1007/978-3-031-19833-5_25

63. Zeng, A., Chen, M., Zhang, L., Xu, Q.: Are transformers effective for time series forecasting? In: Proceedings of the AAAI Conference on Artificial Intelligence, vol. 37, pp. 11121–11128 (2023)

64. Zeng, S., Graf, F., Hofer, C., Kwitt, R.: Topological attention for time series forecasting. In: Advances in Neural Information Processing Systems, vol. 34, pp. 24871–24882 (2021)

65. Zhang, D., Fu, H., Han, J., Borji, A., Li, X.: A review of co-saliency detection algorithms: fundamentals, applications, and challenges. ACM Trans. Intell. Syst. Technol. (TIST) **9**(4), 1–31 (2018)

66. Zhou, H., et al.: Informer: beyond efficient transformer for long sequence time-series forecasting. In: Proceedings of AAAI (2021)

Explaining Taxi Demand Prediction Models Based on Feature Importance

Eric Loff[1(✉)] , Sören Schleibaum[1] , Jörg P. Müller[1] ,
and Benjamin Säfken[2]

[1] Institute for Informatics, Clausthal University of Technology, Julius-Albert-Straße
4, 38578 Clausthal-Zellerfeld, Germany
{eric.loff,soeren.schleibaum,joerg.mueller}@tu-clausthal.de
[2] Institute for Mathematics, Clausthal University of Technology, Erzstraße 1, 38678
Clausthal-Zellerfeld, Germany
benjamin.saefken@tu-clausthal.de

Abstract. The prediction of city-wide taxi demand is used to proactively relocate idle taxis. Often neural network-based models are applied to tackle this problem, which is difficult due to its multivariate input and output space. As these models are composed of multiple layers, their predictions become opaque. This opaqueness makes debugging, optimising, and using the models difficult. To address this, we propose the usage of eXplainable AI (XAI) – feature importance methods.

In this paper, we build and train four city-wide taxi demand prediction models of commonly used neural network types on the New York City Yellow Taxi Trip data set. To explain their predictions, we select three existing XAI techniques – reduced Layerwise Relevance Propagation, Local Interpretable Model-agnostic Explanation, and Shapely Additive Explanations – and enable their usage on the specified problem. In addition, we propose a suite of five quantitative evaluation metrics suitable for explaining models that tackle regression problems with multivariate input and output space. Lastly, we compare the selected XAI techniques through the proposed evaluation metrics along four real-world scenarios.

Keywords: XAI · LRP · LIME · SHAP · Multivariate regression · taxi demand prediction

1 Introduction

Demand-driven industries like taxi services require timely product supply, e.g. taxis at certain locations of a city. The mismatch between demand and supply can be reduced by predicting the demand, i.e. the number of required taxis for each area of a city in the next 30 min, and relocating the product accordingly. Consequently, corresponding demand prediction models can contribute to the optimisation of taxi services, e.g. serving more customers and reducing cruising fuel consumption [18,31].

To predict the taxi demand, typically, a city is divided spatially, e.g. by a 500 m square grid with 20×20 cells, and temporally, e.g. into 30-min time bins. Then, a demand prediction model can use the demand over the last two hours (corresponding shape of $4 \times 20 \times 20$) to predict the demand for each cell of the whole city in the next half an hour (20×20). Typically, neural network-based models, which are considered as black-box models due to their opaqueness, are used for the prediction; see, e.g. [13,38,44,46]. An illustration of such a taxi demand prediction is shown in the upper part of Fig. 1.

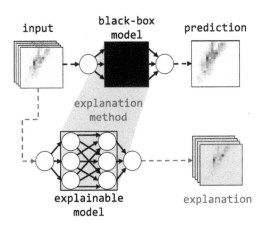

Fig. 1. Illustration of how a neural network-based taxi demand prediction model (black-box model) that receives the demand for taxis of the last four time bins for each cell in the city (green heatmap) and predicts the city-wide demand for the next time bin (blue heatmap) is explained through a local, post-hoc, feature importance-based method (red heatmap is the explanation). (Color figure online)

However, the positive effect of these opaque neural network-based prediction models can only be utilised if the models are reliable, trusted, and understood. To enhance their understanding – which might even be mandatory as humans are affected [11,12] – XAI methods can be utilised. Typically, XAI is applied in high-risk domains, e.g. the medical [32,39] or financial domain [14], where the convenience and accuracy of models based on neural networks are essential [37].

Attempting to explain the predictions of existing taxi demand prediction models, we focus on local, post-hoc XAI methods that explain through feature importance, e.g. SHAP (see [28]). As illustrated in Fig. 1, these XAI methods assign one feature importance value per input feature. Although there are many well-established XAI methods, the explanation of taxi demand prediction – a two-sided multivariate regression problem – is an open research gap.

To investigate this research gap, we enable the use of three commonly used, local, post-hoc, feature importance-based XAI methods for city-wide taxi demand prediction models of four neural network types. To understand the benefits and drawbacks of applying these XAI methods to this two-sided multivariate regression problem, we evaluate them through four scenarios and a novel set of five evaluation metrics specifically designed to match the requirements of the problem class.

2   State of the Art

Taxi Demand Prediction through AI. A straightforward approach to explaining taxi demand prediction models involves simple Artificial Intelligence (AI) models [33], which are interpretable if kept simple [12]. Another approach involves using sophisticated AI models like Support Vector Machines (SVM) [17], Fully Connected Neural Network (FCNN) [38], the spatial Convolutional Neural Network (CNN) [13], the temporal Recurrent Neural Network (RNN), Long-Short-Term Memory (LSTM) [20,42,46], or graph-based models such as Graph Attention Network (GAT) [43,44]. Other researchers use external data, e.g. population, weather, and contextual parameters such as time, temperature, humidity, and weather conditions [16,40] to enhance the training data. Another approach includes the tessellation of grid cells [21]. The sophisticated solutions are complex, making model optimisation and understanding challenging.

Explaining AI Models. XAI has the potential to mitigate risks of complex AI models, i.e. the cost of erroneous predictions, leading to spread and adoption of these AI models in different fields [29]. An overview can be found in [9,26]. Intrinsic and global explanations aim to explain the whole model, e.g. Accumulated Local Effects (ALE) calculate local effects as a global explanation [3], which is complex for multiple input and output features. Local explanations such as gradient-based Layer-wise Relevance Propagation (LRP) [7], surrogate-based Local Interpretable Model-agnostic Explanations (LIME), and SHapley Additive exPlanations (SHAP) [28,34] are often used to explain a single output prediction, reducing the complexity. Other cases include explaining action for multiple agents, e.g. multi-agent systems [22].

Explainable AI in Demand Prediction. XAI is applied to demand predictions, including demand for energy [19,41], bus passengers [30], travel [1], teachers [23], anomaly in oil wells [6], and fashion pre-season decision support [36]. The applied XAI methods use one output dimension and combine global and local explanations. There is no universal XAI metric and no established ground truth [47]. Evaluations of explanations can include Trojan input data [24] or the faithfulness of feature attribution methods [4]. In contrast to a holistic approach, the evaluation can be over four dimensions: the difference between explanation and prediction, complexity, number of features, and stability of the explanation. Qualitative metrics measure different concepts to quantitative metrics [8].

Research Gap and Questions. Even though many well-established XAI methods like SHAP exist, their usage is limited to relatively simple uncorrelated demand prediction problems. We consider the explanation of multivariate regression problems as an open research gap. To tackle this gap, we investigate the following research questions:

(RQ1) *Which XAI methods are feasible for the considered taxi demand prediction models, i.e. a two-sided multivariate regression problem?*

(RQ2) *Which metrics can a developer use to evaluate the soundness of the XAI methods applied to this problem?*

(RQ3) *Given these metrics, which XAI methods satisfactorily explain the taxi demand prediction models?*

3   Methodology

We denote the selected models with prefix M, the explanations with X, and the explanation metrics with MX.

3.1   Dataset

We use the publicly available Yellow Taxi Trip data set for Manhattan from January 2015 to June 2016 [10]. The region is divided into a 20×20 grid and aggregated into 30-min time bins, resulting in 14.49M trips or 18,652 data points – 12,618 for training, 3,154 for validation, and 2,880 for testing. We used standard score normalisation to stabilise the prediction results.

3.2   Demand Prediction Models

Based on the state of the art, we select and adapt four models that represent the most commonly used AI techniques in the prediction of taxi demand: M1-LSTM with three LSTM layers with 20% and 50% dropout; M2-FCNN consisting of five FCNN layers with 1600, 1440, 1280, 1120, 800, and 400 neurons and Rectified Linear Unit (ReLU); M3-CNN with three CNN layers connected through ReLU with kernel sizes of $3 \times 3 \times 4, 5 \times 5 \times 64$, and $7 \times 7 \times 64$; M4-GAT with three GAT layers and multi-head attention, dropout, and ReLU.

Each model receives four 30-min aggregated time bins of the last two hours as input ($4 \times 20 \times 20$) and predicts the demand for the next 30 min (20×20). We train the models for up to 90 epochs to optimise the Mean Squared Error (MSE) and use Adam optimizer with a learning rate of 0.001. The performance over all models is relatively consistent. At the same time, the M1-LSTM achieves a Mean Absolute Error (MAE) of 0.5049. This value is interpreted as a missed prediction against the real value of half a trip on average. The M2-FCNN achieves 0.4926, the M3-CNN 0.4987, and the M4-GAT 0.6472.

3.3 Selection of XAI Methods

Given the constraints of the two-sided multivariate demand prediction problem, not all XAI methods are applicable. As we aim to explain specific predictions rather than a general model behaviour, we focus on local explanation methods and exclude global ones (e.g. ALE). As demand prediction models are typically based on neural networks, the explanation methods need to apply to such. Furthermore, the explanations must be observable quickly, leading to an aggregated visualisation through salience maps [45]. Consequently, we select LRP – referred to as X1-LRP and based on the implementation from Anders et al. [2] – LIME, and SHAP (see Table 1). For LIME, there are implementation derivatives provided by Ribeiro et al. [34] for different data types; only the image- and table-like derivatives are suitable – X2-LIME-Tabular and X3-LIME-Image. For SHAP, we select X4-SHAP-Kernel and X5-SHAP-Deep which were provided by Lundenberg and Lee [28]. The LIME- and SHAP-based explanation methods perturbate the data around the instance to generate the explanation. Table 2 provides an overview of the select XAI-methods. All five chosen explanation methods attribute importance values to features, i.e. feature importance.

Table 1. Available XAI methods

Method	Local/global	Specific/agnostic	Selected
ALE	Global	Agnostic	✗
LRP	Local	Agnostic[†]	✓
LIME	Local	Agnostic	✓
SHAP	Local	Agnostic	✓

† For neural networks

Table 2. Selected XAI methods

Name	XAI method	Type
X1-LRP	LRP [2]	LRP
X2-LIME-Tabular	LIME [34]	LIME Tabular explainer
X3-LIME-Image	LIME [34]	LIME Image explainer
X4-SHAP-Kernel	SHAP [28]	SHAP Kernel explainer
X5-SHAP-Deep	SHAP [28]	SHAP Deep explainer

3.4 Technical Challenges of Explaining

We adopt LRP by using the GuidedBackprop for the activation functions and the AlphaBeta rule for the layers, as the rule allows negative importance values. For

LIME, we adjust parameters such as kernel size to 5, mode to regression, number of samples to 100, and slic for image fragmentation. In the case of SHAP, we use a background size of 1000 by default and modify the configuration for M4-GAT to 100. This step is necessary as the build graph would be too storage-intensive with a more extensive background size.

The previous demand given to the prediction models is normalized to stabilise learning. For the LIME and SHAP derivatives, we include the normalization into the model to receive explanations in the unit trips rather than normalized trips. To enable X2-LIME-Tabular, we reshape the image-like data into table-like data by enhancing each row with the corresponding x, y, and z index. Regarding X3-LIME-Image, we transform the input data into a single-channel or grayscale image.

3.5 Scenarios

To evaluate the generated explanations, i.e. feature importance values, we identify four scenarios in our dataset that have a specific meaning and can occur in a week: (SC1) the lowest point of the demand in a week on Mondays at 11:30pm; (SC2) the lowest demand in times of high demand, i.e. the demand prediction on Thursday at 12:30pm; (SC3) the highest demand during a week is on Fridays at 3pm; (SC4) the highest demand on weekends, i.e. the prediction of the demand on Sundays at 8:30am. Each scenario consists of nine samples per scenario. The scenarios are shown in Fig. 2.

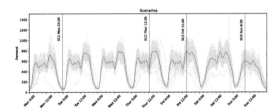

Fig. 2. Scenarios SC1 to SC4 (blue average, gray real values) (Color figure online)

3.6 Evaluation Metrics

Evaluating explanations using human test subjects, e.g. measuring their satisfaction with an explanation with a scale proposed by Hoffman et al. [15], is common. However, our demand prediction problem requires expert users, who are hard to find. Therefore, we need to evaluate the explanations quantitatively. Although some evaluation metrics have been proposed for classification, e.g. by Arras et al. [5], for two-sided multivariate regression, no ground truth exists. To be able to evaluate beyond visually inspecting the explanation, we propose a suite of five quantitative evaluation metrics: *MX1-Unwanted, MX2-Hotspots,*

MX2-Correlation, *MX3-Time*, *MX4-Importance*, and *MX5-Temporal*. The areas of no demand for MX1 and the areas of hotspots for MX2 are shown in Fig. 3. We compute each metric per combination of a demand prediction model, XAI method, and scenario.

MX1-Unwanted. This evaluation metric uses the ground truth available in the data and is inspired by Trojan pixels (proposed by Lin et al. [25] for classification) for evaluating the faithfulness of an explanation method. We identify areas with no demand throughout the dataset and calculate the sum of explanations in these areas. A constant absence of demand cannot influence a prediction, so a nonzero value indicates an undesired attribution of the corresponding explanation method. Consequently, the closer the value is to zero, the better the explanation method is.

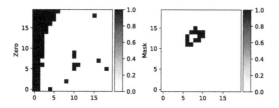

Fig. 3. Area of unwanted attribution for MX1-Unwanted (left) and the demand hotspots of MX2-Hotspots (right)

MX2-Hotspots. When changing the data relevant to a prediction, we expect a proportional change in the corresponding explanation. To evaluate this behaviour, we compare the change in prediction and explanation when the demand in the city's busiest areas is set to zero. We calculate the impact of a change by applying a mask to areas of high demand. The prediction model is evaluated on the masked and original data, and the XAI method explains both cases. We analyse the effect by comparing the masked hotspot to the prediction and dividing it by the stimulus on the prediction [35]. This metric is calculated through

$$m_{\text{hotspot}} := \frac{\sum_i^n |\epsilon_i^m| - |\epsilon_i|}{\sum_i^n |\hat{y}_i^m| - |\hat{y}_i|}. \tag{1}$$

Here, n is the number of features per prediction, ϵ indicates an explanation, $\hat{y}$ is the prediction and m indicates whether a prediction or explanation is masked. If the difference between ϵ_i^m and ϵ_i is marginal, the metric approaches 0 even if the difference of $\hat{y}_i^m$ and $\hat{y}_i$ is substantial. Conversely, if the effect of the explanation drastically differs from the effect of the prediction, the metric would increase rapidly, even if the absolute difference is negligible. A value close to 1 indicates an explanation that faithfully explains a model.

MX3-Correlation. As the input data and the prediction are similar for different samples of one scenario, we expect the explanations to be similar as well – an explanation method should generate a stable explanation. Therefore, we calculate the average correlation between an explanation and a scenario. Next, we use cross-correlation between each method and average the correlation over one row, excluding perfect self-correlation.

MX4-Time. This evaluation metric measures the duration of an explanation generation process for different XAI methods. We use CPU time for all explanations.

MX5-Temporal. To better understand the temporal pattern that a demand prediction model has learned, this evaluation metric analyses the impact of each input time step on the prediction by aggregating the importance values (explanations) and comparing them to the actual demand.

4   Experimental Results

Here, we describe the results of the explanation methods for all evaluation metrics. Sample explanation for each explanation method are shown in Fig. 4. Those of the remaining evaluation metrics are shown in Table 3.

4.1   X1-LRP

As shown in Table 3, all results for X1-LRP and MX1-Unwanted are far away from the desired value of 0. We believe that this relatively poor performance of X1-LRP is caused by catching noise of the gradients. While the values of M3-CNN and M4-GAT are relatively close to 1 for MX2-Hotspots, those of M1-LSTM and M2-FCNN are off to a high degree. This could mean that the AlphaBeta rule used does not fit well with the M1-LSTM and M2-FCNN. However, as shown in Table 3, the MX3-Correlation, MX4-Time, and MX5-Temporal are the strong forts of the X1-LRP, with the latter two metrics achieving the best results among all explanation methods. These results are caused by a relatively close link of the explanation model to the prediction model. Consequently, this method can be used for the M3-CNN and M4-GAT.

4.2   X2-LIME-Tabular

In general, the visual representations of the explanations generated by X2-LIME-Tabular (one visual representation is shown in Fig. 4) are very similar. As shown in Table 3, X2-Lime-Tabular is close to 0 with MX1-Unwanted for all models, achieving the best results for this evaluation metric compared to the other explanation methods. The results regarding MX2-Hotspot are not perfect, but in comparison to the other explanation methods relatively consistent. The correlation between the different explanations over one scenario is good. Unfortunately, the

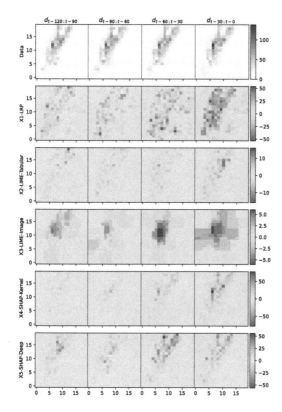

Fig. 4. Input data (first row) and the corresponding explanations generated through the explanation methods X1-LRP to X5-SHAP-Deep (five remaining rows; varying scales) for the M1-LSTM and SC3; e.g. $d_{t-120:t-90}$ refers to the aggregated demand from the current point in time t minus 120 min to t minus 90 min and the heatmaps below show the corresponding feature importances for the different explanation methods.

X2-LIME-Tabular is with an average of around 450 s per explanation one of the slowest explanation methods. Thus, the performance can be considered relatively poor for the MX4-Time. Also, the MX5-Temporal is poor and does not represent the observed predictions for all models.

4.3   X3-LIME-Image

The visual representations of X3-LIME-Image are very granular. Further, the performance on the MX1-Unwanted evaluation metric is rather poor. The explanation method slightly overestimated the role of hotspots and performed the second best on this metric. X3-LIME-Image performs relatively poor on the super pixels used for MX3-Correlation. However, it performs the best on MX4-Time, the time needed for the generation. However, this explanation method performs poorly on the MX5-Temporal as the importance is relatively similar over the four time steps.

Table 3. Mean and standard deviation (M±SD) for each explanation method, model, and evaluation metric; the desired value for each evaluation metric is shown in brackets beside it and the best value per explanation method and metric is highlighted; the values of the evaluation metrics are comparable across the explanation methods.

	MX1-Unwanted (0)	MX2-Hotspots (1)	MX3-Correlation (↑)	MX4-Time (↓)	MX5-Temporal (↑)
X1-LRP					
M1-LSTM	7.24 ± 46.79	10.63 ± 5.88	0.65 ± 0.16	0.01 ± 0	**1.00 ± 0**
M2-FCNN	−69.65 ± 59.13	21.55 ± 21.21	0.63 ± 0.14	**0.00 ± 0**	**1.00 ± 0**
M3-CNN	**9.90 ± 5.67**	0.25 ± 0.07	0.70 ± 0.09	0.01 ± 0	**1.00 ± 0**
M4-GAT	19.34 ± 13.1	**1.47 ± 0.36**	**0.72 ± 0.08**	0.01 ± 0.02	**1.00 ± 0**
X2-LIME-Tabular					
M1-LSTM	−0.01 ± 0.02	4.80 ± 2.26	**0.48 ± 0.23**	451.07 ± 80.12	0.10 ± 0
M2-FCNN	0 ± 0.02	6.98 ± 5.12	0.43 ± 0.22	**447.73 ± 80.07**	0.20 ± 0
M3-CNN	0 ± 0.03	**3.28 ± 1.49**	0.37 ± 0.22	448.78 ± 79.16	0.10 ± 0
M4-GAT	0 ± 0.02	3.82 ± 2.03	0.30 ± 0.21	471.75 ± 80.43	0.10 ± 0
X3-LIME-Image					
M1-LSTM	17.75 ± 15.9	3.82 ± 2.99	0.27 ± 0.1	0.36 ± 0.01	0.20 ± 0
M2-FCNN	24.42 ± 15.68	4.25 ± 3.69	0.24 ± 0.13	**0.19 ± 0.01**	**0.40 ± 0**
M3-CNN	26.47 ± 17.89	**1.49 ± 0.67**	**0.34 ± 0.09**	0.24 ± 0	0.30 ± 0
M4-GAT	**9.22 ± 14.93**	1.50 ± 0.83	0.31 ± 0.12	0.93 ± 0.01	0.30 ± 0
X4-SHAP-Kernel					
M1-LSTM	**3.73 ± 10.03**	5.61 ± 1.7	0.59 ± 0.08	516.20 ± 20.03	**0.80 ± 0**
M2-FCNN	−8.87 ± 9.57	12.53 ± 8.63	0.54 ± 0.12	549.02 ± 31.13	**0.80 ± 0**
M3-CNN	−32.06 ± 5.83	2.78 ± 0.81	**0.69 ± 0.11**	523.83 ± 7.54	**0.80 ± 0**
M4-GAT	14.01 ± 6.65	**1.94 ± 0.48**	0.63 ± 0.16	**479.54 ± 8**	**0.80 ± 0**
X5-SHAP-Deep					
M1-LSTM	−13.05 ± 0	0.72 ± 0.36	**0.75 ± 0.1**	5.03 ± 0.03	**0.60 ± 0**
M2-FCNN	−22.04 ± 0	1.76 ± 1.3	0.73 ± 0.13	**1.48 ± 0.02**	**0.60 ± 0**
M3-CNN	−44.98 ± 0	**0.74 ± 0.21**	0.71 ± 0.13	3.51 ± 0.04	**0.60 ± 0**
M4-GAT	**4.54 ± 0**	0.12 ± 0.05	0.63 ± 0.16	4.54 ± 0.02	**0.60 ± 0**

4.4 X4-SHAP-Kernel

The visual representation of the X4-SHAP-Kernel is excellent for all models. However, the performance of MX1-Unwanted is poor. This could result from the wrong attribution of importance to irrelevant features learned by the corresponding explanation model. This explanation method overvalues the importance of hotspots. The correlation in a scenario is relatively high. However, the method is the slowest one of the selected. On the other hand, the generated MX5-Temporal values are quite diverse and usable.

4.5 X5-SHAP-Deep

This method generates good visual representations of explanations. However, the MX1-Unwanted is poor as the method considers areas without demand as relevant. MX2-Hotspot performs well on the first three models and poorly on the M4-GAT. This method performs the best on the correlation in the scenarios and is relatively fast – on average less than 5.03 s. The MX5-Temporal values are worse than the values from the X1-LRP and X4-SHAP-Kernel, but still high. Due to the fast explanation generation and the usability on all models, we consider this method as the best-selected one.

5   Discussion

We enabled the usage of five model-agnostic explanation methods to the two-sided multivariate regression problem of city-wide taxi demand prediction and were able to explain four corresponding models post-hoc and locally. In particular, we showed that LRP, LIME (derivatives X2-LIME-Tabular and X3-LIME-Image), and SHAP (derivatives X4-SHAP-Kernel and X5-SHAP-Deep) are feasible for these problems (RQ1).

Regarding the metrics to evaluate the soundness of these XAI methods (RQ2), we chose and developed five metrics to evaluate multivariate explanations. The proposed evaluation metrics are quantitative and feasible for our two-sided multivariate regression problem. Especially, the comparison of the explanation to the ground truth available in the data (MX1-Unwanted to measure the influence of unimportant features, MX2-Hotspots to evaluate the influence of influential changes, and MX3-Correlation that measures that similar samples should generate similar explanations) can be beneficial for other regression problems in general.

Table 4 shows an overview of the results when explaining the taxi demand prediction models with the explanation methods and evaluating them with the proposed evaluation metrics. The X1-LRP method was poor for the M1-LSTM and M2-FCNN models, as the rules did not fit well with these models. However, it was usable for the M3-CNN and M4-GAT models, although the interpretation of results differed from those of the other methods. The X2-LIME-Tabular and X3-LIME-Image methods had poor performance due to the local accuracy not guaranteeing fair attribution of important values. However, the X2-LIME-Tabular performed well on the MX1-Unwanted metric, possibly due to similar highlighted areas in the visualisation. The X4-SHAP-Kernel and X5-SHAP-Deep methods showed excellent performance, with the X5-SHAP-Deep method being faster and easier to use. The M1-LSTM and M2-FCNN models had impractical results with the X1-LRP, X2-LIME-Tabular, and X3-LIME-Image methods due to excessive noise. However, the X4-SHAP-Kernel and X5-SHAP-Deep methods provided useful information. For the M3-CNN and M4-GAT models, the X1-LRP, X4-SHAP-Kernel, and X5-SHAP-Deep methods were suitable, with the X1-LRP method having better time performance (see Sect. 4).

Local explanations must cover edge cases from a legal perspective. However, some chosen methods are slow and only suitable for case-based reasoning. SHAP methods approximate Shapely values and provide fair contribution calculations. Visualizations should be more precise and less cluttered for drivers, while developers prefer validation and faster methods. Negative influences in initial input

Table 4. Comparison of XAI methods; $--$ denotes a poor, $-$ a weak, o an acceptable, $+$ a good, and $++$ an excellent performance

Metric	X1-LRP	X2-LIME-Tabular	X3-LIME-Image	X4-SHAP-Kernel	X5-SHAP-Deep
MX1-Unwanted	$-$	$++$	$-$	o	$+$
MX2-Hotspot	o	$-$	o	o	$+$
MX3-Correlation	$+$	o	$-$	$+$	$+$
MX4-Time	$++$	$-$	$++$	$-$	$+$
MX5-Temporal	$++$	$--$	$-$	$++$	$+$

maps can impact explanation aggregation. Noise and shade in models may originate from hidden gradients or incorrect calculations.

Our results are limited as the explanations given by the feature importance values used for this paper do not have ground truth. Further, using homogeneous data made it easier to interpret but harder to generalize. The dataset used, including areas with no demand, limited the applicability of MX1-Unwanted to similar datasets. The limitation of using only feature attribution methods prevents making a general statement about the explainability of taxi demand prediction.

6   Conclusion

Explanations are essential to foster an understanding of the model predictions. They can help to optimize and use a given prediction. We showed a reasonable method to apply explanations to high-dimensional prediction models. Then we evaluated these methods based on a novel suite of quantitative evaluation metrics suitable for two-sided multivariate regression problems. This suite can be applied to optimize and understand prediction models.

Future Work. One idea to improve the perturbation-based methods is to use MX1-Unwanted for better random sampling. Another idea is human evaluation through questionnaires or experiments, which can be used to compare the methods against human understanding. The generated explanations can be used as a component for more straightforward, human-interpretable explanations. Explaining multidimensional input and output models is challenging due to dense explanations. The different methods perform similarly across the proposed metrics despite visual differences. Developers can benefit from the generated explanations for model selection and understanding. The X1-LRP and X5-SHAP-Deep are recommended for real-world scenarios based on their high scores on the metrics. In conclusion, the explanations always depend on the model, even if they are model-agnostic.

References

1. Alwosheel, A., Van Cranenburgh, S., Chorus, C.G.: Why did you predict that? Towards explainable artificial neural networks for travel demand analysis. Transp. Res. C Emerg. Technol. **128**, 103143 (2021). https://doi.org/10.1016/j.trc.2021. 103143

2. Anders, C.J., Neumann, D., Samek, W., Müller, K.R., Lapuschkin, S.: Software for Dataset-wide XAI: From Local Explanations to Global Insights with Zennit, CoRelAy, and ViRelAy, February 2023

3. Apley, D.W., Zhu, J.: Visualizing the effects of predictor variables in black box supervised learning models. J. R. Stat. Soc. Ser. B Stat Methodol. **82**(4), 1059–1086 (2020). https://doi.org/10.1111/rssb.12377

4. Arias-Duart, A., Pares, F., Garcia-Gasulla, D., Gimenez-Abalos, V.: Focus! Rating XAI methods and finding biases. In: 2022 IEEE International Conference on Fuzzy Systems (FUZZ-IEEE), Padua, Italy, pp. 1–8. IEEE, July 2022. https://doi.org/ 10.1109/FUZZ-IEEE55066.2022.9882821

5. Arras, L., Osman, A., Samek, W.: CLEVR-XAI: a benchmark dataset for the ground truth evaluation of neural network explanations. Inf. Fusion **81**, 14–40 (2022). https://doi.org/10.1016/j.inffus.2021.11.008

6. Aslam, N., et al.: Anomaly detection using explainable random forest for the prediction of undesirable events in oil wells. Appl. Comput. Intell. Soft Comput. **2022**, 1–14 (2022). https://doi.org/10.1155/2022/1558381

7. Bach, S., Binder, A., Montavon, G., Klauschen, F., Müller, K.R., Samek, W.: On pixel-wise explanations for non-linear classifier decisions by layer-wise relevance propagation. PLoS ONE **10**(7), e0130140 (2015). https://doi.org/10.1371/journal. pone.0130140

8. Biessmann, F., Refiano, D.: Quality Metrics for Transparent Machine Learning With and Without Humans In the Loop Are Not Correlated, July 2021

9. Carvalho, D.V., Pereira, E.M., Cardoso, J.S.: Machine learning interpretability: a survey on methods and metrics. Electronics **8**(8), 832 (2019). https://doi.org/10. 3390/electronics8080832

10. City of New York: TLC Trip Record Data - TLC (2023). https://www.nyc.gov/ site/tlc/about/tlc-trip-record-data.page

11. Goodman, B., Flaxman, S.: European Union regulations on algorithmic decision making and a "right to explanation." AI Mag. **38**(3), 50–57 (2017). https://doi. org/10.1609/aimag.v38i3.2741

12. Gunning, D., Aha, D.W.: DARPA's explainable artificial intelligence program. AI Mag. **40**(2), 44–58 (2019). https://doi.org/10.1609/aimag.v40i2.2850

13. Haliem, M., Mani, G., Aggarwal, V., Bhargava, B.: A distributed model-free ride-sharing approach for joint matching, pricing, and dispatching using deep reinforcement learning. IEEE Trans. Intell. Transp. Syst. **22**(12), 7931–7942 (2021). https://doi.org/10.1109/TITS.2021.3096537

14. Hoepner, A.G.F., McMillan, D., Vivian, A., Wese Simen, C.: Significance, relevance and explainability in the machine learning age: an econometrics and financial data science perspective. Eur. J. Finance **27**(1–2), 1–7 (2021). https://doi.org/10.1080/ 1351847X.2020.1847725

15. Hoffman, R.R., Mueller, S.T., Klein, G., Litman, J.: Metrics for Explainable AI: Challenges and Prospects, February 2019

16. Ishiguro, S., Kawasaki, S., Fukazawa, Y.: Taxi demand forecast using real-time population generated from cellular networks. In: Proceedings of the 2018 ACM

International Joint Conference and 2018 International Symposium on Pervasive and Ubiquitous Computing and Wearable Computers, Singapore Singapore, pp. 1024–1032. ACM, October 2018. https://doi.org/10.1145/3267305.3274157

17. Jiang, S., Chen, W., Li, Z., Yu, H.: Short-term demand prediction method for online car-hailing services based on a least squares support vector machine. IEEE Access **7**, 11882–11891 (2019). https://doi.org/10.1109/ACCESS.2019.2891825

18. Ke, J., Feng, S., Zhu, Z., Yang, H., Ye, J.: Joint predictions of multi-modal ride-hailing demands: a deep multi-task multi-graph learning-based approach. Transp. Res. C Emerg. Technol. **127**, 103063 (2021). https://doi.org/10.1016/j.trc.2021.103063

19. Kim, J.Y., Cho, S.B.: Explainable prediction of electric energy demand using a deep autoencoder with interpretable latent space. Expert Syst. Appl. **186**, 115842 (2021). https://doi.org/10.1016/j.eswa.2021.115842

20. Kontou, E., Garikapati, V., Hou, Y.: Reducing ridesourcing empty vehicle travel with future travel demand prediction. Transp. Res. C Emerg. Technol. **121**, 102826 (2020). https://doi.org/10.1016/j.trc.2020.102826

21. Korth, M., Schleibaum, S., Müller, J.P., Ehlers, R.: On the influence of grid cell size on taxi demand prediction. In: Pires, I.M., Zdravevski, E., Garcia, N.C. (eds.) Smart Objects and Technologies for Social Goods. LNCIS, vol. 476, pp. 19–36. Springer, Cham (2023). https://doi.org/10.1007/978-3-031-28813-5_2

22. Kraus, S., et al.: AI for explaining decisions in multi-agent environments. In: The Thirty-Fourth AAAI Conference on Artificial Intelligence, AAAI 2020, New York, NY, USA, 7–12 February 2020, pp. 13534–13538. AAAI Press (2020)

23. Lee, K., Eo, M., Jung, E., Yoon, Y., Rhee, W.: Short-term traffic prediction with deep neural networks: a survey. IEEE Access **9**, 54739–54756 (2021). https://doi.org/10.1109/ACCESS.2021.3071174

24. Lin, Q., Xu, W., Chen, M., Lin, X.: A probabilistic approach for demand-aware ride-sharing optimization. In: Proceedings of the Twentieth ACM International Symposium on Mobile Ad Hoc Networking and Computing, Catania Italy, pp. 141–150. ACM, July 2019. https://doi.org/10.1145/3323679.3326512

25. Lin, Y.S., Lee, W.C., Celik, Z.B.: What do you see?: Evaluation of explainable artificial intelligence (XAI) interpretability through neural backdoors. In: Proceedings of the 27th ACM SIGKDD Conference on Knowledge Discovery & Data Mining, Virtual Event Singapore, pp. 1027–1035. ACM, August 2021. https://doi.org/10.1145/3447548.3467213

26. Linardatos, P., Papastefanopoulos, V., Kotsiantis, S.: Explainable AI: a review of machine learning interpretability methods. Entropy **23**(1), 18 (2020). https://doi.org/10.3390/e23010018

27. Loff, E.: Explaining taxi demand prediction models based on feature importance. Bachelor's thesis, Clausthal University of Technology (2023)

28. Lundberg, S.M., Lee, S.I.: A unified approach to interpreting model predictions. In: Proceedings of the 31st International Conference on Neural Information Processing Systems, NIPS 2017, Red Hook, NY, USA, pp. 4768–4777. Curran Associates Inc. (2017)

29. McDermid, J.A., Jia, Y., Porter, Z., Habli, I.: Artificial intelligence explainability: the technical and ethical dimensions. Philos. Trans. Royal Soc. A Math. Phys. Eng. Sci. **379**(2207), 20200363 (2021). https://doi.org/10.1098/rsta.2020.0363

30. Monje, L., Carrasco, R.A., Rosado, C., Sánchez-Montañés, M.: Deep learning XAI for bus passenger forecasting: a use case in Spain. Mathematics **10**(9), 1428 (2022). https://doi.org/10.3390/math10091428

31. Moreira-Matias, L., Gama, J., Ferreira, M., Mendes-Moreira, J., Damas, L.: Predicting taxi-passenger demand using streaming data. IEEE Trans. Intell. Transp. Syst. **14**(3), 1393–1402 (2013). https://doi.org/10.1109/TITS.2013.2262376
32. O'Sullivan, S., et al.: Explainable artificial intelligence (XAI): closing the gap between image analysis and navigation in complex invasive diagnostic procedures. World J. Urol. **40**(5), 1125–1134 (2022). https://doi.org/10.1007/s00345-022-03930-7
33. Pun, L., Zhao, P., Liu, X.: A multiple regression approach for traffic flow estimation. IEEE Access **7**, 35998–36009 (2019). https://doi.org/10.1109/ACCESS.2019.2904645
34. Ribeiro, M.T., Singh, S., Guestrin, C.: "Why should i trust you?" Explaining the predictions of any classifier. In: Proceedings of the ACM SIGKDD International Conference on Knowledge Discovery and Data Mining, vol. 13–17-August, pp. 1135–1144 (2016). https://doi.org/10.1145/2939672.2939778
35. Rosenfeld, A.: Better metrics for evaluating explainable artificial intelligence. In: Proceedings of the 20th International Conference on Autonomous Agents and MultiAgent Systems, AAMAS 2021, pp. 45–50. International Foundation for Autonomous Agents and Multiagent Systems, Richland, SC (2021)
36. Sajja, S., Aggarwal, N., Mukherjee, S., Manglik, K., Dwivedi, S., Raykar, V.: Explainable AI based interventions for pre-season decision making in fashion retail. In: Proceedings of the 3rd ACM India Joint International Conference on Data Science & Management of Data (8th ACM IKDD CODS & 26th COMAD), Bangalore India, pp. 281–289. ACM, January 2021. https://doi.org/10.1145/3430984.3430995
37. Tjoa, E., Guan, C.: A survey on explainable artificial intelligence (XAI): toward medical XAI. IEEE Trans. Neural Netw. Learn. Syst. **32**(11), 4793–4813 (2021). https://doi.org/10.1109/TNNLS.2020.3027314
38. Tong, Y., et al.: The simpler the better: a unified approach to predicting original taxi demands based on large-scale online platforms. In: Proceedings of the 23rd ACM SIGKDD International Conference on Knowledge Discovery and Data Mining, Halifax NS Canada, pp. 1653–1662. ACM, August 2017. https://doi.org/10.1145/3097983.3098018
39. Van Der Velden, B.H., Kuijf, H.J., Gilhuijs, K.G., Viergever, M.A.: Explainable artificial intelligence (XAI) in deep learning-based medical image analysis. Med. Image Anal. **79**, 102470 (2022). https://doi.org/10.1016/j.media.2022.102470
40. Wang, C., Hou, Y., Barth, M.: Data-driven multi-step demand prediction for ride-hailing services using convolutional neural network. In: Arai, K., Kapoor, S. (eds.) Advances in Computer Vision, vol. 944, pp. 11–22. Springer, Cham (2020). https://doi.org/10.1007/978-3-030-17798-0_2
41. Xu, C., Li, C., Zhou, X.: Interpretable LSTM based on mixture attention mechanism for multi-step residential load forecasting. Electronics **11**(14), 2189 (2022). https://doi.org/10.3390/electronics11142189
42. Xu, J., Rahmatizadeh, R., Boloni, L., Turgut, D.: A sequence learning model with recurrent neural networks for taxi demand prediction. In: 2017 IEEE 42nd Conference on Local Computer Networks (LCN), Singapore, pp. 261–268. IEEE, October 2017. https://doi.org/10.1109/LCN.2017.31
43. Xu, Y., Li, D.: Incorporating graph attention and recurrent architectures for city-wide taxi demand prediction. ISPRS Int. J. Geo Inf. **8**(9), 414 (2019). https://doi.org/10.3390/ijgi8090414
44. Ye, J., Sun, L., Du, B., Fu, Y., Xiong, H.: Coupled layer-wise graph convolution for transportation demand prediction. Association for the Advancement of Artificial Intelligence, December 2020

45. Yousif, Y.M., Müller, J.P.: Generating explanatory saliency maps for mixed traffic flow using a behaviour cloning model. In: Lorig, F., Norling, E. (eds.) Multi-Agent-Based Simulation XXIII, vol. 13743, pp. 107–120. Springer, Cham (2023). https://doi.org/10.1007/978-3-031-22947-3_9
46. Zhang, C., Zhu, F., Wang, X., Sun, L., Tang, H., Lv, Y.: Taxi demand prediction using parallel multi-task learning model. IEEE Trans. Intell. Transp. Syst. **23**(2), 794–803 (2022). https://doi.org/10.1109/TITS.2020.3015542
47. Zhou, J., Gandomi, A.H., Chen, F., Holzinger, A.: Evaluating the quality of machine learning explanations: a survey on methods and metrics. Electronics **10**(5), 593 (2021). https://doi.org/10.3390/electronics10050593

Bayesian CAIPI: A Probabilistic Approach to Explanatory and Interactive Machine Learning

Emanuel Slany[1][(✉)] [iD], Stephan Scheele[1] [iD], and Ute Schmid[1,2] [iD]

[1] Fraunhofer Institute for Integrated Circuits IIS Sensory Perception and Analytics, Comprehensible AI, Erlangen, Germany
{emanuel.slany,stephan.scheele}@iis.fraunhofer.de
[2] University of Bamberg – Cognitive Systems Group, Bamberg, Germany
ute.schmid@uni-bamberg.de

Abstract. Explanatory Interactive Machine Learning queries user feedback regarding the prediction and the explanation of novel instances. CAIPI, a state-of-the-art algorithm, captures the user feedback and iteratively biases a data set toward a correct decision-making mechanism using counterexamples. The counterexample generation procedure relies on hand-crafted data augmentation and might produce implausible instances. We propose Bayesian CAIPI that embeds a Variational Autoencoder into CAIPI's classification cycle and samples counterexamples from the likelihood distribution. Using the MNIST data set, where we distinguish ones from sevens, we show that Bayesian CAIPI matches the predictive accuracy of both, traditional CAIPI and default deep learning. Moreover, it outperforms both in terms of explanation quality.

Keywords: Explanatory Interactive Machine Learning · CAIPI · Variational Autoencoders · Image Classification

1 Introduction

Explanatory Interactive Machine Learning (XIML) [19] enables users to be involved in the optimization cycle as well as in the inference step of machine learning (ML) models. Hereby, XIML goes an essential step beyond classical active learning [15], as users are not only asked to correct the prediction of the most informative instance. Moreover, dedicated user feedback regarding local explanations – assuming that they highlight the model's decision-making mechanism – allows to adapt *how* the model conducts decisions. CAIPI [19], a state-of-the-art XIML framework, iteratively trains a model on a small labeled data set, selects the most informative instance from a larger pool of unlabeled data, and queries user feedback regarding its prediction and explanation. Using augmented versions of the most informative instance, so-called counterexamples, CAIPI adapts the model toward correct decision making. Disclosing and shaping the decision-making mechanism is a meaningful step toward robust machine learning models, which ultimately strengthen their trustworthiness [11,19].

S. Nowaczyk et al. (Eds.): ECAI 2023 Workshops, CCIS 1947, pp. 285–301, 2024.
https://doi.org/10.1007/978-3-031-50396-2_16

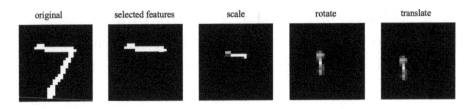

Fig. 1. Data augmentation procedure [17]. Selected features of an image, displaying a seven, are scaled, rotated, and translated.

Crucially, CAIPI overweights so-called decisive features by data augmentation in counterexamples [19]. Although data augmentation procedures require domain-specific knowledge, they are generally more likely to be implemented by ML engineers than by domain experts [17]. Our running example (Fig. 1) shows that this knowledge gap might have serious consequences for XIML procedures, e.g., when a counterexample mimics a one but is supposed to display a seven. To solve this shortcoming, we propose Bayesian CAIPI that extends CAIPI with a novel counterexample generation procedure using the likelihood distribution of Variational Autoencoders. We ask the following research questions:

(R1) Do counterexamples improve the model's predictive quality [19]?
(R2) Do counterexamples contribute to disclose the model's mechanism?
(R3) Is Bayesian CAIPI superior to traditional CAIPI / default deep learning?

Problem. Counterexample generation algorithms in XIML that are using image-specific augmentation techniques might produce implausible results.

Solution. By replacing frequently handcrafted data augmentation procedures by Variational Autoencoders, the counterexample generation procedure is automated to a large extent. High-quality Variational Autoencoders allow us to generate realistic counterexamples by sampling from the likelihood distribution.

Contribution. (i) We propose Bayesian CAIPI, where we embed a Variational Autoencoder into the CAIPI optimization cycle and essentially fit a generative model on all available training examples. Samples from the likelihood distribution replace the iterative execution of data augmentation algorithms. (ii) We integrate the classification task into the Variational Autoencoder. In each optimization iteration, we abstract the input data into a latent distribution, which functions as the classifier's input.

2   Related Work

XIML has first been introduced by Teso and Kersting (2019) [19] with their CAIPI algorithm. CAIPI iteratively optimizes a classification model and queries user feedback regarding prediction and explanation. Since then, CAIPI has been enriched with user interfaces that enable domain experts to interact with ML models, e.g., physicians in the context of cancer detection [17]. The traditional explanatory component within CAIPI is LIME [11], *Local Interpretable Model-agnostic Explanations*, where even CAIPI's name originates, since "CAIPIrinhas are made out of LIMEs" [19]. LIME produces an interpretable model for a specific instance using super-pixels within image classification. CAIPI's core idea is to add synthetic instances, so-called counterexamples, to the data set that move the decision-making mechanism into the presumably correct direction. This idea has been generalized to increase the applicability for deep learning models: Instead of adding counterexamples, indecisive gradients are penalized [14]. XIML has its sources in active learning [15], where an oracle labels instances that were selected from a ML algorithm. The idea of involving humans, or domain experts, *interactively* into model training is even older [21] and has reached the surface again in 2014, where Amershi and co-authors [1] present specific interactive learning case studies that outperform fully-automated learning procedures. Another dedicated XIML approach, called Explanatory Debugging, includes an explanatory component, which lets users interact with the model's underlying mechanism [7]. It has recently been applied to increase the fairness of classification systems [8]. Explanatory Debugging, in contrast to CAIPI, does not align the interaction iteratively in an optimization cycle. Current XIML research has caught attention by the action design research community, where specific architectures are introduced to include human experts in the optimization process [9].

Crucial for CAIPI is the counterexample generation procedure that might be problematic, when ML engineers lack domain knowledge (Fig. 1). We extend CAIPI such that counterexamples are sampled from a Variational Autoencoder, which requires us to embed a classification model into the Variational Autoencoder's latent space. This idea is also not new and Variational Autoencoders have been used to label images and, thus, construct training data for supervised image classification algorithms [10]. Also, vice versa, classification models have been used to improve the quality of the latent space [23]. Let us consider two use cases that closely relate to our architecture, where the combination of supervised ML models and Variational Autoencoders outperform state-of-the-art methods: In [4], a Variational Autoencoder is used to extract robust features from a high-dimensional feature space, applied for anomaly detection where the focus is on classification. Another application is demonstrated in [22] for brain-aging analysis, where the Variational Autoencoder's generation process includes the regression target and hereby allows to execute simulations.

3   Foundations

Bayesian CAIPI replaces the counterexample generation of CAIPI by samples from the likelihood of a Variational Autoencoder. This section covers both, XIML and Variational Autoencoders. But let us first introduce the general notation:

Notation. Formally, let $\mathbf{X}$ be an image matrix of a data set $\mathcal{X} \subseteq \mathbb{R}^{W \times H}$ of fixed width W and height H and let $l : \mathcal{X} \to \mathcal{Y}$ be a labeling function to retrieve corresponding class labels from $\mathcal{Y}$. Let $f : \mathcal{X} \to \mathcal{Y}$ be a differentiable classification model and $\hat{y} = f(\mathbf{X})$ denote model inference. Moreover, let $\mathcal{L} \subseteq \mathcal{X} \times \mathcal{Y}$ and $\mathcal{U} \subseteq \mathcal{X}$ denote subsets of labeled and unlabeled instances, where we write $\mathcal{X}_{\mathcal{L}}$ and $\mathcal{Y}_{\mathcal{L}}$ for the domain and range of $\mathcal{L}$. Further, we write $\mathbf{X}^{(n)}$ $(y^{(n)})$ for the n-th image (label) in $\mathcal{X}$ $(\mathcal{Y})$, when the associated set is clear from the context, or add a subscript like $\mathbf{X}_{\mathcal{L}}^{(n)}$ $(y_{\mathcal{L}}^{(n)})$ and $\mathbf{X}_{\mathcal{U}}^{(n)}$ to explicitly indicate the associated set.

3.1 Explanatory Interactive Machine Learning

Explanatory Interactive Machine Learning (XIML) unifies two components: the tractability of the decision-making mechanism of ML models by explanatory ML techniques and the human-in-the-loop capability of interactive learning [19]. However, in contrast to interactive learning [15,16], XIML allows the user to highlight interactively the important features, and in this sense, the user is able to refine and shape the model's mechanism. There exist three cases for prediction outcomes in the XIML framework CAIPI [19]: (i) **R**ight for the **r**ight reasons (**RRR**), i.e., both, the explanation and the prediction are correct. (ii) **W**rong for the **w**rong reasons (**W**), where both are wrong. (iii) **R**ight for the **w**rong reasons (**RWR**) i.e., the prediction is correct, but the explanation is false.

The two erroneous cases **W** and **RWR** require human intervention. In the former case, we require the user to provide a label correction for the wrong prediction outcome. In the latter case, the user is interactively asked in the role of a human annotator to highlight the correct reasons of a wrong explanation outcome. In our use case using image data from MNIST, the explanation is given by an image mask that highlights relevant pixels, which can be interactively refined by an user. Additional synthetic instances, so-called counterexamples, overweight the human feedback in the classifier's training data set such that the model's mechanism moves into the desirable direction. We assume our explanatory and interactive learner provides a procedure GEN to generate such counterexamples. The resulting counterexample data set contains a fixed amount of novel images that contain only the decisive pixels of an input image for a corresponding class label. The matrix of decisive pixels origins in human feedback.

Definition 1 (Counterexamples). *Let* $\mathbf{D} \in \{0,1\}^{W \times H}$ *be a binary image mask, where 1 encodes a decisive and 0 an indecisive pixel wrt. a label y. Moreover, let* GEN$(\mathbf{X}, y, \mathbf{D}, c)$ *be a procedure that outputs a counterexample data set of size $c \in \mathbb{N}$ in the form $\{(\mathbf{X}', y) \mid \mathbf{X}'$ fresh$\}$ that includes freshly generated images representing decisive features only, taking as input a given image $\mathbf{X}$, input label y and an input mask $\mathbf{D}$ of the same dimensions as $\mathbf{X}$.*

In order to enable users to correct the decision-making mechanism of a classification model in the **RWR** case, CAIPI retrieves local explanations by explanatory ML techniques first. We assume that local explanations correspond to the underlying mechanism of a classification model. Hence, our explanation procedure EXP needs to visualize the reasons why a certain image is associated with a certain prediction. Traditional CAIPI uses LIME [11,19], which fits a simplified surrogate model on aggregated parts of an image, so-called super-pixels. We prefer Integrated Gradients (IG) [18], as LIME is known to be sensitive to the underlying super-pixel segmentation algorithm [13]. IG takes partial derivatives of a classification model to calculate attribution values that represent the importance of pixels for the prediction outcome. This, of course, requires a differentiable classifier, which, in contrast to traditional CAIPI, is a restricting assumption. Out of efficiency reasons, IG approximates gradients with the Riemman summation:

$$
IG_i^{approx} =_{DF} (\mathbf{X}_i - \mathbf{X}_{B_i}) \sum_{k'=1}^{k} \frac{\partial f(\mathbf{X}_B + \frac{k'}{k} \times (\mathbf{X} - \mathbf{X}_B))}{\partial \mathbf{X}_i} \times \frac{1}{k} , \quad (1)
$$

where $\mathbf{X}_i$ indicates a pixel in $\mathbf{X}$, $\mathbf{X}_B$ is a baseline image (a black image with pixel values zero) with the same shape as $\mathbf{X}$, f is a classification model, and k' is a single iteration of k differentiation steps. Intuitively, the gradient is approximated by the sum of small increments between the input $\mathbf{X}$ and the baseline $\mathbf{X}_B$. Thus the resulting attribution values tell us how much a pixel $\mathbf{X}_i$ contributes to a prediction $f(\mathbf{X})$ relative to a baseline pixel $\mathbf{X}_{B_i}$. Our explanation procedure EXP visualizes the attribution values in an explanation mask $\mathbf{M}$.

Definition 2 (Explainer). *The explainer has a procedure* EXP$(\mathbf{X}, \mathbf{X}_B, f, \beta)$ *that takes as input an image* $\mathbf{X}$, *a baseline image* $\mathbf{X}_B$, *a differentiable classification model* f *and a threshold* β. *It returns an explanation mask* $\mathbf{M} \in \{0, 1\}^{W \times H}$ *with shape corresponding to* $\mathbf{X}$, *where* $\mathbf{M}_i = 1$ *indicates high-activated (decisive) and* $\mathbf{M}_i = 0$ *low-activated (indecisive) pixels for a prediction* $\hat{y} = f(\mathbf{X})$. *High-activated pixels have absolute attribution values greater than* β *(1).*

CAIPI shown in Alg. 1 is a cyclic and iterative optimization procedure. It pre-trains a model on a set of labeled images. We assume that the explanatory and interactive learner provides a procedure FIT$(\mathcal{L})$ for training and update of a model. In each iteration, it chooses the most-informative instance from the remaining (unlabeled) images, which is the one whose classification score is closest to the decision boundary. Therefore, we introduce the procedure MII that takes a set of predictions and the decision boundary as input and returns the index of the most-informative instance. We assume to have access to both, the classification scores and the decision boundary. We argue that the instance is *most-informative*, as we associate prediction scores closer to the decision boundary with higher uncertainty. Human feedback will reduce the classifier's uncertainty in the next iteration and, thus, maximize the information gain.

Definition 3 (Most-informative instance). *Consider the set of predictions* $\hat{y} = \{f(\mathbf{X}) \mid \mathbf{X} \in \mathcal{X}\}$. *We assume a procedure* MII$(\hat{y}, \alpha)$ *that returns the index of the most-informative instance from* $\hat{y}$, *whose classification score is closest to a decision boundary* α.

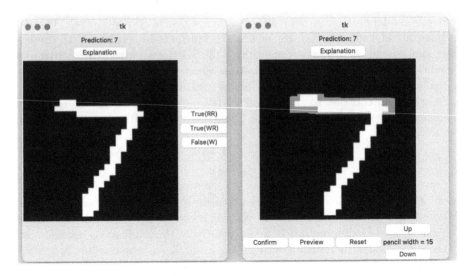

Fig. 2. User interface [17]. CAIPI presents the image and its prediction and explanation (which is empty) to an user (left). The user selects the appropriate prediction outcome state – in this case RWR (True(WR)) – and annotates CAIPI's local explanation (right).

Algorithm 1: CAIPI($\mathcal{L}, \mathcal{U}, c, n, \mathbf{X}_B$) [19]

Input: Labeled data set $\mathcal{L}$, unlabeled data set $\mathcal{U}$, number of counterexamples c, number of iterations n, baseline image $\mathbf{X}_B$

Output: Classification model f

1: **for** $i \leftarrow 1$ **to** n **do**
2:     $f \leftarrow \text{FIT}(\mathcal{L})$
3:     $\hat{\mathcal{Y}} \leftarrow \{f(u) \mid u \in \mathcal{U}\}$
4:     $m \leftarrow \text{MII}(\hat{\mathcal{Y}}, 0.5)$
5:     $y^{(m)} \leftarrow \text{INTERACT}(\mathbf{X}_{\mathcal{U}}^{(m)})$ ▷ *Label retrieved from human annotator*
6:     **if** $\hat{y}^{(m)} \neq y^{(m)}$ **then**
7:        $\mathcal{L} \leftarrow \mathcal{L} \cup \{(\mathbf{X}_{\mathcal{U}}^{(m)}, y^{(m)})\}$ ▷ *Case **W**: label correction*
8:     **else**
9:        $\mathbf{M} \leftarrow \text{EXP}(\mathbf{X}_{\mathcal{U}}^{(m)}, \mathbf{X}_B, f, 0.025)$
10:       $\mathbf{D} \leftarrow \text{INTERACT}(\mathbf{M})$ ▷ *Decisive features retrieved from human annotator*
11:       **if** $\mathbf{M} = \mathbf{D}$ **then**
12:         $\mathcal{L} \leftarrow \mathcal{L} \cup \{(\mathbf{X}_{\mathcal{U}}^{(m)}, \hat{y}^{(m)})\}$ ▷ *Case **RRR**: no further interaction needed*
13:       **else**
14:         $\mathcal{L} \leftarrow \mathcal{L} \cup \text{GEN}(\mathbf{X}_{\mathcal{U}}^{(m)}, \hat{y}^{(m)}, \mathbf{D}, c) \cup \{(\mathbf{X}_{\mathcal{U}}^{(m)}, \hat{y}^{(m)})\}$
          ▷ *Case **RWR**: Explanation correction and generation of counterexamples*
15:     $\mathcal{U} \leftarrow \mathcal{U} \setminus \mathbf{X}_{\mathcal{U}}^{(m)}$
16: **return** f

In the following, we denote interaction with the human annotator by a procedure INTERACT() to query for either a label or an explanation correction. We assume that the human annotator possess sufficient domain knowledge to solve the interaction tasks. We reference to our prior publication [17], where we equip CAIPI with an user interface (Fig. 2). CAIPI presents the most-informative instance together with the classifier's prediction and the corresponding explanation. Here: The prediction is correct, but the explanation is empty. No pixels are considered to be decisive. The user suspects a random guess of the classification model and selects the appropriate prediction outcome state, which is RWR in our example. This opens an annotation prompt, where the user highlights the truly decisive pixels, which are subject of the generated counterexamples.

To finalize this section, let us formalize CAIPI in Alg. 1: In each iteration, CAIPI trains a model on the labeled data sets in line 2 and draws predictions on the unlabeled data set afterwards in line 3. It selects the most-informative instance (l. 4), whose prediction is evaluated by an user. If the prediction is wrong compared to the labeling coming from a human annotator, then CAIPI uses the true label (l. 7). Otherwise, it generates an explanation in line 9. If the explanation is correct, i.e. the decisive features retrieved from the explainer are equal to the perceived decision mechanism $\mathbf{D}$ from a human annotator, then the instance is appended to the labeled data set (l. 12). If not, CAIPI queries an explanation correction and generates counterexamples (l. 14). Finally, the image is removed from the unlabeled data set to prepare the next iteration (l. 15).

3.2 Variational Autoencoders

Autoencoders compress data into a smaller representation that is known as the latent space and reconstruct the input from the latent space afterwards [20]. Variational Autoencoders [6] introduce a so-called prior distribution over the latent space and treat the data itself as probability distribution, also called the marginal distribution. This, in contrast to classical Autoencoders, allows us to generate an unlimited number of novel instances – Variational Autoencoders can therefore be subsumed into the class of *generative models* [3] (Fig. 3).

Definition 4. (Variational Autoencoder *[3]*). *Let a Variational Autoencoder vae : $\mathcal{X} \to \hat{\mathcal{X}}$ consist of an encoder network enc : $\mathcal{X} \to \mathcal{Z}$ and a decoder network dec : $\mathcal{Z} \to \hat{\mathcal{X}}$, where $\mathcal{Z} = \{z_{\mathbf{X}(1)}, ..., z_{\mathbf{X}(n)}\}$ is the latent space representation of $\mathcal{X}$, and $\hat{\mathcal{X}}$ is the reconstruction of $\mathcal{X}$ wrt. $\mathcal{Z}$. We assume a procedure* FITVAE *for fitting the Autoencoder. Further, we define the following probability distributions: the marginal distribution $p(\mathbf{X})$, the latent distribution $p(z)$, also known as prior, the decoder's likelihood distribution $p(\mathbf{X}|z, \theta)$, as well as the posterior $q_\theta(z|\mathbf{X})$ retrieved from the encoder. The parameter θ informally aggregates the inherent parametrization of the Variational Autoencoder.*

Variational Autoencoders are optimized by Variational Inference using the Evidence Lower Bound (ELBO) [2,12]. Therefore, let us introduce the Kullback-Leibler (KL) divergence [3] between a distribution q with known functional form that depends on network parameters θ and the intractable posterior $p(z|\mathbf{X})$ as

$$
\begin{aligned}
KL\left[q_\theta(z|\mathbf{X}) \parallel p(z|\mathbf{X})\right] = &\log p(\mathbf{X}) \\
&+ \mathbb{E}_{q_\theta(z)}\left[\log q_\theta(z|\mathbf{X}) - \log p(\mathbf{X}|z) - \log p(z)\right] ,
\end{aligned}
\tag{2}
$$

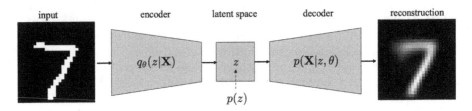

Fig. 3. Variational Autoencoder. The encoder abstracts an input image into the latent space. The decoder reconstructs the image from the latent space.

where the right-hand side expresses the KL divergence under consideration of the Bayes rule and removes $\log p(\mathbf{X})$ from the expectation as it is constant. Since we only observe a subset of the data, the marginal distribution $p(\mathbf{X})$, which reflects the data generating process, remains unknown. Similar to Autoencoders, their variational counterpart aims to reconstruct input data. Hence, Variational Autoencoders for image data approximate $p(\mathbf{X}|z)$ by a loss function – frequently the categorical cross-entropy [3]. Let us now express the difference between the proposal posterior $q_\theta(z|\mathbf{X})$ and the prior $p(z)$ as second KL divergence [2]

$$\begin{aligned}
\log p(\mathbf{X}) = {} & \mathbb{E}_{q_\theta(z)}\left[\log p(\mathbf{X}|z)\right] - KL\left[q_\theta(z|\mathbf{X}) \parallel p(z)\right] \\
& + KL\left[q_\theta(z|\mathbf{X}) \parallel p(z|\mathbf{X})\right] ,
\end{aligned} \quad (3)$$

where we define the first two parts of the right-hand side as ELBO [2]:

$$KL\left[q_\theta(z|\mathbf{X}) \parallel p(z|\mathbf{X})\right] = -ELBO(q) + \log p(\mathbf{X}) . \quad (4)$$

[1] Maximizing the ELBO implies a small KL divergence, which ultimately leaves us with a well-approximated posterior. Additionally, ELBO is a suitable *evidence lower bound* for the marginal, as it is the difference between the marginal distribution and the KL divergence (4). Hence, using ELBO as optimization criteria ensures both, a high latent space and a high marginal approximation quality.

4   The Bayesian CAIPI Algorithm

This section derives Bayesian CAIPI by refining Alg. 1: We embed the classifier into a Variational Autoencoder as depicted in Fig. 4. The adapted architecture has three different paths: an encoding and a decoding path, corresponding to the Variational Autoencoder's encoder and decoder, as well as a classification path, taking a latent space abstraction of an image as input and returning a predicted class. The latter leaves us with a single notational adjustment:

Notation. Let $g : \mathcal{Z} \rightarrow \mathcal{Y}$ be a differentiable binary classification model and let $\hat{y} = g(z)$ for some $z \in \mathcal{Z}$ indicate an inference. We obtain $\mathcal{Z}$ by using the encoder $\mathcal{Z} = enc(\mathcal{X})$ according to Def. 4.

---

[1] Figure adapted from https://danijar.com/building-variational-auto-encoders-in-tensorflow/, 2023/07/11.

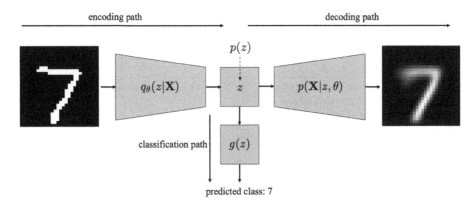

Fig. 4. Bayesian CAIPI backbone. A Variational Autoencoder extended with a classifier that takes an encoded image as input.

The former change in notation has three algorithmic consequences: (i) We train a Variational Autoencoder on all available training images. Of course, this includes the assumption to have a sufficient amount of training images for a high-quality latent abstraction. (ii) The classification model now takes encoded images as input. Hence, we first fit the classification model on the encoded labeled images and afterwards predict encoded unlabeled images to select the most informative instance. (iii) Finally, we refine the counterexample generation procedure (Def. 1) as GEN' in Alg. 2: A priori, the user selects decisive features. We sample repeatedly from the likelihood distribution (l. 3), until the desired amount of counterexamples is met. We element-wise multiply the mask of decisive features $\mathbf{D}$ with the novel image matrix $\hat{\mathbf{X}}$ (l. 4). As a consequence, indecisive features are blacked out and our counterexample contains only decisive features.

Alg. 3 formalizes BAYESIANCAIPI. Different from CAIPI (Alg. 1), we train a Variational Autoencoder prior to optimization (l. 1). We encode labeled (l. 3) as well as unlabeled images (l. 5) and our explainer (Def. 2) propagates the prediction backward to the input – through the classifier and the encoder (l. 12).

5 Experiments

5.1 Architecture

Using a Variational Autoencoder[2], we abstract the images into two latent dimensions. We use a standard normal distribution as prior. Hence, the posterior is also multivariate normally distributed. Our encoder has two convolutional layers with kernel size three and a stride parameter two in each dimension. It has 32 filters in the first convolutional layer and 64 in the second. We flatten the output for the dense layer that ends in the posterior distribution. Practically, the

---

[2] Architecture adapted from https://www.tensorflow.org/tutorials/generative/cvae, 2023/07/11.

encoder's output dimensionality is four, where the first two entries correspond to the first moment and the final entries to the second moment of the posterior.

Algorithm 2: $\mathrm{GEN'}(p(\mathbf{X}|z,\theta), y, D, c)$ (Counterexample Generation)

Input: Decoder's likelihood distribution for $\mathbf{X}$, label y, decisive features $\mathbf{D}$, number of counterexamples c
Output: Data sets of labeled counterexamples $\mathcal{X}', \mathcal{Y}'$
1: $\mathcal{X}' \leftarrow \emptyset; \mathcal{Y}' \leftarrow \emptyset$
2: **for** $i \leftarrow 1$ **to** c **do**
3: $\quad \hat{\mathbf{X}} \leftarrow p(\mathbf{X}|z,\theta)$
4: $\quad \hat{\mathbf{X}} \leftarrow \hat{\mathbf{X}} \cdot \mathbf{D}$
5: $\quad \mathcal{X}' \leftarrow \mathcal{X}' \cup \{\hat{\mathbf{X}}\}; \mathcal{Y}' \leftarrow \mathcal{Y}' \cup \{y\}$
6: **return** $\mathcal{X}', \mathcal{Y}'$

Algorithm 3: $\mathrm{BAYESIANCAIPI}(\mathcal{X}_\mathcal{L}, \mathcal{Y}_\mathcal{L}, \mathcal{U}, c, n, \mathbf{X}_B)$

Input: Labeled data $\mathcal{X}_\mathcal{L}$ and $\mathcal{Y}_\mathcal{L}$, unlabeled data $\mathcal{U}$, number of counterexamples c, iterations n, baseline image $\mathbf{X}_B$
Output: Classification model g
1: $vae, enc, dec \leftarrow \mathrm{FITVAE}(\mathcal{X}_\mathcal{L} \cup \mathcal{U})$
2: **for** $i \leftarrow 1$ **to** n **do**
3: $\quad \mathcal{Z}_\mathcal{L} \leftarrow enc(\mathcal{X}_\mathcal{L})$
4: $\quad g \leftarrow \mathrm{FIT}(\mathcal{Z}_\mathcal{L}, \mathcal{Y}_\mathcal{L})$
5: $\quad \mathcal{Z}_\mathcal{U} \leftarrow enc(\mathcal{U})$
6: $\quad \hat{\mathcal{Y}} \leftarrow \{g(u) \mid u \in \mathcal{Z}_\mathcal{U}\}$
7: $\quad m = \mathrm{MII}(\hat{\mathcal{Y}}, 0.5)$
8: $\quad y^{(m)} \leftarrow \mathrm{INTERACT}(\mathbf{X}_\mathcal{U}^{(m)})$ $\quad\quad\quad \triangleright$ *Label retrieved from human annotator*
9: $\quad$ **if** $\hat{y}^{(m)} \neq y^{(m)}$ **then**
10: $\quad\quad \mathcal{X}_\mathcal{L} \leftarrow \mathcal{X}_\mathcal{L} \cup \{\mathbf{X}_\mathcal{U}^{(m)}\}; \mathcal{Y}_\mathcal{L} \leftarrow \mathcal{Y}_\mathcal{L} \cup \{y^{(m)}\}$ $\quad\quad \triangleright$ *Case W*
11: $\quad$ **else**
12: $\quad\quad \mathbf{M} \leftarrow \mathrm{EXP}(\mathbf{X}_\mathcal{U}^{(m)}, \mathbf{X}_B, g \circ enc, 0.025)$
13: $\quad\quad \mathbf{D} \leftarrow \mathrm{INTERACT}(\mathbf{M})$ $\quad \triangleright$ *Decisive features retrieved from human annotator*
14: $\quad\quad$ **if** $\mathbf{M} = \mathbf{D}$ **then**
15: $\quad\quad\quad \mathcal{X}_\mathcal{L} \leftarrow \mathcal{X}_\mathcal{L} \cup \{\mathbf{X}_\mathcal{U}^{(m)}\}; \mathcal{Y}_\mathcal{L} \leftarrow \mathcal{Y}_\mathcal{L} \cup \{\hat{y}^{(m)}\}$ $\quad \triangleright$ *Case RRR*
16: $\quad\quad$ **else**
17: $\quad\quad\quad \mathcal{X}', \mathcal{Y}' \leftarrow \mathrm{GEN'}(p(\mathbf{X}|z,\theta), \hat{y}^{(m)}, \mathbf{D}, c)$
18: $\quad\quad\quad \mathcal{X}_\mathcal{L} \leftarrow \mathcal{X}_\mathcal{L} \cup \mathcal{X}' \cup \{\mathbf{X}_\mathcal{U}^{(m)}\}; \mathcal{Y}_\mathcal{L} \leftarrow \mathcal{Y}_\mathcal{L} \cup \mathcal{Y}' \cup \{\hat{y}^{(m)}\}$ $\quad \triangleright$ *Case RWR*
19: $\quad \mathcal{X}_\mathcal{U} \leftarrow \mathcal{X}_\mathcal{U} \setminus \mathbf{X}_\mathcal{U}^{(m)}$
20: **return** g

The decoder starts with a dense layer with $1,568$ neurons. After reshaping the image into two dimensions, the following three transposed convolutional layers reconstruct the image. Similar to the encoder, the decoder uses kernel size three and stride parameter two in each dimension. We invert the encoder and start with 64 filters that are reduced to 32 and a single filter in the final layer. All but the final layers of encoder and decoder use rectified linear unit activation functions. We attempt to maximize the ELBO by stochastic optimization for 20 epochs with the Adam optimizer [5] and learning rate 0.0001.

The classifier that is attached to the latent space (Fig. 4) has two dense layers: 512 neurons and rectified linear unit activation in the first and a single neuron with sigmoid activation in the second layer. Similar to the Variational Autoencoder, we use the Adam optimization function. However, we increase the learning rate to 0.001, use the binary cross-entropy loss function, and train for 50 epochs. Whereas the Variational Autoencoder is only fitted once prior to the optimization, we re-train the classification model in each iteration.

5.2 Setup

Using the MNIST data set[3], we distinguish ones from sevens. Our training data size is 12,000 and 2,000 images serve as test data. For the research questions R1 and R2, we start with ten labeled images, where each pixel is sampled from an uniform distribution with lower bound zero and upper bound one. At the start of the optimization cycle, we expect a poor classification and explanation quality. We add $\{0, 1, 3, 5\}$ counterexamples per RWR iteration for 100 iterations. During optimization, we expect the predictive as well as the explanation quality to be improving, where counterexamples should have a positive impact, as we increase the training data set. All experiments are repeated five times.

We measure the predictive quality by the accuracy metric. Distinguishing ones from sevens can presumably be abstracted into distinguishing vertical from horizontal bars – we suspect that sevens have a horizontal bar, whereas ones have a vertical bar. We investigate the position of activation values in the explanation mask with absolute value greater than 0.025. The explanation is correct if at least a single high-activated pixel detects the horizontal bar for a seven and the vertical bar for a one. A horizontal bar is defined as a minimum of five consecutive pixels aligned horizontally. Consequently, a vertical bar has a minimum of five consecutive pixels aligned vertically. The explanation correctness criteria are reflected in the counterexample generation procedure. There, we consider horizontal bars to be decisive for sevens and vertical bars for ones. Counterexamples bias the classification task to horizontal versus vertical bars.

5.3 Benchmark

To evaluate research question R3, we conduct two benchmark tests: First, we execute our encoding and classification path, but replace the counterexample generation procedure with classical image augmentation, where we scale and translate the decisive features. This, in fact, is similar to traditional CAIPI [17, 19]. For the benchmark, we restrict ourselves to five counterexamples per RWR iteration. Second, we compare Bayesian CAIPI to default deep learning, where we use all available training data to train the classification path.

CAIPI with image-specific data augmentation achieves a predictive accuracy of 97.97% and explains 68.67% of the ones in the test data set correctly. However, it fails to explain a single seven wrt. to our defined criteria. With the default deep learning pipeline, we obtain an accuracy of 98.06%, where the correct explanation is retrieved for class one in 36% and for class seven in 0.69%.

---

[3] http://yann.lecun.com/exdb/mnist/, 2023/07/11.

Table 1. Bayesian CAIPI evaluation. We evaluate the accuracy and the ratio of correct explanations for each class wrt. $c = \{0, 1, 3, 5\}$ counterexamples per RWR iteration.

Metric	Counterexamples c			
	0	1	3	5
Predictive Accuracy (%)	98.60 (0.55)	98.40 (0.55)	98.40 (0.55)	98.40 (0.55)
Ratio correct explanations (%)				
Class one	77.70 (10.47)	77.62 (19.83)	44.94 (34.96)	58.63 (17.73)
Class seven	0.30 (0.17)	0.64 (1.26)	1.19 (1.44)	8.38 (1.70)

5.4   Results

The Variational Autoencoder's average ELBO is -28.22 (0.64). Figure 5 visualizes a single Bayesian CAIPI optimization cycle with five counterexamples per RWR iteration: We see that counterexamples are added in only 17 RWR iterations. More often, Bayesian CAIPI queries a prediction correction, which equals 44 W outcomes. In 39 iterations, Bayesian CAIPI predicts and explains the most-informative instance correctly, where we observe that RRR iterations tend to occur more likely in the second half of the optimization cycle.

Table 1 reveals that active learning, which in fact is adding zero counterexamples per RWR iteration, achieves a comparatively high accuracy. The accuracy values are nearly stable over the course of adding counterexamples. Hence, regarding R1, we cannot say that an increasing amount of counterexamples improves the predictive quality. This finding is underpinned by Fig. 6, where the Bayesian CAIPI optimization cycle with five counterexamples per RWR iteration offers only minor accuracy benefits compared to zero counterexamples per RWR iteration. Remarkably, counterexamples contribute to stabilize the predictive performance, as they preserve Bayesian CAIPI from sudden performance shifts over the course of optimization iterations.

Further, we observe a trade-off regarding the explanation quality of the classes one and seven in Table 1. Whereas for zero counterexamples, most explanations for class one are correct, only a few sevens are explained correctly. We observe that the explanation quality of ones plummets, when the explanation quality for class seven increases. Apparently, adding five counterexamples per RWR iteration, breaks the negative trend for class one, where by far the highest ratio of sevens is explained correctly. As we defined the correct decision-making mechanism for distinguishing ones from sevens as a task of identifying vertical versus horizontal bars, we can state for R2 that adding counterexamples improves the explanation quality. Figure 7 visualizes Bayesian CAIPI's explanation mask of a seven wrt. several optimization iterations. Brighter pixels indicate a greater attribution value. Only attribution values in red, which are greater than 0.025, mark a high-activated attribution value. Hence, only red pixels define the explanation correctness. The attribution intensity shifts from vertical and horizontal bars in iteration 1 to the horizontal bar exclusively in iteration 30. In iteration 60, the horizontal bar's attribution values increase and lead to a single high-activated pixel in iteration 100, which yields a correct explanation.

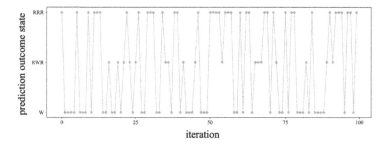

Fig. 5. Prediction outcome states. Visualization of prediction outcome states of a single Bayesian CAIPI run with five counterexamples per RWR iteration.

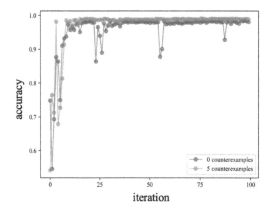

Fig. 6. Accuracy evaluation. Comparison of two experimental iterations of Bayesian CAIPI with zero and five counterexamples per RWR iteration.

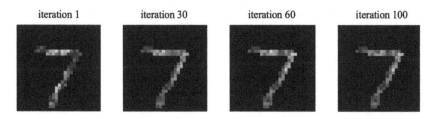

Fig. 7. Explanation quality evaluation. Visualization of an explanation mask for Bayesian CAIPI with five counterexamples per RWR iteration. Brighter values indicate more attribution. Attribution values greater than 0.025 are colored red. (Color figure online)

For R3, we take the benchmark tests into account: We observe that Bayesian CAIPI with five counterexamples per RWR iteration outperforms default deep learning as well as traditional CAIPI in terms of identifying correct explanations for sevens. Bayesian CAIPI even outperforms the explanation quality for class one in the default deep learning setting. Both findings are accompanied by a consistent predictive accuracy, where Bayesian CAIPI requires less than 1% labeling effort compared to default deep learning.

6   Discussion

Bayesian CAIPI samples from the likelihood distribution of a Variational Autoencoder to generate counterexamples. Similar to prior CAIPI publications [14,17,19], we investigate the predictive as well as the explanatory quality in context of an increasing amount of counterexamples per RWR iteration. Whereas, despite of a continuously high predictive accuracy, we cannot observe a positive impact of adding counterexamples, the explanatory quality at least partially profits from more counterexamples – explanations for class seven improve steadily and explanations for class one improve comparing five and three counterexamples per RWR iteration. Our findings are in line with existing CAIPI evaluations, as we match the predictive accuracy of default deep learning [17]. Given that we outperform CAIPI with its traditional data augmentation procedure in terms of explanation quality, we argue that Bayesian CAIPI utilizes a suitable counterexample generation alternative.

In the following, we emphasize four major critical points regarding the experimental setup: (i) The binary MNIST classification task is too simple to observe predictive performance differences. Even standard active learning matches the predictive performance of deep learning optimization with 12,000 labeled images. (ii) Even if the explanation quality of class seven improves by adding counterexamples, it still remains on a low level. Taking into account that the explanation quality is superior to the one of default deep learning and traditional CAIPI, this is an improvement. However, additional experiments are required. (iii) In this context, the concept of correct explanations should also be re-evaluated: Is IG a suitable method? And, can the classification task of ones versus sevens be abstracted by vertical versus horizontal bars? Using IG as explanation method, ones will be explained correctly if the attribution is sufficiently high, as only vertical bars exist. This is an indicator for the highly imbalanced explanation quality. Finally, (iv) the high standard deviations for the explanation quality, especially for three counterexamples per RWR iteration, motivate more sophisticated experiments. This discloses an issue of numerical instability, which might be located in the latent dimension of the Variational Autoencoder.

In summary, the role of counterexample generation for CAIPI has already been investigated [14]. This work is located in the same niche and searches for a substitute for data augmentation. We propose to sample counterexamples from the likelihood distribution of Variational Autoencoders. Therefore, we integrate a classification model into a Variational Autoencoder, which is also strongly related to existing research [4]. The novelty of our approach is to connect Variational Autoencoders with classification models in the context of XIML, where we utilize mostly unlabeled data to generate additional novel training instances.

7   Conclusion and Future Work

CAIPI, a state-of-the-art XIML algorithm, queries user feedback regarding the prediction and explanation of a ML model to move the decision-making mechanism into a presumably correct direction form a user's perspective. Hereby, traditional CAIPI's counterexample generation procedure relies on data augmentation. Depending on the domain, data augmentation might cause unrealistic counterexamples. We propose Bayesian CAIPI that integrates CAIPI's classification task into a Variational Autoencoder and samples counterexamples from the likelihood distribution. This decouples the counterexample generation from domain knowledge and, given a sufficiently high quality of the Variational Autoencoder, creates an unlimited number of realistic counterexamples. The experimental evaluation shows that Bayesian CAIPI achieves a stable high predicative accuracy and adding counterexamples partially benefits the explanations quality. In relation to traditional CAIPI and default deep learning optimization, we observe that Bayesian CAIPI matches the predictive accuracy and outperforms both in terms of explanation quality. Hence, we argue that Variational Autoencoders are a suitable alternative to generate counterexamples for CAIPI.

For future work, we will investigate the role of decisive features. Do we still need their annotation? If not, Bayesian CAIPI would be capable of including implicit knowledge, as users must only be aware of the correct decision-making mechanism without being able to correct it manually. This extends the potential user group from domain experts to novices. Furthermore, we will sharpen our experiments: Powerful generative models, such as Variational Autoencoders, appear to be suitable for complex multi-label classification tasks, where images have larger dimensions and their decisive features might be ambiguous. Probably because of data augmentation limitations, CAIPI still is restricted to classifications. What happens if we apply Bayesian CAIPI to regression tasks? Is the generation ability of Variational Autoencoders still sufficient? In this context, we will also experiment with logical constraints, as especially for tabular data, we suspect implausible results, when we rely on generative models exclusively.

Acknowledgments. This research is funded by BMBF Germany (hKI-Chemie, # 01IS21023A).

References

1. Amershi, S., Cakmak, M., Knox, W.B., Kulesza, T.: Power to the people: the role of humans in interactive machine learning. AI Mag. **35**(4), 105–120 (2014). https://doi.org/10.1609/aimag.v35i4.2513
2. Blei, D.M., Kucukelbir, A., McAuliffe, J.D.: Variational inference: a review for statisticians. J. American Stat. Assoc. **112**(518), 859–877 (Apr 2017). https://doi.org/10.1080/01621459.2017.1285773
3. Doersch, C.: Tutorial on variational autoencoders (2016). https://arxiv.org/abs/1606.05908

4. Ji, T., Vuppala, S.T., Chowdhary, G., Driggs-Campbell, K.R.: Multi-modal anomaly detection for unstructured and uncertain environments. In: Kober, J., Ramos, F., Tomlin, C.J. (eds.) 4th Conference on Robot Learning, CoRL 2020, 16–18 November 2020, Virtual Event / Cambridge, MA, USA. Proceedings of Machine Learning Research, vol. 155, pp. 1443–1455. PMLR (2020). https://proceedings.mlr.press/v155/ji21a.html

5. Kingma, D.P., Ba, J.: Adam: a method for stochastic optimization. In: Bengio, Y., LeCun, Y. (eds.) 3rd International Conference on Learning Representations, ICLR 2015, San Diego, CA, USA, May 7–9, 2015, Conference Track Proceedings (2015). https://arxiv.org/abs/1412.6980

6. Kingma, D.P., Welling, M.: Auto-encoding variational bayes. In: Bengio, Y., LeCun, Y. (eds.) 2nd International Conference on Learning Representations, ICLR 2014, Banff, AB, Canada, April 14–16, 2014, Conference Track Proceedings (2014). https://arxiv.org/abs/1312.6114

7. Kulesza, T., Burnett, M.M., Wong, W., Stumpf, S.: Principles of explanatory debugging to personalize interactive machine learning. In: Brdiczka, O., Chau, P., Carenini, G., Pan, S., Kristensson, P.O. (eds.) Proceedings of the 20th International Conference on Intelligent User Interfaces, IUI 2015, Atlanta, GA, USA, March 29 - April 01, 2015, pp. 126–137. ACM (2015). https://doi.org/10.1145/2678025.2701399

8. Nakao, Y., Stumpf, S., Ahmed, S., Naseer, A., Strappelli, L.: Toward involving end-users in interactive human-in-the-loop AI Fairness. ACM Trans. Interact. Intell. Syst. 12(3), 1–3 (Jul 2022). https://doi.org/10.1145/3514258

9. Pfeuffer, N., et al.: Explanatory interactive machine learning. Business Inform. Syst. Eng. (2023). https://doi.org/10.1007/s12599-023-00806-x

10. Pu, Y., et al.: Variational autoencoder for deep learning of images, labels and captions. In: Lee, D.D., Sugiyama, M., von Luxburg, U., Guyon, I., Garnett, R. (eds.) Advances in Neural Information Processing Systems 29: Annual Conference on Neural Information Processing Systems 2016, December 5–10, 2016, Barcelona, Spain, pp. 2352–2360 (2016)

11. Ribeiro, M.T., Singh, S., Guestrin, C.: "Why should I trust you?": explaining the predictions of any classifier. In: Krishnapuram, B., Shah, M., Smola, A.J., Aggarwal, C.C., Shen, D., Rastogi, R. (eds.) Proceedings of the 22nd ACM SIGKDD International Conference on Knowledge Discovery and Data Mining, San Francisco, CA, USA, August 13–17, 2016, pp. 1135–1144. ACM (2016). https://doi.org/10.1145/2939672.2939778

12. Salimans, T., Kingma, D.P., Welling, M.: Markov chain monte carlo and variational inference: bridging the gap. In: Bach, F.R., Blei, D.M. (eds.) Proceedings of the 32nd International Conference on Machine Learning, ICML 2015, Lille, France, 6–11 July 2015. JMLR Workshop and Conference Proceedings, vol. 37, pp. 1218–1226. JMLR.org (2015). https://ngs.mlr.press/v37/salimans15.html

13. Cellier, P., Driessens, K. (eds.): Machine Learning and Knowledge Discovery in Databases: International Workshops of ECML PKDD 2019, Würzburg, Germany, September 16–20, 2019, Proceedings, Part I. Springer International Publishing, Cham (2020)

14. Schramowski, P., et al.: Making deep neural networks right for the right scientific reasons by interacting with their explanations. Nature Mach. Intell. 2(8), 476–486 (2020). https://doi.org/10.1038/s42256-020-0212-3

15. Settles, B.: Active Learning. Synthesis Lectures on Artificial Intelligence and Machine Learning, Morgan & Claypool Publishers (2012). https://doi.org/10.2200/S00429ED1V01Y201207AIM018

16. Shivaswamy, P., Joachims, T.: Coactive Learning. J. Artif. Intell. Res. **53**, 1–40 (2015). https://doi.org/10.1613/jair.4539

17. Maglogiannis, I., Iliadis, L., Macintyre, J., Cortez, P. (eds.): Artificial Intelligence Applications and Innovations. AIAI 2022 IFIP WG 12.5 International Workshops: MHDW 2022, 5G-PINE 2022, AIBMG 2022, ML@HC 2022, and AIBEI 2022, Hersonissos, Crete, Greece, June 17–20, 2022, Proceedings. Springer International Publishing, Cham (2022)

18. Sundararajan, M., Taly, A., Yan, Q.: Axiomatic attribution for deep networks. In: Precup, D., Teh, Y.W. (eds.) Proceedings of the 34th International Conference on Machine Learning, ICML 2017, Sydney, NSW, Australia, 6–11 August 2017. Proceedings of Machine Learning Research, vol. 70, pp. 3319–3328. PMLR (2017). http://proceedings.mlr.press/v70/sundararajan17a.html

19. Teso, S., Kersting, K.: Explanatory interactive machine learning. In: Conitzer, V., Hadfield, G.K., Vallor, S. (eds.) Proceedings of the 2019 AAAI/ACM Conference on AI, Ethics, and Society, AIES 2019, Honolulu, HI, USA, January 27–28, 2019, pp. 239–245. ACM (2019). https://doi.org/10.1145/3306618.3314293

20. Vincent, P., Larochelle, H., Bengio, Y., Manzagol, P.: Extracting and composing robust features with denoising autoencoders. In: Cohen, W.W., McCallum, A., Roweis, S.T. (eds.) Machine Learning, Proceedings of the Twenty-Fifth International Conference (ICML 2008), Helsinki, Finland, June 5–9, 2008. ACM International Conference Proceeding Series, vol. 307, pp. 1096–1103. ACM (2008). https://doi.org/10.1145/1390156.1390294

21. Ware, M., Frank, E., Holmes, G., Hall, M.A., Witten, I.H.: Interactive machine learning: letting users build classifiers. Int. J. Hum Comput Stud. **55**(3), 281–292 (2001). https://doi.org/10.1006/ijhc.2001.0499

22. Shen, D., et al. (eds.): Medical Image Computing and Computer Assisted Intervention – MICCAI 2019: 22nd International Conference, Shenzhen, China, October 13–17, 2019, Proceedings, Part II. Springer International Publishing, Cham (2019)

23. Zhu, Q., Zhang, R.: A Classification Supervised Auto-Encoder Based on Predefined Evenly-Distributed Class Centroids (2019). https://arxiv.org/abs/1902.00220

Commonsense Reasoning and Explainable Artificial Intelligence Using Large Language Models

Stefanie Krause[✉][iD] and Frieder Stolzenburg[iD]

Automation and Computer Sciences Department, Harz University of Applied Sciences, Friedrichstr. 57–59, 38855 Wernigerode, Germany
{skrause,fstolzenburg}@hs-harz.de
http://artint.hs-harz.de/

Abstract. Commonsense reasoning is a difficult task for a computer, but a critical skill for an artificial intelligence (AI). It can enhance the explainability of AI models by enabling them to provide intuitive and human-like explanations for their decisions. This is necessary in many areas but especially in the field of question answering (QA), which is one of the most important tasks of natural language processing (NLP). Over time, a multitude of methods have emerged for solving commonsense reasoning problems such as knowledge-based approaches using formal logic or linguistic analysis.

In this paper, we investigate the effectiveness of large language models (LLMs) on different QA tasks with focus on their abilities on reasoning and producing explanations. For this, we study the recent and very prominent LLM ChatGPT and evaluate the results by means of a questionnaire. We demonstrate ChatGPT's ability to reason with common sense, and although ChatGPT's accuracy ranges from 56% to 93% on various QA benchmarks, it outperforms human accuracy. Furthermore we can appraise that, in the sense of explainable artificial intelligence (XAI), ChatGPT gives good explanations for its decisions. In our questionnaire we found that 68% of the participants quantify ChatGPT's explanations as "good" or "excellent". Taken together, these findings enrich our understanding of current LLMs and pave the way for future investigations of reasoning and explainability.

Keywords: large language models · explainable AI · commonsense reasoning · question answering · ChatGPT

1 Introduction

LLMs are an important ingredient in developing adaptable, general language systems [3], and scaling up languages models has recently shown great results for various NLP tasks. Lately, a media hype was triggered by the LLM ChatGPT.[1] This new AI model uses an easy interface and performs very well on

---

[1] https://chat.openai.com/.

S. Nowaczyk et al. (Eds.): ECAI 2023 Workshops, CCIS 1947, pp. 302–319, 2024.
https://doi.org/10.1007/978-3-031-50396-2_17

different tasks [9]. The current generation of AI systems offers tremendous benefits, but their effectiveness is limited by the inability of the machine to explain its decisions and actions to users. They perceive the models as black boxes although insights about the decision making are mostly opaque [4]. In response to increasing political, ethical, economical, and curiosity-driven theoretical pressure on ML researchers, the field of XAI tries to solve this black-box problem [36]. According to [2], it is important to focus on the audience for which explainability is sought. They define XAI as follows: "Given an audience, an XAI is one that produces details or reasons to make its functioning clear or easy to understand." They further distinguish between different terms: *explainability* and *interpretability*. Explainability means that a model's outcome can be explained in human-readable form, e.g., by explanatory text. Interpretability of a model on the other hand refers to the design of the model itself, e.g., so-called heatmaps that visualize neural network activity for image recognition helping to understand the (possibly fallacious) behavior of neural networks [18]. We focus in our work on explainability of AI models in the above sense with the goal of XAI to provide human-readable explanations to make users understand the automated decision-making of large language models a posteriori.

There is a strong connection between XAI and commonsense reasoning, as both concepts are concerned with improving the explainability of AI models. Commonsense reasoning can enhance the explainability of AI models by enabling them to provide intuitive and human-like explanations for their decisions. According to [8], starting with a better understanding of human cognition is a solid foundation. Humans use cognitive reasoning to draw meaningful conclusions despite incomplete and inconsistent knowledge [13]. For us, cognitive reasoning is particularly useful when we encounter new situations that are not covered by formal rules or guidelines. In these situations, we rely on our commonsense to make judgments and decisions that are appropriate and effective. Furthermore, commonsense reasoning is essential in interpersonal interactions and communication. It allows us to understand the perspectives of others and to navigate social situations effectively. Commonsense reasoning can help AI models to be more robust in the context of novel situations. A model that can reason based on commonsense principles is better equipped to handle situations that it has not explicitly encountered before, as it can draw on its general understanding of the world to make informed decisions. So far commonsense reasoning is intuitive for humans but has been a long-term challenge for AI models.

We assume that an LLM can reason similar to humans without the need of logical formulas or explicit ontology knowledge. Recent advances in LLMs (e.g. [22]) have pushed machines closer to human-like understanding capabilities. We believe that language comprehension and commonsense reasoning do not require formal structures, although they eventually may provide a better understanding afterwards for humans. Instead we assume LLMs are the appropriate way towards human-like ability to reason as well as explain decisions. To tackle growing demand of explainability for AI systems we aim to prove that generated explanations by LLMs are helpful for users to understand AI decisions. There is no specific structure of learning necessary: LLMs like ChatGPT can generate human-like explanations a posteriori. For this reason we formulate the following **hypotheses**:

1. LLMs like ChatGPT can handle commonsense reasoning in question answering tasks with near-human-level performance.
2. LLMs like ChatGPT are able to generate good, human-understandable explanations for their decisions.

We start our paper by giving an overview of important research directions in Sect. 2. Then, we evaluate the performance of the recent LLM ChatGPT on commonsense reasoning tasks in Sect. 3. Since measuring explainability is still a problem we address this by first testing ChatGPT on eleven QA datasets where commonsense capabilities are required. With a random sample of each benchmark dataset, subsequently we evaluate the quality of ChatGPT's responses with a questionnaire (Sect. 4). The main **contributions** of this paper are described in Sect. 5 and can be summarized as following:

- evaluation of ChatGPT's ability to perform commonsense reasoning
- quality measurement of ChatGPT's explanations by a questionnaire

2   Foundations

2.1   Approaches for Commonsense Reasoning

Commonsense reasoning is a difficult task for a computer to handle [32]. To address this problem, various approaches have been followed in the past. McCarthy [23] was the first who outlined the basic approach of representing commonsense knowledge with predicate logic. Symbolic logic approaches were the main representation type, see e.g. [12,19]. While still in use today [7] for this extremely complex task to work well it requires a large amount of additional logical scaffolding to precisely define the terms used in the statement and their interrelationships [21].

There is a big gap between the logical approach with deductive reasoning and human reasoning, which is largely inductive, associative, and empirical, i.e., based on former experience. Human reasoning, in contrast to formal logical reasoning, does not strictly follow the rules of classical logic. There have been efforts to utilize an approach which uses an automatic theorem prover (that allows to derive new knowledge in an explainable way), large existing ontologies with background knowledge, and recurrent networks with long short-term memory (LSTM) [16] but still did not stand out much from the baseline [32].

Recent efforts to acquire and represent commonsense knowledge resulted in large knowledge graphs, acquired through extractive methods [34] or crowdsourcing [30]. Some approaches use supervised training on a particular knowledge base, e.g., ConceptNet for commonsense knowledge. ConceptNet is a crowd-sourced database that represents commonsense knowledge as a graph of concepts connected by relations [34].

Interestingly, LLMs (cf. Section 2.2) do not contain any explicit semantic knowledge or grammatical let alone logical rules that would allow an explicit reasoning process, not even the large ontologies from the logical knowledge representation like Cyc [19] or Adimen-SUMO [1]. A way out might be to have neural networks learn reasoning explicitly, possibly by focusing on certain sentence forms as in syllogistic reasoning maybe implemented with neural-symbolic cognitive reasoning by specifically structured neural networks [14,15,39]. In contrast to simple deep learning, information from different places and/or documents must be merged here in any case. It does not suffice to investigate any local text properties, e.g., determining the text form.

2.2 Commonsense Reasoning with LLMs

In the past, most deep learning methods used supervised learning and therefore require substantial amounts of manually labeled data. Recent research has shown that learning good representations in an unsupervised fashion can provide a significant performance boost. An example for a premier LLM that can handle a wide range of natural language processing tasks is OpenAI's GPT-3 [3]. GPT-3 (Generative Pre-trained Transformer) is a third-generation, autoregressive language model that uses unsupervised learning to produce human-like text. The language model of ChatGPT is trained on an unlabeled dataset of texts, such as Wikipedia to predict the next word for a given text. The capacity of language model is essential to the success of zero-shot task transfer [28]. ChatGPT performs impressive without the need of finetuning on different natural language processing tasks.

The GPT series focuses on pre-training transformer decoders on language modeling. A similar LLM is the Bidirectional Encoder Representations from Transformers (BERT) which uses the transformer encoder as its backbone architecture [10]. BERT obtained new state-of-the-art results on eleven natural language processing tasks already in October 2018 [10]. As well BERT achieved new state-of-the-art performance for example on the SWAG benchmark [38] that exceeded even that of a human expert [5]. However, BERT does not possess human-level commonsense in general [5]. Therefore BERT has been optimized only one year later to RoBERTa to achieve better results [22]. There is also the Bidirectional Auto-Regressive Transformer (BART) [20], a denoising autoencoder for pretraining sequence-to-sequence models, which can be seen as generalizing BERT due to the bidirectional encoder. In our further investigation we will focus solely on ChatGPT. It is a version of GPT with an easy to use interface and at the moment the most prominent LLM.

3 Evaluating ChatGPT on QA Tasks

We assess ChatGPT twofold: First, we evaluate the accuracy of ChatGPT on QA benchmarks with multiple-choice questions. In the benchmarks we considered, the correct answer is indicated, although it is not always clear whether this answer really is the best one. Second, we take part of the questions from the QA benchmarks for a questionnaire to evaluate the quality of the responses and explanations of ChatGPT and compare the performance of humans and ChatGPT on QA examples.

3.1   Benchmark Datasets

We use 11 benchmark datasets carefully designed to be difficult to solve without commonsense knowledge (see below). From each dataset, we select 30 random examples, covering different QA tasks like text completion or providing cause or effect. In addition, different fields like medicine, physics, and everyday life situations are covered. We evaluate the performance of ChatGPT with the following QA benchmarks:

- Story Cloze Test [25]: is based on ROC Stories for evaluating story understanding and generation. This test requires choosing the correct ending of a four-sentence story.
- Commonsense Reasoning over Entity Knowledge (CREAK) [26]: contains knowledge about specific entities, e.g., deciding the truthfulness of the claim "Harry Potter can teach classes on how to fly on a broomstick.", i.e., including fictional worlds. It is bridging fact-checking about entities with commonsense inferences using 13,000 human-authored English claims about entities that are either true or false.
- COmmonsense Dataset Adversarially-authored by Humans (CODAH) [5]: forms a challenging extension to the SWAG dataset [38] which tests commonsense knowledge using sentence-completion questions that describe situations observed in video.
- COM2SENSE [33]: comprises true/false statements, with each sample paired with its complementary counterpart, resulting in 4,000 sentence pairs.
- Cosmos QA [17]: is constructed to test machine reading comprehension with contextual commonsense reasoning. It is a large-scale dataset of 35,600 multiple-choice questions. It focuses on reading between the lines over a diverse collection of people's everyday narratives.
- Explainable CAusal REasoning dataset (e-CARE) [11]: contains over 21,000 causal reasoning questions, together with natural language formed explanations of the causal questions.
- AI2 Reasoning Challenge (ARC) [6]: covers natural, grade-school science questions that are authored for human tests, and is the largest public-domain set of this kind with 7,787 questions.
- Social IQa [31]: contains 38,000 multiple choice questions for probing emotional and social intelligence in a variety of everyday situations.
- Choice Of Plausible Alternatives (COPA) [29]: is an open-domain commonsense reasoning QA task where each question gives a premise and two plausible causes or effects, where the correct choice is the alternative that is more plausible than the other. The cause category requires backward causal reasoning, while the result category requires forward causal reasoning.

- Multiple-Choice Question Answering (MedMCQA) [27]: is designed to address real-world medical entrance exam questions. It is covering more than 2,400 healthcare topics and 21 medical subjects.
- CommonsenseQA [35]: for this dataset crowd-workers authored multiple-choice questions that mention the source concept extract from ConceptNet [34] multiple target concepts that have the same semantic relation to a single source concept.

3.2 Method

Using all these eleven datasets we randomly selected 30 examples from each dataset and tested the respective QA tasks with ChatGPT. Over all datasets ChatGPT answered 242 out of 330 tasks correctly which equals an accuracy of 73.33%, 77 tasked were answered incorrectly (23.33%), and we did not get a valid response for 11 QA tasks (3.33%). Not valid means that ChatGPT does not respond which answer option is correct and instead asks for further context information, see Fig. 1 for an example. Note that there are tasks with two answer options and tasks with five answer options and everything in between.

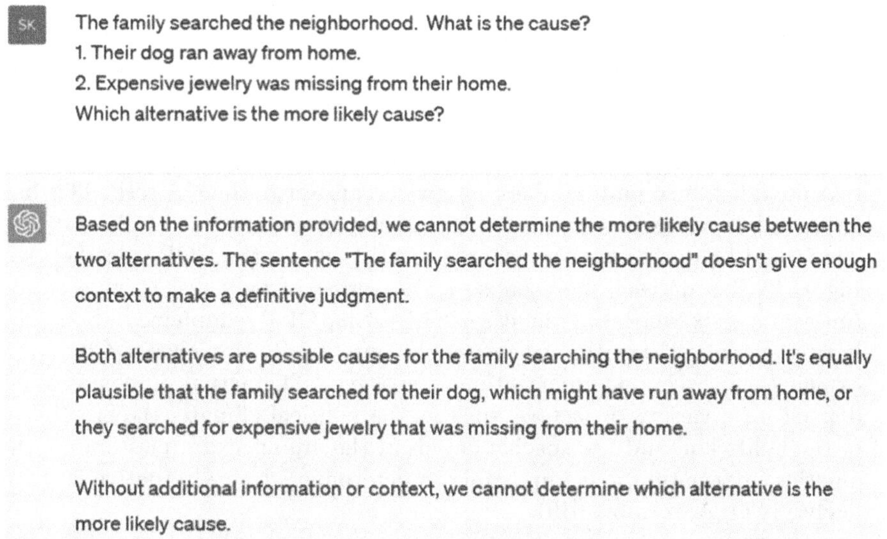

The family searched the neighborhood. What is the cause?
1. Their dog ran away from home.
2. Expensive jewelry was missing from their home.
Which alternative is the more likely cause?

Based on the information provided, we cannot determine the more likely cause between the two alternatives. The sentence "The family searched the neighborhood" doesn't give enough context to make a definitive judgment.

Both alternatives are possible causes for the family searching the neighborhood. It's equally plausible that the family searched for their dog, which might have run away from home, or they searched for expensive jewelry that was missing from their home.

Without additional information or context, we cannot determine which alternative is the more likely cause.

Fig. 1. Example for a not valid response from ChatGPT due to insufficient context information (COPA example 612). While option 1 is correct, the authors agree that option 2 could also be possible as well (but less likely).

A more detailed representation of the performance on each of the eleven datasets is shown in Table 1. We found that ChatGPT has the lowest performance on CommonsenseQA dataset with 56.67% accuracy and the highest accuracy on Story Cloze Test with 93.33%.

Table 1. Overview of eleven publicly available datasets for commonsense reasoning. For each dataset we report the year the dataset was published and the percentage of correct, incorrect and invalid answers of ChatGPT on 30 randomly selected examples per dataset.

dataset	year	correct	incorrect	invalid
Story Cloze Test [25]	2017	93.33%	6.67%	0.00%
CREAK [26]	2021	86.67%	13.33%	0.00%
CODAH [5]	2019	80.00%	20.00%	0.00%
COM2SENSE [33]	2021	76.67%	23.33%	0.00%
CosmosQA [17]	2019	76.67%	23.33%	0.00%
e-CARE [11]	2022	76.67%	23.33%	0.00%
ARC [6]	2018	70.00%	30.00%	0.00%
Social IQa [31]	2019	66.67%	33.33%	0.00%
COPA [29]	2011	63.33%	3.33%	33.33%
MedMCQA [27]	2022	60.00%	40.00%	0.00%
CommonsenseQA [35]	2018	56.67%	43.33%	0.00%

3.3   Analysis

In our error analysis we found that there are six kinds of problems where Chat-GPT still struggles:

1. **missing context**: In cases where ChatGPT has little knowledge of the context provided, it sometimes does not give an answer to the QA task. This has happened 10 times in total and solely with examples of the COPA dataset. This could be due to the very short premise texts in the COPA dataset, see Fig. 1. In this dataset the premise texts consist of only five to nine words (on average six words) in the cases where ChatGPT complained about not having enough information to answer the question. In some cases, ChatGPT explains which context information is missing: "The actual outcome would depend on a variety of factors, such as the political climate, the credibility of the politician, and the specific details of the argument in question. Without this information it is impossible to determine which alternative is more likely." (COPA example 619).
2. **comparative reasoning**: ChatGPT has problems when more than one option is plausible. This is the case in comparative scenarios in the COM2SENSE and Social IQa dataset. In such cases, the commonsense reasoner must explicitly investigate the likelihood of different answer candidates. For the Social IQa example 26823 "Sasha was throwing a party in her new condo which they bought a month ago. What does Sasha need to do before this?" ChatGPT answers "Turn music on" which is likely but the correct and even more likely answer is "needed to buy food for the party".
3. **subjective reasoning**: Some answers depend on the personality of the reasoner, e.g. Social IQa example 18571: "Alex's powers were not as strong since

he was just starting out. Alex used Bailey's powers since hers were stronger. How would Bailey feel as a result?" the correct answer according to the benchmark is "good" but instead ChatGPT answers "upset" and explains "Bailey may feel that her powers are being taken advantage of . . ." which we think is more a personalized subjective inference instead of a commonsense answer.

4. **slang, unofficial abbreviations, and youth language**: ChatGPT has its difficulties to understand slang, unofficial abbreviations and youth language like "subs" for "subscribers" or "yrs" for "years". This could be observed in Cosmos QA examples 6599 and 5748.

5. **social situations**: We identified a lack of understanding social situations correctly especially in the Social IQa dataset. For example, for the question "Kai was visiting from out of state and brought gifts for Quinn's family. What will Kai want to do next?" ChatGPT picked the answer "needed to leave his hometown" instead of the correct answer option "watch the opening of gifts" (Social IQa example 6863).

6. **medical domain**: The analysis of MedMCQA showed that ChatGPT is lacking a deep domain knowledge in the medical field. The answers of ChatGPT were always plausible and explained with a lot of details (on average 43 words per explanation) but 40% were incorrect. This was because of many medical technical terms that are not common knowledge, e.g., "Styloglossus muscle" or "Genioglossus muscle" that are different muscles in the tongue (MedMCQA example 23b363d6-8210–4657-b293-54c9e28bdf31). For a non-medical professional or student, these questions are difficult to answer, too (including the authors of this paper).

Please be aware that for certain questions to be answered correctly, one must possess in-depth knowledge rather than commonsense reasoning ability, e.g., you have to know that "Prison Break" is a television show, not a movie in a theater to tell that "The couple went to the movie theater to watch Prison Break" is a correct or wrong statement (CREAK example 98). Additionally, the authors hold the viewpoint that out of the 78 incorrect answers, 12 of them were very likely to be correct as well and therefore quite hard for an AI to answer correctly.

3.4   Design of the Questionnaire

To evaluate the quality of ChatGPT's responses on different benchmark datasets and to make a comparison to human performance, we created a questionnaire. We used two randomly selected examples for each of the above mentioned datasets – except for MedMCQA because we feel these questions are too difficult for non-medical people to answer.

We created an online survey questionnaire using SoSciSurvey[2] that was open to the public on social media, e.g., LinkedIn, Xing, and platforms like SurveyCircle and we send the questionnaire via e-mail directly to students at the Harz University of Applied Sciences in Germany. Participation was voluntary; participants could not be identified from the material presented and no plausible harm

---

[2] https://www.soscisurvey.de/.

to participating individuals could arise from the study. Survey content validity was reviewed in a pretest by one professor, one academic staff and one non-academic volunteer (business consultant) who did not participate in developing the survey. The questionnaire was structured in three parts, first containing demographic and personal information (gender, age, nationality, English level). The main part then consists of the QA tasks of the different datasets as well an evaluation of ChatGPT's explanations. For each QA task we have the same structure, as follows:

1. The question and answer options for each QA task were given for the survey participants.
2. We ask how comprehensible the question above is using a five-level Likert scale.
3. The question and answer options were repeated and ChatGPT's explanation for one possible answer option is presented (this answer may be incorrect). Then using a five-level Likert scale we ask how good the explanation is.
4. An optional free text field to tell what could be improved in the given explanation.

To see an example of this main questionnaire section, refer to Fig. 2. We used this structure for 10 datasets and randomly selected two examples from every dataset. Therefore we considered $2 \cdot 10 = 20$ QA tasks. In the third part of the questionnaire, the participants should guess how many explanations have been generated by an AI among others. Note that the survey participants did not know that *all* responses have been generated by ChatGPT.

4 Results

4.1 Questionnaire Participants

In total, 103 people participated in the questionnaire, but because of missing data we only used the responses of 49 participants. The time to fully answer the whole questionnaire was about 25 min, that is probably why many participants did not complete the questionnaire until the last question. The participants English level was mainly advanced or excellent so that there is no language barrier in understanding the QA tasks. Among the completed questionnaires, 71% of the participants were male and the average age was 26 years, with a minimum of 19 years and maximum of 49 years. Most of the participants were German with 45% and Indian with 40% and only 5% of Bangladeshi, Pakistan, Finland, Russian Federation and Switzerland.

4.2 Questionnaire Responses

We found that the participants answered 73.72% of the 20 QA tasks correctly compared to ChatGPT's 90.00% on the same questions. Note that these 20 in detail analyzed QA tasks are not as representative as the 330 QA tasks

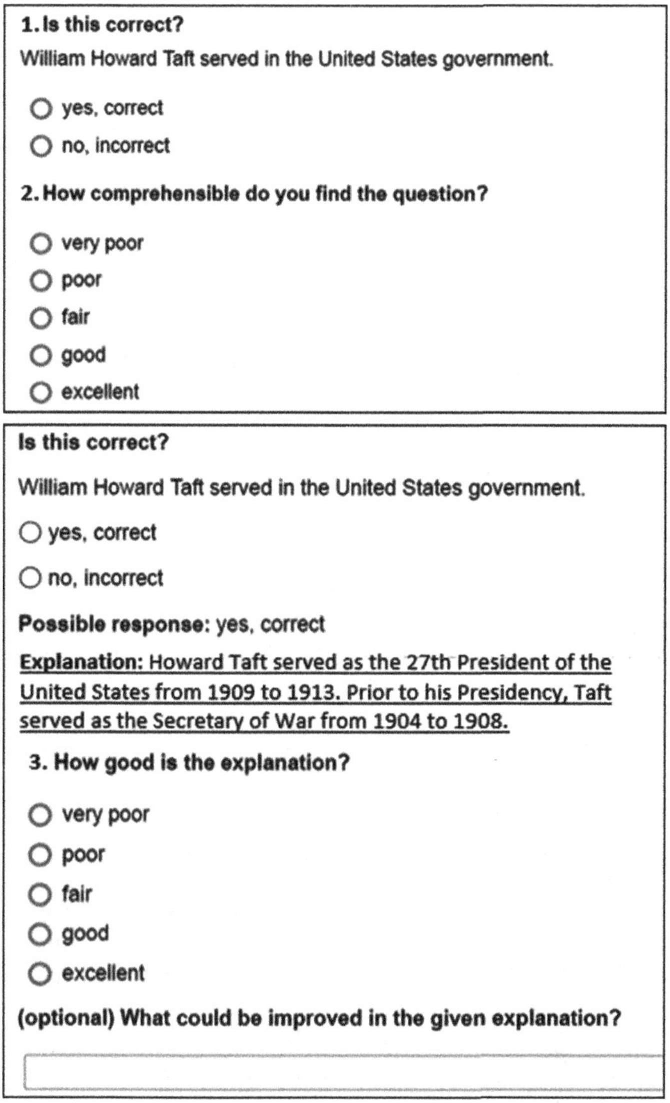

1. Is this correct?

William Howard Taft served in the United States government.

○ yes, correct

○ no, incorrect

2. How comprehensible do you find the question?

○ very poor

○ poor

○ fair

○ good

○ excellent

Is this correct?

William Howard Taft served in the United States government.

○ yes, correct

○ no, incorrect

Possible response: yes, correct

Explanation: Howard Taft served as the 27th President of the United States from 1909 to 1913. Prior to his Presidency, Taft served as the Secretary of War from 1904 to 1908.

3. How good is the explanation?

○ very poor

○ poor

○ fair

○ good

○ excellent

(optional) What could be improved in the given explanation?

Fig. 2. Example of one question answering task with the common structure of four questions per task (CREAK example 1344). After participants answer the first two questions the next two questions with the possible response and explanation are shown.

from Sect. 3.2. Even though we selected the 20 QA tasks randomly, ChatGPT performed much better on these subset than on the overall set of QA tasks. Over all datasets, except MedMCQA, ChatGPT answered 74.67% correct of the $30 \cdot 10 = 300$ tasks. Figure 3 shows a comparison of the performance of ChatGPT and the survey participants on the different datasets. The performance of Chat-

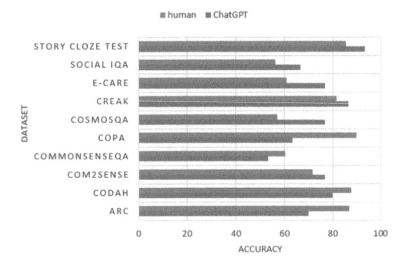

Fig. 3. Comparison of accuracy of ChatGPT (blue) and our survey participants (orange) on ten different QA datasets. (Color figure online)

GPT is better than humans on six datasets and in four datasets humans are superior. The dataset ChatGPT performs worst is also the dataset humans had the most problems (CommonsenseQA). The greatest difference between human and ChatGPT performance is on the COPA and Cosmos QA datasets. In this study, for COPA examples, humans were 26.47% better than ChatGPT and, for the Cosmos QA examples, ChatGPT outperforms humans with 19.53% difference in accuracy. It is quite interesting that ChatGPT performs better on Cosmos QA than the survey participants as contextual commonsense reasoning is needed for this dataset. It focuses on reading between the lines over a diverse collection of people's everyday narratives. In contrast, humans perform a lot better than ChatGPT on COPA where understanding of causes and effects is necessary as well as choosing the most likely alternative. Our study showed that ChatGPT has problems with comparative reasoning in case of more than one likely option. Maybe here explicit traditional reasoning approaches from AI maybe would perform better (cf. Section 1).

We were interested in investigating the relationships between tasks comprehensibility and ChatGPT's explanations. It is worth noting that most questions of the different QA tasks are comprehensible according to the participants. We observed that there is a mean linear positive correlation of 0.58 between the comprehensibility of the QA tasks and that of ChatGPT's explanations. This means that the way the users understand the QA tasks has an impact on the estimated quality of the explanation from ChatGPT. The Social IQa examples 23772 and 11339 were rated 22 times out of 56 total times as very poorly comprehensible. Nevertheless, ChatGPT answered these tasks correctly but only 56.13% survey participants answered these questions correctly.

Furthermore, we found that the explanations for COPA example 610 was often rated "poor" or "very poor", and for this example ChatGPT's answer was invalid as it could not decide for one option saying: "It is not specified in the given information which alternative is the more likely cause." In general, explanations were mostly rated "good" or "excellent" with 67.60% and only 42 times very poor (see Fig. 4). Explanations were rated "fair" or better with 84.80%. In this study, 12 out of 42 times the explanations were rated "very poor" for the undefined responses, where ChatGPT was unable to answer the question due to missing context information (see example above in Fig. 1). The average length of Chat-GPT's explanations is 38 words for both correct and incorrect responses. From the optional free text field we received mostly the same possible improvement for ChatGPT's explanation: ChatGPT should explain why the other answering options are false or less likely and not only focus on explaining why one option is correct. This is in particular important in comparative reasoning tasks.

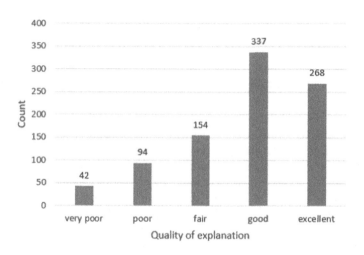

Fig. 4. Participants' rating of all explanations from "very poor" to "excellent".

Figure 5 shows the participants' guess how many responses are created by an AI according to the survey participants. In the chart one can see that the mode is 10 and 15 explanations. While all respondents thinks that at least five explanations are generated by an AI, the mean amount of AI answers is 13. Thus all participants believe that at least 25% of the explanations were AI generated.

To further determine how helpful explanations are, we ask our study partici-pants if they agree that AI tools that give not only a decision but also an expla-nation should be preferred. The majority (52.08%) of the participants agreed to this statement, 31.25% agree strongly and 10.42% are neutral while less than 7% disagree or strongly disagree.

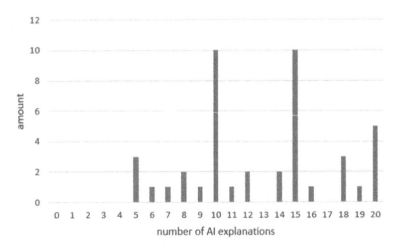

Fig. 5. Bar chart of participants option how many explanations are generated by an AI. The average number of assumed AI answers is 13 while actually all 20 explanations were generated by ChatGPT.

5   Discussion and Future Directions

Over the past, research often focused on logical approaches and large knowledge graphs to deal with commonsense reasoning. Given that we are currently in the era of LLMs which have shown substantial performance improvements across various tasks, we hypothesized that LLMs are capable of handling commonsense reasoning in QA tasks with almost human-level performance (Hypothesis 1). As ChatGPT is trained on a large number of data and produces human-like text, we assume that it can perform commonsense reasoning without explicit semantic knowledge or logical rules. To proof that we evaluated ChatGPT on eleven different QA benchmark datasets which are difficult to solve without commonsense reasoning.

Moreover we evaluated explanations generated with ChatGPT by means on an online questionnaire to investigate how sufficient explanations are to users. Our Hypothesis 2 is that an LLM like ChatGPT is able to provide good explanations to users without the need of explicit formalized knowledge representation. Most participants are content with ChatGPT's explanations. Thereby apparently the problem of explainability of AI decisions can be overcome easily.

5.1   Main Findings

This study shows that ChatGPT reached an overall accuracy of 73.33% on eleven QA datasets that are difficult to handle without commonsense reasoning. While there are still problems (cf. Section 3.3), ChatGPT still outperforms our survey participants in six out of ten datasets (not considering the medical dataset MedMCQA). The results of our questionnaire show that participants answered

73.72% of the 20 QA tasks correctly compared to 90.00% of ChatGPT on the same questions. Although we only compared performance of humans vs. Chat-GPT on a small amount of examples, we beforehand evaluated ChatGPT on eleven different benchmarks on a larger set of examples. Consequently, we believe that the outcome indicates that our Hypothesis 1 is true and LLMs like Chat-GPT can handle commonsense reasoning in QA tasks with near-human-level performance.

This research focused as well on assessing explainability of LLMs, recognizing the significant importance of addressing the black-box problem. This is particularly relevant as users need to understand AI decisions. By means of a web-based questionnaire we evaluated ChatGPT's explanations for 20 QA tasks. We found a mean linear positive correlation of 0.58 between the comprehensibility of the QA tasks and that of ChatGPT's explanations. This observation is relevant for the way ChatGPT's users describe their tasks as it has an impact on the quality of the explanation they receive. In our questionnaire, ChatGPT's explanations were mostly rated "good" or "excellent" with 67.60%. Our Hypothesis 2 that LLMs can generate good explanations could be confirmed. However, to improve explanations, it is recommended to not only focus on explaining why one option is correct but also why the other answering options are false or less likely.

5.2   Impact on the Field

The development of XAI is facing both scientific and social demands [37], and scientists aim to achieve this without sacrificing performance. So far, this grand challenge is mainly dealt by explicit knowledge, such as knowledge graphs. However, we found that implicit knowledge in the form of probabilistic models can generate good explanations. LLMs, such as GPT, made significant advancements in NLP tasks in recent years. Due to the chat function of ChatGPT, users can easily ask for explanations to understand the response of the AI system. This can tackle the lack of explainability and is a quite simple and yet effective way. Using a questionnaire, we could measure and quantify explanations of ChatGPT and investigate the effectiveness of AI explanations.

Moreover, commonsense reasoning is very important for various NLP tasks. It assesses the relative plausibility of different scenarios and recognizes causality. Until now, research focuses on mathematical logic and the formalization of commonsense reasoning knowledge. However, some philosophers, e.g., Wittgenstein, already claimed that commonsense reasoning knowledge is unformalizable or mathematical logic is inappropriate [24]. As seen in our evaluation, the LLM ChatGPT can handle different QA tasks that require commonsense reasoning. Nevertheless, we detected six problems (cf. Section 3.3) where ChatGPT has still problems and further research is necessary. These difficulties are little context information, comparative reasoning, subjective reasoning, slang, unofficial abbreviations and youth language, social situations and knowledge in the medical domain.

Evaluation of the LLM ChatGPT brings AI closer to making a practical impact in the area of XAI and commonsense reasoning. There are still rich opportunities for novel AI research to further measure the quality of explanations as well as opportunities in tackling difficult commonsense reasoning tasks like CommonsenseQA. In future research, one can also investigate other LLMs than ChatGPT, e.g., BERT, BART, RoBERTa, etc.

5.3 Limitations

Our study has limitations that need to be acknowledged. The number of survey participants we included was rather small, which limits generalization of our results. The average age was 26 years with 49 years as maximum, and primarily the participants were university students. In general more participants with diverse gender, age and nationality would help to strengthen the results. Furthermore the key challenge for explainability is to determine what constitutes a "good" explanation, since this is subjective and depends on context. We evaluated explanations using a five-level Likert scale from "very poor" to "excellent". However, we only analyzed 20 explanations of ChatGPT and argue that our Hypothesis 2 (that LLMs can generate good explanations) can be confirmed. Nevertheless, explainability is very important in the medical field, but we did not consider the MedMCQA dataset in our questionnaire due to a supposed lack of participants knowledge in medicine.

6 Conclusion

The field of AI has made considerable progress towards large-scale models, especially for NLP tasks. Although the field requires more testing, we argue that LLMs can be used for commonsense reasoning tasks and as well generate helpful explanations for users to understand AI decisions. The use of LLMs is a promising area of research that offers many opportunities to enhance explainability. However, to unleash their full potential for XAI, it is crucial to approach the use of these models with caution and to critically evaluate their limitations. We have shown important future directions and rich opportunities for novel AI research involving XAI and commonsense reasoning. LLMs have proven capable of human-like performance on a variety of different QA tasks which require commonsense reasoning.

Despite the potential of the field of LLMs, important questions remain for a comprehensive evaluation of ChatGPT's explanations. As these key issues are systematically addressed, the potential of AI to significantly improve the future of XAI may be realized. In particular, the stochastic aspects of LLMs, where repeated queries may lead to different answers, should be considered in future work. This would also allow for a better assessment of the error in the ChatGPT performance estimates.

Acknowledgments. We would like to thank Oliver Obst for sharing our questionnaire on LinkedIn and Osama Siddiqui for his help testing ChatGPT on different datasets. We would also like to thank the anonymous reviewers for their thoughtful reading and comments.

References

1. Álvez, J., Lucio, P., Rigau, G.: Adimen-SUMO: Reengineering an ontology for first-order reasoning. Int. J. Semant. Web Int. Syst. (IJSWIS) 8(4), 80–116 (2012), https://ideas.repec.org/a/igg/jswis0/v8y2012i4p80-116.html
2. Barredo Arrieta, A., et al.: Explainable artificial intelligence (XAI): Concepts, taxonomies, opportunities and challenges toward responsible AI. Inf. Fusion **58**, 82–115 (2020). https://doi.org/10.1016/j.inffus.2019.12.012
3. Brown, T., et al.: Language models are few-shot learners. In: Larochelle, H., Ranzato, M., Hadsell, R., Balcan, M.F., Lin, H. (eds.) Advances in Neural Information Processing Systems 33 (NeurIPS 2020), pp. 1877–1901 (2020). https://proceedings.neurips.cc/paper/2020/file/1457c0d6bfcb4967418bfb8ac142f64a-Paper.pdf
4. Burkart, N., Huber, M.F.: A survey on the explainability of supervised machine learning. J. Artif. Intell. Res. **70**, 245–317 (2021). https://doi.org/10.1613/jair.1.12228
5. Chen, M., D'arcy, M., Liu, A., Fernandez, J., Downey, D.: CODAH: An adversarially-authored question answering dataset for common sense. In: Proceedings of the 3rd Workshop on Evaluating Vector Space Representations for NLP, pp. 63–69 (2019). https://www.jaredfern.com/publication/codah/
6. Clark, P., et al.: Think you have solved question answering? Try ARC, the AI2 reasoning challenge. CoRR - Computing Research Repository abs/1803.05457, Cornell University Library (2018), https://arxiv.org/abs/1803.05457
7. Davis, E.: Logical formalizations of commonsense reasoning: a survey. J. Artif. Intell. Res. **59**, 651–723 (2017). https://doi.org/10.1613/jair.5339
8. Davis, E., Marcus, G.: Commonsense reasoning and commonsense knowledge in artificial intelligence. Commun. ACM **58**(9), 92–103 (2015). https://doi.org/10.1145/2701413
9. Deng, J., Lin, Y.: The benefits and challenges of ChatGPT: An overview. Front. Comput. Intell. Syst. 2(2), 81–83 (2023). https://doi.org/10.54097/fcis.v2i2.4465
10. Devlin, J., Chang, M.W., Lee, K., Toutanova, K.: BERT: Pre-training of deep bidirectional transformers for language understanding. https://arxiv.org/pdf/1810.04805
11. Du, L., Ding, X., Xiong, K., Liu, T., Qin, B.: e-CARE: a new dataset for exploring explainable causal reasoning. In: Proceedings of the 60th Annual Meeting of the Association for Computational Linguistics (Volume 1: Long Papers), pp. 432–446. Association for Computational Linguistics (2022). https://aclanthology.org/2022.acl-long.33/
12. Forbus, K.D.: Qualitative process theory. Artif. Intell. **24**(1–3), 85–168 (1984). https://doi.org/10.1016/0004-3702(84)90038-9
13. Furbach, U., Hölldobler, S., Ragni, M., Schon, C., Stolzenburg, F.: Cognitive reasoning: A personal view. KI 33(3), 209–217 (2019). https://link.springer.com/article/10.1007/s13218-019-00603-3
14. d'Avila Garcez, A.S., Broda, K., Gabbay, D.M.: Symbolic knowledge extraction from trained neural networks: A sound approach. Artificial Intelligence 125(1–2), 155–207 (2001). https://doi.org/10.1016/S0004-3702(00)00077-1
15. d'Avila Garcez, A., Lamb, L., Gabbay, D.: Neural-Symbolic Cognitive Reasoning. Springer, Berlin, Heidelberg (2009). https://doi.org/10.1007/978-3-540-73246-4
16. Hochreiter, S., Schmidhuber, J.: Long short-term memory. Neural Comput. **9**(8), 1735–1780 (1997). https://doi.org/10.1162/neco.1997.9.8.1735

17. Huang, L., Le Bras, R., Bhagavatula, C., Choi, Y.: Cosmos QA: Machine reading comprehension with contextual commonsense reasoning. In: Proceedings of the 2019 Conference on Empirical Methods in Natural Language Processing and the 9th International Joint Conference on Natural Language Processing (EMNLP-IJCNLP), pp. 2391–2401. Association for Computational Linguistics (2019). https://aclanthology.org/D19-1243/

18. Lapuschkin, S., Wäldchen, S., Binder, A., Montavon, G., Samek, W., Müller, K.R.: Unmasking clever hans predictors and assessing what machines really learn. Nature Communications 10(1), 1096 (2019). https://www.nature.com/articles/s41467-019-08987-4

19. Lenat, D.B.: CYC: a large-scale investment in knowledge infrastructure. Commun. ACM **38**(11), 33–38 (1995). https://doi.org/10.1145/219717.219745

20. Lewis, M., et al.: BART: Denoising sequence-to-sequence pre-training for natural language generation, translation, and comprehension (2019). arXiv:1910.13461

21. Liu, Hugo, Singh, Push: Commonsense Reasoning in and Over Natural Language. In: Negoita, Mircea Gh., Howlett, Robert J.., Jain, Lakhmi C.. (eds.) KES 2004. LNCS (LNAI), vol. 3215, pp. 293–306. Springer, Heidelberg (2004). https://doi.org/10.1007/978-3-540-30134-9_40

22. Liu, Y., et al: RoBERTa: A robustly optimized BERT pretraining approach. https://arxiv.org/pdf/1907.11692

23. McCarthy, J.: Programs with common sense (1959). https://www.cs.rit.edu/~rlaz/is2014/files/McCarthyProgramsWithCommonSense.pdf

24. McCarthy, J.: Artificial intelligence, logic and formalizing common sense. In: Thomason, R.H. (ed.) Philosophical Logic and Artificial Intelligence, pp. 161–190. Springer, Netherlands, Dordrecht (1989). https://doi.org/10.1007/978-94-009-2448-2_6

25. Mostafazadeh, N., Roth, M., Louis, A., Chambers, N., Allen, J.: LSDSem 2017 shared task: The Story Cloze Test. In: Proceedings of the 2nd Workshop on Linking Models of Lexical, Sentential and Discourse-level Semantics, pp. 46–51 (2017). https://aclanthology.org/W17-0906.pdf

26. Onoe, Y., Zhang, M.J.Q., Choi, E., Durrett, G.: CREAK: A dataset for commonsense reasoning over entity knowledge. https://arxiv.org/pdf/2109.01653

27. Pal, A., Umapathi, L.K., Sankarasubbu, M.: MedMCQA: A large-scale multi-subject multi-choice dataset for medical domain question answering. ACM Conference on Health (2022). https://arxiv.org/pdf/2203.14371

28. Radford, A., Wu, J., Child, R., Luan, D., Amodei, D., Sutskever, I.: Language models are unsupervised multitask learners. Tech. rep., OpenAI (2019). https://paperswithcode.com/paper/language-models-are-unsupervised-multitask

29. Roemmele, M., Bejan, C.A., Gordon, A.S.: Choice of plausible alternatives: An evaluation of commonsense causal reasoning. In: AAAI Spring Symposium: Logical Formalizations of Commonsense Reasoning, pp. 90–95 (2011), https://aaai.org/papers/02418-choice-of-plausible-alternatives-an-evaluation-of-commonsense-causal-reasoning/

30. Sap, M., et al.: ATOMIC: an atlas of machine commonsense for if-then reasoning. Proc. AAAI Conf. Artif. Intell. **33**(01), 3027–3035 (2019). https://doi.org/10.1609/aaai.v33i01.33013027

31. Sap, M., Rashkin, H., Chen, D., LeBras, R., Choi, Y.: Social IQa: Commonsense reasoning about social interactions. In: Proceedings of the 2019 Conference on Empirical Methods in Natural Language Processing and the 9th International Joint Conference on Natural Language Processing (EMNLP-IJCNLP), pp. 4463–4473.

Association for Computational Linguistics (2019). https://aclanthology.org/D19-1454/

32. Siebert, S., Schon, C., Stolzenburg, F.: Commonsense reasoning using theorem proving and machine learning. In: Holzinger, A., Kieseberg, P., Tjoa, A.M., Weippl, E. (eds.) Machine Learning and Knowledge Extraction - 3rd IFIP TC 5, TC 12, WG 8.4, WG 8.9, WG 12.9 International Cross-Domain Conference, CD-MAKE 2019, pp. 395–413. LNCS 11713, Springer Nature Switzerland, Canterbury, UK (2019). https://doi.org/10.1007/978-3-030-29726-8_25

33. Singh, S., et al.: COM2SENSE: A commonsense reasoning benchmark with complementary sentences. In: Findings of the Association for Computational Linguistics: ACL-IJCNLP 2021, pp. 883–898. Association for Computational Linguistics (2021). https://aclanthology.org/2021.findings-acl.78

34. Speer, R., Chin, J., Havasi, C.: ConceptNet 5.5: An open multilingual graph of general knowledge. Proceedings of the AAAI Conference on Artificial Intelligence 31(1) (2017). https://doi.org/10.1609/aaai.v31i1.11164

35. Talmor, A., Herzig, J., Lourie, N., Berant, J.: CommonsenseQA: A question answering challenge targeting commonsense knowledge. https://arxiv.org/pdf/1811.00937

36. Taylor, J.E.T., Taylor, G.W.: Artificial cognition: how experimental psychology can help generate explainable artificial intelligence. Psychon. Bull. Rev. **28**(2), 454–475 (2021). https://doi.org/10.3758/s13423-020-01825-5

37. Xu, Feiyu, Uszkoreit, Hans, Du, Yangzhou, Fan, Wei, Zhao, Dongyan, Zhu, Jun: Explainable AI: A Brief Survey on History, Research Areas, Approaches and Challenges. In: Tang, Jie, Kan, Min-Yen., Zhao, Dongyan, Li, Sujian, Zan, Hongying (eds.) NLPCC 2019. LNCS (LNAI), vol. 11839, pp. 563–574. Springer, Cham (2019). https://doi.org/10.1007/978-3-030-32236-6_51

38. Zellers, R., Bisk, Y., Schwartz, R., Choi, Y.: SWAG: A large-scale adversarial dataset for grounded commonsense inference. In: Proceedings of the 2018 Conference on Empirical Methods in Natural Language Processing, pp. 93–104. Association for Computational Linguistics (2018). https://aclanthology.org/D18-1009/

39. Zimmer, M., et al.: Differentiable logic machines. CoRR - Computing Research Repository abs/2102.11529, Cornell University Library (2021). https://arxiv.org/abs/2102.11529, latest revision 2023

Post-hoc Rule Based Explanations for Black Box Bayesian Optimization

Tanmay Chakraborty[1,3]($\boxtimes$) (iD), Christian Wirth[2], and Christin Seifert[3] (iD)

[1] Continental AG, Berlin, Germany
`tanmay.chakraborty@continental-corporation.com`
[2] Continental AG, Frankfurt, Germany
`christian.2.wirth@continental-corporation.com`
[3] Philipps-Universität Marburg, Marburg, Germany
`christin.seifert@uni-marburg.de`

Abstract. Explainable Artificial Intelligence (XAI) aims to enhance transparency and trust in AI systems by providing insights into their decision-making processes. While there has been significant progress in developing explainability methods for AI, such advancements do not consider black-box optimization algorithms. In this paper, we present RX-BO (Rule based Explanations for Bayesian Optimization), a novel framework that brings explainability to black-box Bayesian optimization with a Gaussian process (GP) backbone. Leveraging the GP model's approximation and uncertainty estimation capabilities, RX-BO extracts distribution-aware rules through a post-hoc rule based explainability method. These rules shed light on different regions of the posterior distribution, enabling transparent and trustworthy decision making. The framework incorporates a pairwise Mahalanobis distance-based hierarchical agglomerative clustering algorithm with Ward criterion for generating rule proposals. It also employs traditional metrics such as support, coverage, and confidence for selecting high-quality explanations. We evaluate RX-BO on an example optimization problem and six hyperparameter optimization tasks involving three machine learning models (classification and regression) across two datasets. The results demonstrate that RX-BO improves rule confidence and rule granularity control compared to decision trees and Rule based XAI frameworks. Furthermore, RX-BO introduces a novel approach by identifying interesting areas in the search space based on likelihood. This measure allows to rank explanations on how interesting they would be for an end user. Overall, RX-BO enhances the understanding and interpretability of black-box Bayesian optimization algorithm results, contributing to the broader field of XAI.

Keywords: Artificial Intelligence · Black-box Optimization · Explainable Artificial Intelligence (XAI) · Bayesian Optimization

1 Introduction

Recent advances in explainable artificial intelligence (XAI) have improved transparency and interpretability in complex AI systems [36]. These advancements,

S. Nowaczyk et al. (Eds.): ECAI 2023 Workshops, CCIS 1947, pp. 320–337, 2024.
https://doi.org/10.1007/978-3-031-50396-2_18

including rule-based approaches, model-agnostic methods, and visual explanations, enhance user understanding, trust, and compliance with ethical and regulatory requirements [37]. However, a significant gap exists in addressing explainability for black-box optimization algorithms, such as Bayesian optimization (BO).

BO is a sequential, model-based optimization technique that leverages a probabilistic model for optimization, usually a Gaussian Process (GP). Its objective is to find the maximizing solution for a black-box optimization problem with as few evaluations as possible [11]. BO is crucial for various complex tasks, like parameter optimization [39,40], hyperparameter tuning (HPO) in various domains e.g. automotive [17], aerospace engineering [19], machine learning [16,41].

In industry, the challenging task of parameter optimization in cyber-physical systems includes cases where adapting applications to specific environmental conditions is essential. Manual parameterization and tuning are time-consuming and expensive, making optimization algorithms like BO invaluable. Explaining the optimization decisions to engineers in the loop who are not data scientists is safety critical in these scenarios. [44] An explainability method would offer the ability to identify ranges of "good" parameters, providing a broader perspective beyond the single "best" solution obtained from optimization algorithms. This facilitates easy tuning of black-box systems for engineers and narrows down the search space for consecutive BO runs. Despite this importance, explainability of BO optimization algorithms has received limited attention, urging the need to extend explainability methods to cover black-box optimization algorithms and bridge this gap.

Applying existing regression based XAI methods [20] directly to black-box BO is not recommended because of the following differences between BO and regression [11]:

D1: The optimization search space for BO is defined during its initialization. However, regression is usually not subject to such a predefined search space.
D2: BO's "regression" target has an implicit meaning, typically related to the utility.
D3: Unlike regression, BO prioritizes high-quality approximations in costly regions of the search space.
D4: BO employs a biased sample selection/generation process for optimization.
D5: Regression can function without incorporating uncertainty, but uncertainty estimation is crucial in BO.
D6: BO aims to find the minimal utility point without the need for generalization to unseen data.

A tailored explainability method for BO must fulfill the following specific requirements to address its unique characteristics effectively:

R1: The method should handle the bounded optimization space with continuous targets and provide suitable responses when queried beyond these boundaries (D1, D6).

R2: The method should elucidate the underlying data distribution process and the optimization space with the utility (D3, D4).

R3: Given the significance of uncertainty in BO, the method must effectively handle and incorporate this uncertainty into its explanations (D5).

R4: By leveraging the probability distribution inherent in BO, the method should employ appropriate metrics to identify relevant areas and select explanations that respect the implicit meaning (D2).

Existing explainability methods fail to meet these requirements. In this paper, we introduce RX-BO (Rule based Explanations for Bayesian Optimization), a rule-based post-hoc explainability method designed explicitly for black-box BO tasks. RX-BO leverages the GP surrogate model of BO to provide explanations to end users through '*IF-THEN*' rules. RX-BO introduces rule coverage control through a hyperparameter t_s. For evaluation purposes, we utilize the HPO task in AI [46] as a proxy task for the parameter optimization task of cyber-physical systems, as data in the latter task is not public.

In summary, the contributions of this paper are:

- We present a novel method for explaining BO processes, satisfying the requirements R1-R4 stated above. (cf. Sec. 4)
- We show empirically that RX-BO achieves higher rule confidence and rule support when compared with baseline decision tree based rule generation for XAI [9,15,24]. We also show RX-BO is a better fit for the HPO task through an example based comparison with out-of-the-box RuleXAI method [23]. (cf. Sec. 5.2)
- We show in an ablation study that the generated explanations exhibit a decrease in rule length and an increase in interestingness as the hyperparameter t_s is increased. (cf. Sec. 5.3)

In the remainder of our paper we begin with the review of related work, highlighting the inapplicability of various XAI methods to BO. We outline BO and GPs briefly, vital for comprehending RX-BO's design. RX-BO's performance is assessed via a case study and hyperparameter optimization task. We discuss RX-BO's threshold trends. Lastly, we chart future research directions.

2   Related Work

The domain of XAI has witnessed the emergence of various methods aimed at elucidating black-box models. In this Section, we review common rule-based XAI techniques and post-hoc approaches for application in BO domain and discuss why they cannot be directly applied to BO.

Rule-based XAI techniques provide definitive and intuitive rules humans can readily comprehend, thus promoting transparency and understanding of the underlying decision logic [42]. Anchors [35,43], counterfactuals [12,14,27], and decision trees [15,24], offer transparent and interpretable representations of the decision-making process. However, these rule-based explanations are designed for categorical targets. While Rule XAI [23] is a rule-miner for regression cases, it does not incorporate uncertainty and cannot be directly applied to BO (cf. Sec. 1, R3.).

Post-hoc approaches like LIME [34] and SHAP [21,22] aim to provide explanations that are model agnostic, enhancing their versatility. Model specific explanations such as concept highlights [25,29] and GradCAM [4,38], leverage gradients and visualizations to enhance interpretability. While the aforementioned XAI methods share the goal of explaining black-box models, they are not suitable when applied to BO, as they do not explain the full input space but rather find features that maintain a decision boundary (cf. Sec. 1, R2).

Existing literature on **explaining black-box optimization methods** is limited, with Moosbauer et al. [26] utilizing partial dependence plots for HPO. However, these plots are complex and require expert knowledge for interpretation. We draw inspiration from rule-based explainability models, particularly the work by Amoukou et al. [1], which generates rule sets for regression tasks but lacks the incorporation of uncertainty. Additionally, we draw ideas from the conversion of classification models to decision trees [5,10].

In summary, no existing methods satisfy all the requirements for BO explainability (cf. Sect. 1, R1 – R4)

3 Background

In this Section, we provide background for understanding the RX-BO method.

Bayesian Optimization (BO): Given a black-box objective function $f(\mathbf{x})$, the goal of BO is to solve the problem

$$\mathbf{x_{opt}} = \arg\max_{\mathbf{x} \in \mathcal{D}} f(\mathbf{x}), \tag{1}$$

where $\mathbf{x} \in \mathcal{D}$ and $\mathcal{D} \subset \mathcal{R}^d$ is the bounded search space. The black-box function f is assumed to be continuous, expensive to evaluate, noisy, and unknown in the closed form. [3]

BO is employed in these conditions to find the global optimum for the black-box function f. The primary component of BO is a surrogate model for statistical inference, typically employing Gaussian Processes (GPs) [8]. The GP approximates the unknown objective function during the optimization process. BO aims to estimate the optimum for the objective function with limited evaluations, aiming for efficient and effective optimization.

Gaussian Process (GP): A GP consists of a group of random variables where the joint distribution of any finite number of variables follows a Gaussian distribution. A GP describes a distribution over functions, where a mean $m(\mathbf{x})$ and a covariance function $k(\mathbf{x}, \mathbf{x}')$, also known as the kernel function, characterize each function $f(\mathbf{x})$ at location $\mathbf{x}$. If the mean is $m(\mathbf{x}) = \mathbb{E}[f(\mathbf{x})]$, and kernel function is $k(\mathbf{x}, \mathbf{x}') = \mathbb{E}[(f(\mathbf{x}) - m(\mathbf{x}))(f(\mathbf{x}') - m(\mathbf{x}'))]$, then the GP can be described as $f(\mathbf{x}) \sim GP(m(\mathbf{x}), k(\mathbf{x}, \mathbf{x}'))$. [33]

4   Methodology

In this section, we formulate the problem setting, describe RX-BO, and our design choices.

4.1   Problem Setting

We start with a BO setting as given in Eq. 1, where we can access the bounds of the search space $\mathcal{D} = \{\mathbf{x} \in \mathcal{R}^d : lb^j \leq x^j \leq ub^j, \forall j \in 1, 2, ..., d\}$, and the GP model. The posterior distribution of the GP represents the approximation of the black-box objective function. To explain the posterior distribution, we divide the distribution into smaller areas based on the GP uncertainty to construct rules for each area, which allows us to approximate the distribution well. The goal is to find a rule list ρ that can effectively explain the GP posterior distribution. RX-BO assumes a completed BO procedure on an optimization problem, access to the final learned GP model, and the search space.

4.2   Rule Based Explanations for Bayesian Optimization (RX-BO)

RX-BO first constructs an explanation set over a bounded space (R1 & R2). Then it generates a set of candidate rules based on uncertainty (R3), which is filtered to relevant rules (R4). Rule quality metrics (R4) allow the ranking of rules and the generation of the final explanations. We explain the steps in detail in the following, a concise overview is given in Alg. 1.

A rule from RX-BO is a textual representation of concatenation of antecedent $\rho^i_{\dashv}$ and consequent $\rho^i_{\vdash}$:

Rule i:
IF x1 : [lb_{x1}, ub_{x1}], ..., xn : [lb_{xn}, ub_{xn}]
THEN UTILITY (lb_y, ub_y)

where lb and ub are lower bounds and upper bounds of each dimension of the input space respectively, and "UTILITY" is the utility range where the rule is valid.

1. Construction of an Explanation Set over a Bounded Space: In BO all generated samples are used in the training phase of BO. A test set is not available in standard BO procedure. Thus, to create an explanation dataset, additional samples are generated by uniformly sampling the search space. Samples are then represented as sampled set $\mathbf{X_e}$ which is the union of the train set $\mathbf{X}$ and uniformly sampled instances from the search space $\mathcal{U}(\mathcal{D})$, then the GP is queried with $\mathbf{X_e}$ in prediction mode to obtain the posterior distribution over i runs $\mathbf{Y^i_e} = GP_{predict}(\mathbf{X_e})$. The posterior distribution then is represented by the vectors of mean $\boldsymbol{\mu} = m(\mathbf{Y_e})$ and standard deviation $\boldsymbol{\sigma_y} = \sigma(\mathbf{Y_e})$. Then the explanation dataset is $\mathbf{E} = [\mathbf{X_e}; \boldsymbol{\mu}; \boldsymbol{\sigma_y}]$.

Algorithm 1. RX-BO Algorithm

Require: X, $\mathcal{D}$, $N_{samples}$, $P_{samples}$, t_s

1: **procedure** $RX - BO(\mathbf{X}, \mathcal{D}, N_{samples}, P_{samples}, t_s)$
2:     $\mathbf{X_e} \leftarrow \mathbf{X} \bigcup \mathcal{U}(\mathcal{D}, N_{samples})$
3:     **for** $i \in P_{samples}$ **do**
4:         $\mathbf{Y_e^i} \leftarrow GP_{predict}(\mathbf{X_e})$
5:     **end for**
6:     $\mu \leftarrow m(\mathbf{Y_e})$
7:     $\sigma_y \leftarrow \sigma(\mathbf{Y_e})$
8:     $\mathbf{E} \leftarrow [\mathbf{X_e}; \mu; \sigma_y]$ ▷ 1. Creating explanation set over bounded space
9:     $\mathbf{E_{dist}} \leftarrow pdist(\mathbf{E})$ ▷ 2. Computation of pairwise distance
10:     $\rho_{\dashv}, \rho_{\vdash} \leftarrow Ward(\mathbf{E}, \mathbf{E_{dist}}, t_s)$ ▷ (2,3) Proposal & selection of rules
11:     **for** i in $\rho_{\dashv}$ **do**   ▷ 4. Metrics Computation for every rule in rule list
12:         $\rho_{temp}^i \leftarrow find(\mathbf{X_e} \in [\rho_{\dashv}^i; \rho_{\vdash}^i])$ ▷ Find samples from $\mathbf{X_e}$ that agree to a rule
13:         $R^i \leftarrow max(likelihood(GP_{predict}(\rho_{temp}^i)))$ ▷ Computing relevance
14:         $C^i \leftarrow ECDF(\rho_{\dashv}^i, \mathbf{X_e})$ ▷ Computing ECDF for Coverage
15:         $S^i \leftarrow ECDF([\rho_{\dashv}^i; \rho_{\vdash}^i], [\mathbf{X_e}; \mu])$ ▷ Computing ECDF for Support
16:         $\zeta^i \leftarrow S^i / C^i$ ▷ Computing Confidence
17:         $\alpha^i \leftarrow weightedSum(R^i, C^i, S^i, \zeta^i)$ ▷ Computing Interestingness
18:     **end for**
19:     $\rho \leftarrow SortRules([\rho_{\dashv}^i; \rho_{\vdash}^i], \alpha)$ ▷ 5. Explanation ranking
20:     **return** ρ
21: **end procedure**

---

2. Construction of Candidate Rule Set Based on Uncertainty: First, pairwise Mahalanobis distance computation over the dataset **E** is computed and represented as $\mathbf{E_{dist}}$. Then, hierarchical agglomerative clustering based on Ward criterion is employed on $\mathbf{E_{dist}}$ (cf. Sec 4.3)[1] This generates several clusters, which represent all possible rules that can be generated from the dataset **E**. Hierarchical agglomerative clustering generates multiple rules that cover the same space with different degrees of specificity which results in a rule list ρ_{all} containing highly specific rules with very low coverage and highly general rules (one rule for the entire space).

3. Filtering of Candidate Set to Relevant Rules: From candidate rule list, we filter out rules that are in the middle, i.e. not highly specific as well as not highly general. We use a threshold t_s over the distance metric to group data points that are in close proximity. By tuning this parameter, we can control the specificity of the rules. In hierarchical agglomerative clustering based on the Ward criterion, this idea of distance is based on the variance of the data, so the resulting clusters represent the different regions of the posterior space with different levels of uncertainty.

---

[1] The design choices are mentioned here.

For a lower dimensional optimization problem, the threshold t_s can be tuned with the aid of a dendrogram as well. For a higher dimensional problem, this visual aid is complex but still helpful (cf. Sect. 5.1).

4. Computing Rule Quality Metrics: Applying the threshold results in the final rule list ρ which needs to be ranked based on their interest to the end user. To do this, first, we identify interesting areas of the posterior space. We define this area of interest as a space in the posterior distribution where the samples have a high likelihood of being the optimal point because such areas indicate regions of the parameter space that are likely to yield better outcomes or optimal solutions. This can be identified by taking the maximum of the log-likelihood of the examples that satisfy a rule. Let the log-likelihood of examples that satisfy a rule be l_s, and the log-likelihood of the overall dataset be represented by l. The relevance metric then is defined as

$$R_{\rho^i} = max_{l_s \in l}(l_s) \tag{2}$$

Detailed computation of log likelihood $l = log\ p(\mathbf{y}|\mathbf{X})$ is given in [33, Chapter 2].

Furthermore, probabilistic area-based metrics such as coverage, support, and confidence are calculated as well. These metrics, commonly used in traditional rule mining literature, provide measures of the quality and significance of the rules [45]. Coverage represents the extent to which the rule covers the posterior distribution,

$$C = P(\rho_\dashv) = \frac{N_{\rho_\dashv}}{N} \tag{3}$$

where $N_{\rho_\dashv}$ represents the $|\mathbf{E}|$ satisfying $\rho_\dashv$ part of a rule and N represents the total $|\mathbf{E}|$. Support indicates the overlap between $\rho_\dashv$ and $\rho_\vdash$ parts of the rule,

$$S = P(\rho_\dashv \cap \rho_\vdash) = \frac{N_{\rho_\dashv \cap \rho_\vdash}}{N} \tag{4}$$

where $N_{\rho_\dashv \cap \rho_\vdash}$ represents the $|\mathbf{E}|$ satisfying both the antecedent and consequent parts of a rule and N represents the total $|\mathbf{E}|$. Confidence is the ratio of support to coverage

$$\zeta = P(\rho_\dashv|\rho_\vdash) = \frac{S}{C} \tag{5}$$

The aforementioned metrics are calculated using empirical cumulative probability distribution computation [6], offering insights into the areas covered by each rule relative to the entire dataset. Finally, a weighted sum of relevance, support, coverage, and confidence metrics is computed to derive an interestingness rule induction metric, defined as

$$\alpha = w_1 * R + w_2 * S + w_3 * C + w_4 * \zeta \tag{6}$$

The ranges of all metrics are in between (0,1]. Currently, the weights are manually set, allowing the data scientist to divide the overall weight of 1 among the 4 weight values. We recommend putting more weight on R to make sure the metric captures the interesting regions with priority. But for use cases where it is not a priority, an equal weight of 0.25 can be set for all.

5. Rank Rules and Generate Final Explanations: The rules are sorted based on the interestingness metric Eq. 6, and a global explanation is provided. For local explanations, the method matches the user's provided parameter set with the global rules to identify the applicable rule to display as an explanation. RX-BO responds to user queries with arbitrary parameter sets outside the defined search space $\mathcal{D}$ by stating "no rules found", maintaining consistency and avoiding erroneous results.

4.3   Design Choices

This section discusses in detail our design choices for RX-BO.

Choice of Clustering Method: Hierarchical agglomerative clustering with Ward criterion is widely used for finding clusters of data that have minimum variance. It produces compact, evenly-sized clusters, making it suitable for datasets with varying sizes and shapes [28]. The Ward criterion is relevant in the context of explainability in BO as it captures the underlying data distribution by dividing the posterior into smaller subspaces where each subspace has similar characteristics. It identifies different levels of uncertainty present in the posterior distribution and relies on that to cluster samples together. By using the Ward criterion, rules can be generated to capture the entire space by focusing on the model's uncertainty within smaller areas. The method also allows control over rule granularity by setting a distance-based threshold determining the optimal size of smaller areas for rule generation. However, there are drawbacks. The Ward criterion only works with continuous data, requiring one-hot encoding for categorical inputs and resulting in longer rules. Additionally, the choice of threshold t_s affects rule specificity, resembling the challenge of finding optimal clusters in unsupervised learning.

Choice of Rule Based Explanations: Rule based explanations in BO done with RX-BO are faithful by design. Firstly, RX-BO operates by sampling within the bounded search space $\mathcal{D}$ to generate explanations. As a result, the explanations remain faithful to this bounded space. Even if the samples within $\mathcal{D}$ are perturbed, it does not affect the explanations provided by RX-BO. Secondly, traditional fidelity computation methods, i.e. Fidelity $= \frac{1}{N}\sum_{i=1}^{N} \frac{|f(\mathbf{x^i})-\hat{f}(\mathbf{x^i})|}{\max(f(\mathbf{x^i}),\hat{f}(\mathbf{x^i}))}$, where N is the number of evaluation points, $f(\mathbf{x^i})$ represents function output at location $\mathbf{x^i}$ and $\hat{f}(\mathbf{x^i})$ is the explanation based prediction at location $\mathbf{x^i}$, rely on explicit decision boundary. It is not relevant in the context of BO. BO does not rely on defining explicit decision boundaries. Instead, RX-BO focuses on capturing the optimization space. This ensures that the explanations generated by RX-BO faithfully represent the model's behavior within the bounded region.

5   Evaluation

To gain a understanding of RX-BO in practical scenarios, we evaluated RX-BO on a toy optimization problem and on real-world machine learning tasks. The tasks involve HPO with BO for algorithms like Decision Trees (DT), Support Vector Machines (SVM), and Multilayer Perceptron (MLP) for regression and classification [46]. We use the California housing dataset[2] for regression and the MNIST dataset for classification [7]. Additionally, we compared quantitatively with decision trees and qualitatively with RuleXAI [23] highlighting the advantages of RX-BO over baseline approaches. Our evaluation was guided by the following questions:

- How does RX-BO work on an optimization problem? (cf. Sec. 5.1)
- How does RX-BO perform compared to a baseline method? (cf. Sec. 5.2)
- How does the threshold parameter influence rule generation and metrics? (cf. Sec. 5.3)

5.1   Case Study

Given an example black-box objective function as defined in the Bayesian Optimization Python library, $f(x) = e^{-(x-2)^2} + e^{-(x-6)^2/10} + \frac{1}{x^2+1}$ the goal is to find the value of x that maximizes $f(x)$ [31]. We set parameters $N_{samples} = 1000$ & $P_{samples} = 500$.

Figure 1 (a), (b) visually represents the black-box function and the completed BO process. The figure highlights the optimal region with low uncertainty, while the other regions display higher uncertainty. The complete optimization results can be seen here with red marks over the points evaluated by BO while exploring the function space. Figure 1 (c) represents the posterior distribution with an augmented explanation set, which is the approximation of the learned data distribution. In Fig. 1 (d), the generated dendrogram is depicted, and threshold t_s is marked at 5. In this dendrogram, moving up the Y axis indicates greater separation between clusters. Reducing the tree to some height, different numbers of clusters can be formed, i.e. control the rule specificity visually. In RX-BO, the dendrogram can act as an aid for threshold t_s tuning in lower dimensional problems. In higher-dimensional cases, it can be complex but helpful. Finally, Fig. 1 (e) represents the rule rectangles over the complete space. These rectangles are then transformed into textual rules for the end user.

---

[2] https://www.dcc.fc.up.pt/ltorgo/Regression/cal_housing.html, accessed on:2023/ 05/04.

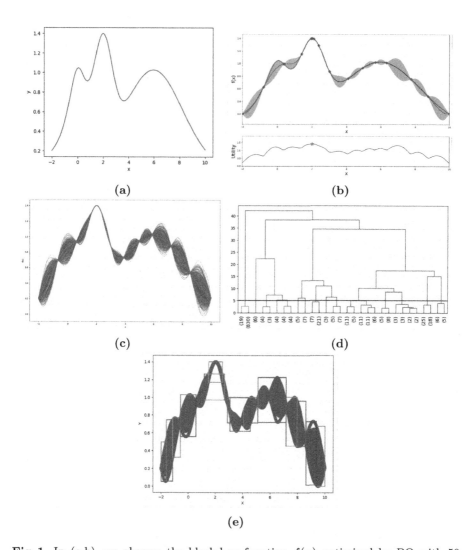

Fig. 1. In (a,b), we observe the black-box function $f(\mathbf{x})$ optimized by BO with 50 iterations, higher uncertainty regions depicted with green highlights (95% confidence interval). Red marks indicate points evaluated by BO during the optimization process. In (c), the posterior distribution generated by 500 GP sampling runs with the explanation dataset is depicted, which is an approximation of the learned data distribution. In (d), we observe the generated dendrogram with a threshold marked at 5 generates the clusters formed over the posterior distribution of the GP. In (e), we observe clusters that are utilized to induce rules, which effectively capture the uncertainty of the model. An example rule for the optimal area *Rule 1: 'IF x : [1.664, 2.296] THEN UTILITY (1.312, 1.401)'*

Table 1. Hyperparameters for regression models optimized

DT-R	SVM-R	MLP-R
max features: Integer$(1, 8)$	C: Real$(1, 50)$	optimizer: adam, rmsprop
max depth: Integer$(5, 5000)$	kernel: poly, rbf, sigmoid	activation: relu, tanh
min sample leaf: Integer$(2, 100)$	epsilon: Real$(0, 1)$	loss: MSE, MAE
min sample split: Integer$(1, 100)$	-	batch-size: $[16, 32, 64]$
criterion: MSE, MAE	-	neurons: Integer$(10, 100)$
-	-	epoch: $[20, 50]$
-	-	patience: Integer$(3, 10)$

5.2   Empirical Evaluation

In this study, we replace our hierarchical agglomerative clustering based rule proposal algorithm with a decision tree based rule proposal which employs the CART algorithm. The decision tree method with CART algorithm, known for its explainability, is a good baseline because a number of other methods of regression XAI build upon it, such as Rulefit [9], TE2Rules [18], Random Forest to rules [2], Skope rules [13]. It is worth noting that the existing body of literature on BO explainability lacks adequate methods for conducting comprehensive comparisons (cf. Sec. 2). Consequently, we compared the performance of the decision tree-based rule proposal method with our method using various metrics from the XAI literature [30].

We will evaluate HPO task on regression and classification models with RX-BO and compare it with the baseline.

Machine Learning Models. We focused on explaining the HPO task for three regression models applied to the California housing dataset The models considered for this analysis were DTR, SVM, and MLP. [46]

Initially, these models were run with their default settings obtained from scikit-learn version 0.24 [32]. Subsequently, a BO method from the skopt library was employed to optimize their hyperparameters and improve their performance in terms of Mean Squared Error (MSE) with 3-fold cross-validation[3]. The skopt library uses the Matern kernel with a length scale of 1 as the default for the backbone GP. Table 1 provides an overview of the parameters optimization for each model. For the categorical parameters in the input, we employ one-hot encoding. In the output, we will get a longer rule with all categories included.

Similar models were used for classification task from sklearn with MNIST dataset [7] with 3-fold cross-validation [46]. In this case, accuracy was utilized as the performance metric. We can see in Table 2 the different parameters optimized with skopt. Like the regression case, we now employ RX-BO to these models and generate explanations. For the categorical parameters in the input, we do a one-hot encoding as well. In the output for these cases, we will get a longer rule similar to the regression set.

---

[3] https://github.com/scikit-optimize/scikit-optimize, accessed on:2023/03/08.

Table 2. Hyperparameters for classification models optimized

DT-C	SVM-C	MLP-C
max features: Integer(1, 64)	C: Real(0.01, 50)	optimizer: adam, rmsprop, sgd
max depth: Integer(5, 50)	kernel: linear, poly, rbf, sigmoid	activation: relu, tanh
min sample leaf: Integer(1, 100)	-	loss: MSE, MAE
min sample split: Integer(2, 100)	-	batch-size: [16, 32, 64]
criterion: gini, entropy	-	neurons: Integer(10, 100)
-	-	epoch: [20, 50]
-	-	patience: Integer(3, 20)

Experimental Setup. Although a direct comparison between the decision tree and RX-BO is not possible due to differences in their approaches, we aimed to make them comparable by enforcing similar rule set lengths for both approaches (similar meaning $|\rho| \pm 5$). This was achieved by tuning the threshold t_s for RX-BO and running the decision tree from the scikit-learn library with default parameters. We observe the mean coverage, mean support, and mean confidence of the rule sets produced by both methods. For the RX-BO method $N_{samples} = 1000$ & $P_{samples} = 500$ was set as default to have sufficient data for the explanation set.

Since decision tree is not inherently capable of incorporating the data uncertainty, an additional preprocessing step was necessary. We performed binning of the explanation dataset **E** utilizing the standard deviation of the targets to account for the data's inherent uncertainty and enable the decision tree to capture this uncertainty. Conversely, RX-BO required no data binning step, as its design inherently facilitated the separation of data based on uncertainty. As a result, RX-BO improved over the baseline approach in data handling, as it effectively handled uncertainty without the need for additional preprocessing steps like binning. (cf. Sec. 1, R1)

Quantitative Results. The results from the comparison are given in Table 3. The research findings reveal that the decision tree variant exhibits higher mean coverage compared to RX-BO. This is because decision tree-based rules consistently capture a similar number of samples per rule, disregarding the data distribution. Consequently, the decision tree variant yields significantly lower mean support, indicating that it generates inconsistent rules that do not always align with the target.

The lower mean rule coverage observed in RX-BO is because RX-BO's rule generation process relies on the variance of the posterior distribution. This suggests that the rule coverage is not solely determined by the number of samples covered by a rule but is also influenced by the data distribution. This achieves consistent rules that represent the data distribution, leading to similar coverage and support metrics for RX-BO. This approach leads to the creation of more consistent rules that better capture the nuances and patterns in the data, resulting in rules that accurately represent the data distribution. (cf. Sect. 1, R4)

Table 3. Comparison between Decision tree-based rule mining and RX-BO averaged over five runs.

Models	Method	Threshold	Rule set length	Mean Coverage↑	Mean Support↑	Mean Confidence↑
opt prob	RX-BO	5	14±1	0.079±0.003	0.079±0.003	**0.99± 0**
-	DT	-	12±0	**0.284±0.001**	**0.096±0**	0.58±0.065
DT-R	RX-BO	20	10.66±1.154	0.087±0.019	0.087±0.019	**0.99±0**
-	DT	-	9.66±2.081	**0.107±0.006**	**0.092±0.004**	0.55±0.141
SVM-R	RX-BO	20	11±1	0.118±0.006	**0.118±0.006**	**0.998±0.001**
-	DT	-	11±1	**0.146±0.044**	0.089±0.009	0.363±0.085
MLP-R	RX-BO	15	9.33±1.154	0.088±0.007	**0.083±0.005**	**0.99±0**
-	DT	-	9.33±2.309	**0.096±0.006**	0.044±0.002	0.371±0.086
DT-C	RX-BO	20	11±1	0.078±0.007	**0.078±0.006**	**0.99±0**
-	DT	-	10.33±2.309	**0.127±0.017**	0.063±0.002	0.315±0.023
SVM-C	RX-BO	20	8.66±1.520	**0.156±0.014**	**0.156±0.014**	**0.998±0.001**
-	DT	-	9.33±0.577	0.115±0.024	0.085±0.011	0.304±0.077
MLP-C	RX-BO	15	9.33±0.570	0.088±0.001	**0.088±0.001**	**0.99±0**
-	DT	-	13±1	**0.101±0.014**	0.059±0.009	0.350±0.033

Regarding the mean confidence metric, several observations can be made. Firstly, RX-BO outperforms the decision tree variant in terms of rule confidence. The decision tree approach disregards the target when proposing rules and instead focuses on segmenting the posterior distribution based on input parameter subsets. RX-BO is purposefully designed to address this limitation by considering the utility while proposing rules. By including the joint relevance of input parameters and the target, RX-BO significantly improves the confidence level in its generated rules. (cf. Sec. 1, R2)

Secondly, the design of decision trees renders them incapable of handling uncertainty even when extensively aided by a preprocessing step (data binning), which is effectively addressed in RX-BO. By separating the optimization space based on uncertainty, RX-BO captures rules for each subspace where data sample characteristics are equivalent. Consequently, the rules generated by RX-BO are more representative of the respective space, thus resulting in higher confidence levels. (cf. Sec. 1, R3)

Therefore, it can be concluded that RX-BO is a superior method for generating explanations in complex spaces compared to decision trees.

Qualitative Comparison to RuleXAI. A qualitative comparison was conducted between RX-BO and RuleXAI [23]. RuleXAI operates by divide and conquer mechanism of rule mining. It then uses feature relevance computation from SHAP [22] method to generate rules containing a subset of the most relevant features based on a decision boundary. Here, individual rules are often smaller in length, containing fewer features as ranked by SHAP. This method is vastly different from RX-BO, where there is no feature relevance, feature ranking, or divide and conquer based rule mining. Thus making a quantitative comparison unfeasible. Below is an example from RuleXAI applied out-of-the-box on an HPO task on the decision tree classifier model. The best parameter that the BO process provides is given below.

Sample: *('criterion':'entropy'), ('max-depth': 38), ('max-features': 30), ('min-samples-leaf': 1), ('min-samples-split': 2)]) - Accuracy:0.795*

The goal is to explain this parameter by providing rule/rules indicating from where in the optimization space this parameter comes. The rules from RuleXAI can be seen below for this case:

Example RuleXAI:

Rule 1: 'IF max-features = <28, 30) THEN UTILITY = 0.78'; Rule 2: 'IF max-features = <28.02, 30.45) AND min-samples-split = <36.89, 40.63) THEN UTILITY = 0.78'

Here, we can see multiple smaller sizer rules for the given sample, and each rule does not incorporate all the input parameters.

Similarly, the rule from RX-BO is seen here: A single rule encompassing all parameters. Example RX-BO:

Rule 1: 'IF entropy : [0.99, 1.00] and gini : [-0.00, 0.00] and max-depth : [35.00, 40.90] and max-features : [29.99, 35.07] and min-samples-leaf : [0.99, 2.10] and min-samples-split : [1.99, 3.00] THEN UTILITY (0.78, 0.81)'

Firstly, It is easier for a user to tune hyperparameters when the "good" ranges of all parameters are known. RuleXAI does not fulfill that; by providing shorter rules, it omits parameters, which might make it difficult for a user of the HPO use case. Secondly, RuleXAI is not fit as a method for BO, for it fails to incorporate the different requirements listed in (Sect. 1 R1-R4). These findings highlight the superiority of RX-BO over regression-based XAI methods in the optimization use case.

5.3   Influence of Threshold Parameter t_s

Two studies were conducted to investigate the impact of the threshold parameter t_s in RX-BO. The first study analyzed the effect of t_s on the number of global rules generated. The second study examined its influence on the average interestingness α of the rules. Weight values of $w_1 = 0.5, w_2 = 0.2, w_3 = 0.1, w_4 = 0.2$ were used for interestingness computation. For this study, the threshold was tuned for $t_s = 1, 10, 20, 30, 40$. This selection was made based on the min/max distance for clusters, as observed in the problems we tackled.

The relationship between t_s, rule length, and interestingness is depicted in Fig. 2. We can observe as t_s increases, the number of rules decreases, indicating a shift from specific to more general rules, which aligns with the expected behavior of a clustering method. Highly general rules tend to have higher interestingness values, but excessively general rules may not provide desirable explanations as they would capture the whole space as one single rule, thereby failing to provide granular information. Since interestingness is a combination metric of different other metrics with higher influence from relevance, we can also say that a higher threshold value would have a higher relevance, which is also expected as the

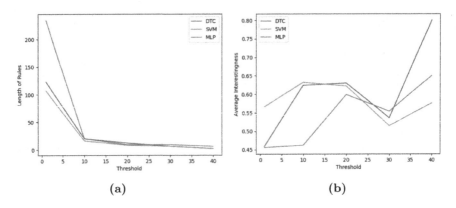

Fig. 2. In (a), we observe a trend in the length of rule list vs. threshold point, and in (b), we observe the trend in interestingness vs. threshold point.

coverage increases for rules. They contain a lot more samples, including the optimal sample, making this value high.

t_s can be tuned with the aid of a dendrogram which can help to identify the range of the threshold variable. An example dendrogram is depicted in Fig. 1 (d), one can observe the possible values t_s can take on the Y axis of this. It can also help in determining the optimal number of clusters and reveals the hierarchical structure of the data distribution, allowing to identify natural clusters and partition in the data effectively. For very high dimensions, it is complex to use this aid. And it is still an open research direction.

6   Conclusion

This research has introduced RX-BO, a novel method that enhances the transparency and interpretability of black-box BO algorithms. By leveraging GP models and a rule-based explainability method, RX-BO extracts distribution-aware rules that provide insights into the decision-making process of BO by elucidating the learned data distribution. Compared to traditional rule-based explainers, RX-BO offers higher rule confidence, improved rule granularity control, and the identification of interesting areas based on likelihood when compared to baseline frameworks like Decision trees and RuleXAI. The framework's contributions to the field of XAI significantly improve the understanding and trustworthiness of black-box BO, making it a valuable tool for researchers and practitioners in various domains. For future work, expanding this framework to explain other probabilistic optimization algorithms would be desirable. While refining the data handling and explanation representation capabilities of RX-BO.

Acknowledgments. This study was supported by BMBF Project hKI-Chemie: humancentric AI for the chemical industry, FKZ 01—S21023D, FKZ 01—S21023G and Continental AG.

References

1. Amoukou, S.I., Brunel, N.J.: Consistent sufficient explanations and minimal local rules for explaining the decision of any classifier or regressor. In: Advances in Neural Information Processing Systems, NeurIPS. Curran Associates, Inc. (2022)
2. Bénard, C., Biau, G., Veiga, S.D., Scornet, E.: Interpretable random forests via rule extraction. In: Proceedings of International Conference on Artificial Intelligence and Statistics, AISTATS, pp. 937–945. PMLR (2021)
3. Brochu, E., Cora, V.M., de Freitas, N.: A tutorial on Bayesian optimization of expensive cost functions, with application to active user modeling and hierarchical reinforcement learning. CoRR abs/1012.2599 (2010)
4. Chakraborty, T., Trehan, U., Mallat, K., Dugelay, J.: Generalizing adversarial explanations with Grad-CAM. In: Proceedings of IEEE/CVF Conference on Computer Vision and Pattern Recognition Workshops, CVPR Workshops, pp. 186–192. Computer Vision Foundation/IEEE (2022)
5. Coppens, Y., et al.: Distilling deep reinforcement learning policies in soft decision trees. In: Proceedings of the Workshop on Explainable Artificial Intelligence, IJCAI Workshop, pp. 1–6. IJCAI (2019)
6. Dekking, F.M., Kraaikamp, C., Lopuhaä, H.P., Meester, L.E.: A Modern Introduction to Probability and Statistics. STS, Springer, London (2005). https://doi.org/10.1007/1-84628-168-7
7. Deng, L.: The MNIST database of handwritten digit images for machine learning research. IEEE Signal Process. Mag. **29**(6), 141–142 (2012)
8. Frazier, P.I.: Bayesian optimization. In: Recent Advances in Optimization and Modeling of Contemporary Problems, pp. 255–278. Informs (2018)
9. Friedman, J.H., Popescu, B.E.: Predictive learning via rule ensembles. Ann. Appl. Stat. **2**(3) (2008)
10. Frosst, N., Hinton, G.E.: Distilling a neural network into a soft decision tree. In: Proceedings of the International Workshop on Comprehensibility and Explanation in AI and ML co-located with International Conference of the Italian Association for Artificial Intelligence, CEUR-WS.org (2017)
11. Garnett, R.: Bayesian Optimization. Cambridge University Press, Cambridge (2023)
12. Geng, Z., Schleich, M., Suciu, D.: Computing rule-based explanations by leveraging counterfactuals. Proc. VLDB Endowment **16**(3), 420–432 (2022)
13. Goix, N., et al.: mrahim: scikit-learn-contrib/skope-rules v1.0.1 (2020). https://doi.org/10.5281/zenodo.4316671
14. Guidotti, R., Monreale, A., Giannotti, F., Pedreschi, D., Ruggieri, S., Turini, F.: Factual and counterfactual explanations for black box decision making. IEEE Intell. Syst. **34**(6), 14–23 (2019)
15. Gulowaty, B., Wozniak, M.: Extracting interpretable decision tree ensemble from random forest. In: Proceedings of International Joint Conference on Neural Networks, IJCNN, pp. 1–8. IEEE (2021)
16. Joy, T.T., Rana, S., Gupta, S., Venkatesh, S.: Hyperparameter tuning for big data using Bayesian optimisation. In: Proceedings of International Conference on Pattern Recognition, ICPR, pp. 2574–2579. IEEE (2016)
17. Khan, F.A., Dietrich, J.P., Wirth, C.: Efficient utility function learning for multi-objective parameter optimization with prior knowledge. CoRR abs/2208.10300 (2022)

18. Lal, G.R., Chen, X., Mithal, V.: TE2Rules: extracting rule lists from tree ensembles. CoRR abs/2206.14359 (2022)
19. Lam, R., Poloczek, M., Frazier, P., Willcox, K.E.: Advances in Bayesian optimization with applications in aerospace engineering. In: Proceedings of Non-Deterministic Approaches Conference, NDA, p. 1656. AIAA (2018)
20. Letzgus, S., Wagner, P., Lederer, J., Samek, W., Müller, K., Montavon, G.: Toward explainable artificial intelligence for regression models: a methodological perspective. IEEE Signal Process. Mag. **39**(4), 40–58 (2022)
21. Lundberg, S.M., et al.: From local explanations to global understanding with explainable AI for trees. Nat. Mach. Intell. **2**(1), 56–67 (2020)
22. Lundberg, S.M., Lee, S.: A unified approach to interpreting model predictions. In: Advances in Neural Information Processing Systems, NeurIPS, pp. 4765–4774. Curran Associates, Inc. (2017)
23. Macha, D., Kozielski, M., Wróbel, L., Sikora, M.: RuleXAI - a package for rule-based explanations of machine learning model. SoftwareX **20**, 101209 (2022)
24. Mahbooba, B., Timilsina, M., Sahal, R., Serrano, M.: Explainable artificial intelligence (XAI) to enhance trust management in intrusion detection systems using decision tree model. Complex, pp. 6634811:1–6634811:11 (2021)
25. Mikriukov, G., Schwalbe, G., Hellert, C., Bade, K.: Evaluating the stability of semantic concept representations in CNNs for robust explainability. CoRR abs/2304.14864 (2023)
26. Moosbauer, J., Herbinger, J., Casalicchio, G., Lindauer, M., Bischl, B.: Explaining hyperparameter optimization via partial dependence plots. In: Advances in Neural Information Processing Systems, NeurIPS, pp. 2280–2291. Curran Associates, Inc. (2021)
27. Mothilal, R.K., Sharma, A., Tan, C.: Explaining machine learning classifiers through diverse counterfactual explanations. In: Proceedings of Conference on Fairness, Accountability, and Transparency, FAT, pp. 607–617. ACM (2020)
28. Murtagh, F., Legendre, P.: Ward's hierarchical clustering method: Clustering criterion and agglomerative algorithm. CoRR abs/1111.6285 (2011)
29. Mutahar, G., Miller, T.: Concept-based explanations using non-negative concept activation vectors and decision tree for CNN models. CoRR abs/2211.10807 (2022)
30. Nauta, M., et al.: From anecdotal evidence to quantitative evaluation methods: a systematic review on evaluating explainable AI. ACM Comput. Surv. (2023)
31. Nogueira, F.: Bayesian Optimization: open source constrained global optimization tool for Python (2014). https://github.com/fmfn/BayesianOptimization
32. Pedregosa, F., et al.: Scikit-Learn: machine learning in Python. J. Mach. Learn. Res. **12**, 2825–2830 (2011)
33. Rasmussen, C.E., Williams, C.K.I.: Gaussian processes for machine learning. MIT Press, Adaptive Computation and Machine Learning (2006)
34. Ribeiro, M.T., Singh, S., Guestrin, C.: "why should I trust you?": explaining the predictions of any classifier. In: Proceedings of the International Conference on Knowledge Discovery and Data Mining, SIGKDD, pp. 1135–1144. ACM (2016)
35. Ribeiro, M.T., Singh, S., Guestrin, C.: Anchors: high-precision model-agnostic explanations. In: Proceedings of the Conference on Artificial Intelligence, AAAI, pp. 1527–1535. AAAI Press (2018)
36. Saeed, W., Omlin, C.W.: Explainable AI (XAI): a systematic meta-survey of current challenges and future opportunities. Knowl. Based Syst. **263**, 110273 (2023)
37. Schwalbe, G., Finzel, B.: A comprehensive taxonomy for explainable artificial intelligence: a systematic survey of surveys on methods and concepts. Data Min. Knowl. Disc., 1–59 (2023)

38. Selvaraju, R.R., Cogswell, M., Das, A., Vedantam, R., Parikh, D., Batra, D.: Grad-CAM: visual explanations from deep networks via gradient-based localization. Int. J. Comput. Vis. **128**(2), 336–359 (2020)
39. Shahriari, B., Swersky, K., Wang, Z., Adams, R.P., de Freitas, N.: Taking the human out of the loop: a review of Bayesian optimization. Proc. IEEE **104**(1), 148–175 (2016)
40. Snoek, J., Larochelle, H., Adams, R.P.: Practical Bayesian optimization of machine learning algorithms. In: Advances in Neural Information Processing Systems, NeurIPS, pp. 2960–2968. Curran Associates, Inc. (2012)
41. Turner, R., Eriksson, D., McCourt, M., Kiili, J., Laaksonen, E., Xu, Z., Guyon, I.: Bayesian optimization is superior to random search for machine learning hyperparameter tuning: Analysis of the black-box optimization challenge 2020. In: Advances in Neural Information Processing Systems Competition and Demonstration Track, NeurIPS, pp. 3–26. Curran Associates, Inc. (2020)
42. van der Waa, J., Nieuwburg, E., Cremers, A.H.M., Neerincx, M.A.: Evaluating XAI: a comparison of rule-based and example-based explanations. Artif. Intell. **291**, 103404 (2021)
43. Wang, J., Chen, K., Yang, S., Loy, C.C., Lin, D.: Region proposal by guided anchoring. In: Proceedings of IEEE/CVF Conference on Computer Vision and Pattern Recognition, CVPR, pp. 2965–2974. Computer Vision Foundation/IEEE (2019)
44. Wirth, C., Schmid, U., Voget, S.: Humanzentrierte Künstliche Intelligenz: Erklärendes interaktives maschinelles Lernen für Effizienzsteigerung von Parametrieraufgaben. In: Hartmann, E.A. (ed.) Digitalisierung souverän gestalten II, pp. 80–92. Springer, Heidelberg (2022). https://doi.org/10.1007/978-3-662-64408-9_7
45. Witten, I.H., Frank, E., Hall, M.A., Pal, C.J.: Chapter 3 - output: knowledge representation. In: Data Mining (Fourth Edition), pp. 67–89. Morgan Kaufmann, fourth edition (2017)
46. Wu, J., Chen, X.Y., Zhang, H., Xiong, L.D., Lei, H., Deng, S.H.: Hyperparameter optimization for machine learning models based on Bayesian optimization. J. Electron. Sci. Technol. **17**(1), 26–40 (2019)

Subgroup Discovery with SD4Py

Dan Hudson[1]([⊠])(iD) and Martin Atzmueller[1,2](iD)

[1] Semantic Information Systems Group, Osnabrück University, Osnabrück, Germany
{daniel.dominic.hudson,martin.atzmueller}@uni-osnabrueck.de
[2] German Research Center for Artificial Intelligence (DFKI), Osnabrück, Germany

Abstract. We present SD4Py, a free open-source Python package for performing subgroup discovery and analysis. SD4Py makes it easy to discover subgroups from data stored in a Pandas data frame, to undertake follow-on analysis to examine the variability in the quality of the subgroups and to visualise important parameters. The core algorithms for discovering subgroups are implemented by an existing well-established and efficient Java back-end, but are exposed through a user-friendly Python interface. SD4Py offers a concise workflow for not only discovering but also comparing subgroups, in order to select those of interest, and for gaining insights into what is distinctive about individual subgroups.

Keywords: Subgroup Discovery · Visualisation · Python Package

1 The SD4Py Package: An Overview

Subgroup discovery [1,27,28,44], an approach closely related to association rule mining [1,40], allows the analyst to extract interpretable patterns according to a given quality function (also called 'interestingness measure'). For instance, it can identify circumstances in which some variable of interest (the 'target') has an extreme distribution of values. When examining a dataset, subgroups of data points are identified through a combination of membership conditions in the form of attribute-value pairs; any data points that meet the conditions count as members. For example, when analysing industrial sensor data, a subgroup might have the conditions "Blade pressure" is Low AND "Vacuum strength" is High. The subgroup consists of all data points matching this description. The most interesting subgroups are identified using a quality function, e.g., quantifying how extreme the values of target variable are within the subgroup and includes some adjustment to favour larger subgroups. Extensions consider, e.g., sets of target variables [17,22,32] or complex network measures [3,12].

Subgroup discovery is applicable to various domains, e.g., medicine [18], industrial [4] as well as business analysis [15], cyber-security [6,13] or social contexts [2,7]. Since subgroups are interpretable, they are highly relevant for knowledge discovery, including hypothesis generation based on existing data. Taking a medical context as an example, subgroup discovery could be used to identify groups of individuals who are especially likely to have a certain medical

S. Nowaczyk et al. (Eds.): ECAI 2023 Workshops, CCIS 1947, pp. 338–348, 2024.
https://doi.org/10.1007/978-3-031-50396-2_19

condition. Each subgroup would specify some factors that potentially combine to increase the risk of the condition; if a subgroup seems promising, follow-on confirmatory research could then establish whether a causal relationship exists.

In another setting the goal may be, say, to predict the selling price of second-hand cars from various properties like the year and brand. Here, subgroup discovery can be used to find simple descriptions of groups of cars that have a high selling price on average. Once subgroups have been identified, they can also be applied to unseen data to decide if a car belongs to a group with a high selling price on average. Thus, each such decision is entirely explainable, being based on a set of explicit rules. Therefore, this directly connects explainable and interpretable machine learning [16, 39], via subgroup discovery as a local pattern mining technique for both *exploratory* and *explanatory* data analysis, in order to provide insights into the data and obtain explanations about its structures and relations.

Although there is a quality function which ranks the subgroups, often many interesting candidate subgroups are discovered. Here, the open-source SD4Py Python package also provides methods to compare and contrast subgroups, and obtain insights into their distinctive characteristics. This aids the analysis process by making it quicker to refine results and form a selection of the most interesting subgroups. Our package provides several novel contributions in this regard, including methods to analyse variability in the 'quality' of subgroups, and visualisation methods to present their important characteristics. In earlier work, we demonstrated the value of applying these visualisations to study teamwork interactions, in order to find moments when a change in group dynamics is especially likely [24]. These visualisation options augment SD4Py, and provide an additional contribution that is specific to our package.

SD4Py is available via several options:

- SD4Py Github: https://github.com/cslab-hub/sd4py,
- the Python Package Index (PYPI), or
- the `pip` package manager.

A Jupyter notebook showcasing SD4Py via several examples can be found at https://github.com/cslab-hub/sd4py/blob/main/sd4py_examples.ipynb Detailed documentation is provided at: https://cslab-hub.github.io/sd4py Furthermore, a brief video is available at https://myshare.uni-osnabrueck.de/f/17689a78ff414cac9f04/

For subgroup discovery, there are implementations in Java (VIKAMINE [5, 9], Cortana [36]), and R (rsubgroup[1], SDEFSR[2]). In Python there is Orange[3] and pysubgroup [31]. Focusing on a light-weight, seamless, extensible and easy-to-use integration into Python for subgroup discovery and analysis, SD4Py provides an alternative based on the efficient, state-of-the-art implementation of

---

[1] https://rsubgroup.org.
[2] https://github.com/SIMIDAT/SDEFSR.
[3] http://kt.ijs.si/petrakralj/SubgroupDiscovery/.

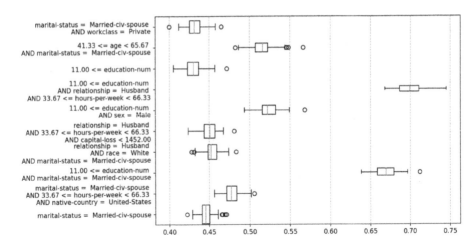

Fig. 1. Income prediction use case: The distribution of mean target values from bootstrapping simulations – assessing variability of subgroup quality and generalisability to new data.

VIKAMINE [5], whilst extending VIKAMINE by introducing a series of new functions to perform additional analysis and visualisation of subgroups.

Compared to pySubgroup and Orange, SD4PY provides a more comprehensive set of state-of-the-art subgroup discovery methods, including in particular the SD-Map/SD-Map* algorithms [10,30], as well as a more comprehensive set of quality functions (for nominal, numeric, ordinal target variables, cf. [1,30]) which we now present through an easy-to-use Python interface. The SD-Map* algorithm in particular is a state-of-the-art method for discovering subgroups, based on the FP-Growth algorithm [21]; SD-Map* specifically applies optimistic estimates in order to provide a performance advantage. This algorithm offers the potential to speed up the subgroup discovery process compared to the available alternatives, and thus is an important addition to SD4PY.

It is important to note that the SD4PY Python interface requires no interaction with Java. Instead, SD4PY offers suitable abstractions as an easy-to-use interface on top of the Java functionality, enabling seamless access via Python. Also, SD4PY extends on previous approaches by providing a number of additional analysis functions that support the analysis workflow after the initial discovery of subgroups. Specifically, this relates to analysis options regarding, for example, subgroup interpretation and analysis via visualisation as well as specific statistical assessment approaches (e. g., boostrapping analytics) described below. Furthermore, different techniques for analysing complex data like time series data [23,24] are provided by SD4PY, integrating into the rich Python software ecosystem, thus enabling sophisticated analytical solutions. These additional analysis options are gathered into a sub-module, which sits alongside and extends the core subgroup search functionality based on VIKAMINE, and which provides a distinguishing characteristic of SD4PY.

2   Example Application Use Cases

Now, we present an example of how subgroup discovery via SD4PY can be applied to a classification scenario. In this example, we use variables gathered from US census data to identify whether an individual is particularly likely to earn more than $50,000 annually. This dataset is freely available from the UCI Machine Learning Repository, under the name 'Adult'[4]. It contains 48842 data points, described by the target variable and 14 additional demographic variables, such as education level and country of birth. The data was obtained from the 1994 US Census, and has been filtered to only include individuals who are older than 16, work, and receive an income. The dataset has been used previously to evaluate machine learning classification algorithms, and although state-of-the-art neural network classifiers are now likely to be evaluated on larger and more complex datasets, it functions well as a nontrivial case study in order to demonstrate subgroup discovery.

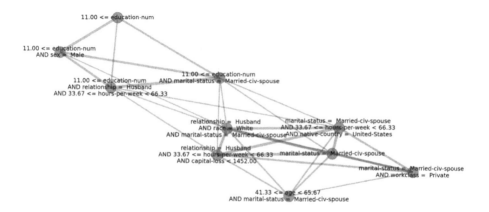

Fig. 2. Income prediction use case: Visualisation of the overlap between subgroups.

In SD4PY, the core operation of discovering subgroups is exposed through a simple function, which is called with a Pandas data frame and the name of the target variable, with additional optional parameters for configuring the search process. This means that subgroup discovery can be performed with a single line of code:

```
subgroups = sd4py.discover_subgroups(
    data, target='target_variable_name')
```

Note that the `discover_subgroups` function is highly flexible, providing an interface into the diverse functionality of the underlying VIKAMINE software.

---

[4] https://archive.ics.uci.edu/ml/datasets/Adult.

Full details of the parameters that can be used to control this functionality can be accessed via the help function, or via the online documentation.[5]

Subgroup discovery was performed with the goal of identifying groups of data points where an income above $50K is especially common. This returns numerous candidate subgroups. To gain a better understanding of these, we first investigate the variability of quality measures, giving an improved understanding of how different subgroups seem likely to generalise. This uses a bootstrapping approach in which the quality of the subgroups is evaluated on repeated over-lapping samples (with replacement) of the dataset. The quality metric to use, such as the average value of the target variable, precision, recall, or F1-score, can be decided by the user. The dataset from which samples are created can also be chosen; it could be the same data used for subgroup discovery or could be a separate validation set. The associated visualisation depicts the average target value (mean for numeric targets, proportion of 'positives' in the subgroup for a nominal target) across bootstrapping samples as a series of boxplots. The size of the subgroups, understood as what fraction of each bootstrapping sample they select on average, is represented in the plot by the thickness of the boxes. All of this functionality is exposed through simple functions in SD4Py. In Fig. 1, various subgroups that were found are displayed. The average likelihood of a subgroup member earning more than $50K varied between subgroups, from around 0.4 on average to approximately 0.7, compared to a likelihood of 0.24 across the full dataset. The size of the subgroups was also variable, with there being fewer members in the subgroups with a higher average target value.

A few attributes appear in many of the subgroup definitions, such as the members being married, working an ordinary number of hours per week, and having a high educational level. This can lead to subgroups having a high overlap, essentially selecting the same data points. When this occurs, it may be desirable to choose a smaller number of more diverse subgroups for further analysis, cf. [1, 8,24,34]. To support this, SD4Py includes a function to operate over an ordered collection of subgroups and remove those that overlap highly with subgroups encountered previously. The threshold used for this is configurable, and expressed in terms of the Jaccard similarity (the size of the intersection divided by the size of the union, a value which varies between 0 and 1). An associated visualisation shows how subgroups cluster together based on their overlap. A weighted network diagram is constructed in which nodes represent subgroups and the weight of an edge connecting two nodes is determined by the Jaccard similarity. This gives a visual basis for selecting subgroups, in which it is possible to see how much subgroups respectively differ (how distant they are in the diagram) and also consider which subgroups are central within a neighbourhood and so likely to be representative. As shown in Fig. 2, although the subgroups often involve similar rules, the amount that they overlap with one another is not consistent – some pairs overlap much more than others. This information could be used by the analyst in selecting subgroups for further investigation.

---

[5] https://cslab-hub.github.io/sd4py/sd4py/sd4py.html#discover_subgroups.

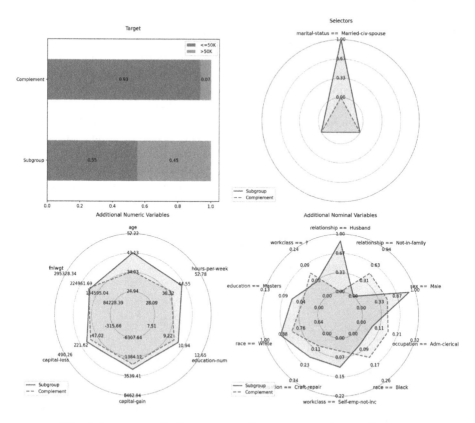

Fig. 3. Income prediction use case: Summary of a single subgroup.

To look more deeply into a single subgroup, we use the 'subgroup overview' visualisation. Once a selection of the most interesting subgroups has been made, it is possible to make a more in-depth examination of individual subgroups, in order to understand how a subgroup characteristically differs from the general tendencies of the dataset. SD4Py provides a visualisation for this purpose. Four panels show important attributes of a single subgroup, presenting the distribution of values for subgroup members compared to the distribution of values for non-subgroup members. In the top-left panel, the target variable is shown; in the top-right, the selector variables used to define the subgroup are shown; in the bottom panels, multiple interesting variables are selected based on estimated effect size (comparing the subgroup to non-subgroup members) and also displayed, with numeric variables on the left and nominal variables on the right. One particular subgroup is shown in Fig. 3, in this case focusing on the subgroup defined by Martial Status is Spouse. Numerous important observations can be made from this visualisation that could be missed otherwise. For one thing, we can see that married people tend to be older than unmarried people. The increased income of married individuals could therefore in part be due to the fact that they are often in a more mature period of their career. Another observation is that the relationship is almost always husband, not wife. It is not clear why this is the case. Perhaps it is because the census was often filled in by the husband on behalf of the whole household, or it could be that data filtering by the dataset creator disproportionately removed wives. The almost exclusively male composition of this subgroup in the data also might be expected to influence income, if it reflects a social bias towards men having higher earnings.

In summary, this case study shows how SD4PY can be applied to analyse data based on a target classification, in this case an income category based on census data. The discovered subgroups provide rules that can be applied to new data, to understand whether individuals are likely to have a higher income. Importantly, the results also gave indications as to which demographic groupings are likely to have a high income, providing a potential starting point for further research. Visualisations provided by the SD4PY package made it possible to quickly gain additional insights, supporting and enriching the interpretable subgroup definitions found through subgroup discovery.

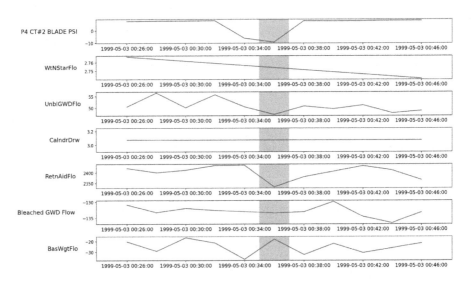

Fig. 4. Paper mill use case: Multiple variables over time, showing when subgroup member occurred.

Besides these visualizations, we also include a visualisation that specifically applies to time series data, when the goal of subgroup discovery is to identify interesting time windows. To demonstrate, we focus upon a second example application, namely the paper mill dataset [41], which contains sensor recordings from a production process for rolls of paper. In this process, a sheet of paper runs through a sequence of mechanical components, and a common cause of faults is that this sheet breaks, making a restart necessary. This is a costly issue for the paper industry, and understanding the circumstances in which it is likely to happen could help to reduce the associated costs. Therefore, we use the occurrence of a fault as a target variable, and search for subgroups of time points in which a fault is especially likely. Measurements are at 2-minute intervals, totalling 18398 time points, of which 124 were faults. Using this data as an input, we search for subgroups where a fault is particularly likely to occur within the next 10 min. After using the box plots and network visualisations to select a single subgroup for further investigation, SD4PY makes it possible to visualise the subgroup members, which represent points in time when a fault is especially likely to occur. One such subgroup member is shown in Fig. 4. Multiple relevant variables, such as raw sensor recordings, derived time-series features, and the target variable, are plotted over time whilst windows belonging to the subgroup are highlighted in the background. This makes it possible to visually inspect the progression of multiple variables and subgroup membership over time, providing additional information that can help an expert review the subgroup and better understand how the system progresses towards a fault state.

3   Conclusion

In this paper, we have presented the SD4PY Python package enabling seamless subgroup discovery implemented in Python via an accessible programming interface. SD4PY enables interpretable local pattern detection, thus enabling explainable and interpretable machine learning. In particular, this also provides for a powerful exploratory but also explanatory data analysis approach. From a technical perspective, for efficiency SD4PY relies on the state-of-the-art VIKAMINE Java implementation for its core subgroup discovery algorithms [1]; SD4PY extends this via a Python API for easy-to-use analysis and integration into the rich Python data analysis environment. It is important to note that the SD4PY Python interface requires no interaction with Java, solely relying on the Python API abstractions. Also, SD4PY specifically extends on previous approaches by providing a number of additional analysis functions that support the analysis workflow after the initial discovery of subgroups. Here, in particular, rich visualisation, post-processing and explanatory functions can be implemented.

We have demonstrated the application of SD4PY in two example use case studies – namely, a task of income prediction, and a task of analysing time series data in the scope of industrial fault analysis. For both, we have demonstrated the applicability and versatile analysis options of SD4PY, in particular highlighting the visualisation and exploratory subgroup analysis approaches, showcasing the overall exploratory and explanatory potential of subgroup discovery via SD4PY.

For future work, we consider to extend SD4PY via more complex quality functions on sets of subgroups [8, 14, 42, 43], e. g., in the spirit of exceptional model mining on such selected (sub-)sets [17, 29], also regarding further algorithmic options, e. g., [35, 37, 38]. Furthermore, we aim to enhance the package further for interactive use by advancing on subgroup (set) visualisation and specifically explanation generation and presentation, e. g., [11, 19, 20, 25, 26, 33].

References

1. Atzmueller, M.: Subgroup Discovery. WIREs Data Min. Knowl. Discovery **5**(1), 35–49 (2015)
2. Atzmueller, M.: Compositional subgroup discovery on attributed social interaction networks. In: Soldatova, L., Vanschoren, J., Papadopoulos, G., Ceci, M. (eds.) DS 2018. LNCS (LNAI), vol. 11198, pp. 259–275. Springer, Cham (2018). https://doi.org/10.1007/978-3-030-01771-2_17
3. Atzmueller, M., Doerfel, S., Mitzlaff, F.: Description-oriented community detection using exhaustive subgroup discovery. Inf. Sci. **329**, 965–984 (2016)
4. Atzmueller, M., Lemmerich, F.: Fast subgroup discovery for continuous target concepts. In: Rauch, J., Raś, Z.W., Berka, P., Elomaa, T. (eds.) ISMIS 2009. LNCS (LNAI), vol. 5722, pp. 35–44. Springer, Heidelberg (2009). https://doi.org/10.1007/978-3-642-04125-9_7
5. Atzmueller, M., Lemmerich, F.: VIKAMINE – open-source subgroup discovery, pattern mining, and analytics. In: Flach, P.A., De Bie, T., Cristianini, N. (eds.) ECML PKDD 2012. LNCS (LNAI), vol. 7524, pp. 842–845. Springer, Heidelberg (2012). https://doi.org/10.1007/978-3-642-33486-3_60
6. Atzmueller, M., Lemmerich, F., Krause, B., Hotho, A.: Who are the spammers? understandable local patterns for concept description. In: Proceedings 7th Conference on Computer Methods and Systems. Oprogramowanie Nauko-Techniczne, Krakow, Poland (2009)
7. Atzmueller, M., Mueller, J.: Subgroup analytics and interactive assessment on ubiquitous data. In: Proceedings of International Workshop on Mining Ubiquitous and Social Environments (MUSE2013), Prague, Czech Republic (2013)
8. Atzmueller, M., Mueller, J., Becker, M.: Exploratory subgroup analytics on ubiquitous data. In: Atzmueller, M., Chin, A., Scholz, C., Trattner, C. (eds.) MSM/MUSE -2013. LNCS (LNAI), vol. 8940, pp. 1–20. Springer, Cham (2015). https://doi.org/10.1007/978-3-319-14723-9_1
9. Atzmueller, M., Puppe, F.: Semi-automatic visual subgroup mining using VIKAMINE. J. Univ. Comput. Sci. **11**(11), 1752–1765 (2005)
10. Atzmueller, M., Puppe, F.: SD-Map – a fast algorithm for exhaustive subgroup discovery. In: Fürnkranz, J., Scheffer, T., Spiliopoulou, M. (eds.) PKDD 2006. LNCS (LNAI), vol. 4213, pp. 6–17. Springer, Heidelberg (2006). https://doi.org/10.1007/11871637_6
11. Atzmueller, M., Roth-Berghofer, T.: The Mining and Analysis Continuum of Explaining Uncovered. In: Proc. Research and Development in Intelligent Systems XXVII. SGAI 2010. pp. 273–278. Springer, London (2010). https://doi.org/10.1007/978-0-85729-130-1_20
12. Atzmueller, M., Soldano, H., Santini, G., Bouthinon, D.: MinerLSD: efficient mining of local patterns on attributed networks. Appl. Network Sci. **4**(43) (2019)
13. Atzmueller, M., Sylvester, S., Kanawati, R.: Exploratory and Explanation-Aware Network Intrusion Profiling using Subgroup Discovery and Complex Network Analysis. In: Proc. European Interdisciplinary Cybersecurity Conference. pp. 153–158. ACM (2023)
14. Belfodil, A., et al.: Fssd-a fast and efficient algorithm for subgroup set discovery. In: 2019 IEEE International Conference on Data Science and Advanced Analytics (DSAA), pp. 91–99. IEEE (2019)

15. Berlanga, F., del Jesus, M.J., González, P., Herrera, F., Mesonero, M.: Multiobjective evolutionary induction of subgroup discovery fuzzy rules: a case study in marketing. In: Perner, P. (ed.) ICDM 2006. LNCS (LNAI), vol. 4065, pp. 337–349. Springer, Heidelberg (2006). https://doi.org/10.1007/11790853_27

16. Biran, O., Cotton, C.: Explanation and justification in machine learning: a survey. In: IJCAI-17 Workshop on Explainable AI (2017)

17. Duivesteijn, W., Feelders, A.J., Knobbe, A.: Exceptional model mining. DMKD 30(1), 47–98 (2016)

18. Gamberger, D., Lavrac, N.: Expert-guided subgroup discovery: methodology and application. J. Artif. Intell. Res. 17, 501–527 (2002)

19. Gilpin, L.H., Bau, D., Yuan, B.Z., Bajwa, A., Specter, M., Kagal, L.: Explaining explanations: an overview of interpretability of machine learning. In: 2018 IEEE 5th International Conference on data science and advanced analytics (DSAA), pp. 80–89. IEEE (2018)

20. Guven, C., Seipel, D., Atzmueller, M.: Applying ASP for knowledge-based link prediction with explanation generation in feature rich networks. IEEE Trans. Network Sci. Eng. 8(2), 1305–1315 (2021)

21. Han, J., Pei, J., Yin, Y.: Mining frequent patterns without candidate generation. In: Chen, W., Naughton, J., Bernstein, P.A. (eds.) 2000 ACM SIGMOD Intl. Conference on Management of Data, pp. 1–12. ACM Press (05 2000)

22. Hendrickson, A.T., Wang, J., Atzmueller, M.: Identifying exceptional descriptions of people using topic modeling and subgroup discovery. In: Ceci, M., Japkowicz, N., Liu, J., Papadopoulos, G.A., Raś, Z.W. (eds.) ISMIS 2018. LNCS (LNAI), vol. 11177, pp. 454–462. Springer, Cham (2018). https://doi.org/10.1007/978-3-030-01851-1_44

23. Hudson, D., Wiltshire, T.J., Atzmueller, M.: Local exceptionality detection in time series using subgroup discovery: an approach exemplified on team interaction data. In: Soares, C., Torgo, L. (eds.) DS 2021. LNCS (LNAI), vol. 12986, pp. 435–445. Springer, Cham (2021). https://doi.org/10.1007/978-3-030-88942-5_34

24. Hudson, D., Wiltshire, T.J., Atzmueller, M.: Visualization methods for exploratory subgroup discovery on time series data. In: Ferrández Vicente, J.M., Álvarez-Sánchez, J.R., de la Paz López, F., Adeli, H. (eds.) Bio-inspired Systems and Applications: from Robotics to Ambient Intelligence, pp. 34–44. Springer, Cham (2022). https://doi.org/10.1007/978-3-031-06527-9_4

25. Iferroudjene, M., Lonjarret, C., Robardet, C., Plantevit, M., Atzmueller, M.: Methods for explaining top-n recommendations through subgroup discovery. Data Min. Knowl. Disc. 37(2), 833–872 (2023)

26. Jorge, A.M., Pereira, F., Azevedo, P.J.: Visual interactive subgroup discovery with numerical properties of interest. In: Todorovski, L., Lavrač, N., Jantke, K.P. (eds.) DS 2006. LNCS (LNAI), vol. 4265, pp. 301–305. Springer, Heidelberg (2006). https://doi.org/10.1007/11893318_31

27. Klösgen, W.: Explora: a multipattern and multistrategy discovery assistant. In: Advances in Knowledge Discovery and Data Mining, pp. 249–271. AAAI Press (1996)

28. Klösgen, W.: Handbook of Data Mining and Knowledge Discovery, chap. 16.3: Subgroup Discovery. Oxford University Press, New York (2002)

29. Leman, D., Feelders, A., Knobbe, A.: Exceptional model mining. In: Daelemans, W., Goethals, B., Morik, K. (eds.) ECML PKDD 2008. LNCS (LNAI), vol. 5212, pp. 1–16. Springer, Heidelberg (2008). https://doi.org/10.1007/978-3-540-87481-2_1

30. Lemmerich, F., Atzmueller, M., Puppe, F.: Fast exhaustive subgroup discovery with numerical target concepts. Data Min. Knowl. Disc. **30**(3), 711–762 (2016)
31. Lemmerich, F., Becker, M.: pysubgroup: Easy-to-use subgroup discovery in python. In: Proc. European Conference on Machine Learning and Principles and Practice of Knowledge Discovery in Databases (ECML PKDD), pp. 658–662. Springer, Heidelberg (2018)
32. Lemmerich, F., Becker, M., Atzmueller, M.: Generic pattern trees for exhaustive exceptional model mining. In: Flach, P.A., De Bie, T., Cristianini, N. (eds.) ECML PKDD 2012. LNCS (LNAI), vol. 7524, pp. 277–292. Springer, Heidelberg (2012). https://doi.org/10.1007/978-3-642-33486-3_18
33. Li, P., Boubrahimi, S.F., Hamdi, S.M.: Motif-guided time series counterfactual explanations. In: International Conference on Pattern Recognition. pp. 203–215. Springer, Cham (2022). https://doi.org/10.1007/978-3-031-37731-0_16
34. Li, R., Perneczky, R., Drzezga, A., Kramer, S.: Efficient redundancy reduced subgroup discovery via quadratic programming. J. Intell. Inf. Syst. **44**, 271–288 (2015)
35. Lopez-Martinez-Carrasco, A., Juarez, J.M., Campos, M., Canovas-Segura, B.: Vlsd-an efficient subgroup discovery algorithm based on equivalence classes and optimistic estimate. Algorithms **16**(6), 274 (2023)
36. Meeng, M., Knobbe, A.: Flexible enrichment with cortana-software demo. In: Proceedings of BeneLearn, pp. 117–119 (2011)
37. Meeng, M., Knobbe, A.: For real: a thorough look at numeric attributes in subgroup discovery. Data Min. Knowl. Disc. **35**(1), 158–212 (2021)
38. Millot, A., Mathonat, R., Cazabet, R., Boulicaut, J.-F.: Actionable subgroup discovery and urban farm optimization. In: Berthold, M.R., Feelders, A., Krempl, G. (eds.) IDA 2020. LNCS, vol. 12080, pp. 339–351. Springer, Cham (2020). https://doi.org/10.1007/978-3-030-44584-3_27
39. Mollenhauer, D., Atzmueller, M.: Sequential exceptional pattern discovery using pattern-growth: an extensible framework for interpretable machine learning on sequential data. In: Proc. First International Workshop on Explainable and Interpretable Machine Learning (XI-ML 2020). University of Bamberg (2020)
40. Proença, H.M., Grünwald, P., Bäck, T., van Leeuwen, M.: Robust subgroup discovery: discovering subgroup lists using mdl. Data Min. Knowl. Disc. **36**(5), 1885–1970 (2022)
41. Ranjan, C., Reddy, M., Mustonen, M., Paynabar, K., Pourak, K.: Dataset: rare event classification in multivariate time series. arXiv preprint arXiv:1809.10717 (2018)
42. van Leeuwen, M., Knobbe, A.: Non-redundant subgroup discovery in large and complex data. In: Gunopulos, D., Hofmann, T., Malerba, D., Vazirgiannis, M. (eds.) ECML PKDD 2011. LNCS (LNAI), vol. 6913, pp. 459–474. Springer, Heidelberg (2011). https://doi.org/10.1007/978-3-642-23808-6_30
43. Van Leeuwen, M., Knobbe, A.: Diverse subgroup set discovery. Data Min. Knowl. Disc. **25**(2), 208–242 (2012)
44. Wrobel, S.: An algorithm for multi-relational discovery of subgroups. In: Komorowski, J., Zytkow, J. (eds.) PKDD 1997. LNCS, vol. 1263, pp. 78–87. Springer, Heidelberg (1997). https://doi.org/10.1007/3-540-63223-9_108

Exploring Multi-Task Learning
for Explainability

Foivos Charalampakos[✉] and Iordanis Koutsopoulos[✉]

Department of Informatics, Athens University of Economics and Business, Athens,
Greece
phoebuschar@aueb.gr, jordan@aueb.gr

Abstract. Machine Learning (ML) model understanding and interpretation is an essential component of several applications in different
domains. Several explanation techniques have been developed in order
to provide insights about decisions of complex ML models. One of the
most common explainability methods, Feature Attribution, assigns an
importance score to each input feature that denotes its contribution (relative significance) to the complex (black-box) ML model's decision. Such
scores can be obtained through another model that acts as a surrogate,
e.g., a linear one, which is trained after the black-box model so as to
approximate its predictions. In this paper, we propose a training procedure based on Multi-Task Learning (MTL), where we *concurrently* train
a black-box neural network and a surrogate linear model whose coefficients can then be used as feature significance scores. The two models exchange information through their predictions via the optimization
objective which is a convex combination of a predictive loss function for
the black-box model and of an explainability metric which aims to keep
the predictions of the two models close together. Our method manages
to make the surrogate model achieve a more accurate approximation of
the black-box one, compared to the baseline of separately training the
black-box and surrogate models, and therefore improves the quality of
produced explanations, both global and local ones. We also achieve a
good trade-off between predictive performance and explainability with
minimal to negligible accuracy decrease. This enables black-box models
acquired from the MTL training procedure to be used instead of normally
trained models whilst being more interpretable.

Keywords: Multi-Task Leaning · Explainable Artificial Intelligence ·
Feature Attribution methods

1 Introduction

Contemporary, complex Deep Neural Networks (DNNs) are increasingly used in
order to assist the decision-making process. Despite their impressive predictive
abilities, these networks provide a very limited understanding of the reasoning
behind their decisions [15]. In domains with high-stakes applications such as
law, finance and healthcare, model understanding and therefore interpretation
is essential so that the model's predictions can be trusted [15]. Interpretability

© The Author(s), under exclusive license to Springer Nature Switzerland AG 2024
S. Nowaczyk et al. (Eds.): ECAI 2023 Workshops, CCIS 1947, pp. 349–365, 2024.
https://doi.org/10.1007/978-3-031-50396-2_20

of ML algorithms has thus become a pressing issue, and the field of eXplainable - or Interpretable - Artificial Intelligence (XAI) has emerged and constitutes an important component of Trustworthy AI.

XAI methods can be arranged to several categories according to different criteria. The most apparent distinction is the one of 'transparent' versus 'opaque' models. The former category concerns models like Linear/Logistic Regression and Decision Trees whose structure is simple, and their decision-making process is understandable by humans. Unfortunately, the simplicity of these models often comes with an unsatisfactory performance in real-world applications. This caveat is known as the accuracy-interpretability trade-off. XAI aims to fill this gap by providing explainability for 'opaque' models such as Neural Networks and Random Forests which require the development of separate specialized algorithms in order to render their predictions interpretable [15]. Usually, these algorithms make use of the predictions produced by the model after its training, and are referred to as *post-hoc* explainability methods.

Post-hoc methods can be further categorized into global and local methods. The former aim at explaining the general machinery of the ML model, by describing its average behavior over the entire dataset [5], while local methods focus on explaining predictions for individual data instances [5]. Another categorization is based on whether the algorithm is model-agnostic (i.e., it does not require access to the model architecture) or model-specific.

One well-known class of explainability algorithms are the Feature Attribution (FA) methods [6] which rely on a score that captures how much the input features contribute to the model's output. FA methods can be used in both global and local settings, as well as in model-specific [2] and model-agnostic [6] contexts. On the other hand, the class of counterfactual explanations [7] concerns local model-agnostic methods that describe the smallest changes to the feature values that change the output of the prediction for a given instance, while decision rule-based explanations are simple IF-THEN natural language hypothetical statements, consisting of a condition which contains one or more input features, and a corresponding prediction based on the values of the features involved in the condition [5].

Real-world problems are multi-objective ones, which means that ML training should address multiple tasks simultaneously, possibly belonging to different data modalities. For example, an autonomous vehicle should be able to segment the lane markings, detect humans, locate road signs, and identify their meaning [21]. In the medical sector, prediction accuracy and prediction explainability are simultaneously required, e.g., when a patient should be informed about potential side-effect risks for a particular tretment plan. Such problems motivate the development of Deep Learning models that, given an input, can infer several desired task outputs [21]. This kind of models can be trained using the *Multi-Task Learning (MTL)* paradigm that permits multiple tasks to be concurrently learned by a single model, enabling the different tasks to share potential common underlying information, and removing the need for training different models for each task. In the case of XAI, a way to use MTL is to *think of prediction and explainability as two distinct tasks*, and to simultaneously solve for these tasks in order to allow information exchange between the two tasks and to produce more specific and accurate explanations for the predictions.

In this work, we utilize the MTL paradigm, which has recently been used in the field of XAI [8,24,37], in order to develop a framework that concurrently solves a ML prediction task and an explainability task. We focus on surrogate models and employ them to produce FA explanations. We aim at finding a black-box neural network model f along with a surrogate approximation model g, by forcing the former to take into account, during training, how well it is approximated by the latter. To that end, we optimize a loss function that includes a term for predictive training loss and an explainability-based metric. For the latter, we use a known explainability metric such as fidelity, which measures the difference between the predictions of g and f. This component aims to improve f's approximation through g and to enhance the quality of post-hoc explanations of the black-box model. Furthermore, the combined objective acts as the information-sharing 'channel' between the two models in the course of back-propagation [18] during the *joint* training. In another point of view, g could be considered as an explainability-regularizing model that constrains the values of f's predictions to being similar to those of the interpretable model g. In order to demonstrate the concept of our approach, we choose g to be a parameterized linear model which can be trained along with the black-box, but other choices are possible as well. Using such linear models, feature importance explanations for the predictions of f can be acquired through the coefficients of g [5].

We experiment with a variety of regression and binary classification tasks, where we compare models trained with and without MTL. We show that, our approach that uses MTL to concurrently train f and g, results in a more accurate approximation of the black-box by the surrogate linear model, compared to the standard practice where the two models are trained sequentially and separately. Therefore, the global explanation's fidelity is very much improved and in addition, only a minimal drop in the predictive performance is observed as a trade-off. Furthermore, we show that the same black-box model can be more accurately approximated by local linear explainers (like Local Interpretable Model-Agnostic Explanations (LIME) [6]), thus resulting on a lower-fidelity local explanation.

2   Related Work

2.1   Feature Attribution (FA) Methods for Explainability

FA algorithms are most commonly used as local explainers and assign importance scores to how much a given input feature contributes to the model's prediction result for a single instance of interest. Much work has been done on model-specific techniques that are gradient-based and work for DNNs by computing the significance of input features based on the gradient values of the model's parameters [2,25]. Another line of research works create a local neighborhood around the instance of interest $\mathbf{x}$ based on perturbations of $\mathbf{x}$'s feature values and measure the change in the model's output in order to calculate the significance of each feature [6, 29, 35], based on a surrogate model. One of the most popular FA explanation systems, LIME [6], results to a local surrogate model-based explanation by optimizing the following objective, given the instance of interest $\mathbf{x}$ and a trained black-box model f:

$$e(\mathbf{x}, f) = \underset{g \in \mathcal{G}}{\arg\min} \left[\sum_{\mathbf{x}' \in N_{\mathbf{x}}} \mathbf{w}_{\mathbf{x}} \left(f(\mathbf{x}') - g(\mathbf{x}') \right)^2 + \Omega(g) \right] \tag{1}$$

where $N_{\mathbf{x}}$ is the neighborhood around $\mathbf{x}$, consisting of synthetic perturbations of $\mathbf{x}$. The class of surrogate models is denoted by $\mathcal{G}$ (e.g., linear models or decision trees), and $\Omega(g)$ is a measure of complexity that encourages desirable properties of g such as sparsity, i.e., using a small number of features [6]. LIME also weighs each neighbor of $\mathbf{x}$ to denote its importance, using a proximity measure (e.g., ℓ_2-distance from $\mathbf{x}$) and solves a *weighted linear regression objective*, using a weight vector $\mathbf{w}_{\mathbf{x}}$. The form of the resulting explanation $e(\mathbf{x}, f)$ depends on $\mathcal{G}$. For instance, if $\mathcal{G}$ includes all possible linear functions, then $e(\mathbf{x}, f)$ will consist of the coefficients of the learned linear function g, while in the case of decision trees, $e(\mathbf{x}, f)$ will consist of decision rules based on the trained tree.

In addition to local explainability, FA methods have also been used for global explainability through global surrogate models which aim to approximate (mimic) the predictions of the underlying black-box model [5, 10]. Global surrogate models are similar to local surrogate models, except that they are trained by using the whole dataset and not just a generated neighborhood of a specific instance $\mathbf{x}$. The most common way to learn a global surrogate model is to train it on the predictions $\{\mathbf{x}_i, f(\mathbf{x}_i)\}_{i=1}^{N}$ of the black-box model, where $\mathbf{x}_i$, $f(\mathbf{x}_i)$ respectively are the i-th input training feature vector and the corresponding black-box model's output. This is also the baseline that we use in our experiments for global explainability.

2.2 Multi-Task Learning

MTL has been extensively studied for training a model on multiple tasks at the same time. This formulation can result in both improved training efficiency and better model performance for each task [14]. The most widely used multi-task learning architecture comprises a shared-parameter model structure, where the first (representation learning) layers are shared across tasks [21] and N task-specific parallel heads are added on top, one for each task. This approach is called a hard parameter-sharing one, where essentially the parameters are divided into shared and task-specific [21]. In an alternative approach, the soft parameter-sharing one, there are no shared layers, and each task is assigned its own set of parameters, a subset of weights of the DNN corresponds to a certain task. In addition, a mechanism is employed to allow information flow among tasks (i.e., soft sharing) [21, 22]. For example, individual (task) modules could exchange information by sharing a segment of their learned latent features (also see Fig. 1). Clearly, the soft parameter-sharing approach requires more training time and computational resources due to the larger number of task-specific parameters.

However, it can prove more useful in settings where the tasks at hand are not so closely related.

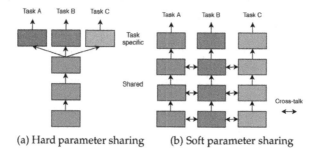

(a) Hard parameter sharing   (b) Soft parameter sharing

Fig. 1. Two widely used MTL architectures. Each box represents a layer. In (a), the hard parameter-sharing approach is depicted. Grey boxes denote shared layers while colored ones denote task-specific heads. In (b), the soft parameter-sharing approach is shown with no shared layers. Three dedicated subsets of the model's parameters correspond to the three different tasks. Figure is taken from [21] (Color figure online).

In this work, a soft sharing-based approach is utilized, where the surrogate model g does not share parameters with the black-box f in order to preserve the former model's transparency (by keeping its linear structure), and the two models exchange information only through their respective predictions which we aim to make as similar as possible. In other words, we treat the black-box model f and the surrogate model g as two separate sets of parameters, one for each task, which however communicate through the optimization of the joint training loss function which includes both f and g.

MTL has recently been used as a facilitator of XAI in specific settings. Some works propose its use in the design of explainable recommendation systems, either by producing accompanying textual explanations about the recommendation [8] or by solving joint tensor factorization objectives of *"user preference modeling for recommendation"* and *"opinionated content modeling for explanation"* that involve tensors regarding the user, the items and the users' preferences on individual items' features [37]. Another line of work, related to ours [24], considers MTL for weakly-supervised concept-based explainability. In a fraud detection setting, the authors employ *distant supervision* using domain knowledge and a rule-based database in order to acquire imprecise (noisy) concept explainability labels. They map rule descriptions present in the database that hold for specific data instances to concepts which stem from a concept taxonomy (related to the task). For instance: {Rule: Order contains risky product styles. → Concepts: Suspicious Items}.

They also explore various training strategies for jointly training ML models for two classification tasks, one about a prediction task and one based on the concept labels which is essentially a multi-label classification task.

Following a rationale similar to that of [8, 24], in this work, we jointly solve a prediction and an explainability task. However, our approach differs in the following. First, instead of solving an additional supervised learning task such as text generation [8] or classification of concept categories [24], we make use of a quantitative explainability-related metric as one of the two objectives, corresponding to the task of explainablity, and we incorporate it into the loss function. Additionally, we focus on surrogate models that produce feature importance values without the need for any additional labeled data (e.g., text reviews or interpretable concepts). Our method aims at obtaining an accurate black-box model while at the same time learning a better approximation of it through the surrogate model. On the contrary, in the baseline, currently used method, a surrogate is obtained separately, after the training of the black-box is completed. Thus, the adoption of MTL allows us to achieve this improved approximation as the parameters of the black-box model are updated through the shared optimization objective with respect to the performance of the explainability task which quantitatively measures how accurate the approximation is between the black-box and the surrogate models.

2.3   Explainability Through Regularization

Some works consider the direction of explainability-based model optimization, which we also address in this work. However, they use various types of regularizers in the optimization scheme of the black-box model. The method of Functional Transparency for Structured Data (FTSD) [33] uses a non-differentiable game-theoretic approach to regularize black-box models so that they become more locally interpretable. It focuses on graph and time-series data, and thus requires domain knowledge to define the neighborhood N_x. Self-Explaining Neural Networks (SENN) [31] generalize linear models, enriching them with complex features and maintaining interpretability via gradient regularization and an autoencoder network. The Right for the Right Reasons (RRR) method [11] and some similar works [4, 30, 36] use domain knowledge to decide on the features that are used by the underlying model through a loss regularizer. This regularization affects the model's explanations. Regularization for tree-based approximation was proposed in [12, 13]. Finally, Explanation-based Optimization (ExPO) [1] uses a model-agnostic regularizer based on XAI metrics aiming at improving the quality of local post-hoc explanations of the black-box model.

Our work is related to these methods on the aspect of explainability-based optimization. However, different from these works, we utilize MTL, which allows us to obtain a more interpretable black-box model as well as an explainer without affecting the black-box architecture. Furthermore, our approach does not require access to domain knowledge, thus removing the need for costly feature engineering and supplementary data.

3   MTL-Inspired Explainability

In this section, we present our proposed framework that leverages MTL in order to enhance explainability. Our approach addresses both a prediction and an explainability task, each characterized by a distinct loss function. We use a formulation in which these two losses are fused using a convex combination. The goal is to *jointly* train a black-box model and a surrogate model that tries to approximate the predictions of the former. We concurrently update the parameters of the two models using the combined loss objective that consists of the two loss components. The first component represents the predictive training loss of the black-box model, while the second one utilizes an explainability metric to assess the quality of the surrogate model's approximation.

3.1   Background

We consider a supervised learning setting [34], where the objective is to learn a ML model f, namely a mapping from a vector space $\mathcal{X}$ to a target space $\mathcal{Y}$, with $f \in \mathcal{F} : \mathcal{X} \rightarrow \mathcal{Y}$, where $\mathcal{F}$ is the function family, and the target variable $y \in \mathcal{Y}$ can be either a real value (in regression problems) or a categorical value (in classification problems). In ML settings, f is modeled as a DNN parameterized by a set of parameters θ (henceforth f_θ) that is trained with data $\mathcal{D} = \{\mathbf{x}_i, \mathbf{y}_i\}_{i=1}^N$ using a loss function $\mathcal{L}_{STL}$ in the single-task scenario (e.g., cross-entropy for a classification task - note that STL stands for Single-Task Loss).

In MTL, f_θ is learned with respect to multiple objectives which are most commonly combined in a weighted linear sum:

$$\mathcal{L}_{MTL} = \sum_{j=1}^m \alpha_j \mathcal{L}_{STL_j} \qquad (2)$$

where $\alpha_j \in \mathbb{R}$ is the weight for the j-th task and m is the number of distinct tasks. In addition, the model is trained using data in the form of $\mathcal{D} = \{\mathbf{x}_i, [\mathbf{y}_{i1}, \ldots, \mathbf{y}_{ij}, \ldots, \mathbf{y}_{im}]\}_{i=1}^N$ where $\mathbf{y}_{ij}$ is the target for the i-th training example and the j-th task.

In this work, we aim to generate explanations in the form of feature importances. Therefore, one of the objectives will be responsible for the explainability, while the other will be responsible for the prediction task. A system that produces such explanations is denoted as $e : \mathcal{X} \times \mathcal{F} \rightarrow \mathcal{E}$, where $\mathcal{E}$ is the family of possible explanations and is defined as $\mathcal{E} = \{g_q \in \mathcal{G} \mid g_q : \mathcal{X} \rightarrow \mathcal{Y}\}$. In this work, $\mathcal{G}$ is the set of linear functions which are suitable for producing feature-based explanations. Therefore, since the explanations will be based on the coefficients of the learned linear function, we have that $\mathcal{E} = \mathcal{G}$. Moreover, q denotes the parameter set (i.e., the coefficients) of g_q.

3.2   Explainability Metrics: Fidelity

Several metrics have been developed to objectively assess the quality of explanations according to different criteria [3]. A common choice for the evaluation of feature-based explanations is to estimate how accurately g_q approximates the behavior of f_θ for each target sample $\mathbf{x}$ [1,23]. This can be captured through the squared difference:

$$\text{PF}(f_\theta, g_q, \mathbf{x}) = (g_q(\mathbf{x}) - f_\theta(\mathbf{x}))^2 \tag{3}$$

which is referred to as Point Fidelity [6,29]. The Global Fidelity is obtained as the average of Point Fidelity values, across all N samples,

$$\text{GF}(f_\theta, g_q) = \frac{1}{N} \sum_{i=1}^{N} [\text{PF}(f_\theta, g_q, \mathbf{x}_i)] \ . \tag{4}$$

Fidelity is also used in cases that involve *locality*, where it is used to measure how good g_q is in modeling f_θ in a local neighborhood $N_\mathbf{x}$ of point $\mathbf{x}$, which consists of synthetically generated perturbations of $\mathbf{x}$'s feature values [1,23],

$$\text{NF}(f_\theta, g_q, \mathbf{x}) = \frac{1}{|N_\mathbf{x}|} \sum_{\mathbf{x}' \in N_\mathbf{x}} \left[(g_q(\mathbf{x}') - f_\theta(\mathbf{x}'))^2 \right] \tag{5}$$

and is called Neighborhood Fidelity [1]. Similar to Point Fidelity, we can average across all data points to get a 'global' Neighborhood Fidelity (GNF) measure for the entire dataset:

$$\text{GNF}(f_\theta, g_q) = \frac{1}{N} \sum_{i=1}^{N} [\text{NF}(f_\theta, g_q, \mathbf{x}_i)] \ . \tag{6}$$

3.3   Optimization Objective

As mentioned above, the intention is to compute the parameters of both the black-box and the explainable models in a way that g_q's predictions are as close as possible to f_θ's ones, while also catering for the latter model's predictive performance.

Specifically, we want to train f_θ and g_q by solving the following optimization problem:

$$(\hat{f}_\theta, \hat{g}_q) = \underset{(f_\theta, g_q) \in \mathcal{F} \times \mathcal{E}}{\arg\min} \frac{1}{N} \sum_{i=1}^{N} [\alpha \cdot \mathcal{L}_{base}(f_\theta(\mathbf{x}_i), y_i) + (1 - \alpha) \cdot PF(f_\theta, g_q, \mathbf{x}_i)] \tag{7}$$

where $\hat{f}_\theta, \hat{g}_q$ are the acquired black-box and surrogate models respectively, after the MTL training process. The function $\mathcal{L}_{base}(\cdot)$ is a prediction loss function (e.g., squared error loss for regression, cross-entropy loss for classification, etc.), PF is the point fidelity metric (3) and $\alpha \in (0,1)$ is a hyper-parameter that controls the relative weight of the two loss functions (Fig. 2). The optimization problem in (7) can be solved using a gradient-based optimization algorithm. The obtained surrogate model $\hat{g}_q$ can be used as a global explanation method regarding the obtained $\hat{f}_\theta$.

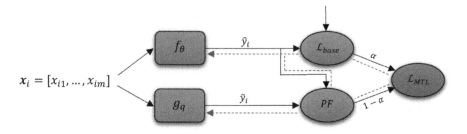

Fig. 2. The proposed MTL framework. We represent a data point as a feature vector $\mathbf{x}_i$ with f_θ and g_q being the black-box and explainable models respectively. Ground-truth response is denoted by $\mathbf{y}_i$, while the black-box's and the linear model's predictions are denoted by $\hat{\mathbf{y}}_i$ and $\tilde{\mathbf{y}}_i$ respectively. Red dashed lines denote the back-propagated gradients which allow the information exchange between the two tasks via the joint optimization of the parameter sets θ and q. (Color figure online)

4 Experimental Results

This section provides results and insights from the experiments that we carried out in order to assess the performance of the MTL-based framework and compare it with state-of-the-art, single-task (STL) approaches. We experimented with global and local explainability performance metrics. For simplicity, we considered experiments on tabular datasets in which attribution is directly awarded on the input features without further processing (e.g., formation of super-pixels for imaging data [6]).

4.1 Model Architectures and Training

For the black-box f_θ, we experimented with Multi-Layer Perceptrons (MLPs). We acquired the final architecture through a tuning process in which the number of hidden layers as well as the number of neurons per layer were selected based on the performance in a held-out validation set. We set *ReLU* [19] as the activation function of the hidden layers. For training, we used SGD with Adam [17] and starting learning rate $\eta = 10^{-3}$. Additionally, we used the *binary cross-entropy* loss for binary classification tasks, the *logarithm of the hyperbolic cosine* for regression tasks and an early stopping criterion. For the MTL paradigm, a linear model was used for g_q.

4.2 Datasets

We tested our models on a variety of regression and binary classification problems from the UCI database [20], the California Housing dataset[1] [27] and the Titanic dataset[2] [32]. Information about characteristics of these datasets can be found

---

[1] https://www.dcc.fc.up.pt/~ltorgo/Regression/cal_housing.html.
[2] https://www.openml.org/search?type=data&sort=runs&id=40945&status=active.

in Table 1. For each dataset, we standardized numerical features to have mean zero and variance one.

Table 1. Statistics of the datasets.

Dataset	# samples	# features	Type
(Red) Wine Quality [16]	1,599	12	regression
Adult [26]	48,842	14	classification
California Housing [27]	20,640	8	regression
Titanic [32]	1,309	14	classification
AutoMPG [28]	398	7	regression

4.3   Evaluation Measures

For the prediction tasks, we relied on traditional metrics such as *Accuracy* and the F_1 *score* for classification, and *Mean Squared Error (MSE)* for regression, in order to measure the predictive performance of the models. For the explainability task, we used the GF and GNF metrics, defined in (4) and (6), in the experiments regarding global and local explainability respectively.

4.4   Global Explainability Evaluation

Our method provides global explanations through the coefficients of $\hat{g}_q$ in the form of feature importance scores. We compared the models trained in the MTL fashion to the ones obtained using separate, single-task training. For the single-task scenario, we used a global surrogate model to approximate the single-task trained model *after the end of its training*. For classification tasks, the comparison in predictive performance is made based on *Accuracy*, while in regression tasks, *MSE* is used. Table 3 shows the results of the experiments on the test set of each dataset. For α, we experimented with *step* = 0.1 in the range $(0, 1)$, resulting in 9 values. Additionally, for the sake of completeness, we present prediction test scores from a linear model baseline trained with STL in Table 2 in order to justify the use of a non-linear black-box model.

The results show that training by using the MTL setting improves the GF metric. Lower GF is better as it measures the difference of predictions. The improvement holds for all values of α, but especially for the lower values of α it does so by a large margin, compared to STL. This is expected, since for low values of α, the Fidelity loss component has a large coefficient, and the optimization process is highly influenced by it. However, for low values of α, we see that the predictive performance of $\hat{f}_\theta$ decreases only by a small margin. This effect diminishes as α takes on higher values, but so does the margin of the decrease of GF, compared to the STL baseline. This is also anticipated as

Table 2. Comparison of single-task trained MLP and linear models.

Metric	Dataset	Linear	Non-linear (MLP)
ACCURACY/MSE	WINE (MSE)	0.598	0.541
	ADULT (ACC.)	0.824	0.850
	HOUSING (MSE)	0.410	0.237
	TITANIC (ACC.)	0.774	0.785
	AUTOMPG (MSE)	0.176	0.098

Table 3. Comparison of a single-task trained MLP model (STL) with MTL training for various values of α based on the corresponding metric for the predictive task performance and GF for the global explainability task. Results are shown across 5 runs.

Metrics	Datasets	STL	MTL - parameter α								
		-	0.1	0.2	0.3	0.4	0.5	0.6	0.7	0.8	0.9
ACCURACY/	WINE (MSE)	0.541	0.569	0.558	0.544	0.544	0.540	0.539	0.536	0.540	0.547
MSE	ADULT (ACC.)	0.850	0.836	0.839	0.842	0.844	0.848	0.849	0.850	0.849	0.850
	HOUSING (MSE)	0.237	0.403	0.381	0.381	0.340	0.307	0.279	0.262	0.221	0.204
	TITANIC (ACC.)	0.785	0.764	0.767	0.775	0.781	0.776	0.776	0.781	0.780	0.776
	AUTOMPG (MSE)	0.098	0.153	0.148	0.137	0.126	0.117	0.110	0.104	0.096	0.105
Global	WINE	0.034	0.001	0.003	0.005	0.009	0.014	0.025	0.036	0.056	0.086
Fidelity (GF)	ADULT	0.033	0.001	0.004	0.007	0.010	0.013	0.016	0.018	0.021	0.021
	HOUSING	0.199	0.0006	0.002	0.006	0.015	0.025	0.038	0.056	0.100	0.152
	TITANIC	0.048	0.001	0.004	0.007	0.011	0.017	0.020	0.026	0.026	0.028
	AUTOMPG	0.093	0.001	0.001	0.004	0.008	0.013	0.024	0.039	0.055	0.083

a higher weight for the predictive loss allows it to affect training to a greater extent and thus increase the predictive performance.

This accuracy-interpretability trade-off for the different values of α is depicted in Fig. 3 for each dataset. The larger sized (circled) points represent the Pareto optimal points (i.e., the optimal trade-offs between the two tasks). The behavior is consistent for all the datasets where a monotonicity of GF is observed, except for the Wine Quality dataset where the fidelity metric is slightly worse than the single-task baseline for large values of α (e.g., $0.7, 0.8, 0.9$). This could be explained by the fact that we treat the target variable of the dataset as continuous, thus solving a regression problem. It could be possible that since the linear model cannot predict the target as accurately as the neural network model, and since for large values of α the Fidelity component takes a small weight in the loss function, the result of the approximation is less accurate.

4.5 Local Explainability Evaluation

We additionally experimented with local explainability, in order to assess if the acquired black-box $\hat{f}_\theta$ could be better explained by local surrogate models. We used a post-hoc local explainability method and specifically, LIME [6]. We evaluated the explanations produced by LIME based on the acquired black-box $\hat{f}_\theta$

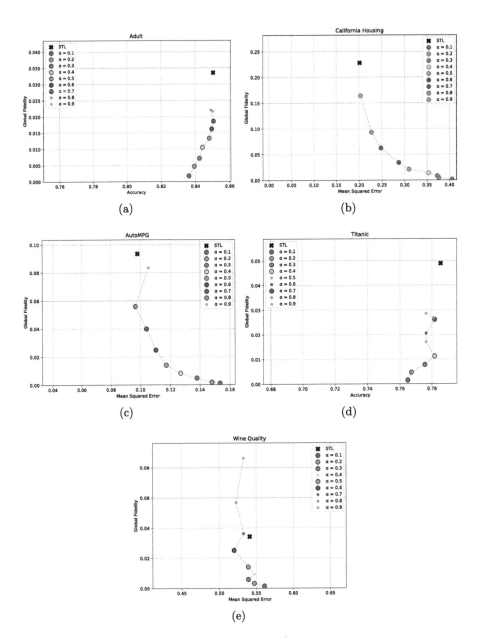

Fig. 3. Visualization of the predictivity-explainability trade-off. Prediction accuracy vs. Global Fidelity results for different values of α on different datasets. Datasets: (a) Adult, (b) California Housing (c) AutoMPG, (d) Titanic, (e) Wine Quality.

using the GNF metric. We again compared a single-task trained black-box model against black-box models trained with MTL ($\alpha \in (0, 1), step = 0.1$).

After the training procedure of $\hat{f}_\theta$ was completed, we used LIME to produce local explanations for each instance in the test set. For the GNF metric, we generated neighbors for $N_{\mathbf{x}}$ using perturbations stemmed from $\mathcal{N}(\mathbf{x}, \mu, \sigma^2)$ with $\mu = 0, \sigma^2 = 0.1$ and used 10 neighbors ($|N_{\mathbf{x}}| = 10$) for the evaluation.

Table 4 contains the results of the experiments for all datasets.

Table 4. Comparison of a single-task trained (STL) MLP model with MTL training for various values of α based on the corresponding metric for the predictive task performance and GNF for the local explainability task. Because calculation of GNF is slow due to a separate training of a surrogate model for each instance, results are shown for a single run. In addition, for the ADULT and HOUSING datasets, 500 test points were used.

Metrics	Datasets	STL	MTL - parameter α								
		-	0.1	0.2	0.3	0.4	0.5	0.6	0.7	0.8	0.9
ACCURACY/ MSE	WINE (MSE)	0.541	0.584	0.557	0.545	0.537	0.551	0.529	0.518	0.509	0.540
	ADULT (ACC.)	0.850	0.834	0.838	0.842	0.843	0.845	0.850	0.852	0.851	0.852
	HOUSING (MSE)	0.237	0.403	0.391	0.355	0.334	0.348	0.264	0.251	0.234	0.195
	TITANIC (ACC.)	0.785	0.778	0.774	0.774	0.770	0.774	0.767	0.782	0.774	0.771
	AUTOMPG (MSE)	0.098	0.156	0.141	0.135	0.123	0.118	0.113	0.103	0.104	0.112
Global Neighborhood Fidelity (GNF)	WINE	0.019	0.001	0.002	0.003	0.008	0.008	0.014	0.031	0.018	0.029
	ADULT	0.084	0.048	0.047	0.057	0.061	0.067	0.078	0.074	0.051	0.083
	HOUSING	1.260	0.003	0.052	0.085	0.134	0.369	0.230	0.937	0.242	0.616
	TITANIC	0.131	0.048	0.120	0.140	0.164	0.119	0.009	0.153	0.225	0.105
	AUTOMPG	0.111	0.027	0.039	0.016	0.022	0.035	0.033	0.041	0.047	0.126

Results show that GNF is also improved when MTL is employed. This shows that the acquired black-box model $\hat{f}_\theta$ which was trained with regard to having similar predictions to those of a linear model $\hat{g}_q$ can also be more accurately approximated by *local* linear explanations. However, local explainability results seems to be independent regarding the value of α which could be explained by the fact that the objective (7) does not involve a local explainability optimization component. A possible solution would be the incorporation of a component similar to [1] that will also account for local explainability performance during the training process.

4.6   Lessons Learned from the Experiments

Overall, our results showcase that using the proposed MTL training procedure allows the surrogate linear model $\hat{g}_q$ to better approximate the black-box model $\hat{f}_\theta$, compared to the standard baseline of training them sequentially and separately. We also appose Table 5 which contains the R^2 score between the predictions of $\hat{f}_\theta$ and $\hat{g}_q$ in the single-task and multi-task settings on the ADULT dataset.

Table 5. R^2 score between the predictions of the black-box and the surrogate models on ADULT, in single-task and multi-task settings.

Approach	STL	$\alpha = 0.1$	$\alpha = 0.2$	$\alpha = 0.3$	$\alpha = 0.4$	$\alpha = 0.5$	$\alpha = 0.6$	$\alpha = 0.7$	$\alpha = 0.8$	$\alpha = 0.9$
R^2	0.57	0.97	0.93	0.89	0.85	0.83	0.78	0.77	0.72	0.73

The following key points can be observed from our experiments:

- The produced global and local explanations are more accurate than the explanations produced by the single-task trained black-box model. This means that $\hat{f}_\theta$ can be more accurately approximated even from local explainability methods compared to a black-box trained with STL.
- For global explainability, we observe a high improvement in the Global Fidelity metric for low values of α and a slight decrease in the predictive performance of $\hat{f}_\theta$, compared to the baseline of the single-task training. The decrease diminishes as α gets larger and *even disappears on certain datasets*.
- For local explainability, we also observe an improvement on the Fidelity of the local explanations produced by LIME [6], compared to the Fidelity of the same explanations when the black-box neural network is trained in a traditional single-task fashion, but the improvement seems to be independent of the value of α. This could be explained by the fact that the optimization objective manages to make $\hat{f}_\theta$ more 'interpretable' but does not account for local explainability performance per se.

5 Conclusions

In this work, we propose and evaluate a novel Multi-Task Learning framework in which we train a black-box neural network model together with a surrogate linear model in order to obtain Feature Attribution explanations. We use a convex combination of two loss components. The first component assesses the black-box's predictive performance in terms of a training loss function, while the second one evaluates the surrogate's approximation quality through the fidelity metric. We demonstrate that this paradigm improves the quality of the surrogate model's approximation to the black-box, thus resulting in more accurate (fidelity-wise) global explanations on unseen test data compared to the standard used method, which is to train the surrogate model separately from, rather than concurrently with the black-box one. Finally, we also showcase the effectiveness of the framework on a local explainability setting where again, more accurate (fidelity-wise) local explanations are produced.

Future work could generalize the current setting through more explainability metrics such as faithfulness, complexity [9] and stability [1] to the training procedure. We could also consider other forms of optimization like constrained optimization, namely minimize the prediction accuracy subject to a constraint on an explainability metric. The objective would be to optimize the predictive training loss while enforcing a constraint on the value taken by the fidelity metric in order to keep it below a desired threshold.

Lastly, an area we would like to study is related to user-perception based explainability metrics. In the current work, we use a quantitative metric for explainability, however, the real perceived experience on the end-user is not clear. As explainability of ML models touches upon the end-users more than any other ML model property, the grand objective would be to translate metrics such as fidelity to new ones that are closer to the user perception of what explainability means to them and how it is perceived, and at the same time continue to follow a systematic optimization approach, similar to what we describe in this paper. This of course necessitates that the new metrics are differentiable or can be approximated by differentiable functions, so that they can be incorporated in a Deep Learning-based framework. Learning this mapping from the set of quantitative explainability metrics such as fidelity, faithfulness, complexity, to perceived user experience is a challenging goal which calls for ML methods on crowdsourced datasets collected from human feedback that we intend to pursue in the future.

Acknowledgements. This work was supported by the CHIST-ERA grant CHIST-ERA-18-SDCDN-004 (project LeadingEdge, grant number T11EPA4- 00056) through the General Secretariat for Research and Innovation (GSRI). It was also supported by the Horizon Europe PRE-ACT project, supported by the European Commission through the Horizon Europe Program (Grant Agreement number 101057746), by the Swiss State Secretariat for Education, Research and Innovation (SERI) under contract number 22 00058, and by the UK government (Innovate UK application number 10061955).

References

1. Plumb, G., Al-Shedivat, M., Cabrera, Á. A., Perer, A., Xing, E., Talwalkar, A.: Regularizing black-box models for improved interpretability. Adv. Neural Inf. Process. Syst. **33**, 10526–10536 (2020). Curran Associates Inc.
2. Shrikumar, A., Greenside, P., Kundaje, A.: Learning important features through propagating activation differences. In: Proceedings of the 34th International Conference on Machine Learning (ICML 2017), vol. 70, pp. 3145–3153 (2017)
3. Zhou, J., Gandomi, A.H., Chen, F., Holzinger, A.: Evaluating the quality of machine learning explanations: a survey on methods and metrics. Electronics **10**(5) (2021)
4. Rieger, L., Singh, C., Murdoch, W., Yu, B.: Interpretations are useful: penalizing explanations to align neural networks with prior knowledge. In: Proceedings of the 37th International Conference on Machine Learning, volume 119 of Proceedings of Machine Learning Research, pp. 8116–8126 (2020)
5. Molnar, C.: Interpretable Machine Learning, 2nd edn. (2022)
6. Ribeiro, M.T., Singh, S., Guestrin, C.: Why should i trust you?: explaining the predictions of any classifier. In: Proceedings of the 22nd ACM SIGKDD International Conference on Knowledge Discovery and Data Mining, San Francisco, 13–17 August 2016, pp. 1135–1144 (2016)

7. Wachter, S., Mittelstadt, B., Russell, C.: Counterfactual explanations without opening the black box: automated decisions and the GDPR. Harvard J. Law Technol. **2**(31), 841–887 (2018)
8. Chen, Z., et al.: Co-attentive multi-task learning for explainable recommendation. In: Proceedings of the Twenty-Eighth International Joint Conference on Artificial Intelligence (IJCAI 2019), pp. 2137–2143. International Joint Conferences on Artificial Intelligence Organization (2019)
9. Bhatt, U., Weller, A., Moura, J.M.F.: Evaluating and aggregating feature-based model explanations. In: Proceedings of the Twenty-Ninth International Joint Conference on Artificial Intelligence (IJCAI 2020) (2020)
10. Burkart, N., Huber, M.F.: A survey on the explainability of supervised machine learning. J. Artif. Int. Res. **70**, 245–317 (2021)
11. Ross, A.S., Hughes, M.C., Doshi-Velez, F.: Right for the right reasons: training differentiable models by constraining their explanations. In: Proceedings of the Twenty-Sixth International Joint Conference on Artificial Intelligence (IJCAI 2017), Melbourne, pp. 2662–2670 (2017)
12. Wu, M., Hughes, M.C., Parbhoo, S., Zazzi, M., Roth, V., Doshi-Velez, F.: Beyond sparsity: tree regularization of deep models for interpretability. In: Proceedings of the Thirty-Second AAAI Conference on Artificial Intelligence and Thirtieth Innovative Applications of Artificial Intelligence Conference and Eighth AAAI Symposium on Educational Advances in Artificial Intelligence, AAAI 2018/IAAI 2018/EAAI 2018 (2018)
13. Wu, M., Parbhoo, S., Hughes, M., Kindle, R., Celi, L., Zazzi, M., Roth, V., Doshi-Velez, F.: Regional tree regularization for interpretability in deep neural networks. Proc. AAAI Conf. Artif. Intell. **34**(04), 6413–6421 (2020)
14. Ma, J., Zhao, Z., Yi, X., Chen, J., Hong, L., Chi, E.H.: Modeling task relationships in multi-task learning with multi-gate mixture-of-experts. In: Proceedings of the 24th ACM SIGKDD International Conference on Knowledge Discovery and Data Mining (KDD 2018), 19–23 August 2018, pp. 1930–1939. ACM, London (2018)
15. Belle, V.I., Papantonis, I.: Principles and practice of explainable machine learning. Front. Big Data **4** (2021)
16. Cortez, P., Cerdeira, A., Almeida, F., Matos, T., Reis, J.: Wine Quality. UCI Machine Learning Repository (2009)
17. Kingma, D.P., Ba, J.: Adam: a method for stochastic optimization. In: 3rd International Conference on Learning Representations (ICLR 2015), San Diego, 7–9 May 2015, Conference Track Proceedings (2015)
18. Rumelhart, D., Hinton, G.E., Williams, R.J.: Learning representations by back-propagating errors. Nature **323**, 533–536 (1986)
19. Fukushima, K.: Visual feature extraction by a multilayered network of analog threshold elements. IEEE Trans. Syst. Sci. Cybernet. **5**(4), 322–333 (1969)
20. Kelly, M., Longjohn, R., Nottingham, K.: The UCI Machine Learning Repository. https://archive.ics.uci.edu. Accessed June 2023
21. Vandenhende, S., et al.: Multi-task learning for dense prediction tasks: a survey. IEEE Trans. Pattern Anal. Mach. Intell. **44**(07), 3614–3633 (2022)
22. Misra, I., Shrivastava A., Gupta, A., Hebert, M.: Cross-stitch networks for multi-task learning. In: Proceedings of the IEEE Conference on Computer Vision and Pattern Recognition (CVPR) (2016)
23. Amparore, E.G., Perotti, A., Bajardi, P.: To trust or not to trust an explanation: using LEAF to evaluate local linear XAI methods. PeerJ Comput. Sci. **7**, e479 (2021)

24. Belém, C., Balayan, V., Saleiro, P., Bizarro, P.: Weakly supervised multi-task learning for concept-based explainability. In: Proceedings of the 1st Workshop on Weakly Supervised Learning (WeaSuL) - 38th International Conference on Machine Learning (ICML), Online (2021)
25. Sundararajan, M., Taly, A., Yan, Q.: Axiomatic attribution for deep networks. In: Proceedings of the 34th International Conference on Machine Learning (ICML 2017), vol. 70, pp. 3319–3328 (2017)
26. Becker, B., Kohavi, R.: Adult. UCI Machine Learning Repository (1996)
27. Pace, K., Barry, R.: Sparse spatial autoregressions. Statist. Prob. Lett. **33**(3), 291–297 (1997)
28. Quinlan, R.: Auto MPG. UCI Machine Learning Repository (1993)
29. Lundberg, S., Lee, S.: A unified approach to interpreting model predictions. Adv. Neural Inf. Process. Syst. **30**, 4765–4774 (2017)
30. Weinberger, E., Janizek, J., Lee, S.: Learning deep attribution priors based on prior knowledge. Adv. Neural Inf. Process. Syst. **33**, 14034–14045 (2020)
31. Alvarez-Melis, D., Jaakkola, T.: Towards robust interpretability with self-explaining neural networks. Adv. Neural Inf. Process. Syst. **31** (2018)
32. Harrell Jr., F.E., Cason, T.: Titanic dataset. https://www.openml.org/d/40945 (2017)
33. Lee, G., Jin, W., Alvarez-Melis, D., Jaakkola, T.: Functional transparency for structured data: a game-theoretic approach. In: Proceedings of the 36th International Conference on Machine Learning, Volume 97 of Proceedings of Machine Learning Research, pp. 3723–3733 (2019)
34. Mitchell, T.N.: Machine Learning, 1st edn. McGraw-Hill Inc., USA (1997)
35. Štrumbelj, E., Kononenko, I.: Explaining prediction models and individual predictions with feature contributions. Knowl. Inf. Syst. **41**(3), 647–665 (2014)
36. Du, M., Liu, N., Yang, F., Hu, X.: Learning credible deep neural networks with rationale regularization. In: 2019 IEEE International Conference on Data Mining (ICDM), Los Alamitos, pp. 150–159 (2019)
37. Wang, N., Wang, H., Jia, Y., Yin, Y.: Explainable recommendation via multi-task learning in opinionated text data. In: 41st International ACM SIGIR Conference on Research and Development in Information Retrieval, pp. 165–174. Association for Computing Machinery (2018)

Optimizing Decision Trees for Enhanced Human Comprehension

Ruth Cohen Arbiv[1], Laurence Lovat[2], Avi Rosenfeld[3(✉)], and David Sarne[1]

[1] Department of Computer Science, Bar Ilan University, Ramat Gan, Israel
[2] University of College London, London, UK
[3] Department of Computer Science, Jerusalem College of Technology, 91160 Jerusalem, Israel
rosenfa@jct.ac.il

Abstract. This paper studies a novel approach for training people to perform complex classification tasks using decision trees. The main objective of this study is to identify the most effective subset of rules for instructing users on how to excel in classification tasks themselves. The paper addresses the challenge of striking a balance between maximizing knowledge by incorporating numerous rules and the need to limit rules to prevent cognitive overload. To investigate this matter, a series of experiments were conducted, training users using decision trees to identify cases where cancer is suspected, and further testing is required. Notably, the study revealed a correlation between the decision tree characteristics and users' comprehension levels. Building on these experimental outcomes, a machine learning model was developed to predict users' comprehension levels based on different decision trees, thereby facilitating the selection of the most appropriate tree. To further assess the machine learning model's performance, additional experiments were carried out using an alternative dataset focused on Crohn's disease. The results demonstrated a significant enhancement in user understanding and classification performance. These findings emphasize the potential to improve human understanding and decision rule explainability by effectively modeling users' comprehension.

Keywords: Explainable Artificial Intelligence · Adaptive User Modeling · Medical Diagnoses

1 Introduction

As human beings, we are inherently inclined to make classifications in our daily lives, as we encounter a multitude of situations where accurate categorization is crucial [1]. Consider for instance the act of distinguishing between safe and potentially harmful technology, such as determining whether a link is safe to click. Similarly, the ability to discern fraudulent financial behavior is of paramount importance to safeguard our personal information and assets. In the context of medical diagnosis, correctly classifying various diseases or conditions based

S. Nowaczyk et al. (Eds.): ECAI 2023 Workshops, CCIS 1947, pp. 366–381, 2024.
https://doi.org/10.1007/978-3-031-50396-2_21

on symptoms, test results, and patient information is critical for appropriate treatment and care. Furthermore, even during a seemingly simple field trip, the identification of poisonous plants becomes essential for ensuring personal safety and well-being.

Undoubtedly, while expert guidance or accessing relevant resources on the internet can aid in making accurate classifications for most tasks, there are numerous situations where the ability to make prompt decisions or the disruption caused by seeking advice become a significant factor. Moreover, when faced with repetitive classification tasks, developing sufficient competency to make accurate judgments proves far more efficient than repeatedly seeking guidance. By acquiring the skill to classify different events effectively, individuals can enhance their autonomy, streamline decision-making processes, and minimize reliance on external sources for every instance of classification.

This paper aims to provide an effective method for teaching and training people in classification tasks in which they have no prior experience, focusing primarily in medical classification and diagnosis. In medical domains there is much merit in studying decision models, especially for purposes of training and evaluating the competence of interns. Here, rules produced through Machine Learning (potentially based on expert opinions) can substantially shortened the intern's learning curve, resulting in a relatively accurate diagnosis which improves the detection rates of diseases such as cancer. This has been successfully demonstrated by Sehgal et al. [15] who used decision trees for training medical interns in the diagnosis of esophageal dysplasia by performing endoscopy. This approach has been successfully used also in non-medical domains, e.g., for the purpose of training helicopter pilots in cockpit operation [10].

Our motivation is to strike a balance between incorporating more rules to enhance user knowledge and on the other hand to limiting these rules to prevent overwhelming them. This balance is crucial not only for learning new tasks but also for the field of explainable artificial intelligence (XAI). Previous studies have suggested that the number of rules a system generates can serve as an effective metric for objectively measuring the effectiveness of XAI [12]. However, the question of how many rules can be learned and how to optimize this balance with performance has remained unanswered. We present a machine learning approach to learn this value.

There are various machine learning methods that can be used for generating the classification guidelines to train people. Some models, such as decision trees, provide explicit classification rules [6]. Others, like Random Forest, Support Vector Machines (SVM), Naive Bayes classifiers and Neural Networks do not directly provide explicit decision rules, however it is possible to derive decision rules based on the output [14]. Taking SVM as an example, one can gain insights into the important features and their contributions to the classification decision by analyzing the support vectors and their associated weights. Similarly, decision rules can be derived based on the relationships between the features as reflected by the decision boundary and its representation as a hyperplane in the feature space. Additionally, techniques like feature importance or feature ranking can be applied to guide the formulation of decision rules by considering the relative importance and thresholds associated with different features.

In this paper we produce decision rules using decision trees due to their numerous advantages which make this method highly popular in XAI-based systems. Decision trees generate rules in a clear and interpretable format, i.e., can be easily understood and followed by humans [2,4–6,9,14]. This transparency makes decision trees particularly useful when the interpretability of the classification rules is important, such as in domains where explanations are required or legal and ethical considerations come into play. Furthermore, decision trees naturally form a hierarchy of rules, with higher-level rules capturing broader patterns and lower-level rules handling more specific conditions [5]. This hierarchical structure allows decision trees to effectively handle complex classification tasks by breaking them down into a series of simpler decision rules. Decision trees can provide insights into the importance of different features in the classification process, which aids in understanding the underlying factors driving the classification decisions and can be valuable for the training process. Finally, decision trees are robust to noise and outliers in the data, can handle missing values by utilizing surrogate splits and are less sensitive to irrelevant features.

The main contribution of this paper is the learning process presented in Sect. 3. Here we present a task-independent framework for identifying which decision tree rules should be presented to trainees as part of the training process, using machine learning. In Sect. 4 we present details for how this process was successful in learning what rules were necessary to teach for a cancer prediction task and also show how the same learning process can be validated on a second medical dataset– Crohn's prediction. In Sect. 5 we present results detailing the effectiveness of this approach, demonstrating how XAI can be created based on the outputted rules. Section 6 concludes.

2   Related Work

While this paper focuses on the set of rules that a user should be presented for a learning task, previous works have primarily focused more on the learning process itself: what the learning order should look like, whether the learning process should be based on examples [18], whether the learning should be visual or verbal. Instead, we focus on what explanation should be given, emphasizing finding the size and content that will be effective for the person's learning.

Our problem is directly connected to Explainable artificial intelligence (XAI) - to date, XAI is a relatively young field and some confusion exists about terminology. The terms explainability and interpretability are often used interchangeably with the machine learning community often focusing on the system's machine learning logic while the human-agent communities often focusing on how understandable the system's logic is to the intended user [4,14,17]. The opposite of explainable or interpretable systems are "opaque" or "black box" systems that do not provide insight into their decisions and it is not possible to understand how the inputs led to the system's decision [3]. Following previous definitions, [14] we refer to **Explicitness** as the extent to which the system's logic is understandable to the intended user, **Faithfulness** as the extent to which the explanation's logic is similar to the actual logic being used, and **Transparency** as the case for which the explanation is both explicit and faithful. We chose to present the system's logic using a decision tree because it is transparent - that is, both explicit and faithful, making it the most understandable for the human user to learn and apply [2, 4, 11].

The hierarchical structure inherent in decision trees yields itself to understanding which attributes are most important, of second-most importance, etc. [11]. Furthermore, assuming the size of the tree is relatively small due to Occam's Razor [16], the if-then rules that can be derived directly from decision trees are both particularly explicit and faithful [11]. However, in practice not all decision trees are easily understood. Large decision trees with hundreds of nodes and leaves are often more accurate than smaller ones, despite the assumption inherent within Occam's Razor [7]. Such trees are less explicit, especially if they contain many attributes and/or multiple instances of nodes using the same attribute for different conditions. As we now describe the goal of our paper is to find the optimal subset of decision tree rules to maximize a person's ability to learn and apply those rules, thus demonstrating its explainability.

3 Problem Statement and Proposed Solution

We consider a model for a problem where a continuous stream of instances from the same application domain needs to be classified according to a predefined set of k target class values. The classification is being performed by an untrained person (i.e., with no preliminary knowledge related to classification rules). Training is based on a decision tree - the human learner is presented with a decision tree that captures some of the classification rules and the system iterates over several examples (paths) and the resulting classification for each. The underlying decision tree can either be picked from a set of given trees (and their accuracy measures) or produced based on a given set of annotated (i.e., correctly classified) instances. The goal of this research is thus to come up with an effective method for picking the tree based on which training will take place in a way that maximizes the percentage of correct classification made by the human classifier for their task.

Figure 1 depicts the logical flow of the proposed solution. The process can be initiated either based on a set of trees provided by a domain expert or based on a labeled database (i.e., with cases that need to be classified and their correct classification). In the latter case, we produce the set of potential trees using standard libraries such as Sklearn by controlling parameters such as min_samples_leaf or max_depth of the tree. We emphasize that with both methods we only need a small initial set of decision trees, as we can substantially augment that set by including different variants of each tree, resulting from the removal of some of its sub-trees. For each tree, we predict the percentage of cases the user will be able to correctly classify with respect to the classification rules defined by that tree.

This can be done either by developing the prediction model based on trees (i.e., provide a training set in the form of trees used and the percentage of correct classifications obtained for each tree) or based on paths (provide a training set in which each record represents a path within a tree and whether or not the user provided the correct classification) and aggregating according[1]

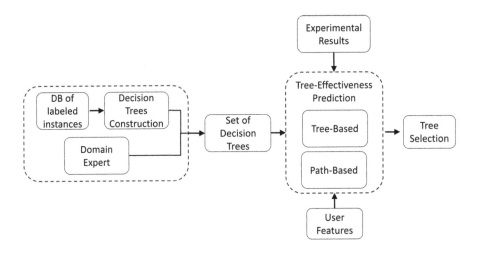

Fig. 1. The proposed solution architecture.

We incorporate features pertaining to the specific user that needs to be trained, such as age, gender and education in both methods. To create the prediction model, we must conduct some initial experiment in which different users are trained with different trees to record the percentage of correct classifications they achieve. Once the prediction models are established, we can use them as-is in different domains, without the overhead of running new experiments for collecting the training data. It is important to note that using pre-established models in new domains may lead to a slight decrease in accuracy compared to developing fresh models from scratch because there's no assurance that the distribution of paths or cases in the new domain matches the one used for training in the original domain. Nevertheless, our experimental evaluation demonstrates impressive performance, particularly when the prediction is based on tree paths.

Once we have gained the ability to predict the ability of the user to replicate the logic encapsulated in a given tree, we can calculate her predicted performance in classifying the stream of instances that she is about to encounter next. The calculation takes into account the fact that even when correctly classifying according to the learned tree, a misclassification is still possible as the tree

---

[1] We do not include the underlying distribution of paths while doing the training, as this is already implicitly encapsulated in the label provided to each record in the training set (e.g., when doing this based on paths we know that this path was used for training according to its frequency in the population).

its does not have perfect, 100%, accuracy. We can quantify this expected mis-classification by noting the original tree's accuracy error. When using a prediction model based on trees, the user's expected absolute performance (i.e., with respect to the ground truth) when using a tree T_i with accuracy $accuracy(T_i)$ and predicted recollection $P_m(T_i)$ which is the prediction of how well the user will remember the tree, denoted $P_a(T_i)$, is thus:

$$P_a(T_i) = accuracy(T_i) \cdot P_m(T_i) + \frac{(1 - accuracy(T_i)) \cdot (1 - P_m(T_i))}{k - 1} \quad (1)$$

where the first product relates to the case of where the model's rule is correct and the user manages to successfully follow it and the second relates to the case where the model's rule is incorrect however the user did not follow that rule and picked the correct classification. The probability of the latter event is $1/(k - 1)$ (assuming the user randomly picks one of the remaining $k - 1$ classification values). When using a prediction model based on paths, we rely on the accuracy of each path p_j which represents the portion of cases correctly classified by the rule captured by that path. The user's expected absolute performance of using a tree T_i is given by:

$$P_a(T_i) = \sum_{p_j \in T_i} f(p_j) \left(accuracy(p_j) \cdot P_m(p_j) + \frac{(1 - accuracy(p_j)) \cdot (1 - P_m(p_j))}{k - 1} \right)$$

$$(2)$$

where $f(p_j)$ is the portion of cases that match the decision rule represented by path p_j. The selected tree is thus the one associated with the maximum expected absolute performance, formally: $\arg\max_{T_i} P_a(T_i)$.

The specific steps of this process were as follows:

1. **Experimental Framework:** Using the cancer dataset, we generated many decision trees. We then constructed an initial experiment in which we attempted to teach human participants without cancer diagnostic background the correct diagnosis for the database instances. The results of the experiment were saved in the learning repository.

2. **Machine Learning:** We then applied different machine learning (ML) algorithms to the repository to create a general predictive model P_m as to which decision trees are worth presenting in future cases. The prediction model was based on learning the expected probability a person would remember a given tree and correctly learning a set of tree rules against the expected value (utility) for the prediction value of that tree. We successfully modeled this task with machine learning for regression (e.g. the expected utility value) and classification (e.g. the likelihood the person would remember a given tree).

3. **Independent Validation:** To confirm the result of these models, we applied the prediction models learning from the cancer database to another medical disease– Crohn's. As we present in the results section, this model was successful here as well.

Each of these steps are further detailed in Subsect. 4.1, 4.2, 4.3 respectively.

4   Experimental Setup and Methods

4.1   Experiment Research Framework

In order to develop methods and algorithms to improve XAI within Human-Agent Learning Systems, we built an application called "Learn how to diagnose cancer" using an ASP.NET interactive web-based application for conducting experiments with human participants. Data was collected through the use of Amazon Mechanical Turk (AMT, MTurk). AMT has proven to be a well-established method for data collection in tasks which require human intelligence [8]. We recruited 200 participants from the United States equally divided between 5 decision trees that we generated. The average participant age was 40.29 (ranging between 18–76), of which 50% were men and 50% were women. Each of the five decision tree models were built from oncological data from patients that had or did have suspected esophageal cancer. Our decision tree model was based on important features for the patient's final diagnosis of cancer/not cancer. The features were selected according to previous work done [13] which investigated what important features can be extracted to diagnose cancer.

Five different decision trees were built in order of most simple to most complex. The more complex models had higher accuracy, but also more rules (symptoms/characteristics) which was reflected in the size of the tree. We took care to not include overfitted trees to isolate the relationship between increased rules and a person's ability to perform better. Two examples of these decision trees are presented in Fig. 2. The complete list of trees used, as well as their differentiating characteristics is given in Sect. 4.2.

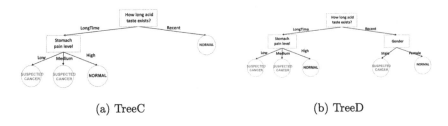

(a) TreeC   (b) TreeD

Fig. 2. Two examples of learning trees for diagnosing suspected cancer given to learning in our experiment

The experiment consisted of a learning phase and test phase. In the learning phase, participants were shown patient data along with a system-generated diagnosis, which included a decision tree explaining the decision-making process. Each participant encountered 12 different cases, each with varying tree sizes. The participant's objective was to "learn" to diagnose cancer based on the rules he was taught. After completing the learning phase, participants moved on to the test phase, where they were presented with 12 new real-world patient cases. They were then asked to make their own diagnoses based on what they had learned during the learning phase from the provided explanations. The cases presented to participants in both the learning and test phases were selected based on the distribution of cases in the database. Additionally, the labeling of cases was designed so that each tree represented the percentage of successful classifications for the model accurately. To assess the participants' understanding, the researchers measured the percentage of cases that each participant correctly labeled during the test phase.

4.2 Machine Learning-Prediction Model

Based on the results of this experiment, we created repository that would be used for machine learning to identify which trees are generally best to present to future users to maximizes their performance in new classification tasks. We recorded three types data to build the repository for the machine learning model – specific information about the structure of the decision tree, user demographic information, and user performance information. Tree structure information included properties such as the number of nodes, depth, and theoretical accuracy of the tree. User demographic information included peoples' gender, age, education level, and medical knowledge. User performance information was related to logged information about their task progress, such as the amount of time they spent for each question in the learning and testing phases. Twelve questions were presented in both the learning and testing phases. The participant's response was stored in the learning repository for both the **correct_model** value which is the true/false value indicating whether the participant's classification answer is correct compared to the model's classification answer, and the **correct_truth** value which is the true/false value indicating whether the participant's classification answer is correct compared to the true label of the case, e.g. the ground truth. It should be noted that at times the participant's answer was wrong according to what the presented model attempted to teach (**correct_model**) but actually correct according to the objective labelled data (correct_truth). As such, these two variables help catch this nuanced difference. Based on the **correct_truth** and (**correct_model**) values, we created two different accuracy metrics used for building the repository for effectively decision the best tree size required for a given user, **Accuracy_model** and **Accuracy_truth**. **Accuracy_model** represents the percent of the 12 questions answered correctly. In other words, the percentage of the tree a person will remember through the learning process. This can numerically be represented as:

$$Accuracy\_model = \sum_{i=1}^{N} \frac{correct\_model}{N} * 100 \qquad (3)$$

Accuracy_truth measures the success of the participant's diagnosis in relation to ground truth based on the labeled data. It is an indication of the level of his success in classifying instances in relation to the real world. It can be numerically represented as:

$$Accuracy\_truth = \sum_{i=1}^{N} \frac{correct\_truth}{N} * 100 \tag{4}$$

For example, assume a user received a decision tree with an accuracy level of 80%, and successfully memorized the entire model and correctly classifying all presented cases according to the learned model. This user would receive a score of 100% according to the first metric, and a score of 80% according to the second metric, as the model itself had an error rate of 20%. The prediction model was based on learning the expected probability a person would remember a given tree and correctly learning a set of tree rules against the expected value (utility) for the prediction value of that tree. We successfully modeled this task with machine learning for regression (e.g. the expected utility value) and classification (e.g. the likelihood the person would remember a given tree).

Based on these metrics collected from the experiment and saved in the repository, we built the $P_m(T_i)$ learning model. As we mentioned earlier, we examined two learning methods: tree-based learning and path-based learning. In the tree-based learning method we examined the Linear Regression, Stacking and Random Forest algorithms, denoting them as: $P_{m_{Linear regression(T_i)}}$, $P_{m_{Stacking(T_i)}}$ and $P_{m_{Random Forest(T_i)}}$ respectively. These algorithms were utilized to effectively tackle the regression problem of predicting the score of the entire tree, e.g. the results of "Accuracy_model," for the entire tree. The path-based prediction model used logistic regression, denoted as $P_{m_{Logistic regression(T_i)}}$, to use each user decision labeled with a binary classification, "correct_model." By analyzing the experiment results, the algorithm measures and predicts the probability that a user will recall a specific path. While the tree-based learning had a numeric target (e.g. the percentage of the tree learned), the path-based repository used a binary classification target variable to represent if the participant succeed in remembering the branch or not.

An advantage of path-based learning over tree-based learning is the ability to utilize a much larger repository of data. As each participant answered 12 questions, we now have 12 times more data available for learning compared to the tree-based repository. Additionally, the path-based repository includes branch-specific information such as the number of nodes in the branch and its size relative to the tree. While the tree-based learning had a numeric target (e.g., the percentage of the tree learned), the path-based repository employed a binary classification target variable to indicate whether the participant successfully remembered the branch or not.

4.3   Independent Validation

In order to properly test the system's performance, we conducted another experiment in which we built decision trees based on a Crohn's dataset independent of the cancer dataset used in the previous experiment. The experiment protocol

was similar to the first experiment except that here we created 4 decision trees
of different sizes as we eliminated validating the most complicated tree as it was
overfitted. We again recruited groups of 40 participants which were each given
a different sized trees for a total of another 160 participants in this experiment.
Here too, the experiment was carried out in two phases: The training phase and
the testing phase, and scores were given to each participant. We present two
generated trees for the validation experiment in Fig. 3.

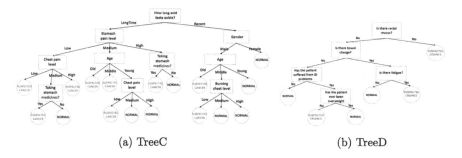

(a) TreeC   (b) TreeD

Fig. 3. Two examples of learning trees for diagnosing suspected cancer-on left side and
Crohn's disease given to learning in our experiment

5   Results and Analysis

In this section we detail the results from the experiment and machine learning in
this study, including what performance metrics were used to measure the user's
ability to learn the classification rules. We then present the results from the
validation study from Crohn's disease to highlight the generality of this work.

5.1   Experiment Results

Table 1. Table showing that were generated for diagnosis of suspected Esophageal
Cancer in order of the most simple (TreeA) to most complex (TreeE) tree.

	TreeA	TreeB	TreeC	TreeD	TreeE
SIZE (Number of nodes = rules):	3	5	6	8	26
ACCURACY:	60%	77%	75%	80%	89%
Accuracy_model:	90.10	83.72	83.10	74.81	57.31
Accuracy_truth:	55.18	56.58	62.96	68.41	53.40

As expected, we found that the more complex decision trees built for cancer
prediction were harder for people to remember, thus impacting their ability to

remember and apply the model. This in turn negatively impacted their ability to successfully classifying new cases in the real world. Our result analysis relies on the two metrics Accuracy_model and Accuracy_truth mentioned in the previous section. As previously mentioned, we generated 5 trees with different sizes with different levels of accuracy, shown in Table 1. Note the values for these trees relative to the model (Accuracy_model) and to the truth (Accuracy_truth). In the following figure we present the result of the two metrics explained in Sect. 4.2.

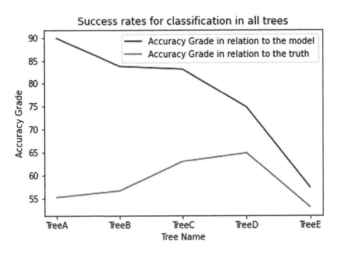

Fig. 4. The success rates of each group to classify correctly, in relation to the model (blue) and in relation to the truth (red). (Color figure online)

Figure 4 shows the success rates of each group to correctly classify new instances. The X-axis represents the tree name and Y-axis represents the accuracy grade per each group of participants. It can be seen that the group that received the small tree - TreeA (with 2 nodes-size 2), was able to remember the model and classify according to this model 90.1% of the time, but its success in classifying cases in the real world is only 55.18% because of the low accuracy of that tree. The group that received the medium tree, TreeD (size 8), was able to remember and apply the model 74.81% of the time and their real-world case classification increased significantly to 68.41%. As expected, the group that received the big tree, TreeE (size 26), was able to remember and apply the model only 57.31% of the time, and their ability to classify cases in the real world was also low at 53.04%.

5.2   Machine Learning Results

Recall that P_m is a prediction model for the percentage of the tree a human person will remember. We took two learning approaches to learn this value: a **prediction model based on full tree learning** and a **prediction model based on tree path learning**.

The prediction model based on full tree learning- gives a numeric prediction for the percentage of the tree the user is predicted to remember. To solve this regression problem, we tested different ML models, such as: Linear regression, Random Forest and Stacking. We found that the simple regression model:

$$P\_m\_Simple\_Linear\ Regression(T\_i) = -0.0124 * Number\_of\_nodes + 0.877$$

had a **Correlation coefficient** $= 0.46$, and **Mean absolute error** $= 0.164$.

While this simple model quantified the relationship between tree complexity and predicted success, we studied what additional variables collected from learning repository could improve the results. After studying different ML algorithms and testing them with cross-validation, we found that the relationship between the variables: Gender, Learning_Phase_Time_Minutes, Number_of_nodes, Tree_Depth and the variable we wanted to predict, Accuracy_model was slightly better with a **Correlation coefficient** $= 0.48$, and **Mean absolute error** $= 0.161$. This model was:

$$
\begin{aligned}
P\_m\_Linear\_Regression(T\_i) = {}& 0.8747 \\
& + 0.0445 * Gender = Female \\
& + 0.034 * Learning\_Phase\_Time\_Minutes \\
& - 0.0186 * Number\_of\_nodes \\
& - 0.0505 * depth
\end{aligned}
$$

Note that per this relationship females were slightly better than males at remembering the learning tree, people who spent more time in the learning phase typically remembered the tree better, but on the other hand people had a harder time remembering trees with more nodes and greater depths. We considered more complex models with slightly improved results. A Random Forest model yielded a correlation coefficient $= 0.58$ and Mean absolute error $= 0.143$. An Ensemble-Stacking Algorithm with a LinearRegression meta learner and the weak learners of LinearRegression and Random Forest yielded similar results with a correlation coefficient $= 0.58$ and Mean absolute error $= 0.144$. The results of the categorical prediction model based on logistic regression for modeling how well people remembered individual paths of the tree. We found that this approach was overall successful with a ROC Area of 0.703 after performing 10-fold cross validation.

5.3   External Validation Results

We now present the results of the experiment for predicting suspected Crohn's disease, which was used to validate the proposed machine learning model similar to the previous cancer diagnosis experiment. As we mentioned, we created 4 trees of different sizes with different levels of accuracy, and in Table 2 you can see for each tree how many of the participants were able to remember the tree model - this is a measure Accuracy_model we mentioned earlier, and how well the participants were able to classify new cases that were presented to them, which is measure Accuracy_truth. It can be seen from the table that trees with fewer vertebrae showed success in the model recall, but the accuracy of the tree is low and anyway the value of the second index is also low.

Table 2. Table showing the accuracies of the decision trees that were generated for diagnosis of suspected Crohn's disease in order of the most simple (TreeA) to the most complex (TreeD) tree.

	TreeA	TreeB	TreeC	TreeD
SIZE (Number of nodes = rules):	3	5	7	11
ACCURACY:	72%	80%	81%	82%
Accuracy_model:	89.41	83.83	76.33	65.59
Accuracy_truth:	69.14	71.46	69.00	61.29

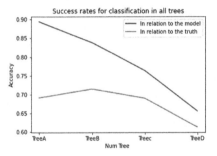

Fig. 5. The success rates of each group to classify correctly, in relation to the model (blue) and in relation to the truth (red). (Color figure online)

Figure 5 shows the success rates of each group to correctly classify new instances of Crohn's disease. The X-axis again represents the tree name and Y-axis represents the accuracy grade per each group of participants. It can again be seen that the group that received the small tree - TreeA (with 2 nodes-size 2), was able to remember the model and classify according to this model 89.41% of the time, but its success in classifying cases in the real world is only 69.14% because of the low accuracy of that tree. Conversely, the group that received the big tree, TreeD (size 11), was able to remember and apply the model 65.59% of the time, and their ability to classify cases in the real world was also relatively low at 61.29%. It can be seen that the tree in which the participants were most successful in the classification performance in relation to the ground truth is TreeB (its Accuracy_truth is: 71.46%), therefore, according to the experiment we did, this is the most useful tree to teach human users.

We then examined how successful our prediction models were in predicting the classification success of participants in the real world (P_a), versus the success of the participants in classifying in the real world as measured by the Accuracy_truth metric. The first row in Table 3 shows the Accuracy_truth for each of the four trees (also the last row in Table 2). The next four rows show the P_a prediction for the different models (Linear Regression, Stacking, Random Forest, and Logistic Regression).

Table 3. The results of the P_a_i model for predicting the success of learning each tree by a human user according to i = 4 different learning algorithms, this when trained over Crohn's and the prediction is over Crohn's database.

Tree Used:	TreeA	TreeB	TreeC	TreeD	MAE to Accuracy_truth
1. Accuracy_truth:	69.14	71.46	69.00	61.29	0
2. P_a_Linear Regression:	65.75	67.88	63.62	58.53	3.77
3. P_a _Stacking:	65.45	68.07	65.56	60.76	2.76
4. P_a _ Random Forest:	65.64	68.42	66.88	61.63	2.25
5. P_a _Logistic regression:	68.91	69.61	65.17	59.10	2.02

Our objective was twofold: to compare these prediction models with the actual values (Accuracy_truth) and to determine if they could recommend the best tree among the options (TreeB). To illustrate, let's focus on the fifth row of Table 3, where we analyze the Logistic Regression (RL) model's performance compared to Accuracy_truth (row 1). The RL model predicted a classification success rate of 68.91% in the real world, while the actual value was 69.14% (corresponding to the value in the first row under the TreeA column). Similarly, for TreeB, the RL model predicted a 69.61% success rate compared to the actual value of 71.46%. For TreeC, the model expected a 65.17% success rate compared to the actual value of 69.00%, and for TreeD, the model predicted a 59.10% success rate compared to the actual value of 61.29%. To quantify these differences, we calculated the Mean Absolute Error (MAE), presented in the last column, which amounted to 2.02 for this model across the four trees. The LR model had the smallest MAE and performed the best in predicting the experimental results.

It's worth noting that all the other models also achieved impressive results, unanimously recommending TreeB for the user as it received the highest success prediction (highlighted in red). This aligns with the experiment's findings, where TreeB proved to be the most effective in facilitating user learning.

6   Conclusions and Future Work

In this paper we proposed a model for optimizing how many rules could be comprehended by people learning new information. This model is critical not only for this specific application, but is generally applicable to many other problems, such as learning the number of rules an XAI should present to a user. The learned model used tree general information such as the size and number of nodes in the tree and general demographic data to determine how many rules to present. We built this model using extensive human trials from a dataset of esophageal cancer to build a repository of information about when additional rules were useful. Not only did this repository help us accurate model human behavior within this task, but we were able to externally validate the model on a second medical dataset – diagnosing Crohn's disease.

In theory, more complex variations of the problem could be considered such as how to order specific rules importance. For example, it could be that certain rules, such as well-known differences based on age or gender, might be easier to remember than obscure rules such medical rules based on specific enzyme marker levels in blood tests. However, for purposes of this work, we assume that all rules are of equal importance and difficulty to learn, similar to previous XAI work [12].

For future work, we hope to extent this success by considering additional task and tree features. We hope to both demonstrate the success of this approach in new tasks and consider if additional information about decision trees may be incorporated. For example, this work considered all rule information as being equally hard for users to learn. It is likely this is not always the case, and as such the learning algorithm should learn which rules are better to present to a given user based on previous experience with other users or even previous experience with this specific user. It is possible that users can and should be modeled differently over time, and such elements will be considered in future versions of this work. For example, it seems reasonable that during a learning process one might initially begin with a small set of rules, but add them as the user seems ready based on previous experience and as knowledge is acquired. In theory this process could be either implicit or explicit, learning either implicitly based on a user's previous responses or by incorporating feedback within the system. Last, we are studying how these results can be directly applied to XAI applications. As the number of rules or the amount of information an XAI outputs is often a critical component, we believe that many possible improvements to XAI are possible based on this work – something we are currently studying.

References

1. Basu, S., Christensen, J.: Teaching classification boundaries to humans. In: Proceedings of the AAAI Conference on Artificial Intelligence, vol. 27, pp. 109–115 (2013)
2. Dam, H.K., Tran, T., Ghose, A.: Explainable software analytics. In: Proceedings of the 40th International Conference on Software Engineering: New Ideas and Emerging Results, pp. 53–56 (2018)
3. Doran, D., Schulz, S., Besold, T.R.: What does explainable AI really mean? A new conceptualization of perspectives. arXiv preprint arXiv:1710.00794 (2017)

4. Doshi-Velez, F., Kim, B.: Towards a rigorous science of interpretable machine learning. arXiv preprint arXiv:1702.08608 (2017)
5. Freitas, A.A.: Comprehensible classification models: a position paper. ACM SIGKDD Explor. Newsl. **15**(1), 1–10 (2014)
6. Gunning, D.: Explainable artificial intelligence (XAI) volume 2 defense advanced research projects agency (DARPA), Arlington, VA, USA (2017)
7. Murphy, P.M., Pazzani, M.J.: Exploring the decision forest: an empirical investigation of Occam's Razor in decision tree induction. J. Artif. Intell. Res. **1**, 257–275 (1993)
8. Paolacci, G., Chandler, J., Ipeirotis, P.G.: Running experiments on amazon mechanical turk. Judgm. Decis. Mak. **5**(5), 411–419 (2010)
9. Quinlan, J.R.: Induction of decision trees. Mach. Learn. **1**(1), 81–106 (1986)
10. Richards, R.A.: Principle hierarchy based intelligent tutoring system for common cockpit helicopter training. In: Cerri, S.A., Gouardères, G., Paraguaçu, F. (eds.) ITS 2002. LNCS, vol. 2363, pp. 473–483. Springer, Heidelberg (2002). https://doi.org/10.1007/3-540-47987-2_50
11. Rosemarin, H., Rosenfeld, A., Kraus, S.: Emergency department online patient-caregiver scheduling. In: Proceedings of the AAAI Conference on Artificial Intelligence, vol. 33, pp. 695–701 (2019)
12. Rosenfeld, A.: Better metrics for evaluating explainable artificial intelligence. In: Proceedings of the 20th International Conference on Autonomous Agents and Multiagent Systems, pp. 45–50 (2021)
13. Rosenfeld, A., et al.: Development and validation of a risk prediction model to diagnose Barrett's oesophagus (MARK-BE): a case-control machine learning approach. Lancet Digit. Health **2**(1), e37–e48 (2020)
14. Rosenfeld, A., Richardson, A.: Explainability in human-agent systems. Auton. Agent. Multi-Agent Syst. **33**(6), 673–705 (2019)
15. Sehgal, V., et al.: Machine learning creates a simple endoscopic classification system that improves dysplasia detection in Barrett's oesophagus amongst non-expert endoscopists. Gastroenterol. Res. Pract. **2018** (2018)
16. Smith, J.: Applying Occam's razor in machine learning: a comparative study. J. Data Sci. **15**(3), 123–145 (2020)
17. Tomsett, R., Braines, D., Harborne, D., Preece, A., Chakraborty, S.: Interpretable to whom? A role-based model for analyzing interpretable machine learning systems. arXiv preprint arXiv:1806.07552 (2018)
18. van der Waa, J., Nieuwburg, E., Cremers, A., Neerincx, M.: Evaluating XAI: a comparison of rule-based and example-based explanations. Artif. Intell. **291**, 103404 (2021)

ChatGPT-HealthPrompt. Harnessing the Power of XAI in Prompt-Based Healthcare Decision Support using ChatGPT

Fatemeh Nazary, Yashar Deldjoo[(✉)], and Tommaso Di Noia

Polytechnic University of Bari, Bari, Italy
{fatemeh.nazary,yashar.deldjoo,tommaso.dinoia}@poliba.it

Abstract. This study presents an innovative approach to the application of large language models (LLMs) in clinical decision-making, focusing on OpenAI's ChatGPT. Our approach introduces the use of *contextual prompts*-strategically designed to include task description, feature description, and crucially, integration of domain knowledge-for high-quality binary classification tasks even in data-scarce scenarios. The novelty of our work lies in the utilization of domain knowledge, obtained from high-performing interpretable ML models, and its seamless incorporation into prompt design. By viewing these ML models as medical experts, we extract key insights on feature importance to aid in decision-making processes. This interplay of domain knowledge and AI holds significant promise in creating a more insightful diagnostic tool.

Additionally, our research explores the dynamics of zero-shot and few-shot prompt learning based on LLMs. By comparing the performance of OpenAI's ChatGPT with traditional supervised ML models in different data conditions, we aim to provide insights into the effectiveness of prompt engineering strategies under varied data availability. In essence, this paper bridges the gap between AI and healthcare, proposing a novel methodology for LLMs application in clinical decision support systems. It highlights the transformative potential of effective prompt design, domain knowledge integration, and flexible learning approaches in enhancing automated decision-making.

Keywords: Healthcare · LLM · ChatGPT · XAI

1 Introduction

Motivation. The ever-evolving field of Natural Language Processing (NLP) has opened the door for potential advancements in a variety of sectors, the medical and healthcare field being no exception. The latest breakthroughs achieved by large language models (LLMs) such as OpenAI's GPT [3], Google's PALM [4], and Facebook's LaMDA [11], has sparked intriguing speculation about the integration of AI in clinical decision-making and healthcare analytic. Consider a

S. Nowaczyk et al. (Eds.): ECAI 2023 Workshops, CCIS 1947, pp. 382–397, 2024.
https://doi.org/10.1007/978-3-031-50396-2_22

scenario where a healthcare professional, seeking a second opinion on a complex case, turns to an AI-powered system such as ChatGPT instead of consulting another colleague. With the provision of all relevant medical data and context, the model could provide a comprehensive interpretation of the information, potentially suggesting diagnoses or treatment options. This application is no longer purely speculative; models such as OpenAI's ChatGPT have already demonstrated their potential to understand and generate contextually relevant responses, indicating a potential to become supportive aids in clinical decision-making.

Notwithstanding their great promise, it is important to underline that LLMs gain their power from being trained on billions of documents on internet data, allowing them to identify connections between words in various settings and formulate the most likely word sequences in a given new context. As promising as this might seem, the application of LLMs in the healthcare field is not *without risks*, including potential inaccuracies due to a lack of specific medical training, misinterpretation of context, or data privacy concerns, all of which could have serious consequences in this critical domain. Enhancing the performance of LLMs for specific applications typically involves two major strategies, namely *fine-tuning* and *prompt design* [9,13,15]. Both serve similar goals in LLM enhancement to accomplish desired tasks, however, they differ significantly in their approaches. Prompting manipulates the model at inference time by providing context, instruction, and examples within the prompt, leaving the model's parameters unchanged. In contrast, fine-tuning modifies the model parameters according to a representative dataset, demanding more resources, however resulting in more specialized and consistent outcomes across similar tasks.

Prompt-design strategies for LLMs can be categorized based on task complexity and the degrees of contextual examples provided. These categories include *zero-shot*, *one-shot*, and *few-shot prompting*. Zero-shot prompting is ideal for straightforward, well-defined tasks that do not require multiple examples. It involves providing a single, concise prompt and relying on the model's preexisting knowledge to generate responses. For instance, in the medical field, zero-shot prompting could be employed to provide a broad overview of common diseases. On the other hand, the techniques of one-shot and few-shot prompting involve guiding the model with one or more examples or queries to steer it toward generating desired outputs. An example prompt might be, *"Consider a 57-year-old male with high cholesterol, abnormal ECG, and exercise-induced angina, who shows signs of heart disease. Conversely, a 48-year-old male experiencing typical angina, but maintaining normal blood sugar levels and ECG, and without exercise-induced angina, is likely not suffering from heart disease. Based on these examples, predict the presence or absence of heart disease for a newly presented individual with specified medical conditions, using the narratives provided as guidance."* Historically, GPT-1 was evaluated for its zero-shot capabilities, demonstrating encouraging results. As language models evolved, however, there was a shift towards the use of few-shot prompting in subsequent iterations such as GPT-2 and GPT-3 [1]. Despite the success of these models, the format of the prompt and the sequence of examples can have a substantial impact on task performance [2]. As a result, optimizing the use of prompts in these models continues to be an area of active research. While tasks requiring specialized skills often benefit from fine-tuning, this methodology is beyond the scope of our current research. Instead, our focus lies in employing **guided prompt-design** to improve decision-making processes within the medical domain.

Contributions. This paper aims to explore the application of OpenAI's Chat-GPT to tackle binary classification tasks within clinical decision support systems, utilizing contextual prompts for high-quality predictions with minimal data. Our method underscores the incorporation of "**domain-specific knowledge**," extracted from interpretable ML models, to enhance prediction tasks and foster few-shot (and also zero-shot) learning. We showcase how OpenAI models can handle downstream tasks, matching the performance of traditional supervised ML models with ample data, even in data-scarce scenarios. We further discuss the relative advantages of zero-shot and few-shot prompts engineering.

Figure 1 symbolically presents our novel approach to enhancing medical decision-making by leveraging interpretable ML. The core novelty of our work lies in crafting effective prompts that will function as inputs for OpenAI's ChatGPT. To generate these prompts, we start with a basic version containing the task description. To provide more context, we integrate a feature description, which highlights key features relevant to the classification task at hand. Crucially, we also incorporate domain knowledge, obtained by separately training ML models and using their feature-based explanations as a source of expert insights. These ML models can be metaphorically seen as doctors, each emphasizing specific features deemed important for diagnosing particular diseases. This integration of expert-driven knowledge aims to enrich the diagnostic process. Further, we study the dynamics of zero-shot versus few-shot prompt engineering by varying the number of examples supplied to the prompt, thus enabling us to evaluate the system's adaptability to different data volumes. In summary, our contributions are summarized as follows:

- **Utilizing OpenAI's ChatGPT for Clinical Decision Support.** We exploit the potential of OpenAI's ChatGPT in clinical decision support systems, specifically for binary classification tasks, demonstrating its practical application in this domain.
- **Advancing Prompt Engineering and Domain Knowledge Integration.** Our study introduces a novel approach to prompt engineering using "contextual prompts" and underscores the integration of domain-specific knowledge. These carefully crafted prompts lead to high-quality predictions even in scenarios with limited data. We further enhance this process by creating **a domain knowledge generator**, which leverages high-performing ML tasks. We treat these ML models as metaphorical medical experts, enhancing prediction tasks and facilitating these models to operate as few-shot learners.
- **Exploring Few-Shot vs. Zero-Shot Learning:** Our work contrasts the few-shot learning capability of OpenAI's ChatGPT with traditional supervised ML models, trained with ample data. We highlight the benefits of zero-

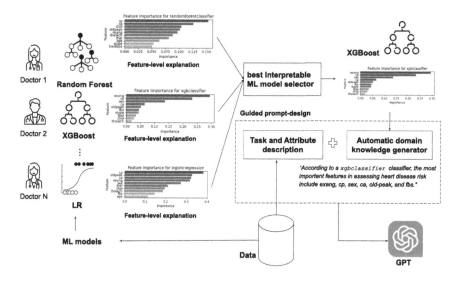

Fig. 1. Flowchart illustrating the conceptual framework of the paper

shot and few-shot prompt engineering, shedding light on the interplay between data availability and prediction quality.

The structure of this paper is as follows: Sect. 2 presents the related work, detailing the history of Transformers and Large Language Models, prompt engineering, and the use of LLMs in clinical decision-making. Section 3 introduces our novel OpenAI-ML framework. Section 4 outlines our experiments and methodology, followed by Sect. 5, which discusses the performance outcomes and risks associated with our proposed system.

2   Related Work

2.1   History of Transformers and Large Language Models

The evolution of language models has been marked by the ongoing pursuit of more complex, versatile, and human-like machine representations of language. Prior to 2017, Natural Language Processing (NLP) models were largely trained on supervised learning tasks, limiting their generalizability [9]. However, the advent of the transformer architecture by Vaswani et al. [12], a self-attention network, led to the development of ground-breaking models such as Generative Pretrained Transformers (GPT) and Bidirectional Encoder Representations from Transformers (BERT) [7]. These models use a semi-supervised approach, combining unsupervised pre-training with supervised fine-tuning, to achieve superior generalization capabilities. In recent years, we have witnessed a rapid progression in GPT models, resulting in the creation of GPT-3, a behemoth model with

175 billion parameters. Notwithstanding, these models still face significant challenges, including alignment with human values and the potential for generating biased or incorrect information. Efforts have been made to mitigate these issues, with the introduction of reinforcement learning from human feedback (RLHF) for improved model fine-tuning and alignment, as exemplified in the evolution of GPT-3 into ChatGPT [10].

2.2   Prompt Engineering

Prompts play a crucial role in controlling and guiding the application of Large Language Models (LLMs). Essentially, a prompt is a set of instructions given to the model using natural, human language to define the task to be performed and the desired output. Prompts can be broadly categorized into two main types: *manual prompts* and *automated prompts* [13]. Manual prompts are carefully designed by human specialists to provide models with precise instructions. However, their creation requires substantial expertise and time, and even minor adjustments can significantly affect the model's predictions. To overcome these limitations, various automated methods for prompt design have been developed.

Automated prompts, including discrete and continuous prompts, have gained popularity due to their efficiency and adaptability. They are generated using a variety of algorithms and techniques, thereby reducing the need for human intervention. Continuous prompts consider the current conversation context to generate accurate responses, while discrete prompts depend on predefined categories to produce responses. There are also both static and dynamic prompts that interpret the historical context differently. Ultimately, the performance and effectiveness of LLMs are significantly influenced by the quality and efficiency of these prompts [9].

2.3   Use of LLMs in Clinical Decision Making

Prompt engineering and LLMs such as ChatGPT and GPT-4 have shown promising performance in advancing the medical field. Their diverse applications in various tasks, including unique prompt designs, multi-modal data processing, and deep reinforcement learning, are discussed comprehensively in Wang et al. [13]. The LLMs demonstrate promising potential for clinical decision-making due to their adaptive abilities, enabling zero-shot and few-shot in-context learning despite the scarcity of labeled data. They contribute to offering diagnostic insights, treatment suggestions, and risk assessments. However, while these advancements demonstrate the transformative potential of LLMs in healthcare, it underlines the need for additional research to address prompt engineering limitations and ensure the ethical, reliable, safe, and effective use of LLMs in healthcare settings.

3   OpenAI-ML Framework for Health Risk Assessment

Overview of the Proposed System. We propose a system for health risk assessment that leverages OpenAI's advanced language model, `ChatGPT-3.5`

Guided Prompt Design

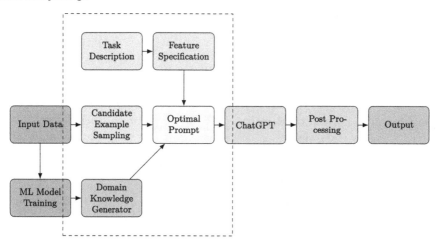

Fig. 2. Flowchart illustrating the proposed guided prompt design process for integrating contextual information in the medical field, emphasizing the sequential steps involved in designing effective prompts.

-Turbo. This system employs a conversation-based strategy to predict the risk of heart disease. It is designed to output binary responses ('1' or '0'), which correspond to high and low risk of heart disease, respectively. A detailed flowchart of our proposed system can be seen in Fig. 2.

- **Part 1: Task Instruction:** The model is provided a task to assess heart disease risk based on given attributes. Here, the degree of diameter narrowing in the blood vessels informs the risk assessment, where less than 50% narrowing indicates low risk ('0') and more than 50% indicates high risk ('1');
- **Part 2: Attribute Description:** The model is informed about the meaning of each attribute involved in the risk assessment. This ranges from the individual's age, sex, and chest pain type (cp), to their cholesterol levels (chol), among others. Each attribute is clearly defined, aiding the model to understand its relevance and role in the task at hand;
- **Part 3: In-context Examples:** The model is given example scenarios with specific attribute inputs and corresponding risk assessment answers, aiding it to understand the pattern and relationship between the attributes and the risk level;
- **Part 4: Integration of Domain Knowledge:** The model is given domain knowledge which is simulated by best-performing interpretable ML models, such as RandomForestClassifier, LogisticRegression, and XGBClassifier. These models offer an ordered list of feature importance, which can aid the ChatGPT model in making a more informed assessment;
- **Part 5: Formulation of a Question/Problem:** The model is presented with an test instance. The instance involves specific inputs for each attribute

Table 1. Summary of Domain Knowledge Types

	dk0	Odd dk (MLFI)	Even dk (MLFI-ord)
Name	N/A	ML defines feature importance	Similar to MLFI, includes feature order
Description	No extra domain knowledge	Feature importance defined by ML algorithms	Includes both feature importance and order
Focus	N/A	Feature Attribution	Feature Attribution with order-awareness
Implementation	Solely data-driven	XGB, RF, AdaBoost, LR	XGB, RF, AdaBoost,LR
Usage Scenarios	*Zero-shot* scenarios; Simple tasks with no specific domain knowledge required	*Few-shot* scenarios; Tasks requiring the understanding of feature importance;	*Few-shot* scenarios; Tasks requiring the understanding of both feature importance and order;

and the model is asked to assess the risk level based on the prior instructions, examples, attribute descriptions, and domain knowledge. This allows for the practical application of the instruction in a real-world example.

Domain Knowledge Integration. Domain knowledge integration is categorized into three types as shown in Table 1. These types are designed to handle different tasks based on the requirements of domain knowledge and the order of features.

- **dk0:** This scenario involves no additional domain knowledge, where learning is purely data-driven. It is most suitable for simple tasks that do not require specific domain knowledge, making it an effective choice for testing *zero-shot* scenarios;
- **Odd dk or MLFI:** This category identifies the importance of features as determined by various ML algorithms such as XGB, RF, Ada, and LR. It is particularly useful in tasks requiring the understanding of feature importance, and it is used to test *few-shot* scenarios (MLFI is short for Machine learning Feature Importance);
- **Even dk or MLFI-ord:** This category not only considers the importance of features but also their order, as determined by ML algorithms. It is ideal

for tasks that require an understanding of both feature importance and their order, and it is also used to test *few-shot* scenarios (MLFI is short for Machine learning Feature Importance-*ordered*).

More detailed information regarding the conversation used is depicted below.

Part 1: Task Instruction

Given the provided input attributes, evaluate the risk of heart disease for the individual. The diagnosis of heart disease (angiographic disease status) is based on the degree of diameter narrowing in the blood vessels:

- 0: Less than 50% diameter narrowing, implying a lower risk.
- 1: More than 50% diameter narrowing, indicating a higher risk.

If the assessment determines a high risk, the output should be '1'. If the risk is determined to be low, the output should be '0'. Evaluate the heart risk based on given attributes. If good, respond with '1', if bad, respond with '0'.

Part 2: Attribute Description

The explanation of each attribute is as follows:

- Age: Age of the individual
- Sex: Sex of the individual (1 = Male, 0 = Female)
- Cp: Chest pain type (1 = typical angina, 2 = atypical angina, 3 = non-anginal pain, 4 = asymptomatic)
- Trestbps: Resting blood pressure (in mm Hg on admission to the hospital)
- Chol: Serum cholesterol in mg/dl
- Fbs: Fasting blood sugar > 120 mg/dl (1 = true, 0 = false)
- Restecg: Resting electrocardiographic results (0 = normal, 1 = having ST-T wave abnormality, 2 = showing probable or definite left ventricular hypertrophy)
- Thalach: Maximum heart rate achieved
- Exang: Exercise-induced angina (1 = yes, 0 = no)
- Oldpeak: ST depression induced by exercise relative to rest
- Slope: The slope of the peak exercise ST segment (1 = upsloping, 2 = flat, 3 = downsloping)
- Ca: Number of major vessels (0-3) colored by fluoroscopy
- Thal: Thalassemia (3 = normal, 6 = fixed defect, 7 = reversible defect)

Part 3: In-Context Example

Example 1:

<Inputs 1>: age: 57, sex: 1, cp: 2, trestbps: 140, chol: 265, fbs: 0, restecg: 1, thalach: 145, exang: 1, oldpeak: 1, slope: 2, ca: 0.2, thal: 5.8

<Answer 1>: 1

Example 2:

<Inputs 2>: age: 48, sex: 1, cp: 2, trestbps: 130, chol: 245, fbs: 0, restecg: 0, thalach: 160, exang: 0, oldpeak: 0, slope: 1.4, ca: 0.2, thal: 4.6

<Answer 2>: 0

Example 3:

<Inputs 3>: age: 44, sex: 1, cp: 4, trestbps: 112, chol: 290, fbs: 0, restecg: 2, thalach: 153, exang: 0, oldpeak: 0, slope: 1, ca: 1, thal: 3

<Answer 3>: 1

Part 4: Domain Knowledge Integration using Interpretable ML

Domain Knowledge:

- **dk0**: None

- **dk1**: According to a `randomforestclassifier` classifier, the most important features in assessing heart disease risk include cp, ca, chol, oldpeak, exang, and thalach. Features like fbs and restecg have relatively lower importance;

- **dk2**: The **order of features** is critically important when evaluating heart disease risk. The sequence of features according to their importance starts with cp, followed by ca, then chol, oldpeak, exang, thalach, thal, age, slope, trestbps, sex, fbs, and finally restecg;

- **dk3**: According to a `logisticregression` classifier, the most important features in assessing heart disease risk include cp, oldpeak, ca, exang, sex, and thal. Features like restecg and trestbps have relatively lower importance;

- **dk4**: The **order of features** is critically important when evaluating heart disease risk. The sequence of features according to their importance starts with cp, followed by oldpeak, then ca, exang, sex, thal, chol, thalach, fbs, age, slope, restecg, and finally trestbps;

- **dk5**: According to a `xgbclassifier` classifier, the most important features in assessing heart disease risk include exang, cp, sex, ca, oldpeak, and fbs. Features like trestbps and restecg have relatively lower importance;

- **dk6**: The **order of features** is critically important when evaluating heart disease risk. The sequence of features according to their importance starts with exang, followed by cp, then sex, ca, oldpeak, fbs, slope, thal, chol, thalach, age, trestbps, and finally restecg;

Part 5: Final Task Question

Now, given the following inputs, please evaluate the risk of heart disease:
<Inputs>: age: 46.0, sex: 1.0, cp: 3.0, trestbps: 150.0, chol: 163.0, fbs: 0.2, restecg: 0.0, thalach: 116.0, exang: 0.0, oldpeak: 0.0, slope: 2.2, ca: 0.4, thal: 6.2
<Answer>: ?

4 Experimental Setup

Task. This work focuses on binary classification within a health risk assessment context in machine learning (ML). The task involves learning a function $f : \mathcal{X} \rightarrow \{0, 1\}$, predicting a binary outcome $y \in \{0, 1\}$ for each feature instance $x \in \mathcal{X}$.

Dataset. We used the Heart Disease dataset [8] was collected from four hospitals located in the USA, Switzerland, and Hungary. The task associated with this dataset is binary classification, aimed at determining the presence or absence of heart disease. The dataset initially contains 621 out of 920 samples with missing values, which were all successfully *imputed* using the KNN method, resulting in no samples with missing values. The distribution of males to females in the dataset is approximately 78% to 21%, while the disease prevalence ratio between males and females is approximately 63% to 28% in the given population, males tend to suffer from heart disease more frequently than females).

Baseline Prediction Models. To assess the performance of our model under varying levels of dataset skewness, we implemented three baseline prediction models that operate independently of features. These include, Maj Class-1 Prediction: generates predictions with 90% of them belonging to class 1, chosen randomly; Maj Class-0 Prediction: generates predictions with 90% of them belonging to class 0, chosen randomly; Random Prediction: Generates predictions by randomly.

Table 2. Summary of ML models and their Hyper-parameters

Algorithm	Parameters	Total
RF	n_estimators, max_depth, min_samples_split, min_samples_leaf, bootstrap	5
LR	C, penalty, solver	3
MLP	hidden_layer_sizes, activation, solver, alpha, learning_rate, learning_rate_init, tol, max_iter	8
KNN	n_neighbors, weights, algorithm, leaf_size, p	5
XGB	use_label_encoder, eval_metric, n_estimators, learning_rate, max_depth, colsample_bytree	6
AdaBoost	n_estimators, learning_rate	2

Hyperparameters and ML Models. We employed six ML models, each with a distinct set of hyperparameters. These were optimized using a randomized search cross-validation (CV) strategy, with a total of 29 unique hyperparameters across all models. This led to an extensive model tuning process involving numerous model iterations. We used a 5-fold CV (0.8, 0.2) with *RandomizedSearchCV* over 20 iterations. The exact hyperparameters depended on the specific model and are listed in Table 2.

OpenAI Model. We utilized the OpenAI's `GPT-3.5-turbo` model to perform heart disease risk assessment based on patient health data. The model interacts through a chat-like interface, taking a sequence of messages and user inputs as prompts and generating corresponding output responses. The model was configured with a temperature setting of 0, dictating no randomness of the model's responses. The usage of the OpenAI model involved the generation of requests, comprising individual patient data features. Each request was processed by the model, returning an output prediction. For efficiency, these requests were sent in batches. The Python code made use of the OpenAI API, the tenacity library for retrying failed requests, and other common data processing libraries such as pandas. The code is available for reproducibility at this link.[1]

5   Results

Table 3 provides an in-depth comparison of heart health risk prediction performance using traditional ML models and OpenAI-based predictions. We have excluded results from `Random`, `Maj0`, and `Maj1` for average calculations and highlighted utilized values in the table for better tracking. We evaluated OpenAI predictions against conventional models such as `RF`, `LR` , `MLP`, `KNN`, `XGB`, `AdaBoost`, with prompts categorized based on the integration of extra domain knowledge or without it. We also considered the number of examples used in prompt formulation (represented as N_{ex}). The results are presented in two main dimensions: *overall performance* (F1 and Acc.) and *risks* (FPC, FNC, and cost-sensitive accuracy). In this context, a particular emphasis was placed on false-negative costs due to the significant health risk of incorrectly diagnosing a healthy individual as sick. Lastly, we introduced a new metric, cost-sensitive accuracy, with specific weights (FP=0.2, FN=0.8) that may vary based on the scenario.

5.1   Overall Performance

The section sheds light on the comparative performance between classical machine learning (ML) models and OpenAI-based models, with and without the incorporation of domain knowledge as proposed in this paper (cf. Section 3).

Classical ML vs. OpenAI Without Domain Knowledge. From the provided table, it is clear that the OpenAI-based models using prompts have produced varied results depending on the number of examples used in their construction (denoted by N_{ex}). Specifically, looking at `prompt-0` which uses no

---

[1] Source code.https://github.com/atenanaz/ChatGPT-HealthPrompt.

extra domain knowledge, we see that its performance significantly improves as N_{ex} increases. At '$N_{ex} = 0$', the F1 score is 0.7402 and the Accuracy is 0.6413, which are better than those of Maj-1, Maj-0, and random, indicating an advancement of OpenAI-ML in *zero-shot scenarios* over those basic models. Yet, they are still below the average of classical Machine Learning models.

Progressing forward, in *few-shot scenarios*, there is a noticeable improvement in the performance of prompt-0, which does not leverage any domain knowledge. As N_{ex} (the number of examples) increases, this model even surpasses some traditional machine learning counterparts. At 'n=16', it reaches an F1 score of 0.8241 and an Accuracy of 0.7935, which are closely comparable to the average F1 (0.8576) and Accuracy (0.8203) of classical ML models. This showcases the robustness and potential of the OpenAI-based prediction model when a larger number of examples are used for prompt construction. It demonstrates that while classical machine learning methods have more consistent performance, the OpenAI models have the ability to learn and improve from more example prompts, achieving competitive performance with an increasing number of examples.

The study underscores the potential of prediction models based on OpenAI. Even though these models initially perform at a lower level compared to traditional ML models, the inherent iterative learning and enhancement capabilities of OpenAI models become increasingly clear as the number of examples used for prompt construction increases.

Classical ML vs. OpenAI-ML with Domain Knowledge. The comparison between OpenAI's GPT-3.5 and classical machine learning models reveals intriguing insights. The OpenAI prediction prompts adopt two strategies: some without extra domain knowledge, while others integrate results from classical ML models (RF, LR , XGB). We selected these models due to their capability to yield attribute-based explanation outcomes, as illustrated in Fig. 1, and their inherent diversity. The sequence of features is contemplated in half of these prompts, particularly the even-numbered ones (prompt-2, prompt-4, and prompt-6). Moving forward to the analysis, in the second type of prompts (prompt-1, prompt-3, and prompt-5) that utilize the prediction results of classical ML models without considering their order of importance, there is a noticeable improvement as n increases, similar to prompt-0, however, the increase is more drastic. For instance, at 'n=8', prompt-5 outperforms all models, yielding the highest F1 score (0.8711), Accuracy (0.8424), clearly surpassing all the baseline ML models. Note that here, using just 8 examples (about 2–3% of the total training data) seems to be enough for the model to significantly outperform the average results of classical ML models, particularly in terms of cost-sensitive accuracy.

Lastly, the prompts where the order of features was considered (prompt-2, prompt-4, and prompt-6) generally show a similar pattern, with performance improving as n increases. However, their results appear to be slightly lower than the prompts using classical ML model results without considering feature order. This may suggest that for certain tasks, the added complexity of considering feature order does not always translate into a clear performance advantage.

Summary. This study contrasted the performance of classical Machine Learning (ML) models and OpenAI-based models, with and without the integration of domain knowledge. The initial performance of OpenAI models is lower than classical ML models in *zero-shot scenarios*, but exhibits substantial enhancement with an increase in the number of examples, i.e., in *few-shot scenarios*, eventually attaining comparable metric values. Upon **domain knowledge** integration, particularly the prediction results of classical ML models, OpenAI models show **significant performance** improvement, with some surpassing all baseline ML models. However, the benefit of incorporating feature order is not always clear.

5.2 Risks

It can be observed that on average, False Negatives (FN) in a majority of experimental cases of OpenAI remain below those of the classical Machine Learning (ML) models. For example, OpenAI models recorded FN of 3.08, 10.7, 8.6, and 9.37 compared to an average FN of 10.9 for ML models. This advantage, however, comes with a trade-off of higher False Positives (FP). OpenAI models on average scored higher in FP with values such as 12.77, 8.971, 80.578, and 6.4571, compared to the classical ML models.

Interestingly, the best-performing prompts within the OpenAI models demonstrated very low FP and FN rates (e.g., 4.6 and 4.8), which in terms of FN, remain much lower than even the best ML models. Summarizing the key observations, it can be stated that while OpenAI models may present better results in specific cases, care should be taken when discussing the risk of these models' predictions in clinical decision support. This caution is due to the high variability and variance these models show (e.g., in one case, FN reaches 20.8), and simply considering average statistics may not provide an accurate representation of their performance. On the other hand, ML models show more homogeneous performance. This phenomenon might be attributed to the tendency of prompt-based predictions to produce more 1s than 0s, thereby decreasing FN. However, considering the accuracies, it is evident that the results are not randomly generated, and OpenAI models are indeed capable of making sense of the data. This demonstrates the potential power of these models but also the need for careful design and implementation in clinical decision-making scenarios.

Table 3. Performance comparison: Green boxes highlight key values, **bold** and *italics* denote top results in classical and OpenAI models.

Model	DK Type	DK source	N_{ex}	Pre.↑	Rec↑	F1↑	Acc.↑	FP Cost↓	FN Cost↓	Cost-Sens Acc.↑
RF				0.8585	0.875	0.8667	0.8478	3.0	10.4	0.9208
LR				0.8241	0.8558	0.8396	0.8152	3.8	12.0	0.9047
MLP				0.8381	0.8462	0.8421	0.8207	3.4	12.8	0.9031
KNN				0.8654	0.8654	0.8654	0.8478	2.8	11.2	0.9176
XGB				0.8667	0.875	**0.8708**	**0.8533**	2.8	10.4	0.9224
AdaBoost				0.8304	0.8942	0.8611	0.8370	3.8	8.8	**0.9243**
Maj1				0.5576	0.8846	0.6840	0.5380	14.6	9.6	0.8035
Maj0				0.6842	0.125	0.2114	0.4728	1.2	72.8	0.5403
random				0.5326	0.4712	0.5	0.4674	8.6	44.0	0.6204
Avg.				0.8472	0.8686	0.8576	0.8368	3.26	10.9	0.9155
prompt-0	NO	-	0	0.6267	0.9038	0.7402	0.6413	11.2	8.0	0.8600
prompt-1	MLFI	RF	0	0.6121	0.9712	0.7509	0.6359	12.8	2.4	0.8850
prompt-2	MLFI-ord	RF	0	0.5976	0.9712	0.7399	0.6141	13.6	2.4	0.8759
prompt-3	MLFI	LR	0	0.6242	0.9904	0.7658	0.6576	12.4	0.8	0.9016
prompt-4	MLFI-ord	LR	0	0.6111	0.9520	0.7444	0.6304	12.6	4.0	0.8748
prompt-5	MLFI	XGB	0	0.6108	0.9808	0.7528	0.6359	13.0	1.6	0.8890
prompt-6	MLFI-ord	XGB	0	0.5941	0.9712	0.7372	0.6087	13.8	2.4	0.8736
Avg.	-	-	2	0.6109	0.9629	0.7473	0.6319	12.77	3.08	0.8799
prompt-0	NO	-	2	0.6375	0.9808	0.7727	0.6739	11.6	1.6	0.9037
prompt-1	MLFI	RF	2	0.6415	0.9808	0.7757	0.6793	11.4	1.6	0.9057
prompt-2	MLFI-ord	RF	2	0.6358	0.9904	0.7744	0.6739	11.8	0.8	0.9077
prompt-3	MLFI	LR	2	0.6159	0.9712	0.7537	0.6413	12.6	2.4	0.8872
prompt-4	MLFI-ord	LR	2	0.6711	0.9615	0.7905	0.7120	9.8	3.2	0.9097
prompt-5	MLFI	XGB	2	0.8548	0.5096	0.6386	0.6739	1.8	40.8	0.7442
prompt-6	MLFI-ord	XGB	2	0.7935	0.7019	0.7449	0.7283	3.8	24.8	0.8241
Avg.	-	-	2	0.6928	0.8708	0.7500	0.6832	8.971	10.74	0.8689
prompt-0	NO	-	4	0.6978	0.9327	0.7984	0.7337	8.4	5.6	0.9060
prompt-1	MLFI	RF	4	0.8659	0.6827	0.7634	0.7609	2.2	26.4	0.8303
prompt-2	MLFI-ord	RF	4	0.5886	0.9904	0.7384	0.6033	14.4	0.8	0.8795
prompt-3	MLFI	LR	4	0.8257	0.8654	0.8451	0.8207	3.8	11.2	0.9096
prompt-4	MLFI-ord	LR	4	0.6375	0.9808	0.7727	0.6739	11.6	1.6	0.9037
prompt-5	MLFI	XGB	4	0.6205	0.9904	0.7630	0.6522	12.6	0.8	0.8995
prompt-6	MLFI-ord	XGB	4	0.8350	0.8269	0.8309	0.8098	3.4	14.4	0.8932
Avg.	-	-	4	0.7244	0.8956	0.7874	0.7220	8.058	8.6857	0.8888
prompt-0	NO	-	8	0.8041	0.7500	0.7761	0.7554	3.8000	20.8000	0.8496
prompt-1	MLFI	RF	8	0.8515	0.8269	0.8390	0.8207	3.0000	14.4000	0.8967
prompt-2	MLFI-ord	RF	8	0.6944	0.9615	0.8065	0.7391	8.8000	3.2000	0.9189
prompt-3	MLFI	LR	8	0.6242	0.9904	0.7658	0.6576	12.4000	0.8000	0.9016
prompt-4	MLFI-ord	LR	8	0.6776	0.9904	0.8047	0.7283	9.8000	0.8000	0.9267
prompt-5	MLFI	XGB	8	0.8099	0.9423	*0.8711*	*0.8424*	4.6000	4.8000	*0.9428*
prompt-6	MLFI-ord	XGB	8	0.8478	0.7500	0.7959	0.7826	2.8000	20.8000	0.8592
Avg.	-	-	8	0.7585	0.8873	0.8084	0.7608	6.4571	9.3714	0.8993
prompt-0	NO	-	16	0.7946	0.8558	0.8241	0.7935	4.6000	12.0000	0.8979
prompt-1	MLFI	RF	16	0.7965	0.8654	0.8295	0.7989	4.6000	11.2000	0.9029
prompt-2	MLFI-ord	RF	16	0.7538	0.9423	0.8376	0.7935	6.4000	4.8000	0.9288
prompt-3	MLFI	LR	16	0.8554	0.6827	0.7594	0.7554	2.4000	26.4000	0.8284
prompt-4	MLFI-ord	LR	16	0.7339	0.8750	0.7982	0.7500	6.6000	10.4000	0.8903
prompt-5	MLFI	XGB	16	0.7638	0.9327	0.8398	0.7989	6.0000	5.6000	0.9269
prompt-6	MLFI-ord	XGB	16	0.8198	0.8750	0.8465	0.8207	4.0000	10.4000	0.9129
Avg.	-	-	16	0.7884	0.8612	0.8193	0.7872	4.9429	11.54	0.8983

Summary. The study of risk and false predictions shows that while OpenAI models on average produced fewer False Negatives (FN) compared to traditional Machine Learning (ML) models, they came with a significant trade-off of higher False Positives (FP). Notably, the OpenAI models demonstrated high variability in their results, indicating that relying on average statistics may not provide a comprehensive view of their performance. The observations underscore the need for careful design and implementation of OpenAI models in clinical decision-making scenarios, especially considering their potentially higher risk of incorrect predictions.

6   Conclusion

In this work, we investigated the utility and implications of employing large language models, particularly OpenAI's ChatGPT, within the healthcare sector. We aimed to demonstrate their potential role in enhancing decision-making processes, drawing particular attention to the use of contextual prompts for high-quality predictions and the value of integrating domain-specific knowledge from interpretable Machine Learning (ML) models.

Our analysis affirmed the strength and promise of OpenAI's ChatGPT for clinical decision-making. In *zero-shot scenarios*, its initial performance was found to lag behind classical ML models. However, with an increase in the number of examples used for prompt construction, i.e., in *few-shot scenarios*, ChatGPT showcased the ability to improve significantly, reaching, and in some instances surpassing, the performance of traditional supervised ML models. This capacity to learn and adapt with additional examples emphasizes the potential of these models in contexts with limited data.

A key finding from our study was the notable performance improvement in ChatGPT when domain knowledge was integrated, specifically prediction outcomes from high-performing ML models such as XGB. This underscores the value of harnessing domain knowledge information and corroborates our hypothesis that expert knowledge (here obtained through XGB) provides the beneficial domain knowledge input. Such integration of AI with medical expertise holds immense potential for healthcare applications, illustrating the ability of AI models to leverage traditional ML insights.

However, we identified considerable variability in the performance of OpenAI models, along with the potential risk of higher False Positives (FP) even though False Negatives (FN) were generally lower compared to traditional ML models. n the medical field, both types of errors have serious implications, *however, the cost of FN can sometimes be particularly high,* such as in critical diagnoses like cancer, where a missed detection could lead to dire consequences. On the other hand, a higher rate of FP, as seen in the OpenAI models, while concerning, could be viewed as a safer error direction in these high-stakes situations. In general, both types of incorrect predictions bear significant implications within a medical context, introducing over-diagnosis, and unnecessary treatments, causing physical, emotional, and financial burdens to patients.

Looking ahead, future endeavors should persist in refining the design of prompts, mitigating social and ethical risks [5,6,14], and optimizing performance. An in-depth examination of zero-shot and few-shot learning dynamics would offer valuable insights for designing more reliable AI systems. Expanding the application of these techniques to different healthcare realms could broaden the impact of AI-assisted decision-making tools. Given the potential risks, we suggest the cautious use of these models in clinical settings, accentuating the importance of careful model design and implementation. Ultimately, the seamless blending of AI with domain-specific expertise will be the key to successfully deploying large language models within the healthcare sector.

References

1. Agrawal, M., Hegselmann, S., Lang, H., Kim, Y., Sontag, D.: Large language models are few-shot clinical information extractors. In: Proceedings of the 2022 Conference on Empirical Methods in Natural Language Processing, pp. 1998–2022 (2022)
2. Bhatti, B.M.: The art and science of crafting effective prompts for llms (2023). https://thebabar.medium.com/the-art-and-science-of-crafting-effective-prompts-for-llms-e04447e8f96a
3. Brown, T., et al.: Language models are few-shot learners. Adv. Neural. Inf. Process. Syst. **33**, 1877–1901 (2020)
4. Chowdhery, A., et al.: Palm: scaling language modeling with pathways. arXiv preprint arXiv:2204.02311 (2022)
5. Deldjoo, Y.: Fairness of chatgpt and the role of explainable-guided prompts. arXiv preprint arXiv:2307.11761 (2023), https://arxiv.org/abs/2307.11761
6. Deldjoo, Y., Jeunen, O., Zamani, H., McAuley, J.: Navigating the harms from recommender systems in the era of large language models. arxiv (2023)
7. Devlin, J., Chang, M.W., Lee, K., Toutanova, K.: Bert: pre-training of deep bidirectional transformers for language understanding. arXiv preprint arXiv:1810.04805 (2018)
8. Janosi, A., Steinbrunn, W., Pfisterer, M., Detrano, R.: Heart disease data set. The UCI KDD Archive (1988)
9. Liu, P., Yuan, W., Fu, J., Jiang, Z., Hayashi, H., Neubig, G.: Pre-train, prompt, and predict: a systematic survey of prompting methods in natural language processing. ACM Comput. Surv. **55**(9), 1–35 (2023)
10. Liu, Z., et al.: Deid-gpt: zero-shot medical text de-identification by gpt-4. arXiv preprint arXiv:2303.11032 (2023)
11. Thoppilan, R., et al.: Lamda: Language models for dialog applications. CoRR abs/2201.08239 (2022). https://arxiv.org/abs/2201.08239
12. Vaswani, A., et al.: Attention is all you need. In: Advances in neural information processing systems 30 (2017)
13. Wang, J., et al.: Prompt engineering for healthcare: Methodologies and applications. arXiv preprint arXiv:2304.14670 (2023)
14. Weidinger, L., et al.: Ethical and social risks of harm from language models (2021)
15. White, J., et al.: A prompt pattern catalog to enhance prompt engineering with chatgpt. arXiv preprint arXiv:2302.11382 (2023)

Simple Framework for Interpretable Fine-Grained Text Classification

Munkhtulga Battogtokh[1]([✉]) [iD], Michael Luck[1] [iD], Cosmin Davidescu[2] [iD], and Rita Borgo[1] [iD]

[1] King's College London, London, UK
{munkhtulga.battogtokh,michael.luck,rita.borgo}@kcl.ac.uk
[2] ContactEngine, Southampton, UK
cosmin.davidescu@nice.com

Abstract. Fine-grained text classification with similar and many labels is a challenge in practical applications. Interpreting predictions in this context is particularly difficult. To address this, we propose a simple framework that disentangles feature importance into more fine-grained links. We demonstrate our framework on the task of intent recognition, which is widely used in real-life applications where trustworthiness is important, for state-of-the-art Transformer language models using their attention mechanism. Our human and semi-automated evaluations show that our approach better explains fine-grained input-label relations than popular feature importance estimation methods LIME and Integrated Gradient and that our approach allows faithful interpretations through simple rules, especially when model confidence is high.

Keywords: Interpretability · Text understanding · Language models

1 Introduction

In practical applications, text classification tasks often have fine-grained labels that are difficult to distinguish from each other [3,25,37], which make interpreting predictions particularly challenging. Overcoming this challenge is important to trustworthiness, which is indispensable for automated systems to be deployed in production where business relationships, user experience, and valuable resources are at stake. Interpretability provides reassurance that predictions are right for the right reasons, allows debugging and continuous development, and ultimately enables developers to gauge their trust in a system by revealing what to expect.

Existing approaches in explainable AI (XAI) for interpreting text classification models are ill-equipped for explaining distinctions between highly similar labels. The most common paradigm for explaining predictions is feature importance [20,26,32], which ranks input features in terms of importance to a given label. It falls under the category of extractive explanations, whose expressiveness is fundamentally limited to the input features only, which unfortunately means that they cannot draw links from those features to the fine-grained nuances of

S. Nowaczyk et al. (Eds.): ECAI 2023 Workshops, CCIS 1947, pp. 398–425, 2024.
https://doi.org/10.1007/978-3-031-50396-2_23

the labels or reveal any implicit knowledge such as common sense that influenced a prediction. On the other hand, more emerging approaches such as natural language explanations generated using large language models (LMs), often together with the predictions by the same model [21], are theoretically expressive enough to reveal common sense reasoning or accommodate fine-grained explanations, but they can be unfaithful to actual model reasoning and have been shown to be unreliable in practice [43]. Furthermore, generative large LMs are expensive, especially if label-specific explanations are required as prompt context and if there are many labels [30], while smaller bidirectional Transformer encoder [38] LMs like BERT [6], DeBERTa [7] and RoBERTa [19] still achieve state-of-the-art performance on classification tasks more cost-effectively.

In this work, we first identify the key problems with current methodologies in text classification for predicting and explaining, which hinder those methodologies from being interpretable, especially for fine-grained practical tasks that require trustworthiness. Then, we propose our simple framework for interpretable fine-grained classification, which allows fine-grained links to be drawn between input features and labels by requiring the labels to be broken down into meaningful constituents. Our framework can be seen as extending the feature importance paradigm by disentangling a given feature importance score into multiple links, which explain input-label correspondence more precisely. We demonstrate our framework with the white-box attention mechanism of state-of-the-art LMs, as we prefer intrinsic interpretability to black-box post-hoc explanations because how to evaluate explanations is still an open question and it is thus unverifiable to what extent black-box explanations truly reflect model reasoning, whereas white-box mechanisms directly show at least some parts of a model's actual prediction process. We evaluate on the task of intent recognition, which is well-known to be fine-grained and is widely used in real-life task-oriented dialogue systems across application domains such as banking [3] and customer service [24] where trustworthiness is crucial.[1]

Our human evaluation, head-to-head comparisons between feature importance explanations and ours, show that our explanations better explain predictions on two well-known intent recognition datasets, which recent work has identified as especially fine-grained [30]. Furthermore, our semi-automated evaluation of explanation faithfulness, the degree to which they accurately represent model reasoning, shows that our explanations are faithful across three intent recognition datasets, especially when the model is confident in its prediction.

In summary, our main findings include 1) an understanding of the limitations of current methodologies including the feature importance paradigm and importance of task formulation in interpretability, 2) a simple framework for interpretable fine-grained classification, and 3) a demonstration and evaluation of our framework, which show that our explanations are faithful and better explain predictions with fine-grained labels than feature importance.

---

[1] Intent recognition remains important in high-responsibility applications despite generative LM-based conversational tools like ChatGPT, which suffer from issues like hallucination, unpredictability, difficulty to control, and privacy concerns [2,28,39].

2   Related Work

2.1   Fine-Grained Text Classification

Fine-grained text classification involves a high number of class labels with subtle differences between them [34]. This is an emerging challenge driven by techno-logical progress in natural language processing (NLP) and practical needs across different tasks, including emotion recognition [25], sentiment analysis [37], and intent recognition [3]. Previous work tailoring to this challenge, especially those focusing on interpretability, is severely limited.

Our focus, intent recognition, is the practical task of assigning an intent label to a user utterance. The intent labels in this task are well-known to be fine-grained and challenging to distinguish, especially in practical applications [3], even for recent very large LMs like GPT-3 [30]. For this work, we consider two different text classification approaches that have been applied to intent recogni-tion, primarily in terms of their intrinsic interpretability (see Sect. 3.1).

The traditional approach is to formulate the task as a single-sentence clas-sification problem and use neural encoder models like BERT with classification heads [3]. The lack of interpretability in this approach is broadly attributed to the black-box nature of the models. Interestingly, this approach is also known to be limited in its ability to generalize to new labels due to its convention of *label encoding*, which means that the intent labels are encoded into arbitrary numeric indices [44]. Surprisingly, previous works have not considered its effect on interpretability. Nevertheless, a different approach [44] has shown that adopt-ing lexicalized natural language representations of the labels and reformulating classification tasks as sentence-pair classification enables zero-shot generaliza-tion. This approach has also been shown to be effective for intent recognition, which has complex and fine-grained labels that can benefit from being explicitly described [14]. The explicit human-readable descriptions can also be useful for interpretability, but previous works have not explored that opportunity.

2.2   XAI for NLP

Existing explanation methods have been categorized along many axes in previous literature [5]. Firstly, they can be either local or global depending on whether they aim to explain the output of a model for a specific input instance or if they aim to explain the general model behavior. We focus on local explanations in this work, as we require the ability to explain certain input instances for practical purposes such as understanding and debugging specific errors. Examples of local explanation methods include the well-known LIME [26] or Integrated Gradient [32], whereas those of global explanations include probing classifiers [4].

Along another important taxonomy axis, explanations can be black-box or white-box. Black-box explanations do not require access to the internal compo-nents or intermediate outputs of their target model. They explain a model *from the outside* by analyzing model output with respect to different inputs. Exam-ples include testing the model with counterfactual perturbations and analyzing the output (e.g., change in prediction probability in the case of a classification model [26]), or presenting a historical example based on output similarity (e.g., outputs of an encoder model [33]) in the case of example-based explanations. On the other hand, white-box explanations or interpretations of self-explaining models rely on intrinsically interpretable mechanisms of the models, e.g., attention mechanism in language models [4].

The former, black-box explanations, have the advantage of being model-agnostic, but they can lack robustness to small perturbations [31], and are costly, especially for use on LMs [43]. More importantly, they infer an explanation for a given input instance *indirectly* based on other similar instances without ever directly explaining how the given instance itself was processed by the model. This is problematic considering that how to evaluate explanation faithfulness [8] is still an open question and it is thus currently impossible to fully verify a given local explanation. On the other hand, white-box explanations directly rely on mechanisms that are part of a model's actual prediction process. While they too can be misinterpreted in an unfaithful way by humans and any interpretations of white-box mechanisms should also be validated as much as possible [8], they at least do not have the problem of potentially misrepresenting the model's prediction process as they themselves are the process, whereas black-box explanations can both misrepresent the model and be misinterpreted by humans.

Finally, recent work on natural language explanations has categorized explanations into extractive versus free-text based on expressiveness [40]. The former includes discrete rationales and continuous feature importance explanations, which are limited in expressiveness to the input features only. On the other hand, the latter refers to natural language explanations that are highly expressive and intuitive to understand. Unfortunately, free-text explanations are far from applicable in high-responsibility practical tasks, as they can be unreliable (inconsistent with the prediction and not factually grounded in the input instance [43]).

3 Feature Relation Framework

3.1 Interpretability Bottleneck in Existing Conventions

In this section, we describe an interpretability bottleneck in existing conventions of *single-sentence* text classification and extractive explanations. Conventionally, text classification tasks are formulated as *single-sentence* classification [3,45], in which labels are traditionally encoded into arbitrary numeric indices. A previous work [44] argued that this *label-encoding* prevents models from "understanding" a label. We agree and add that label-encoding also prevents *us* humans from understanding what the model understands about labels.

The convention obscures the fine-grained aspects of the labels and sets a bottleneck on how fine-grained an explanation can be, i.e., how fine-grained the links drawn between an input and a label can be. The underlying problem is treating the labels as if they were atomic (see Fig. 1a). As a result, explanations cannot explain *how* features relate to the different aspects of labels, and *why* features relate to the labels in the ways they do (unlike in Fig. 1b), which leads

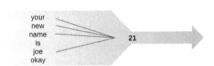
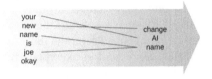

(a) Atomic label: an explanation can only link input features to the label as a whole.

(b) Fine-grained label: an explanation can link input features to label constituents.

Fig. 1. Fine-grained label representations can enable fine-grained explanations.

to explanations that are ambiguous for similar fine-grained labels. Unfortunately, this bottleneck applies to extractive (e.g., feature importance) explanations in general, the predominant paradigm in XAI, which goes hand in hand with the traditional classification approach.

For example, Fig. 2 shows results by existing extractive methods. The explanations seek to answer why an incorrect label was predicted rather than the ground truth. Figures 2a and 2b show LIME-based [26] importance of each word to each label, which lack clarity as to *why* certain words have negative importance while others have positive. For example, although both labels are about verifying identity, "verify" confusingly has negative importance for the label why_verify_identity but positive importance for verify_my_identity while "identity" has positive importance for both. Figure 2c shows an explanation by a method from a different work [9], which can be seen in a sense as more fine-grained, as it aims to highlight only the most contrastive word that distinguishes between two labels. It highlights the word "identity" as the most contrastive word, but also leaves unclear *why*, as it does not reveal *how* "identity" (or other words) relates to each label.

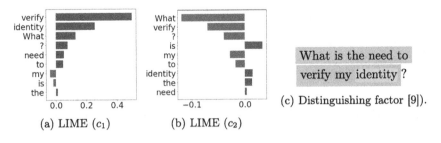

(a) LIME (c_1)   (b) LIME (c_2)

(c) Distinguishing factor [9]).

Fig. 2. Extractive explanations of "Why c_1 rather than c_2?" for a text x where c_1 is an erroneous label (verify_my_identity) and c_2 (why_verify_identity) is the ground-truth label. The text x and the labels c_1 and c_2 are from a public fine-grained text classification dataset for banking domain [3].

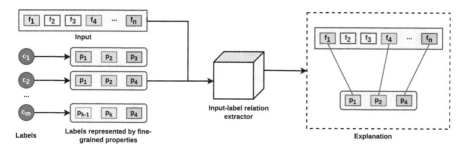

Fig. 3. Given an input and its corresponding label, our *feature relation* explanation framework treats each of them as a collection of features and explains the input-label correspondence in terms of links between the two collections.

3.2 Beyond Feature Importance: Feature Relations as Fine-Grained Explanation

To overcome the interpretability bottleneck described in Sect. 3.1, which stems from neglecting fine-grained label-specific information, we propose our input-label feature relation framework (see Fig. 3). Intuitively, our framework aims to dissect a label into its fine-grained constituents and then to disentangle the importance of features with respect to those. Our simple but powerful *feature relation* framework is generalizable across all data types just like feature importance but more fine-grained thanks to our formulation based on *relations* rather than the coarse-grained idea of *importance*.

Relations. We define *relation* as a mapping $R : A \times B \to \mathbb{R}$ that assigns a strength score l to each $(a \in A, b \in B)$ pair/link where A and B are collections of features. Figure 3 illustrates this as lines between input features $\{f_1, f_2, ..., f_n\}$ and label features $\{p_1, p_2, ..., p_k\}$. In text classification, f_i would be a word or a token of an input text x whereas p_i could be any type of feature that can characterize the labels. For example, the labels could be represented simply by their label names, which distinguish the labels from each other in a human-readable manner (e.g., "verify my identity" versus "why verify identity" in Fig. 2), or they could even be represented with free-text descriptions or representative examples. In those cases, p_i would be words or tokens but our *relation* concept is generalizable beyond text processing to all data types as long as the data instances and the labels/targets are *collections of features*, e.g., sequences of tokens like the above, or tabular data entries, or even image patches. The process of inferring a relation R is not limited to any specific method, which means different methods (e.g., attention, or mutual information between contextual encodings [16]) can be used for this.

Feature. Our general framework is not tied to a specific type of feature either. In existing *feature importance* explanations, a feature can be of a wide variety

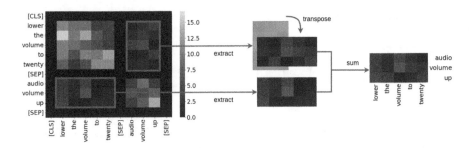

Fig. 4. The process of inferring a relation $R(x, c_i)$ (rightmost) from the attention outputs of a sentence-pair model m. It involves extracting the cross-sentence attention between x and c_i and aggregating them.

of types, e.g., lexical (words/tokens, n-grams, etc.), feature-engineered, graphic (pixels), or even latent [5]. By combining this general definition of features and our above definition of relations, our general framework extends the feature *importance* paradigm to a more fine-grained paradigm of feature *relations*. Instead of considering the importance of only input features (like in Fig. 1a), our framework considers the relations from input features to target/output features (like in Fig. 1b). In general, the relations may be between even different types of features (e.g., n-grams of text x to tokens of label c_i) depending on task and implementation.

3.3   Input-Label Cross Attention

We demonstrate our framework based on attention between input text tokens and label tokens (when the label is represented in natural language), using the sentence-pair approach [14] and state-of-the-art Transformer encoder models [6, 7], for which the attention mechanism is fundamental.

Broadly, interpreting the attention outputs of models is common [4,27,36].[2] However, exactly in what scenarios attention serves as useful explanations is not fully understood and existing works that use attention for interpretability often lack rigorous evaluation of the attention-based explanations [1,10,41]. Unlike such existing works, we evaluate our interpretations thoroughly using human and automated evaluations in the next section.

We extract explanations from attention as follows. Firstly, we concatenate the input pair (x, c_i) together with a special token "[SEP]" as a delimiter, where x is an example of an input text and c_i is the label name, and input the result into the sentence-pair model m, which in turn outputs the prediction score p_i,

---

[2] A concurrent work has used cross-attention of text-to-image stable diffusion models to interpret which parts of images correspond to which words [35]. This fits our general framework but our work differs in that we apply our framework to identify text-label relations for practical fine-grained classification tasks.

to obtain the intermediate attention outputs. Then, we sum them together the attention outputs (matrices) into a single aggregate attention matrix.

Figure 4 (leftmost) shows an example of such an attention matrix, which consists of four quadrants, separated by two crossing lines that correspond to the " [SEP]" token. Two quadrants (top left and bottom right) represent the intra-sentence attention within each of x and c_i, while the other two (circled) represent the *cross-sentence* attention between x and c_i.

We extract a relation $R(x, c_i)$ from the cross-sentence quadrants by summing them together (with one transposed), which results in a matrix $[l_{ij}] \in \mathbb{R}^{m \times n}$ where l_{ij} is the strength value of the *link* between the ith of the m tokens in x and jth of the n tokens in c_i (see Fig. 4).

4 Evaluation

In this section, we present qualitative results and evaluate our framework by comparing it against feature importance and measuring how faithful our explanations are. The rest of this section details our evaluation methods and results.

4.1 Qualitative Results

Figure 5 shows examples of our feature relation explanations next to feature importance explanations. We visualize our explanations similarly to the saliency

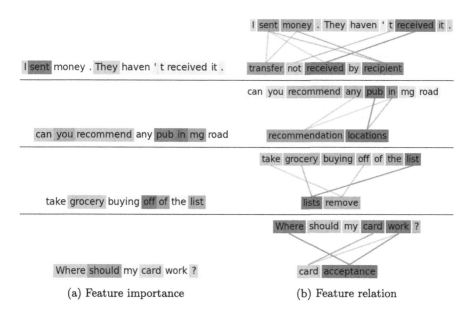

(a) Feature importance   (b) Feature relation

Fig. 5. Feature importance versus feature relation explanations. The labels and the texts are from intent recognition datasets BANKING77 [3] and HWU64 [18]. In each feature relation explanation (Fig. 5b), the label is placed *below* the text. (Color figure online)

visualization of LIME (opacity of the input token highlights corresponds to the total attention they receive from the label tokens and vice versa) and self-attention visualization of BertViz [4]. Unlike feature importance, which can have positive and negative importance (encoded by blue and red highlights respectively), attention values can only be positive (hence only blue highlights). To prevent visual clutter, we only show up to the three strongest links of each token if their strengths exceed a fixed threshold. Our explanations leave less to guess even if the same words are highlighted as important by both explanations (e.g., "pub", "off", "list", "Where", etc.), as the links clarify what fine-grained aspects of the label those words correspond to.

4.2   Head-to-Head Comparison with Feature Importance

Following previous work [29,40], we compare our framework with feature importance in head-to-head comparisons of explanations of each paradigm on examples from two well-known intent recognition datasets employing crowdworkers. The two datasets are BANKING77 [3] and HWU64 [18], which are known to be especially fine-grained [30]. First, we randomly sample 300 test examples from each of the datasets. Then, we visualize two explanations for each sample (a prediction is made using a fine-tuned sentence-pair BERT model) using feature importance (half the time with LIME and the other half with Integrated Gradient) and our feature relations framework (with the same type of visualizations as in Fig. 5). We presented each sample's text and corresponding correct label along with the two alternative visualizations to our study participants and asked them which one best explained the correspondence between the text and the label. For each sample, we asked three different annotators. Appendix B provides further details on our crowdsourcing method. Figure 6 below shows the overall results.

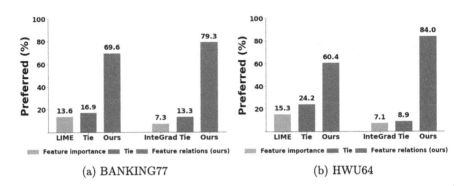

(a) BANKING77   (b) HWU64

Fig. 6. Head-to-head comparison between feature importance explanations, obtained using LIME or Integrated Gradient (InteGrad), and our feature relation explanations across two fine-grained classification datasets.

Do Humans Prefer Feature Relations to Feature Importance? Figure 6 shows the head-to-head comparison results on BANKING77 and HWU64. Across both datasets and both feature importance methods, crowdworkers strongly preferred our feature relation explanations (60.4% to 84.0%) to feature importance (7.1% to 15.3%). In the strongest case, on HWU64, our explanations topped Integrated Gradient explanations with roughly a 12 to 1 win-rate ratio, whereas in the weakest case, our explanations topped LIME with roughly a 4 to 1 win-rate ratio (also on HWU64). LIME was relatively more competitive than Integrated Gradient on both datasets but its win rate against our framework was at best 15.3% and always lower than its tie rate.

Inter-annotator Agreement. Table 1 shows the agreement levels among the annotators in terms of the percentages of examples for which the three annotators had full agreements (3/3), partial agreements (2/3), and full disagreements, as well as Krippendorff's α, which indicates agreement among judges with a value between -1 (systematic disagreement) and 1 (full agreement) [12].

Table 1. Levels of agreement among annotators across conditions.

	BANKING77				HWU64			
	Agree	Partial	Disagree	α	Agree	Partial	Disagree	α
LIME	32.0	60.7	7.3	0.1	19.3	64.7	16.0	0.0
InteGrad	53.3	39.3	7.3	0.2	62.7	33.3	4.0	0.3

Comparisons against Integrated Gradient had moderate agreements, as the annotators fully agreed on more than half of the samples from both datasets and fully disagreed on only 4–7% of the samples. Agreements were lower in the comparisons against LIME, as annotators only partially agreed on the majority of the samples (roughly 60%) and fully agreed on 19–32% of the samples. Krippendorff's α indicated low agreement in general, which could be due to the subjectivity of preferences. However, both full and partial agreements were on strongly preferring our explanations.

Figure 7 shows that more than 90% of the full agreements were on preferring our explanations to both LIME and Integrated Gradient on both datasets. In each combination of a dataset and a feature importance method, there was at most only one full agreement on preferring the feature importance explanation to our explanation. On BANKING against Integrated Gradient and on HWU against LIME, there were zero full agreements on preferring feature importance. This shows that feature importance is highly unlikely to definitively win against our framework, whereas our framework is highly likely to definitively win. Similarly, at least about three-quarters (up to 86.8%) of the partial agreements agreed on preferring our explanations, which further supports that humans prefer feature relations as explanations to feature importance.

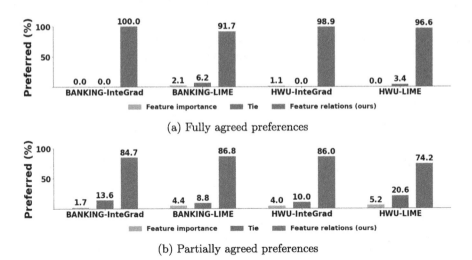

(a) Fully agreed preferences

(b) Partially agreed preferences

Fig. 7. Preferences with different levels of agreement

4.3 Faithfulness

We measure the faithfulness of our attention-based feature relation explanations using a semi-automated evaluation. Faithfulness refers to how accurately explanations represent the reasoning behind model predictions. Previous work has outlined the various evaluation methods in existing works by which faithfulness has been measured and the general reasoning behind those methods [8]. We especially emphasize the reasoning among those that an explanation is unfaithful if it disagrees with the decision of the model that it is explaining. We agree that this is a minimum requirement of a local explanation's faithfulness regardless of the explanation's form (e.g., feature importance, feature relations, natural language, etc.).

A broadly applicable way to measure faithfulness based on the above reasoning is to reproduce model predictions from the explanations [8,13,17,23]. This can be done by tasking humans to guess (predict) model predictions from explanations [23], or using another model or the model itself to do so [13].

In our case, as we utilize attention outputs, which the model is already relying on to make its predictions, we sought to answer how humans can interpret those outputs faithfully, i.e., such that they can guess the model prediction. Toward answering this question, we manually analyzed a few dozen misclassified examples for which we were presented with label-specific attention heatmaps for the predicted and the gold label. As a result, we observed a few simple rules that allowed us to guess model predictions fairly well. From this point, to verify our hypothesis that these rules faithfully predict model predictions for a larger set of examples, we automated them and measured their reproduction accuracy (see Table 2). Unlike tasking humans (or other black-box models) to guess model predictions from explanations without clarifying how they interpreted the explanations, automatically evaluating the faithfulness of human-friendly rules allows us to make clear exactly how the explanations should be interpreted by humans and how and how much they can trust the explanations.

Our two main rules based on our manual analysis, which take two label-specific explanations $R(x, c_1)$ and $R(x, c_2)$ as inputs and predict $c_i \in \{c_1, c_2\}$, are as follows:

1. **Magnitude.** A higher total magnitude of link strength in input-label relation indicates a higher probability of the label. Predicts c_1 if Inequality 1 holds (c_2 otherwise).

$$\sum l_i \in R(x, c_1) > \sum l_j \in R(x, c_2) \tag{1}$$

2. **Concentration (on top-K links).** An input-label relation with a higher concentration of link strength (regardless of total magnitude) indicates a higher probability of the label. Predicts c_1 Inequality 2 holds (c_2 otherwise).

$$\frac{\sum_{i=1}^{K} l_i^1}{\sum l^1} > \frac{\sum_{i=1}^{K} l_i^2}{\sum l^2} \tag{2}$$

where $l^1 \in R^*(x, c_1)$, $l^2 \in R^*(x, c_2)$ while $R^*(x, c_i)$ denotes $R(x, c_i)$ that is flattened and sorted from the largest to smallest value.

Experiments

Datasets and Model. Our results are reported on the previous two datasets BANKING77 [3], HWU64 [18], and an additional intent recognition dataset CLINC150 [15]. Our main results are based on sentence-pair BERT models fine-tuned on each of the datasets (see Appendix A for training details).

Main Evaluation Loop. Algorithm 1 describes how we measure reproduction accuracy on error sets (misclassified examples) in pseudo-code. Given a collection F of rules, we calculate how often each rule f_i successfully reproduces a prediction p_n. We say that f_i reproduces p_n if and only if f_i predicts p_n from each possible pair (p_n, c_j) (where $p_n \in C$, $c_j \in C \setminus \{p_n\}$, and C is the set of all possible intents) given the explanations $R(x_n, p_n)$ and $R(x_n, c_j)$.

Can Our Explanations Faithfully Reproduce Model Predictions?

Table 2 shows the reproduction accuracy of our rules. We used the parameter $K = 1$ in the *concentration* rule, based on additional experiments (see Appendix C.4). In addition to the two main rules from earlier, we evaluated a "Mean" rule, which compares two relations by the mean link strength (added as an alternative to "Magnitude"), and compound rules such as "*Mag. + Con.*" that combine the individual rules by conjugating their Boolean conditions with the logical operator OR. We do so motivated by our observation that the cross-sentence attention for the predicted intent often tends to be *either* higher across all links or strongly

Algorithm 1: Main evaluation loop

input : $C = \{c_i\}$, $D = \{x_i\}$, $P = \{p_i \in C\}$, $F = \{f_i\}$
output: $S = \{s_i \in [0,1]\}$
$S \leftarrow$ sequence of zeros repeated $|F|$ times ;
for $x_n \in D$ **do**
    for $f_i \in F$ **do**
        $P_{f_i} \leftarrow \{\}$;
        for $c_j \in C \setminus \{p_n\}$ **do**
            $p \leftarrow f_i(R(x_n, p_n), R(x_n, c_j))$;
            $P_{f_i}.add(p)$;
        end
        if $\forall_{p \in P_{f_i}}(p = p_n)$ **then**
            $S[i] \leftarrow S[i] + \frac{1}{|D|}$;
        end
    end
end
return S

concentrated on a few links between the keywords. We also include a "Reference" baseline, which compares two relations $R(x, c_1)$ and $R(x, c_2)$ by randomly picking a single value from each and comparing those values with one another, and a "Random" baseline, which makes a random guess between two relations.

Table 2. Reproduction accuracy (%)

	BANKING77	HWU64	CLINC150
Mag.+ Con.+ Mean	**72.8**	**58.4**	**68.0**
Mag. + Con.	63.8	54.0	63.6
Mag. + Mean	34.8	30.1	48.1
Mean + Con.	28.8	28.3	22.5
Mean	14.8	17.7	14.9
Mag.	5.8	15.9	16.5
Con.	0.9	2.7	1.6
Reference	0.0	0.0	0.9
Random	0.0	0.0	0.0

As expected, reproducing model predictions with the random rule is highly improbable as there are many labels in each dataset (the chance is $2^{-(|C|-1)}$ where $|C|$ is the number of labels; see Algorithm 1). Considering this, each non-compound rule was able to reproduce a significant (though low) percentage of

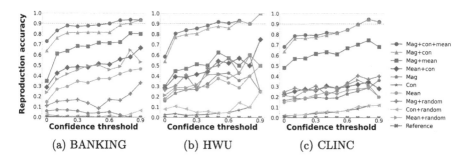

(a) BANKING   (b) HWU   (c) CLINC

Fig. 8. Relation between confidence threshold and reproduction accuracy for different rules (Color figure online)

model predictions. Compound rules from combining two individual rules performed better than both their individual counterparts and those combined with the random rule. Furthermore, in line with our manual analysis, the combination of the magnitude and concentration rules led to a fair reproduction accuracy (54%–63.8%) that is the highest by far among the other two-way combinations. Combining the three rules (magnitude, concentration, and mean) resulted in a higher reproduction accuracy (up to 72.8%). In summary, these results show that cross-sentence attention relations can be interpreted fairly faithfully through simple rules.

Does Model Confidence Correlate with Faithfulness? To understand why reproduction sometimes failed, we investigated how reproduction success is related to relative prediction scores. Therefore, we experimented with different *confidence* thresholds (the minimum *confidence* $|p_{c_1} - p_{c_2}|$ with which to filter

Table 3. Spearman correlations

	BANKING77	HWU64	CLINC150
Mag.+ Con.+ Mean	0.952	0.915	0.964
Mag. + Con.	0.952	**0.976**	0.988
Mag. + Mean	0.964	0.632	0.927
Mean + Con.	0.976	0.903	0.770
Mean + Random	0.891	0.948	0.491
Mag. + Random	0.685	0.345	0.721
Mean	**0.988**	0.855	0.733
Mag.	−0.875	0.564	0.952
Con. + Random	0.261	0.285	0.988
Con.	−0.792	0.867	**1.000**

out examples from our main evaluation loop) based on our observation that when a reproduction failed, the model often had low prediction scores for both c_1 and c_2, i.e., the confidence was also low.

Figure 8 shows that the reproduction rate of our best rules "Mag. + Con. + Mean" and "Mag. + Con." increased up to perfect accuracy as the confidence threshold was increased. These rules achieved strong faithfulness (above 90% reproduction accuracy, indicated by the gray dotted line in Fig. 8) across all datasets (with a confidence threshold of as little as 0.5). Additional experiments further show that our approach achieves highly faithful explanations, even with a different BERT-like model (see Appendix C and D).

Indeed, there was a strong tendency for a positive monotonic correlation between confidence threshold and reproduction accuracy (see Table 3). The reproduction accuracy of the "Mag. + Con." rule had the highest average correlation with confidence threshold across the three datasets, while "Mean" was the only non-compound rule that consistently had a strong positive correlation score. These results show that when model confidence is high, our cross-sentence attention relations can be interpreted with high faithfulness using just simple rules.

5   Conclusion and Future Work

Firstly, we found that conventions of single-sentence classification and extractive explanations suffer from a fundamental interpretability bottleneck, as they ignore fine-grained label information. Based on this insight, we proposed a general framework that prevents the said bottleneck. Subsequently, we demonstrated our framework using the attention mechanism of state-of-the-art Transformer encoder models and evaluated our explanations by comparing them against feature importance explanations and measuring faithfulness. Our results showed that crowdworkers strongly preferred feature relation explanations to feature importance and that our attention-based explanations can be faithfully interpreted through simple rules, especially when model confidence is high.

In future work, we are interested in exploring feature relation explanations in the context of free-text label descriptions (rather than label names). We are also interested in exploring explanations that are expressive enough to not only incorporate the input features and the label but also implicit or external knowledge. In this direction, we find natural language explanations promising (but with its own set of challenges).

Acknowledgement. This work was supported by UK Research and Innovation [grant number EP/S023356/1], in the UKRI Centre for Doctoral Training in Safe and Trusted Artificial Intelligence (www.safeandtrustedai.org).

A   Model Fine-Tuning

For each of the three datasets (BANKING77, CLINC150, and HWU64), we train two models: a conventional single-sentence (1sent) model and a sentence-pair

(2sent) model. The default initial model checkpoint (which we fine-tune) in the main body of this paper is `BERT-base` [6], distributed on Huggingface's Transformers library [42] with `apache-2.0` license. The datasets BANKING, CLINC, and HWU were accessed from Amazon Alexa AI's DialoGLUE benchmark's repository [22] with CC-BY-4.0, CC-BY-SA 3.0, and CC-BY-SA 3.0 licenses respectively.[3]

For both formulations, we fine-tuned `BERT-base` on all examples in the training splits and evaluated on the test sets. The training script was run on NVIDIA Quadro T1000 4GB GPU, which allowed for a batch size of 8 (for both 1sent and 2sent) for the `BERT-base` model with nearly 110 million parameters. The 1sent models took approximately 20 min *to train* on average across the three datasets, while the 2sent models took approximately one hour on average. For each dataset, we optimized using an Adam optimizer [11] with learning rate 3×10^{-5} for 3 epochs, with the rest of the training hyperparameters set to default (by the Transformers library version 4.8.2).

Given an example x from the test or the training set, the 1sent model m_1 calculates $|C|$ (the number of intents in the set of all candidate intents C) prediction scores $[y_i] \in \mathbb{R}^{|C|}$ and outputs the index i with the highest prediction score. On the other hand, the 2sent model m_2 outputs a *match* score (m_2 makes a binary prediction; we treat the prediction score for the positive class as this match score) given x and the natural language name c_i of the intent concatenated together with a special separator token "`[SEP]`". During the *evaluation*, we generate $|C|$ inputs per x, pairing x with each intent c_j, and identify the intent with the highest match score as the 2sent prediction.

However, during *training*, it is not required to pair an example x with all intents. Therefore, given an example x annotated with an intent c_{true}, we generate $2 \times N + 1$ inputs, where $N < |C|$. The N of those are x paired with N random intents (negative labels) that are not c_{true}. Another N are random N example texts from the training split that do not have the intent c_{true} (negative examples), paired with c_{true}. We set N equal to 5 to limit training time according to our resource constraints.

Table 5 reports the accuracy achieved by our main sentence-pair model (BERT-2sent) along with benchmark performances (BERT-fixed and BERT-tuned) from [3] and the accuracy of a single-sentence BERT model (BERT-1sent) that we trained for reference. BERT-2sent is on par with the benchmark model BERT-fixed[4] and approaches BERT-1sent in accuracy (Table 4).

B   Crowdsourcing Details

Our study design followed those of previous work [29,40]. We presented crowdworkers (on Prolific) with two alternative types of explanations and asked them

---

[3] https://github.com/alexa/dialoglue.

[4] BERT-fixed uses mean-pooling of the token encodings as sentence embedding unlike BERT-tuned, which instead uses the encoding of the special token "`[CLS]`".

Table 4. Overview of the datasets

	BANKING77	HWU64	CLINC150
Train examples	8622	8954	15000
Test examples	3080	1076	4500
Num. intents	77	64	150
Domains	1	21	10

Table 5. Accuracy on the three datasets

Model	BANKING77	HWU64	CLINC150
BERT-fixed	87.2	85.8	91.8
BERT-tuned	93.7	92.1	96.9
BERT-1sent	91.5	90.8	95.4
BERT-2sent	85.6	89.5	93.0

to select their preference. We screened participants based on their English language proficiency and location (also as a proxy of language proficiency following [40]) because our evaluation datasets were in English, and based on their education level (at least undergraduate level) because our study involved non-trivial language understanding and familiarity with visualizations. We employed participants from the United Kingdom, the United States, Canada, Australia, and New Zealand with a minimum approval rate of 98% and a minimum of 100 previous submissions on Prolific. All submissions were anonymous and all participants were presented with an information sheet providing the details of our study and were asked for their consent at the beginning of our study.

Quality Control. Before our main head-to-head comparisons, we selected participants based on two preliminary rounds of questions. In the first preliminary round, we presented the crowdworkers with 12 multiple-choice questions based on example texts from fine-grained classification datasets (intent recognition and sentiment analysis) in order to test their ability to understand the fine-grained differences between English texts. We only selected participants who answered at least 11 questions correctly. In the second preliminary round, we presented the participants with 12 explanations, half of them feature importance and the other half feature relation (ours), and asked them to rate how well those explanations explained the correspondence between a given text and its label. We acknowledged that subjectivity can play a significant role here and participants can disagree with us on non-trivial cases or be more or less generous than us (but with similar relative ratings of the different explanations). Therefore, we passed participants through this round based on manually checking their submissions mostly for only low-quality responses (same choice for all questions, too short time spent per question, obvious random clicking on trivial cases, etc.).

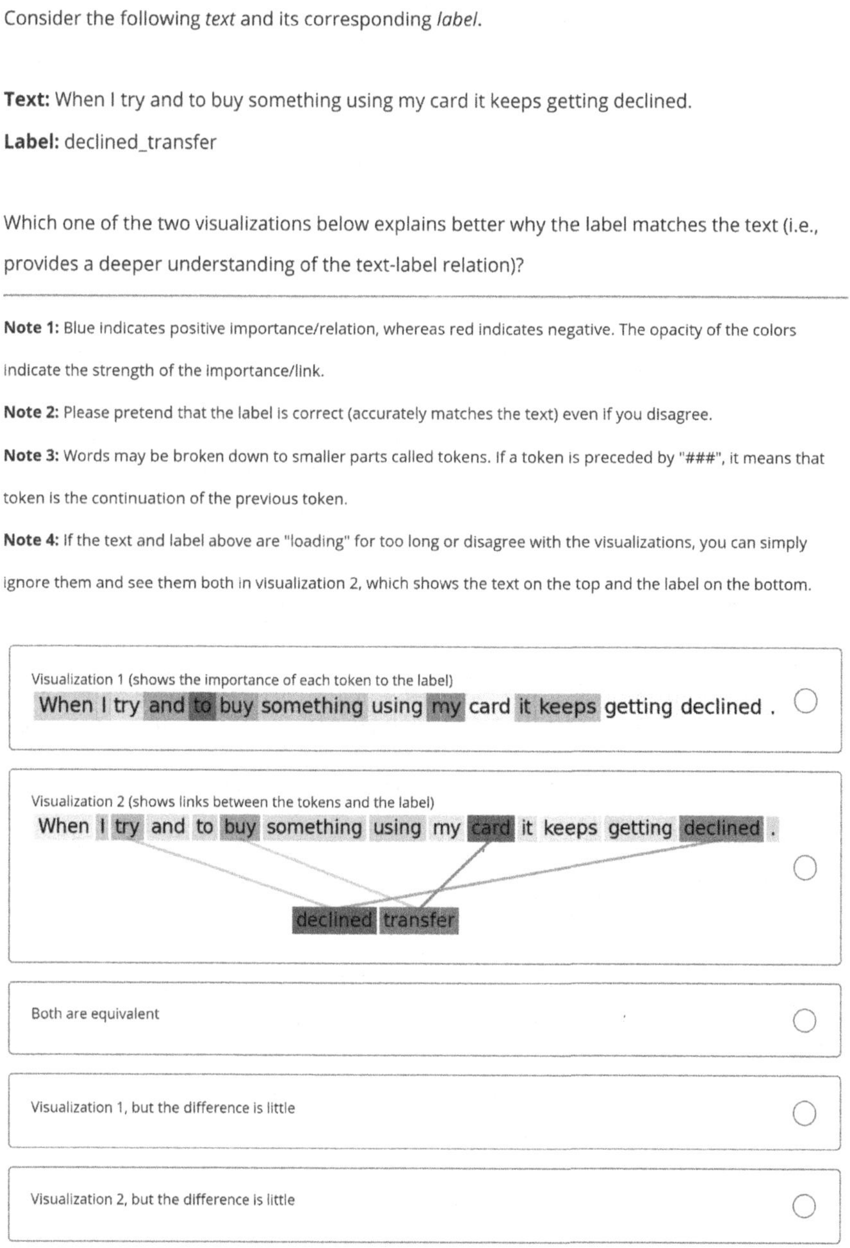

Consider the following *text* and its corresponding *label*.

Text: When I try and to buy something using my card it keeps getting declined.

Label: declined_transfer

Which one of the two visualizations below explains better why the label matches the text (i.e., provides a deeper understanding of the text-label relation)?

Note 1: Blue indicates positive importance/relation, whereas red indicates negative. The opacity of the colors indicate the strength of the importance/link.

Note 2: Please pretend that the label is correct (accurately matches the text) even if you disagree.

Note 3: Words may be broken down to smaller parts called tokens. If a token is preceded by "###", it means that token is the continuation of the previous token.

Note 4: If the text and label above are "loading" for too long or disagree with the visualizations, you can simply ignore them and see them both in visualization 2, which shows the text on the top and the label on the bottom.

Visualization 1 (shows the importance of each token to the label)
When I try and to buy something using my card it keeps getting declined .   ○

Visualization 2 (shows links between the tokens and the label)
When I try and to buy something using my card it keeps getting declined .

declined transfer

○

Both are equivalent   ○

Visualization 1, but the difference is little   ○

Visualization 2, but the difference is little   ○

Fig. 9. User-interface of our head-to-head comparison study (example)

Payment. Our two preliminary rounds paid £1 (20£/h) and £1.5 (15£/h) for 3 and 6 min respectively. Our main survey was expected to take 8–13 minutes and participants were paid £3 (at least 12£/h).

User Interface. Figure 9 shows the user interface of our study, which is implemented on Qualtrics.

C   Further Evaluation

In this section, we report the results from our initial (less computationally expensive) evaluation setting, which we refer to as the *lite* evaluation setting. The results from this setting are on both full test splits and the error sets (the subset of misclassified examples) of the three datasets BANKING77, HWU64, and CLINC150. The key difference from the main evaluation setting is that the *lite* setting asks the contrastive question "Why c_1 rather than c_2?" only once per example whereas the main setting asks it for all possible values of c_2. Moreover, the *lite* setting only evaluates the subset of the rules.

Within the *lite* setting, for each example in the error set, we aim to explain why the model made an error, i.e., "Why c_1 rather than c_2?", where c_1 is the predicted intent and c_2 is the *correct* (ground-truth) intent. On the full sets, our aim is the same for misclassified examples, but for correctly classified examples, it is to explain "why not c_2?", i.e., "Why c_1 rather than c_2?" where c_1 is predicted and c_2 is an intent similar to c_1. For this work, we pick such c_2 from the set of all intents other than c_1, by the highest vector similarity between the intent names (using the spaCy library).

C.1   Faithfulness

Tables 6 and 7 show the *lite* reproduction accuracy of our rules on the error and full sets respectively. We used the parameter $K = 1$ in the *concentration* rule since reproduction rate has a strong negative and monotonic correlation with K (see Appendix C.4).

Table 6. Reproduction accuracy (error set)

	BANKING77	HWU64	CLINC150
Random	49.2	53.1	49.1
Magnitude	59.6	65.5	63.3
Concentration	57.1	52.2	47.8
Mag. + con.	**94.6**	**83.2**	**89.6**

Table 7. Reproduction accuracy (full set)

	BANKING77	HWU64	CLINC150
Random	48.0	49.5	50.7
Magnitude	82.5	83.7	81.3
Concentration	57.6	65.0	59.8
Mag. + con.	**98.6**	**96.2**	**98.7**

All rules consistently achieved higher reproduction accuracy than random guesses. *Magnitude* consistently outperformed *concentration* with an average of 62.8% on the error sets and 82.5% on the full sets. Combining *magnitude* and *concentration* (mag. + con.) achieved the highest values with an average of 89.1% on the error sets and 97.8% on the full sets. The highest reproduction accuracy scores were 98.7% and 98.6%, which were on the full sets of CLINC150 and BANKING77 respectively. These high values suggest that our explanations faithfully explain model predictions.

Table 8. Spearman correlations

	BANKING77		HWU64		CLINC150	
	error	full	error	full	error	full
Mag.+con	−0.10	0.98	**0.93**	0.98	0.99	**1.**
Mag.	**0.94**	**1.**	0.70	**1.**	0.95	**1.**
Con.	−0.39	−0.39	0.85	0.85	**1.**	**1.**

C.2   Correlation between Confidence and Reproduction Accuracy

Figure 10 shows that the reproduction rate of our best rule *mag. + con.* increased up to perfect accuracy on the error sets and near perfect on the full sets as we filtered out evaluation examples with increasing confidence threshold. This was the case despite decreasing number of examples, i.e., a higher drop in accuracy with each failure (see Fig. 11).

Just like in our main results, there was a strong tendency for positive and monotonic correlation (see Table 8, in which most correlation values are close to +1) between the two variables: reproduction accuracy and confidence threshold. The error set of BANKING77 had a weak correlation (value near 0) against this tendency, but Fig. 10a shows that the reproduction accuracy increased even for this case, though *non-monotonically.*

C.3   Importance of Special Tokens

We also hypothesized that certain reproductions may have failed because our cross-sentence relations did not always fully capture model reasoning. Impor-

418   M. Battogtokh et al.

tantly, we ignored the special tokens " [CLS]" and " [SEP]", which are known for aggregating the input and receiving high levels of attention [4], to focus only on human-readable tokens (see Fig. 4). There are three special tokens in each concatenated input that we feed into our model: " [CLS]" as the first token, and two " [SEP]" tokens (one for delimiting the input pairs and one at the end of the input). We experimented with treating the " [CLS]" and the first " [SEP]" as features of text x, while treating the last " [SEP]" as a feature of intent c_i. This led to higher reproduction rates on all datasets (see Table 9).

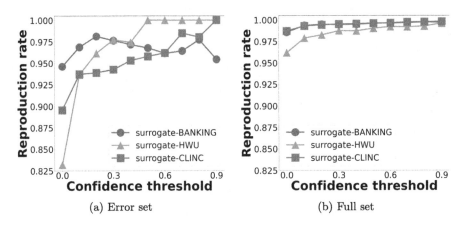

Fig. 10. Graphs showing the correlation between confidence threshold and reproduction accuracy

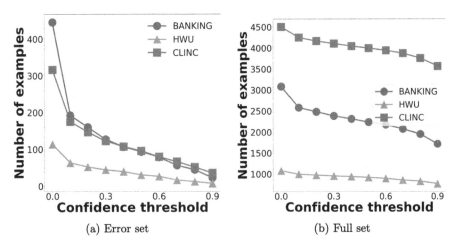

Fig. 11. Graphs showing the correlation between confidence threshold and number of examples

C.4   Correlation Between Concentration Parameter K and Reproduction Accuracy

Figure 12 shows the relation between the parameter K (see Sect. 4.3) in our *concentration* rule and the reproduction accuracy (under the *lite* evaluation setting; see Appendix C.1) of the rule.

As Table 10 shows, there is a strong negative and monotonic correlation between the parameter K and reproduction accuracy.

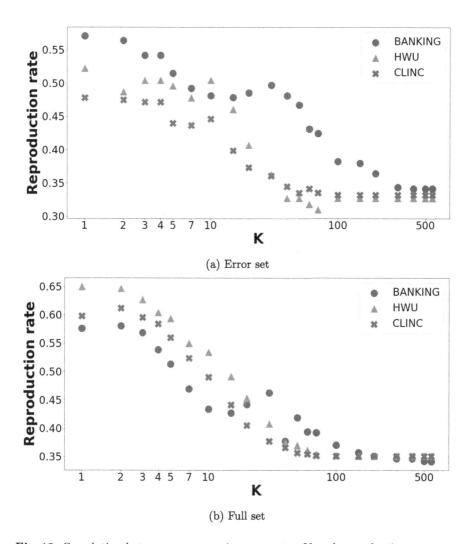

(a) Error set

(b) Full set

Fig. 12. Correlation between concentration parameter K and reproduction accuracy

Table 9. Reproduction accuracy (full set) when special tokens are treated as features of text x and intent c_i (with confidence threshold) under *lite* evaluation setting (see Appendix C.1)

Min. confidence	BANKING77	HWU64	CLINC150
0	99.81	99.91	99.87
0.1	99.96	100	99.95
0.2	99.96	100	99.95
0.3	99.96	100	99.98
0.4	99.96	100	99.98
0.5	99.95	100	99.98
0.6	99.95	100	99.97
0.7	100	100	99.97
0.8	100	100	99.97
0.9	100	100	99.97

Table 10. Spearman correlations between K and reproduction accuracy. There is a strong negative correlation between K and reproduction accuracy across all datasets.

BANKING77		HWU64		CLINC150	
error	full	error	full	error	full
-0.975	-0.979	-0.833	-0.989	-0.975	-0.980

D   Experiments with DeBERTa

Model training followed. Model training followed the same process for both DeBERTa and BERT except for a few details (see Appendix A). We used `microsoft/deberta-base` [7] with approximately 140 million parameters, distributed on Huggingface's Transformers library [42] with an MIT license. We used learning rates of 1×10^{-2} or 2×10^{-2} selected by greedy search (due to resource constraints), and batch size of 1 or 2 with our DeBERTa models. *Training* took approximately one hour for the 1sent models across the three datasets, and 4–6 h for the 2sent models. On the other hand, our main *evaluation loop* takes approximately less than 5 min on the full set for both 1sent and 2sent models. The DeBERTa model trained with single-sentence formulation (DeBERTa-1sent) achieved the highest accuracy among the models we trained. However, DeBERTa trained with the sentence-pair formulation (DeBERTa-2sent) achieved scores lower than BERT-2sent, possibly due to non-optimal choices of hyperparameters (especially learning rate). Nevertheless, we proceeded to use this DeBERTa-2sent model since its performance is adequate for our primary purpose of evaluating interpretability (Table 11).

Table 11. Accuracy of our fine-tuned models including DeBERTa trained with single-sentence (DeBERTa-1sent) and sentence-pair (DeBERTa-2sent) approaches

Model	BANKING77	HWU64	CLINC150
BERT-1sent	91.5	90.8	95.4
BERT-2sent	85.6	89.5	93.0
DeBERTa-1sent	**92.8**	**91.0**	**96.0**
DeBERTa-2sent	75.3	84.5	90.7

Faithfulness Results. The faithfulness results with DeBERTa-2sent were similar to those with BERT-2sent (under the *lite* evaluation setting; see Appendix C), since the *mag. + con.* rule achieved high reproduction accuracy on both the error and full sets (see Tables 12 and 13). However, an interesting difference was that *magnitude* was better at reproducing model prediction than *concentration* with BERT, but it was the other way around with DeBERTa.

Table 12. Reproduction accuracy (error set) with DeBERTa

	BANKING77	HWU64	CLINC150
Random	53.0	47.0	46.0
Magnitude	47.0	56.0	44.4
Concentration	58.6	65.7	56.8
Mag. + con.	**93.6**	**93.4**	**86.3**

Table 13. Reproduction accuracy (full set) with DeBERTa

	BANKING77	HWU64	CLINC150
Random	50.6	51.7	49.0
Magnitude	63.9	76.0	58.3
Concentration	57.9	63.8	70.6
Mag. + con.	**96.1**	**97.3**	**95.9**

References

1. Bastings, J., Filippova, K.: The elephant in the interpretability room: why use attention as explanation when we have saliency methods? In: Proceedings of the Third BlackboxNLP Workshop on Analyzing and Interpreting Neural Networks for NLP, pp. 149–155. Association for Computational Linguistics, November 2020. https://doi.org/10.18653/v1/2020.blackboxnlp-1.14

2. Brown, T.B., et al.: Language models are few-shot learners. In: Proceedings of the 34th International Conference on Neural Information Processing Systems, NIPS 2020, Curran Associates Inc., Red Hook, NY, USA (2020). https://dl.acm.org/doi/abs/10.5555/3495724.3495883

3. Casanueva, I., Temčinas, T., Gerz, D., Henderson, M., Vulić, I.: Efficient intent detection with dual sentence encoders. In: Proceedings of the 2nd Workshop on Natural Language Processing for Conversational AI, pp. 38–45. Association for Computational Linguistics, July 2020. https://doi.org/10.18653/V1/2020.NLP4CONVAI-1.5

4. Clark, K., Khandelwal, U., Levy, O., Manning, C.D.: What does BERT look at? An analysis of BERT's attention. In: Proceedings of the Second BlackboxNLP Workshop on Analyzing and Interpreting Neural Networks for NLP, pp. 276–286. Association for Computational Linguistics (2019). https://doi.org/10.18653/v1/W19-4828

5. Danilevsky, M., Qian, K., Aharonov, R., Katsis, Y., Kawas, B., Sen, P.: A survey of the state of explainable AI for natural language processing. In: Proceedings of the 1st Conference of the Asia-Pacific Chapter of the Association for Computational Linguistics and the 10th International Joint Conference on Natural Language Processing, pp. 447–459. Association for Computational Linguistics, Suzhou, China, December 2020. https://aclanthology.org/2020.aacl-main.46

6. Devlin, J., Chang, M.W., Lee, K., Toutanova, K.: BERT: pre-training of deep bidirectional transformers for language understanding. In: Proceedings of the 2019 Conference of the North American Chapter of the Association for Computational Linguistics: Human Language Technologies, Volume 1 (Long and Short Papers), pp. 4171–4186. Association for Computational Linguistics, Minneapolis, Minnesota, June 2019. https://doi.org/10.18653/v1/N19-1423

7. He, P., Liu, X., Gao, J., Chen, W.: DeBERTa: decoding-enhanced BERT with disentangled attention. In: International Conference on Learning Representations (2021). https://openreview.net/forum?id=XPZIaotutsD

8. Jacovi, A., Goldberg, Y.: Towards faithfully interpretable NLP systems: how should we define and evaluate faithfulness? In: Proceedings of the 58th Annual Meeting of the Association for Computational Linguistics, pp. 4198–4205. Association for Computational Linguistics, Online, July 2020. https://doi.org/10.18653/v1/2020.acl-main.386

9. Jacovi, A., Swayamdipta, S., Ravfogel, S., Elazar, Y., Choi, Y., Goldberg, Y.: Contrastive explanations for model interpretability. In: Proceedings of the 2021 Conference on Empirical Methods in Natural Language Processing, pp. 1597–1611. Association for Computational Linguistics, Online and Punta Cana, Dominican Republic, November 2021. https://doi.org/10.18653/v1/2021.emnlp-main.120

10. Jain, S., Wallace, B.C.: Attention is not explanation. In: Proceedings of the 2019 Conference of the North American Chapter of the Association for Computational Linguistics: Human Language Technologies, Volume 1 (Long and Short Papers), pp. 3543–3556. Association for Computational Linguistics, Minneapolis, Minnesota, June 2019. https://doi.org/10.18653/v1/N19-1357

11. Kingma, D.P., Ba, J.L.: Adam: a method for stochastic optimization. In: International Conference on Learning Representations (2015). https://arxiv.org/abs/1412.6980v9

12. Krippendorff, K.: Computing Krippendorff's alpha-reliability (2011)

13. Kumar, S., Talukdar, P.: NILE: natural language inference with faithful natural language explanations. In: Proceedings of the 58th Annual Meeting of the Associa-

tion for Computational Linguistics, pp. 8730–8742. Association for Computational Linguistics, Online, July 2020. https://doi.org/10.18653/v1/2020.acl-main.771

14. Lamanov, D., Burnyshev, P., Artemova, K., Malykh, V., Bout, A., Piontkovskaya, I.: Template-based approach to zero-shot intent recognition. In: Proceedings of the 15th International Conference on Natural Language Generation, pp. 15–28. Association for Computational Linguistics, Waterville, Maine, USA and Virtual Meeting, July 2022. https://aclanthology.org/2022.inlg-main.2

15. Larson, S., et al.: An evaluation dataset for intent classification and out-of-scope prediction. In: Proceedings of the 2019 Conference on Empirical Methods in Natural Language Processing and the 9th International Joint Conference on Natural Language Processing (EMNLP-IJCNLP), pp. 1311–1316. Association for Computational Linguistics, Hong Kong, China, November 2019. https://doi.org/10.18653/v1/D19-1131

16. Li, Z., et al.: A unified understanding of deep NLP models for text classification. IEEE Trans. Visual Comput. Graphics **28**(12), 4980–4994 (2022). https://doi.org/10.1109/TVCG.2022.3184186

17. Liu, H., Yin, Q., Wang, W.Y.: Towards explainable NLP: a generative explanation framework for text classification. In: Proceedings of the 57th Annual Meeting of the Association for Computational Linguistics, pp. 5570–5581. Association for Computational Linguistics, Florence, Italy, July 2019. https://doi.org/10.18653/v1/P19-1560

18. Liu, X., Eshghi, A., Swietojanski, P., Rieser, V.: Benchmarking natural language understanding services for building conversational agents. In: Marchi, E., Siniscalchi, S.M., Cumani, S., Salerno, V.M., Li, H. (eds.) Increasing Naturalness and Flexibility in Spoken Dialogue Interaction. LNEE, vol. 714, pp. 165–183. Springer, Singapore (2021). https://doi.org/10.1007/978-981-15-9323-9_15

19. Liu, Y., et al.: RoBERTa: a robustly optimized BERT pretraining approach. arXiv (2019). https://arxiv.org/abs/1907.11692

20. Lundberg, S.M., Lee, S.I.: A unified approach to interpreting model predictions. In: Guyon, I., et al. (eds.) Advances in Neural Information Processing Systems, vol. 30. Curran Associates, Inc. (2017). https://dl.acm.org/doi/10.5555/3295222.3295230

21. Marasovic, A., Beltagy, I., Downey, D., Peters, M.: Few-shot self-rationalization with natural language prompts. In: Findings of the Association for Computational Linguistics: NAACL 2022, pp. 410–424. Association for Computational Linguistics, Seattle, United States, July 2022. https://doi.org/10.18653/v1/2022.findings-naacl.31

22. Mehri, S., Eskenazi, M.: DialoGLUE: a natural language understanding benchmark for task-oriented dialogue. arXiv (2020). https://arxiv.org/abs/2009.13570

23. Nguyen, D.: Comparing automatic and human evaluation of local explanations for text classification. In: Proceedings of the 2018 Conference of the North American Chapter of the Association for Computational Linguistics: Human Language Technologies, Volume 1 (Long Papers), pp. 1069–1078. Association for Computational Linguistics, New Orleans, Louisiana, June 2018. https://doi.org/10.18653/v1/N18-1097

24. Nuruzzaman, M., Hussain, O.K.: A survey on chatbot implementation in customer service industry through deep neural networks. In: 2018 IEEE 15th International Conference on e-Business Engineering (ICEBE), pp. 54–61 (2018). https://doi.org/10.1109/ICEBE.2018.00019

25. Rashkin, H., Smith, E.M., Li, M., Boureau, Y.L.: Towards empathetic open-domain conversation models: a new benchmark and dataset. In: Proceedings of the 57th Annual Meeting of the Association for Computational Linguistics, pp. 5370–5381. Association for Computational Linguistics, Florence, Italy, July 2019. https://doi.org/10.18653/v1/P19-1534

26. Ribeiro, M.T., Singh, S., Guestrin, C.: "Why Should I Trust You?": explaining the predictions of any classifier. In: Proceedings of the 22nd ACM SIGKDD International Conference on Knowledge Discovery and Data Mining, KDD 2016, pp. 1135–1144. Association for Computing Machinery, New York, NY, USA (2016). https://doi.org/10.1145/2939672.2939778

27. Rogers, A., Kovaleva, O., Rumshisky, A.: A primer in BERTology: what we know about how BERT works. Trans. Assoc. Comput. Linguist. **8**, 842–866 (2021). https://doi.org/10.1162/tacl_00349

28. Roller, S., et al.: Recipes for building an open-domain chatbot. In: Proceedings of the 16th Conference of the European Chapter of the Association for Computational Linguistics: Main Volume, pp. 300–325. EACL, April 2021. https://doi.org/10.18653/v1/2021.eacl-main.24

29. Saha, S., Hase, P., Rajani, N., Bansal, M.: Are hard examples also harder to explain? A study with human and model-generated explanations. In: Proceedings of the 2022 Conference on Empirical Methods in Natural Language Processing, pp. 2121–2131. Association for Computational Linguistics, Abu Dhabi, United Arab Emirates, December 2022. https://aclanthology.org/2022.emnlp-main.137

30. Sahu, G., Rodriguez, P., Laradji, I., Atighehchian, P., Vazquez, D., Bahdanau, D.: Data augmentation for intent classification with off-the-shelf large language models. In: Proceedings of the 4th Workshop on NLP for Conversational AI, pp. 47–57. Association for Computational Linguistics, Dublin, Ireland, May 2022. https://doi.org/10.18653/v1/2022.nlp4convai-1.5

31. Slack, D., Hilgard, A., Lakkaraju, H., Singh, S.: Counterfactual explanations can be manipulated. In: Ranzato, M., Beygelzimer, A., Dauphin, Y., Liang, P., Vaughan, J.W. (eds.) Advances in Neural Information Processing Systems, vol. 34, pp. 62–75. Curran Associates, Inc. (2021). https://proceedings.neurips.cc/paper/2021/hash/009c434cab57de48a31f6b669e7ba266-Abstract.html

32. Sundararajan, M., Taly, A., Yan, Q.: Axiomatic attribution for deep networks. In: Proceedings of the 34th International Conference on Machine Learning - Volume 70, ICML 2017, pp. 3319–3328 (2017). https://dl.acm.org/doi/10.5555/3305890.3306024

33. Suresh, H., Lewis, K.M., Guttag, J., Satyanarayan, A.: Intuitively assessing ML model reliability through example-based explanations and editing model inputs. In: 27th International Conference on Intelligent User Interfaces, IUI 2022, pp. 767–781. Association for Computing Machinery, New York, NY, USA (2022). https://doi.org/10.1145/3490099.3511160

34. Suresh, V., Ong, D.: Not all negatives are equal: label-aware contrastive loss for fine-grained text classification. In: Proceedings of the 2021 Conference on Empirical Methods in Natural Language Processing, pp. 4381–4394. Association for Computational Linguistics, Online and Punta Cana, Dominican Republic, November 2021. https://doi.org/10.18653/v1/2021.emnlp-main.359

35. Tang, R., et al.: What the DAAM: interpreting stable diffusion using cross attention. In: Proceedings of the 61st Annual Meeting of the Association for Computational Linguistics (Volume 1: Long Papers), pp. 5644–5659. Toronto, Canada, July 2023. https://aclanthology.org/2023.acl-long.310

36. Tenney, I., Das, D., Pavlick, E.: BERT rediscovers the classical NLP pipeline. In: Proceedings of the 57th Annual Meeting of the Association for Computational Linguistics, pp. 4593–4601. Association for Computational Linguistics, Florence, Italy, July 2019. https://doi.org/10.18653/v1/P19-1452
37. Theodoropoulos, P., Alexandris, C.: Fine-grained sentiment analysis of multidomain online reviews. In: Kurosu, M. (ed.) Human-Computer Interaction. Technological Innovation, vol. 13303, pp. 264–278. Springer, Cham (2022). https://doi.org/10.1007/978-3-031-05409-9_20
38. Vaswani, A., et al.: Attention is all you need. In: Guyon, I., et al. (eds.) Advances in Neural Information Processing Systems, vol. 30. Curran Associates, Inc. (2017). https://proceedings.neurips.cc/paper/2017/file/3f5ee243547dee91fbd053c1c4a845aa-Paper.pdf
39. Weidinger, L., et al.: Taxonomy of risks posed by language models. In: Proceedings of the 2022 ACM Conference on Fairness, Accountability, and Transparency, FAccT 2022, pp. 214–229. Association for Computing Machinery, New York, NY, USA (2022). https://doi.org/10.1145/3531146.3533088
40. Wiegreffe, S., Hessel, J., Swayamdipta, S., Riedl, M., Choi, Y.: Reframing human-AI collaboration for generating free-text explanations. In: Proceedings of the 2022 Conference of the North American Chapter of the Association for Computational Linguistics: Human Language Technologies, pp. 632–658. Association for Computational Linguistics, Seattle, United States, July 2022. https://doi.org/10.18653/v1/2022.naacl-main.47
41. Wiegreffe, S., Pinter, Y.: Attention is not not explanation. In: Proceedings of the 2019 Conference on Empirical Methods in Natural Language Processing and the 9th International Joint Conference on Natural Language Processing (EMNLP-IJCNLP), pp. 11–20. Association for Computational Linguistics, Hong Kong, China, November 2019. https://doi.org/10.18653/v1/D19-1002
42. Wolf, T., et al.: Transformers: state-of-the-art natural language processing. In: Proceedings of the 2020 Conference on Empirical Methods in Natural Language Processing: System Demonstrations, pp. 38–45. Association for Computational Linguistics, Online, October 2020. https://doi.org/10.18653/v1/2020.emnlp-demos.6
43. Ye, X., Durrett, G.: The unreliability of explanations in few-shot prompting for textual reasoning. In: NeurIPS (2022). https://proceedings.neurips.cc/paper_files/paper/2022/file/c402501846f9fe03e2cac015b3f0e6b1-Paper-Conference.pdf
44. Yin, W., Hay, J., Roth, D.: Benchmarking zero-shot text classification: datasets, evaluation and entailment approach. In: Proceedings of the 2019 Conference on Empirical Methods in Natural Language Processing and the 9th International Joint Conference on Natural Language Processing (EMNLP-IJCNLP), pp. 3914–3923. Association for Computational Linguistics, Hong Kong, China, November 2019. https://doi.org/10.18653/v1/D19-1404
45. Zhang, X., Wang, H.: A joint model of intent determination and slot filling for spoken language understanding. In: Proceedings of the Twenty-Fifth International Joint Conference on Artificial Intelligence, IJCAI 2016, pp. 2993–2999. AAAI Press (2016). https://dl.acm.org/doi/10.5555/3060832.3061040

Mark My Words: Dangers
of Watermarked Images in ImageNet

Kirill Bykov[1,2(✉)] ⓘ, Klaus-Robert Müller[1,3,4,5] ⓘ,
and Marina M.-C. Höhne[2,5,6,7] ⓘ

[1] Technische Universität Berlin, Berlin, Germany
[2] Understandable Machine Intelligence Lab, Leibniz Institute for Agricultural
Engineering and Bioeconomy, Potsdam, Germany
kbykov@atb-potsdam.de
[3] Department of Artificial Intelligence, Korea University, Seoul, Korea
[4] Max Planck Institute for Informatics, Saarbrücken, Germany
[5] BIFOLD – Berlin Institute for the Foundations of Learning and Data, Berlin,
Germany
[6] Department of Computer Science, University of Potsdam, Potsdam, Germany
[7] UiT the Arctic University of Norway, Tromsø, Norway

Abstract. The utilization of pre-trained networks, especially those
trained on ImageNet, has become a common practice in Computer
Vision. However, prior research has indicated that a significant number of
images in the ImageNet dataset contain watermarks, making pre-trained
networks susceptible to learning artifacts such as watermark patterns
within their latent spaces. In this paper, we aim to assess the extent
to which popular pre-trained architectures display such behavior and to
determine which classes are most affected. Additionally, we examine the
impact of watermarks on the extracted features. Contrary to the popular belief that the Chinese logographic watermarks impact the "carton"
class only, our analysis reveals that a variety of ImageNet classes, such as
"monitor", "broom", "apron" and "safe" rely on spurious correlations.
Finally, we propose a simple approach to mitigate this issue in fine-tuned
networks by ignoring the encodings from the feature-extractor layer of
ImageNet pre-trained networks that are most susceptible to watermark
imprints.

Keywords: Explainable AI · Representation Analysis · Spurious
correlation identification

1 Introduction

In recent years, the utilization of ImageNet [5] pre-trained models has become
a standard practice in Computer Vision applications [13]. Trained on the large
and diverse collection of images, these models obtain the ability to extract high-
level visual features that later could be transferred to a different task. This
technique, referred to as transfer learning (see e.g. [27] for a review), has proven

S. Nowaczyk et al. (Eds.): ECAI 2023 Workshops, CCIS 1947, pp. 426–434, 2024.
https://doi.org/10.1007/978-3-031-50396-2_24

to be highly effective, leading to significant advancements in various computer vision applications, such as object detection [24], semantic segmentation [26] and classification [30].

Deep Neural Networks (DNNs), despite being highly effective across a variety of applications, are prone to learning spurious correlations, i.e., erroneous relationships between variables that seem to be associated based on a given dataset but in reality lack a causal relationship [12]. This phenomenon, referred to as the "Clever-Hans effect" [15] or "shortcut-learning" [7], impairs the model's ability to generalize. In Computer Vision (CV), such correlations may manifest as DNNs' dependence on background information for image classification [28], textural information [8], secondary objects [18], or unintended artifacts, such as human pen markings in skin cancer detection [1] and patient information in X-ray images for pneumonia detection [32].

Recent studies have uncovered the presence of spurious correlations in the ImageNet dataset, specifically, the connection of the Chinese logographic watermarks (illustrated in the Fig. 1) to the "carton" class [1,3,16]. Such correlations potentially render networks trained on ImageNet susceptible to developing watermark detectors within their latent space, which can result in inaccurate predictions when confronted with similar patterns in the data. Alarmingly, this tendency persists even post fine-tuning on diverse datasets [3], suggesting that the susceptibility to watermarks may not be confined to ImageNet networks, but could possibly extend to all models that undergo fine-tuning.

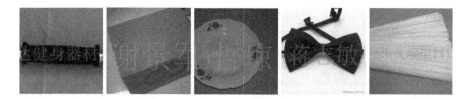

Fig. 1. A number of watermarked images have been identified within the ImageNet training dataset.

In this study, we investigate the specific ImageNet classes that are impacted by the artifact-driven behavior of watermarks. We provide evidence that models trained on ImageNet display a considerable dependency on Chinese watermarks, extending beyond the previously considered "carton" class to include various other classes. Remarkably, in some models, the proportion of high-level representations that are able to detect watermarks exceeds 10%. Finally, we suggest a simple solution to mitigate such behavior during transfer learning, which involves the elimination of the most artifact-sensitive representations, while maintaining the model's performance with negligible impact.

| Baseline | Chinese | Latin | Hindi | Numerals |

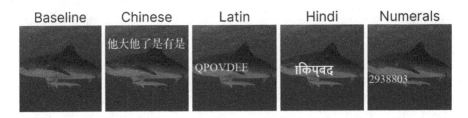

Fig. 2. The illustration shows the image in the baseline dataset and its corresponding watermarked versions.

2   Method

In this work, we define neural representations as sub-functions of a model that map the input domain to a scalar value indicating the activation of a specific neuron. Our analysis focuses on two primary scenarios: scalar representations of output classes and *feature-extractor* representations, which correspond to the layer preceding the output logit layer[1].

To evaluate the susceptibility of individual representations to watermarks, we created binary classification datasets between normal and watermarked images and assessed their ability to distinguish between the two classes. We followed the approach outlined in [3] and used a baseline dataset of 998 ImageNet images[2]. We created four probing datasets by inserting random textual watermarks in the three most popular languages (Chinese, Latin, Hindi) [19] and Arabic numerals, as illustrated in Fig. 2. For each image in the baseline dataset, we inserted a random string of 7 symbols, selected from the set of the 20 most frequently occurring characters in each language [4,25] (for Arabic numerals we sample digits out of 10 available numbers). The watermark was placed randomly within the image, subject to the requirement of full visibility. The font size for all watermarks has been set to 30, while the image dimensions remain standard at 224 × 224 pixels.

We evaluated the representations' ability to differentiate between watermarked and normal classes using AUC ROC, a widely used performance metric for binary classifiers. To do so, we utilized the true labels provided by the two datasets, where class 1 represents images with a watermark and class 0 represents those without. We first calculated the scalar activations from a specific neural representation for all images from both classes. Then, utilizing the binary labels, we calculated the AUC ROC classification score based on the differences in activations. AUC ROC score of 1 indicates a perfect classifier, ranking the watermarked images consistently higher than normal ones, and 0.5 a random classifier.

---

[1] In the case of neurons that produce multi-dimensional activations, such as convolutional neurons, the channel neurons were analyzed by taking the average of the activation maps per each channel.

[2] Images were obtained from https://github.com/EliSchwartz/imagenet-sample-images, excluding 2 images that already contained Chinese logographic watermarks.

However, we can also observe scores less than 0.5, such as the score of 0 illustrating the perfect classifier, that is de-activated by the watermarked images. To measure the general ability of representations to differentiate between the two classes and provide evidence that the concept has been learned, we defined a *differentiability* measure $d = \max(A, 1 - A)$, where A is the AUC ROC score of the representation in the particular binary classification problem.

3   Results

To analyze the effects of watermarked images on learned representations, we employed 20 popular ImageNet-pre-trained Computer Vision architectures, namely AlexNet [14], ResNet 18, 50, 101, and 152 [10], ResNext 101 [29], WideResNet 101 [31], ViT [6], BEiT [2], Inception V3 [23], DenseNet 121, 161, and 201 [11], GoogLeNet [22], MobileNet V2 [20], ShuffleNet V2 [17], VGG 11, 13, 16, and 19 [21].

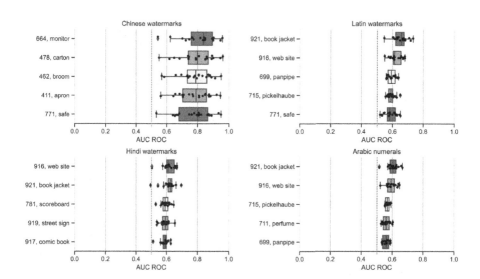

Fig. 3. ImageNet classes with the highest mean AUC ROC scores across the models analyzed in 4 different scenarios (Chinese, Latin, Hindi, and Numeric watermarks). Each dot represents the AUC ROC performance of the class representation for a single model.

For the 4 different scenarios, we collected the AUC ROC scores for every class logit representation across all 20 ImageNet pre-trained networks. Figure 3 illustrates the top-5 ImageNet classes by the highest average AUC ROC across the 20 models. We can observe the clear distinction between the different scenarios – Chinese watermarks show significantly higher average classification scores, compared to the other three watermarks, namely Latin, Hindi, and Arabic numerals.

Furthermore, it can be observed that classes with a high capability for detecting Chinese watermarks are not inherently linked to textual objects, whereas classes for other watermarks have a natural association with text, such as "web site" or "book jacket". This observation supports the conclusion that the ability of DNNs to detect Chinese logograms results from the Clever-Hans effect and is not desirable, whereas this cannot be said for other text detectors. Interestingly, by analyzing the classes with the lowest average AUC ROC we could even reveal—for the first time—the ability of ImageNet classes to detect the absence of the Chinese watermarks in images, which was not given for the other types of watermarks, illustrated in the Fig. 4.

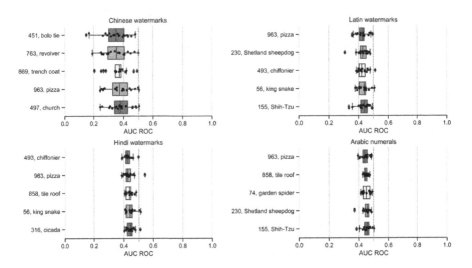

Fig. 4. Top-5 ImageNet classes ranked by the lowest average AUC ROC across 20 analyzed models for 4 different scenarios.

Figure 5 illustrates the number of representations that are sensitive to the Chinese symbols, across the logit and feature-extractor layers (layers of representations, preceding the last prediction layer) of different networks. From the left figure, which represents the sensitivity of output logits, we can observe that nearly all of the networks exhibit sensitive logit representations. This could be the reason for the average drop of 10.6% in model performance when transparent Chinese watermarks are added to the ImageNet validation dataset, as reported in [16]. Some networks, such as GoogleNet, have up to 285 output classes (out of 1000) that are susceptible to Chinese watermarks. The right figure, which represents the ratio of sensitive representations to the total number of representations in the feature-extractor layers, reveals a significant proportion of representations that have a high degree of differentiability toward the Chinese watermarks. Furthermore, we can observe that several networks, including DenseNet-161, ResNet-18, and GoogLeNet exhibit at least several representations with very high watermark differentiability scores ($d > 0.95$), which is in line with the reported high number of Chinese-sensitive class representations across output logit layer.

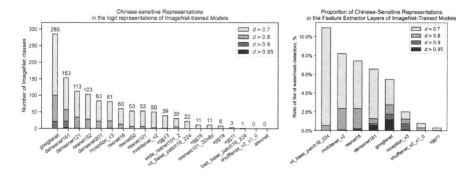

Fig. 5. *Left*: Number of output class representations that exhibit a high degree of differentiability towards Chinese watermarks across various ImageNet models. *Right*: Percentage of representations in the feature-extractor layers of various networks that demonstrate a high degree of differentiability towards Chinese watermarks.

4 Ignoring Sensitive Embeddings During Fine-Tuning

Pre-trained ImageNet models are frequently utilized as feature extractors, where the pre-trained weights are kept fixed and only the final layer of the network is trained on a new task-specific dataset. To disable the undesired, but inherent correlations of the classes in fine-tuned networks, we propose the method that simply ignores the most sensitive representations from the feature-extractor model.

To demonstrate this, we conduct an experiment, where we employed a pre-trained DenseNet-161 model as a fixed feature-extractor and fine-tuned the last linear layer on the CalTech-256 image classification dataset [9] while varying the amount of the most sensitive representations omitted from the embeddings. Specifically, we ranked the representations from the DenseNet-161 [11] feature-extractor layer based on the *differentiability* towards Chinese watermarks and retrained the last linear layer while ignoring a varying amount of the most sensitive representations. To determine the effect of this procedure, we evaluated both the accuracy of each fine-tuned model, as well as the distribution of AUC ROC and differentiability scores across 256 output representations. The results of the experiment, displayed in Fig. 6, demonstrate that by excluding 0.5% of the most sensitive representations from the DenseNet-161 feature extractor, the dependence of the newly learned logit representations on Chinese watermarks can be significantly reduced. Furthermore, omitting up to 10% of the most sensitive embeddings has no significant impact on the performance of the fine-tuned model while significantly suppressing the Clever-Hans effect of the new model.

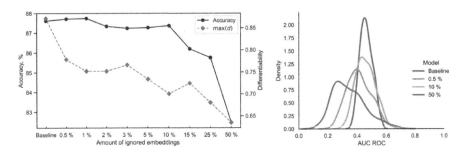

Fig. 6. *Left*: The accuracy of the fine-tuned model and the maximum differential ability towards Chinese symbols across output representations, with respect to the number of representations ignored in the DenseNet-161 feature-extractor layer. *Right*: The distribution of AUC ROC scores across output representations, with respect to the number of representations omitted from the feature extractor.

Additionally, it can be observed that excluding the most sensitive representations from the feature-extractor layer narrows the distribution of AUC ROC scores, making the output classes less likely to be highly differentiable towards spurious concepts.

5   Discussion and Conclusion

With this paper, we aim to bring awareness to the potential risks of watermarked images present in ImageNet and their impact on popular DNNs trained on this dataset. It is known that the "carton" class is impacted by the Chinese watermarks - however, we were able for the first time to demonstrate and identify the significant amount of other ImageNet classes, which are affected by the Chinese watermarks across popular ImageNet pre-trained models. Our results indicate that the sensitivity to watermarks is a common trait among all studied networks and this poses significant risks for transfer learning, as new models could be also vulnerable to unintended concepts. We demonstrate that by simply omitting the most watermark-sensitive representations, fine-tuned networks can suppress the reliance on the watermarks without incurring a significant decline in model performance. Overall, this study highlights the importance of paying attention to the presence of watermarks in image datasets and their impact on the performance of machine learning models.

Acknowledgements. This work was partly funded by the German Ministry for Education and Research through the project Explaining 4.0 (ref. 01IS200551), the German Research Foundation (ref. DFG KI-FOR 5363), the Investitionsbank Berlin through BerDiBa (grant no. 10174498). KRM was partly funded by the German Ministry for Education and Research (under refs 01IS14013A-E, 01GQ1115, 01GQ0850, 01IS18056A, 01IS18025A and 01IS18037A) and BBDC/BZML and BIFOLD and by the Institute of Information & Communications Technology Planning & Evaluation (IITP) grants funded by the Korea Government (MSIT) (No. 2019-0-00079, Artificial Intelligence Graduate School Program, Korea University and No. 2022-0-00984, Development of Artificial Intelligence Technology for Personalized Plug-and-Play Explanation and Verification of Explanation).

References

1. Anders, C.J., Weber, L., Neumann, D., Samek, W., Müller, K.R., Lapuschkin, S.: Finding and removing clever hans: using explanation methods to debug and improve deep models. Information Fusion **77**, 261–295 (2022)
2. Bao, H., Dong, L., Wei, F.: BEIT: BERT pre-training of image transformers. arXiv preprint arXiv:2106.08254 (2021)
3. Bykov, K., Deb, M., Grinwald, D., Muller, K.R., Höhne, M.M.: DORA: exploring outlier representations in deep neural networks. Trans. Mach. Learn. Res. (2023). https://openreview.net/forum?id=nfYwRIezvg
4. Da, J.: A corpus-based study of character and bigram frequencies in chinese e-texts and its implications for chinese language instruction. In: Proceedings of the Fourth International Conference on New Technologies in Teaching and Learning Chinese, pp. 501–511. Citeseer (2004)
5. Deng, J., Dong, W., Socher, R., Li, L.J., Li, K., Fei-Fei, L.: Imagenet: a large-scale hierarchical image database. In: 2009 IEEE Conference on Computer Vision and Pattern Recognition, pp. 248–255. IEEE (2009)
6. Dosovitskiy, A., et al.: An image is worth 16x16 words: transformers for image recognition at scale. arXiv preprint arXiv:2010.11929 (2020)
7. Geirhos, R., Jacobsen, J.H., Michaelis, C., Zemel, R., Brendel, W., Bethge, M., Wichmann, F.A.: Shortcut learning in deep neural networks. Nat. Mach. Intell. **2**(11), 665–673 (2020)
8. Geirhos, R., Rubisch, P., Michaelis, C., Bethge, M., Wichmann, F.A., Brendel, W.: ImageNet-trained CNNs are biased towards texture; increasing shape bias improves accuracy and robustness. arXiv preprint arXiv:1811.12231 (2018)
9. Griffin, G., Holub, A., Perona, P.: Caltech-256 object category dataset (2007)
10. He, K., Zhang, X., Ren, S., Sun, J.: Deep residual learning for image recognition. In: Proceedings of the IEEE Conference on Computer Vision and Pattern Recognition, pp. 770–778 (2016)
11. Huang, G., Liu, Z., Van Der Maaten, L., Weinberger, K.Q.: Densely connected convolutional networks. In: Proceedings of the IEEE Conference on Computer Vision and Pattern Recognition, pp. 4700–4708 (2017)
12. Izmailov, P., Kirichenko, P., Gruver, N., Wilson, A.G.: On feature learning in the presence of spurious correlations. arXiv preprint arXiv:2210.11369 (2022)
13. Kornblith, S., Shlens, J., Le, Q.V.: Do better imagenet models transfer better? In: Proceedings of the IEEE/CVF Conference on Computer Vision and Pattern Recognition, pp. 2661–2671 (2019)
14. Krizhevsky, A.: One weird trick for parallelizing convolutional neural networks. arXiv preprint arXiv:1404.5997 (2014)
15. Lapuschkin, S., Wäldchen, S., Binder, A., Montavon, G., Samek, W., Müller, K.R.: Unmasking clever hans predictors and assessing what machines really learn. Nat. Commun. **10** (2019). https://doi.org/10.1038/s41467-019-08987-4
16. Li, Z., et al.: A whac-a-mole dilemma: shortcuts come in multiples where mitigating one amplifies others (2022). https://doi.org/10.48550/ARXIV.2212.04825

17. Ma, N., Zhang, X., Zheng, H.-T., Sun, J.: ShuffleNet V2: practical guidelines for efficient CNN architecture design. In: Ferrari, V., Hebert, M., Sminchisescu, C., Weiss, Y. (eds.) ECCV 2018. LNCS, vol. 11218, pp. 122–138. Springer, Cham (2018). https://doi.org/10.1007/978-3-030-01264-9_8

18. Rosenfeld, A., Zemel, R., Tsotsos, J.K.: The elephant in the room. arXiv preprint arXiv:1808.03305 (2018)

19. Sanches, E.R.: The community of portuguese language speaking countries: the role of language in a globalizing world. In: Workshop, University of Pretoria (South Africa) (2014)

20. Sandler, M., Howard, A., Zhu, M., Zhmoginov, A., Chen, L.C.: Mobilenetv 2: inverted residuals and linear bottlenecks. In: Proceedings of the IEEE Conference on Computer Vision and Pattern Recognition, pp. 4510–4520 (2018)

21. Simonyan, K., Zisserman, A.: Very deep convolutional networks for large-scale image recognition. arXiv preprint arXiv:1409.1556 (2014)

22. Szegedy, C., et al.: Going deeper with convolutions. In: Proceedings of the IEEE Conference on Computer Vision and Pattern Recognition, pp. 1–9 (2015)

23. Szegedy, C., Vanhoucke, V., Ioffe, S., Shlens, J., Wojna, Z.: Rethinking the inception architecture for computer vision. In: Proceedings of the IEEE Conference on Computer Vision and Pattern Recognition, pp. 2818–2826 (2016)

24. Talukdar, J., Gupta, S., Rajpura, P., Hegde, R.S.: Transfer learning for object detection using state-of-the-art deep neural networks. In: 2018 5th International Conference on Signal Processing and Integrated Networks (SPIN), pp. 78–83. IEEE (2018)

25. Trost, S.: Wordcreator (2023). https://www.sttmedia.com/characterfrequency-latin

26. Van Opbroek, A., Achterberg, H.C., Vernooij, M.W., De Bruijne, M.: Transfer learning for image segmentation by combining image weighting and kernel learning. IEEE Trans. Med. Imaging 38(1), 213–224 (2018)

27. Weiss, K., Khoshgoftaar, T.M., Wang, D.: A survey of transfer learning. J. Big data 3(1), 1–40 (2016)

28. Xiao, K., Engstrom, L., Ilyas, A., Madry, A.: Noise or signal: the role of image backgrounds in object recognition. arXiv preprint arXiv:2006.09994 (2020)

29. Xie, S., Girshick, R., Dollár, P., Tu, Z., He, K.: Aggregated residual transformations for deep neural networks. In: Proceedings of the IEEE Conference on Computer Vision and Pattern Recognition, pp. 1492–1500 (2017)

30. Yuan, Z., Yan, Y., Sonka, M., Yang, T.: Large-scale robust deep AUC maximization: a new surrogate loss and empirical studies on medical image classification. In: Proceedings of the IEEE/CVF International Conference on Computer Vision, pp. 3040–3049 (2021)

31. Zagoruyko, S., Komodakis, N.: Wide residual networks. arXiv preprint arXiv:1605.07146 (2016)

32. Zech, J.R., Badgeley, M.A., Liu, M., Costa, A.B., Titano, J.J., Oermann, E.K.: Variable generalization performance of a deep learning model to detect pneumonia in chest radiographs: a cross-sectional study. PLoS Med. 15(11), e1002683 (2018)

Towards Evaluating Policy Optimisation Agents Using Algorithmic Intelligence Quotient Test

Ondřej Vadinský[(✉)]🆔 and Petr Zeman

Department of Information and Knowledge Engineering,
Prague University of Economics and Business, Prague, Czech Republic
ondrej.vadinsky@vse.cz

Abstract. With the advent of more powerful AI systems, the issue of theoretically well-founded and more robust methods for general evaluation of intelligence in (not only) artificial systems increases in importance. The Algorithmic Intelligence Quotient Test (AIQ test) is an example of a reasonably well-founded yet practically feasible test of intelligence. Deep Reinforcement Learning offers a powerful framework that enables artificial agents to learn how to act in unknown environments of realistic complexities. Vanilla Policy Gradient (VPG) and Proximal Policy Optimisation (PPO) are two examples of model-free on-policy deep reinforcement learning agents. In this paper, a computational experiment with the AIQ test is conducted that evaluates VPG and PPO agents and compares them to classical off-policy Q-learning. An initial analysis of the results indicates that while the maximum AIQ achieved is comparable for the tested agents given sufficient training time, large differences show with short training times. Corresponding to previous research, on-policy methods have lower starting positions than off-policy methods, and PPO learns faster than VPG. This further depends on steps-per-epoch parameter setting of PPO and VPG agents. These findings indicate the utility of the AIQ test as an AI evaluation method.

Keywords: Reinforcement learning · Vanilla Policy Gradient · Proximal Policy Optimisation · Evaluating intelligence of artificial systems · Universal Intelligence definition · Algorithmic Intelligence Quotient test

1 Introduction

As we are witnessing the recent bloom of powerful AI systems (aptly coined as Multimodal Models [26]) that manifest unprecedented levels of generality, thus furthering the advent of Artificial General Intelligence [10], let us take a sidestep towards the question of AI evaluation and, specifically, the issue of artificial agent evaluation.

Historically, artificial intelligence evaluation has been focused on a few selected tasks. While this was natural since AI has been mostly viewed as a

S. Nowaczyk et al. (Eds.): ECAI 2023 Workshops, CCIS 1947, pp. 435–451, 2024.
https://doi.org/10.1007/978-3-031-50396-2_25

means to solve particular tasks or problems [39], such evaluation does not inform us about the intelligence of evaluated systems or even about their broader capabilities. More recently, a shift towards more general AI benchmarks and competitions, such as Arcade Learning Environment (ALE) [4], OpenAI Gym [5], and General Game Competition [8,9], can be seen. However, mainstream AI evaluation still lacks solid theoretical foundations.

Since the pioneering work of Hernández-Orallo on C-test [13], an increasing effort can be seen that tries to base artificial intelligence evaluation on algorithmic information theory (AIT), see e.g. [6,7]. Resulting methods for general evaluation of intelligence in (not only) artificial systems [11] consist of a wide range of tools such as formal definitions of intelligence and measures of some of its aspects [14,20], as well as test proposals and prototypes of practically feasible tests [12,17,22]. While these methods are theoretically well-founded and, in some cases, also practically feasible, they have not seen an extended use apart from brief demonstrations with a few simple agents. An opportunity arises to extend this evaluation to more advanced agents.

Reinforcement learning (RL) [34] offers a powerful framework based on feedback (in the form of rewards) that the artificial agent receives from an environment in which it performs actions. Deep learning techniques [32] can be used to approximate (action-)value functions and/or policies of RL agents and thus enable them to scale well to some realistically complex problems [23]. There are many different RL architectures (both classical and deep) that were applied to various tasks of differing levels of difficulty [27]. A theoretically well-founded general evaluation of advanced RL architectures is missing.

An example of a feasible yet sufficiently general and theoretically well-founded test is Algorithmic Intelligence Quotient test (AIQ test) [22]. As an in-depth analysis shown [37,38], AIQ test is not without its limits, yet since some of them were addressed, we chose this test to evaluate further agents.

Since the AIQ test was originally demonstrated with classical off-policy Q-learning and its variants [16,40], we see merit in applying it to on-policy deep RL agents, namely Vanilla Policy Gradient [3] and Proximal Policy Optimisation [31].

More details on the AIQ test will be given in Sect. 2. Section 3 will cover the chosen Policy Optimisation agents. Section 4 will give an initial comparison of these agents using the AIQ test. The paper will be concluded, and a possible future work will be discussed in Sect. 5.

2   Algorithmic Intelligence Quotient Test

In an attempt to give a definition of intelligence meaningful for AI, Legg and Hutter [19] surveyed a broad variety of existing definitions, tests and theories from many scientific fields. They abstracted the following informal definition: "Intelligence measures an agent's ability to achieve goals in a wide range of environments." The main contribution of Legg and Hutter [20] is, however, the *definition of Universal Intelligence*, where they formalize the working definition above into a form rooted in AIT concepts such as algorithmic probability and Kolmogorov complexity [18]. Since they strove to define intelligence as broadly as possible, their definition is uncomputable, requiring a practical test to be some kind of approximation.

Legg and Veness [22] introduced such an approximation of *the Universal Intelligence* [20] that also includes some of the ideas from *the Anytime Intelligence Test proposal* [12]. The resulting practically feasible test is called *the Algorithmic Intelligence Quotient*, and its main idea is described in Eq. 1.

Three main components make *the AIQ test* [22] computable in contrast to *the Universal Intelligence definition* [20]:

1. limiting *episode length* at finite k steps,
2. using a finite sample of N environment programs p_i that describe environments,
3. and switching from *Kolmogorov Complexity* [18] to a related Solomonoff's *Universal Distribution* [33] that is used to sample environment programs. Multiple programs can, however, describe the same environment.

Putting these together, Legg and Veness [22] give the following Equation of *the Algorithmic Intelligence Quotient*:

$$\hat{\Upsilon}(\pi) := \frac{1}{N} \sum_{i=1}^{N} \hat{V}_{p_i}^{\pi}, \text{ where } \qquad \hat{V}_{p_i}^{\pi} := \frac{1}{k} \sum_{j=1}^{k} r_j, \tag{1}$$

where *the AIQ estimate of Universal Intelligence* $\hat{\Upsilon}$ of an agent π is given by its ability to achieve goals as described by the empirical value function $\hat{V}_{p_i}^{\pi}$ as an average reward achieved by the agent over k interactions with an environment program p_i from a finite sample of N environment programs that are sampled according to Solomonoff's *Universal Distribution* [33]: $M_{\mathcal{U}}(x) := \sum_{p:\mathcal{U}(p)=x*} 2^{-l(p)}$.

Solomonoff's *Universal Distribution* [33] prefers short environment programs over long ones with respect to a particular *reference machine* $\mathcal{U}$. As a result, the choice of the language of the environment programs in the AIQ test determines the classes of programs that are likely to be included in the sample [22]. Legg and Veness attempted to minimise this issue by using a minimalist *BF reference machine* [24]. The BF (as implemented in the AIQ test) is a low-level language that only uses ten instructions which are closely related to operating a Turing machine, yet the programs can be nondeterministic [21]. Environment programs of the selected minimum length can be sampled in the updated version of the test [37] that implements a possible solution given by Hibbard [15].

Since the AIQ test is a practical test, it needs to deal with limited resources that are available to test the agents [21,22]. This, in turn, introduces further requirements, as analysed by Hernández-Orallo and Dowe [12]. The AIQ test meets them in the following way:

1. Since the interaction sequence is limited to k steps and received rewards are simply averaged, environments need to be *balanced* [12]. Legg and Veness

[21,22] normalize the rewards to an interval $[-100, +100]$. As each program is tested twice (once with negative and once with positive rewards), this also ensures that a randomly behaving agent will reach AIQ close to 0 [21,22].

2. Since the sample of the environment programs has a fixed size, environments should be *discriminative* so that they can meaningfully contribute to the evaluation of intelligence of the tested agent [12]. Legg and Veness [21,22] partially fulfil the requirement by excluding programs without read or write instructions as well as by excluding programs that return constant rewards. In an updated version of the test [38], further programs without discriminative power can be omitted from the sample.

For the purpose of practical testing of selected agents with respect to available resources, a reasonable *episode length* of k steps and *sample size* of N programs has to be decided. Setting the episode length increases the "learning time" available to the agent. As previous results suggest [22,37,38], this is very much agent dependent, and $k = 100000$ was often used for simple agents. Setting the sample size influences the precision of the estimate. Legg and Veness [21,22] employed several variance reduction techniques to speed up the AIQ estimation. While $N = 10000$ gives small confidence intervals, it may not be practically feasible for demanding agents [22,37,38].

Finally, the complexity of the interaction space of the BF reference machine can be influenced by two parameters [21,22]: The number of symbols used by the machine directly translates into the number of available actions for the agent to choose from, as well as it determines the granularity of rewards and observations. Number of output observations can be further increased independently.

3   Reinforcement Learning Using Policy Optimisation

Various approaches to Reinforcement learning [34] exist that can be categorised according to several criteria. In this paper, we focus on model-free on-policy methods that are also called Policy Optimisation [2]. Such methods do not have a known model of the environment, nor do they learn one. Instead, they learn policies (explicit prescriptions of how to act), which they optimise directly based on information from a value function. As both policies and value functions can get impractically large for interesting environments, they are often approximated usually using some kind of a neural network.

In Sect. 3.1, the Vanilla Policy Gradient agent will be introduced. Section 3.2 will cover the Proximal Policy Optimisation agent.

3.1   Vanilla Policy Gradient Agent

Vanilla Policy Gradient (VPG) [3] is an example of a simple policy gradient algorithm. It is a more advanced and robust variant of Williams' classical REINFORCE agent [41]. VPG extends the original REINFORCE agent by incorporating ideas from [28,30,35], most notably utilising Generalised Advantage Estimation, allowing for better computation of required policy gradient.

Vanilla Policy Gradient is an on-policy agent without an internal model of the environment directly optimising its policy through Gradient methods. VPG utilises two neural networks. A policy network (Actor) is the main part of the agent responsible for deciding which actions to take. By updating this network, the agent works towards maximising the reward received by actions done by this network. This network is trained with the help of a baseline in the form of advantage estimation based on the value network, which informs the policy on how well it did in its last action. Value network (Critic) is trained to minimise the mean squared error between the estimated value to be received in the state and the actual value received. Together, these two networks work to improve the performance of the agent. The actor selects actions with the highest probability of maximising reward based on the current state, and Critic informs about the quality of the selected action to allow for improving the agent's policy. By optimising both policy and value networks, agents can achieve an optimal policy that maximises the expected total reward over time.

The code of the VPG agent used in our experiments draws heavily from [3] introducing only minimal changes needed for the AIQ test. These changes concern a different design of agent-environment interaction. While in the AIQ test implementation [21], the test and its environments are central and direct the communication to the agent, in the implementation by [3] the agent is central and directs the communication towards environments. The behaviour of the resulting agent can be influenced by setting the following hyperparameters (where applicable, default values were taken from [3]):

- *SPE* – number of environment interaction steps per epoch,
- *VFTI* – number of gradient descent iterations for value function optimisation per epoch (80),
- γ – discount factor (0.99),
- *PLR* – policy learning rate (0.0003),
- *VFLR* – value function learning rate (0.001),
- Λ – balances variance (0) and bias (1) in generalised advantage estimation (0.97).

Number of gradient ascent iterations for policy optimisation per epoch (*PTI*) is fixed at a single iteration for the VPG agent.

3.2   Proximal Policy Optimisation Agent

Proximal Policy Optimisation (PPO) [1,31] is an example of a more advanced policy gradient algorithm that enables larger steps in policy optimisation compared to VPG [3]. PPO utilises the idea behind Trust Region Policy Optimisation (TRPO) [29] in a different, more efficient way, most notably by using Clipped Surrogate Objective.

Proximal Policy Optimisation is an agent without an internal model of the environment directly optimising its policy through Gradient methods. Like TRPO, PPO focuses on improving the performance of simple Policy Gradient agents by allowing larger steps in policy optimisation. Unlike TRPO, which uses a hard constraint based on relative entropy (KL-Divergence) calculated through multiple complex equations, PPO elegantly introduces a new method of constraining policy changes without introducing any additional complex equations. This method, called Clipped Surrogate Objective *"relies on specialised clipping in the objective function to remove incentives for the new policy to get far from the old policy."* [2]. This is achieved by keeping two separate policy networks, one to refine and one to collect samples. While keeping both policies also allows evaluating new policies with samples collected from older policies, the main reason for this change happens every few iterations where synchronisation between policies happens to avoid inaccuracy. During this synchronisation, a ratio between the old and the new policy is computed to find the difference between the two policies. If the difference falls outside the specified range $[1 - \epsilon, 1 + \epsilon]$, a new objective function is constructed to clip the estimated advantage function. This discourages large policy changes and allows multiple optimisation steps during policy updates.

The code of the PPO agent used in our experiments draws heavily from [1], introducing only minimal changes needed for the AIQ test. As is the case with VPG described in Sect. 3.1, these changes concern a different design of agent-environment interaction. The behaviour of the resulting agent can be influenced by setting the following hyperparameters (where applicable, default values were taken from [1]):

- *SPE* – number of environment interaction steps per epoch,
- *PTI* – maximum number of gradient ascent iterations for policy optimisation per epoch (80),
- *VFTI* – number of gradient descent iterations for value function optimisation per epoch (80),
- γ – discount factor (0.99),
- *PLR* – policy learning rate (0.0003),
- *VFLR* – value function learning rate (0.001),
- Λ – balances variance (0) and bias (1) in generalised advantage estimation (0.97),
- ϵ – clip ratio for new policy clipping (0.2),
- *TKL* – (approximate) KL-Divergence between new and old policy that triggers early-stopping of policy gradient update (0.01).

4   Initial Comparison of Policy Optimisation Agents

For the initial comparison, the default settings of the AIQ test [22] with improved discriminative power of environments [38] was used. While these settings create rather low-dimensional action and observation spaces that may not give prominence to the ability of deep RL agents to approximate complex functions, it is still a necessary first step in any more extensive evaluation which brings informational value even in itself.

4.1   Hypotheses

Experiments with the AIQ test in [22,37] show that it is not only the final AIQ score at a chosen episode length that is of interest when evaluating agents, but also the characteristics of AIQ convergence. Experiments conducted in [31] suggest, that PPO should perform better than VPG. Increasing the *SPE* hyperparameter of VPG and PPO agents (given a constant episode length in the AIQ test) effectively decreases the number of possible policy updates [1,3] impacting the ability of the agent to learn about its environment. While off-policy algorithms tend to be less stable than on-policy methods, they also tend to learn better, as off-policy methods can also utilise experience gained beyond currently followed policy [2,34].

Based on the above-mentioned considerations, we formulated the following hypotheses:

1. AIQ scores of tested agents are significantly different.
2. There are significant differences in the AIQ convergence of tested agents.
3. AIQ scores of PPO are significantly higher than those of VPG.
4. AIQ of PPO converges significantly faster than VPG.
5. Increasing the values of *SPE* hyperparameter decreases AIQ scores of both PPO and VPG.
6. Increasing the values of *SPE* hyperparameter slows down AIQ convergence of both PPO and VPG.
7. AIQ scores of on-policy agents are significantly lower than off-policy agents.
8. AIQ of on-policy agents converges significantly slower than off-policy agents.

4.2   Experiment Settings

We noticed (and fixed) a typo in one of the regular expressions of the *SEP-ext* method of [38]. As expected due to the nature of the typo, testing revealed a negligible yet statistically significant decrease in AIQ score. Thus, the results achieved with *patched SEP-ext* cannot be directly compared to the results of [38].

For the experiment, we generated 200,000 new environment programs using the improved version of the BF sampler [38]. We employed the *(patched) SEP-ext* and *SDP* options suggested by [38] to increase the discriminative power of the environment programs. Descriptive statistics according to a program length, as well as the number of the unique programs in the new sample, correspond well with the statistics reported in [38]. Only a few minor differences among the samples were identified by a semantic analysis conducted with a tool provided by [38]. The newly generated sample, as well as the results of the conducted analysis, is included in the Appendix.

Since our *patched SEP-ext* has an impact on the AIQ scores of agents, we retested the configurations of *freq*, Q_0, Q_λ and HLQ_λ used by [37,38]. For the newly implemented *VPG* and *PPO* agents, we used (except for *SPE*) the default hyperparameter values as described in Sect. 3.1 and 3.2 respectively. For the *SPE* hyperparameter, we varied its values in the following way: 10, 50, 100, 500, 1000 and 5000. This gives us the opportunity to observe the agents both with relatively short as well as with relatively long epoch lengths, enabling us to analyse the trade-off between the number of policy updates during the test and times to discover environment under the given policy. Full configurations of all tested agents are given in the Appendix.

To estimate the AIQ score of all the mentioned configurations of agents, the episode length of 100,000 interactions and sample size of 10,000 programs were used as suggested by [22,37,38]. Intermediate results were saved every 1,000 interactions to enable an analysis of the AIQ score convergence. BF reference machine with 5 symbol action and observation spaces was used that returns 1 reward symbol and 1 observation symbol each interaction. A script that can run our setting of the experiment with the AIQ test is included in the Appendix.

4.3   Results

Figure 1 shows the highest achieved AIQ score estimates for each agent after the tested number of interactions. The best configuration of each agent was selected based on the highest AIQ score achieved at the episode length of 100,000 interactions. Detailed results of all tested VPG and PPO configurations are shown by Fig. 2. Full results of all tested agent configurations are part of the Appendix.

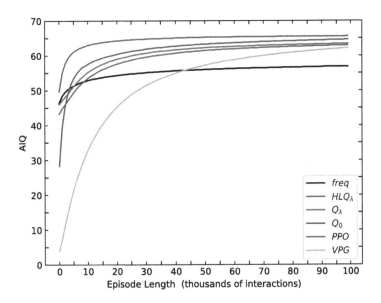

Fig. 1. Highest achieved estimated AIQ scores of agents as a function of episode length on BF 5 reference machine with patched SEP-ext and SDP functionality.

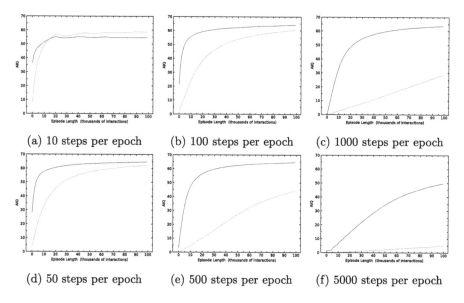

(a) 10 steps per epoch   (b) 100 steps per epoch   (c) 1000 steps per epoch

(d) 50 steps per epoch   (e) 500 steps per epoch   (f) 5000 steps per epoch

Fig. 2. An impact of modifying *SPE* of VPG and PPO on achieved estimated AIQ scores as a function of episode length on BF 5 reference machine with patched SEP-ext and SDP.

All the tested agent configurations successfully finished the test with the exception of *PPO* with *SPE* = 10. We noticed that this configuration often experienced NaN errors, most likely due to the advantages between policy changes being almost 0 in some environments. In order to understand the issue, we extended the test to log the cases when an agent fails and reset the agent. We then recomputed all the *PPO* and *VPG* configurations. The resulting number of environments that caused the agent to fail is listed in Table 1. Nevertheless, given the limited computational resources, we only managed to test *PPO* with *SPE* = 10 on a sample size of 5,000 programs. The high number of errors in the case of *SPE* = 10 and the resulting agent resets are most likely responsible for the AIQ score fluctuations in Fig. 2a.

Table 1. The impact of *SPE* hyperparameter on the number of errors of VPG and PPO (PPO with *SPE* = 10 tested on 5,000 programs, the other configurations tested on 10,000 programs).

Agent	Number of Errors for SPE					
	10	*50*	*100*	*500*	*1000*	*5000*
PPO	2186	435	49	25	16	7
VPG	3697	348	23	16	8	6

4.4 Data Analysis

To evaluate hypotheses 1 and 2, we will look at the results of the highest performing configuration for each agent. For the remaining hypotheses, we will consider
all the tested agent configurations, in order to understand their performance in
more detail.

Hypothesis 1. As can be seen in Fig. 1, the AIQ estimates of the tested agents
at the episode length of 100,000 differ. In some cases, however, these estimates
are within confidence intervals. Two-sample t statistics were computed to determine the significance of the differences. In most cases, the differences indeed are
significant, the exception being: Q_0 vs. Q_λ, and Q_0 vs. VPG, see Appendix for
details. Thus, the highest AIQ of 65.6 ± 0.5 was achieved by HLQ_λ, closely followed by PPO with 64.6 ± 0.4. Q_λ, Q_0 and VPG closely follow bundled around
the AIQ of 63. Finally, *freq* has a far lower AIQ of $56.8 \pm 0,5$. Overall, the
hypothesis has been rejected.

Hypothesis 2. As can be seen from the shape of curves in Fig. 1, there are some
pronounced differences in AIQ convergence among agents. HLQ_λ still performs
the highest on all episode lengths. The curves of Q_λ and Q_0 are rather similar,
with PPO starting far lower with the AIQ of 28.3 ± 0.3 but getting significantly
above both of them quickly at EL of 5,000 interactions. VPG starts the lowest
with AIQ of 4 ± 0.1 and converges the slowest significantly outperforming *freq*
only at EL of 49,000 and getting on par with Q_0 at EL of 97,000 interactions.
This is further confirmed by the area under the curve (AUC) analysis computed
according to the Simpson's rule as listed in Table 2a. Thus, the hypothesis holds.

Hypothesis 3. As can be seen in Fig. 3, the AIQ estimates of the PPO agent are
not always higher than that of VPG at the episode length of 100,000. Further,
Fig. 2 suggests that the AIQ of both VPG and (to a lesser degree) PPO depends
on the SPE hyperparameter. Looking at the results with SPE hyperparameter
fixed, the AIQ of PPO is significantly higher than that of VPG for all but one
SPE configuration. In the case of 10 steps per epoch, however, the AIQ of PPO
is significantly lower that the AIQ of VPG. Overall, the hypothesis has been
rejected.

Hypothesis 4. As can be seen from the shape of curves in Fig. 3, it is not always
the case, that PPO converges faster that VPG. Again, Fig. 2 suggests there is
a dependence of the AIQ convergence on the SPE hyperparameter. Looking at
the results with this hyperparameter fixed, PPO performs higher than VPG
in all cases except for ten steps for an epoch. Even then, PPO starts with a
significantly higher AIQ than VPG, but it is overcome rather swiftly at the EL
of 20,000. Overall, the hypothesis has been rejected.

Hypothesis 5. As can be seen in Fig. 3, the AIQ estimates of VPG at the episode length of 100,000 decrease with increasing values of SPE hyperparameter except for $SPE = 10$. In all cases, the estimates lie outside the confidence intervals, so the differences are significant. In the case of PPO, the AIQ scores at the episode length of 100,000 are mostly within confidence intervals, and only the configurations with extreme values of SPE 10 and 5,000 achieved noticeably (and significantly) lower AIQ. Overall, the hypothesis has been rejected.

Hypothesis 6. As can be seen from the shape of curves in Fig. 3, increasing the values of SPE hyperparameter slows down the convergence of both VPG and PPO. While the curves with $SPE = 10$ are not the highest for all episode lengths, they start the highest for both agents. In the case of PPO, it is outperformed quickly at the episode length of 3,000, while for VPG it is only significantly outperformed at EL of 59,000. This is further confirmed by AUC analysis computed according to Simpson's rule as listed in Table 2b. Thus, the hypothesis holds.

Hypothesis 7. As can be seen in Fig. 1, the AIQ estimate of the highest performing on-policy algorithm (PPO) at the episode length of 100,000 is indeed significantly slightly lower than the estimate of the highest-performing off-policy algorithm (HLQ_λ). Further, the lowest AIQ score was achieved by VPG (with SPE of 5,000). However, there is no clear-cut difference among all the tested agent configurations, and we consider their number to be too small to warrant a meaningful t-test between the groups. Thus, the results are inconclusive.

Hypothesis 8. As can be seen from the shape of curves in Fig. 1, both PPO and VPG start (significantly) far lower than the off-policy agents. This holds for all the tested agent configurations, as can be seen from full results in the Appendix. Apart from this clear-cut difference, the other parts of the curves are not so clearly differentiated, and the same limitations apply as with the hypothesis 7. Overall, the results are inconclusive.

4.5   Discussion

Based on the data analysis above, we will now interpret the findings with respect to hypotheses from Sect. 4.1 and discuss the limits of the research so far. The main considerations are as follows:

1. The number of configurations tested for each agent is rather limited. Instead of statistical testing over a "population" of agent configurations, we used as a proxy the current highest performing configuration. This allows for a statistical comparison of AIQ scores with respect to their confidence intervals that are robust due to a large sample size of environment programs. However, as most of the agents have many hyperparameters, the results of particular configurations may not be representative of the agent's performance.

Table 2. Area under the curve of the AIQ scores acquired through Simpson's rule.

(a) Highest performing agent configurations

Agent	AUC
HLQ_λ	6388.77
PPO	6102.47
Q_λ	5999.79
Q_0	5904.27
freq	5472.47
VPG	5131.48

(b) The impact of *SPE* hyperparameter on VPG and PPO.

Agent	AUC for Steps Per Epoch					
	10	50	100	500	1000	5000
PPO	5318.38	6102.47	5977.23	5756.87	5307.15	3006.89
VPG	5441.08	5131.48	4714.94	2470.08	1374.39	212.70

2. A suitable method to formally evaluate hypotheses concerning the speed of AIQ score convergence is missing. We tried to supplement the visual analysis of the shape of AIQ curves with the area under the curve analysis, however, AUC is, in this case, strongly dependent on the episode length.

3. Further limitations when comparing deep and classical RL techniques stem from the chosen BF 5 reference machine that has rather low-dimensional action and observation spaces. While this setting will likely not show the power of deep RL agents, it can serve as a baseline for future experiments that would test changes in agent performance when increasing the dimensionality of action and observation spaces.

With these considerations in mind, we can now formulate some insights with respect to the hypotheses.

Differences Among Tested Agents (hypotheses 1 and 2). While the maximum achieved AIQ scores of tested agents are significantly different in most of the cases, the scores are also quite comparable given the sufficiently high episode length. Only *freq* (a very basic learning agent) achieves notably lower maximal score. It is the short episode length and the speed of AIQ convergence that show the most pronounced differences between the agents.

The Case of HLQ_λ and PPO. From the overall comparison, HLQ_λ seems to be a more capable agent (both with respect to its maximum AIQ as well as its speed of convergence) than *PPO*. This might come as a surprise since *PPO* is a rather popular state-of-the-art deep RL agent [31], and HLQ_λ is just an improved version of tabular Q-learning (albeit with automatic learning rate) [16]. But these might actually be the causes of these results. As the BF 5 settings used for our initial evaluation of the agents has a rather low dimensionality, strong points of a deep RL technique may not show, and a tabular solution is still feasible (and possibly even more accurate than an approximation learned by the deep technique). If this is the case, increasing the dimensionality of BF reference machine should impede HLQ_λ more than *PPO*. Further, the automatic learning rate might make HLQ_λ more adaptive with respect to a sample of different environments than *PPO* (and all other agents) that has all hyperparameters fixed for all the environments in the sample.

Comparison of VPG and PPO (hypotheses 3–6). In case of *PPO* and *VPG* comparison it is also the speed of convergence that distinguishes the agents most clearly and shows that *PPO* is a more capable learning agent. Apart from the slower convergence, *VPG* also achieves notably lower AIQ with higher values of *SPE* hyperparameter than *PPO*, and overall, it seems to be more impacted by changing its values.

On-Policy Vs. Off-Policy Agents (hypotheses 7 and 8). The differences between the on-policy and off-policy agents also show the most in the speed of AIQ convergence and, especially in their AIQ at the EL of 1,000, which is noticeably lower than that of off-policy agents.

These insights are consistent with the observations made in previous works with the AIQ test [22, 37, 38] as well as with the existing experiments with *VPG* and *PPO* [31] and the general knowledge of on-policy and off-policy agents [2, 34].

5 Conclusion and Future Work

In this paper, we presented the initial results of Vanilla Policy Gradient [3] and Proximal Policy Optimisation [31] evaluation using the Algorithmic Intelligence Quotient test [22] including a comparison of these agents to a classical off-policy Q-learning and its variants [16, 40]. An initial analysis of the results indicates that while the maximum AIQ achieved is comparable for the tested agents given sufficient training time, large differences show with short training times and the speed of AIQ convergence. Corresponding to previous research [2, 31, 34], on-policy methods have lower starting positions than off-policy methods, and PPO learns faster than VPG. This further depends on steps-per-epoch hyperparameter setting of PPO and VPG agents. While only initial insights were drawn from a relatively small number of tested agent configurations, these findings indicate the utility of the AIQ test as an AI evaluation method.

As part of future work, we would like to focus on the following areas:

- Finding a suitable method to formally compare the speed of AIQ convergence.
- Testing a higher number of agent configurations in a more systematic way to get a better picture of agents' performance.
- Analysing the results of various agents on particular environment programs to get a better understanding of the AIQ test limits.
- Comparing deep and classical RL agents in a more robust way using larger action and observation spaces of the BF reference machine.

In the field of explainable reinforcement learning [25], the AIQ test might be used as a more robust measure of both the black box as well as the derived interpretable model capabilities, thus ensuring the same level of performance is attained. Furthermore, the insights gained from the interpretable models would be beneficial to the AIQ test development since a better understanding of the environments used in the test is also needed.

Acknowledgements. This work was funded by the Internal Grant Agency of Prague University of Economics and Business (F4/41/2023). Computational resources were kindly provided by the project "e-Infrastruktura CZ" (e-INFRA CZ LM2018140) supported by the Ministry of Education, Youth and Sports of the Czech Republic.

Appendix

A compact view of the results of all tested VPG and PPO configurations to facilitate visual comparison is shown by Fig. 3.

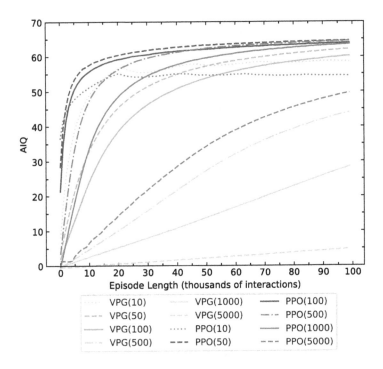

Fig. 3. Achieved estimated AIQ scores of VPG and PPO as a function of episode length on BF 5 reference machine with patched SEP-ext and SDP.

Full experiment settings, as well as results of the conducted analyses and experiments, are available from: https://github.com/xvado00/TEPOA/archive/refs/tags/XI-ML23.zip.

Full sources of the AIQ test (a Python 3 conversion of [36]), including the implementation of VPG and PPO agents, are available from: https://github.com/zemp02/AIQ/archive/refs/tags/v2.1.zip.

References

1. Achiam, J.: Proximal policy optimization. In: Spinning Up in Deep RL (2018). https://spinningup.openai.com/en/latest/algorithms/ppo.html
2. Achiam, J.: Spinning up in deep RL (2018). https://spinningup.openai.com/en/latest/
3. Achiam, J.: Vanilla policy gradient. In: Spinning Up in Deep RL (2018). https://spinningup.openai.com/en/latest/algorithms/vpg.html
4. Bellemare, M.G., Naddaf, Y., Veness, J., Bowling, M.: Arcade learning environment: an evaluation platform for general agents. J. Artifi. Intell. Res. **47**, 253–279 (2013)
5. Brockman, G., et al.: Openai gym. Tech. Rep. **1606**, 01540 (2016)
6. Chaitin, G.J.: Algorithmic Information Theory, Cambridge Tracts in Theoretical Computer Science, vol. 1. Cambridge University Press, Cambridge, 3 edn. (1987)
7. Chaitin, G.J.: Information, 2nd edn. Randomness and Incompleteness. World Scientific, Singapore (1990)
8. Genesereth, M., Love, N., Pell, B.: General game playing: overview of the AAAI competition. AI Mag. **26**(2), 62–72 (2005)
9. Genesereth, M., Thielscher, M.: General Game Playing, Synthesis Lectures on Artificial Intelligence and Machine Learning, vol. 24. 1 edn. (2014)
10. Goertzel, B., Pennachin, C. (eds.): Artificial General Intelligence, Cognitive Technologies, vol. 8. Springer, Berlin (2007). https://doi.org/10.1007/978-3-540-68677-4
11. Hernández-Orallo, J.: Measure of All Minds, The. Cambridge University Press, Cambridge, 1 edn. (2017). https://doi.org/10.1017/9781316594179
12. Hernández-Orallo, J., Dowe, D.L.: Measuring universal intelligence: towards an anytime intelligence test. Artif. Intell. **174**(18), 1508–1539 (2010). https://doi.org/10.1016/j.artint.2010.09.006
13. Hernández-Orallo, J.: Beyond the turing test. J. Logic Lang. Inform. **9**(4), 447–466 (2000). https://doi.org/10.1023/A:1008367325700
14. Hernández-Orallo, J., Loe, B.S., Cheke, L., Martínez-Plumed, F., hÉigeartaigh, S.: General intelligence disentangled via a generality metric for natural and artificial intelligence. Nat. Sci. Rep. **11**(1), 1–16 (2021). https://doi.org/10.1038/s41598-021-01997-7
15. Hibbard, B.: Bias and no free lunch in formal measures of intelligence. J. Artifi. Gen. Intell. **1**(1), 54–61 (2009). https://doi.org/10.2478/v10229-011-0004-6
16. Hutter, M., Legg, S.: Temporal difference updating without a learning rate. In: Platt, J.C., Koller, D., Singer, Y., Roweis, S.T. (eds.) Proceedings of the 21st Annual Conference on Advances in Neural Information Processing Systems, NIPS 2007, pp. 705–712. Curran Associates Inc, New York (2007)
17. Insa-Cabrera, J., Dowe, D.L., España-Cubillo, S., Hernández-Lloreda, M.V., Hernández-Orallo, J.: Comparing humans and AI agents. In: Schmidhuber, J., Thórisson, K.R., Looks, M. (eds.) AGI 2011. LNCS (LNAI), vol. 6830, pp. 122–132. Springer, Heidelberg (2011). https://doi.org/10.1007/978-3-642-22887-2_13
18. Kolmogorov, A.N.: On tables of random numbers. Sankhyā: Indian J. Stat. Ser. A **4**(25), 369–376 (1963). https://doi.org/10.1016/S0304-3975(98)00075-9
19. Legg, S., Hutter, M.: A collection of definitions of intelligence. In: Goertzel, B., Wang, P. (eds.) Advances in Artificial General Intelligence: Concepts, Architectures and Algorithms, Frontiers in Artificial Intelligence and Applications, vol. 157, pp. 17–24. IOS Press, Amsterdam (2007)

20. Legg, S., Hutter, M.: Universal intelligence: a definition of machine intelligence. Mind. Mach. **17**(4), 391–444 (2007). https://doi.org/10.1007/s11023-007-9079-x

21. Legg, S., Veness, J.: AIQ: Algorithmic intelligence quotient [source codes] (2011). https://github.com/mathemajician/AIQ

22. Legg, S., Veness, J.: An approximation of the universal intelligence measure. In: Dowe, D.L. (ed.) Algorithmic Probability and Friends. Bayesian Prediction and Artificial Intelligence. LNCS, vol. 7070, pp. 236–249. Springer, Heidelberg (2013). https://doi.org/10.1007/978-3-642-44958-1_18

23. Mnih, V., et al.: Human-level control through deep reinforcement learning. Nature **518**(7540), 529–533 (2015). https://doi.org/10.1038/nature14236

24. Müller, U.: Dev/lang/brainfuck-2.lha in aminet (1993). http://aminet.net/package.php?package=dev/lang/brainfuck-2.lha

25. Saeed, W., Omlin, C.: Explainable AI (XAI): a systematic meta-survey of current challenges and future opportunities. Knowl.-Based Syst. **263**, 110273 (2023). https://doi.org/10.1016/j.knosys.2023.110273

26. Schellaert, W., et al.: Your prompt is my command: on assessing the human-centred generality of multimodal models. J. Artifi. Intell. Res. **2023**(77), 377–394 (2023)

27. Schrittwieser, J., et al.: Mastering Atari, go, chess and shogi by planning with a learned model. Nature **588**, 604–609 (2020). https://doi.org/10.1038/s41586-020-03051-4

28. Schulman, J.: Optimizing Expectations: From Deep Reinforcement Learning to Stochastic Computation Graphs. Ph.D. thesis, University of California, Berkeley (2016)

29. Schulman, J., Levine, S., Moritz, P., Jordan, M.I., Abbeel, P.: Trust region policy optimization. In: Proceedings of the 32nd International Conference on Machine Learning, PMLR 37, pp. 1889–1897 (2015)

30. Schulman, J., Moritz, P., Levine, S., Jordan, M., Abbeel, P.: High-dimensional continuous control using generalized advantage estimation. In: Bengio, Y., LeCun, Y. (eds.) 4th International Conference on Learning Representations, ICLR 2016 (2016)

31. Schulman, J., Wolski, F., Dhariwal, P., Radford, A., Klimov, O.: Proximal policy optimization algorithms. Tech. Rep. 1707.06347, OpenAI (2017)

32. Skansi, S.: Introduction to Deep Learning?: From Logical Calculus to Artificial Intelligence. Springer, Cham (2018). https://doi.org/10.1007/978-3-319-73004-2

33. Solomonoff, R.J.: A formal theory of inductive inference, part 1 and part 2. Inf. Control **7**(1–22), 224–254 (1964). https://doi.org/10.1016/S0019-9958(64)90131-7

34. Sutton, R.S., Barto, A.G.: Reinforcement Learning: An Introduction, 2nd edn. MIT Press, Cambridge (2018)

35. Sutton, R.S., McAllester, D., Singh, S., Mansour, Y.: Policy gradient methods for reinforcement learning with function approximation. In: Solla, S.A., Leen, T.K., Müller, K. (eds.) NIPS 1999: Proceedings of the 12th International Conference on Neural Information Processing Systems, pp. 1057–1063. MIT Press, Cambridge (1999)

36. Vadinský, O.: AIQ: Algorithmic intelligence quotient [source codes] (2018). https://github.com/xvado00/AIQ/archive/v1.3.zip

37. Vadinský, O.: Towards general evaluation of intelligent systems: lessons learned from reproducing AIQ test results. J. Artifi. Gen. Intell. **9**(1), 1–54 (2018). https://doi.org/10.2478/jagi-2018-0001

38. Vadinský, O.: Towards general evaluation of intelligent systems: using semantic analysis to improve environments in the AIQ test. In: Iklé, M., Franz, A., Rzepka, R., Goertzel, B. (eds.) AGI 2018. LNCS (LNAI), vol. 10999, pp. 248–258. Springer, Cham (2018). https://doi.org/10.1007/978-3-319-97676-1_24
39. Wang, P.: On defining artificial intelligence. J. Artifi. Gen. Intell. **2**(10), 1–37 (2019). https://doi.org/10.2478/jagi-2019-0002
40. Watkins, C.: Learning from Delayed Rewards. Ph.D. thesis, University of Cambridge, Kings College, Cambridge (1989)
41. Williams, R.J.: Simple statistical gradient-following algorithms for connectionist reinforcement learning. Mach. Learn. **8**, 229–256 (1992). https://doi.org/10.1007/BF00992696

Author Index

Printed in the United States
by Baker & Taylor Publisher Services